AMPED 3

ALL SLEDS

Select Cheat Codes from the Options menu and press Right Trigger, X, Left Trigger, Down, Right, Left Bumper, Left Trigger, Right Trigger, Y, X.

ALL GEAR

Select Cheat Codes from the Options menu and press Y, Down, Up, Left, Right, Left Bumper, Right, Right Trigger, Right Trigger, Right Bumper.

ALL TRICKS
Select Cheat Codes from the Options menu and press Left Bumper, Right Trigger, Y, Up, Down, X, Left Trigger, Left, Right Bumper, Right Trigger.

ALL LEVELS
Select Cheat Codes from the Options menu and press X, Y, Up, Left, Left Bumper, Left Bumper, Right Trigger, X, Y, Left Trigger.

ALL CONFIGS
Select Cheat Codes from the Options menu and press Down, X, Right, Left Bumper, Right, Right Bumper, X, Right Trigger, Left Trigger, Y.

SUPER SPINS
Select Cheat Codes from the Options menu and press X (x4), Y (x3), X.

AWESOME METER ALWAYS FULL
Select Cheat Codes from the Options menu and press Up, Right Trigger, X, Y, Left Bumper, X, Down, Left Bumper, Right Trigger, Right Bumper.

ALL AWESOMENESS
Select Cheat Codes from the Options menu and press Right Bumper, Right Bumper, Down, Left, Up, Right Trigger, X, Right Bumper, X, X.

ALL BUILD LICENSES
Select Cheat Codes from the Options menu and press Left, Right Trigger, Left Bumper, Right Trigger, X, X, Y, Down, Up, X.

ALL BUILD OBJECTS
Select Cheat Codes from the Options menu and press Left Trigger, Right Trigger, Up, Up, Right Bumper, Left, Right, X, Y, Left Bumper.

ALL CHALLENGES
Select Cheat Codes from the Options menu and press Right, Left Bumper, Left Trigger, X, Left, Right Bumper, Right Trigger, Y, Left Trigger, X.

LOUD SPEAKERS
Select Cheat Codes from the Options menu and press Y, Right Trigger, Right Trigger, Left Bumper, Down, Down, Left, Left, Right, Left Bumper.

LOW GRAVITY BOARDERS
Select Cheat Codes from the Options menu and press Right Trigger, Down, Down, Up, X, Left Bumper, Y, Right Trigger, Y, Down.

NO AI
Select Cheat Codes from the Options menu and press X, X, Left Bumper, Down, Right, Right, Up, Y, Y, Left Trigger.

ALL MUSIC
Select Cheat Codes from the Options menu and press Up, Left, Right Trigger, Right Bumper, Right Trigger, Up, Down, Left, Y, Left Trigger.

AVATAR: THE LAST AIRBENDER — THE BURNING EARTH

UNLIMITED HEALTH
Select Code Entry from the Extras menu and enter 65049.

DOUBLE DAMAGE
Select Code Entry from the Extras menu and enter 90210.

MAXIMUM LEVEL
Select Code Entry from the Extras menu and enter 89121.

UNLIMITED SPECIALS
Select Code Entry from the Extras menu and enter 66206.

ONE-HIT DISHONOR
Select Code Entry from the Extras menu and enter 28260.

ALL BONUS GAMES
Select Code Entry from the Extras menu and enter 99801.

UNLOCKS GALLERY
Select Code Entry from the Extras menu and enter 85061.

BAJA: EDGE OF CONTROL

ALL VEHICLES AND TRACKS
Select Cheat Codes from the Options menu and enter SHOWTIME.

ALL PARTS
Select Cheat Codes from the Options menu and enter SUPERMAX.

BANJO-KAZOOIE

In Treasure Trove Cove, enter the Sandcastle and spell CHEAT by using your Beak Buster on the desired letter. A sound will confirm the entry of the letter. The following cheats will now be available for you. Two things to keep in mind: First, no sound will confirm the correct letter. Secondly, ignore the spaces in the phrases—]just spell the entire phrase out.

AREA OPENING CHEATS

ACCESS CLANKER'S CAVERN
THERES NOWHERE DANKER THAN IN WITH CLANKER

ACCESS MAD MONSTER MANSION
THE JIGGYS NOW MADE WHOLE INTO THE MANSION YOU CAN STROLL

ACCESS GOBI'S VALLEY
GOBIS JIGGY IS NOW DONE TREK ON IN AND GET SOME SUN

ACCESS RUSTY BUCKET BAY
WHY NOT TAKE A TRIP INSIDE GRUNTYS RUSTY SHIP

ACCESS CLICK CLOCK WOOD
THIS ONES GOOD AS YOU CAN ENTER THE WOOD

ACCESS FREEZEEZY PEAK
THE JIGGYS DONE SO OFF YOU GO INTO FREEZEEZY PEAK AND ITS SNOW

ACCESS BUBBLEGLOOP SWAMP
NOW INTO THE SWAMP YOU CAN STOMP

HIDDEN EGG CHEATS

The Hidden Egg cheats will only work if you have been to the level previously.

REVEAL THE BLUE EGG IN GOBI'S VALLEY BEHIND THE LOCKED GATE IN THE ROCK WALL
A DESERT DOOR OPENS WIDE ANCIENT SECRETS WAIT INSIDE

REVEAL THE PURPLE EGG IN TREASURE TROVE COVE IN SHARKFOOD ISLAND
OUT OF THE SEA IT RISES TO REVEAL MORE SECRET PRIZES

REVEAL THE ICE KEY IN FREEZEEZY PEAK IN THE ICE CAVE
NOW YOU CAN SEE A NICE ICE KEY WHICH YOU CAN HAVE FOR FREE

REVEAL THE LIGHT BLUE EGG IN GRUNTILDA'S LAIR—YOU'LL FIND IT IN THE CASK MARKED WITH AN X
DONT YOU GO AND TELL HER ABOUT THE SECRET IN HER CELLAR

REVEAL THE GREEN EGG IN MAD MONSTER MANSION IN THE SAME ROOM AS LOGGO THE TOILET
AMIDST THE HAUNTED GLOOM A SECRET IN THE BATHROOM

REVEAL THE YELLOW EGG IN CLICK CLOCK WOOD IN NABNUTS' TREE HOUSE
NOW BANJO WILL BE ABLE TO SEE IT ON NABNUTS TABLE

REVEAL THE RED EGG IN RUSTY BUCKET BAY IN THE CAPTAIN'S CABIN
THIS SECRET YOULL BE GRABBIN IN THE CAPTAINS CABIN

NOTE DOOR CHEATS

These codes will pop the note doors open without having to find the required notes.

DOOR 2
THESE GO RIGHT ON THROUGH NOTE DOOR TWO

DOOR 3
NOTE DOOR THREE GET IN FOR FREE

DOOR 4
TAKE A TOUR THROUGH NOTE DOOR FOUR

DOOR 5
USE THIS CHEAT NOTE DOOR FIVE IS BEAT

DOOR 6
THIS TRICKS USED TO OPEN NOTE DOOR SIX

DOOR 7
THE SEVENTH NOTE DOOR IS NOW NO MORE

SWITCH AND OBSTACLE CHEATS FOR GRUNTILDA'S LAIR

These will allow you to alter certain obstacles throughout Gruntilda's Lair. Sometimes, the cheat will even remove them completely.

RAISE THE PIPES NEAR CLANKER'S CAVERN
BOTH PIPES ARE THERE TO CLANKERS LAIR

RAISE THE LARGE PIPE NEAR CLANKER'S CAVERN
YOULL CEASE TO GRIPE WHEN UP GOES A PIPE

UNLOCK THE PATH NEAR CLANKER'S CAVERN THAT LEADS TO THE CLICK CLOCK WOOD PICTURE
ONCE IT SHONE BUT THE LONG TUNNEL GRILLE IS GONE

REVEAL THE PODIUM FOR THE CLICK CLOCK WOOD JIGGY
DONT DESPAIR THE TREE JIGGY PODIUM IS NOW THERE

UNLOCK THE PATH INSIDE THE GIANT WITCH STATUE, NEAR BUBBLEGLOOP SWAMP (OPEN THE GRILL)
SHES AN UGLY BAT SO LETS REMOVE HER GRILLE AND HAT

UNLOCK THE PATH TO THE FREEZEEZY PEAK PICTURE BEHIND THE ICE CUBE
ITS YOUR LUCKY DAY AS THE ICE BALL MELTS AWAY

UNLOCK PASSAGES BLOCKED BY COBWEBS
WEBS STOP YOUR PLAY SO TAKE THEM AWAY

REVEAL A JIGGY IN GRUNTILDA'S STATUE BY SMASHING THE EYE NEAR MAD MONSTER MANSION
GRUNTY WILL CRY NOW YOUVE SMASHED HER EYE

RAISE THE WATER LEVEL NEAR RUSTY BUCKET BAY
UP YOU GO WITHOUT A HITCH UP TO THE WATER LEVEL SWITCH

UNLOCK THE PATH TO THE CRYPT NEAR MAD MONSTER MANSION (REMOVE THE GATE)
YOU WONT HAVE TO WAIT NOW THERES NO CRYPT GATE

REMOVE THE COFFIN LID IN THE CRYPT
THIS SHOULD GET RID OF THE CRYPT COFFIN LID

CRUMBLE ALL BREAKABLE WALLS
THEY CAUSE TROUBLE BUT NOW THEYRE RUBBLE

ACTIVATE SPECIAL PADS

Skip the lesson from Bottles by entering these codes.

ACTIVATE THE FLY PAD
YOU WONT BE SAD NOW YOU CAN USE THE FLY PAD

ACTIVATE THE SHOCK JUMP PAD
YOULL BE GLAD TO SEE THE SHOCK JUMP PAD

EXTRA HEALTH CHEAT

Skip the note-hunt and get that extra health by entering this cheat.

AN ENERGY BAR TO GET YOU FAR

Remember, to enter a code you must first enter the word CHEAT in the Sandcastle.

BATTLEFIELD 2: MODERN COMBAT

ALL WEAPONS
During a game, hold Right Bumper + Left Bumper and quickly press Right, Right, Down, Up, Left, Left.

BATTLEFIELD: BAD COMPANY

M60

Select Unlocks from the Multiplayer menu, press Start, and enter try4ndrunf0rcov3r.

QBU88

Select Unlocks from the Multiplayer menu, press Start, and enter your3mynextt4rget.

UZI

Select Unlocks from the Multiplayer menu, press Start, and enter cov3r1ngthecorn3r.

FIND ALL FIVE WEAPONS

SNIPER RIFLE

You received a weapon unlock code for this gun if you pre-ordered the game.

MACHINE GUN

Receive a weapon unlock code for this gun after signing up for the newsletter at www.findallfive.com.

SUB-MACHINE GUN

Download the demo and reach rank 4 to receive an unlock code for this weapon.

ASSAULT RIFLE

Go to veteran.battlefield.com and register your previous Battlefield games to receive an unlock code for this weapon.

SEMI-AUTOMATIC SHOTGUN

Check your online stats at www.findallfive.com to get an unlock code for this weapon.

BATTLESTATIONS: MIDWAY

ALL CAMPAIGN AND CHALLENGE MISSIONS

At the mission select, hold Right Bumper + Left Bumper + Right Trigger + Left Trigger and press X.

BEAT'N GROOVY

ALTERNATE CONTROLS

At the Title screen, press Up, Up, Down, Down, Left, Right, Left, Right, B, A.

BIONIC COMMANDO REARMED

The following challenge rooms can be found in the Challenge Room list. Only one code can be active at a time.

AARON SEDILLO'S CHALLENGE ROOM (CONTEST WINNER)

At the Title screen, press Right, Down, Left, Up, Left Bumper, Right Bumper, Y, Y, X, X, Start.

EUROGAMER CHALLENGE ROOM:

At the Title screen, press Down, Up, Down, Up, Left, Left Bumper, X, Left Bumper, X, Y, Start.

GAMESRADAR CHALLENGE ROOM:

At the Title screen, press Right Bumper, Y, X, X, Up, Down, Left Bumper, Left Bumper, Up, Down, Start.

IGN CHALLENGE ROOM:

At the Title screen, press Up, Down, Y, X, X, Y, Down, Up, Left Bumper, Left Bumper, Start.

MAJOR NELSON CHALLENGE ROOM

At the Title screen, press Left Bumper, X, X, X, Right, Down, Left Bumper, Left, Y, Down, Start.

BLAZING ANGELS: SQUADRONS OF WWII

ALL MISSIONS, MEDALS, & PLANES

At the Main menu hold Left Trigger + Right Trigger and press X, Left Bumper, Right Bumper, Y, Y, Right Bumper, Left Bumper, X.

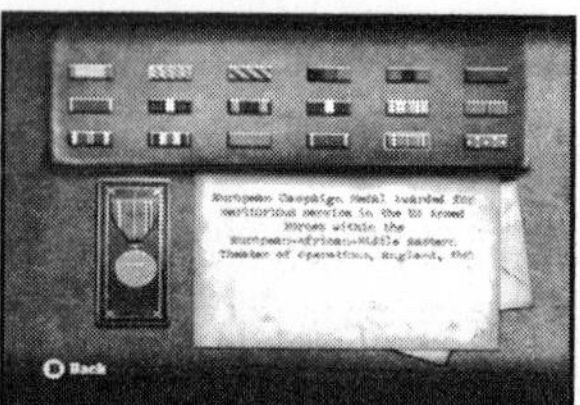

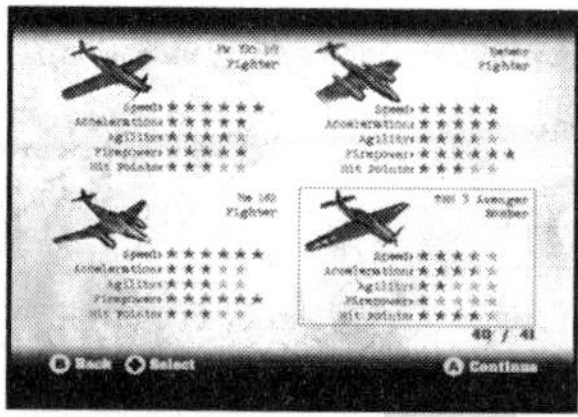

GOD MODE

Pause the game, hold Left Trigger and press X, Y, Y, X. Release Left Trigger, hold Right Trigger and press Y, X, X, Y. Re-enter the code to disable it.

INCREASED DAMAGE

Pause the game, hold Left Trigger and press Left Bumper, Left Bumper, Right Bumper. Release Left Trigger, hold Right Trigger and press Right Bumper, Right Bumper, Left Bumper. Re-enter the code to disable it.

BLAZING ANGELS 2: SECRET MISSIONS OF WWII

Achievements are disabled when using these codes.

ALL MISSIONS AND PLANES UNLOCKED

At the Main menu, hold Left Trigger + Right Trigger, and press X, Left Bumper, Right Bumper, Y, Y, Right Bumper, Left Bumper, X.

GOD MODE

Pause the game, hold Left Trigger, and press X, Y, Y, X. Release Left Trigger, hold Right Trigger and press Y, X, X, Y. Re-enter the code to disable it.

INCREASED DAMAGE WITH ALL WEAPONS

Pause the game, hold Left Trigger, and press Left Bumper, Left Bumper, Right Bumper. Release Left Trigger, hold Right Trigger, and press Right Bumper, Right Bumper, Left Bumper. Re-enter the code to disable it.

BLITZ: THE LEAGUE

The following codes work for Quick Play mode:

UNLIMITED UNLEASH

Select Codes from Extras and enter BIGDOGS.

STAMINA OFF

Select Codes from Extras and enter NOTTIRED.

DOUBLE UNLEASH ICONS

Select Codes from Extras and enter PIPPED.

UNLIMITED CLASH ICONS

Select Codes from Extras and enter CLASHY.

TWO PLAYER CO-OP

Select Codes from Extras and enter CHUWAY.

BALL TRAIL ALWAYS ON

Select Codes from Extras and enter ONFIRE.

BEACH BALL

Select Codes from Extras and enter BOUNCY.

BLITZ: THE LEAGUE II

TOUCHDOWN CELEBRATIONS

Press these button combinations when given the chance after scoring a touchdown

CELEBRATION	CODE
Ball Spike	A, A, A, B
Beer Chug	A, A, B, B
Dance Fever	Y, Y, Y, A
Get Down	B, A, B, Y
Golf Putt	A, X, Y, B
Helmet Fling	A, X, A, X
Knockout	X, X, Y, Y
Man Crush	X, X, X, Y
Nut Shot	Y, Y, B, A
Pylon Darts	A, B, A, B
The Pooper	Y, X, A, B

BROTHERS IN ARMS: HELL'S HIGHWAY

ALL CHAPTERS

Select Enter Codes from the Options and enter GIMMECHAPTERS.

ALL RECON POINTS

Select Enter Codes from the Options and enter 0ZNDRBICRA.

KILROY DETECTOR

Select Enter Codes from the Options and enter SH2VYIVNZF.

TWO MULTIPLAYER SKINS

Select Enter Codes from the Options and enter HI9WTPXSUK.

BULLY: SCHOLARSHIP EDITION

FULL HEALTH

During a game and with a second controller, hold Left Bumper and press Right Trigger, Right Trigger, Right Trigger.

MONEY

During a game and with a second controller, hold Left Bumper and press Y, X, B, A.

INFINITE AMMO

During a game and with a second controller, hold Left Bumper and press Up, Down, Up, Down. Re-enter code to disable.

ALL WEAPONS

During a game and with a second controller, hold Left Bumper and press Up, Up, Up, Up.

ALL GYM GRAPPLE MOVES

During a game and with a second controller, hold Left Bumper and press Up, Left, Down, Down, Y, X, A, A.

ALL HOBO MOVES

During a game and with a second controller, hold Left Bumper and press Up, Left, Down, Right, Y, X, A, B

BURNOUT PARADISE

BEST BUY CAR

Pause the game and select Sponsor Product Code from the Under the Hood menu. Enter Bestbuy. Need A License to use this car offline.

CIRCUIT CITY CAR

Pause the game and select Sponsor Product Code from the Under the Hood menu. Enter Circuitcity. Need Burnout Paradise License to use this car offline.

GAMESTOP CAR

Pause the game and select Sponsor Product Code from the Under the Hood menu. Enter Gamestop. Need A License to use this car offline.

WALMART CAR

Pause the game and select Sponsor Product Code from the Under the Hood menu. Enter Walmart. Need Burnout Paradise License to use this car offline.

"STEEL WHEELS" GT

Pause the game and select Sponsor Product Code from the Under the Hood menu. Enter G23X 5K8Q GX2V 04B1 or E60J 8Z7T MS8L 51U6.

LICENSES

LICENSE	NUMBER OF WINS NEEDED
D	2
C	7
B	16
A	26
Burnout Paradise	45
Elite License	All events

CABELA'S DANGEROUS HUNTS 2009

.470 NITRO EXPRESS HIGH CALIBER RIFLE

Select Enter Special Code from the Extras menu and enter 101987.

CALL OF DUTY 3

ALL CHAPTERS AND BONUS CONTENT

At the Chapter Select screen, hold Back and press Right, Right, Left, Left, X, X.

CALL OF DUTY 4: MODERN WARFARE

ARCADE MODE

After a complete playthrough of the game, Arcade Mode becomes available from the Main menu.

UNLOCKABLE CHEATS

After completing the game, cheats are unlocked based on how many intelligence pieces were gathered. These cheats cannot be used during Arcade Mode. They may also disable the ability to earn Achievements.

CHEAT	INTEL ITEMS	DESCRIPTION
CoD Noir	2	Black and white
Photo-Negative	4	Inverses colors
Super Contrast	6	Increases contrast
Ragtime Warfare	8	Black and white, scratches fill screen, double speed, piano music
Cluster Bombs	10	Four extra grenade explosions after frag grenade explodes
A Bad Year	15	Enemies explode into a bunch of old tires when killed
Slow-Mo Ability	20	Melee button enables/disables slow-motion mode
Infinite Ammo	30	Unlimited ammo and no need to reload. Doesn't work for single-shot weapons such as RPG.

CARS

UNLOCK EVERYTHING
Select Cheat Codes from the Options and enter IF900HP.

ALL CHARACTERS
Select Cheat Codes from the Options and enter YAYCARS.

ALL CHARACTER SKINS
Select Cheat Codes from the Options and enter R4MONE.

ALL MINI-GAMES AND COURSES
Select Cheat Codes from the Options and enter MATTL66.

FAST START
Select Cheat Codes from the Options and enter IMSPEED.

INFINITE BOOST
Select Cheat Codes from the Options and enter VROOOOM.

ART
Select Cheat Codes from the Options and enter CONC3PT.

VIDEOS
Select Cheat Codes from the Options and enter WATCHIT.

CARS MATER-NATIONAL

ALL ARCADE RACES, MINI-GAMES, AND WORLDS
Select Codes/Cheats from the options and enter PLAYALL.

ALL CARS
Select Codes/Cheats from the options and enter MATTEL07.

ALTERNATE LIGHTNING MCQUEEN COLORS
Select Codes/Cheats from the options and enter NCEDUDZ.

ALL COLORS FOR OTHERS
Select Codes/Cheats from the options and enter PAINTIT.

UNLIMITED TURBO
Select Codes/Cheats from the options and enter ZZOOOOM.

EXTREME ACCELERATION
Select Codes/Cheats from the options and enter 0TO200X.

EXPERT MODE
Select Codes/Cheats from the options and enter VRYFAST.

ALL BONUS ART
Select Codes/Cheats from the options and enter BUYTALL.

CASTLEVANIA: SYMPHONY OF THE NIGHT

Before using the following codes, complete the game with 170%.

PLAY AS RICHTER BELMONT
Enter RICHTER as your name.

ALUCARD WITH AXELORD ARMOR
Enter AXEARMOR as your name.

ALUCARD WITH 99 LUCK AND OTHER STATS ARE LOW
Enter X-X!V"Q as your name.

CONDEMNED: CRIMINAL ORIGINS

ALL LEVELS
Enter ShovelFighter as a profile name.

CONDEMNED 2: BLOODSHOT

ALL BONUS ART

Create a profile with the name ShovelFighter. Use this profile to start a game and all of the bonus art is unlocked.

CRASH BANDICOOT: MIND OVER MUTANT

A cheat can be deactivated by re-entering the code.

FREEZE ENEMIES WITH TOUCH

Pause the game, hold Right Trigger and press Down, Down, Down, Up.

ENEMIES DROP X4 DAMAGE

Pause the game, hold Right Trigger and press Up, Up, Up, Left.

ENEMIES DROP PURPLE FRUIT

Pause the game, hold Right Trigger and press Up, Down, Down, Up.

ENEMIES DROP SUPER KICK

Pause the game, hold Right Trigger and press Up, Right, Down, Left.

ENEMIES DROP WUMPA FRUIT

Pause the game, hold Right Trigger and press Right, Right, Right, Up.

SHADOW CRASH

Pause the game, hold Right Trigger and press Left, Right, Left, Right.

DEFORMED CRASH

Pause the game, hold Right Trigger and press Left, Left, Left, Down.

CRASH OF THE TITANS

BIG HEAD CRASH

Pause the game, hold the Right Trigger, and press X, X, Y, A.

SHADOW CRASH

Pause the game, hold the Right Trigger, and press Y, X, Y, A.

DARK MESSIAH OF MIGHT AND MAGIC: ELEMENTS

EXCLUSIVE MAP

Select Exclusive content from the Main menu. Select Exclusivity code and enter 5684219998871395. You can access it through Aranthir's office, in chapter 8.

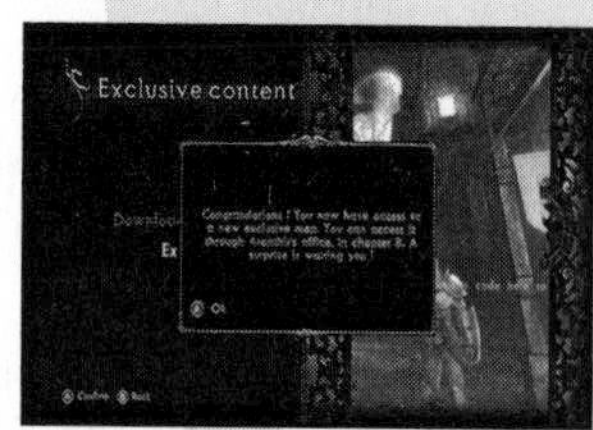

THE DARKNESS

DARKLING OUTFITS

Even Darklings can make a fashion statement. Support your mini minions with an ensemble fit for murderous monsters by collecting these fun and colorful outfits.

OUTFIT	MENTIONED IN	AREA	LOCATION
Potato Sack	Chapter 1	Chinatown	Sitting against alley wall near metro exit
Jungle	Chapter 1	Hunters Point Alley	Inside hidden room
Roadworker	Chapter 3	City Hall station	Inside train car
Lumberjack	Side Objectives	Cutrone objective	Inside Cutrone's apartment
Fireman	Side Objectives	Pajamas objective	Inside room 261
Construction	Side Objectives	Mortarello objective	Inside room of last mission
Baseball	N/A	Dial: 555-4263	N/A
Golfshirt	N/A	Dial: 555-5664	N/A

PHONE NUMBERS

Dialing 'D' for Darkness isn't the only number to punch on a telephone. Sure, you called every number you found on those hard-to-get Collectibles, but you certainly haven't found *all* of the phone numbers. Pay close to attention to the environment as you hunt down Uncle Paulie. Chances are, you overlooked a phone number or two without even knowing it as you ripped out a goon's heart. All 25 'secret' phone numbers are scattered throughout New York and can be seen on anywhere from flyers and storefronts to garbage cans and posters. Dial 18 of the 25 numbers on a phone—in no specific order—to unlock the final secret of the game.

PHONE NUMBERS

555-6118	555-1847	555-6667	555-4569
555-9985	555-1037	555-1206	555-9528
555-3285	555-5723	555-8024	555-6322
555-9132	555-6893	555-2402	555-6557
555-2309	555-4372	555-9723	555-5289
555-6205	555-7658	555-1233	555-3947
555-9562	555-7934	555-7892	555-8930
555-3243	555-3840	555-2349	555-6325
555-4565	555-9898	555-7613	555-6969

DEAD SPACE

REFILL STASIS AND KINESIS ENERGY

Pause the game and press X, Y, Y, X, Y.

REFILL OXYGEN

Pause the game and press X, X, Y (x3).

ADD 2 POWER NODES

Pause the game and press Y, X (x3), Y. This code can only be used once.

ADD 5 POWER NODES

Pause the game and press Y, X, Y, X, X, Y, X, X, Y, X, X, Y. This code can only be used once.

1,000 CREDITS

Pause the game and press X (x3), Y, X. This code can only be used once.

2,000 CREDITS

Pause the game and press X (x3), Y, Y. This code can only be used once.

5,000 CREDITS

Pause the game and press X (x3), Y, X, Y. This code can only be used once.

10,000 CREDITS

Pause the game and press X, Y (x3), X, X, Y. This code can only be used once.

DEF JAM: ICON

IT'S GOING DOWN BY YUNG JOC

At the Title Screen, after "Press Start Button" appears, press Down, B, A, Right.

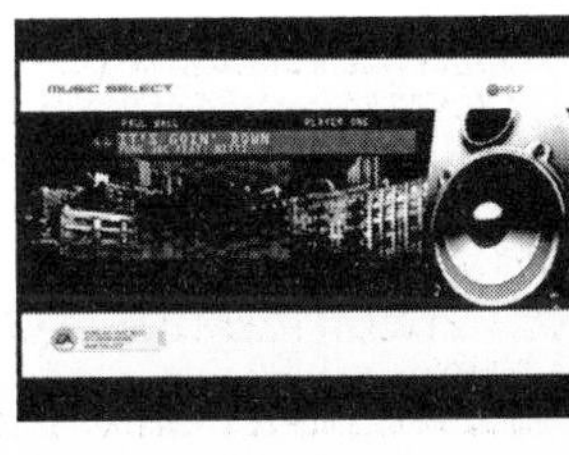

MAKE IT RAIN BY FAT JOE AND FIGHT AS FAT JOE

At the Title Screen, after "Press Start Button" appears, press B, Up, Right, Left, Y.

DESTROY ALL HUMANS! PATH OF THE FURON

After entering the following codes, select Customize from the Options to activate them.

60'S APPEARANCE

Select Unlock Content from Extras and enter M13Ni95L.

70'S APPEARANCE

Select Unlock Content from Extras and enter S63bf2kd.

BIKER OUTFIT

Select Unlock Content from Extras and enter 1gb57M2x.

CHEF OUTFIT

Select Unlock Content from Extras and enter 51c24KiW.

GANGSTER OUTFIT

Select Unlock Content from Extras and enter J5d99bPz.

KUNG FU OUTFIT

Select Unlock Content from Extras and enter Ly11r98H.

MIME OUTFIT

Select Unlock Content from Extras and enter 7qd33J1n.

VELVET OUTFIT

Select Unlock Content from Extras and enter F9sT5v88.

SAUCER ATTACHMENTS

Select Unlock Content from Extras and enter V81fvUW3.

SAUCER SKINS

Select Unlock Content from Extras and enter X91mw7zp.

DON KING PRESENTS: PRIZEFIGHTER

UNLOCK RICARDO MAYORGA

Select Enter Unlock Code from the Extras menu and enter potsemag.

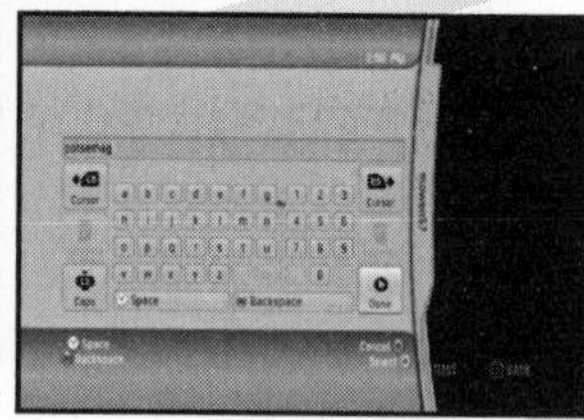

EXCLUSIVE BEST BUY FIGHT FOOTAGE

Select Enter Unlock Code from the Extras menu and enter 1bestbuybest. Select Watch Videos from the Extras menu to find video.

EAT LEAD: THE RETURN OF MATT HAZARD

MAXIMUM HAZARD DIFFICULTY

At the difficulty select, press Up, Up, Down, Down, Left, Right, Left, Right.

ERAGON

FURY MODE

Pause the game, hold Left Bumper + Right Bumper + Left Trigger + Right Trigger and press X, X, B, B.

EVERY EXTEND EXTRA EXTREME

FINE ADJUSTMENT MENU

At the Start screen, press Left Bumper, Right Bumper, Left Bumper, Right Bumper, Left Bumper, Right Bumper, Left Bumper, Right Bumper.

FAR CRY INSTINCTS PREDATOR

EVOLUTION GAME

Select the Cheat menu option from the Main menu or the pause menu and enter GiveMeltAll.

HEAL

Select the Cheat menu option from the Main menu or the pause menu and enter ImJackCarver.

INFINITE ADRENALINE

Select the Cheat menu option from the Main menu or the pause menu and enter Bloodlust.

INFINITE AMMO

Select the Cheat menu option from the Main menu or the pause menu and enter UnleashHell.

ENABLE EVOLUTIONS

Select the Cheat menu option from the Main menu or the pause menu and enter FeralAttack.

ALL MAPS

Select the Cheat menu option from the Main menu or the pause menu and enter GiveMeTheMaps.

FAR CRY 2

BONUS MISSIONS

Select Promotional Content from the Additional Content menu and enter the following codes. Each code gives four or six extra missions.

6aPHuswe
Cr34ufrE
2Eprunef
JeM8SpaW
tr99pUkA

FATAL FURY SPECIAL

CHEAT MENU

During a game, hold Start and push A + X + Y.

F.E.A.R.

ALL MISSIONS

Sign in with F3ARDAY1 as your Profile Name. Using this cheat will disable Achievements.

XBOX 360

FIGHT NIGHT ROUND 3

ALL VENUES

Create a champ with a first name of NEWVIEW.

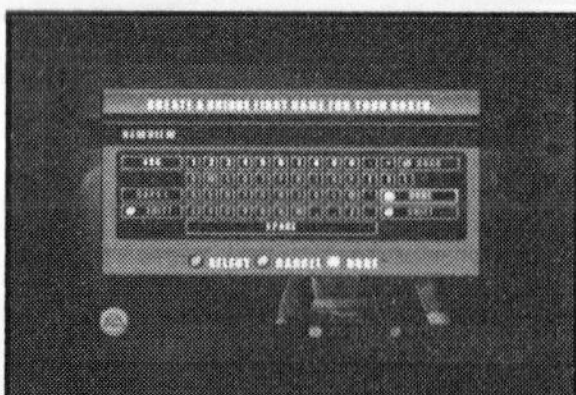

FLATOUT: ULTIMATE CARNAGE

MOB CAR IN SINGLE EVENTS

Select Enter Code from Extras and enter BIGTRUCK.

PIMPSTER IN SINGLE EVENTS

Select Enter Code from Extras and enter RUTTO.

ROCKET IN SINGLE EVENTS

Select Enter Code from Extras and enter KALJAKOPPA.

FRACTURE

EXCLUSIVE PRE-ORDER SKIN

Pause the game and press Up, Right, Left, Down, Up, Left, Right, Down.

FROGGER

BIG FROGGER

At the One/Two-Player screen, press Up, Up, Down, Down, Left, Right, Left, Right, B, A.

FULL AUTO

ALL TRACKS, VEHICLES, & WEAPONS

Create a new profile with the name magicman.

OVERLOAD

THE GODFATHER: THE GAME

FULL AMMO
Pause the game and press Y, Left, Y, Right, X, Right Thumbstick.

FULL HEALTH
Pause the game and press Left, X, Right, Y, Right, Left Thumbstick.

UNLOCK ENTIRE FILM ARCHIVE
After loading a game and before joining the family, press Y, X, Y, X, X, Left Thumbstick. Select Film Archive to view the films.

THE GODFATHER II

These codes can only be used once every few minutes.

$5,000
While in Don view, press X, Y, X, X, Y, click Left Analog Stick.

FULL HEALTH
While in Don view, press Left, X, Right, Y, Right, click Left Analog Stick.

FULL AMMO
While in Don view, press Y, Left, Y, Right, X, click Right Analog Stick.

GRAND THEFT AUTO IV

CHEATS
Call the following phone numbers with Niko's phone to activate the cheats. Some cheats may affect the missions and achievements.

VEHICLE	PHONE NUMBER
Change weather	468-555-0100
Get weapons	486-555-0100
Get different weapons	486-555-0150
Raise wanted level	267-555-0150
Remove wanted level	267-555-0100
Restore armor	362-555-0100
Restore health	482-555-0100
Restore armor, health, and ammo	482-555-0100

SPAWN VEHICLES
Call the following phone numbers with Niko's phone to spawn the corresponding vehicle.

VEHICLE	PHONE NUMBER
Annihilator	359-555-0100
Cognoscenti	227-555-0142
Comet	227-555-0175
FIB Buffalo	227-555-0100
Jetmax	938-555-0100
NRG-900	625-555-0100
Sanchez	625-555-0150
SuperGT	227-555-0168
Turismo	227-555-0147

MAP LOCATIONS
Access a computer in game and enter the following URL: www.whattheydonotwantyoutoknow.com.

GRID

ALL DRIFT CARS

Select Bonus Codes from the Options. Then choose Enter Code and enter TUN58396.

ALL MUSCLE CARS

Select Bonus Codes from the Options. Then choose Enter Code and enter MUS59279.

BUCHBINDER EMOTIONAL ENGINEERING BMW 320SI

Select Bonus Codes from the Options. Then choose Enter Code and enter F93857372. You can use this in Race Day or in GRID World once you've started your own team.

EBAY

Select Bonus Codes from the Options. Then choose Enter Code and enter DAFJ55E01473M0. You can use this in Race Day or in GRID World once you've started your own team.

GAMESTATION BMW 320SI

Select Bonus Codes from the Options. Then choose Enter Code and enter G29782655. You can use this in Race Day or in GRID World once you've started your own team.

MICROMANIA PAGANI ZONDA R

Select Bonus Codes from the Options. Then choose Enter Code and enter M38572343. You can use this in Race Day or in GRID World once you've started your own team.

PLAY.COM ASTON MARTIN DBR9

Select Bonus Codes from the Options. Then choose Enter Code and enter P47203845. You can use this in Race Day or in GRID World once you've started your own team.

GRAND THEFT AUTO IV: THE LOST AND DAMNED

CHEATS

Call the following phone numbers with your phone to activate the cheats. Some cheats may affect the missions and achievements.

BONUS	PHONE NUMBER
Get weapons	486-555-0100
Get different weapons	486-555-0150
Raise wanted level	267-555-0150
Remove wanted level	267-555-0100
Restore armor	362-555-0100
Restore armor, health, and ammo	482-555-0100

SPAWN VEHICLES

Call the following phone numbers with your phone to spawn the corresponding vehicle.

VEHICLE	PHONE NUMBER
Annihilator	359-555-0100
Burrito	826-555-0150
Double T	245-555-0125
FIB Buffalo	227-555-0100
Hakuchou	245-555-0199
Hexer	245-555-0150
Innovation	245-555-0100
Slamvan	826-555-0100

GUITAR HERO II

ALL SONGS
At the Main menu, press Blue, Yellow, Orange, Red, Yellow, Orange, Blue, Yellow, Blue, Yellow, Blue, Yellow, Blue, Yellow, Blue, Yellow.

HYPER SPEED
At the Main menu, press Blue, Orange, Yellow, Orange, Blue, Orange, Yellow, Yellow.

PERFORMANCE MODE
At the Main menu, press Blue, Blue, Yellow, Blue, Blue, Orange, Blue, Blue.

AIR GUITAR
At the Main menu, press Yellow, Blue, Yellow, Orange, Yellow, Blue.

EYEBALL HEAD CROWD
At the Main menu, press Yellow, Orange, Blue, Blue, Blue, Orange, Yellow.

MONKEY HEAD CROWD
At the Main menu, press Orange, Yellow, Blue, Blue, Yellow, Orange, Blue, Blue.

FLAME HEAD
At the Main menu, press Orange, Yellow, Yellow, Orange, Yellow, Yellow, Orange, Yellow, Yellow, Blue, Yellow, Yellow, Blue, Yellow, Yellow.

GUITAR HERO III: LEGENDS OF ROCK

To enter the following cheats, strum the guitar with the given buttons held. For example, if it says Yellow + Orange, hold Yellow and Orange as you strum. Air Guitar, Precision Mode, and Performance Mode can be toggled on and off from the Cheats menu. You can also change between five different levels of Hyperspeed at this menu.

UNLOCK EVERYTHING
Select Cheats from the Options. Choose Enter Cheat and enter Green + Red + Blue + Orange, Green + Red + Yellow + Blue, Green + Red + Yellow + Orange, Green + Yellow + Blue + Orange, Green + Red + Yellow + Blue, Red + Yellow + Blue + Orange, Green + Red + Yellow + Blue, Green + Yellow + Blue + Orange, Green + Red + Yellow + Blue, Green + Red + Yellow + Orange, Green + Red + Yellow + Orange, Green + Red + Yellow + Blue, Green + Red + Yellow + Orange. No sounds play while this code is entered.

An easier way to show this code is by representing Green as 1 down to Orange as 5. For example, if you have 1345, you would hold down Green + Yellow + Blue + Orange while strumming. 1245 + 1234 + 1235 + 1345 + 1234 + 2345 + 1234 + 1345 + 1234 + 1235 + 1235 + 1234 + 1235.

ALL SONGS
Select Cheats from the Options. Choose Enter Cheat and enter Yellow + Orange, Red + Blue, Red + Orange, Green + Blue, Red + Yellow, Yellow + Orange, Red + Yellow, Red + Blue, Green + Yellow, Green + Yellow, Yellow + Blue, Yellow + Blue, Yellow + Orange, Yellow + Orange, Yellow + Blue, Yellow, Red, Red + Yellow, Red, Yellow, Orange.

NO FAIL
Select Cheats from the Options. Choose Enter Cheat and enter Green + Red, Blue, Green + Red, Green + Yellow, Blue, Green + Yellow, Red + Yellow, Orange, Red + Yellow, Green + Yellow, Yellow, Green + Yellow, Green + Red.

AIR GUITAR
Select Cheats from the Options. Choose Enter Cheat and enter Blue + Yellow, Green + Yellow, Green + Yellow, Red + Blue, Red + Blue, Red + Yellow, Red + Yellow, Blue + Yellow, Green + Yellow, Green + Yellow, Red + Blue, Red + Blue, Red + Yellow, Red + Yellow, Green + Yellow, Green + Yellow, Red + Yellow, Red + Yellow.

HYPERSPEED
Select Cheats from the Options. Choose Enter Cheat and enter Orange, Blue, Orange, Yellow, Orange, Blue, Orange, Yellow.

Red, Green + Red, Green + Red, Red + Yellow, Red + Yellow, Red + Blue, Red + Blue, Yellow + Blue, Yellow + Orange, Yellow + Orange.

PERFORMANCE MODE

Select Cheats from the Options. Choose Enter Cheat and enter Red + Yellow, Red + Blue, Red + Orange, Red + Blue, Red + Yellow, Green + Blue, Red + Yellow, Red + Blue.

EASY EXPERT

Select Cheats from the Options. Choose Enter Cheat and enter Green + Red, Green + Yellow, Yellow + Blue, Red + Blue, Blue + Orange, Yellow + Orange, Red + Yellow, Red + Blue.

PRECISION MODE

Select Cheats from the Options. Choose Enter Cheat and enter Green + Red, Green + Red, Green + Red, Red + Yellow, Red + Yellow, Red + Blue, Red + Blue, Yellow + Blue, Yellow + Orange, Yellow + Orange, Green + Red, Green + Red, Green + Red, Red + Yellow, Red + Yellow, Red + Blue, Red + Blue, Yellow + Blue, Yellow + Orange, Yellow + Orange.

BRET MICHAELS SINGER

Select Cheats from the Options. Choose Enter Cheat and enter Green + Red, Green + Red, Green + Red, Green + Blue, Green + Blue, Green + Blue, Red + Blue, Red, Red, Red, Red + Blue, Red, Red, Red, Red + Blue, Red, Red, Red.

GUITAR HERO: AEROSMITH

To enter the following cheats, strum the guitar with the given buttons held. For example, if it says Yellow + Orange, hold Yellow and Orange as you strum. Air Guitar, Precision Mode, and Performance Mode can be toggled on and off from the Cheats menu. You can also change between five different levels of Hyperspeed at this menu.

ALL SONGS

Red + Yellow, Green + Red, Green + Red, Red + Yellow, Red + Yellow, Green + Red, Red + Yellow, Red + Yellow, Green + Red, Green + Red, Red + Yellow, Red + Yellow, Green + Red, Red + Yellow, Red + Blue.

AIR GUITAR

Red + Yellow, Green + Red, Red + Yellow, Red + Yellow, Red + Blue, Red + Blue, Red + Blue, Red + Blue, Red + Blue, Yellow + Blue, Yellow + Blue, Yellow + Orange

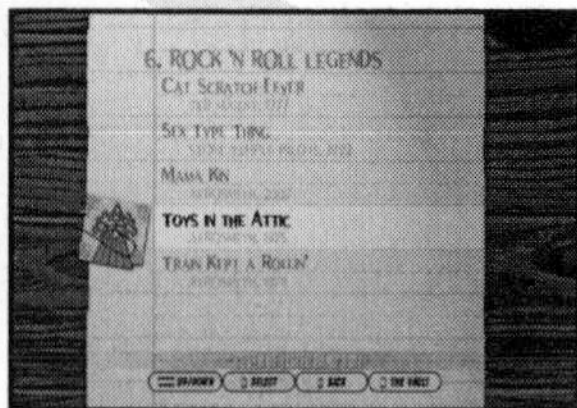

HYPERSPEED

Yellow + Orange, Yellow + Orange, Yellow + Orange, Yellow + Orange, Yellow + Orange, Red + Yellow, Red + Yellow, Red + Yellow, Red + Yellow, Red + Blue, Red + Blue, Red + Blue, Red + Blue, Red + Blue, Yellow + Blue, Yellow + Orange, Yellow + Orange.

NO FAIL

Select Cheats from the Options. Choose Enter Cheat and enter Green + Red, Blue, Green + Red, Green + Yellow, Blue, Green + Yellow, Red + Yellow, Orange, Red + Yellow, Green + Yellow, Yellow, Green + Yellow, Green + Red.

PERFORMANCE MODE

Green + Red, Green + Red, Red + Orange, Red + Blue, Green + Red, Green + Red, Red + Orange, Red + Blue

PRECISION MODE

Red + Yellow, Red + Blue, Red + Blue, Red + Yellow, Red + Yellow, Yellow + Blue, Yellow + Blue, Yellow + Blue, Red + Blue, Red + Yellow, Red + Blue, Red + Blue, Red + Yellow, Red + Yellow, Yellow + Blue, Yellow + Blue, Yellow + Blue, Red + Blue.

GUITAR HERO: METALLICA

Once entered, the cheats must be activated in the Cheats menu.

METALLICA COSTUMES

Select Cheats from Settings and enter Green, Red, Yellow, Blue, Blue, Yellow, Red, Green.

HYPERSPEED

Select Cheats from Settings and enter Green, Blue, Red, Yellow, Yellow, Red, Green, Green.

PERFORMANCE MODE

Select Cheats from Settings and enter Yellow, Yellow, Blue, Red, Blue, Green, Red, Red.

INVISIBLE ROCKER

Select Cheats from Settings and enter Green, Red, Yellow (x3), Blue, Blue, Green.

AIR INSTRUMENTS

Select Cheats from Settings and enter Red, Red, Blue, Yellow, Green (x3), Yellow.

ALWAYS DRUM FILL

Select Cheats from Settings and enter Red (x3), Blue, Blue, Green, Green, Yellow.

AUTO KICK

Select Cheats from Settings and enter Yellow, Green, Red, Blue (x4), Red. With this cheat activated, the bass pedal is automatically hit.

ALWAYS SLIDE

Select Cheats from Settings and enter Green, Green, Red, Red, Yellow, Red, Yellow, Blue. All Guitar Notes Become Touch Pad Sliding Notes.

BLACK HIGHWAY

Select Cheats from Settings and enter Yellow, Red, Green, Red, Green, Red, Red, Blue.

FLAME COLOR

Select Cheats from Settings and enter Green, Red, Green, Blue, Red, Red, Yellow, Blue.

GEM COLOR

Select Cheats from Settings and enter Blue, Red, Red, Green, Red, Green, Red, Yellow.

STAR COLOR

Select Cheats from Settings and enter Press Red, Red, Yellow, Red, Blue, Red, Red, Blue.

ADDITIONAL LINE 6 TONES

Select Cheats from Settings and enter Green, Red, Yellow, Blue, Red, Yellow, Blue, Green.

VOCAL FIREBALL

Select Cheats from Settings and enter Red, Green, Green, Yellow, Blue, Green, Yellow, Green.

GUITAR HERO WORLD TOUR

The following cheats can be toggled on and off at the Cheats menu.

QUICKPLAY SONGS

Select Cheats from the Options menu, choose Enter New Cheat and press Blue, Blue, Red, Green, Green, Blue, Blue, Yellow.

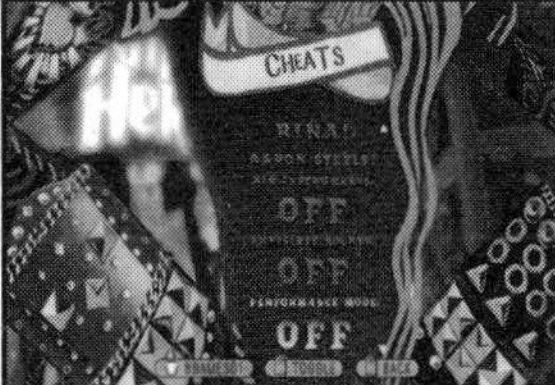

ALWAYS SLIDE

Select Cheats from the Options menu, choose Enter New Cheat and press Green, Green, Red, Red, Yellow, Red, Yellow, Blue.

AT&T BALLPARK

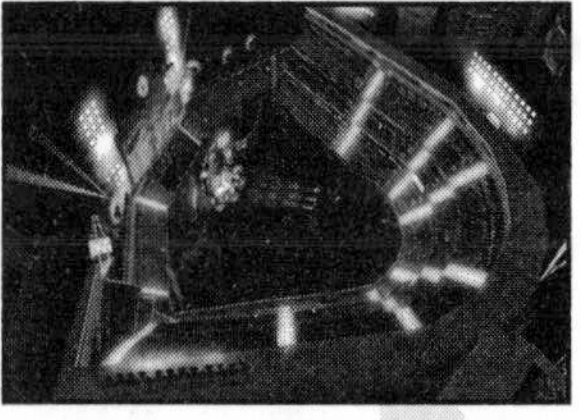

Select Cheats from the Options menu, choose Enter New Cheat and press Yellow, Green, Red, Red, Green, Blue, Red, Yellow.

AUTO KICK

Select Cheats from the Options menu, choose Enter New Cheat and press Yellow, Green, Red, Blue (x4), Red.

EXTRA LINE 6 TONES

Select Cheats from the Options menu, choose Enter New Cheat and press Green, Red, Yellow, Blue, Red, Yellow, Blue, Green.

FLAME COLOR

Select Cheats from the Options menu, choose Enter New Cheat and press Green, Red, Green, Blue, Red, Red, Yellow, Blue.

GEM COLOR

Select Cheats from the Options menu, choose Enter New Cheat and press Blue, Red, Red, Green, Red, Green, Red, Yellow.

STAR COLOR

Select Cheats from the Options menu, choose Enter New Cheat and press Red, Red, Yellow, Red, Blue, Red, Red, Blue.

AIR INSTRUMENTS

Select Cheats from the Options menu, choose Enter New Cheat and press Red, Red, Blue, Yellow, Green (x3), Yellow.

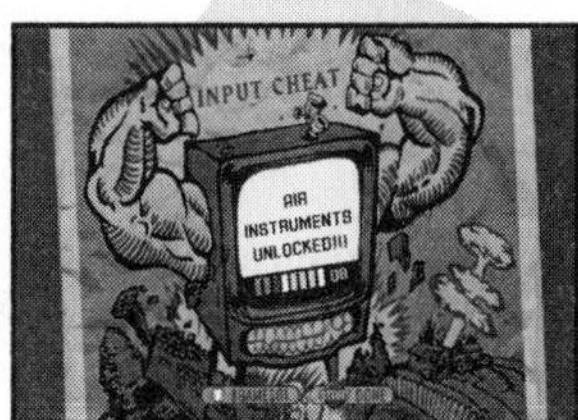

HYPERSPEED

Select Cheats from the Options menu, choose Enter New Cheat and press Green, Blue, Red, Yellow, Yellow, Red, Green, Green. These show up in the menu as HyperGuitar, HyperBass, and HyperDrums.

PERFORMANCE MODE

Select Cheats from the Options menu, choose Enter New Cheat and press Yellow, Yellow, Blue, Red, Blue, Green, Red, Red.

INVISIBLE ROCKER

Select Cheats from the Options menu, choose Enter New Cheat and press Green, Red, Yellow (x3), Blue, Blue, Green.

VOCAL FIREBALL

Select Cheats from the Options menu, choose Enter New Cheat and press Red, Green, Green, Yellow, Blue, Green, Yellow, Green.

AARON STEELE!

Select Cheats from the Options menu, choose Enter New Cheat and press Blue, Red, Yellow (x5), Green.

JONNY VIPER

Select Cheats from the Options menu, choose Enter New Cheat and press Blue, Red, Blue, Blue, Yellow (x3), Green.

NICK

Select Cheats from the Options menu, choose Enter New Cheat and press Green, Red, Blue, Green, Red, Blue, Blue, Green.

RINA
Select Cheats from the Options menu, choose Enter New Cheat and press Blue, Red, Green, Green, Yellow (x3), Green.

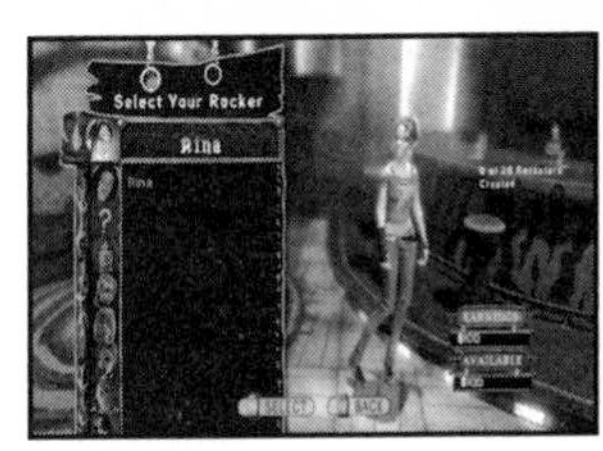

HALO 3

TOGGLE HIDE WEAPON
During a local game, hold Left Bumper + Right Bumper + Left Stick + A + Down.

TOGGLE SHOW COORDINATES
During a local game, hold Left Bumper + Right Bumper + Left Stick + A + Up.

TOGGLE BETWEEN PAN-CAM AND NORMAL
During a local game, hold Left Stick + Right Stick and press Left when Show Coordinates is active.

IDOLMASTER: LIVE FOR YOU!

MAMI
At the character select, press R3 while on Ami.

SHORT-HAIRED MIKI
At the character select, press R3 while on Miki.

IRON MAN

CLASSIC ARMOR
Clear One Man Army vs. Mercs.

EXTREMIS ARMOR
Clear One Man Army vs. Maggia.

MARK II ARMOR
Clear One Man Army vs. Ten Rings.

HULKBUSTER ARMOR
Clear One Man Army vs. AIM-X. Can also be unlocked when clear game save data from Incredible Hulk is stored on the same console.

SILVER CENTURION ARMOR
Clear Mission 13: Showdown.

CLASSIC MARK I ARMOR
Clear One Man Army vs. AIM.

JUICED 2: HOT IMPORT NIGHTS

HIDDEN CHALLENGE AND AN AUDI TT 1.8 QUATTRO
Select Cheats and Codes from the DNA Lab menu and enter YTHZ. Defeat the challenge to earn the Audi TT 1.8 Quattro.

HIDDEN CHALLENGE AND A BMW Z4
Select Cheats and Codes from the DNA Lab menu and enter GVDL. Defeat the challenge to earn the BMW Z4.

HIDDEN CHALLENGE AND A HOLDEN MONARO
Select Cheats and Codes from the DNA Lab menu and enter RBSG. Defeat the challenge to earn the Holden Monaro.

HIDDEN CHALLENGE AND A HYUNDAI COUPE 2.7 V6
Select Cheats and Codes from the DNA Lab menu and enter BSLU. Defeat the challenge to earn the Hyundai Coupe 2.7 V6.

HIDDEN CHALLENGE AND AN INFINITY G35
Select Cheats and Codes from the DNA Lab menu and enter MRHC. Defeat the challenge to earn the Infinity G35.

HIDDEN CHALLENGE AND A KOENIGSEGG CCX
Select Cheats and Codes from the DNA Lab menu and enter KDTR. Defeat the challenge to earn the Koenigsegg CCX.

HIDDEN CHALLENGE AND A MITSUBISHI PROTOTYPE X

Select Cheats and Codes from the DNA Lab menu and enter DOPX. Defeat the challenge to earn the Mitsubishi Prototype X.

HIDDEN CHALLENGE AND A NISSAN 350Z

Select Cheats and Codes from the DNA Lab menu and enter PRGN. Defeat the challenge to earn the Nissan 350Z.

HIDDEN CHALLENGE AND A NISSAN SKYLINE R34 GT-R

Select Cheats and Codes from the DNA Lab menu and enter JWRS. Defeat the challenge to earn the Nissan Skyline R34 GT-R.

HIDDEN CHALLENGE AND A SALEEN S7

Select Cheats and Codes from the DNA Lab menu and enter WIKF. Defeat the challenge to earn the Saleen S7.

HIDDEN CHALLENGE AND A SEAT LEON CUPRA R

Select Cheats and Codes from the DNA Lab menu and enter FAMQ. Defeat the challenge to earn the Seat Leon Cupra R.

KUNG FU PANDA

INFINITE CHI

Select Cheats from the Extra menu and press Down, Right, Left, Up, Down.

INVINCIBILITY

Select Cheats from the Extra menu and press Down, Down, Right, Up, Left.

FULL UPGRADES

Select Cheats from the Extra menu and press Left, Right, Down, Left, Up.

4X DAMAGE MULTIPLAYER

Select Cheats from the Extra menu and press Up, Down, Up, Right, Left.

ALL MULTIPLAYER CHARACTERS

Select Cheats from the Extra menu and press Left, Down, Left, Right, Down.

DRAGON WARRIOR OUTFIT IN MULTIPLAYER

Select Cheats from the Extra menu and press Left, Down, Right, Left, Up.

ALL OUTFITS

Select Cheats from the Extra menu and press Right, Left, Down, Up, Right.

THE LEGEND OF SPYRO: DAWN OF THE DRAGON

UNLIMITED LIFE

Pause the game, hold Left Bumper and press Right, Right, Down, Down, Left with the Left Control Stick.

UNLIMITED MANA

Pause the game, hold Right Bumper and press Up, Right, Up, Left, Down with the Left Control Stick.

MAXIMUM XP

Pause the game, hold Right Bumper and press Up, Left, Left, Down, Up with the Left Control Stick.

ALL ELEMENTAL UPGRADES

Pause the game, hold Left Bumper and press Left, Up, Down, Up, Right with the Left Control Stick.

LEGENDS OF WRESTLEMANIA

ANIMAL'S SECOND COSTUME

Select Cheat Codes from the Options menu and enter TheRoadWarriorAnimal.

BRUTUS BEEFCAKE'S SECOND COSTUME

Select Cheat Codes from the Options menu and enter BrutusTheBarberShop!.

IRON SHIEK'S SECOND COSTUME

Select Cheat Codes from the Options menu and enter IronSheikCamelClutch.

JIMMY HART'S SECOND COSTUME

Select Cheat Codes from the Options menu and enter WithManagerJimmyHart.

KOKO B WARE'S SECOND COSTUME

Select Cheat Codes from the Options menu and enter TheBirdmanKokoBWare!.

THE ROCK'S SECOND COSTUME

Select Cheat Codes from the Options menu and enter UnlockTheRockBottom!.

SGT. SLAUGHTER'S SECOND COSTUME

Select Cheat Codes from the Options menu and enter CobraClutchSlaughter.

SHAWN MICHAEL'S SECOND COSTUME

Select Cheat Codes from the Options menu and enter ShawnsSweetChinMusic.

UNDERTAKER'S SECOND COSTUME

Select Cheat Codes from the Options menu and enter UndertakersTombstone.

LEGO BATMAN

BATCAVE CODES

Using the computer in the Batcave, select Enter Code and enter the following codes.

CHARACTERS

CHARACTER	CODE
Alfred	ZAQ637
Batgirl	JKR331
Bruce Wayne	BDJ327
Catwoman (Classic)	M1AAWW
Clown Goon	HJK327
Commissioner Gordon	DDP967
Fishmonger	HGY748
Freeze Girl	XVK541
Joker Goon	UTF782
Joker Henchman	YUN924
Mad Hatter	JCA283
Man-Bat	NYU942
Military Policeman	MKL382
Nightwing	MVY759
Penguin Goon	NKA238
Penguin Henchman	BJH782
Penguin Minion	KJP748
Poison Ivy Goon	GTB899

CHARACTER	CODE
Police Marksman	HKG984
Police Officer	JRY983
Riddler Goon	CRY928
Riddler Henchman	XEU824
S.W.A.T.	HTF114
Sailor	NAV592
Scientist	JFL786
Security Guard	PLB946
The Joker (Tropical)	CCB199
Yeti	NJL412
Zoo Sweeper	DWR243

VEHICLES

VEHICLE	CODE
Bat-Tank	KNTT4B
Bruce Wayne's Private Jet	LEA664
Catwoman's Motorcycle	HPL826
Garbage Truck	DUS483
Goon Helicopter	GCH328
Harbor Helicopter	CHP735
Harley Quinn's Hammer Truck	RDT637
Mad Hatter's Glider	HS000W
Mad Hatter's Steamboat	M4DM4N
Mr. Freeze's Iceberg	ICYICE
The Joker's Van	JUK657
Mr. Freeze's Kart	BCT229
Penguin Goon Submarine	BTN248
Police Bike	LJP234
Police Boat	PLC999
Police Car	KJL832
Police Helicopter	CWR732
Police Van	MAC788
Police Watercraft	VJD328
Riddler's Jet	HAHAHA
Robin's Submarine	TTF453
Two-Face's Armored Truck	EFE933

CHEATS

CHEAT	CODE
Always Score Multiply	9LRGNB
Fast Batarangs	JRBDCB
Fast Walk	ZOLM6N
Flame Batarang	D8NYWH
Freeze Batarang	XPN4NG
Extra Hearts	ML3KHP
Fast Build	EVG26J
Immune to Freeze	JXUDY6
Invincibility	WYD5CP
Minikit Detector	ZXGH9J
More Batarang Targets	XWP645
Piece Detector	KHJ554
Power Brick Detector	MMN786
Regenerate Hearts	HJH7HJ
Score x2	N4NR3E
Score x4	CX9MAT
Score x6	MLVNF2
Score x8	WCCDB9
Score x10	18HW07

LEGO INDIANA JONES: THE ORIGINAL ADVENTURES

CHARACTERS

Approach the blackboard in the Classroom and enter the following codes.

CHARACTER	CODE
Bandit	12N68W
Bandit Swordsman	1MK4RT
Barranca	04EM94
Bazooka Trooper (Crusade)	MK83R7
Bazooka Trooper (Raiders)	S93Y5R
Belloq	CHN3YU
Belloq (Jungle)	TDR197
Belloq (Robes)	VEO29L
British Commander	B73EUA
British Officer	VJ5TI9
British Soldier	DJ5I2W
Captain Katanga	VJ3TT3
Chatter Lal	ENW936
Chatter Lal (Thuggee)	CNH4RY
Chen	3NK48T
Colonel Dietrich	2K9RKS
Colonel Vogel	8EAL4H
Dancing Girl	C7EJ21
Donovan	3NFTU8
Elsa (Desert)	JSNRT9
Elsa (Officer)	VMJ5US
Enemy Boxer	8246RB
Enemy Butler	VJ48W3
Enemy Guard	VJ7R51
Enemy Guard (Mountains)	YR47WM
Enemy Officer	572E61
Enemy Officer (Desert	2MK45O
Enemy Pilot	B84ELP
Enemy Radio Operator	1MF94R
Enemy Soldier (Desert)	4NSU7Q
Fedora	V75YSP
First Mate	0GIN24
Grail Knight	NE6THI
Hovitos Tribesman	H0V1SS
Indiana Jones (Desert Disguise)	4J8S4M
Indiana Jones (Officer)	VJ85OS
Jungle Guide	24PF34
Kao Kan	WMO46L
Kazim	NRH23J
Kazim (Desert)	3M29TJ
Lao Che	2NK479
Maharajah	NFK5N2
Major Toht	13NS01
Masked Bandit	N48SF0
Mola Ram	FJUR31
Monkey Man	3RF6YJ
Pankot Assassin	2NKT72
Pankot Guard	VN28RH
Sherpa Brawler	VJ37WJ
Sherpa Gunner	ND762W
Slave Child	0E3ENW
Thuggee	VM683E
Thuggee Acolyte	T2R3F9
Thuggee Slave Driver	VBS7GW
Village Dignitary	KD48TN
Village Elder	4682E1
Willie (Dinner Suit)	VK93R7

CHARACTER	CODE
Willie (Pajamas)	MEN4IP
Wu Han	3NSLT8

EXTRAS

Approach the blackboard in the Classroom and enter the following codes. Some cheats need to be enabled by selecting Extras from the pause menu.

CHEAT	CODE
Artifact Detector	VIKED7
Beep Beep	VNF59Q
Character Treasure	VIES2R
Disarm Enemies	VKRNS9
Disguises	4ID1N6
Fast Build	V83SLO
Fast Dig	378RS6
Fast Fix	FJ59WS
Fertilizer	B1GW1F
Ice Rink	33GM7J
Parcel Detector	VUT673
Poo Treasure	WWQ1SA
Regenerate Hearts	MDLP69
Secret Characters	3X44AA
Silhouettes	3HE85H
Super Scream	VN3R7S
Super Slap	0P1TA5
Treasure Magnet	H86LA2
Treasure x10	VI3PS8
Treasure x2	VM4TS9
Treasure x4	VLWEN3
Treasure x6	V84RYS
Treasure x8	A72E1M

LEGO STAR WARS: THE COMPLETE SAGA

The following still need to be purchased after entering the codes.

CHARACTERS

ADMIRAL ACKBAR

At the bar in Mos Eisley Cantina, select Enter Code and enter ACK646.

BATTLE DROID (COMMANDER)

At the bar in Mos Eisley Cantina, select Enter Code and enter KPF958.

BOBA FETT (BOY)

At the bar in Mos Eisley Cantina, select Enter Code and enter GGF539.

BOSS NASS

At the bar in Mos Eisley Cantina, select Enter Code and enter HHY697.

CAPTAIN TARPALS

At the bar in Mos Eisley Cantina, select Enter Code and enter QRN714.

COUNT DOOKU

At the bar in Mos Eisley Cantina, select Enter Code and enter DDD748.

DARTH MAUL

At the bar in Mos Eisley Cantina, select Enter Code and enter EUK421.

EWOK

At the bar in Mos Eisley Cantina, select Enter Code and enter EWK785.

GENERAL GRIEVOUS

At the bar in Mos Eisley Cantina, select Enter Code and enter PMN576.

GREEDO

At the bar in Mos Eisley Cantina, select Enter Code and enter ZZR636.

IG-88

At the bar in Mos Eisley Cantina, select Enter Code and enter GIJ989.

IMPERIAL GUARD

At the bar in Mos Eisley Cantina, select Enter Code and enter GUA850.

JANGO FETT

At the bar in Mos Eisley Cantina, select Enter Code and enter KLJ897.

KI-ADI MUNDI

At the bar in Mos Eisley Cantina, select Enter Code and enter MUN486.

LUMINARA

At the bar in Mos Eisley Cantina, select Enter Code and enter LUM521.

PADMÉ

At the bar in Mos Eisley Cantina, select Enter Code and enter VBJ322.

R2-Q5
At the bar in Mos Eisley Cantina, select Enter Code and enter EVILR2.

STORMTROOPER
At the bar in Mos Eisley Cantina, select Enter Code and enter NBN431.

TAUN WE
At the bar in Mos Eisley Cantina, select Enter Code and enter PRX482.

VULTURE DROID
At the bar in Mos Eisley Cantina, select Enter Code and enter BDC866.

WATTO
At the bar in Mos Eisley Cantina, select Enter Code and enter PLL967.

ZAM WESELL
At the bar in Mos Eisley Cantina, select Enter Code and enter 584HJF.

SKILLS

DISGUISE
At the bar in Mos Eisley Cantina, select Enter Code and enter BRJ437.

FORCE GRAPPLE LEAP
At the bar in Mos Eisley Cantina, select Enter Code and enter CLZ738.

VEHICLES

DROID TRIFIGHTER
At the bar in Mos Eisley Cantina, select Enter Code and enter AAB123.

IMPERIAL SHUTTLE
At the bar in Mos Eisley Cantina, select Enter Code and enter HUT845.

TIE INTERCEPTOR
At the bar in Mos Eisley Cantina, select Enter Code and enter INT729.

TIE FIGHTER
At the bar in Mos Eisley Cantina, select Enter Code and enter DBH897.

ZAM'S AIRSPEEDER
At the bar in Mos Eisley Cantina, select Enter Code and enter UUU875.

LEGO STAR WARS II: THE ORIGINAL TRILOGY

BEACH TROOPER
At Mos Eisley Canteena, select Enter Code and enter UCK868. You must still select Characters and purchase this character for 20,000 studs.

BEN KENOBI (GHOST)
At Mos Eisley Canteena, select Enter Code and enter BEN917. You must still select Characters and purchase this character for 1,100,000 studs.

BESPIN GUARD
At Mos Eisley Canteena, select Enter Code and enter VHY832. You must still select Characters and purchase this character for 15,000 studs.

BIB FORTUNA
At Mos Eisley Canteena, select Enter Code and enter WTY721. You must still select Characters and purchase this character for 16,000 studs.

BOBA FETT
At Mos Eisley Canteena, select Enter Code and enter HLP221. You must still select Characters and purchase this character for 175,000 studs.

DEATH STAR TROOPER
At Mos Eisley Canteena, select Enter Code and enter BNC332. You must still select Characters and purchase this character for 19,000 studs.

EWOK
At Mos Eisley Canteena, select Enter Code and enter TTT289. You must still select Characters and purchase this character for 34,000 studs.

GAMORREAN GUARD
At Mos Eisley Canteena, select Enter Code and enter YZF999. You must still select Characters and purchase this character for 40,000 studs.

GONK DROID
At Mos Eisley Canteena, select Enter Code and enter NFX582. You must still select Characters and purchase this character for 1,550 studs.

GRAND MOFF TARKIN
At Mos Eisley Canteena, select Enter Code and enter SMG219. You must still select Characters and purchase this character for 38,000 studs.

GREEDO

At Mos Eisley Canteena, select Enter Code and enter NAH118. You must still select Characters and purchase this character for 60,000 studs.

HAN SOLO (HOOD)

At Mos Eisley Canteena, select Enter Code and enter YWM840. You must still select Characters and purchase this character for 20,000 studs.

IG-88

At Mos Eisley Canteena, select Enter Code and enter NXL973. You must still select Characters and purchase this character for 30,000 studs.

IMPERIAL GUARD

At Mos Eisley Canteena, select Enter Code and enter MMM111. You must still select Characters and purchase this character for 45,000 studs.

IMPERIAL OFFICER

At Mos Eisley Canteena, select Enter Code and enter BBV889. You must still select Characters and purchase this character for 28,000 studs.

IMPERIAL SHUTTLE PILOT

At Mos Eisley Canteena, select Enter Code and enter VAP664. You must still select Characters and purchase this character for 29,000 studs.

IMPERIAL SPY

At Mos Eisley Canteena, select Enter Code and enter CVT125. You must still select Characters and purchase this character for 13,500 studs.

JAWA

At Mos Eisley Canteena, select Enter Code and enter JAW499. You must still select Characters and purchase this character for 24,000 studs.

LOBOT

At Mos Eisley Canteena, select Enter Code and enter UUB319. You must still select Characters and purchase this character for 11,000 studs.

PALACE GUARD

At Mos Eisley Canteena, select Enter Code and enter SGE549. You must still select Characters and purchase this character for 14,000 studs.

REBEL PILOT

At Mos Eisley Canteena, select Enter Code and enter CYG336. You must still select Characters and purchase this character for 15,000 studs.

REBEL TROOPER (HOTH)

At Mos Eisley Canteena, select Enter Code and enter EKU849. You must still select Characters and purchase this character for 16,000 studs.

SANDTROOPER

At Mos Eisley Canteena, select Enter Code and enter YDV451. You must still select Characters and purchase this character for 14,000 studs.

SKIFF GUARD

At Mos Eisley Canteena, select Enter Code and enter GBU888. You must still select Characters and purchase this character for 12,000 studs.

SNOWTROOPER

At Mos Eisley Canteena, select Enter Code and enter NYU989. You must still select Characters and purchase this character for 16,000 studs.

STORMTROOPER

At Mos Eisley Canteena, select Enter Code and enter PTR345. You must still select Characters and purchase this character for 10,000 studs.

THE EMPEROR

At Mos Eisley Canteena, select Enter Code and enter HHY382. You must still select Characters and purchase this character for 275,000 studs.

TIE FIGHTER

At Mos Eisley Canteena, select Enter Code and enter HDY739. You must still select Characters and purchase this item for 60,000 studs.

TIE FIGHTER PILOT

At Mos Eisley Canteena, select Enter Code and enter NNZ316. You must still select Characters and purchase this character for 21,000 studs.

TIE INTERCEPTOR

At Mos Eisley Canteena, select Enter Code and enter QYA828. You must still select Characters and purchase this item for 40,000 studs.

TUSKEN RAIDER

At Mos Eisley Canteena, select Enter Code and enter PEJ821. You must still select Characters and purchase this character for 23,000 studs.

UGNAUGHT

At Mos Eisley Canteena, select Enter Code and enter UGN694. You must still select Characters and purchase this character for 36,000 studs.

LOONEY TUNES: ACME ARSENAL

UNLIMITED AMMO

At the Cheat menu, press Down, Left, Up, Right, Down, Left, Up, Right, Down.

LOST PLANET: EXTREME CONDITION

The following codes are for Single Player Mode on Easy Difficulty only.

500 THERMAL ENERGY

Pause the game and press Up, Up, Down, Down, Left, Right, Left, Right, X, Y, Right Bumper + Left Bumper.

INFINITE AMMUNITION

Pause the game and press Right Trigger, Right Bumper, Y, X, Right, Down, Left, Left Bumper, Left Trigger, Right Trigger, Right Bumper, Y, X, Right, Down, Left, Left Bumper, Left Trigger, Right Trigger, Left Trigger, Left Bumper, Right Bumper, Y, Left, Down, X, Right Bumper + Left Bumper.

INFINITE HEALTH

Pause the game and press Down (x3), Up, Y, Up, Y, Up, Y, Up(x3), Down, X, Down, X, Down, X, Left, Y, Right, X, Left, Y, Right, X, Right Bumper + Left Bumper.

CHANGE CAMERA ANGLE IN CUT SCENES

During a cut scene, press B, A, X, Y, B, A, X, Y, B, A, X, Y.

LOST PLANET: EXTREME CONDITION COLONIES EDITION

The following cheats only work for Easy Campaign, Score Attack, and Trial Battle. Each code must be reentered for every level.

+500 THERMAL ENERGY

Pause the game and enter: Up, Up, Down, Down, Left, Right, Left, Right, X, Y, RB + LB. This code can be used more than once.

INFINITE AMMUNITION

Pause the game and enter: RT, RB, Y, X, Right, Down, Left, LB, LT, RT, RB, Y, X, Right, Down, Left, LB, LT, RT, LT, LB, RB, Y, Left, Down, X, RB + LB

INFINITE HEALTH

Pause the game and enter: Down (x3), Up, Y, Up, Y, Up, Y, Up (x3), Down, X, Down, X, Down, X, Left, Y, Right, X, Left, Y, Right, X, RB + LB

USE WAYNE'S FINAL VS DURING END CREDITS

During the ending credits, before the words TEST PLAYER comes on screen, press and hold the following buttons to control Wayne's LP-9999 VS during credits.

Left Trigger, Left Bumper, Right Trigger, Right Bumper, X, Y, B.

MAJOR LEAGUE BASEBALL 2K6

UNLOCK EVERYTHING

Select Enter Cheat Code from the My 2K6 menu and enter Derek Jeter.

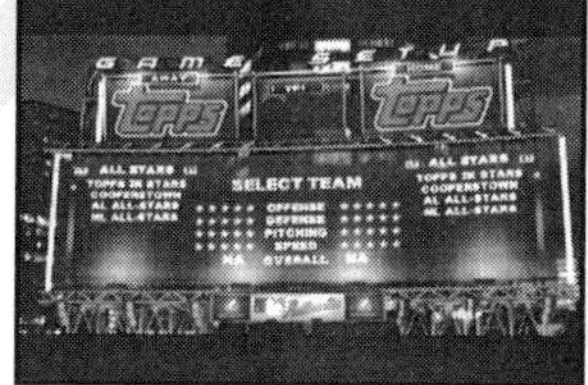

TOPPS 2K STARS

Select Enter Cheat Code from the My 2K6 menu and enter Dream Team.

SUPER WALL CLIMB

Select Enter Cheat Code from the My 2K6 menu and enter Last Chance. Enable the cheats by selecting My Cheats or selecting Cheat Codes from the in-game Options screen.

SUPER PITCHES

Select Enter Cheat Code from the My 2K6 menu and enter Unhittable. Enable the cheats by selecting My Cheats or selecting Cheat Codes from the in-game Options screen.

ROCKET ARMS

Select Enter Cheat Code from the My 2K6 menu and enter Gotcha. Enable the cheats by selecting My Cheats or selecting Cheat Codes from the in-game Options screen.

BOUNCY BALL

Select Enter Cheat Code from the My 2K6 menu and enter Crazy Hops. Enable the cheats by selecting My Cheats or selecting Cheat Codes from the in-game Options.

MAJOR LEAGUE BASEBALL 2K7

MICKEY MANTLE ON THE FREE AGENTS LIST

Select Enter Cheat Code from the My 2K7 menu and enter themick.

ALL CHEATS

Select Enter Cheat Code from the My 2K7 menu and enter Black Sox.

ALL EXTRAS

Select Enter Cheat Code from the My 2K7 menu and enter Game On.

UNLOCK EVERYTHING

Select Enter Cheat Code from the My 2K7 menu and enter Derek Jeter. This does not unlock the Topps cheats.

MIGHTY MICK CHEAT

Select Enter Cheat Code from the My 2K7 menu and enter mightymick.

TRIPLE CROWN CHEAT

Select Enter Cheat Code from the My 2K7 menu and enter triplecrown.

PINCH HIT MICK CHEAT

Select Enter Cheat Code from the My 2K7 menu and enter phmantle.

BIG BLAST CHEAT

Select Enter Cheat Code from the My 2K7 menu Rand enter m4murder.

MARVEL ULTIMATE ALLIANCE

UNLOCK ALL SKINS

At the Team menu, press Up, Down, Left, Right, Left, Right, Start.

UNLOCKS ALL HERO POWERS

At the Team menu, press Left, Right, Up, Down, Up, Down, Start.

ALL HEROES TO LEVEL 99

At the Team menu, press Up, Left, Up, Left, Down, Right, Down, Right, Start.

UNLOCK ALL HEROES

At the Team menu, press Up, Up, Down, Down, Left, Left, Left, Start.

UNLOCK DAREDEVIL

At the Team menu, press Left, Left, Right, Right, Up, Down, Up, Down, Start.

UNLOCK SILVER SURFER

At the Team menu, press Down, Left, Left, Up, Right, Up, Down, Left, Start.

GOD MODE

During gameplay, press Up, Down, Up, Down, Up, Left, Down, Right, Start.

TOUCH OF DEATH

During gameplay, press Left, Right, Down, Down, Right, Left, Start.

SUPER SPEED

During gameplay, press Up, Left, Up, Right, Down, Right, Start.

FILL MOMENTUM

During gameplay, press Left, Right, Right, Left, Up, Down, Down, Up, Start.

UNLOCK ALL COMICS

At the Review menu, press Left, Right, Right, Left, Up, Up, Right, Start.

UNLOCK ALL CONCEPT ART

At the Review menu, press Down, Down, Down, Right, Right, Left, Down, Start.

UNLOCK ALL CINEMATICS

At the Review menu, press Up, Left, Left, Up, Right, Right, Up, Start.

UNLOCK ALL LOAD SCREENS

At the Review menu, press Up, Down, Right, Left, Up, Up Down, Start.

UNLOCK ALL COURSES

At the Comic Missions menu, press Up, Right, Left, Down, Up, Right, Left, Down, Start.

MEDAL OF HONOR: AIRBORNE

Using the following cheats disables saves and achievements. During a game, hold Left Bumper + Right Bumper, and press X, B, Y, A, A. This brings up an Enter Cheat screen. Now you can enter the following:

FULL AMMO

Hold Left Bumper + Right Bumper and press B, B, Y, X, A, Y.

FULL HEALTH

Hold Left Bumper + Right Bumper and press Y, X, X, Y, A, B.

MERCENARIES 2: WORLD IN FLAMES

These codes work with the updated version of Mercenaries 2 only. The cheats will keep you from earning achievements, but anything earned up to that point remains. You can still save with the cheats, but be careful if you want to earn trophies. Quit the game without saving to return to normal.

CHEAT MODE

Access your PDA by pressing Back. Press Left Bumper, Right Bumper, Right Bumper, Left Bumper, Right Bumper, Left Bumper, Left Bumper, Right Bumper, Right Bumper, Right Bumper, Left Bumper and close the PDA. You then need to accept the agreement that says achievements are disabled. Now you can enter the following cheats.

INVINCIBILITY

Access your PDA and press Up, Down, Left, Down, Right, Right. This activates invincibility for you and anyone that joins your game.

INFINITE AMMO

Access your PDA and press Up, Down, Left, Right, Left, Left.

GIVE ALL VEHICLES

Access your PDA and press Up, Down, Left, Right, Right, Left.

GIVE ALL SUPPLIES

Access your PDA and press Left, Right, Right, Left, Up, Up, Left, Up.

GIVE ALL AIRSTRIKES (EXCEPT NUKE)

Access your PDA and press Right, Left, Down, Up, Right, Left, Down, Up.

GIVE NUKE

Access your PDA and press Up, Up, Down, Down, Left, Right, Left, Right.

FILL FUEL

Access your PDA and press Up, Up, Up, Down, Down, Down.

ALL COSTUMES

Access your PDA and press Up, Right, Down, Left, Up.

GRAPPLING HOOK

Access your PDA and press Up, Left, Down, Right, Up.

MONSTER MADNESS: BATTLE FOR SUBURBIA

Pause the game and press Up, Up, Down, Down, Left, Right, Left, Right, B, A. This brings up a screen where you can enter the following cheats. With the use of some cheats profile saving, level progression, and Xbox Live Achievements are disabled until you return to the Main menu.

EFFECT	CHEAT
Animal Sounds	patrickdugan
Disable Tracking Cameras	ihatefunkycameras
Faster Music	upthejoltcola
First Person	morgythemole
Infinite Secondary Items	stevebrooks
Objects Move Away from Player	southpeak
Remove Film Grain	reverb

MOTOGP 06

USA EXTREME BIKE
At the Game Mode screen, press Right, Up, B, B, A, B, Up, B, B, A.

MOTOGP 07

ALL CHALLENGES
At the Main menu, press Right, Up, B, A, B, A, Left, Down, Y.

ALL CHAMPIONSHIPS
At the Main menu, press Right, Up, B, Y, Right, Up, B, Y, Right, Up, B, Y.

ALL LIVERIES
At the Main menu, press Right, A, Left, Left, Y, Left, A, Down, Y.

ALL RIDERS
At the Main menu, press Right, Up, B, B, A, Down, Up, B, Down, Up, B.

ALL TRACKS
At the Main menu, press Left, A, Right, Down, Y, B, A, B, Y.

MX VS. ATV UNTAMED

ALL RIDING GEAR
Select Cheat Codes from the Options and enter crazylikea.

ALL HANDLEBARS
Select Cheat Codes from the Options and enter nohands.

27 GRAPHICS
Select Cheat Codes from the Options and enter STICKERS.

NARUTO: THE BROKEN BOND

NINE TAILS NARUTO
At the Character Select press X, X, Y, Y, X, Y, X, Y, X, X.

NASCAR 08

ALL CHASE MODE CARS
Select cheat codes from the options menu and enter checkered flag.

EA SPORTS CAR
Select cheat codes from the options menu and enter ea sports car.

FANTASY DRIVERS
Select cheat codes from the options menu and enter race the pack.

WALMART CAR AND TRACK
Select cheat codes from the options menu and enter walmart everyday.

NASCAR 09

ALL FANTASY DRIVERS

Select EA Extras from My NASCAR, choose Cheat Codes and enter CHECKERED FLAG.

WAL-MART TRACK AND THE WAL-MART CAR

Select EA Extras from My Nascar, choose Cheat Codes and enter Walmart Everyday.

NBA 2K6

CELEBRITY STREET OPTION

Select Codes from the Features menu and enter ballers.

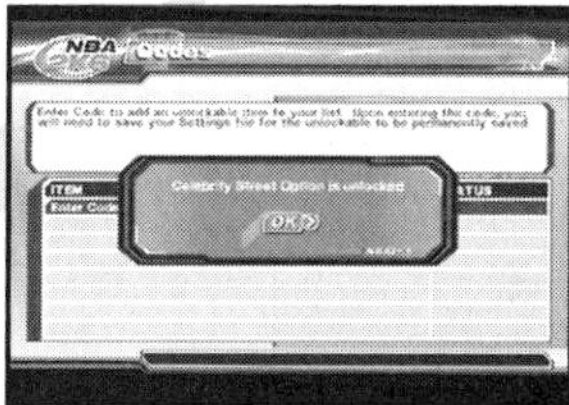

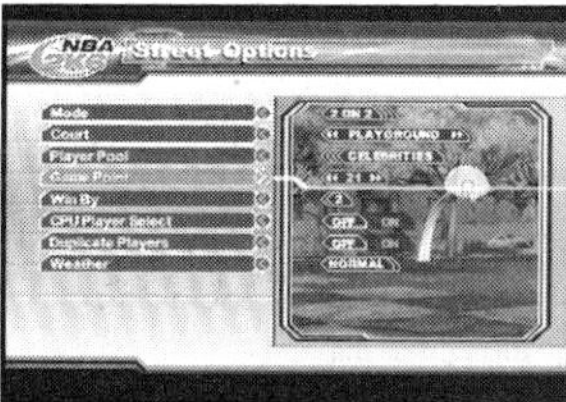

2KSPORTS TEAM

Select Codes from the Features menu and enter 2ksports.

2K6 TEAM

Select Codes from the Features menu and enter nba2k6.

VC TEAM

Select Codes from the Features menu and enter vcteam.

NIKE SHOX MTX SHOES

Select Codes from the Features menu and enter crazylift.

NIKE ZOOM 20-5-5 SHOES

Select Codes from the Features menu and enter lebronsummerkicks.

NIKE ZOOM KOBE 1 SHOES

Select Codes from the Features menu and enter kobe.

NIKE ZOOM LEBRON III ALL-STAR COLORWAY SHOES

Select Codes from the Features menu and enter lb allstar.

NIKE ZOOM LEBRON III BLACK/CRIMSON SHOES

Select Codes from the Features menu and enter lb crimsonblack.

NIKE ZOOM LEBRON III SPECIAL BIRTHDAY EDITION SHOES

Select Codes from the Features menu and enter lb bday.

NIKE ZOOM LEBRON III WHITE/GOLD SHOES

Select Codes from the Features menu and enter lb whitegold.

NIKE UP TEMPO PRO SHOES

Select Codes from the Features menu and enter anklebreakers.

NIKE UP TEMPO PRO SHOES

Select Codes from the Features menu and enter anklebreakers.

2006 ALL-STAR UNIFORMS

Select Codes from the Features menu and enter fanfavorites.

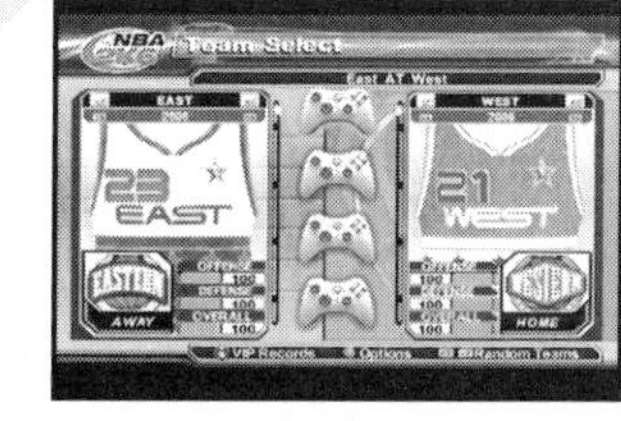

ST. PATRICK'S DAY UNIFORMS

Select Codes from the Features menu and enter gogreen.

BULLS RETRO UNIFORM

Select Codes from the Features menu and enter chi retro.

CAVALIERS ALTERNATE UNIFORM
Select Codes from the Features menu and enter cle 2nd.

CELTICS ALTERNATE UNIFORM
Select Codes from the Features menu and enter bos 2nd.

CLIPPERS RETRO UNIFORM
Select Codes from the Features menu and enter lac retro.

GRIZZLIES RETRO UNIFORM
Select Codes from the Features menu and enter mem retro.

HEAT RETRO UNIFORM
Select Codes from the Features menu and enter mia retro.

HORNETS RETRO UNIFORM
Select Codes from the Features menu and enter no retro.

KINGS ALTERNATE UNIFORM
Select Codes from the Features menu and enter sac 2nd.

KNICKS RETRO UNIFORM
Select Codes from the Features menu and enter ny retro.

MAGIC RETRO UNIFORM
Select Codes from the Features menu and enter orl retro.

NETS RETRO UNIFORM
Select Codes from the Features menu and enter nj retro.

NUGGETS ALTERNATE UNIFORM
Select Codes from the Features menu and enter den 2nd.

2005-06 PACERS UNIFORM
Select Codes from the Features menu and enter 31andonly.

PISTONS ALTERNATE UNIFORM
Select Codes from the Features menu and enter det 2nd.

ROCKETS RETRO UNIFORM
Select Codes from the Features menu and enter hou retro.

SONICS RETRO UNIFORM
Select Codes from the Features menu and enter sea retro.

SUNS RETRO UNIFORM
Select Codes from the Features menu and enter phx retro.

WIZARDS RETRO UNIFORM
Select Codes from the Features menu and enter was retro.

+10 BONUS FOR DEFENSIVE AWARENESS
Find the PowerBar vending machine in The Crib. Select Enter Code and enter lockdown.

+10 BONUS FOR OFFENSIVE AWARENESS
Find the PowerBar vending machine in The Crib. Select Enter Code and enter getaclue.

MAX DURABILITY
Find the PowerBar vending machine in The Crib. Select Enter Code and enter noinjury.

UNLIMITED STAMINA
Find the PowerBar vending machine in The Crib. Select Enter Code and enter nrgmax.

POWERBAR TATTOO
Find the PowerBar vending machine in The Crib. Select Enter Code and enter pbink. You can now use it in the game's Create Player feature.

NBA 2K7

MAX DURABILITY
Select Codes from the Features menu and enter ironman.

UNLIMITED STAMINA
Select Codes from the Features menu and enter norest.

+10 DEFFENSIVE AWARENESS
Select Codes from the Features menu and enter getstops.

+10 OFFENSIVE AWARENESS
Select Codes from the Features menu and enter inthezone.

TOPPS 2K SPORTS ALL-STARS
Select Codes from the Features menu and enter topps2ksports.

ABA BALL
Select Codes from the Features menu and enter payrespect.

NBA 2K8

ABA BALL
Select Codes from the Features menu and enter Payrespect.

2KSPORTS TEAM
Select Codes from the Features menu and enter 2ksports.

NBA DEVELOPMENT TEAM
Select Codes from the Features menu and enter nba2k.

SUPERSTARS TEAM
Select Codes from the Features menu and enter llmohffaae.

VISUAL CONCEPTS TEAM
Select Codes from the Features menu and enter Vcteam.

2008 ALL STAR NBA JERSEYS
Select Codes from the Features menu and enter haeitgyebs.

BOBCATS RACING JERSEY
Select Codes from the Features menu and enter agtaccsinr.

PACERS SECOND ROAD JERSEY
Select Codes from the Features menu and enter cpares.

ST. PATRICK'S DAY JERSEYS
Select Codes from the Features menu and enter uclerehanp.

VALENTINE'S DAY JERSEYS
Select Codes from the Features menu and enter amcnreo.

NBA 2K9

2K SPORTS TEAM
Select Codes from the Features menu and enter 2ksports.

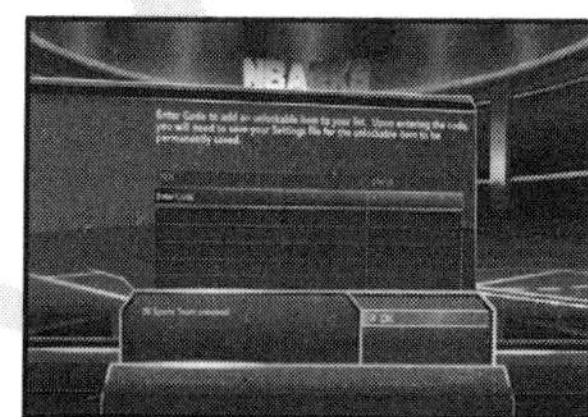

NBA 2K TEAM
Select Codes from the Features menu and enter nba2k.

2K CHINA TEAM
Select Codes from the Features menu and enter 2kchina.

SUPERSTARS
Select Codes from the Features menu and enter llmohffaae.

VC TEAM
Select Codes from the Features menu and enter vcteam.

ABA BALL
Select Codes from the Features menu and enter payrespect.

2009 ALL-STAR UNIFORMS
Select Codes from the Features menu and enter llaveyfonus.

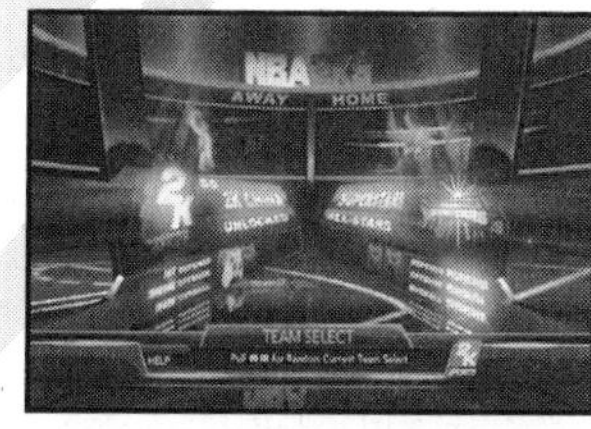

NBA LIVE 07

ADIDAS ARTILLERY II BLACK AND THE RBK ANSWER 9 VIDEO
Select NBA Codes from My NBA Live and enter 99B6356HAN.

ADIDAS ARTILLERY II
Select NBA Codes and enter NTGNFUE87H.

ADIDAS BTB LOW AND THE MESSAGE FROM ALLEN IVERSON VIDEO
Select NBA Codes and enter 7FB3KS9JQ0.

ADIDAS C-BILLUPS
Select NBA Codes and enter BV6877HB9N.

ADIDAS C-BILLUPS BLACK
Select NBA Codes and enter 85NVLDMWS5.

ADIDAS CAMPUS LT
Select NBA Codes and enter CLT2983NC8.

ADIDAS CRAZY 8
Select NBA Codes and enter CC98KKL814.

ADIDAS EQUIPMENT B-BALL
Select NBA Codes and enter 22OIUJKMDR.

ADIDAS GARNETT BOUNCE
Select NBA Codes and enter HYIOUHCAAN.

ADIDAS GARNETT BOUNCE BLACK
Select NBA Codes and enter KDZ2MQL17W.

ADIDAS GIL-ZERO
Select NBA Codes and enter 23DN1PPOG4.

ADIDAS GIL-ZERO BLACK
Select NBA Codes and enter QQQ3JCUYQ7.

ADIDAS GIL-ZERO MID
Select NBA Codes and enter 1GSJC8JWRL.

ADIDAS GIL-ZERO MID BLACK
Select NBA Codes and enter 369V6RVU3G.

ADIDAS STEALTH
Select NBA Codes and enter FE454DFJCC.

ADIDAS T-MAC 6
Select NBA Codes and enter MCJK843NNC.

ADIDAS T-MAC 6 WHITE
Select NBA Codes and enter 84GF7EJG8V.

CHARLOTTE BOBCATS 2006-07 ALTERNATE JERSEY
Select NBA Codes and enter WEDX671H7S.

UTAH JAZZ 2006-07 ALTERNATE JERSEY
Select NBA Codes and enter VCBI89FK83.

NEW JERSEY NETS 2006-07 ALTERNATE JERSEY
Select NBA Codes and enter D4SAA98U5H.

WASHINGTON WIZARDS 2006-07 ALTERNATE JERSEY
Select NBA Codes and enter QV93NLKXQC.

EASTERN ALL-STARS 2006-07 AWAY JERSEY
Select NBA Codes and enter WOCNW4KL7L.

EASTERN ALL-STARS 2006-07 HOME JERSEY
Select NBA Codes and enter 5654ND43N6.

WESTERN ALL-STARS 2006-07 AWAY JERSEY
Select NBA Codes and enter XX93BVL20U.

WESTERN ALL-STARS 2006-07 HOME JERSEY
Select NBA Codes and enter 993NSKL199.

NBA LIVE 08

ADIDAS GIL-ZERO - ALL-STAR EDITION
Select NBA Codes from My NBA and enter 23DN1PPOG4.

ADIDAS TIM DUNCAN STEALTH - ALL-STAR EDITION
Select NBA Codes from My NBA and enter FE454DFJCC.

NBA LIVE 09

SUPER DUNKS MODE
Use the Sprite vending machine in the practice area and enter spriteslam.

NBA STREET HOMECOURT

ALL TEAMS
At the Main menu, hold Right Bumper + Left Bumper and press Left, Right, Left, Right.

ALL COURTS
At the Main menu, hold Right Bumper + Left Bumper and press Up, Right, Down, Left.

BLACK/RED BALL
At the Main menu, hold Right Bumper + Left Bumper and press Up, Down, Left, Right.

NCAA FOOTBALL 07

#16 BAYLOR
Select Pennant Collection from My NCAA, then press SELECT and enter Sic Em.

#16 NIKE SPEED TD
Select Pennant Collection from My NCAA, then press SELECT and enter Light Speed.

#63 ILLINOIS
Select Pennant Collection from My NCAA, then press SELECT and enter Oskee Wow.

#160 TEXAS TECH
Select Pennant Collection from My NCAA, then press SELECT and enter Fight.

#200 FIRST AND FIFTEEN
Select Pennant Collection from My NCAA, then press SELECT and enter Thanks.

#201 BLINK
Select Pennant Collection from My NCAA, then press SELECT and enter For.

#202 BOING
Select Pennant Collection from My NCAA, then press SELECT and enter Registering.

#204 BUTTER FINGERS
Select Pennant Collection from My NCAA, then press SELECT and enter With EA.

#205 CROSSED THE LINE
Select Pennant Collection from My NCAA, then press SELECT and enter Tiburon.

#206 CUFFED
Select Pennant Collection from My NCAA, then press SELECT and enter EA Sports.

#207 EXTRA CREDIT
Select Pennant Collection from My NCAA, then press SELECT and enter Touchdown.

#208 HELIUM
Select Pennant Collection from My NCAA, then press SELECT and enter In The Zone.

#209 HURRICANE
Select Pennant Collection from My NCAA, then press SELECT and enter Turnover.

#210 INSTANT FREEPLAY
Select Pennant Collection from My NCAA, then press SELECT and enter Impact.

#211 JUMBALAYA
Select Pennant Collection from My NCAA, then press SELECT and enter Heisman.

#212 MOLASSES
Select Pennant Collection from My NCAA, then press SELECT and enter Game Time.

#213 NIKE FREE
Select Pennant Collection from My NCAA, then press SELECT and enter Break Free.

#214 NIKE MAGNIGRIP
Select Pennant Collection from My NCAA, then press SELECT and enter Hand Picked.

#215 NIKE PRO
Select Pennant Collection from My NCAA, then press SELECT and enter No Sweat.

#219 QB DUD
Select Pennant Collection from My NCAA, then press SELECT and enter Elite 11.

#221 STEEL TOE
Select Pennant Collection from My NCAA, then press SELECT and enter Gridiron.

#222 STIFFED
Select Pennant Collection from My NCAA, then press SELECT and enter NCAA.

#223 SUPER DIVE
Select Pennant Collection from My NCAA, then press SELECT and enter Upset.

#224 TAKE YOUR TIME
Select Pennant Collection from My NCAA, then press SELECT and enter Football.

#225 THREAD & NEEDLE
Select Pennant Collection from My NCAA, then press SELECT and enter 06.

#226 TOUGH AS NAILS
Select Pennant Collection from My NCAA, then press SELECT and enter Offense.

#227 TRIP
Select Pennant Collection from My NCAA, then press SELECT and enter Defense.

#228 WHAT A HIT
Select Pennant Collection from My NCAA, then press SELECT and enter Blitz.

#229 KICKER HEX
Select Pennant Collection from My NCAA, then press SELECT and enter Sideline.

#273 2004 ALL-AMERICANS
Select Pennant Collection from My NCAA, then press SELECT and enter Fumble.

#274 ALL-ALABAMA
Select Pennant Collection from My NCAA, then press SELECT and enter Roll Tide.

#276 ALL-ARKANSAS
Select Pennant Collection from My NCAA, then press SELECT and enter Woopigsooie.

#277 ALL-AUBURN
Select Pennant Collection from My NCAA, then press SELECT and enter War Eagle.

#278 ALL-CLEMSON
Select Pennant Collection from My NCAA, then press SELECT and enter Death Valley.

#279 ALL-COLORADO
Select Pennant Collection from My NCAA, then press SELECT and enter Glory.

#280 ALL-FLORIDA
Select Pennant Collection from My NCAA, then press SELECT and enter Great To Be.

#281 ALL-FSU
Select Pennant Collection from My NCAA, then press SELECT and enter Uprising.

#282 ALL-GEORGIA
Select Pennant Collection from My NCAA, then press SELECT and enter Hunker Down.

#283 ALL-IOWA
Select Pennant Collection from My NCAA, then press SELECT and enter On Iowa.

#284 ALL-KANSAS STATE
Select Pennant Collection from My NCAA, then press SELECT and enter Victory.

#285 ALL-LSU
Select Pennant Collection from My NCAA, then press SELECT and enter Geaux Tigers.

#286 ALL-MIAMI
Select Pennant Collection from My NCAA, then press SELECT and enter Raising Cane.

#287 ALL-MICHIGAN
Select Pennant Collection from My NCAA, then press SELECT and enter Go Blue.

#288 ALL-MISSISSIPPI STATE
Select Pennant Collection from My NCAA, then press SELECT and enter Hail State.

#289 ALL-NEBRASKA
Select Pennant Collection from My NCAA, then press SELECT and enter Go Big Red.

#290 ALL-NORTH CAROLINA
Select Pennant Collection from My NCAA, then press SELECT and enter Rah Rah.

#291 ALL-NOTRE DAME
Select Pennant Collection from My NCAA, then press SELECT and enter Golden Domer.

#292 ALL-OHIO STATE
Select Pennant Collection from My NCAA, then press SELECT and enter Killer Nuts.

#293 ALL-OKLAHOMA
Select Pennant Collection from My NCAA, then press SELECT and enter Boomer.

#294 ALL-OKLAHOMA STATE
Select Pennant Collection from My NCAA, then press SELECT and enter Go Pokes.

#295 ALL-OREGON
Select Pennant Collection from My NCAA, then press SELECT and enter Quack Attack.

#296 ALL-PENN STATE
Select Pennant Collection from My NCAA, then press SELECT and enter We Are.

#297 ALL-PITTSBURGH
Select Pennant Collection from My NCAA, then press SELECT and enter Lets Go Pitt.

#298 ALL-PURDUE
Select Pennant Collection from My NCAA, then press SELECT and enter Boiler Up.

#299 ALL-SYRACUSE
Select Pennant Collection from My NCAA, then press SELECT and enter Orange Crush.

#300 ALL-TENNESSEE
Select Pennant Collection from My NCAA, then press SELECT and enter Big Orange.

#301 ALL-TEXAS
Select Pennant Collection from My NCAA, then press SELECT and enter Hook Em.

#302 ALL-TEXAS A&M
Select Pennant Collection from My NCAA, then press SELECT and enter Gig Em.

#303 ALL-UCLA
Select Pennant Collection from My NCAA, then press SELECT and enter MIGHTY.

#304 ALL-USC
Select Pennant Collection from My NCAA, then press SELECT and enter Fight On.

#305 ALL-VIRGINIA
Select Pennant Collection from My NCAA, then press SELECT and enter Wahoos.

#306 ALL-VIRGINIA TECH
Select Pennant Collection from My NCAA, then press SELECT and enter Tech Triumph.

#307 ALL-WASHINGTON
Select Pennant Collection from My NCAA, then press SELECT and enter Bow Down.

#308 ALL-WISCONSIN
Select Pennant Collection from My NCAA, then press SELECT and enter U Rah Rah.

#311 ARK MASCOT
Select Pennant Collection from My NCAA, then press SELECT and enter Bear Down.

#329 GT MASCOT
Select Pennant Collection from My NCAA, then press SELECT and enter RamblinWreck.

#333 ISU MASCOT
Select Pennant Collection from My NCAA, then press SELECT and enter Red And Gold.

#335 KU MASCOT
Select Pennant Collection from My NCAA, then press SELECT and enter Rock Chalk.

#341 MINN MASCOT
Select Pennant Collection from My NCAA, then press SELECT and enter Rah Rah Rah.

#344 MIZZOU MASCOT
Select Pennant Collection from My NCAA, then press SELECT and enter Mizzou Rah.

#346 MSU MASCOT
Select Pennant Collection from My NCAA, then press SELECT and enter Go Green.

#349 NCSU MASCOT
Select Pennant Collection from My NCAA, then press SELECT and enter Go Pack.

#352 NU MASCOT
Select Pennant Collection from My NCAA, then press SELECT and enter Go Cats.

#360 S CAR MASCOT
Select Pennant Collection from My NCAA, then press SELECT and enter Go Carolina.

#371 UK MASCOT
Select Pennant Collection from My NCAA, then press SELECT and enter On On UK.

#382 WAKE FOREST
Select Pennant Collection from My NCAA, then press SELECT and enter Go Deacs Go.

#385 WSU MASCOT
Select Pennant Collection from My NCAA, then press SELECT and enter All Hail.

#386 WVU MASCOT
Select Pennant Collection from My NCAA, then press SELECT and enter Hail WV.

NEED FOR SPEED CARBON

CASTROL CASH
At the main menu, press Down, Up, Left, Down, Right, Up, X, B. This will give you 10,000 extra cash.

INFINITE CREW CHARGE
At the main menu, press Down, Up, Up, Right, Left, Left, Right, X.

INFINITE NITROUS
At the main menu, press Left, Up, Left, Down, Left, Down, Right, X.

INFINITE SPEEDBREAKER
At the main menu, press Down, Right, Right, Left, Right, Up, Down, X.

NEED FOR SPEED CARBON LOGO VINYLS
At the main menu, press Right, Up, Down, Up, Down, Left, Right, X.

NEED FOR SPEED CARBON SPECIAL LOGO VINYLS
At the main menu, press Up, Up, Down, Down, Down, Down, Up, X.

NEED FOR SPEED PROSTREET

$2,000
Select Career and then choose Code Entry. Enter 1MA9X99.

$4,000
Select Career and then choose Code Entry. Enter W2IOLL01.

$8,000
Select Career and then choose Code Entry. Enter L1IS97A1.

$10,000
Select Career and then choose Code Entry. Enter 1MI9K7E1.

$10,000
Select Career and then choose Code Entry. Enter CASHMONEY.

$10,000
Select Career and then choose Code Entry. Enter REGGAME.

AUDI TT
Select Career and then choose Code Entry. Enter ITSABOUTYOU.

CHEVELLE SS
Select Career and then choose Code Entry. Enter HORSEPOWER.

COKE ZERO GOLF GTI
Select Career and then choose Code Entry. Enter COKEZERO.

DODGE VIPER
Select Career and then choose Code Entry. Enter WORLDSLONGESTLASTING.

MITSUBISHI LANCER EVOLUTION
Select Career and then choose Code Entry. Enter MITSUBISHIGOFAR.

UNLOCK ALL BONUSES
Select Career and then choose Code Entry. Enter UNLOCKALLTHINGS.

5 REPAIR MARKERS
Select Career and then choose Code Entry. Enter SAFETYNET.

ENERGIZER VINYL
Select Career and then choose Code Entry. Enter ENERGIZERLITHIUM.

CASTROL SYNTEC VINYL
Select Career and then choose Code Entry. Enter CASTROLSYNTEC. This also gives you $10,000.

NEED FOR SPEED MOST WANTED

BURGER KING CHALLENGE
At the Title screen, press Up, Down, Up, Down, Left, Right, Left, Right.

CASTROL SYNTEC VERSION OF THE FORD GT
At the Title screen, press Left, Right, Left, Right, Up, Down, Up, Down.

MARKER FOR BACKROOM OF THE ONE-STOP SHOP
At the Title screen, press Up, Up, Down, Down, Left, Right, Up, Down.

JUNKMAN ENGINE
At the Title screen, press Up, Up, Down, Down, Left, Right, Up, Down.

PORSCHE CAYMAN
At the Title screen, press L, R, R, R, Right, Left, Right, Down.

NEED FOR SPEED UNDERCOVER

$10,000
Select Secret Codes from the Options menu and enter $EDSOC.

DIE-CAST BMW M3 E92
Select Secret Codes from the Options menu and enter)B7@B=.

DIE-CAST LEXUS IS F
Select Secret Codes from the Options menu and enter 0;5M2;.

NEEDFORSPEED.COM LOTUS ELISE
Select Secret Codes from the Options menu and enter -KJ3=E.

DIE-CAST NISSAN 240SX (S13)
Select Secret Codes from the Options menu and enter ?P:COL.

DIE-CAST PORSCHE 911 TURBO
Select Secret Codes from the Options menu and enter >8P:I;.

SHELBY TERLINGUA
Select Secret Codes from the Options menu and enter NeedForSpeedShelbyTerlingua.

DIE-CAST VOLKSWAGEN R32
Select Secret Codes from the Options menu and enter!2ODBJ:.

NHL 08

ALL RBK EDGE JERSEYS

At the RBK Edge Code option, enter h3oyxpwksf8ibcgt.

NHL 2K6

CHEAT MODE

Select Manage Profiles from the Options menu. Create a new profile with the name Turco813.

NHL 2K8

2007-2008 NHL REEBOK EDGE JERSEYS

From the Features menu, select Unlock 2007-2008/Enter Password. Enter S6j83RMk01.

NHL 2K9

3RD JERSEYS

From the Features menu, enter R6y34bsH52 as a code.

NPPL CHAMPIONSHIP PAINTBALL 2009

TIPPMANN X-7 AK-47 SCENARIO PAINTBALL MARKER

Select Field Gear and press Up, Up, Right, Right, Down, Down, Left, Left.

THE ORANGE BOX

HALF-LIFE 2

The following codes work for Half-Life 2, Half-Life 2: Episode One, and Half-Life 2: Episode Two.

CHAPTER SELECT

While playing, press Left, Left, Left, Left, Left Bumper, Right, Right, Right, Right, Right Bumper. Pause the game and select New Game to skip to another chapter.

RESTORE HEALTH (25 POINTS)

While playing, press Up, Up, Down, Down, Left, Right, Left, Right, B, A.

RESTORE AMMO FOR CURRENT WEAPON

While playing, press Y, B, A, X, Right Bumper, Y, X, A, B, Right Bumper.

INVINCIBILITY

While playing, press Left Shoulder, Up, Right Shoulder, Up, Left Shoulder, Left Shoulder, Up, Right Shoulder, Right Shoulder, Up.

PORTAL

CHAPTER SELECT

While playing, press Left, Left, Left, Left, Left Bumper, Right, Right, Right, Right, Right Bumper. Pause the game and select New Game to skip to another chapter.

GET A BOX
While playing, press Down, B, A, B, Y, Down, B, A, B, Y.

ENERGY BALL
While playing, press Up, Y, Y, X, X, A, A, B, B, Up.

PORTAL PLACEMENT ANYWHERE
While playing, press Y, A, B, A, B, Y, Y, A, Left, Right.

PORTALGUN ID 0
While playing, press Up, Left, Down, Right, Up, Left, Down, Right, Y, Y.

PORTALGUN ID 1
While playing, press Up, Left, Down, Right, Up, Left, Down, Right, X, X.

PORTALGUN ID 2
While playing, press Up, Left, Down, Right, Up, Left, Down, Right, A, A.

PORTALGUN ID 3
While playing, press Up, Left, Down, Right, Up, Left, Down, Right, B, B.

UPGRADE PORTALGUN
While playing, press X, B, Left Bumper, Right Bumper, Left, Right, Left Bumper, Right Bumper, Left Trigger, Right Trigger.

PETER JACKSON'S KING KONG: THE OFFICIAL GAME OF THE MOVIE

At the Main menu hold Left Bumper + Right Bumper + Left Trigger + Right Trigger and press Down, Up, Y, X, Down, Down, Y, Y. Release the buttons to access the Cheat option. The Cheat option is also available on the pause menu. Note that you cannot record your scores using cheat codes.

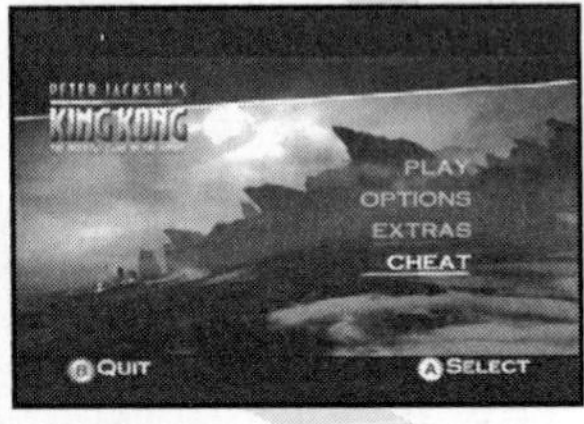

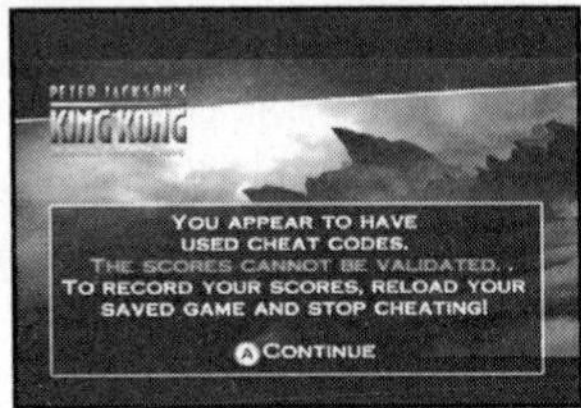

GOD MODE
Select Cheat and enter 8wonder.

ALL CHAPTERS
Select Cheat and enter KKst0ry.

AMMO 999
Select Cheat and enter KK 999 mun.

MACHINE GUN
Select Cheat and enter KKcapone.

REVOLVER
Select Cheat and enter KKtigun.

SNIPER RIFLE
Select Cheat and enter KKsn1per.

INFINITE SPEARS
Select Cheat and enter lance 1nf.

1-HIT KILLS
Select Cheat and enter GrosBras.

EXTRAS

Select Cheat and enter KKmuseum.

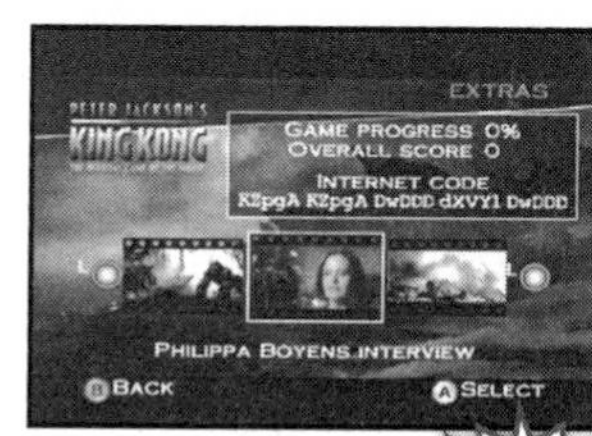

PRINCE OF PERSIA

SANDS OF TIME PRINCE/FARAH SKINS

Select Skin Manager from the Extras menu. Press Y and enter 52585854. This gives you the Sands of Time skin for the Prince and Farah from Sands of Time for the Princess. Access them from the Skin Manager

PRINCE ALTAIR IBN LA-AHAD SKIN

At the Main menu, press Y for Exclusive Content. Create an Ubisoft account. Then select "Altair Skin for Prince" to unlock.

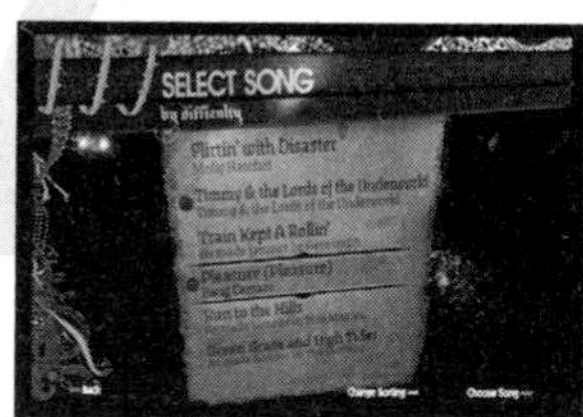

QUAKE 4

ALL WEAPONS, FULL ARMOR, HEALTH & AMMO

Press the Back button to access the Objectives, then press Up, Up, Down, Down, Left, Right, Left, Right, B, A.

FULL AMMO

Press the Back button to access the Objectives, then press B, A, X, Y, Left, Right, Left.

FULL HEALTH

Press the Back button to access the Objectives, then press B, A, B, A, Up, Up, Down, X.

RATATOUILLE

UNLIMITED RUNNING

At the cheat code screen, enter SPEEDY.

ALL MULTIPLAYER AND SINGLE PLAYER MINI GAMES

At the cheat code screen, enter MATTELME.

ROBERT LUDLUM'S THE BOURNE CONSPIRACY

LIGHT MACHINE GUNS HAVE SILENCERS

Select Enter Code from the Cheats screen and enter whattheymakeyougive.

EXTRAS UNLOCKED – CONCEPT ART

Select Enter Code from the Cheats screen and enter lastchancemarie. Select Concept Art from the Extras menu.

EXTRAS UNLOCKED – MUSIC TRACKS

Select Enter Code from the Cheats screen and enter jasonbourneisdead. This unlocks Treadstone Appointment and Manheim Suite in the Music Selector found in the Extras menu.

ROCK BAND

ALL SONGS

At the title screen, press Red, Yellow, Blue, Red, Red, Blue, Blue, Red, Yellow, Blue. Saving and all network features are disabled with this code.

TRANSPARENT INSTRUMENTS

Complete the hall of fame concert with that instrument.

GOLD INSTRUMENT

Complete the solo tour with that instrument.

SILVER INSTRUMENT

Complete the bonus tour with that instrument.

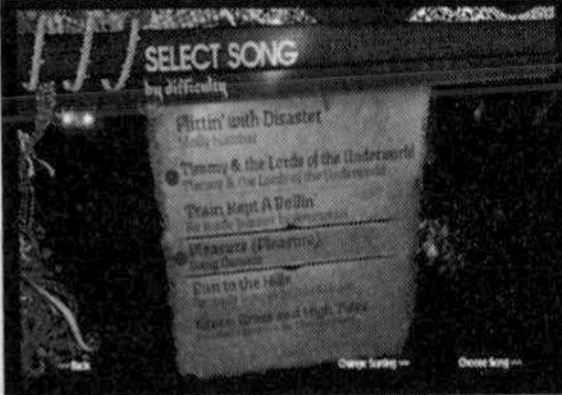

ROCK BAND 2

Most of these codes disable saving, achievements, and Xbox LIVE play.

UNLOCK ALL SONGS

Select Modify Game from the Extras menu, choose Enter Unlock Code and press Red, Yellow, Blue, Red, Red, Blue, Blue, Red, Yellow, Blue or Y, B, X, Y, Y, X, X, Y, B, X. Toggle this cheat on or off from the Modify Game menu.

SELECT VENUE SCREEN

Select Modify Game from the Extras menu, choose Enter Unlock Code and press Blue, Orange, Orange, Blue, Yellow, Blue, Orange, Orange, Blue, Yellow or X, Left Bumper, Left Bumper, X, B, X, Left Bumper, Left Bumper, X, B. Toggle this cheat on or off from the Modify Game menu.

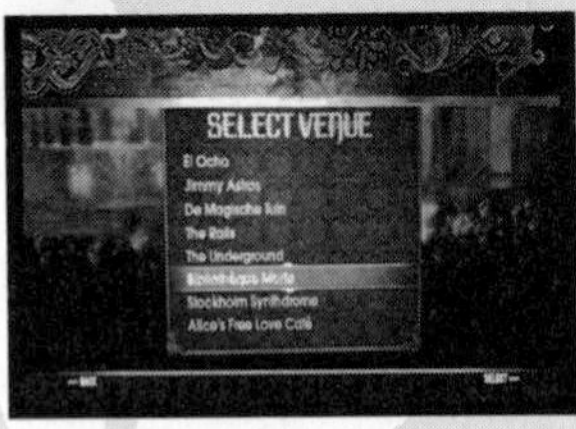

NEW VENUES ONLY

Select Modify Game from the Extras menu, choose Enter Unlock Code and press Red, Red, Red, Red, Yellow, Yellow, Yellow, Yellow or Y (x4), B (x4). Toggle this cheat on or off from the Modify Game menu.

PLAY THE GAME WITHOUT A TRACK

Select Modify Game from the Extras menu, choose Enter Unlock Code and press Blue, Blue, Red, Red, Yellow, Yellow, Blue, Blue or X, X, Y, Y, B, B, X, X. Toggle this cheat on or off from the Modify Game menu.

AWESOMENESS DETECTION

Select Modify Game from the Extras menu, choose Enter Unlock Code and press Yellow, Blue, Orange, Yellow, Blue, Orange, Yellow, Blue, Orange or B, X, Left Bumper, B, X, Left Bumper, B, X, Left Bumper. Toggle this cheat on or off from the Modify Game menu.

STAGE MODE

Select Modify Game from the Extras menu, choose Enter Unlock Code and press Blue, Yellow, Red, Blue, Yellow, Red, Blue, Yellow, Red or X, B, Y, X, B, Y, X, B, Y. Toggle this cheat on or off from the Modify Game menu.

ROCKSTAR GAMES PRESENTS TABLE TENNIS

Use of the following codes will disable achievements.

SWEATY CHARACTER VIEWER

After loading the map and before accepting the match, press Right Trigger, Up, Down, Left Trigger, Left, Right, Y, X, X, Y.

SMALL CROWD AUDIO

After loading the map and before accepting the match, press Down, Down, Down, Left Bumper, Left Trigger, Left Bumper, Left Trigger.

BIG BALL

After loading the map and before accepting the match, press Left, Right, Left, Right, Up, Up, Up, X.

COLORBLIND SPINDICATOR (ONLY IN NEWER PATCH)

After loading the map and before accepting the match, press Up, Down, X, X, Y, Y.

SILHOUETTE MODE

After loading the map and before accepting the match, press Up, Down, Y, Y, Left Bumper, Left Trigger, Right Trigger, Right Bumper.

BIG PADDLES CHEAT (ONLY IN NEWER PATCH)

After loading the map and before accepting the match, press Up, Left, Up, Right, Up, Down, Up, Up, X, X.

UNLOCK ALL

After loading the map and before accepting the match, press Up, Right, Down, Left, Left Bumper, Right, Up, Left, Down, Right Bumper.

VINTAGE AUDIO

After loading the map and before accepting the match, press Up, Up, Down, Down, Left, Right, Left, Right, Left Bumper, Right Bumper.

BIG CROWD AUDIO

After loading the map and before accepting the match, press Up, Up, Up, Right Bumper, Right Trigger, Right Bumper, Right Trigger.

OFFLINE GAMERTAGS

After loading the map and before accepting the match, press X, Y, X, Y, X, Y, Left Trigger, Right Trigger, Down, Down, Down.

SAINTS ROW

Pause the game and select Dial from your phone. Enter the following codes and then press Call. Select Cheats to enable the first set of codes, the ones that start with "#." You cannot earn achievements if using these cheats. Note that vehicles are delivered to your garage.

CODE NAME	DIAL
Give Cash	#MONEY
Full Health	#FULLHEALTH
Repair Car	#778
Infinite Ammo	#AMMO
Infinite Sprint	#SPRINT
No Cop Notoriety	#NOCOPS
No Gang Notoriety	#NOGANGS
Evil Cars	#EVILCARS
Clear Skies	#SUNNY
Wrath of God	#10
44	#SHEPHERD
12 Gauge	#12GAUGE
Ambulance	#AMBULANCE
Anchor	#ANCHOR
Ant	#ANT
Aqua	#A7UA

CODE NAME	DIAL
Hannibal	#42664225
Hollywood	#HOLLYWOOD
Jackrabbit	#JACKRABBIT
The Job	#THEJOB
K6	#K6KRUKOV
Keystone	#KEYSTONE
Knife	#KNIFE
Komodo	#KOMODO
La Fuerza	#LAFUER9A
Mag	#MAG
McManus	#MACMANUS
Mockingbird	#MOCKINGBIRD
Molotov	#MOLOTOV
Nelson	#635766
Newman	#NEWMAN
Nightstick	#NIGHTSTICK

CODE NAME	DIAL
AR40	#AR40XTND
AS12	#AS12RIOT
Baron	#BARON
Baseball Bat	#BASEBALL
Betsy	#BETSY
Bulldog	#BULLDOG
Cavallaro	#CAVALLARO
Compton	#COMPTON
Cosmos	#COSMOS
Destiny	#DESTINY
Justice	#JUSTICE
FBI	#FBI
Ferdelance	#FERDELANCE
Gdhc	#GDHC50
Grenade	#GRENADE
Gunslinger	#GUNSLINGER
Halberd	#HALBERD
Hammerhead	#HAMMERHEAD
Hannibal	#42664225
Zenith	#9ENITH
Zimos	#9IMOS
Zircon	#9IRCON

CODE NAME	DIAL
Nordberg	#NORDBERG
NR4	#NR4
Pimp Cane	#PIMPCANE
Pipebomb	#PIPEBOMB
Quasar	#7UASAR
Quota	#7UOTA
Rattler	#RATTLER
Reaper	#REAPER
RPG	#ROCKET
Shogun	#SHOGUN
SKR7	#SKRSPREE
T3K	#T3KURBAN
Taxi	#TAXI
Titan	#TITAN
Tombstone	#TOMBSTONE
Traxxmaster	#TRAXXMASTER
VICE9	#Vice9
Vortex	#VORTEX
Voxel	#VOXEL
GameStop	#42637867
Chicken Ned	5552445 (select Homies from your Phone to access Chicken Ned)

For the following codes, select the Phone Book to call.

CODE NAME	DIAL
EagleLine Yellow	5550180174
Big Willy's Cab	5558198415
Brown Baggers	5553765
Crash Landing	5556278
The Dead Cow	5556238
Emergency	911
Eye for an Eye	5555966
Freckle Bitch's	5556328
Grounds for Divorce	5559473
Impression	5553248
Legal Lee's	5559467
Lik-a-Chick	5553863
On the Fence	5557296
On the Rag	5555926
On Thin Ice	5552564
Rim Jobs	5553493
$tock$	5552626
Suicide Hotline	5554876837
TNA Taxis	5554558008

SAINTS ROW 2

CHEAT CODES

Select Dial from the Phone menu and enter these numbers followed by the Call button. Activate the cheats by selecting Cheats from the Phone menu. Enabling a cheat prevents the acquisition of Achievements

PLAYER ABILITY

CHEAT	NUMBER
Give Cash	#2274666399
No Cop Notoriety	#50
No Gang Notoriety	#51
Infinite Sprint	#6
Full Health	#1
Player Pratfalls	#5
Milk Bones	#3
Car Mass Hole	#2
Infinite Ammo	#11
Heaven Bound	#12
Add Police Notoriety	#4
Add Gang Notoriety	#35
Never Die	#36
Unlimited Clip	#9

VEHICLES

CHEAT	NUMBER
Repair Car	#1056
Venom Classic	#1079
Five-0	#1055
Stilwater Municipal	#1072
Baron	#1047
Attrazione	#1043
Zenith	#1081
Vortex	#1080
Phoenix	#1064
Bootlegger	#1049
Raycaster	#1068
Hollywood	#1057
Justice	#1058
Compton	#1052
Eiswolf	#1053
Taxi	#1074
Ambulance	#1040
Backhoe	#1045
Bagboy	#1046
Rampage	#1067
Reaper	#1069
The Job	#1075
Quota	#1066
FBI	#1054
Mag	#1060
Bulldog	#1050
Quasar	#1065
Titan	#1076
Varsity	#1078
Anchor	#1041
Blaze	#1044
Sabretooth	#804
Sandstorm	#805
Kaneda	#801
Widowmaker	#806
Kenshin	#802
Melbourne	#803
Miami	#826

CHEAT	NUMBER
Python	#827
Hurricane	#825
Shark	#828
Skipper	#829
Mongoose	#1062
Superiore	#1073
Tornado	#713
Horizon	#711
Wolverine	#714
Snipes 57	#712
Bear	#1048
Toad	#1077
Kent	#1059
Oring	#1063
Longhauler	#1061
Atlasbreaker	#1042
Septic Avenger	#1070
Shaft	#1071
Bulldozer	#1051

WEAPONS

CHEAT	NUMBER
AR-50	#923
K6	#935
GDHC	#932
NR4	#942
44	#921
Tombstone	#956
T3K	#954
VICE9	#957
AS14 Hammer	#925
12 Gauge	#920
SKR-9	#951
McManus 2010	#938
Baseball Bat	#926
Knife	#936
Molotov	#940
Grenade	#933
Nightstick	#941
Pipebomb	#945
RPG	#946
Crowbar	#955
Pimp Cane	#944
AR200	#922
AR-50/Grenade Launcher	#924
Chainsaw	#927
Fire Extinguisher	#928
Flamethrower	#929
Flashbang	#930
GAL43	#931
Kobra	#934
Machete	#937
Mini-gun	#939
Pepperspray	#943
Annihilator RPG	#947
Samurai Sword	#948
Satchel Charge	#949
Shock Paddles	#950
Sledgehammer	#952
Stungun	#953
XS-2 Ultimax	#958
Pimp Slap	#969

WEATHER

CHEAT	NUMBER
Clear Skies	#78669
Heavy Rain	#78666
Light Rain	#78668
Overcast	#78665
Time Set Midnight	#2400
Time Set Noon	#1200
Wrath Of God	#666

WORLD

CHEAT	NUMBER
Super Saints	#8
Super Explosions	#7
Evil Cars	#16
Pedestrian War	#19
Drunk Pedestrians	#15
Raining Pedestrians	#20
Low Gravity	#18

SAMURAI SHODOWN 2

PLAY AS KUROKO IN 2-PLAYER

At the character select, press Up, Down, Left, Up, Down, Right + X.

SEGA SUPERSTARS TENNIS

UNLOCK CHARACTERS

Complete the following missions to unlock the corresponding character.

CHARACTER	COMPLETE THIS MISSION
Alex Kidd	Mission 1 of Alex Kidd's World
Amy Rose	Mission 2 of Sonic the Hedgehog's World
Gilius	Mission 1 of Golden Axe's World
Gum	Mission 12 of Jet Grind Radio's World
Meemee	Mission 8 of Super Monkey Ball's World
Pudding	Mission 1 of Space Channel 5's World
Reala	Mission 2 of NiGHTs' World
Shadow The Hedgehog	Mission 14 of Sonic the Hedgehog's World

SHREK THE THIRD

10,000 GOLD COINS

At the gift shop, press Up, Up, Down, Up, Right, Left.

SILENT HILL: HOMECOMING

YOUNG ALEX COSTUME

At the Title screen, press Up, Up, Down, Down, Left, Right, Left, Right, B.

THE SIMPSONS GAME

After unlocking the following, the outfits can be changed at the downstairs closet in the Simpson's house. The Trophies can be viewed at different locations in the house: Bart's room, Lisa's room, Marge's room, and the garage.

BART'S OUTFITS AND TROPHIES (POSTER COLLECTION)

At the Main menu, press Right, Left, X, X, Y, Right Thumb Stick.

HOMER'S OUTFITS AND TROPHIES (BEER BOTTLE COLLECTION)

At the Main menu, press Left, Right, Y, Y, X, Left Thumb Stick.

LISA'S OUTFITS AND TROPHIES (DOLLS)

At the Main menu, press X, Y, X, X, Y, Left Thumb Stick.

MARGE'S OUTFITS AND TROPHIES (HAIR PRODUCTS)

At the Main menu, press Y, X, Y, Y, X, Right Thumb Stick.

SKATE

EXCLUSIVE BEST BUY CLOTHES

At the Main menu, press Up, Down, Left, Right, X, Right Bumper, Y, Left Bumper. You can get the clothes at Reg's or Slappy's Skate Shop. Find it under Skate.

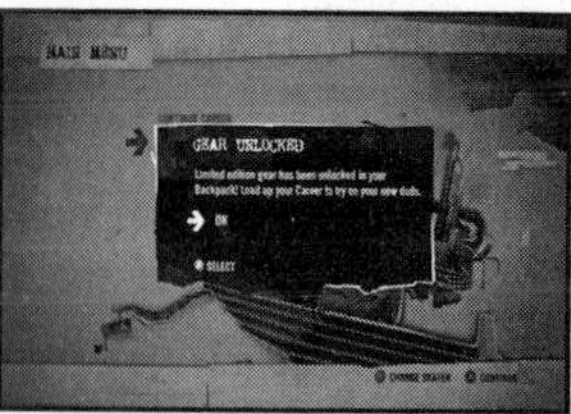

DEM BONES CHARACTER

Break each bone in your body at least three times.

SKATE 2

BIG BLACK

Select Enter Cheat from the Extras menu and enter letsdowork.

3D MODE

Select Enter Cheat from the Extras menu and enter strangeloops. Use glasses to view in 3D.

SOLDIER OF FORTUNE: PAYBACK

ACR-2 SNIPER RIFLE

At the difficulty select, press Up, Up, Down, Left, Right, Right, Down.

SPIDER-MAN: FRIEND OR FOE

NEW GREEN GOBLIN AS A SIDEKICK

While standing in the Helicarrier between levels, press Left, Down, Right, Right, Down, Left.

SANDMAN AS A SIDEKICK

While standing in the Helicarrier between levels, press Right, Right, Right, Up, Down, Left.

VENOM AS A SIDEKICK

While standing in the Helicarrier between levels, press Left, Left, Right, Up, Down, Down.

5000 TECH TOKENS

While standing in the Helicarrier between levels, press Up, Up, Down, Down, Left, Right.

STAR WARS: THE FORCE UNLEASHED

CHEAT CODES

Pause the game and select Input Code. Here you can enter the following codes. Activating any of the following cheat codes will disable some unlockables, and you will be unable to save your progress.

CHEAT	CODE
All Force Powers at Max Power	KATARN
All Force Push Ranks	EXARKUN
All Saber Throw Ranks	ADEGAN
All Repulse Ranks	DATHOMIR
All Saber Crystals	HURRIKANE
All Talents	JOCASTA
Deadly Saber	LIGHTSABER

COMBOS

Pause the game and select Input Code. Here you can enter the following codes. Activating any of the following cheat codes will disable some unlockables, and you will be unable to save your progress.

COMBO	CODE
All Combos	MOLDYCROW
Aerial Ambush	VENTRESS
Aerial Assault	EETHKOTH
Aerial Blast	YADDLE
Impale	BRUTALSTAB
Lightning Bomb	MASSASSI

COMBO	CODE
Lightning Grenade	RAGNOS
Saber Slam	PLOKOON
Saber Sling	KITFISTO
Sith Saber Flurry	LUMIYA
Sith Slash	DARAGON
Sith Throw	SAZEN
New Combo	FREEDON
New Combo	MARAJADE

ALL DATABANK ENTRIES

Pause the game and select Input Code. Enter OSSUS.

MIRRORED LEVEL

Pause the game and select Input Code. Enter MINDTRICK. Re-enter the code to return level to normal.

SITH MASTER DIFFICULTY

Pause the game and select Input Code. Enter SITHSPAWN.

COSTUMES

Pause the game and select Input Code. Here you can enter the following codes.

COSTUME	CODE
All Costumes	SOHNDANN
Bail Organa	VICEROY
Ceremonial Jedi Robes	DANTOOINE
Drunken Kota	HARDBOILED
Emperor	MASTERMIND
Incinerator Trooper	PHOENIX
Jedi Adventure Robe	HOLOCRON
Kashyyyk Trooper	TK421GREEN
Kota	MANDALORE
Master Kento	WOOKIEE
Proxy	PROTOTYPE
Scout Trooper	FERRAL
Shadow Trooper	BLACKHOLE
Sith Stalker Armor	KORRIBAN
Snowtrooper	SNOWMAN
Stormtrooper	TK421WHITE
Stormtrooper Commander	TK421BLUE

STREET FIGHTER IV

ALTERNATE STAGES

At the stage select, hold L1 or R1 and select a stage.

STUNTMAN IGNITION

3 PROPS IN STUNT CREATOR MODE

Select Cheats from Extras and enter COOLPROP.

ALL ITEMS UNLOCKED FOR CONSTRUCTION MODE

Select Cheats from Extras and enter NOBLEMAN.

MVX SPARTAN

Select Cheats from Extras and enter fastride.

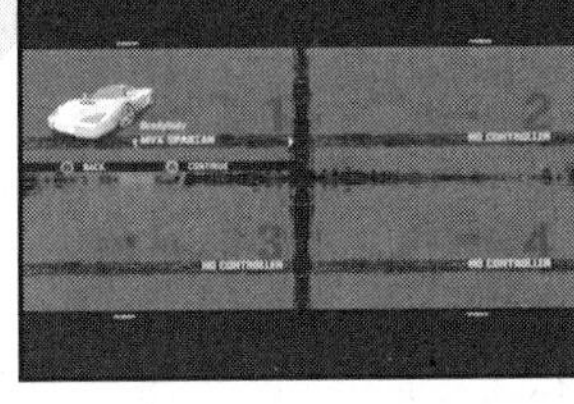

ALL CHEATS

Select Cheats from Extras and enter Wearefrozen. This unlocks the following cheats: Slo-mo Cool, Thrill Cam, Vision Switcher, Nitro Addiction, Freaky Fast, and Ice Wheels.

ALL CHEATS

Select Cheats from Extras and enter Kungfoopete.

ICE WHEELS CHEAT
Select Cheats from Extras and enter IceAge.

NITRO ADDICTION CHEAT
Select Cheats from Extras and enter TheDuke.

VISION SWITCHER CHEAT
Select Cheats from Extras and enter GFXMODES.

SUPERMAN RETURNS: THE VIDEOGAME

GOD MODE
Pause the game, select Options and press Up, Up, Down, Down, Left, Right, Left, Right, Y, X.

INFINITE CITY HEALTH
Pause the game, select Options and press Y, Right, Y, Right, Up, Left, Right, Y.

ALL POWER-UPS
Pause the game, select Options and press Left, Y, Right, X, Down, Y, Up, Down, X, Y, X.

ALL UNLOCKABLES
Pause the game, select Options and press Left, Up, Right, Down, Y, X, Y, Up, Right, X.

FREE ROAM AS BIZARRO
Pause the game, select Options and press Up, Right, Down, Right, Up, Left, Down, Right, Up.

SUPER PUZZLE FIGHTER II TURBO HD REMIX

PLAY AS AKUMA
At the character select, highlight Hsien-Ko and press Down.

PLAY AS DAN
At the character select, highlight Donovan and press Down.

PLAY AS DEVILOT
At the character select, highlight Morrigan and press Down.

PLAY AS ANITA
At the character select, hold Left Bumper + Right Bumper and choose Donovan.

PLAY AS HSIEN-KO'S TALISMAN
At the character select, hold Left Bumper + Right Bumper and choose Hsien-Ko.

PLAY AS MORRIGAN AS A BAT
At the character select, hold Left Bumper + Right Bumper and choose Morrigan.

PLAY AS ANITA
At the character select, hold Left Bumper + Right Bumper and choose Donovan.

PLAY AS HSIEN-KO'S TALISMAN
At the character select, hold Left Bumper + Right Bumper and choose Hsien-Ko.

PLAY AS MORRIGAN AS A BAT
At the character select, hold Left Bumper + Right Bumper and choose Morrigan.

SUPER STREET FIGHTER II TURBO HD REMIX

The following codes give you the classic fighters in Classic Arcade Mode. Select the character, quickly enter the given code, and select him/her again.

CLASSIC BALROG
Right, Left, Left, Right

CLASSIC BLANKA
Left, Right (x3)

CLASSIC CAMMY
Up, Up, Down, Down

CLASSIC CHUN-LI
Down (x3), Up

CLASSIC DEE JAY
Down, Down, Up, Up

CLASSIC DHALSIM
Down, Up (x3)

CLASSIC E. HONDA
Up (x3), Down

CLASSIC FEI LONG
Left, Left, Right, Right

CLASSIC GUILE
Up, Down (x3)

CLASSIC KEN
Left (x3), Right

CLASSIC M. BISON
Down, Up, Up, Down

CLASSIC RYU
Right (x3), Left

CLASSIC SAGAT
Up, Down (x3), Up

CLASSIC T. HAWK
Right, Right, Left, Left

CLASSIC VEGA
Left, Right, Right, Left

CLASSIC ZANGIEF
Left, Right (x3)

SURF'S UP

ALL CHAMPIONSHIP LOCATIONS
Select Cheat Codes from the Extras menu and enter FREEVISIT.

ALL LEAF SLIDE STAGES
Select Cheat Codes from the Extras menu and enter GOINGDOWN.

ALL MULTIPLAYER LEVELS
Select Cheat Codes from the Extras menu and enter MULTIPASS.

ALL BOARDS
Select Cheat Codes from the Extras menu and enter MYPRECIOUS.

ASTRAL BOARD
Select Cheat Codes from the Extras menu and enter ASTRAL.

MONSOON BOARD
Select Cheat Codes from the Extras menu and enter MONSOON.

TINE SHOCKWAVE BOARD
Select Cheat Codes from the Extras menu and enter TINYSHOCKWAVE.

ALL CHARACTER CUSTOMIZATIONS
Select Cheat Codes from the Extras menu and enter TOPFASHION.

PLAY AS ARNOLD
Select Cheat Codes from the Extras menu and enter TINYBUTSTRONG.

PLAY AS ELLIOT
Select Cheat Codes from the Extras menu and enter SURPRISEGUEST.

PLAY AS GEEK
Select Cheat Codes from the Extras menu and enter SLOWANDSTEADY.

PLAY AS TANK EVANS
Select Cheat Codes from the Extras menu and enter IMTHEBEST.

PLAY AS TATSUHI KOBAYASHI
Select Cheat Codes from the Extras menu and enter KOBAYASHI.

PLAY AS ZEKE TOPANGA
Select Cheat Codes from the Extras menu and enter THELEGEND.

ALL VIDEOS AND SPEN GALLERY
Select Cheat Codes from the Extras menu and enter WATCHAMOVIE.

ART GALLERY
Select Cheat Codes from the Extras menu and enter NICEPLACE.

THRILLVILLE: OFF THE RAILS

$50,000
While in a park, press X, B, Y, X, B, Y, A.

500 THRILL POINTS
While in a park, press B, X, Y, B, X, Y, X.

ALL PARKS
While in a park, press X, B, Y, X, B, Y, X.

ALL RIDES IN CURRENT PARK
While in a park, press X, B, Y, X, B, Y, Y.

MISSION UNLOCK
While in a park, press X, B, Y, X, B, Y, B.

ALL MINI-GAMES IN PARTY PLAY
While in a park, press X, B, Y, X, B, Y, Right.

TIGER WOODS PGA TOUR 06

ALL GOLFERS
Select Password from the Options menu and enter itsinthegame.

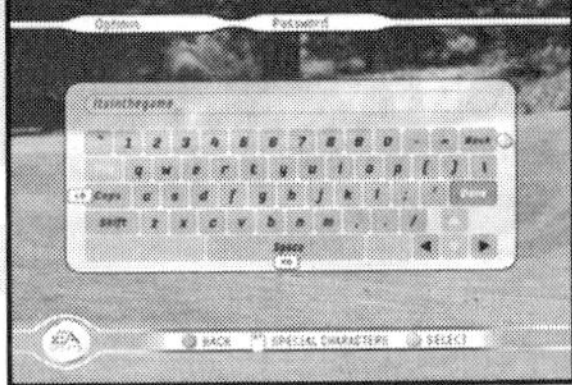

XBOX 360

XBOX 360

ALL CLUBS

Select Password from the Options menu and enter clubs11.

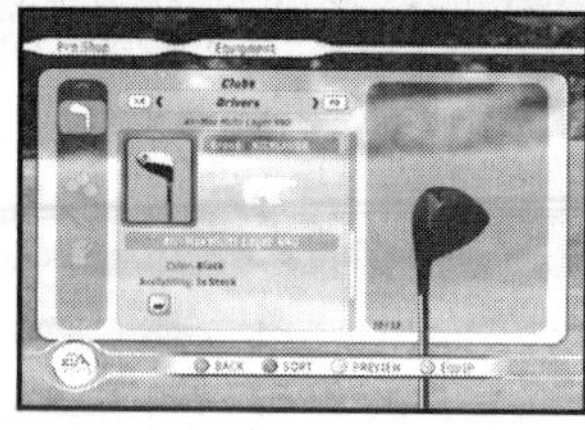

GOLD COLLECTION EA SPORTS BALL

Select Password from the Options menu and enter golfisfun.

NICKLAUS ITEMS

Select Password from the Options menu and enter goldenbear.

ALL COURSES

Select Password from the Options menu and enter eyecandy.

VIJAY SINGH

Select Password from the Options menu and enter victory.

WAYNE ROONEY

Select Password from EA Sports Extras and enter playfifa08.

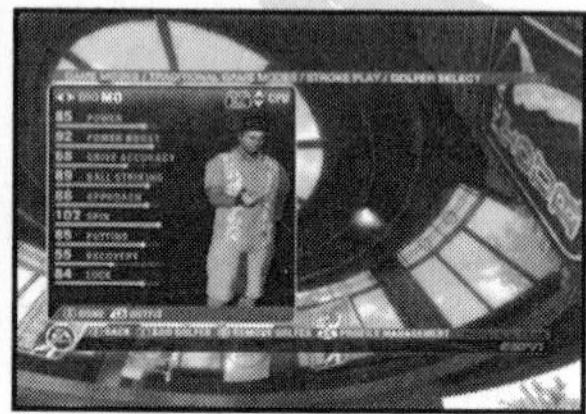

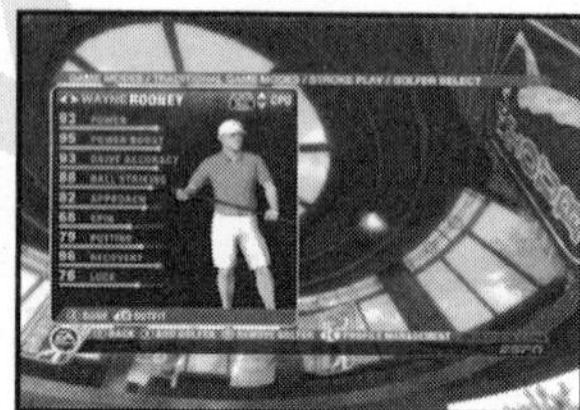

INFINITE MONEY

Select Password from EA Sports Extras and enter cream.

TIGER WOODS PGA TOUR 07

BIG HEAD MODE FOR CROWDS

Select Password and enter tengallonhat.

TIGER WOODS PGA TOUR 08

ALL COURSES

Select Password from EA Sports Extras and enter greensfees.

ALL GOLFERS

Select Password from EA Sports Extras and enter allstars.

TIGER WOODS PGA TOUR 09

SPECTATORS BIG HEAD MODE

Select EA SPORTS Extras from My Tiger '09, choose Password and enter cephalus.

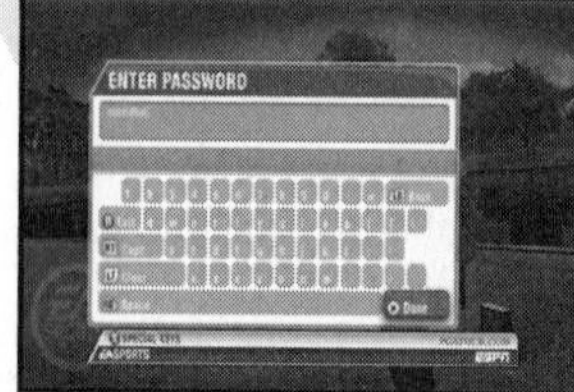

TIMESHIFT

KRONE IN MULTIPLAYER

Select Multiplayer from the Options menu. Highlight Model and press Left to get to Krone. Press Y and enter RXYMCPENCJ.

TMNT

CHALLENGE MAP 2

At the Main menu, hold the Left Bumper and press A, A, B, A.

DON'S BIG HEAD GOODIE

At the Main menu, hold the Left Bumper and press B, Y, A, X.

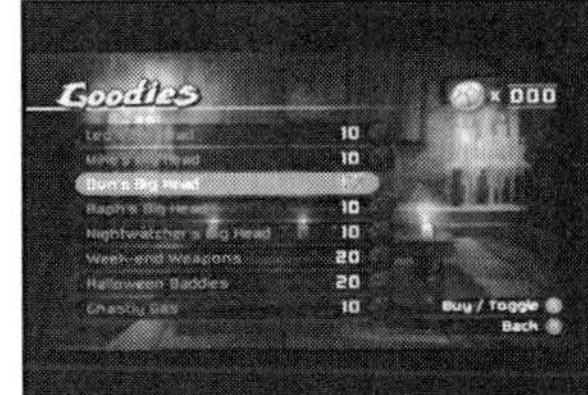

TOMB RAIDER: LEGEND

You must unlock the following codes in the game before using them.

BULLETPROOF

During a game, hold Left Trigger and press A, Right Trigger, Y, Right Trigger, X, Left Bumper.

DRAIN ENEMY HEALTH

During a game, hold Left Trigger and press X, B, A, Left Bumper, Right Trigger, Y.

INFINITE ASSAULT RIFLE AMMO

During a game, hold Left Bumper and press A, B, A, Left Trigger, X, Y.

INFINITE GRENADE LAUNCHER AMMO

During a game, hold Left Bumper and press Left Trigger, Y, Right Trigger, B, Left Trigger, X.

INFINITE SHOTGUN AMMO

During a game, hold Left Bumper and press Right Trigger, B, X, Left Trigger, X, A.

INFINITE SMG AMMO

During a game, hold Left Bumper and press B, Y, Left Trigger, Right Trigger, A, B.

EXCALIBUR

During a game, hold Left Bumper and press Y, A, B, Right Trigger, Y, Left Trigger.

SOUL REAVER

During a game, hold Left Bumper and press A, Right Trigger, B, Right Trigger, Left Trigger, X.

1-SHOT KILL

During a game, hold Left Trigger and press Y, A, Y, X, Left Bumper, B.

TEXTURELESS MODE

During a game, hold Left Trigger and press Left Bumper, A, B, A, Y, Right Trigger.

TOMB RAIDER: UNDERWORLD

BULLETPROOF LARA

During a game, hold Left Trigger and press A, Right Trigger, Y, Right Trigger, X, LB.

ONE-SHOT KILL

During a game, hold Left Trigger and press Y, A, Y, X, Left Bumper, B.

SHOW ENEMY HEALTH

During a game, hold Left Trigger and press X, B, A, Left Bumper, Right Trigger, Y.

TOM CLANCY'S ENDWAR

EUROPEAN ENFORCER CORPS

Go to Community and Extras, highlight Downloadable Content and press Y. Enter EUCA20.

RUSSIAN SPETZNAZ BATTALION

Go to Community and Extras, highlight Downloadable Content and press Y. Enter SPZT17.

RUSSIAN SPETZNAZ GUARD BRIGADE

Go to Community and Extras, highlight Downloadable Content and press Y. Enter SPZA39.

US JOINT STRIKE FORCE BATTALION

Go to Community and Extras, highlight Downloadable Content and press Y. Enter JSFA35.

TOM CLANCY'S GHOST RECON ADVANCED WARFIGHTER

ALL MISSIONS

At the Mission Select screen, hold Back + Left Trigger + Right Trigger and press Y, Right Bumper, Y, Right Bumper, X.

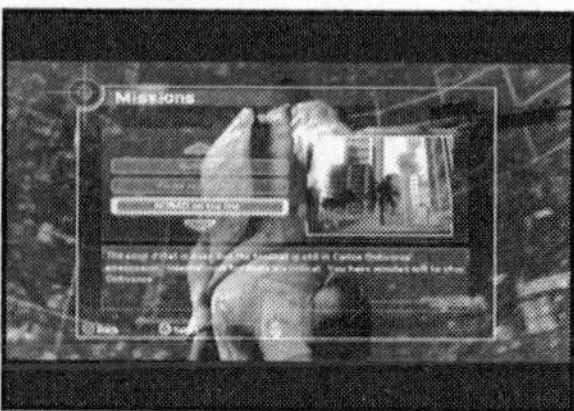

INVINCIBLE

Pause the game, hold Back + Left Trigger + Right Trigger and press Y, Y, X, Right Bumper, X, Left Bumper.

TEAM INVINCIBLE

Pause the game, hold Back + Left Trigger + Right Trigger and press X, X, Y, Right Bumper, Y, Left Bumper.

UNLIMITED AMMO

Pause the game, hold Back + Left Trigger + Right Trigger and press Right Bumper, Right Bumper, Left Bumper, X, Left Bumper, Y.

FULL HEALTH

Pause the game, hold Back + Left Trigger + Right Trigger and press Left Bumper, Left Bumper, Right Bumper, X, Right Bumper, Y.

TOM CLANCY'S GHOST RECON ADVANCED WARFIGHTER 2

FAMAS IN QUICK MISSION MODE

Create a new campaign with the name: GRAW2QUICKFAMAS.

TOM CLANCY'S HAWX

A-12 AVENGER II

At the hangar, hold Left Trigger and press X, Left Bumper, X, Right Bumper, Y, X.

F-18 HARV

At the hangar, hold Left Trigger and press Left Bumper, Y, Left Bumper, Y, Left Bumper, X.

FB-22 STRIKE RAPTOR

At the hangar, hold Left Trigger and press Right Bumper, X, Right Bumper, X, Right Bumper, Y.

TOM CLANCY'S RAINBOW SIX VEGAS

The following codes work in single player only.

BIG HEADS

Pause the game, hold Left Trigger and press B, X, A, Y, Left Thumbstick, Y, A, X, B, Right Thumbstick.

CHANGE BULLET TRACER COLOR

Pause the game, hold Left Trigger and press Left Thumbstick, Left Thumbstick, A, Right Thumbstick, Right Thumbstick, B, Left Thumbstick, Left Thumbstick, X, Right Thumbstick, Right Thumbstick, Y.

ONE SHOT KILLS

Pause the game, hold the Left Bumper and press Left Thumbstick, Right Thumbstick, Left Thumbstick, Right Thumbstick, A, B, Left Thumbstick, Right Thumbstick, Left Thumbstick, Right Thumbstick, X, Y.

THIRD PERSON VIEW

Pause the game, hold Left Trigger and press X, B, X, B, Left Thumbstick, Left Thumbstick, Y, A, Y, A, Right Thumbstick, Right Thumbstick.

TOM CLANCY'S RAINBOW SIX VEGAS 2

GI JOHN DOE MODE

Pause the game, hold the Right Bumper and press Left Thumbstick, Left Thumbstick, A, Right Thumbstick, Right Thumbstick, B, Left Thumbstick, Left Thumbstick, X, Right Thumbstick, Right Thumbstick, Y.

SUPER RAGDOLL

Pause the game, hold the Right Bumper and press A, A, B, B, X, X, Y, Y, A, B, X, Y.

THIRD PERSON MODE

Pause the game, hold the Right Bumper and press X, B, X, B, Left Thumbstick, Left Thumbstick, Y, A, Y, A, Right Thumbstick, Right Thumbstick.

TAR-21 ASSAULT RIFLE

At the Character Customization screen, hold Right Bumper and press Down, Down, Up, Up, X, B, X, B, Y, Up, Up, Y.

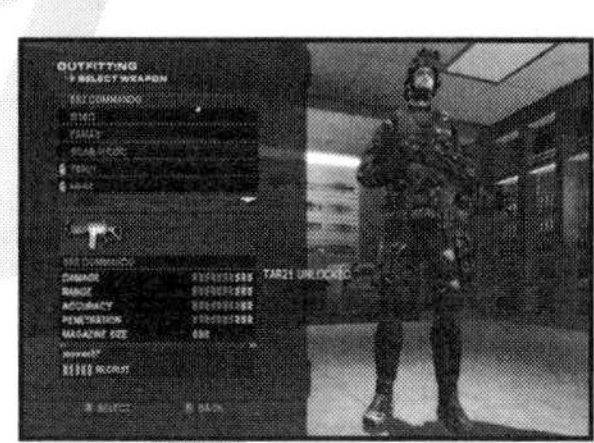

MULTIPLAYER MAP: COMCAST EVENT

Select Extras from the Main menu. Choose Comcast Gift and enter Comcast Faster.

M468 ASSAULT RIFLE

While customizing your character, hold down RB and press Up, Y, Down, A, Left, X, Right, B, Left, Left, Right, X

TONY HAWK'S AMERICAN WASTELAND

ALWAYS SPECIAL

Select Cheat Codes from the Options menu and enter uronfire. Pause the game and select Cheats from the Game Options to enable the code.

PERFECT RAIL

Select Cheat Codes from the Options menu and enter grindxpert. Pause the game and select Cheats from the Game Options to enable the code.

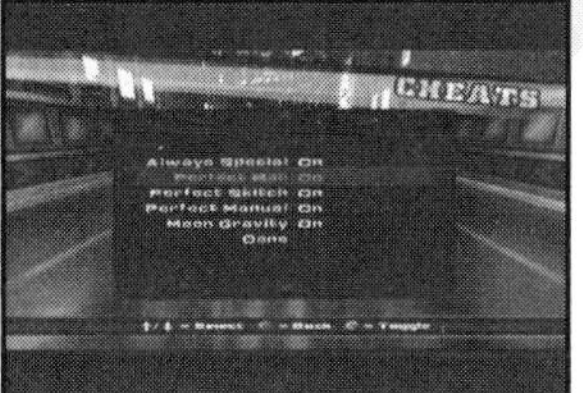

PERFECT SKITCH

Select Cheat Codes from the Options menu and enter h!tchar!de. Pause the game and select Cheats from the Game Options to enable the code.

PERFECT MANUAL

Select Cheat Codes from the Options menu and enter 2wheels!. Pause the game and select Cheats from the Game Options to enable the code.

MOON GRAVITY

Select Cheat Codes from the Options menu and enter 2them00n. Pause the game and select Cheats from the Game Options to enable the code.

MAT HOFFMAN

Select Cheat Codes from the Options menu and enter the_condor.

TONY HAWK'S PROJECT 8

SPONSOR ITEMS

As you progress through Career mode and move up the rankings, you gain sponsors. Each sponsor comes with its own Create-a-Skater item.

RANK	CAS ITEM UNLOCKED
Rank 040	Adio Kenny V2 Shoes
Rank 050	Quiksilver_Hoody_3
Rank 060	Birdhouse Tony Hawk Deck
Rank 080	Vans No Skool Gothic Shoes
Rank 100	Volcom Scallero Jacket
Rank 110	eS Square One Shoes
Rank 120	Almost Watch What You Say Deck
Rank 140	DVS Adage Shoe
Rank 150	Element Illuminate Deck
Rank 160	Etnies Sheckler White Lavender Shoes
Complete Skateshop Goal	Stereo Soundwave Deck

SKATERS

You must unlock all of the skaters, except for Tony Hawk, by completing challenges in the Career Mode. They are playable in Free Skate and 2-Player modes.

SKATER	HOW TO UNLOCK
Tony Hawk	Always unlocked
Lyn-z Adams Hawkins	Complete Pro Challenge
Bob Burquist	Complete Pro Challenge
Dustin Dollin	Complete Pro Challenge
Nyjah Huston	Complete Pro Challenge
Bam Margera	Complete Pro Challenge
Rodney Mullen	Complete Pro Challenge
Paul Rodriguez	Complete Pro Challenge
Ryan Sheckler	Complete Pro Challenge
Daewon Song	Complete Pro Challenge
Mike Vallely	Complete Pro Challenge
Stevie Willams	Complete Pro Challenge
Travis Barker	Complete Pro Challenge
Kevin Staab	Complete Pro Challenge
Zombie	Complete Pro Challenge
Christaian Hosoi	Rank #1
Jason Lee	Complete Final Tony Hawk Goal
Photographer	Unlock Shops
Security Guard	Unlock School
Bum	Unlock Car Factory
Beaver Mascot	Unlock High School
Real Estate Agent	Unlock Downtown
Filmer	Unlock High School
Skate Jam Kid	Rank #4
Dad	Rank #1
Colonel	All Gaps
Nerd	Complete School Spirit Goal

CHEAT CODES

Select Cheat Codes from the Options menu to enter the following codes. You can access some of these codes from the Options menu.

CODE	WHAT IT UNLOCKS
plus44	Travis Barker
hohohosoi	Christian Hosoi
notmono	Jason Lee
mixitup	Kevin Staab
strangefellows	Dad & Skater Jam Kid
themedia	Photog Girl & Filmer
militarymen	Colonel & Security Guard
jammypack	Always Special

CODE	WHAT IT UNLOCKS
balancegalore	Perfect Rail
frontandback	Perect Manual
shellshock	Unlimited Focus
shescaresme	Big Realtor
birdhouse	Inkblot Deck
allthebest	Full Stats
needaride	All Decks unlocked and free, except for Inkblot Deck and Gamestop Deck
yougotitall	All specials unlocked and in player's special list and set as owned in Skate Shop
wearelosers	Nerd and a Bum
manineedadate	Beaver Mascot
suckstobedead	Officer Dick
HATEDANDPROUD	The Vans unlockable item

TONY HAWK'S PROVING GROUND

Select Cheat Codes from the Options and enter the following cheats. Some codes need to be enabled by selecting Cheats from the Options during a game.

UNLOCK	CHEAT
Unlocks Boneman	CRAZYBONEMAN
Unlocks Bosco	MOREMILK
Unlocks Cam	NOTACAMERA
Unlocks Cooper	THECOOP
Unlocks Eddie X	SKETCHY
Unlocks El Patinador	PILEDRIVER
Unlocks Eric	FLYAWAY
Unlocks Mad Dog	RABBIES
Unlocks MCA	INTERGALACTIC
Unlocks Mel	NOTADUDE
Unlocks Rube	LOOKSSMELLY
Unlocks Spence	DAPPER
Unlocks Shayne	MOVERS
Unlocks TV Producer	SHAKER
Unlock FDR	THEPREZPARK
Unlock Lansdowne	THELOCALPARK
Unlock Air & Space Museum	THEINDOORPARK
Unlocks all Fun Items	OVERTHETOP
Unlocks all CAS items	GIVEMESTUFF
Unlocks all Decks	LETSGOSKATE
Unlock all Game Movies	WATCHTHIS
Unlock all Lounge Bling Items	SWEETSTUFF
Unlock all Lounge Themes	LAIDBACKLOUNGE
Unlock all Rigger Pieces	IMGONNABUILD
Unlock all Video Editor Effects	TRIPPY
Unlock all Video Editor Overlays	PUTEMONTOP
All specials unlocked and in player's special list	LOTSOFTRICKS
Full Stats	BEEFEDUP
Give player +50 skill points	NEEDSHELP
THE FOLLOWING CHEATS LOCK YOU OUT OF THE LEADERBOARDS:	
Unlocks Perfect Manual	STILLAINTFALLIN
Unlocks Perfect Rail	AINTFALLIN
Unlock Super Check	BOOYAH
Unlocks Unlimited Focus	MYOPIC
Unlock Unlimited Slash Grind	SUPERSLASHIN
Unlocks 100% branch completion in NTT	FOREVERNAILED
No Bails	ANDAINTFALLIN
YOU CAN NOT USE THE VIDEO EDITOR WITH THE FOLLOWING CHEATS:	
Invisible Man	THEMISSING
Mini Skater	TINYTATER
No Board	MAGICMAN

TRANSFORMERS: THE GAME

The following cheats disable saving and achievements:

INFINITE HEALTH
At the Main menu, press Left, Left, Up, Left, Right, Down, Right.

INFINITE AMMO
At the Main menu, press Up, Down, Left, Right, Up, Up, Down.

NO MILITARY OR POLICE
At the Main menu, press Right, Left, Right, Left, Right, Left, Right.

ALL MISSIONS
At the Main menu, press Down, Up, Left, Right, Right, Right, Up, Down.

BONUS CYBERTRON MISSIONS
At the Main menu, press Right, Up, Up, Down, Right, Left, Left.

GENERATION 1 SKIN: JAZZ
At the Main menu, press Left, Up, Down, Down, Left, Up, Right.

GENERATION 1 SKIN: MEGATRON
At the Main menu, press Down, Left, Left, Down, Right, Right, Up.

GENERATION 1 SKIN: OPTIMUS PRIME
At the Main menu, press Down, Right, Left, Up, Down, Down, Left.

GENERATION 1 SKIN: ROBOVISION OPTIMUS PRIME
At the Main menu, press Down, Down, Up, Up, Right, Right, Right.

GENERATION 1 SKIN: STARSCREAM
At the Main menu, press Right, Down, Left, Left, Down, Up, Up.

UNDERTOW

GAMER PIC 1 - SCUBA DIVER
Total 100 kills.

GAMER PIC 2 - ATLANTIS MAN
Total 10,000 kills.

VIRTUA TENNIS 3

KING & DUKE
At the Main menu, press Up, Up, Down, Down, Left, Right, LB, RB.

ALL GEAR
At the Main menu, press Left, Right, B, Left, Right, B, Up, Down.

ALL COURTS
At the Main menu, press Up, Up, Down, Down, Left, Right, Left, Right.

WIN ONE MATCH TO WIN TOURNAMENT
At the Main menu, press B, Left, B, Right, B, Up, B, Down.

VIVA PINATA

NEW ITEMS IN PET STORE
Select New Garden and enter chewnicorn as the name.

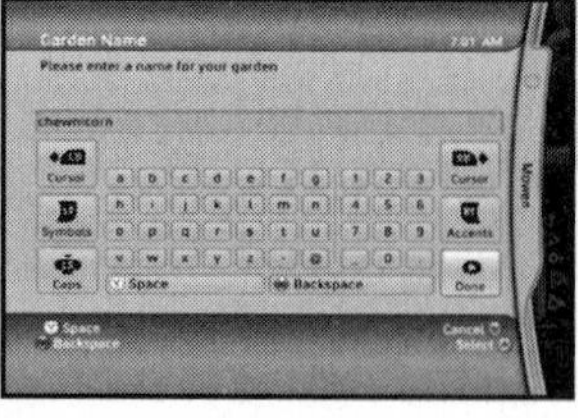

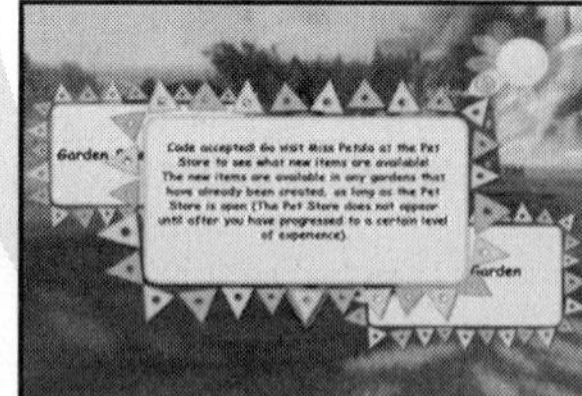

NEW ITEMS IN PET STORE
Select New Garden and enter bullseye as the name.

NEW ITEMS IN PET STORE
Select New Garden and enter goobaa as the name.

NEW ITEMS IN PET STORE
Select New Garden and enter kittyfloss as the name.

VIVA PINATA: PARTY ANIMALS

CLASSIC GAMER AWARD ACHIEVEMENT

At the START screen, press Up, Up, Down, Down, Left, Right, Left, Right, B, A. This earns you 10 points toward your Gamerscore.

VIVA PINATA: TROUBLE IN PARADISE

CREDITS

Select Play Garden and name your garden Piñata People. This unlocks the ability to view the credits on the Main menu.

WALL-E

The following cheats will disable saving. The five possible characters starting with Wall-E and going down are: Wall-E, Auto, EVE, M-O, GEL-A Steward.

ALL BONUS FEATURES UNLOCKED

Select Cheats from the Bonus Features menu and enter Wall-E, Auto, EVE, GEL-A Steward.

ALL GAME CONTENT UNLOCKED

Select Cheats from the Bonus Features menu and enter M-O, Auto, GEL-A Steward, EVE.

ALL SINGLE PLAYER LEVELS UNLOCKED

Select Cheats from the Bonus Features menu and enter Auto, GEL-A Steward, M-O, Wall-E.

ALL MULTIPLAYER MAPS UNLOCKED

Select Cheats from the Bonus Features menu and enter EVE, M-O, Wall-E, Auto.

ALL HOLIDAY COSTUMES UNLOCKED

Select Cheats from the Bonus Features menu and enter Auto, Auto, GEL-A Steward, GEL-A Steward.

ALL MULTIPLAYER COSTUMES UNLOCKED

Select Cheats from the Bonus Features menu and enter GEL-A Steward, Wall-E, M-O, Auto.

UNLIMITED HEALTH UNLOCKED

Select Cheats from the Bonus Features menu and enter Wall-E, M-O, Auto, M-O.

WALL-E: MAKE ANY CUBE AT ANY TIME

Select Cheats from the Bonus Features menu and enter Auto, M-O, Auto, M-O.

WALL-EVE: MAKE ANY CUBE AT ANY TIME

Select Cheats from the Bonus Features menu and enter M-O, GEL-A Steward, EVE, EVE.

WALL-E WITH A LASER GUN AT ANY TIME

Select Cheats from the Bonus Features menu and enter Wall-E, EVE, EVE, Wall-E.

WALL-EVE WITH A LASER GUN AT ANY TIME

Select Cheats from the Bonus Features menu and enter GEL-A Steward, EVE, M-O, Wall-E.

WALL-E: PERMANENT SUPER LASER UPGRADE

Select Cheats from the Bonus Features menu and enter Wall-E, Auto, EVE, M-O.

EVE: PERMANENT SUPER LASER UPGRADE

Select Cheats from the Bonus Features menu and enter EVE, Wall-E, Wall-E, Auto.

CREDITS

Select Cheats from the Bonus Features menu and enter Auto, Wall-E, GEL-A Steward, M-O.

WANTED: WEAPONS OF FATE

HEALTH IMPROVEMENT
Select Secret Codes and enter 0100 1100.

ONE SHOT ONE KILL
Select Secret Codes and enter 0111 0010.

PLAY WITH SPECIAL SUIT
Select Secret Codes and enter 0110 0001.

SUPER WEAPONS
Select Secret Codes and enter 0100 1111.

UNLIMITED ADRENALINE
Select Secret Codes and enter 0110 1101.

UNLIMITED AMMO
Select Secret Codes and enter 0110 1111.

PLAY AS AIRPLANE BODYGUARD
Select Secret Codes and enter 0101 0111.

PLAY AS CROSS
Select Secret Codes and enter 0101 0100.

PLAY AS JANICE
Select Secret Codes and enter 0100 0100.

PLAY AS WESLY
Select Secret Codes and enter 0100 0011.

CINEMATIC MODE
Select Secret Codes and enter 0111 0100.

CLOSE COMBAT MODE
Select Secret Codes and enter 0110 0101.

HEADSHOT MODE
Select Secret Codes and enter 0110 0111.

WWE SMACKDOWN! VS. RAW 2008

HBK AND HHH'S DX OUTFIT
Select Cheat Codes from the Options and enter DXCostume69K2.

KELLY KELLY'S ALTERNATE OUTFIT
Select Cheat Codes from the Options and enter KellyKG12R.

BRET HART
Complete the March 31, 1996 Hall of Fame challenge by defeating Bret Hart with Shawn Michaels in a One-On-One 30-Minute Iron Man Match on Legend difficulty. Purchase from WWE Shop for $210,000.

MICK FOLEY
Complete the June 28, 1998 Hall of Fame challenge by defeating Mick Foley with The Undertaker in a Hell In a Cell Match on Legend difficulty. Purchase from WWE Shop for $210,000.

MR. MCMAHON
Win or successfully defend a championship (WWE or World Heavyweight) at WrestleMania in WWE 24/7 GM Mode. Purchase from WWE Shop for $110,000.

THE ROCK
Complete the April 1, 2001 Hall of Fame challenge by defeating The Rock with Steve Austin in a Single Match on Legend Difficulty. Purchase from WWE Shop for $210,000.

STEVE AUSTIN
Complete the March 23, 1997 Hall of Fame challenge by defeating Steve Austin with Bret Hart in a Submission Match on Legend Difficulty. Purchase from WWE Shop for $210,000.

TERRY FUNK
Complete the April 13, 1997 Hall of Fame challenge by defeating Tommy Dreamer, Sabu and Sandman with any Superstar in an ECW Extreme Rules 4-Way Match on Legend difficulty. Purchase from WWE Shop for $210,000.

MR. MCMAHON BALD
Must unlock Mr. McMahon as a playable character first. Purchase from WWE Shop for $60,000.

WWE SMACKDOWN VS. RAW 2009

BOOGEYMAN
Select Cheat Codes from My WWE and enter BoogeymanEatsWorms!!.

GENE SNITSKY
Select Cheat Codes from My WWE and enter UnlockSnitskySvR2009.

HAWKINS & RYDER
Select Cheat Codes from My WWE and enter Ryder&HawkinsTagTeam.

JILLIAN HALL
Select Cheat Codes from My WWE and enter PlayAsJillianHallSvR.

LAYLA
Select Cheat Codes from My WWE and enter UnlockECWDivaLayla09.

RIC FLAIR
Select Cheat Codes from My WWE and enter FlairWooooooooooooo.

TAZZ
Select Cheat Codes from My WWE and enter UnlockECWTazzSvR2009.

VINCENT MCMAHON
Select Cheat Codes from My WWE and enter VinceMcMahonNoChance.

HORNSWOGGLE AS MANAGER
Select Cheat Codes from My WWE and enter HornswoggleAsManager.

CHRIS JERICHO COSTUME B
Select Cheat Codes from My WWE and enter AltJerichoModelSvR09.

CM PUNK COSTUME B
Select Cheat Codes from My WWE and enter CMPunkAltCostumeSvR!.

REY MYSTERIO COSTUME B
Select Cheat Codes from My WWE and enter BooyakaBooyaka619SvR.

SATURDAY NIGHT'S MAIN EVENT ARENA
Select Cheat Codes from My WWE and enter SatNightMainEventSvR.

YOU'RE IN THE MOVIES

ALL TRAILERS AND DIRECTOR'S MODE
At the options screen, press Left Bumper, Right Bumper, Left Bumper, Right Bumper, Y.

XBOX 360® ACHIEVEMENTS

GAMES

AFRO SAMURAI

ACHIEVEMENTS

NAME	GOAL/REQUIREMENT	POINT VALUE
A Secret History	Complete "THE DAIMYO'S STORY".	10
The Death of Innocence	Complete "SCHOOL INVASION".	15
The Price for Vengeance	Complete "SWORD MASTER'S STORY".	20
Love Lost	Complete "OKIKU'S STORY".	25
The Path to Godhood	Complete "THE LOWDOWN EAST PASS".	30
And so it begins	Complete "PRELUDE".	5
Copy-Cat Killer	Complete "THE DOPPELGANGER".	35
The Past Laid to Rest	Complete "KUMA'S STORY".	40
All That Stood Are Gone	Complete "THE EMPTY SEVEN'S STORY".	45
Revenge Served?	Complete "JUSTICE'S STORY".	50
Completionist	Complete the game on both difficulties.	200
Closer to God	Slice an enemy using a Vertical Attack with a bonus.	5
This Little Piggy	Slice off fingers and toes at the same time.	10
Give Me a Hand	Slice off an enemy's hand.	10
Two Birds One Sword	Slice 2 enemies at once.	5
Three-way	Slice 3 enemies at once.	5
Four to the Floor	Slice 4 enemies at once.	10
The Child Without a Name	Collect 5 mementos in "THE DAIMYO'S STORY".	5
Afro Samurai	Collect 5 mementos in "SCHOOL INVASION".	5
The Demon of Vengeance	Collect 5 mementos in "OKIKU'S STORY".	5
The Number Two	Collect 5 mementos in "THE LOWDOWN EAST PASS".	5
The Death Bringer	Collect 5 mementos in "THE DOPPELGANGER".	5
Widow Maker	Collect 5 mementos in "KUMA'S STORY".	5
The Samurai Ghost	Collect 5 mementos in "THE EMPTY SEVEN'S STORY".	5
The Number One	Unlock all skills.	100
Hundred Head Hunter	Slice off 100 heads with a bonus.	20
Head to Toe	Slice 50 enemies using a Vertical Attack with a bonus.	25
Meijin	Achieve 100 kills.	5
Kengo	Achieve 1000 kills.	20
Kensei	Achieve 2000 kills.	50
Made Hand Ronin	Complete a Ronin Straight Flush.	5

NAME	GOAL/REQUIREMENT	POINT VALUE
No Limit Ninjas	Complete a Ninja Straight Flush.	10
Kunoichi Suicide Queens	Complete a Kunoichi Straight Flush.	10
Gutshot Android Straight	Complete an Android Straight Flush.	15
Off Suit Samurai	Complete a Samurai Straight Flush.	25
Hip Hop	Slice off an enemy's foot.	10
Slow Your Roll	Slice an enemy during their attack.	5
You Are Glue	Kill an enemy with a sliced bullet.	10
I Am Rubber	Kill an enemy with a reflected bullet.	10
Mash Medley	Achieve a 20 hit combo.	5
Rhythm Section	Achieve a total of 3000 combos.	20
Let It Flow	Spill 2000 gallons of blood.	15
Bushi	Unlock 40 skills.	30
Ashigaru	Unlock 10 skills.	10
Hatamoto	Unlock 25 skills.	20
F*!# Gravity	Slice an enemy in the air.	5
Hats Off to You	Slice off a head with a bonus.	5
Torso From Tail	Slice 50 bellies.	15

ASSASSIN'S CREED

ACHIEVEMENTS

NAME	GOAL/REQUIREMENT	POINTS
The Eagle and The Apple - 1191	Complete Assassin's Creed.	100
Personal Vendetta	Kill every Templar.	40
Keeper of the Lions Passant	Find All of Richard's Flags in the Kingdom.	25
Keeper of the Creed	Find All Flags in Masyaf.	10
Keeper of the Four Gospels	Find All Flags in Jerusalem.	20
Keeper of the Crescent	Find All Flags in Damascus.	20
Absolute Symbiosis	Have a complete Synchronization bar.	45
Fearless	Complete all Reach High Points.	25
Hungerer of Knowledge	See 85% of all the memory glitches.	20
Defender of the People: Acre	Complete every free mission in Acre.	20
Defender of the People:Jerusalem	Complete every free mission in Jerusalem.	20
Defender of the People: Damascus	Complete every free mission in Damascus.	20
Conversationalist	Go through every dialog with Lucy.	20
Disciple of the Creed	Assassinate all your targets with a full DNA bar.	30
Eagle's Will	Defeat 100 opponents without dying.	20
Eagle's Flight	Last 10 minutes in open conflict.	20
Eagle's Prey	Assassinate 100 guards.	20
Blade in the Crowd	Kill one of your main targets like a true assassin.	30
Eagle's Challenge	Defeat 25 guards in a single fight.	20
Eagle's Swiftness	Perform 100 Counter Kill in Fights.	20
Eagle's Dive	Perform 50 Combo Kills in Fights.	20
Eagle's Talon	Perform 50 stealth assassinations.	15
Eagle's Dance	Perform 50 leap of faith.	10
The hands of a Thief	Pickpocket 200 throwing knives.	15
March of the Pious	Use Scholar blending 20 times.	5
Eagle's Eye	Kill 75 guards by throwing knives.	15
Enemy of the Poor	Grab and Throw 25 Harassers.	5
Gifted Escapist	Jump through 20 merchant stands.	5
Keeper of the Black Cross	Find All Teutonic Flags in Acre.	10
Keeper of the Order	Find all Templar Flags in Acre.	10
Keeper of the 8 Virtues	Find All Hospitalier Flags in Acre.	10

SECRET ACHIEVEMENTS

NAME	GOAL/REQUIREMENT	POINTS
Visions of the Future	A strange vision has appeared to you. What could it mean?	50
The Blood of a Corrupt Merchant	You've slain Tamir, Black Market Merchant in Damascus.	25
The Blood of a Slave Trader	You've slain Talal, Slave Trader of Jerusalem.	25
The Blood Of A Doctor	You've slain Garnier de Naplouse, Hospitlier Leader in Acre.	25
The Blood of a Regent	You've slain Majd Addin, Regent of Jerusalem.	25
The Blood of the Merchant King	You've slain Abul Nuqoud, Merchant King of Damascus.	25
The Blood of a Liege-Lord	You've slain William of Montferrat, Liege-Lord of Acre.	25
The Blood of a Scribe	You've slain Jubair, the Scribe of Damascus.	25
The Blood of a Teutonic Leader	You've slain Sibrand, the Teutonic Leader of Acre.	25
The Blood of a Nemesis	You've slain Robert de Sable, but there is one more...	25
Welcome to the Animus	You've successfully completed the Animus tutorial.	20
Hero of Masyaf	You've protected Masyaf from the Templar invasion.	20
The Punishment for Treason	You have found the traitor and have brought him before Al Mualim.	20

CALL OF DUTY: WORLD AT WAR

ACHIEVEMENTS

NAME	GOAL/REQUIREMENT	POINT VALUE
Carlson's Raiders	Complete 'Semper Fi' on any difficulty. (Solo only)	10
Stormed Peleliu	Establish a beachhead on the island of Peleliu on any difficulty. (Solo only)	15
The Last Stand	Survive the land and air conflict surrounding Okinawa on any difficulty. (Solo only)	20
Stabbed in the Heart	Complete all missions on the Eastern Front on any difficulty setting. (Solo only)	20
Get Your Hands Dirty	Complete 'Semper Fi' on Veteran difficulty. (Solo only)	30
Saved Private Ryan	Save the soldier before he burns to death. (Solo or co-op)	10
Bloody Peleliu	Complete 'Little Resistance' on Veteran difficulty. (Solo only)	30
Weapon of Mass Destruction	Radio in a naval bombardment that kills at least 4 Japanese soldiers. (Solo or co-op)	15
The Sword Is Broken	Complete 'Hard Landing' on Veteran difficulty. (Solo only)	30
No Safe Place	Burn an enemy out of a tree with the flamethrower in 'Hard Landing' (Solo or co-op)	15
Architect	Complete 'Vendetta' on Veteran difficulty. (Solo only)	30
The Professional	Shoot all of Amsel's henchmen, including their attack dog, without reloading. (Solo only)	15
Gunslinger	Assassinate General Amsel with a pistol shot. (Solo only)	15
The Hammer Strikes	Complete 'Their Land, Their Blood' on Veteran difficulty. (Solo only)	30
Scorched Earth	Complete 'Burn`em Out' on Veteran difficulty. (Solo only)	30
Firestarter	Complete a mission using only the flamethrower. (Melee, grenades, & explosives are okay.) (Solo or co-op)	15
Fearless	Complete 'Relentless' on Veteran difficulty. (Solo only)	30
Hell on Wheels	Complete 'Blood and Iron' on Veteran difficulty. (Solo only)	30
Iron Fist	Destroy all towers and bunkers in 'Blood and Iron'. (Solo or co-op)	15

NAME	GOAL/REQUIREMENT	POINT VALUE
No Return	Complete 'Ring of Steel' on Veteran difficulty. (Solo only)	30
Ruthless	Kill 15 enemies while mounted on a tank in 'Ring of Steel'. (Solo or co-op)	15
When It Rains, It Pours	Complete 'Eviction' on Veteran difficulty. (Solo only)	30
Shot in the Dark	Kill 10 enemies while the lights are out in the subway in 'Eviction'. (Solo or co-op)	10
One Bad Gato	Complete 'Black Cats' on Veteran difficulty. (Solo only)	30
The Sum of All Zeros	Down 45 Japanese Zeros in 'Black Cats'. (Solo only)	15
Lights Out!	In 'Black Cats', blast out all of the spot lights in the Japanese cargo convoy. (Solo only)	10
Blowtorch & Corkscrew	Complete 'Blowtorch & Corkscrew' on Veteran difficulty. (Solo only)	30
Setting of the Sun	Complete 'Breaking Point' on Veteran difficulty. (Solo only)	30
Mortar-dom	Kill 8 Japanese with thrown mortars in 'Breaking Point'. (Solo or co-op)	10
Guardian Angel	In the final battle for Okinawa, save Sergeant Roebuck. (Solo or co-op)	10
For the Motherland	Complete 'Heart of the Reich' on Veteran difficulty. (Solo only)	30
Bearing the Burden	Complete 'Downfall' on Veteran difficulty. (Solo only)	30
Rough Economy	Kill 3 enemies with a single bullet. (Solo or co-op)	15
Close Shave	Survive a Banzai attack. (Solo only)	10
Snake in the Grass	Take out a Japanese soldier while he is lying in wait in the grass. (Solo or co-op)	15
Grave Robber	Collect all Death Cards in the game. (Solo only)	15
Kamikaze	Complete any level on Regular difficulty or higher using only melee and grenades. (Solo only)	15
Throw a Six and a Half	On Hardened or Veteran difficulty, complete a level without dying. (Solo only)	15
Purple Heart	When staring into the face of adversity, show courage and persevere.	5
War Hero	Complete the game on any difficulty. (Solo only)	40
Hardened War Hero	Complete the game on Hardened or Veteran difficulty. (Solo only)	100
Get Your Left Foot Wet	Complete a match in Campaign Co-Op mode over Xbox LIVE. (Online co-op only)	30
Get Your Right Foot Wet	Complete a match in Competitive Co-Op mode over Xbox LIVE. (Online co-op only)	30
Blue Ribbon	Complete a 4-player Competitive Co-Op match in 1st place over Xbox LIVE. (Online co-op only)	25

SECRET ACHIEVEMENTS

NAME	GOAL/REQUIREMENT	POINT VALUE
It's All about Prestige	You achieved the first level of Prestige. Only 9 more to go.	0
Go Get Some Sun	You achieved the highest level in the game. Time to go outside and find some things to do...	0

CONAN

ACHIEVEMENTS

NAME	GOAL/REQUIREMENT	POINTS
Hands-On	5 Grapple Kills	10
Man Handle	50 Grapple Kills	15
Death Grip	250 grapple kills	20
Fatal Touch	500 grapple kills	30
Shish Kabob	Impale an enemy	10
Enemy Appetizers	Impale 100 enemies	30
Now You See It, Now You Don't	Disarm an enemy	10
Master Looter	Disarm 100 enemies	30
Rock of Ages	Kill 100 enemies by boulder throw	30
Free Fall	Kill an enemy by death fall	10
Death Rain	Kill 100 enemies by death fall	30

NAME	GOAL/REQUIREMENT	POINTS
Slice 'n Dice	100 dismemberments	10
Chop Shop	500 dismemberments	20
Meat Market	1000 dismemberments	30
Parry Farm	Perform every parry kill move	10
Parry Assassin	100 parry kills	15
Parry King	200 parry kills	20
Chained Attacker	Combo Counter reaches 100	10
Chain of Fools	Combo Counter reaches 325	20
Mob Massacre	Kill 5 or more enemies simultaneously	15
Treasure Seeker	Find 5 treasure chests	10
Treasure Hunter	Find 50 treasure chests	20
Filthy Rich	Find all treasure chests	30
Noble Conan	Save a Maiden	10
Triumvirate Seeker	Activate 5 rune triumvirates	10
Triumvirates United	Activate all rune triumvirates	20
The Legendary Set	Collect all armor pieces	10
Mighty Conan	Complete the game on Hard mode	30
Master Conan	Complete the game on King mode	50
Bill of Health	Find all Health Meter powerups	20
Armored Up	Find all Power Meter powerups	20
Adrenaline Rush	Find all Song of Death meter powerups	20
Master Swordsman	All one-handed blade attacks mastered	10
Master Dual Wielder	All dual wield attacks mastered	10
Master Two-Handed Swordsman	All two-handed blade attacks mastered	10
Bring out the Gimp	Kill at least 25 enemies during the Giant Squid boss battle	15
Losing His Mind	Decapitate a captain with a shield	20
Untouchable	Complete a mission without taking any damage	40
High and Mighty	Score 20000 points in a level	10
The Bloody Crown	Score 100000 total points	40

SECRET ACHIEVEMENTS

NAME	GOAL/REQUIREMENT	POINTS
Rest In Peace	Send Graven into the Netherworld in the Ocean Ruins and complete the game	40
My Hero	Save all maidens	20
Defeat Cleaver's Army	Defeat the Bone Cleaver and his army in Barachan Isles and obtain The Ward of Fire	10
Dragon Slayer	Defeat the Sand Dragon in the lost city of Shem and obtain The Ward of the Earth	10
Demon Slayer	Defeat the Elephant Demon in the Kush caves and obtain The Ward of the Abyss	20
Snake Charmer	Defeat the Sorceress Queen in Stygia and obtain The Ward of Souls	20
Sink the Squid	Defend the ship and defeat the Giant Squid	30
Who's your Daddy?	Defeat the Bone Cleaver in Argos and obtain The Ward of the Departed	30
Strength of 10 Men	Kill 10 or more enemies simultaneously	40

CRACKDOWN

ACHIEVEMENTS

NAME	GOAL/REQUIREMENT	POINTS
Agency Explosives Expert	Bomb your way to a 4-star Explosives rating.	20
Agency Athlete	Run & jump your way to a 4-star Agility rating.	20
Agency Wheelman	Accelerate and slide your way to a 4-star Driving rating.	20
Agency Brawler	Punch, jab, kick, and throw your way to a 4-star Strength rating.	20
Agency Marksman	Hit your target every time to achieve a 4-star Firearms rating.	20
Master Agent	Earn 4-star ratings in all five skill areas and then max out your Skills Status meters.	40

NAME	GOAL/REQUIREMENT	POINTS
Roadkill King	Mow down and massacre 175 gang members while driving.	15
High Flyer	Make your way to the top of the Agency Tower.	10
Firing Squad	Fire away - shoot and kill 500 gang members using firearms.	15
Bare-Knuckle Brawler	Kill 150 gang members with your bare hands (or thrown objects).	15
Mad Bomber	Show your explosive personality - kill 500 gang members using explosives.	15
Untouchable Agent	Kill 200 gang members without dying yourself.	15
Body Juggler	Use explosives to keep a body up in the air for 10 seconds.	20
Car Juggler	Use explosives to keep a car up in the air for seven seconds.	20
Hazardous Hangtime	Execute a 6-second jump in a vehicle.	10
Driving High	Achieve a height of 115 feet or more in a vehicle.	10
Front Flipper	Execute two forward flips in a single jump in a moving vehicle.	20
Timed Stunt Driver	Execute six car stunts in 60 seconds.	20
Base Jumper	Jump from the top of the Agency Tower and land in the water below.	10
Stunt Driver	Successfully execute five car stunts - front & back flips, barrel rolls, a long jump.	20
Orb Hunter	Collect 300 Hidden Orbs.	50
Free Runner	Collect 500 Agility Orbs.	50
Repo Man	Commandeer 100 gang-controlled vehicles.	10
Los Muertos Intel Master	Locate all Los Muertos dossier targets.	10
Volk Intel Master	Locate all Volk dossier targets.	10
Shai-Gen Intel Master	Locate all Shai-Gen dossier targets.	10
First Blood	Eliminate the first of 21 gang bosses.	10
Los Muertos Cleanser	Murder Los Muertos - kill all Los Muertos gang members.	20
Volk Cleanser	Eviscerate the Volk - take out all Volk gang members.	40
Shai-Gen Cleanser	Assassinate Shai-Gen - kill all Shai-Gen gang members.	50
The Trifecta	Wipe the city clean by taking out all members of all three gangs.	50
Rampage	Wreak havoc in 60-second increments.	20
Take Me To Your Supply Point	Unlock your first Supply Point.	10
It's Good To Be Connected	Unlock all Supply Points.	30
Airtime Assassin	Shoot and kill 5 gang members in a single jump (while airborne).	10
Shot-putter	Throw any object (other than a grenade) 205 feet or more.	10
Global Impact	Kill 15 gang members using the Observatory Globe.	15
Ring Leader	Drive through all of the unique Stunt Markers.	20
Chain Banger	Blow up 100 explosive objects in 60 seconds.	10
Double Trouble	Double your fun - complete your first mission in Co-op mode.	10
Tag Teamer	Partner up and complete every mission in Co-op mode.	40
Road Warrior	Successfully complete all 14 Road Races.	30
Over Our Heads	Successfully complete all 12 Rooftop Races.	30

GEARS OF WAR 2

ACHIEVEMENTS

NAME	GOAL/REQUIREMENT	POINT VALUE
Green as Grass	Train the rook (any difficulty)	10
It's a Trap!	Story progression in Act 1, Chapter 2	10
Escort Service	Story progression in Act 1, Chapter 4	10
Girl About Town	Story progression in Act 1, Chapter 6	10
That Sinking Feeling	Story progression in Act 2, Chapter 4	10
Freebaird!	Story progression in Act 2, Chapter 5	10
Heartbroken	Story progression in Act 2, Chapter 6	10

NAME	GOAL/REQUIREMENT	POINT VALUE
Longitude and Attitude	Story progression in Act 3, Chapter 3	10
Tanks for the Memories	Story progression in Act 3, Chapter 4	10
Water Sports	Story progression in Act 3, Chapter 6	10
There's a Time for Us	Story progression in Act 4, Chapter 2	10
Better Wrapped in Beacon	Story progression in Act 4, Chapter 3	10
Have Fun Storming the Castle	Story progression in Act 4, Chapter 6	10
And the Horse You Rode in On	Story progression in Act 5, Chapter 1	10
You Are the Support, Son	Story progression in Act 5, Chapter 2	10
Brumak Rodeo	Story progression in Act 5, Chapter 4	10
Does This Look Infected to You?	Story progression in Act 5, Chapter 5	10
Tourist of Duty	Complete all campaign acts on Casual Difficulty	25
Guerilla Tactician	Complete all campaign acts on Normal Difficulty	50
Artist of War	Complete all campaign acts on Hardcore Difficulty	75
Suicide Missionary	Complete all campaign acts on Insane Difficulty	150
Collector	Recover 5 collectibles (any difficulty)	5
Pack Rat	Recover 20 collectibles (any difficulty)	15
Completionist	Recover all 41 collectibles (any difficulty)	30
One-Night Stand	Complete 1 chapter in co-op on any difficulty (Marcus or Dom)	10
Open Relationship	Complete 10 chapters in co-op on any difficulty (Marcus or Dom)	30
Friends with Benefits	Complete all acts in co-op on any difficulty (Marcus or Dom)	50
Once More, With Feeling	Perform 30 perfect active reloads (any mode)	10
Takes a Licking	Melee 30 Tickers (any mode)	30
Organ Grinder	Kill 30 enemies with a cover mounted Mulcher (any mode)	10
Shock and Awe	Kill 30 enemies with the heavy Mortar (any mode)	10
Said the Spider to the Fly	Kill 10 enemies with a planted grenade (any mode)	10
Crowd Control	Melee 10 enemies down with the Boomshield equipped (any mode)	10
Smells Like Victory	Kill 30 enemies with the Scorcher Flamethrower (any mode)	10
Variety is the Spice of Death	Kill an enemy with every weapon in the game (any mode)	30
Seriously 2.0	Kill 100,000 enemies (any mode)	50
Standing Here, Beside Myself	Win 3 matches of Wingman (public)	10
Beat the Meatflag	Capture 10 meatflags in Submission (public)	10
It's Good to be the King	Win 10 rounds of Guardian as the leader (public)	10
You Go Ahead, I'll Be Fine	Win three matches of King of the Hill (public)	10
Back to Basic	Successfully complete the 5 lessons of multiplayer Training Grounds	10
Party Like It's 1999	Play 1999 rounds of multiplayer (any mode)	30
Around the World, Again	Win a multiplayer match on each map (any mode)	30
Dirty, Dirty Horde	Survive the first 10 waves of Horde (any difficulty, any map)	20
Hoard the Horde	Survive all 50 waves of Horde (any difficulty, any map)	30
Crossed Swords	Win 10 chainsaw duels (any mode)	10
A Parting Gift	Kill 10 enemies with a grenade while down but not out (any mode)	20
Pound of Flesh	Use a meatshield to save your life 10 times (any mode)	10
Photojournalist	Submit a spectator photo	10
Kick 'Em When They're Down	Perform all 11 unique executions on a downed enemy	10

GAME COMPLETION ON HARDCORE

CAMPAIGN ACHIEVEMENTS	TYPE	DIFFICULTY	POINTS	DESCRIPTION
Completed Act 1 on Hardcore	Campaign	Medium	20	Complete Act 1 on Hardcore Difficulty.
Completed Act 2 on Hardcore	Campaign	Medium	20	Complete Act 2 on Hardcore Difficulty.
Completed Act 3 on Hardcore	Campaign	Medium	20	Complete Act 3 on Hardcore Difficulty.
Completed Act 4 on Hardcore	Campaign	Medium	20	Complete Act 4 on Hardcore Difficulty.
Completed Act 5 on Hardcore	Campaign	Medium	20	Complete Act 5 on Hardcore Difficulty.
Soldier (unlocks Gamer Pic)	Campaign	Medium	20	Complete all Acts on Hardcore Difficulty.

GAME COMPLETION ON INSANE

CAMPAIGN ACHIEVEMENTS	TYPE	DIFFICULTY	POINTS	DESCRIPTION
Completed Act 1 on Insane	Campaign	Hard	30	Complete Act 1 on Insane Difficulty.
Completed Act 2 on Insane	Campaign	Hard	30	Complete Act 2 on Insane Difficulty.
Completed Act 3 on Insane	Campaign	Hard	30	Complete Act 3 on Insane Difficulty.
CAMPAIGN ACHIEVEMENTS	TYPE	DIFFICULTY	POINTS	DESCRIPTION
Completed Act 4 on Insane	Campaign	Hard	30	Complete Act 4 on Insane Difficulty.
Completed Act 5 on Insane	Campaign	Hard	30	Complete Act 5 on Insane Difficulty.
Commando (unlocks Gamer Pic)	Campaign	Hard	30	Complete all Acts on Insane Difficulty.

COG TAGS

CAMPAIGN ACHIEVEMENTS	TYPE	DIFFICULTY	POINTS	DESCRIPTION
Time to Remember	Campaign	Easy	10	Recover 10 COG Tags (on any difficulty).
Honor Bound	Campaign	Medium	20	Recover 20 COG Tags (on any difficulty).
For the Fallen	Campaign	Hard	30	Recover 30 COG Tags (on any difficulty).

KILLING BOSSES

CAMPAIGN ACHIEVEMENTS	TYPE	DIFFICULTY	POINTS	DESCRIPTION
My Love for You is Like a Truck	Campaign	Hard	30	Defeat a Berserker on Hardcore Difficulty.
Broken Fingers	Campaign	Hard	30	Defeat a Corpser on Hardcore Difficulty.
A Dish Best Served Cold	Campaign	Hard	30	Defeat General RAAM on Hardcore Difficulty.

GAME SKILLS

CAMPAIGN ACHIEVEMENTS	TYPE	DIFFICULTY	POINTS	DESCRIPTION
Zen and the Art of Reloading	Campaign	Easy	10	Perform 25 Perfect Active Reloads (on any difficulty).
Zen and the Art Part 2	Campaign	Medium	20	Perform 5 Perfect Active Reloads in a row (on any difficulty).
Clusterluck	Campaign	Medium	20	Kill 3 enemies at once 10 different times (on any difficulty).

CO-OP ACHIEVEMENTS

CO-OP SPECIFIC ACHIEVEMENTS	TYPE	DIFFICULTY	POINTS	DESCRIPTION
Dom-curious	Co-op	Easy	10	Complete 1 chapter as Dominic Santiago on any difficulty.
Domination	Co-op	Medium	20	Complete 10 chapters as Dominic Santiago on any difficulty.

CO-OP SPECIFIC ACHIEVEMENTS	TYPE	DIFFICULTY	POINTS	DESCRIPTION
I Can't Quit You Dom	Co-op	Hard	30	Complete all Acts in Co-Op on any difficulty.

VERSUS ACHIEVEMENTS

VERSUS ACHIEVEMENTS	TYPE	DIFFICULTY	POINTS	DESCRIPTION
Don't You Die on Me	Versus	Easy	10	Revive 100 teammates in Ranked Matches.
A Series of Tubes	Versus	Medium	20	Host 50 complete Ranked Matches.

WEAPON MASTERY

CAMPAIGN ACHIEVEMENTS	TYPE	DIFFICULTY	POINTS	DESCRIPTION
Fall Down Go Boom	Versus	Easy	10	Kill 100 enemies in Ranked Matches with the Boomshot.
Pistolero	Versus	Medium	20	Kill 100 enemies in Ranked Matches with a Pistol.
The Nuge	Versus	Medium	20	Kill 100 enemies in Ranked Matches with the Torquebow.
I Spy With My Little Eye	Versus	Medium	20	Kill 100 enemies in Ranked Matches with the Longshot.
Don't Hurt 'Em	Versus	Medium	20	Kill 100 enemies in Ranked Matches with the Hammer of Dawn.

HUMILIATION MASTERY

CAMPAIGN ACHIEVEMENTS	TYPE	DIFFICULTY	POINTS	DESCRIPTION
It's a Massacre	Versus	Easy	10	Kill 100 enemies in Ranked Matches with the Chainsaw.
Curb Appeal	Versus	Medium	20	Kill 100 enemies in Ranked Matches with the Curb Stomp.
Capital Punishment	Versus	Medium	20	Kill 100 enemies in Ranked Matches with an Execution.
Crackdown	Versus	Medium	20	Kill 100 enemies in Ranked Matches with Melee.
Is it a Spider?	Versus	Medium	20	Kill 100 enemies in Ranked Matches with Grenade Tag.
The Money Shot	Versus	Medium	20	Kill 100 enemies in Ranked Matches with a Head Shot.

VERSUS SUCCESS

CAMPAIGN ACHIEVEMENTS	TYPE	DIFFICULTY	POINTS	DESCRIPTION
Always Remember Your First	Versus	Easy	10	Finish playing a Versus Ranked Match.
Don't Hate the Player	Versus	Easy	10	Finish with the highest points in a Ranked Match.
Mix it Up	Versus	Medium	20	Win a Ranked Match in every Versus game type.
Can't Touch Us	Versus	Medium	20	Win 10 Ranked Matches without losing a Round.
Around the World	Versus	Hard	30	Win a Ranked Match on every Versus map.
Seriously… (unlocks Gamer Pic)	Versus	Hard	50	Kill 10,000 people in Versus Ranked Match total.

GRAND THEFT AUTO IV: THE LOST AND DAMNED

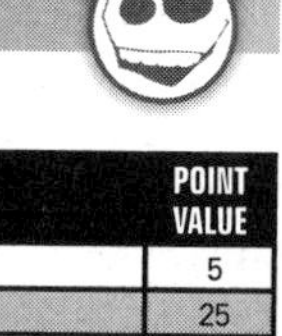

ACHIEVEMENTS

NAME	GOAL/REQUIREMENT	POINT VALUE
TLAD: One Percenter	Help Billy get his bike back.	5
TLAD: The Lost Boy	Become leader of The Lost.	25
TLAD: Easy Rider	Finish the story.	100
TLAD: Get Good Wood	In the bike races, whack off 69 bikers with a bat.	50
TLAD: Full Chat	Build Terry and Clay's toughness to 100%.	70

GUITAR HERO: METALLICA

ACHIEVEMENTS

NAME	GOAL/REQUIREMENT	POINT VALUE
The More I See	Complete the Tutorials	5
Metallica	Complete any instrument career on Expert (Guitar, Bass, Vocals, Drums or Band)	75
James Hetfield	Complete the career as the vocalist	25
Lars Ulrich	Complete the career as the drummer	25
Kirk Hammett	Complete the career as the guitarist	25
Robert Trujillo	Complete the career as the bassist	25
Holier Than Thou	Complete all instrument careers	150
One	Complete a song with any instrument on Hard or Expert in local Quickplay or Career	10
...And Justice for All	Earn 100 stars in Band Career or any single instrument Career	50
The Ecstasy of Gold	Earn $15,000	50
Ride the Lightning	You triggered star power simultaneously (4 player band)	10
2 X 4	Earn a band Hot Streak (4 player band)	10
Metal Militia	100% a song (4 player band)	30
The Struggle Within	Complete a song in a band in Quickplay or Career (4 players)	10
The Four Horsemen	Complete a song with all band members on expert in Quickplay or Career (4 player band)	20
Nothing Else Matters	Complete the career in a band (2-4 player band)	50
Better Than You	Win an online Pro Face-Off match	10
Blitzkrieg	Win an online Band v Band match (8 players)	10
Seek & Destroy	Play 20 online matches	25
The Unforgiven	Win an online Face-Off match	10
Reload	Download a song from GHTunes	5
Hero of the Day	Complete a song on Expert + in Quickplay or Career (drums only)	30
Wherever I May Roam	Complete a song in every venue	15
The Memory Remains	View a Metallifacts video	5
Black	Win an online battle match with the Fade to Black power up	10

SECRET ACHIEVEMENTS

NAME	GOAL/REQUIREMENT	POINT VALUE
Trapped Under Ice	You completed a song at the Ice Cave venue	5
Lemmy	You rocked out as Lemmy	5
Invisible Kid	You performed as the bassist	5
Some Kind of Monster	You performed as the guitarist	5
The House Jack Built	You completed a song in every In-the-Round venue	10
Astronomy	You hit every star power phrase in the song Orion	10
Stone Dead Forever	You completed a song at The Stone venue	5
Cure	You recovered from a poor performance in Quickplay or Career	5
Eye of the Beholder	You created a new custom band logo	5
Fixxxer	You created a new custom instrument	5
Blackened	You created a custom tattoo	5

NAME	GOAL/REQUIREMENT	POINT VALUE
Master of Puppets	You scored the highest individual score on a song in a band	10
Disposable Heroes	You created a new custom rocker	5
Damage Inc.	You performed as the drummer	5
Motorbreath	You performed as the vocalist	5
King Diamond	You rocked out as King Diamond	5
Enter Sandman	You scored 330,000 on the song Enter Sandman on guitar	30
Dyer's Eve	You scored 450,000 on the song Dyer's Eve as the drummer	30
Fight Fire with Fire	You scored 340,000 on the song Fight Fire with Fire as the bassist	30
Stone Cold Crazy	You scored 65,000 on Stone Cold Crazy as the vocalist	30
Creeping Death	You scored 575,000 on the song Creeping Death as the guitarist	30
Battery	You scored 1,000,000 on the song Battery as a band	30
The Unforgiven II	You won an online Face-Off match by 25,000 points or more	10
Green Hell	Drummed every green note and finished the song Blood and Thunder with the rock meter in green	15
The Unforgiven III	You won an online Pro Face-Off match by 25,000 points or more	10

LEGO BATMAN

ACHIEVEMENTS

NAME	GOAL/REQUIREMENT	POINT VALUE
Hero.	Complete the first episode - Hero.	25
Super Hero.	Complete the second episode - Hero.	25
Crusader.	Complete the third episode - Hero.	25
Villain.	Complete the first episode - Villain.	25
Super-villain.	Complete the second episode - Villain.	25
Crime Lord.	Complete the third episode - Villain.	25
Sidekick.	Complete a level in co-op.	15
Memorabilia.	Collect all Memorabilia.	35
League of Assassins.	Unlock all the Villain characters.	30
Justice League.	Unlock all the Hero characters.	30
It's the car, right?	Unlock all Vehicles (Hero/Villain).	30
1007 Mountain Drive.	Complete Wayne Manor bonus level.	30
Unbreakable.	Finish a level without dying (Character) with no extras.	30
0000001 00000011.	Build the giant LEGO Robot.	20
The city is safe... for now.	100% game completion.	50
Cobblepot School of Driving.	Smash all the cars in the robot level.	20
Vigilante.	Rescue 25 civilians.	25
Be a Hero.	Super Hero on every level.	40
Super Builder.	Build 50 LEGO build-its.	20
Nice Outfit!	Collect all suits.	20
Dressed to Impress.	Get all suit upgrades.	20
The Richest Man in Gotham.	Max out the stud counter.	40
The Most Dangerous Man on Earth.	Defeat Joker, Two-Face, Riddler and Catwoman as Batman.	20
Heads I win, tails you lose.	Defeat 10 goons and 10 police officers with Two-Face in a level.	20
Who needs curiosity?	Defeat Catwoman 9 times.	20
Shot to the goon.	Defeat 8 goons in 8 seconds.	20
Throwing up.	Throw 50 policemen with superstrength.	20
Atomic Backbreaker.	As Bane do the Backbreaker on Batman.	20
Oh, I got a live one here!	Shock 30 people with Joker's hand buzzer.	10
Kill-a moth.	Defeat Killer Moth.	20
Smash Gordon.	Defeat Commissioner Gordon with Harley Quinn's Hammer.	20

NAME	GOAL/REQUIREMENT	POINT VALUE
Start of something wonderful.	Shock the Joker with the Joker.	15
Boy Wonder.	Perform 20 backflips in a row with Robin.	10
Thanks a million.	Complete Arkham Bonus level.	30
Is it a bird? Is it a plane?	Glide for 9 seconds.	10
Gentlemen, start your screaming.	Knock 5 people into the ground with a vehicle at once.	15
Natural Habitat.	Smash all street lights in Episode 1 Chapter 1.	10
Make it snappy.	Build the Croc ride on.	20
The Destroyer of Worlds.	Destroy 12 objects at once with Bat Bombs.	15
There and back.	Destroy 10 objects in one Batarang throw.	10
Kiss from a Rose.	Eat 15 enemies with the Venus ride on .	15
Ice to see you.	Freeze 50 enemies as Mr. Freeze.	15
Say hello to my little friends.	Destroy 20 policemen with penguin bombers.	15
Scare Tactics.	Scare 5 enemies with Scarecrow.	10
Down the rabbit hole.	Use Mad Hatter's mind control to walk 5 enemies to their deaths.	20
Eat floor... High fiber.	Slam 20 goons into the floor with Batman.	15

MADDEN NFL 09

ACHIEVEMENTS

NAME	GOAL/REQUIREMENT	POINT VALUE
2 TD Kickoff Returns in a game	Return 2 Kickoffs for a TD in a game (non co-op)	75
Shut out Rival in a Franchise	Shut out Rival in a Franchise game (non co-op)	50
Kick a FG for over 50 yards	Kick a FG for over 50 yards in a Franchise game (non co-op)	15
Complete a game without an INT	Complete a game without an interception, 5 min+ quarter length (non co-op)	30
6 Rush TDs with the Dolphins	6 Rush TDs in a game with the Dolphins (non co-op)	50
Catch 10 passes in a game	Catch 10 passes in a game with one receiver (non co-op)	50
Complete game without fumbling	Complete a game without fumbling, 5 min+ quarter length (non co-op)	25
2 TD Punt Returns in a game	2 TD Punt Returns in a game (non co-op)	65
Intercept 6 passes in a game	Intercept 6 passes in a game (non co-op)	50
Hold a Rival to under 300 yards	Hold a Rival to under 300 yards total offense in a game (non co-op)	50
Score 60 points in a Rival game	Score 60 points in a Rival game (non co-op)	30
Score 40 points in a Rival game	Score 40 points in a Rival game (non co-op)	20
Record 12 sacks in a game	Record 12 sacks in a game (non co-op)	50
6 sacks with 1 player in a game	6 sacks with 1 player in a game (non co-op)	50
80% completion for a game	80% pass completion in a Franchise game, 5 min+ quarter length (non co-op)	50
7 Pass TDs with the Falcons	Throw 7 pass TDs in a game with the Falcons (non co-op)	50
550 Pass Yds with the Titans	550 Pass Yds in a game with the Titans (non co-op)	50
300 Rush Yds with the Jets	300 Rush Yds in a game with the Jets (non co-op)	10
Hold a Rival to under 20 points	Hold a Rival team to under 20 points in a game (non co-op)	10
Midway Monster	Create a legendary player from the past.	50
Can You Believe These Seats?!	Celebrate a touchdown in a wall hotspot	30
Steal Their Thunder	Steal an opposing player's touchdown celebration	30

NAME	GOAL/REQUIREMENT	POINT VALUE
Slam Dunk All-Star	Dunk the ball over the goalpost (or at least attempt to) after a touchdown	30
Shine In The Spotlight	Celebrate a touchdown in an endzone hotspot	30

SECRET ACHIEVEMENTS

NAME	GOAL/REQUIREMENT	POINT VALUE
Now Here's a Guy...	Thank you for purchasing Madden NFL 09. Here's to another 20 years!	50

MAJOR LEAGUE BASEBALL 2K9

ACHIEVEMENTS

NAME	GOAL/REQUIREMENT	POINT VALUE
Grand Poobah	Unlock all Achievements	150
Long Balls	Hit 25 Home Runs with your User Profile	5
Even More Long Balls	Hit 50 Home Runs with your User Profile	10
The Most Long Balls	Hit 100 Home Runs with your User Profile	20
Feel the Heat	Strike out 25 batters with your User Profile	5
That guy's not throwing it nice	Strike out 50 batters with your User Profile	10
There's a hole in my bat	Strike out 100 batters with your User Profile	20
Catch me if you can	Steal 25 bases with your User Profile	10
Slippery when Wet	Steal 50 bases with your User Profile	20
Good things always happen in 3's	Hit three Home Runs in a game	10
It's a good day to be a hitter	Hit four Home Runs in a game	20
Grab some pine	Strike out 12 batters in one game	10
Pining Away	Strike out 15 batters in one game	20
Unstoppable	Score 10 Runs in a game	10
Has anyone seen the Fat Lady?	Score 15 Runs in a game	20
Sticky Fingers	Steal 4 bases in one game	10
Cat Burglar	Steal 6 bases in one game	20
Flawless	Win a game without allowing any runs scored	20
Unhittable	Don't give up any hits in a game	30
It's Alive!	Create a Player	10
Man-Crush	Hit a Home Run with Tim Lincecum	10
Chicks dig the long ball	Win the Classic Home Run Derby®	10
I could have been a contender	Play a Ranked Online Exhibition game	10
Two turn tables...	Create a 2K beats Playlist	10
Absolute Power	Hit 40 Home Runs in a season with one player (play at least 20 games)	20
May the best man...	Win 20 Games in a season with one pitcher (play at least 20 games)	20
Centennial Man	Drive in 100 runs in a season with one player (play at least 20 games)	20
Show Stopper	Save 40 games in a season with one player (play at least 20 games)	20
Bicentennial Man	Strike out 200 batters in a season with one player (play at least 20 games)	20
There can be only one	Win the World Series® in Franchise mode (play at least 20 games)	20
If you build it...	Create a Card Team	5
Spring Training	Try all 4 Practice Modes	5
King of the Hill	Get to the top of the Best of the Best ladder in Home Run Derby® Mode	5
Alone at the top	Win the World Series® in Postseason Mode (Play Final Game)	5
Team 2K	Beat a Team 2K member or someone that has unlocked this achievement in an online game	60
Hurlers	Unlock all the pitcher cards in the game	10

NAME	GOAL/REQUIREMENT	POINT VALUE
Crushers	Unlock all the batter cards in the game	10
Teamwork	Unlock all nine cards for one team	5
Spread the wealth	Unlock one card on each of the 30 MLB teams	5
A man for all seasons	Unlock 10 Classic Player Cards	10
One Hundo	Unlock 100 cards	10
Two Hundo	Unlock 200 cards	10
All the Tea...	Unlock all 320 Cards	10

SECRET ACHIEVEMENTS

NAME	GOAL/REQUIREMENT	POINT VALUE
Hard Knocks	Hit three batters in a row	5
Vicious Cycle	Hit a Home Run, a Triple, a Double and a Single in one game with one player	50
This old man came rolling home	Steal home	50
Expect the Unexpected	Drive in a run with a pitcher during a game	5
That's all folks	Hit a home run to win a game	50
Untouchable	Throw a No Hitter with one pitcher in a game	50
Ya Can't Get Fooled Again	Strike out a batter and throw out a runner on the same play	50

MIRROR'S EDGE

ACHIEVEMENTS

NAME	GOAL/REQUIREMENT	POINT VALUE
Access all areas	Unlock all Time Trial stretches.	20
Tango down	Knock out 20 enemies in melee combat.	15
Mine!	Perform 15 successful disarms (outside of the tutorial).	15
Packrat	Find all 30 hidden bags.	80
Back on the job	Complete the Tutorial.	10
Prologue Complete	Complete the Prologue in story mode.	20
Chapter 1 Complete	Complete Chapter 1 in story mode.	20
Chapter 2 Complete	Complete Chapter 2 in story mode.	20
Chapter 3 Complete	Complete Chapter 3 in story mode.	20
Chapter 4 Complete	Complete Chapter 4 in story mode.	20
Chapter 5 Complete	Complete Chapter 5 in story mode.	20
Chapter 6 Complete	Complete Chapter 6 in story mode.	20
Chapter 7 Complete	Complete Chapter 7 in story mode.	20
Chapter 8 Complete	Complete Chapter 8 in story mode.	20
That's a wrap	Complete the story mode on any difficulty.	60
Bag lady	Find all three hidden bags in one chapter.	20
Pro runner	Complete story mode on hard difficulty.	80
Ran out of fingers	Find 11 hidden bags.	30
On the clock	Beat the qualifier time on any Time Trial stretch.	10
Baby steps	Attain a Time Trial star rating of 20.	20
A for effort	Attain a Time Trial star rating of 35.	25
Still counting	Attain a Time Trial star rating of 50	30
Prologue Speedrun	Complete a Speedrun of the Prologue below the target time.	10
Chapter 1 Speedrun	Complete a Speedrun of Chapter 1 below the target time.	10
Chapter 2 Speedrun	Complete a Speedrun of Chapter 2 below the target time.	10
Chapter 3 Speedrun	Complete a Speedrun of Chapter 3 below the target time.	10
Chapter 4 Speedrun	Complete a Speedrun of Chapter 4 below the target time.	10
Chapter 5 Speedrun	Complete a Speedrun of Chapter 5 below the target time.	10
Chapter 6 Speedrun	Complete a Speedrun of Chapter 6 below the target time.	10
Chapter 7 Speedrun	Complete a Speedrun of Chapter 7 below the target time.	10

NAME	GOAL/REQUIREMENT	POINT VALUE
Chapter 8 Speedrun	Complete a Speedrun of Chapter 8 below the target time.	10
Chapter 9 Speedrun	Complete a Speedrun of Chapter 9 below the target time.	10
Vrooom!	Maintain sprint speed for 30 seconds.	40
Up, over, under, onwards	String together the following: jump, coil (over obstacle), slide (under obstacle).	25
Free flowing	String together the following: wallrun, jump, speedvault.	25
May I have this dance?	String together the following: wallrun, turn, jump, wallclimb, turn, jump.	30
aaaand safe!	String together the following: wallrun, jump, coil (over obstacle), skill roll.	30
Head over heels	Complete a chapter of the game without ending up in a heavy landing.	20
Untouchable	Complete a chapter without getting shot.	15
Pacifist	Complete a chapter without firing a gun.	15
Test of Faith	Complete the game without shooting an enemy.	80
Martial artist	Perform a melee hit from a wallrun.	10
U-turn	String together: wallrun, wallrun, turn, swing, jump. [Pure Time Trials].	30
Dicey launch	String together: slide, wallrun, wall climb, turn, jump. [Pure Time Trials].	30
Surreptitious swing	String together: springboard, wallrun, turn, swing, jump. [Pure Time Trials].	30
The twister	String together: wallclimb, turn, swing, wallclimb, turn, swing, jump. [Pure Time Trials].	30
To explore strange new worlds	Attain a Time Trial star rating of 75. [Pure Time Trials].	30
Superstar	Attain a Time Trial star rating of 90. [Pure Time Trials].	100

SECRET ACHIEVEMENTS

NAME	GOAL/REQUIREMENT	POINT VALUE
Hey, it's-a-me!	Execute a stomp move on an enemy.	10
Sweet goodbye	Trigger the flip-off move.	5

NBA 2K9

ACHIEVEMENTS

NAME	GOAL/REQUIREMENT	POINT VALUE
30 Assists	Record 30 assists or more with any team.	20
10 Blocks	Record 10 blocks or more with any team.	20
15 Steals	Record 15 steals or more with any team.	20
Rebound Margin +7	Win the rebound battle by a margin of +7 with any team.	20
15 Threes	Make 15 three pointers or more with any team.	15
Defensive FG%	Hold the opposing team's FG% below 40% with any team.	15
Lights Out	FG% over 55% for the game [minimum 40 FGA's] with any team.	15
Track Meet	Score at least 15 fastbreak points with any team.	15
Second Unit	Score at least 40 bench points with any team.	15
Inside Domination	Score at least 60 points in the paint with any team.	20
Good Hands	Record 20 assists with no more than 5 turnovers with any team.	20
All-Hustle	Record at least 10 offensive rebounds, 5 blocks and 5 steals with any team.	15
All-Heart	Start the 4th period losing by 10 or more points and win the game with any team.	15
3-For-All	Make at least 10 3pt FG's while shooting at least 45% from 3pt range with any team.	20
Ice Water	FT% over 85% with at least 15 FTA's with any team.	15
Lockdown	Record at least 10 blocks and 10 steals with any team.	20
Celtics vs Lakers	User controlled team must win this matchup on All-Star difficulty.	15

NAME	GOAL/REQUIREMENT	POINT VALUE
Spurs vs Suns	User controlled team must win this matchup on All-Star difficulty.	15
Cavaliers vs Wizards	User controlled team must win this matchup on All-Star difficulty.	15
Suns vs Mavericks	User controlled team must win this matchup on All-Star difficulty.	15
Lakers vs Clippers	User controlled team must win this matchup on All-Star difficulty.	15
East vs West	User controlled team must win this matchup on All-Star difficulty.	15
LeBron James	Record at least 35 points, 9 rebounds and 9 assists with LeBron James.	25
Dwyane Wade	Record at least 26 points, 5 rebounds and 7 assists with Dwyane Wade.	25
Kobe Bryant	Record at least 40 points, 5 rebounds and 5 assists with Kobe Bryant.	25
Allen Iverson	Record at least 30 points, 8 assists and 3 steals with Allen Iverson.	25
Steve Nash	Record at least 20 points and 15 assists with Steve Nash.	25
Dwight Howard	Record at least 20 points, 15 rebounds and 3 blocks with Dwight Howard.	25
Gilbert Arenas	Record at least 35 points, 3 steals and 5 threes with Gilbert Arenas.	25
Carmelo Anthony	Record at least 40 points and 8 rebounds with Carmelo Anthony.	25
Chris Paul	Record at least 20 points, 10 assists and 3 steals with Chris Paul.	25
Kevin Garnett	Record at least 20 points, 13 rebounds and 5 assists with Kevin Garnett.	25
Yao Ming	Record at least 30 points, 12 rebounds and 4 blocks with Yao Ming.	25
Chris Bosh	Record at least 30 points, 10 rebounds and 2 blocks with Chris Bosh.	25
Sprite Slam Dunk	Win the Sprite Slam Dunk Contest using LeBron James.	35
Dunk-Off	Defeat any challenger in a Dunk-Off.	35
Trivia	Answer 15 trivia questions correctly.	35
3pt Shootout	Win the 3pt Shootout.	15
Create Player	Use the Create Player feature.	10
2K Beats Playlist	Create a 2K Beats playlist.	10
Online Ranked Game	Win one online ranked game.	15
3 Online Ranked Streak	Win 3 online ranked games in a row.	15
5 Online Ranked Streak	Win 5 online ranked games in a row.	20
5 Online Ranked Wins	Win 5 online ranked games.	15
10 Online Ranked Wins	Win 10 online ranked games.	25
20 Online Ranked Wins	Win 20 online ranked games.	30
Team 2K	Beat a Team 2K member in an online game.	20
Good Teammate	Earn a positive "teammate rating" in the online Team-Up Mode.	20
Better to Give	Share any file type through 2K Share.	20
Reel Critic	Download a reel from ReelViewer and rate it.	10

NBA LIVE 09

ACHIEVEMENTS

NAME	GOAL/REQUIREMENT	POINT VALUE
Ice Water	Win a solo game in overtime vs. the CPU.	30
Well Rounded Player	Get a 'triple double' with your player in a solo Be a Pro game vs. the CPU.	50
Super GM	Fully upgrade your Dynasty Mode™ team staff.	100
Perimeter Man	Fully complete all of the 'Guard Station' challenges in the NBA LIVE Academy.	50

NAME	GOAL/REQUIREMENT	POINT VALUE
BMOC	Fully complete all of the 'Big Man Station' challenges in the NBA LIVE Academy.	50
Team Player	Fully complete all of the 'Team-Play Station' challenges in the NBA LIVE Academy.	50
Created a Monster	Score over 60 points with a created player in a solo game vs. the CPU.	25
The Past is Present	Play and win a solo NBA LIVE Rewind Game vs. the CPU.	25
Game of the Week	Play and win a 'Game of the Week' ranked match online.	30
BAP MVP	Win a Be a Pro game, receiving an 80 or higher Be a Pro rating with your player solo vs. the CPU.	30
David and Goliath	Defeat any team rated 10 points or higher in a solo match on Superstar difficulty vs. the CPU.	50
MVP	A player on your Dynasty Mode™ team wins the MVP of the regular season.	30
NBA Finals MVP	A player on your Dynasty Mode™ teams wins the NBA Finals MVP.	30
All-Star	A player on your Dynasty Mode™ team makes the NBA All-Star Game.	20
All-NBA	A player on your Dynasty Mode™ team makes the All-NBA team.	20
Clutch	On Superstar difficulty vs. the CPU, make two free throws in a row with under two minutes remaining.	20
G.O.A.T.	Win by at least 20 points in solo game on Superstar difficulty vs. the CPU.	60
The Comeback Kid	Win a solo game after being down by 20 points vs. the CPU.	40
Shock the World	Defeat Team USA in a solo match in the FIBA World Championship tournament vs. the CPU.	30
The Grinder	Play 20 ranked matches online.	100
Club Victory	Play and win a Team Play Club match.	50
Cool Off	Shut down a hot 'Shot Streak' by keeping his point total under 10 vs. the CPU (minimum 10 min. Q).	50
Old School	Win a game with no dunks or 3 point shots in a solo game vs. the CPU.	60

NHL 09

ACHIEVEMENTS

NAME	GOAL/REQUIREMENT	POINT VALUE
Position Player	As the lead NHL® 09 Profile win a Ranked Versus Match locked as the goalie.	25
Shut the Door	As the lead NHL® 09 Profile get a shutout in a ranked versus match locked as the goalie.	50
Streaker	As the lead NHL® 09 Profile win 5 ranked matches in a row.	25
People Person	As the lead NHL® 09 Profile complete an OTP game with 10 players.	25
Team Player	As the lead NHL® 09 Profile play 25 OTP Ranked Matches.	25
Be A Pro	As the lead NHL® 09 Profile play EA Sports™ Hockey League with a random team.	25
Play Like The Pros	As the lead NHL® 09 Profile execute a created play online.	25
EA Sports™ Hockey League	As the lead NHL® 09 Profile play EA Sports™ Hockey League with your team.	50
Big Club	As the lead NHL® 09 Profile be part of an online team with 15 players.	25
Online All The Time	As the lead NHL® 09 Profile play 30 Versus Ranked Matches.	30
Enforcer Extraordinaire	As the lead NHL® 09 Profile win a fight against a non user controlled player.	25
Media Man	As the lead NHL® 09 Profile assign any playlist to a game area with the Custom Audio feature.	25
Show Off	As the lead NHL® 09 Profile create and upload a video.	50

NAME	GOAL/REQUIREMENT	POINT VALUE
Say Cheese	As the lead NHL® 09 Profile take and upload a screenshot.	50
Build Your Legend	As the lead NHL® 09 Profile apply a new screenshot to your hockey card.	50
Be A Pro Legend	As the lead NHL® 09 Profile unlock your Be A Pro Legend hockey card.	100
EA Sports™ Hockey League Legend	As the lead NHL® 09 Profile unlock your EA Sports™ Hockey League Legend card.	100
Complete Legend	As the lead NHL® 09 Profile unlock both the Be A Pro and EA Sports™ Hockey League Legend cards	75
DEL Victory	As the lead NHL® 09 Profile win a game with a German DEL team on Pro Level.	30
Russian Superliga Victory	As the lead NHL® 09 Profile win a game with a Russian Superliga team on Pro Level.	30
A Defense Pro	As the lead NHL® 09 Profile achieve an overall Be A Pro rank of A as a Defenseman on Pro Level.	25
A Center Pro	As the lead NHL® 09 Profile achieve an overall Be A Pro rank of A as a Center on Pro Level.	25
A Winger Pro	As the lead NHL® 09 Profile achieve an overall Be A Pro rank of A as a Winger on Pro Level.	25
A Goalie Pro	As the lead NHL® 09 Profile achieve an overall Be A Pro rank of A as a Goalie on Pro Level.	25
Hat Trick	As the lead NHL® 09 Profile score a Hat Trick with your Be A Pro Character.	30
Passing Machine	As the lead NHL® 09 Profile get 3 assists in a game with your Be A Pro Character.	30

SECRET ACHIEVEMENT

NAME	GOAL/REQUIREMENT	POINT VALUE
Bully	As the lead NHL® 09 Profile win a fight against another user.	0

NHL 2K9

ACHIEVEMENTS

NAME	GOAL/REQUIREMENT	POINT VALUE
5 Goals	Achieve a total of 5 User Goals.	5
25 Goals	Achieve a total of 25 User Goals.	10
75 Goals	Achieve a total of 75 User Goals.	20
150 Goals	Achieve a total of 150 User Goals.	40
1000 Goals	Achieve a total of 1000 User Goals.	100
10 Assists	Achieve a total of 10 User Assists.	5
40 Assists	Achieve a total of 40 User Assists.	10
100 Assists	Achieve a total of 100 User Assists.	20
200 Assists	Achieve a total of 200 User Assists.	40
1500 Assists	Achieve a total of 1500 User Assists.	100
10 PIMs	Achieve a total of 10 User PIMs (Penalties in Minutes).	5
50 PIMs	Achieve a total of 50 User PIMs (Penalties in Minutes).	10
100 PIMs	Achieve a total of 100 User PIMs (Penalties in Minutes).	20
150 PIMs	Achieve a total of 150 User PIMs (Penalties in Minutes).	40
500 PIMs	Achieve a total of 500 User PIMs (Penalties in Minutes).	100
1 Win	Achieve a total of 1 User Wins.	5
15 Wins	Achieve a total of 15 User Wins.	10
50 Wins	Achieve a total of 50 User Wins.	20
100 Wins	Achieve a total of 100 User Wins.	40
150 Wins	Achieve a total of 150 User Wins.	100
Powerplay Specialist	Score three powerplay goals in one game.	20
Boom Goes the Dynamite	Score a goal from behind the blue line.	10
Kill It	Kill a full 2 minute 5 on 3 powerplays.	10

NAME	GOAL/REQUIREMENT	POINT VALUE
Skillful Skater	Score a goal after performing a 1-on-1 deke special move.	10
Masterful Scorer	Score a goal using a goalie deke special move.	10
Wraparound	Score on a wraparound goal.	5
Ride the Zamboni	Win the Zamboni mini-game.	40
Marty Turco	Get a shutout with Marty Turco in net while facing a minimum of 20 shots.	10
Jason Spezza	Get at least 6 points with Jason Spezza in a single game.	10
Joe Thornton	Get at least 2 goals, 3 assists and 4 PIMs with Joe Thornton in a single game.	10
Rick Nash	Get at least 3 points and a shootout goal in a win with Rick Nash.	10
Undisputed Champion	Win the Presidents' Trophy and Stanley Cup in a single season.	45
Reel Him In	Resign a Superstar (95+ overall) to your team.	15
Lumberjack	Get a hat trick with a player that's fully-bearded in the Stanley Cup playoffs.	15
Team 2K	Beat a Team 2K member or someone that has unlocked this achievement in an online game.	20
Good Teammate	Average an A teammate grade.	20
Alter Ego	Customize your Online Avatar.	20
Critic	Download and rate a reel from ReelViewer.	20

PRINCE OF PERSIA

ACHIEVEMENTS

NAME	GOAL/REQUIREMENT	POINT VALUE
Wallrunner	Completing the Canyon.	10
Compass	Use the Compass.	10
Heal the Land	First Healing.	30
Saviour of the City of Light	Final Healing.	50
Explorer	Explore every part of every region.	20
Block Master	Block 50 attacks.	20
Deflect Master	Deflect 20 attacks.	20
Sword Master	Perform 14 hits in one combo.	20
Be gentle with her	Elika saves you fewer than 100 times in the whole game.	100
Improviser	Use the environment against an enemy.	10
Up against it	Win a wall mini-game in combat.	10
Ruined Citadel Runner	Run from the Sun Temple's Fertile Ground to the Fertile Ground in Windmills in 5 minutes.	10
Vale Runner	Run between the Fertile Grounds in the Construction Yards and Heaven's Stair in 6 minutes.	20
Royal Palace Runner	Run between the Fertile Grounds in the Royal Gardens and Coronation Halls in 4 minutes.	30
City of Light Runner	Run between the Fertile Grounds in the Tower of Ahriman and City of Light in 7 minutes.	40
Warrior Special	Dodge the Warrior's attacks 20 times in one battle.	20
Hunter Special	Deflect the Hunter's attacks 5 times in one battle.	20
Alchemist Special	Defeat the Alchemist without using the acrobatic button.	20
Concubine Special	Defeat the Concubine without using grab.	20
Light Seeds Finder	Collect 100 Light Seeds.	10
Light Seeds Collector	Collect 200 Light Seeds.	10
Light Seeds Provider	Collect 300 Light Seeds.	10
Light Seeds Locator	Collect 400 Light Seeds.	10
Light Seeds Harvester	Collect 500 Light Seeds.	10
Light Seeds Hoarder	Collect 600 Light Seeds.	10
Light Seeds Gatherer	Collect 700 Light Seeds.	10
Light Seeds Accumulator	Collect 800 Light Seeds.	10
Light Seeds Protector	Collect 900 Light Seeds.	10
Light Seeds master	Collect 1001 Light Seeds.	50

NAME	GOAL/REQUIREMENT	POINT VALUE
Speed Kill	Kill 10 generic enemies before they spawn.	10
Throw Master	Throw 10 Soldiers of Ahriman into pits.	10
Assassin View	Find the Assassin's view.	10
Titanic view	Find the Titanic View.	10
In Harmony	500 coop jumps.	10
Precious Time	Take one minute to think.	10
Where's that Temple?	Talk to Elika.	10
Getting to Know You	Get to know Elika by talking to her.	10
Good Company	Learn about the world, and Elika's history.	10
Climbing to New Heights!	Find the highest point in the world.	10
Sinking to New Depths!	Find the lowest point in the world.	10
Speed Demon	Finish the game in under 12 hours.	10
Combo Specialist	Find every combo in the game.	50
Leaving the Storm	Complete the Epilogue.	30
Bouncing From Here to There	Complete the puzzle with rebound in the Epilogue.	20
The Best Offence Is Good Defense	Defeat any enemy of the Epilogue by only starting a combo with a Deflect and Counter-Attack.	20
Change Once, Then Die	In the Epilogue, defeat the Shapeshifter with only one shape change.	20
A Fresco Of Light	Reach one Ormazd's fresco in the Epilogue.	10
All The Frescos	Reach all Ormazd's Frescos in the Epilogue.	20
Born Dead	Kill all the soldiers of the Epilogue before they spawn.	40

SECRET ACHIEVEMENTS

NAME	GOAL/REQUIREMENT	POINT VALUE
Into the Storm... Saved!	Congratulations, you have unlocked Elika's saving ability.	10
Death of a Concubine	Congratulations, you have killed the Concubine.	20
Now who's the Hunter?	Congratulations, you have killed the Hunter.	20
Death of a Warrior King	Congratulations, you have killed the Warrior.	20
Traitor's End	Congratulations, you have killed the Alchemist.	20
From Darkness...Light!	Congratulations, you have reimprisoned Ahriman.	30
To be continued...	Congratulations, the game is complete... the story has only just begun...	80
I Only Need a Hand or Twenty	Elika saves you fewer than 20 times in the whole Epilogue.	40
No Time to Waste	Complete the Epilogue in less than 2 hours.	40
What Once was There	First use of Energize in the Epilogue.	10

ROCK BAND 2

ACHIEVEMENTS

NAME	GOAL/REQUIREMENT	POINT VALUE
Solid Gold, Baby!	Gold Star a song	25
The Bachman-Turner Award	Maintain deployed Overdrive for 90 seconds	25
Flawless Fretwork	Score 100% notes hit as a guitarist on Expert	25
Flawless Guitar Solo	100% a guitar solo on Expert, using only the solo buttons	20
Flawless Drumming	Score 100% notes hit as a drummer on Expert	25
Flawless Singing	Score a 100% rating as a vocalist on Expert	25
Flawless Groove	Score 100% notes hit as bassist, up-strums only, on Expert	25
Comeback Kid	Defeat the last player that defeated you over Xbox LIVE in either Score Duel or Tug of War.	15
Victory!	Defeat a player in either Score Duel or Tug of War.	15
Band Savior	Be a savior three times during a single song	20
Overdrive Overdose	Achieve an 8x Band Multiplier	25

NAME	GOAL/REQUIREMENT	POINT VALUE
Hello Cleveland!	Deploy Vocal Overdrive 4 times in a single song	20
Million Point Club	Earn more than 1,000,000 points in a single song.	25
You're Hired!	Hire a staff member	10
Needs more Umlauts!	Make a band logo	10
The San Dimas 4th Annual Award	Compete in a Battle of the Bands event	15
You Killed the Radio Star	Make a music video in World Tour	15
Clothes to the Edge	Buy over $100,000 worth of items from the Rock Shop	20
Along for the Ride	Beat an instrument-specific challenge while playing another instrument	10
Challenge Novice	Complete either 25 challenges on Medium, 10 challenges on Hard, or 5 challenges on Expert	10
Challenge Master	Complete 25 Challenges on Hard Difficulty or 10 Challenges on Expert Difficulty	15
Challenge Savant	Complete 25 Challenges on Expert Difficulty	25
The Final Countdown	Unlock an Impossible Challenge	15
Groove Assassin	Beat the Impossible Bass Challenge	20
Lord of the Strings	Beat the Impossible Guitar Challenge	25
Stage Igniters	Beat the Impossible Band Challenge	25
AN-I-MAL!!!	Beat the Impossible Drum Challenge	25
Virtuoso	Beat the Impossible Vocal Challenge	25
West Coast Performer	Play a set on the West Coast of North America	10
Heartland Performer	Play a set in Middle America	10
East Coast Performer	Play a set on the East Coast of North America	10
God Save the Band	Play a set in the United Kingdom	10
Western Europe Performer	Play a set in Western Europe.	10
Eastern European Performer	Play a set in Eastern Europe	10
Worldwide Sensation	Gain access to every venue in the world	25
Road Dog	Play in every venue in the world	30
One Million Fans	Reach 1 million fans in World Tour	30
Open Road	Win a Bus in World Tour	20
Got Wheels	Win a Van in World Tour	20
Jet Setter	Win a Jet in World Tour	20
Beat It!	Complete all beats at 60 BPM or higher or half of the beats at 140 BPM or higher	10
The Beat Goes On	Complete all beats at 100 BPM or higher or half of the beats at 180 BPM or higher	20
Fill Me In	Complete all fills at 60 BPM or higher or half of the fills at 140 BPM or higher	10
Fill Legend	Complete all fills at 100 BPM or higher or half of the fills at 180 BPM or higher	20

SECRET ACHIEVEMENTS

NAME	GOAL/REQUIREMENT	POINT VALUE
Buy a Real Instrument Already!	Beat an "Impossible" Challenge with all players on Expert Difficulty	35
Rock Immortal Inductee	Joined the Rolling Stone Rock Immortals list	20
Vinyl Artist	Finished the Endless Setlist 2 in World Tour on Medium	20
Gold Artist	Finished the Endless Setlist 2 in World Tour on Hard	30
Platinum Artist	Finished the Endless Setlist 2 in World Tour on Expert	50
The Bladder of Steel Award	Completed the Endless Setlist 2 without pausing or failing.	25

SKATE 2

ACHIEVEMENTS

NAME	GOAL/REQUIREMENT	POINT VALUE
On Top Of The World	Perform an invert on one of the highest points in the city in career mode.	20
Skater Evolved	Get off your board in career mode.	5
I Like To Move It	Move your first object in career mode.	5
That's the Way	Beat all of Danny Way's film challenges.	20
GVR Champ	Win the GVR Contest.	20
Big Air Champ	Win the San Van-a-Slamma.	50
Still Alive?	Win a Deathrace in career mode.	5
Race Hero	Win all races in career mode.	20
Where's my TV show?	Beat all Rob Dyrdek challenges.	20
SBM Cover	Get the cover of The Skateboard Mag.	30
Thrasher Cover	Get the cover of Thrasher.	30
Meet Slappy	Meet Slappy.	5
How you like them apples?	Acquire all phone numbers for the pros.	20
Anyone Else?	Beat all the pros at Throwdown challenges.	20
New San Van Hero	Call Mikey 10 times.	20
Perfectionist	Complete all paths in career mode.	50
Pull the Plug	Drain every pool and fountain in career mode.	15
Real Estate Mogul	Purchase all property in career mode.	50
Spare Parts	All Hall Of Meat paths complete.	50
Fully Sponsored	Obtain all sponsorships.	50
Urban Legend Too	Own all spots in career mode.	40
The Architect	Upload a created spot.	5
The Critic	Rate 10 community videos and photos.	10
Pwn some n00bs	Win an online ranked match.	15
Active Skater	Successfully complete all online freeskate activities with your created skater.	20
Online Legend	Achieve Legend Rank Online.	50
Online Pro	Achieve Pro Rank Online.	25
Amateur Skater	Achieve Amateur Rank Online.	15
Graphically Extreme	Add a custom graphic to your skater.	5
Dethrowned	Download and own a community-created spot	20
Skater's Choice	Win the Skater's choice award in an online ranked match.	20
Juggling Chainsaws	Wipeout at high speed in career mode.	20
Skitched Up	Skitch for 1000 meters or 3000 feet in career mode.	5
Make it Big!	Use Big Black's service 10 times in career mode.	15
Running Man	Escape a chase off board in career mode.	5
DIY	Spend 30 minutes moving objects in career mode	35
Good Samaritan	Knock down a security guard chasing another skater in career mode.	20
Need for Speed	Maintain maximum speed for 5 seconds in career mode.	50
Sandbag	Break at least 15 bones in a single wipeout in career mode.	20
Gender Bender	Change your skater's gender	5
Grasshopper	Perform one grass gap of at least 10 meters or 30 feet in career mode.	20
Stairmaster	Perform one stair gap of at least 12 meters or 36 feet in career mode.	20
Uninsurable	Break 100 bones in career mode	20
Playing Nice Together	Complete your first online freeskate activity with your created skater.	5
Cooperation is key	Complete 50 online freeskate activities with your created skater.	10
Film School Dropout	Complete all film and photo challenges at Oliver Elementary.	25
Parking Lot Attendant	Complete all film and photo challenges at the Parkade.	25
Center of Attention	Complete all film challenges at the Community Center.	25
Best in Class	Win the Best Trick Contest at Oliver Elementary.	25

NAME	GOAL/REQUIREMENT	POINT VALUE
Best Trick Valet	Win the Best Trick Contest at the Parkade.	25
Community Jammer	Win the Jam Contest at the Community Center.	25
A Budding Star	Complete all film challenges at Rob's Fantasy Factory.	25
Jam Fantasy	Win the Jam Contest at Rob's Fantasy Factory.	25

SECRET ACHIEVEMENTS

NAME	GOAL/REQUIREMENT	POINT VALUE
Taste The Mongo	Mongo Push 5000 times in career mode.	20
Skylight Superstar	Drop into Rob's plaza through the skylight.	25
No Hard Hat Required	Touch the top of the construction full-pipe.	25

SPIDER-MAN: WEB OF SHADOWS

ACHIEVEMENTS

NAME	GOAL/REQUIREMENT	POINT VALUE
Complete Story, Act One	Complete Act One	50
Complete Story, Act Two	Complete Act Two	50
Complete Web of Shadows	Complete Game	75
Ultimate Spider-Man	Purchase all Upgrades	50
Obsessive Spider-Man	Complete 60 Bonus Goals	25
Excessive Spider-Man	Complete Half of All Optional Goals	15
Max Out Spider-Man	Max Out Spider-Man	75
Heroic Accumulation	Find Half of all Collectibles	25
First One Hundred	Find 100 Collectibles	15
50 Hit Combo - Spider Silk	Execute 50 Hit Combo "Spider Silk"	10
100 Hit Combo - Ownership	Execute 100 Hit Combo "Ownership"	25
250 Hit Combo - Neighborly	Execute 250 Hit Combo "Neighborly"	50
Great Power	Thwart 25 City Crimes	10
Great Responsibility	Thwart 100 City Crimes	25
Defeat 100 Enemies	Defeat 100 Enemies	20
Defeat 500 Enemies	Defeat 500 Enemies	35
No Sweat	Defeat 1000 Enemies	50
The Bigger They Come...	Defeat First Tech Mech	5
Eviction	Pull Tech Mech Pilot from his seat	5
Encountered	Parry then Counter Attack one enemy	5
Over the Counter	Parry then Counter Attack 100 enemies	10
Bowling Ball	Web Swing-Kick 5 Enemies in a single pass	5
Trampoline	Web-Strike Bounce 20 Enemies in succession	25
Overkill	Perform all three types of attacks (Ground, Air, Wall) on a single enemy 10 times	20
Ground Combo Skill	Defeat 50 Enemies using only Ground Combos	15
Air Combo Skill	Defeat 50 Enemies using only Air Combos	15
Wall Combo Skill	Defeat 50 Enemies using only Wall Combos	15

SECRET ACHIEVEMENTS

NAME	GOAL/REQUIREMENT	POINT VALUE
Hero	Red Suit Conclusion earned	20
Mary Jane and Spider-Man	Mary Jane Conclusion achieved	20
Black Cat and Spider-Man	Black Cat Conclusion achieved	20
Antihero	Black Suit Conclusion earned	20
Bad Kitty	Black Cat defeated	15
Defeat Venom, Round One	Defeated Venom once	15
Grounded	Electro defeated	15

NAME	GOAL/REQUIREMENT	POINT VALUE
Declawed	Wolverine defeated	15
Defeat Symbiote Vulture	Symbiote Vulture Defeated	20
Defeat Symbiote Black Cat	Symbiote Black Cat defeated	20
Defeat Symbiote Wolverine	Symbiote Wolverine Defeated	20
Defeat Symbiote Electro	Symbiote Electro defeated	20
Winged	Vulture defeated	15
Defeat Venom, Round Two	Defeated Venom twice	20
Id	Spent time with Black Cat	5
Vice	First Black Suit Choice	5
Super-ego	Black Cat Spurned	5
Virtue	First Red Suit Choice	5

STAR OCEAN: THE LAST HOPE

ACHIEVEMENTS

NAME	GOAL/REQUIREMENT	POINT VALUE
Rookie Battler	Obtain 10% of all battle trophies.	10
Novice Battler	Obtain 20% of all battle trophies.	10
Practiced Battler	Obtain 30% of all battle trophies.	10
Skilled Battler	Obtain 40% of all battle trophies.	10
Accomplished Battler	Obtain 50% of all battle trophies.	10
Seasoned Battler	Obtain 60% of all battle trophies.	10
Advanced Battler	Obtain 70% of all battle trophies.	10
Expert Battler	Obtain 80% of all battle trophies.	10
Master Battler	Obtain 90% of all battle trophies.	10
Ultimate Battler	Obtain 100% of all battle trophies.	10
Ship Savant	Collect 100% of all spaceship data.	20
Arms Addict	Collect 100% of all weapon data.	30
Creature Collector	Collect 50% of all monster data.	20
Monster Master	Collect 100% of all monster data.	30
Dilettante Designer	Create 20% of all possible items.	20
Aspiring Architect	Create 40% of all possible items.	20
Creative Craftsman	Create 60% of all possible items.	20
Inspired Inventor	Create 80% of all possible items.	20
World's Biggest Welch Fan	Create 100% of all possible items.	20
Treasure Hunter	Open 50% of all treasure chests.	20
Treasure Hoarder	Open 100% of all treasure chests.	30
Errand Boy	Complete 30% of all quests.	20
Potential Postman	Complete 60% of all quests.	20
Dutiful Deliverer	Complete 100% of all quests.	30

SECRET ACHIEVEMENTS

NAME	GOAL/REQUIREMENT	POINT VALUE
Abolished Armaros	Defeated Armaros on the northern coast of Aeos.	20
Butchered Barachiel	Defeated Barachiel in the engine room of the celestial ship.	20
Squelched Sahariel	Defeated Sahariel in the Cardianon control tower's central isolation chamber.	30
Escaped from Earth	Narrowly escaped from the alternate Earth before its untimely demise…	20
Trounced Tamiel	Defeated Tamiel and his Sydonaist henchmen in the hallowed halls of the Purgatorium.	30
Massacred Manifest	Defeated Armaros Manifest in the grimy depths of the Miga Insect Warren.	30
Quelled Kokabiel	Defeated Kokabiel and her spawn in the sacred En II Sanctuary.	30
Silenced Satanail	Defeated Satanail in the Palace of Creation on Nox Obscurus.	40

NAME	GOAL/REQUIREMENT	POINT VALUE
Abolished Armaros	Defeated Armaros on the northern coast of Aeos.	20
Universal Victor	Completed the game on the Universe difficulty level.	30
Chaotic Conqueror	Completed the game on the Chaos difficulty level.	70
Reimi's Ending	Viewed Reimi's ending sequence.	10
Lymle's Ending	Viewed Lymle's ending sequence.	10
Bacchus's Ending	Viewed Bacchus's ending sequence.	10
Meracle's Ending	Viewed Meracle's ending sequence.	10
Myuria's Ending	Viewed Myuria's ending sequence.	10
Sarah's Ending	Viewed Sarah's ending sequence.	10
Arumat's Ending	Viewed Arumat's ending sequence.	10
Faize's Ending	Viewed Faize's ending sequence.	10
Crowe's Ending	Viewed Crowe's ending sequence.	10
Colosseum Charter	Broke into the top 30 in solo or team battle rankings.	10
Colosseum Challenger	Broke into the top 10 in solo or team battle rankings.	20
Colosseum Champion	Took over the top spot in solo or team battle rankings.	30
Hasty Hare Handler	Earned 50 victories in class 100 bunny racing.	10
Rapid Rabbit Wrangler	Earned 100 victories in class 100 bunny racing.	20
Celestial Slayer	Defeated Gabriel Celeste.	40
Ethereal Executioner	Defeated the Ethereal Queen.	40.

STORMRISE

ACHIEVEMENTS

NAME	GOAL/REQUIREMENT	POINT VALUE
Epic Saga	Complete Story Mode on Hard.	50
Scrap Metal	Destroy 27 Stalkers.	20
Decked Out	Win 10 ranked matches fully equipped.	35
Totaled Eclipse	Destroy 9 Eclipses.	25
Veteran's Affair	Win 99 ranked matches.	40
Eradicator	Beat the AI on all Skirmish maps.	30
Epic Campaign	Complete Story Mode on Easy or Normal.	30
The Other Side	Complete Act 1 of Story Mode.	25
The Other Path	Complete Act 2 of Story Mode.	25
Qualify for Duty	Complete the Tutorial.	15
Clean Sweep	Destroy all hiding Sai insurgents in the Tutorial.	10
Ulterior Motives	Use the playbook to switch weapons.	10
First Assault	Complete Mission 1: Domestic Disturbance.	20
In Transit	Secure the Control Node powering the turrets in Mission 2: Assault Charge.	20
Telepathic	Establish a portal in Mission 3: Double Jeopardy.	20
H.Y.D.R.A.	Defeat the Hydra in Mission 4: Multiple Counts.	20
Hammer Time	Take out the Arc-Hammers in Mission 5: Self Defense.	20
Evacuation	Rescue Vantage in Mission 6: Innocent Victim.	20
A Bridge Not Too Far	Secure all 3 bridges in Mission 7: Unfair Surprise.	20
Power Up	Secure all 3 power junctions in Mission 8: Reasonable Doubt.	20
Fur Coat	Defeat Sable in Mission 9: Shock Verdict.	20
Rite of Passage	Rescue Eona in Mission 10: Prison Break	25
In Pursuit	Secure the AA Turrets in Mission 11: Hot Pursuit.	25
Reverse Polarity	Recalibrate the airfield station in Mission 12: Natural Justice.	25
Spray and Pray	Use the Matriarch's Acid Rain ability.	15
Demolisher	Destroy 55 Control Nodes with the Demo Bomb ability.	25
Puppet Master	Destroy an enemy unit with one you have Mind-Controlled.	20
Unleashed	Use the Rage Smash ability.	15
Playing Both Sides	Win 8 ranked matches with each faction.	15
Demoraliser	Destroy 11 enemy units in the first 5 minutes of a ranked match.	20
First Down and Ten	Win a ranked match in under 10 minutes.	20

NAME	GOAL/REQUIREMENT	POINT VALUE
Winning Streak	Win 6 consecutive ranked matches.	25
Feeding the Habit	Play 16 ranked matches.	15
Calling all Units	Recruit one of every unit type in any game mode	15
Gone Shopping	Lose a multiplayer match while the deployment queue is open.	20
Maximum Firepower	Upgrade a Control Node to have level 3 turrets (multiplayer or skirmish).	20
Slice and Dice	Use the Spectre's Rapid Slice ability to kill an enemy commander (multiplayer or skirmish).	15
False Sense of Security	Attack 24 cloaked Spectres while using the Infiltrator's Thermal Vision.	25
Appetite for Destruction	Destroy 77 units using the Stalker's SAMs.	25
Pest Control	Kill 80 Broodlings.	20

SECRET ACHIEVEMENTS

NAME	GOAL/REQUIREMENT	POINT VALUE
Full Repertoire	You have used all unit abilities at least once.	50
Formidable	You destroyed 500 units.	50
Whip it Good	You whipped 250 times during a map or match.	20

WHEELMAN

ACHIEVEMENTS

NAME	GOAL/REQUIREMENT	POINT VALUE
Venga Venga!	Complete the Mission - Frantic.	20
Salute from Stavo	Complete the Mission - Finding Family.	20
Respect from Radu	Complete the Mission - Letting Off Steam.	20
Praise from Paulo	Complete the Mission - Stand and Deliver.	20
The Target Revealed	Complete the Mission - Recover the Documents.	20
The Best of the Best	Complete the Mission - Defeat Felipe.	20
Stavo's Swansong	Defeat Stavo, the boss of the Chulos Canallas.	30
The Spanish Job	Complete the Mission - Getting the Job Done.	20
A Real Wheelman	Complete the Mission - Get Gallo.	50
Leap of Faith	Perform an Airjack successfully.	5
Finish Him!	Perform a Finishing Move on an enemy vehicle.	5
Riding on Rims	Shoot out the tyre of an enemy vehicle.	5
Ready, Aim, Fire!	Kill an enemy vehicle using the Aimed Shot.	5
Spin Spin Shooter	Kill an enemy vehicle using the Cyclone.	5
Speedy and Angry	Achieve ANY rank on ONE Street Showdown side mission.	5
Furious and Fast	Achieve ANY rank on FIVE Street Showdown side missions.	10
Barcelona Drift	Achieve ANY rank on ALL Street Showdown side missions.	20
Taxi	Achieve ANY rank on ONE Taxi side mission.	5
Krazy Taxi	Achieve ANY rank on FIVE Taxi side missions.	10
The Knowledge	Achieve ANY rank on ALL Taxi side missions.	20
Making a Mess	Achieve ANY rank on ONE Rampage side mission.	5
Disturbing the Peace	Achieve ANY rank on FIVE Rampage side missions.	10
Anti Social Behaviour Order	Achieve ANY rank on ALL Rampage side missions.	20
Road Warrior	Achieve ANY rank on ONE Contracts side mission.	5
Road Rage	Achieve ANY rank on FIVE Contracts side missions.	10
Road Rash	Get any Rank on ALL Contracts side missions.	20
Delivery Boy	Achieve ANY rank on ONE Hot Potato side mission.	5
The Courier	Achieve ANY rank on FIVE Hot Potato side missions.	10
Man In Brown	Achieve ANY rank on ALL Hot Potato side missions.	20
Made to Order	Achieve ANY rank on ONE Made to Order side mission.	5
Gone In One Minute	Achieve ANY rank on FIVE Made to Order side missions.	10

NAME	GOAL/REQUIREMENT	POINT VALUE
Gone In 59 Seconds	Achieve ANY rank on ALL Made to Order side missions.	20
Run, Milo, Run	Achieve ANY rank on ONE Fugitive side mission.	5
Getaway in Barcelona	Achieve ANY rank on FIVE Fugitive side missions.	10
Can't Catch Me!	Achieve ANY rank on ALL Fugitive side missions.	20
Diesel Powered!	Complete ALL side missions with an "A" rank or better.	50
I Live For this Stuff!	Complete ALL side missions with an "S" rank.	100
Jump in My Car	Perform a cinematic stunt jump.	10
Dukes of Barcelona	Perform TWENTY FIVE cinematic stunt jumps.	25
White Men Can Jump	Perform ALL FIFTY cinematic stunt jumps.	50
Art Critic	Destroy ONE cat statue.	10
Cat Hater	Destroy FIFTY cat statues.	25
Wreaking Havok!	Destroy ONE HUNDRED cat statues.	50
Radu's Requiem	Defeat Radu, the boss of the Romanians.	30
Paulo's Peace	Defeat Paulo, the boss of the Los Lantos.	30
Is It A Bird?	Use the Airjack FIFTY times.	25
Sharpshooter	Destroy three vehicles during a single Cyclone or Aimed Shot move.	25
Mission Improbable	Complete a Fugitive side mission on a motorcycle.	25
Mission From God	Survive a five star police response for 5 minutes.	25
Accidental Tourist	Visit every district in Barcelona.	30

WWE LEGENDS OF WRESTLEMANIA

ACHIEVEMENTS

NAME	GOAL/REQUIREMENT	POINT VALUE
Chain Struggle	Win a match using a Chain Struggle.	30
Tag Chain Struggle	Win a match using a Tag Chain Struggle.	30
Grapplemania	Win a match using only grapple attacks.	30
Technician	Win by using five or more reversals in a single match.	30
Royal Rumble Winner	Win a 30-Man Royal Rumble.	90
Dive Attack	Successfully perform a dive attack from all four corners.	30
First Medal	Obtain a medal in WrestleMania Tour Mode.	30
Medal Collector	Obtain all of the medals in WrestleMania Tour Mode.	100
WrestleMania Tour	Clear all "Relive" matches in WrestleMania Tour Mode.	90
Memory Serves Me Well	Complete any match without pausing in the "Relive" section of WrestleMania Tour Mode.	30
New Legend	Defeat 10 opponents with a Created Legend in a single tier in Legend Killer Mode.	30
Legend Killer	Obtain a medal in Legend Killer Mode.	30
True Legend Killer	Obtain all of the medals in Legend Killer Mode.	100
Invincible Created Legend	Max out a Created Legend's attributes.	30
Super Fast Legend Killer	Become a Legend Killer in Legend Killer Mode in 30 minutes or less.	90
You're #1	Have your Created Legend reach the Top rank in Hall of Fame Mode.	100
Created a Legend	Make a Created Legend.	20

SECRET ACHIEVEMENTS

NAME	GOAL/REQUIREMENT	POINT VALUE
Manager	Win a match using a manager in an Exhibition match.	20
King of Kings	Defeat the Favorite Legends Tier in Legend Killer Mode.	90

X-MEN ORIGINS: WOLVERINE

ACHIEVEMENTS

NAME	GOAL/REQUIREMENT	POINT VALUE
Getting Started	Killed 100 enemies	10
A Day's Work	Killed 500 enemies	20
What I Do Best	Killed 2000 enemies	30
You Can't Hide	Lunged to 250 enemies	20
Lunge	Lunged to 25 enemies	10
Pounce	Lunged to 100 enemies	15
Piggy Back Ride	Lunged to a W.E.N.D.I.G.0 prototype's back	10
Quick Killer	Quick Killed 1 enemy	10
Efficient Killer	Quick Killed 20 enemies	15
Perfect Killer	Quick Killed 3 enemies in a row	20
Drop Dead	Killed 10 enemies by throwing them off high areas	10
Apprentice	Raised One Combat Reflex to Master Level	10
Samurai	Raised All Combat Reflexes to Master Level	25
Mutant Lover	Raised one Mutagen to level 3	15
Astonishing	Found 1/2 of all Dog Tags in the game	20
Devil's Brigade	Found all Dog Tags in the game	30
Defensive	Performed 1 Counter move	10
Untouchable	Performed 25 Counter moves	20
Catch!	Killed 1 enemy with a reflected projectile	10
Boomerang	Killed 25 enemies with a reflected projectile	20
Aerial Assault	Performed 10 Air Grabs	10
Ultimate Wolverine	Fought 4 W.E.N.D.I.G.0 prototypes at the same time and defeated them at Alkali lake.	15
Hot Potato	Light 20 enemies on fire	20
Shotgun Epic Fail	Killed 25 Ghosts with their own weapon	15
James Howlett	Performed a Wolverine to Wolverine Lunge	15
WoW!	You feel cold as you examine the skeleton and read the name "Arthas" etched into the nearby sword	15
Aerial Master	Got 6 enemies airborne at once	15
Fully Loaded	Maxed out all upgrades	35
Slice n' Dice	Killed 6 enemies with a single attack	15
Found!	You found a mysterious hatch!	15
Slaughter House	Dismembered 100 enemies	15
Blender	Killed 200 enemies with Claw Spin	25
Walking Death	Beat the game on Hard Difficulty	50
Heightened Senses	Killed 200 enemies in Feral Sense	20
Environmentally Friendly	Killed 10 enemies using objects in the environment	15
Whatever it Takes	Killed 30 enemies using objects in the environment	20
Bloodlust	Killed 50 enemies while in Berserker mode	20
Weapon X	Killed 150 enemies while in Berserker mode	25
The Cake	You found the cake, yummy!	15

SECRET ACHIEVEMENTS

NAME	GOAL/REQUIREMENT	POINT VALUE
Bar Fight	Defeated Victor Creed (Sabretooth)	30
Spillway Escape	Escapes from Weapon X	30
Helicopter Ride	Defeated David Nord (Agent Zero)	30
Secret Achievement	Continue playing to unlock this secret achievement.	30
Secret Achievement	Continue playing to unlock this secret achievement.	30
Secret Achievement	Continue playing to unlock this secret achievement.	50
Secret Achievement	Continue playing to unlock this secret achievement.	30
Secret Achievement	Continue playing to unlock this secret achievement.	15
Secret Achievement	Continue playing to unlock this secret achievement.	30
Secret Achievement	Continue playing to unlock this secret achievement.	10
Secret Achievement	Continue playing to unlock this secret achievement	10

NINTENDO Wii™

GAMES

WII VIRTUAL CONSOLE

AVATAR: THE LAST AIRBENDER

UNLIMITED HEALTH
Select Code Entry from Extras and enter 94677.

UNLIMITED CHI
Select Code Entry from Extras and enter 24463.

UNLIMITED COPPER
Select Code Entry from Extras and enter 23637.

NEVERENDING STEALTH
Select Code Entry from Extras and enter 53467.

1 HIT DISHONOR
Select Code Entry from Extras and enter 54641.

DOUBLE DAMAGE
Select Code Entry from Extras and enter 34743.

ALL TREASURE MAPS
Select Code Entry from Extras and enter 37437.

THE CHARACTER CONCEPT ART GALLERY
Select Code Entry from Extras and enter 97831.

AVATAR: THE LAST AIRBENDER— THE BURNING EARTH

DOUBLE DAMAGE
Go to the code entry section and enter 90210.

INFINITE LIFE
Go to the code entry section and enter 65049.

INFINITE SPECIAL ATTACKS
Go to the code entry section and enter 66206.

MAX LEVEL
Go to the code entry section and enter 89121.

ONE-HIT DISHONOR
Go to the code entry section and enter 28260.

ALL BONUS GAMES
Go to the code entry section and enter 99801.

ALL GALLERY ITEMS
Go to the code entry section and enter 85061.

AVATAR: THE LAST AIRBENDER— INTO THE INFERNO

After you have defeated the first level, The Awakening, go to Ember Island. Walk to the left, past the volleyball net, to a red and yellow door. Select Game Secrets and then Code Entry. Now you can enter the following cheats:

MAX COINS
Enter 66639224.

ALL ITEMS AVAILABLE FROM SHOP
Enter 34737253.

ALL CHAPTERS
Enter 52993833.

UNLOCK CONCEPT ART IN GALLERY
Enter 27858343.

BEN 10: PROTECTOR OF EARTH

INVINCIBILITY
Select a game from the Continue option. Go to the Map Selection screen, press Plus and choose Extras. Select Enter Secret Code and enter XLR8, Heatblast, Wildvine, Fourarms.

ALL COMBOS

Select a game from the Continue option. Go to the Map Selection screen, press Plus and choose Extras. Select Enter Secret Code and enter Cannonblot, Heatblast, Fourarms, Heatblast.

ALL LOCATIONS

Select a game from the Continue option. Go to the Map Selection screen, press Plus and choose Extras. Select Enter Secret Code and enter Heatblast, XLR8, XLR8, Cannonblot.

DNA FORCE SKINS

Select a game from the Continue option. Go to the Map Selection screen, press Plus and choose Extras. Select Enter Secret Code and enter Wildvine, Fourarms, Heatblast, Cannonbolt.

DARK HEROES SKINS

Select a game from the Continue option. Go to the Map Selection screen, press Plus and choose Extras. Select Enter Secret Code and enter Cannonbolt, Cannonbolt, Fourarms, Heatblast.

ALL ALIEN FORMS

Select a game from the Continue option. Go to the Map Selection screen, press Plus and choose Extras. Select Enter Secret Code and enter Wildvine, Fourarms, Heatblast, Wildvine.

MASTER CONTROL

Select a game from the Continue option. Go to the Map Selection screen, press Plus and choose Extras. Select Enter Secret Code and enter Cannonbolt, Heatblast, Wildvine, Fourarms.

BLAZING ANGELS: SQUADRONS OF WWII

ALL AIRCRAFT AND CAMPAIGNS

After you have chosen a pilot, hold Minus + Plus and press Left, Right, 1, 2, 2, 1.

GOD MODE

Pause the game, hold Minus and press 1, 2, 1, 2.

WEAPON DAMAGE INCREASED

Pause the game, hold Minus and press 2, 1, 1, 2.

BOOM BLOX

ALL TOYS IN CREATE MODE

At the Title screen, press Up, Right, Down, Left to bring up a cheats menu. Enter Tool Pool.

SLOW-MO IN SINGLE PLAYER

At the Title screen, press Up, Right, Down, Left to bring up a cheats menu. Enter Blox Time.

CHEERLEADERS BECOME PROFILE CHARACTER

At the Title screen, press Up, Right, Down, Left to bring up a cheats menu. Enter My Team.

FLOWER EXPLOSIONS

At the Title screen, press Up, Right, Down, Left to bring up a cheats menu. Enter Flower Power.

JINGLE BLOCKS

At the Title screen, press Up, Right, Down, Left to bring up a cheats menu. Enter Maestro.

BUILD-A-BEAR WORKSHOP: A FRIEND FUR ALL SEASONS

ALL ISLANDS, MINIGAMES, OUTFITS, AND ACCESSORIES

At the Main menu, press Up, Down, Left, Right, A, B.

CABELA'S DANGEROUS HUNTS 2009

.470 NITRO EXPRESS HIGH CALIBER RIFLE

Select Enter Special Code from the Extras menu and enter 101987.

CALL OF DUTY 3

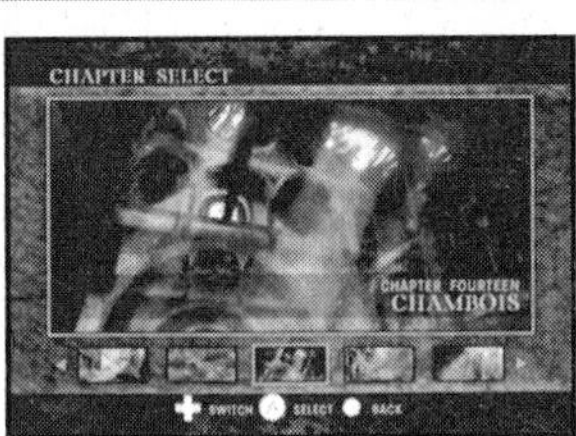

ALL CHAPTERS AND BONUS CONTENT

At the Chapter Select screen, hold Plus and press Right, Right, Left, Left, 2 Button, 2 Button.

CARS MATER-NATIONAL

ALL ARCADE RACES, MINI-GAMES, AND WORLDS

Select Codes/Cheats from the options and enter PLAYALL.

ALL CARS

Select Codes/Cheats from the options and enter MATTEL07.

ALTERNATE LIGHTNING MCQUEEN COLORS

Select Codes/Cheats from the options and enter NCEDUDZ.

ALL COLORS FOR OTHERS

Select Codes/Cheats from the options and enter PAINTIT.

UNLIMITED TURBO

Select Codes/Cheats from the options and enter ZZOOOOM.

EXTREME ACCELERATION

Select Codes/Cheats from the options and enter 0TO200X.

EXPERT MODE

Select Codes/Cheats from the options and enter VRYFAST.

ALL BONUS ART

Select Codes/Cheats from the options and enter BUYTALL.

CODE LYOKO: QUEST FOR INFINITY

UNLOCK EVERYTHING

Pause the game and press 2, 1, C, Z, 2, 1.

UNLIMITED HEALTH AND POWER

Pause the game and press 2, 2, Z, Z, 1, 1.

INCREASE SPEED

Pause the game and press Z, 1, 2, 1 (x3).

INCREASE DAMAGE

Pause the game and press 1, Z, Z, C (x3).

CONFIGURATION A

Pause the game and press 2, Z, 1, Z, C, Z.

CONFIGURATION B

Pause the game and press C, C, 1, C, Z, C.

ALL ABILITIES

Pause the game and press Z, C, Z, C (x3).

ALL BONUSES

Pause the game and press 1, 2, C, 2 (x3).

ALL GOODIES

Pause the game and press C, 2, 2, Z, C, Z.

CORALINE

UNLIMITED LEVEL SKIP

Select Cheats from the Options menu and enter beldam.

UNLIMITED HEALTH

Select Cheats from the Options menu and enter beets.

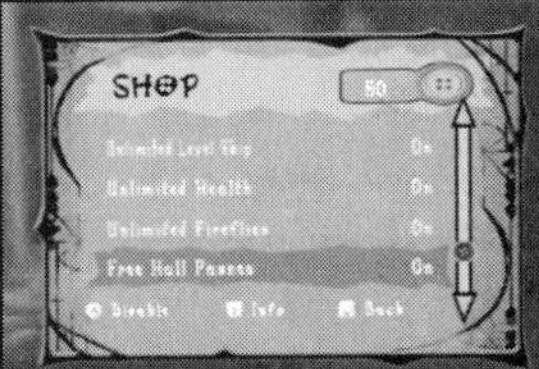

UNLIMITED FIREFLIES

Select Cheats from the Options menu and enter garden.

FREE HALL PASSES

Select Cheats from the Options menu and enter well.

BUTTON EYE CORALINE

Select Cheats from the Options menu and enter cheese.

DEADLY CREATURES

ALL CHAPTERS

At the chapter select, press Right, Right, Up, Down, 2, 1, 1, 2. When you jump to a later chapter, you get any move upgrades you would have, but not health upgrades.

DE BLOB

INVULNERABILITY

During a game, hold C and press 1, 1, 1, 1. Re-enter the code to disable.

LIFE UP

During a game, hold C and press 1, 1, 2, 2.

TIME BONUS

During a game, hold C and press 1, 2, 1, 2. This adds 10 minutes to your time.

ALL MOODS

At the Main menu, hold C and press B, B, 1, 2, 1, 2, B, B.

ALL MULTIPLAYER LEVELS

At the Main menu, hold C and press 2, 2, B, B, 1, 1, B, B.

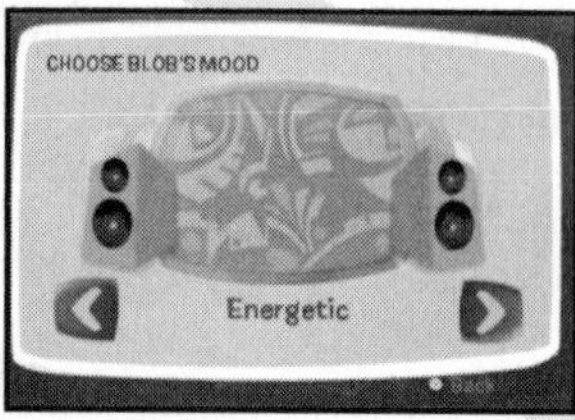

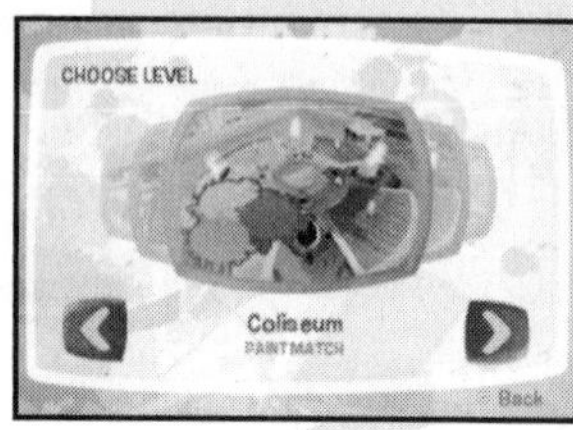

DEFEND YOUR CASTLE

GIANT ENEMIES

Select Credits and click SMB3W4 when it appears.

TINY UNITS

Select Credits and click Chuck Norris when it appears.

EASY LEVEL COMPLETE

Pause the game and wait for the sun to set. Unpause to complete the level.

DESTROY ALL HUMANS! BIG WILLY UNLEASHED

Pause the game and go to the Unlockables screen. Hold the analog stick Up until a Enter Unlock Code window appears. You can now enter the following cheats with the directional-pad. Press A after entering a code.

Use this menu to toggle cheats on and off.

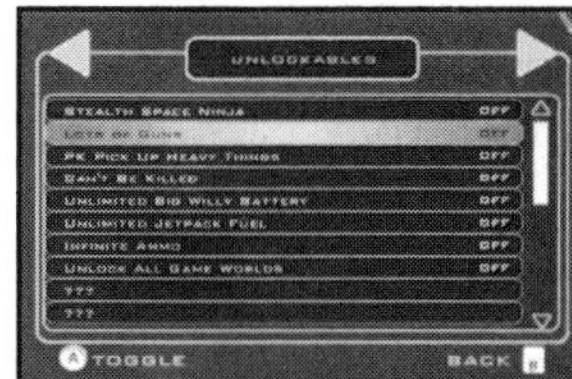

UNLOCK ALL GAME WORLDS
Up, Right, Down, Right, Up

CAN'T BE KILLED
Left, Down, Up, Right, Up

LOTS OF GUNS
Right, Left, Down, Left, Up

INFINITE AMMO
Right, Up, Up, Left, Right

UNLIMITED BIG WILLY BATTERY
Left, Left, Up, Right, Down

UNLIMITED JETPACK FUEL
Right, Right, Up, Left, Left

PK PICK UP HEAVY THINGS
Down, Up, Left, Up, Right

STEALTH SPACE NINJA
Up, Right, Down, Down, Left

CRYPTO DANCE FEVER SKIN
Right, Left, Right, Left, Up

KLUCKIN'S CHICKEN BLIMP SKIN
Left, Up, Down, Up, Down

LEISURE SUIT SKIN
Left, Down, Right, Left, Right

PIMP MY BLIMP SKIN
Down, Up, Right, Down, Right

DISNEY'S CHICKEN LITTLE: ACE IN ACTION

ALL LEVELS
Select the Cheats option and enter Right, Up, Left, Right, Up.

ALL WEAPONS
Select the Cheats option and enter Right, Down, Right, Left.

UNLIMITED SHIELD
Select the Cheats option and enter Right, Down, Right, Down, Right.

DISNEY PRINCESS: ENCHANTED JOURNEY

BELLE'S KINGDOM
Select Secrets and enter GASTON.

GOLDEN SET
Select Secrets and enter BLUEBIRD.

FLOWER WAND
Select Secrets and enter SLEEPY.

HEART WAND
Select Secrets and enter BASHFUL.

SHELL WAND
Select Secrets and enter RAJAH.

SHIELD WAND
Select Secrets and enter CHIP.

STAR WAND
Select Secrets and enter SNEEZY.

DRAGON BALL Z: BUDOKAI TENKAICHI 3

SURVIVAL MODE

Clear 30 missions in Mission 100 mode.

DRAGON BLADE: WRATH OF FIRE

ALL LEVELS

At the Title screen, hold Plus + Minus and select New Game or Load game. Hold the buttons until the stage select appears.

EASY DIFFICULTY

At the Title screen, hold Z + 2 when selecting "New Game."

HARD DIFFICULTY

At the Title screen, hold C + 2 when selecting "New Game."

To clear the following codes, hold Z at the stage select.

DRAGON HEAD

At the stage select, hold Z and press Plus. Immediately Swing Wii-mote Right, swing Wii-mote Down, swing Nunchuck Left, swing Nunchuck Right.

DRAGON WINGS

At the stage select, hold Z and press Plus. Immediately Swing Nunchuck Up + Wii-mote Up, swing Nunchuck Down + Wii-mote Down, swing Nunchuck Right + Wii-mote Left, swing Nunchuck Left + Wii-mote Right.

TAIL POWER

At the stage select, hold Z and press Plus. Immediately Swing your Wii-mote Down, Up, Left, and Right

DOUBLE FIST POWER

At the stage select, hold Z and press Plus. Immediately swing your Nunchuck Right, swing your Wii-mote left, swing your Nunchuck right while swinging your Wii-mote left, then swing both Wii-mote and Nunchuck down

DRIVER: PARALLEL LINES

ALL VEHICLES

Pause the game, select cheats and enter carshow.

ALL WEAPONS

Pause the game, select cheats and enter gunrange.

INVINCIBILITY

Pause the game, select cheats and enter steelman.

INFINITE AMMUNITION

Pause the game, select cheats and enter gunbelt.

INFINITE NITROUS

Pause the game, select cheats and enter zoomzoom.

INDESTRUCTIBLE CARS

Pause the game, select cheats and enter rollbar.

WEAKER COPS

Pause the game, select cheats and enter keystone.

ZERO COST

Pause the game, select cheats and enter tooledup. This gives you free upgrades.

FAR CRY VENGEANCE

ALL MAPS

Select Cheats Menu from the Options menu and enter GiveMeTheMaps.

GHOST SQUAD

COSTUMES

Reach the following levels in single player to unlock the corresponding costume.

LEVEL	COSTUME
07	Desert Camouflage
10	Policeman
15	Tough Guy
18	Sky Camouflage
20	World War II
23	Cowboy
30	Urban Camouflage
34	Virtua Cop
38	Future Warrior
50	Ninja
60	Panda Suit
99	Gold Uniform

NINJA MODE

Play through Arcade Mode.

PARADISE MODE

Play through Ninja Mode.

THE GODFATHER: BLACKHAND EDITION

The following pause screen codes can be used only once every five minutes.

$5000

Pause the game and press Minus, 2, Minus, Minus, 2, Up.

FULL AMMO

Pause the game and press 2, Left, 2, Right, Minus, Down.

FULL HEALTH

Pause the game and press Left, Minus, Right, 2, Right, Up.

FILM CLIPS

After loading your game, before selecting Play Game, press 2, Minus, 2, Minus, Minus, Up.

GODZILLA UNLEASHED

UNLOCK ALL

At the Main menu, press A + Up to bring up the cheat entry screen. Enter 204935.

90000 STORE POINTS

At the Main menu, press A + Up to bring up the cheat entry screen. Enter 031406.

SET DAY

At the Main menu, press A + Up to bring up the cheat entry screen. Enter 0829XX, where XX represents the day. Use 00 for day one.

SHOW MONSTER MOVES

At the Main menu, press A + Up to bring up the cheat entry screen. Enter 411411.

VERSION NUMBER

At the Main menu, press A + Up to bring up the cheat entry screen. Enter 787321.

MOTHERSHIP LEVEL

Playing as the Aliens, destroy the mothership in the Invasion level.

GRADIUS REBIRTH

4 OPTIONS

Pause the game and press Up, Up, Down, Down, Left, Right, Left, Right, Fire, Powerup. This code can be used once for each stage you have attempted.

THE GRIM ADVENTURES OF BILLY & MANDY

CONCEPT ART

At the Main menu, hold 1 and press Up, Up, Down, Down, Left, Right, Left, Right.

GUITAR HERO III: LEGENDS OF ROCK

To enter the following cheats, strum the guitar with the given buttons held. For example, if it says Yellow + Orange, hold Yellow and Orange as you strum. Air Guitar, Precision Mode and Performance Mode can be toggled on and off from the Cheats menu. You can also change between five different levels of Hyperspeed at this menu.

UNLOCK EVERYTHING

Select Cheats from the Options. Choose Enter Cheat and enter Green + Red + Blue + Orange, Green + Red + Yellow + Blue, Green + Red + Yellow + Orange, Green + Yellow + Blue + Orange, Green + Red + Yellow + Blue, Red + Yellow + Blue + Orange, Green + Red + Yellow + Blue, Green + Yellow + Blue + Orange, Green + Red + Yellow + Blue, Green + Red + Yellow + Orange, Green + Red + Yellow + Orange, Green + Red + Yellow + Blue, Green + Red + Yellow + Orange. No sounds play while this code is entered.

An easier way to show this code is by representing Green as 1 down to Orange as 5. For example, if you have 1345, you would hold down Green + Yellow + Blue + Orange while strumming. 1245 + 1234 + 1235 + 1345 + 1234 + 2345 + 1234 + 1345 + 1234 + 1235 + 1235 + 1234 + 1235.

ALL SONGS

Select Cheats from the Options. Choose Enter Cheat and enter Yellow + Orange, Red + Blue, Red + Orange, Green + Blue, Red + Yellow, Yellow + Orange, Red + Yellow, Red + Blue, Green + Yellow, Green + Yellow, Yellow + Blue, Yellow + Blue, Yellow + Orange, Yellow + Orange, Yellow + Blue, Yellow, Red, Red + Yellow, Red, Yellow, Orange.

NO FAIL

Select Cheats from the Options. Choose Enter Cheat and enter Green + Red, Blue, Green + Red, Green + Yellow, Blue, Green + Yellow, Red + Yellow, Orange, Red + Yellow, Green + Yellow, Yellow, Green + Yellow, Green + Red.

AIR GUITAR

Select Cheats from the Options. Choose Enter Cheat and enter Blue + Yellow, Green + Yellow, Green + Yellow, Red + Blue, Red + Blue, Red + Yellow, Red + Yellow, Blue + Yellow, Green + Yellow, Green + Yellow, Red + Blue, Red + Blue, Red + Yellow, Red + Yellow, Green + Yellow, Green + Yellow, Red + Yellow, Red + Yellow.

HYPERSPEED

Select Cheats from the Options. Choose Enter Cheat and enter Orange, Blue, Orange, Yellow, Orange, Blue, Orange, Yellow.

PERFORMANCE MODE

Select Cheats from the Options. Choose Enter Cheat and enter Red + Yellow, Red + Blue, Red + Orange, Red + Blue, Red + Yellow, Green + Blue, Red + Yellow, Red + Blue.

EASY EXPERT

Select Cheats from the Options. Choose Enter Cheat and enter Green + Red, Green + Yellow, Yellow + Blue, Red + Blue, Blue + Orange, Yellow + Orange, Red + Yellow, Red + Blue.

PRECISION MODE

Select Cheats from the Options. Choose Enter Cheat and enter Green + Red, Green + Red, Green + Red, Red + Yellow, Red + Yellow, Red + Blue, Red + Blue, Yellow + Blue, Yellow + Orange, Yellow + Orange, Green + Red, Green + Red, Green + Red, Red + Yellow, Red + Yellow, Red + Blue, Red + Blue, Yellow + Blue, Yellow + Orange, Yellow + Orange.

LARGE GEMS

Select Cheats from the Options. Choose Enter Cheat and enter Green, Red, Green, Yellow, Green, Blue, Green, Orange, Green, Blue, Green, Yellow, Green, Red, Green, Green + Red, Red + Yellow, Green + Red, Yellow + Blue, Green + Red, Blue + Orange, Green + Red, Yellow + Blue, Green + Red, Red + Yellow, Green + Red, Green + Yellow.

GUITAR HERO: AEROSMITH

Select Cheats from the Options menu and enter the following. To do this, strum the guitar while holding the indicated buttons. For example, if it says Yellow + Orange, hold Yellow and Orange as you strum. Air Guitar, Precision Mode, and Performance Mode can be toggled on and off from the Cheats menu. You can also change between five different levels of Hyperspeed at this menu.

ALL SONGS

Red + Yellow, Green + Red, Green + Red, Red + Yellow, Red + Yellow, Green + Red, Red + Yellow, Red + Yellow, Green + Red, Green + Red, Red + Yellow, Red + Yellow, Green + Red, Red + Yellow, Red + Blue. This code does not unlock Pandora's Box.

AIR GUITAR

Red + Yellow, Green + Red, Red + Yellow, Red + Yellow, Red + Blue, Red + Blue, Red + Blue, Red + Blue, Red + Blue, Yellow + Blue, Yellow + Blue, Yellow + Orange

HYPERSPEED

Yellow + Orange, Yellow + Orange, Yellow + Orange, Yellow + Orange, Yellow + Orange, Red + Yellow, Red + Yellow, Red + Yellow, Red + Yellow, Red + Blue, Red + Blue, Red + Blue, Red + Blue, Red + Blue, Yellow + Blue, Yellow + Orange, Yellow + Orange.

NO FAIL

Select Cheats from the Options. Choose Enter Cheat and enter Green + Red, Blue, Green + Red, Green + Yellow, Blue, Green + Yellow, Red + Yellow, Orange, Red + Yellow, Green + Yellow, Yellow, Green + Yellow, Green + Red.

PERFORMANCE MODE

Green + Red, Green + Red, Red + Orange, Red + Blue, Green + Red, Green + Red, Red + Orange, Red + Blue.

PRECISION MODE

Red + Yellow, Red + Blue, Red + Blue, Red + Yellow, Red + Yellow, Yellow + Blue, Yellow + Blue, Yellow + Blue, Red + Blue, Red + Yellow, Red + Blue, Red + Blue, Red + Yellow, Red + Yellow, Yellow + Blue, Yellow + Blue, Yellow + Blue, Red + Blue.

GUITAR HERO: METALLICA

METALLICA COSTUMES

Select Cheats from Settings and enter Green, Red, Yellow, Blue, Blue, Yellow, Red, Green.

HYPERSPEED

Select Cheats from Settings and enter Green, Blue, Red, Yellow, Yellow, Red, Green, Green.

PERFORMANCE MODE

Select Cheats from Settings and enter Yellow, Yellow, Blue, Red, Blue, Green, Red, Red.

INVISIBLE ROCKER

Select Cheats from Settings and enter Green, Red, Yellow (x3), Blue, Blue, Green.

AIR INSTRUMENTS

Select Cheats from Settings and enter Red, Red, Blue, Yellow, Green (x3), Yellow.

ALWAYS DRUM FILL

Select Cheats from Settings and enter Red (x3), Blue, Blue, Green, Green, Yellow.

AUTO KICK

Select Cheats from Settings and enter Yellow, Green, Red, Blue (x4), Red. With this cheat activated, the bass pedal is automatically hit.

ALWAYS SLIDE

Select Cheats from Settings and enter Green, Green, Red, Red, Yellow, Red, Yellow, Blue. All Guitar Notes Become Touch Pad Sliding Notes.

BLACK HIGHWAY

Select Cheats from Settings and enter Yellow, Red, Green, Red, Green, Red, Red, Blue.

FLAME COLOR

Select Cheats from Settings and enter Green, Red, Green, Blue, Red, Red, Yellow, Blue.

GEM COLOR

Select Cheats from Settings and enter Blue, Red, Red, Green, Red, Green, Red, Yellow.

STAR COLOR

Select Cheats from Settings and enter Press Red, Red, Yellow, Red, Blue, Red, Red, Blue.

ADDITIONAL LINE 6 TONES

Select Cheats from Settings and enter Green, Red, Yellow, Blue, Red, Yellow, Blue, Green.

VOCAL FIREBALL

Select Cheats from Settings and enter Red, Green, Green, Yellow, Blue, Green, Yellow, Green.

GUITAR HERO WORLD TOUR

The following cheats can be toggled on and off at the Cheats menu.

QUICKPLAY SONGS

Select Cheats from the Options menu, choose Enter New Cheat and press Blue, Blue, Red, Green, Green, Blue, Blue, Yellow.

ALWAYS SLIDE

Select Cheats from the Options menu, choose Enter New Cheat and press Green, Green, Red, Red, Yellow, Red, Yellow, Blue.

AT&T BALLPARK

Select Cheats from the Options menu, choose Enter New Cheat and press Yellow, Green, Red, Red, Green, Blue, Red, Yellow.

AUTO KICK

Select Cheats from the Options menu, choose Enter New Cheat and press Yellow, Green, Red, Blue (x4), Red.

EXTRA LINE 6 TONES

Select Cheats from the Options menu, choose Enter New Cheat and press Green, Red, Yellow, Blue, Red, Yellow, Blue, Green.

FLAME COLOR

Select Cheats from the Options menu, choose Enter New Cheat and press Green, Red, Green, Blue, Red, Red, Yellow, Blue.

GEM COLOR

Select Cheats from the Options menu, choose Enter New Cheat and press Blue, Red, Red, Green, Red, Green, Red, Yellow.

STAR COLOR

Select Cheats from the Options menu, choose Enter New Cheat and press Red, Red, Yellow, Red, Blue, Red, Red, Blue.

AIR INSTRUMENTS

Select Cheats from the Options menu, choose Enter New Cheat and press Red, Red, Blue, Yellow, Green (x3), Yellow.

HYPERSPEED

Select Cheats from the Options menu, choose Enter New Cheat and press Green, Blue, Red, Yellow, Yellow, Red, Green, Green. These show up in the menu as HyperGuitar, HyperBass, and HyperDrums.

PERFORMANCE MODE

Select Cheats from the Options menu, choose Enter New Cheat and press Yellow, Yellow, Blue, Red, Blue, Green, Red, Red.

INVISIBLE ROCKER

Select Cheats from the Options menu, choose Enter New Cheat and press Green, Red, Yellow (x3), Blue, Blue, Green.

VOCAL FIREBALL

Select Cheats from the Options menu, choose Enter New Cheat and press Red, Green, Green, Yellow, Blue, Green, Yellow, Green.

AARON STEELE!

Select Cheats from the Options menu, choose Enter New Cheat and press Blue, Red, Yellow (x5), Green.

JONNY VIPER

Select Cheats from the Options menu, choose Enter New Cheat and press Blue, Red, Blue, Blue, Yellow (x3), Green.

NICK

Select Cheats from the Options menu, choose Enter New Cheat and press Green, Red, Blue, Green, Red, Blue, Blue, Green.

RINA

Select Cheats from the Options menu, choose Enter New Cheat and press Blue, Red, Green, Green, Yellow (x3), Green.

ICE AGE 2: THE MELTDOWN

INFINITE PEBBLES

Pause the game and press Down, Down, Left, Up, Up, Right, Up, Down.

INFINITE ENERGY

Pause the game and press Down, Left, Right, Down, Down, Right, Left, Down.

INFINITE HEALTH

Pause the game and press Up, Right, Down, Up, Left, Down, Right, Left.

IRON MAN

ARMOR SELECTION

Iron Man's different armor suits are unlocked by completing certain missions. Refer to the following tables for when each is unlocked. After selecting a mission to play, you get the opportunity to pick the armor you wish to use.

COMPLETE MISSION	SUIT UNLOCKED
1: Escape	Mark I
2: First Flight	Mark II
3: Fight Back	Mark III
6: Flying Fortress	Comic Tin Can
9: Home Front	Classic
13: Showdown	Silver Centurion

CONCEPT ART

Concept Art is unlocked after finding certain numbers of Weapon Crates.

CONCEPT ART UNLOCKED	NUMBER OF WEAPON CRATES FOUND
Environments Set 1	6
Environments Set 2	12
Iron Man	18
Environments Set 3	24
Enemies	30
Environments Set 4	36
Villains	42
Vehicles	48
Covers	50

KUNG FU PANDA

INFINITE CHI
Select Cheats from the Extra menu and press Down, Right, Left, Up, Down.

INVINCIBILITY
Select Cheats from the Extra menu and press Down, Down, Right, Up, Left.

4X DAMAGE MULTIPLIER
Select Cheats from the Extra menu and press Up, Down, Up, Right, Left.

ALL MULTIPLAYER CHARACTERS
Select Cheats from the Extra menu and press Left, Down, Left, Right, Down.

DRAGON WARRIOR OUTFIT IN MULTIPLAYER
Select Cheats from the Extra menu and press Left, Down, Right, Left, Up.

THE LEGEND OF SPYRO: DAWN OF THE DRAGON

INFINITE HEALTH
Pause the game, hold Z and move the Nunchuk Right, Right, Down, Down, Left.

INFINITE MANA
Pause the game, hold Z and move the Nunchuk Up, Right, Up, Left, Down.

MAX XP
Pause the game, hold Z and move the Nunchuk Up, Left, Left, Down, Up.

ALL ELEMENTAL UPGRADES
Pause the game, hold Z and move the Nunchuk Left, Up, Down, Up, Right.

LEGO BATMAN

BATCAVE CODES
Using the computer in the Batcave, select Enter Code and enter the following codes.

CHARACTERS

CHARACTER	CODE
Alfred	ZAQ637
Batgirl	JKR331
Bruce Wayne	BDJ327
Catwoman (Classic)	M1AAWW
Clown Goon	HJK327
Commissioner Gordon	DDP967
Fishmonger	HGY748
Freeze Girl	XVK541
Joker Goon	UTF782
Joker Henchman	YUN924
Mad Hatter	JCA283
Man-Bat	NYU942
Military Policeman	MKL382
Nightwing	MVY759
Penguin Goon	NKA238
Penguin Henchman	BJH782
Penguin Minion	KJP748
Poison Ivy Goon	GTB899
Police Marksman	HKG984
Police Officer	JRY983
Riddler Goon	CRY928
Riddler Henchman	XEU824
S.W.A.T.	HTF114
Sailor	NAV592
Scientist	JFL786
Security Guard	PLB946
The Joker (Tropical)	CCB199
Yeti	NJL412
Zoo Sweeper	DWR243

VEHICLES

VEHICLE	CODE
Bat-Tank	KNTT4B
Bruce Wayne's Private Jet	LEA664
Catwoman's Motorcycle	HPL826
Garbage Truck	DUS483
Goon Helicopter	GCH328
Harbor Helicopter	CHP735
Harley Quinn's Hammer Truck	RDT637
Mad Hatter's Glider	HS000W
Mad Hatter's Steamboat	M4DM4N
Mr. Freeze's Iceberg	ICYICE
The Joker's Van	JUK657
Mr. Freeze's Kart	BCT229
Penguin Goon Submarine	BTN248
Police Bike	LJP234
Police Boat	PLC999
Police Car	KJL832
Police Helicopter	CWR732
Police Van	MAC788
Police Watercraft	VJD328
Riddler's Jet	HAHAHA
Robin's Submarine	TTF453
Two-Face's Armored Truck	EFE933

CHEATS

CHEAT	CODE
Always Score Multiply	9LRGNB
Fast Batarangs	JRBDCB
Fast Walk	ZOLM6N
Flame Batarang	D8NYWH
Freeze Batarang	XPN4NG
Extra Hearts	ML3KHP
Fast Build	EVG26J
Immune to Freeze	JXUDY6
Invincibility	WYD5CP
Minikit Detector	ZXGH9J
More Batarang Targets	XWP645
Piece Detector	KHJ554
Power Brick Detector	MMN786
Regenerate Hearts	HJH7HJ
Score x2	N4NR3E
Score x4	CX9MAT
Score x6	MLVNF2
Score x8	WCCDB9
Score x10	18HW07

LEGO INDIANA JONES: THE ORIGINAL ADVENTURES

EXTRAS

Approach the blackboard in the Classroom and enter the following codes. Pause the game and select Extras. Here you can enable the cheat.

EXTRA	CODE
Artifact Detector	VIKED7
Beep Beep	VNF59Q
Character Treasure	VIES2R
Disarm Enemies	VKRNS9
Disguises	4ID1N6
Fast Build	V83SLO
Fast Dig	378RS6

EXTRA	CODE
Fast Fix	FJ59WS
Fertilizer	B1GW1F
Ice Rink	33GM7J
Parcel Detector	VUT673
Poo Treasure	WWQ1SA
Regenerate Hearts	MDLP69
Secret Characters	3X44AA
Silhouettes	3HE85H
Super Scream	VN3R7S
Super Slap	0P1TA5
Treasure Magnet	H86LA2
Treasure x2	VM4TS9
Treasure x4	VLWEN3
Treasure x6	V84RYS
Treasure x8	A72E1M
Treasure x10	VI3PS8

CHARACTERS

Approach the blackboard in the Classroom and enter the following codes.

CHARACTER	CODE
Bandit	12N68W
Bandit Swordsman	1MK4RT
Barranca	04EM94
Bazooka Trooper (Crusade)	MK83R7
Bazooka Trooper (Raiders)	S93Y5R
Belloq	CHN3YU
Belloq (Jungle)	TDR197
Belloq (Robes)	VEO29L
British Commander	B73EUA
British Officer	VJ5TI9
British Soldier	DJ5I2W
Captain Katanga	VJ3TT3
Chatter Lal	ENW936
Chatter Lal (Thuggee)	CNH4RY
Chen	3NK48T
Colonel Dietrich	2K9RKS
Colonel Vogel	8EAL4H
Dancing Girl	C7EJ21
Donovan	3NFTU8
Elsa (Desert)	JSNRT9
Elsa (Officer)	VMJ5US
Enemy Boxer	8246RB
Enemy Butler	VJ48W3
Enemy Guard	VJ7R51
Enemy Guard (Mountains)	YR47WM
Enemy Officer	572E61
Enemy Officer (Desert	2MK45O
Enemy Pilot	B84ELP
Enemy Radio Operator	1MF94R
Enemy Soldier (Desert)	4NSU7Q
Fedora	V75YSP
First Mate	0GIN24
Grail Knight	NE6THI
Hovitos Tribesman	H0V1SS
Indiana Jones (Desert Disguise)	4J8S4M
Indiana Jones (Officer)	VJ85OS
Jungle Guide	24PF34
Kao Kan	WMO46L
Kazim	NRH23J
Kazim (Desert)	3M29TJ
Lao Che	2NK479
Maharajah	NFK5N2
Major Toht	13NS01

CHARACTER	CODE
Masked Bandit	N48SF0
Mola Ram	FJUR31
Monkey Man	3RF6YJ
Pankot Assassin	2NKT72
Pankot Guard	VN28RH
Sherpa Brawler	VJ37WJ
Sherpa Gunner	ND762W
Slave Child	0E3ENW
Thuggee	VM683E
Thuggee Acolyte	T2R3F9
Thuggee Slave Driver	VBS7GW
Village Dignitary	KD48TN
Village Elder	4682E1
Willie (Dinner Suit)	VK93R7
Willie (Pajamas)	MEN4IP
Wu Han	3NSLT8

EXTRAS

Approach the blackboard in the Classroom and enter the following codes. Some cheats must be enabled by selecting Extras from the Pause menu.

CHEAT	CODE
Artifact Detector	VIKED7
Beep Beep	VNF59Q
Character Treasure	VIES2R
Disarm Enemies	VKRNS9
Disguises	4ID1N6
Fast Build	V83SLO
Fast Dig	378RS6
Fast Fix	FJ59WS
Fertilizer	B1GW1F
Ice Rink	33GM7J
Parcel Detector	VUT673
Poo Treasure	WWQ1SA
Regenerate Hearts	MDLP69
Secret Characters	3X44AA
Silhouettes	3HE85H
Super Scream	VN3R7S
Super Slap	0P1TA5
Treasure Magnet	H86LA2
Treasure x10	VI3PS8
Treasure x2	VM4TS9
Treasure x4	VLWEN3
Treasure x6	V84RYS
Treasure x8	A72E1M

LEGO STAR WARS: THE COMPLETE SAGA

The following must still be purchased after entering the codes.

CHARACTERS

ADMIRAL ACKBAR
At the bar in Mos Eisley Cantina, select Enter Code and enter ACK646.

BATTLE DROID (COMMANDER)
At the bar in Mos Eisley Cantina, select Enter Code and enter KPF958.

BOBA FETT (BOY)
At the bar in Mos Eisley Cantina, select Enter Code and enter GGF539.

BOSS NASS
At the bar in Mos Eisley Cantina, select Enter Code and enter HHY697.

CAPTAIN TARPALS
At the bar in Mos Eisley Cantina, select Enter Code and enter QRN714.

COUNT DOOKU
At the bar in Mos Eisley Cantina, select Enter Code and enter DDD748.

DARTH MAUL
At the bar in Mos Eisley Cantina, select Enter Code and enter EUK421.

EWOK
At the bar in Mos Eisley Cantina, select Enter Code and enter EWK785.

GENERAL GRIEVOUS
At the bar in Mos Eisley Cantina, select Enter Code and enter PMN576.

GREEDO
At the bar in Mos Eisley Cantina, select Enter Code and enter ZZR636.

IG-88
At the bar in Mos Eisley Cantina, select Enter Code and enter GIJ989.

IMPERIAL GUARD
At the bar in Mos Eisley Cantina, select Enter Code and enter GUA850.

JANGO FETT
At the bar in Mos Eisley Cantina, select Enter Code and enter KLJ897.

KI-ADI MUNDI
At the bar in Mos Eisley Cantina, select Enter Code and enter MUN486.

LUMINARA
At the bar in Mos Eisley Cantina, select Enter Code and enter LUM521.

PADMÉ
At the bar in Mos Eisley Cantina, select Enter Code and enter VBJ322.

R2-Q5
At the bar in Mos Eisley Cantina, select Enter Code and enter EVILR2.

STORMTROOPER
At the bar in Mos Eisley Cantina, select Enter Code and enter NBN431.

TAUN WE
At the bar in Mos Eisley Cantina, select Enter Code and enter PRX482.

VULTURE DROID
At the bar in Mos Eisley Cantina, select Enter Code and enter BDC866.

WATTO
At the bar in Mos Eisley Cantina, select Enter Code and enter PLL967.

ZAM WESELL
At the bar in Mos Eisley Cantina, select Enter Code and enter 584HJF.

SKILLS

DISGUISE
At the bar in Mos Eisley Cantina, select Enter Code and enter BRJ437.

FORCE GRAPPLE LEAP
At the bar in Mos Eisley Cantina, select Enter Code and enter CLZ738.

VEHICLES

DROID TRIFIGHTER
At the bar in Mos Eisley Cantina, select Enter Code and enter AAB123.

IMPERIAL SHUTTLE
At the bar in Mos Eisley Cantina, select Enter Code and enter HUT845.

TIE INTERCEPTOR
At the bar in Mos Eisley Cantina, select Enter Code and enter INT729.

TIE FIGHTER
At the bar in Mos Eisley Cantina, select Enter Code and enter DBH897.

ZAM'S AIRSPEEDER
At the bar in Mos Eisley Cantina, select Enter Code and enter UUU875.

MADDEN NFL 07

MADDEN CARDS
Select Madden Cards from My Madden. Then select Madden Codes and enter the following:

CARD	PASSWORD
#199 Gold Lame Duck Cheat	5LAWO0
#200 Gold Mistake Free Cheat	XL7SP1
#210 Gold QB on Target Cheat	WROA0R
#220 Super Bowl XLI Gold	RLA9R7
#221 Super Bowl XLII Gold	WRLUF8
#222 Super Bowl XLIII Gold	NIEV4A
#223 Super Bowl XLIV Gold	M5AB7L
#224 Aloha Stadium Gold	YI8P8U
#225 1958 Colts Gold	B57QLU
#226 1966 Packers Gold	1PL1FL
#227 1968 Jets Gold	MIE6WO
#228 1970 Browns Gold	CL2TOE
#229 1972 Dolphins Gold	NOEB7U
#230 1974 Steelers Gold	YO0FLA
#231 1976 Raiders Gold	MOA11I
#232 1977 Broncos Gold	C8UM7U
#233 1978 Dolphins Gold	VIU0O7

CARD	PASSWORD
#234 1980 Raiders Gold	NLAPH3
#235 1981 Chargers Gold	COAGI4
#236 1982 Redskins Gold	WL8BRI
#237 1983 Raiders Gold	H0EW71
#238 1984 Dolphins Gold	M1AM1E
#239 1985 Bears Gold	QOETO8
#240 1986 Giants Gold	ZI8S2L
#241 1988 49ers Gold	SP2A8H
#242 1990 Eagles Gold	2L4TRO
#243 1991 Lions Gold	J1ETRI
#244 1992 Cowboys Gold	W9UVI9
#245 1993 Bills Gold	DLA3I7
#246 1994 49ers Gold	DR7EST
#247 1996 Packers Gold	F8LUST
#248 1998 Broncos Gold	FIES95
#249 1999 Rams Gold	S9OUSW
#250 Bears Pump Up the Crowd	B1OUPH
#251 Bengals Cheerleader	DRL2SW
#252 Bills Cheerleader	1PLUYO
#253 Broncos Cheerleader	3ROUJO
#254 Browns Pump Up the Crowd	T1UTOA
#255 Buccaneers Cheerleader	S9EWRI
#256 Cardinals Cheerleader	57IEPI
#257 Chargers Cheerleader	F7UHL8
#258 Chiefs Cheerleader	PRI5SL
#259 Colts Cheerleader	1R5AMI
#260 Cowboys Cheerleader	Z2ACHL
#261 Dolphins Cheerleader	C5AHLE
#262 Eagles Cheerleader	PO7DRO
#263 Falcons Cheerleader	37USPO
#264 49ers Cheerleader	KL0CRL
#265 Giants Pump Up the Crowd	C4USPI
#266 Jaguars Cheerleader	MIEH7E
#267 Jets Pump Up the Crowd	C0LUXI
#268 Lions Pump Up the Crowd	3LABLU
#269 Packers Pump Up the Crowd	4HO7VO
#270 Panthers Cheerleader	F2IASP
#282 All AFC Team Gold	PRO9PH
#283 All NFC Team Gold	RLATH7

MANHUNT 2

INFINITE AMMO

At the Main menu, press Up, Up, Down, Down, Left, Right, Left, Right.

LEVEL SELECT

At the Main menu, press Up, Down, Left, Right, Up, Down, Left, Right.

MARBLE SAGA: KORORINPA

MASTER HIGGINS BALL

Select ??? from the Options. Press A on the right lamp, the left lamp twice, and the right lamp again. Now select the right icon and enter TV, Car, Sunflower, Bike, Helicopter, Strawberry.

MIRROR MODE

Select ??? from the Options. Press A on the right lamp, the left lamp twice, and the right lamp again. Now select the right icon and enter Beetle, Clover, Boy, Plane, Car, Bike.

MARIO & SONIC AT THE OLYMPIC GAMES

UNLOCK 4X100M RELAY EVENT
Medal in Mercury, Venus, Jupiter, and Saturn.

UNLOCK SINGLE SCULLS EVENT
Medal in Mercury, Venus, Jupiter, and Saturn.

UNLOCK DREAM RACE EVENT
Medal in Mercury, Venus, Jupiter, and Saturn.

UNLOCK ARCHERY EVENT
Medal in Moonlight Circuit.

UNLOCK HIGH JUMP EVENT
Medal in Stardust Circuit.

UNLOCK 400M EVENT
Medal in Planet Circuit.

UNLOCK DREAM FENCING EVENT
Medal in Comet Circuit.

UNLOCK DREAM TABLE TENNIS EVENT
Medal in Satellite Circuit.

UNLOCK 400M HURDLES EVENT
Medal in Sunlight Circuit.

UNLOCK POLE VAULT EVENT
Medal in Meteorite Circuit.

UNLOCK VAULT EVENT
Medal in Meteorite Circuit.

UNLOCK DREAM PLATFORM EVENT
Medal in Cosmos Circuit.

CROWNS
Get all gold medals in all events with a character to unlock their crown.

MARIO KART WII

CHARACTERS

CHARACTER	UNLOCK BY...
Baby Daisy	Earn 1 Star in 50cc for Mushroom, Flower, Star, and Special Cups.
Baby Luigi	Unlock 8 Expert Staff Ghost Data in Time Trials.
Birdo	Race 16 different courses in Time Trials or win 250 versus races.
Bowser Jr.	Earn 1 Star in 100cc for Shell, Banana, Leaf, and Lightning Cups.
Daisy	Win 150cc Special Cup.
Diddy Kong	Win 50cc Lightning Cup.
Dry Bones	Win 100cc Leaf Cup.
Dry Bowser	Earn 1 Star in 150cc for Mushroom, Flower, Star, and Special Cups.
Funky Kong	Unlock 4 Expert Staff Ghost Data in Time Trials.
King Boo	Win 50cc Star Cup.
Mii Outfit A	Win 100cc Special Cup.
Mii Outfit B	Unlock all 32 Expert Staff Ghost Data in Time Trials.
Mii Outfit C	Get 15,000 points in Versus Mode.
Rosalina	Have a Super Mario Galaxy save file and she is unlocked after 50 races or earn 1 Star in all Mirror Cups.
Toadette	Race 32 different courses in Time Trials.

KARTS

KART	UNLOCK BY...
Blue Falcon	Win Mirror Lightning Cup.
Cheep Charger	Earn 1 Star in 50cc for Mushroom, Flower, Star, and Special Cups.
Rally Romper	Unlock an Expert Staff Ghost Data in Time Trials.
B Dasher Mk. 2	Unlock 24 Expert Staff Ghost Data in Time Trials.
Royal Racer	Win 150cc Leaf Cup.
Turbo Blooper	Win 50cc Leaf Cup.
Aero Glider	Earn 1 Star in 150cc for Mushroom, Flower, Star, and Special Cups.
Dragonetti	Win 150cc Lightning Cup.
Piranha Prowler	Win 50cc Special Cup.

BIKES

BIKE	UNLOCK BY...
Bubble Bike	Win Mirror Leaf Cup.
Magikruiser	Race 8 different courses in Time Trials.
Quacker	Win 150cc Star Cup.
Dolphin Dasher	Win Mirror Star Cup.
Nitrocycle	Earn 1 Star in 100cc for all cups.
Rapide	Win 100cc Lightning Cup.
Phantom	Win Mirror Special Cup.
Torpedo	Unlock 12 Expert Staff Ghost Data in Time Trials.
Twinkle Star	Win 100cc Star Cup.

MARVEL ULTIMATE ALLIANCE

UNLOCK ALL SKINS

At the Team menu, press Up, Down, Left, Right, Left, Right, Plus.

UNLOCKS ALL HERO POWERS

At the Team menu, press Left, Right, Up, Down, Up, Down, Plus.

ALL HEROES TO LEVEL 99

At the Team menu, press Up, Left, Up, Left, Down, Right, Down, Right, Plus.

UNLOCK ALL HEROES

At the Team menu, press Up, Up, Down, Down, Left, Left, Left, Plus.

UNLOCK DAREDEVIL

At the Team menu, press Left, Left, Right, Right, Up, Down, Up, Down, Plus.

UNLOCK SILVER SURFER

At the Team menu, press Down, Left, Left, Up, Right, Up, Down, Left, Plus.

GOD MODE

During gameplay, press Up, Down, Up, Down, Up, Left, Down, Right, Plus.

TOUCH OF DEATH

During gameplay, press Left, Right, Down, Down, Right, Left, Plus.

SUPER SPEED

During gameplay, press Up, Left, Up, Right, Down, Right, Plus.

FILL MOMENTUM

During gameplay, press Left, Right, Right, Left, Up, Down, Down, Up, Plus.

UNLOCK ALL COMICS

At the Review menu, press Left, Right, Right, Left, Up, Up, Right, Plus.

UNLOCK ALL CONCEPT ART

At the Review menu, press Down, Down, Down, Right, Right, Left, Down, Plus.

UNLOCK ALL CINEMATICS

At the Review menu, press Up, Left, Left, Up, Right, Right, Up, Plus.

UNLOCK ALL LOAD SCREENS

At the Review menu, press Up, Down, Right, Left, Up, Up Down, Plus.

UNLOCK ALL COURSES

At the Comic Missions menu, press Up, Right, Left, Down, Up, Right, Left, Down, Plus.

MEDAL OF HONOR: VANGUARD

EXTRA ARMOR

Pause the game and press Up, Down, Up, Down to display the words Enter Cheat Code. Then press Right, Left, Right, Down, Up, Right.

DECREASE ENEMY ACCURACY

Pause the game and press Up, Down, Up, Down to display the words Enter Cheat Code. Then press Right, Left, Right, Down, Up, Right.

INVISIBLE

Pause the game and press Up, Down, Up, Down to display the words Enter Cheat Code. Then press Up, Right, Left, Down, Down, Up.

MLB POWER PROS

EXTRA FORMS

At the Main menu, press Right, Left, Up, Down, Down, Right, Right, Up, Up, Left, Down, Left.

VIEW MLB PLAYERS AT CUSTOM PLAYER MENU

Select View or Delete Custom Players/Password Display from My Data and press Up, Up, Down, Down, Left, Right, Left, Right, 1, 2.

MONSTER JAM

TRUCKS

As you collect monster points, they are tallied toward your Championship Score. Trucks are unlocked when you reach certain point totals.

TRUCK	POINTS
Destroyer	10,000
Blacksmith	50,000
El Toro Loco	70,000
Suzuki	110,000
Maximum Destruction	235,000

MORTAL KOMBAT: ARMAGEDDON

The following codes are for the Wii Remote and Nunchuck. Directions are input with the Nunchuck stick, except where noted to use the Wii Remote's D-pad. You need to use a Classic Controller to input ZL and ZR where called for.

You can also use the Classic Controller alone to input the codes with the following chart:

REMOTE/NUNCHUCK	CLASSIC CONTROLLER
Nunchuck Directions	D-pad
Down on Wii Remote D-pad	B
Up on Wii Remote D-pad	X
Left on Wii Remote D-pad	Y
Right on Wii Remote D-pad	A
A	R
C	L
ZL on Classic Controller	Same
ZR on Classic Controller	Same

BLAZE CHARACTER

While in The Krypt, select the "?" and press Up on D-pad, Left on D-pad, Left, C, Left, Right on D-pad.

DAEGON CHARACTER

While in The Krypt, select the "?" and press A, C, Up on D-pad, Down, Down, Left on D-pad.

MEAT CHARACTER

While in The Krypt, select the "?" and press Up, Left on D-pad, Left on D-pad, Right on D-pad, Right on D-pad, Up.

TAVEN CHARACTER

While in The Krypt, select the "?" and press C, Left, ZR, Up, Right on D-pad, Down.

DRAHMIN'S ALTERNATE COSTUME

While in The Krypt, select the "?" and press C, Right, Down on D-pad, A, Up, Up.

FROST'S ALTERNATE COSTUME

While in The Krypt, select the "?" and press Down, A, A, C, Right on D-pad, C.

NITARA'S ALTERNATE COSTUME

While in The Krypt, select the "?" and press Down, C, Up, C, C, Right.

SHANG TSUNG'S ALTERNATE COSTUME

While in The Krypt, select the "?" and press C, Left, Up, Right on D-pad, Up, L (or ZL).

FALLING CLIFFS ARENA

While in The Krypt, select the "?" and press ZR, Right on D-pad, Left on D-pad, Down on D-pad, Right on D-pad, Up on D-pad.

KRIMSON FOREST ARENA

While in The Krypt, select the "?" and press Right on D-pad, C, Up, Left on D-pad, Right on D-pad, Down.

NETHERSHIP INTERIOR ARENA

While in The Krypt, select the "?" and press A, Left, Left, Down, C, Left on D-pad.

THE PYRAMID OF ARGUS ARENA

While in The Krypt, select the "?" and press A, C, Left on D-pad, Down on D-pad, A, Up.

REIKO'S WAR ROOM ARENA

While in The Krypt, select the "?" and press A, Up on D-pad, A, Up, Down on D-pad, Down on D-pad.

SHINNOK'S SPIRE ARENA

While in The Krypt, select the "?" and press Left, Left, Right on D-pad, Up, Up on D-pad, C.

ARMAGEDDON PROMO MOVIE
While in The Krypt, select the "?" and press Up, Up, Down, Up, ZL, Right on D-pad.

CYRAX FATALITY BLOOPER MOVIE
While in The Krypt, select the "?" and press Right, C, ZR, Down, Up, C.

MOTOR GAMEPLAY MOVIE
While in The Krypt, select the "?" and press Up on D-pad, Up, ZR, L (or ZL), A, ZR.

BLAZE BOSS SKETCH KONCEPT ART
While in The Krypt, select the "?" and press C, Up on D-pad, C, C, A, Left on D-pad.

COLOR STUDY FOR OPENING MOVIE 3 KONCEPT ART
While in The Krypt, select the "?" and press Up on D-pad, Left, Left, Down on D-pad, Down, Right on D-pad.

FIREWELL SKETCH 3 KONCEPT ART
While in The Krypt, select the "?" and press Up, Left on D-pad, R (or ZR), L (or ZL), Right on D-pad, C.

GAUNTLET TRAP SKETCH KONCEPT ART
While in The Krypt, select the "?" and press Right on D-pad, RZ, Up on D-pad, Down, Right on D-pad, Left.

HERO SKETCHES 1 KONCEPT ART
While in The Krypt, select the "?" and press Up, Down on D-pad, RZ, Down, L (or LZ), Down on D-pad.

MILEENA'S CAR SKETCH KONCEPT ART
While in The Krypt, select the "?" and press R (or ZR), Right, Up, R (or ZR), Up on D-pad, Up.

SCORPION THROW SKETCH KONCEPT ART
While in The Krypt, select the "?" and press L (or ZL), Left, Up, Right on D-pad, R (or ZR), C.

SEKTOR'S 2-HAND PULSE BLADE SKETCH KONCEPT ART
While in The Krypt, select the "?" and press A, C, Left, Down on D-pad, Up, A.

ARMORY FIGHT TUNE
While in The Krypt, select the "?" and press Down on D-pad, Left on D-pad, Left, Up on D-pad, Left on D-pad, Down on D-pad.

LIN KUEI PALACE TUNE
While in The Krypt, select the "?" and press L (or ZL), Left, Right on D-pad, Down on D-pad, RZ, Right.

PYRAMID OF ARGUS TUNE
While in The Krypt, select the "?" and press Down, Left, A, C, Up, C.

TEKUNIN WARSHIP TUNE
While in The Krypt, select the "?" and press Up, Right on D-pad, C, A, A, Down on D-pad.

MYSIMS

PASSWORD SCREEN
Press the – Button to bring up the pause screen. Then enter the following with the Wii Remote: 2, 1, Down, Up, Down, Up, Left, Left, Right, Right. Now you can enter the following passwords:

OUTFITS	PASSWORD
z	N10ng5g
Diamond vest	Tglg0ca
Genie outfit	Gvsb3k1
Kimono dress	I3hkdvs
White jacket	R705aan

FURNITURE	PASSWORD
Bunk bed	F3nevr0
Hourglass couch	Ghtymba
Modern couch	T7srhca
Racecar bed	Ahvmrva
Rickshaw bed	Itha7da

MYSIMS KINGDOM

DETECTIVE OUTFIT

Pause the game and press Left, Right, Left, Right, Left, Right.

SWORDSMAN OUTFIT

Pause the game and press Down, Up, Down, Up, Down, Up, Down, Up.

TATTOO VEST OUTFIT

Pause the game and press C, Z, C, Z, B, A, B, A.

NASCAR KART RACING

JOEY LOGANO

Select Enter Cheat from the Profile Info menu and enter 426378.

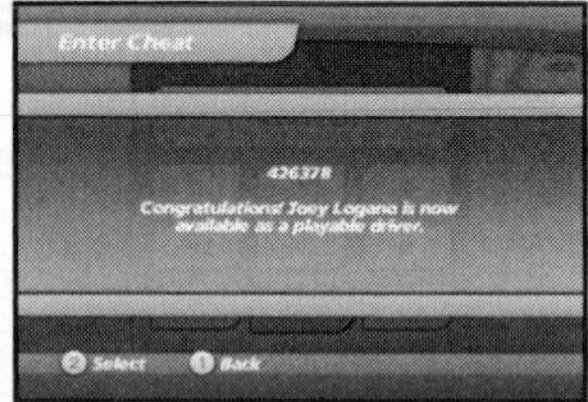

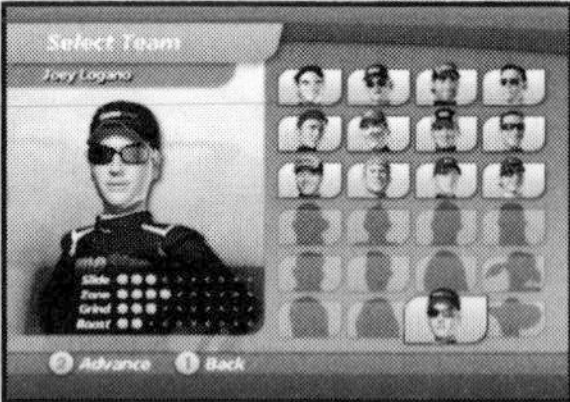

NBA LIVE 08

AGENT ZERO SHOES

At the Extras menu, enter ADGILLIT6BE as a code.

CUBA SHOES

At the Extras menu, enter ADGILLIT4BC as a code.

CUSTOMIZE SHOES

At the Extras menu, enter ADGILLIT5BD as a code.

DUNCAN ALL STAR SHOES

At the Extras menu, enter FE454DFJCC as a code.

GIL WOOD SHOES

At the Extras menu, enter ADGILLIT1B9 as a code.

GIL ZERO ALL STAR SHOES

At the Extras menu, enter 23DN1PPOG4 as a code.

TS LIGHTSWITCH AWAY SHOES

At the Extras menu, enter ADGILLIT0B8 as a code.

TS LIGHTSWITCH HOME SHOES

At the Extras menu, enter ADGILLIT2BA as a code.

NEED FOR SPEED CARBON

CASTROL CASH

At the Main menu, press Down, Up, Left, Down, Right, Up, Button 1, B. This gives you 10,000 extra cash.

INFINITE CREW CHARGE

At the Main menu, press Down, Up, Up, Right, Left, Left, Right, Button 1.

INFINITE NITROUS

At the Main menu, press Left, Up, Left, Down, Left, Down, Right, Button 1.

INFINITE SPEEDBREAKER

At the Main menu, press Down, Right, Right, Left, Right, Up, Down, Button 1.

NEED FOR SPEED CARBON LOGO VINYLS

At the Main menu, press Right, Up, Down, Up, Down, Left, Right, Button 1.

NEED FOR SPEED CARBON SPECIAL LOGO VINYLS

At the Main menu, press Up, Up, Down, Down, Down, Down, Up, Button 1.

NEED FOR SPEED PROSTREET

$2,000
Select Career and then choose Code Entry. Enter 1MA9X99.

$4,000
Select Career and then choose Code Entry. Enter W2IOLL01.

$8,000
Select Career and then choose Code Entry. Enter L1IS97A1.

$10,000
Select Career and then choose Code Entry. Enter 1MI9K7E1.

$10,000
Select Career and then choose Code Entry. Enter CASHMONEY.

$10,000
Select Career and then choose Code Entry. Enter REGGAME.

AUDI TT
Select Career and then choose Code Entry. Enter ITSABOUTYOU.

CHEVELLE SS
Select Career and then choose Code Entry. Enter HORSEPOWER.

COKE ZERO GOLF GTI
Select Career and then choose Code Entry. Enter COKEZERO.

DODGE VIPER
Select Career and then choose Code Entry. Enter WORLDSLONGESTLASTING.

MITSUBISHI LANCER EVOLUTION
Select Career and then choose Code Entry. Enter MITSUBISHIGOFAR.

UNLOCK ALL BONUSES
Select Career and then choose Code Entry. Enter UNLOCKALLTHINGS.

5 REPAIR MARKERS
Select Career and then choose Code Entry. Enter SAFETYNET.

ENERGIZER VINYL
Select Career and then choose Code Entry. Enter ENERGIZERLITHIUM.

CASTROL SYNTEC VINYL
Select Career and then choose Code Entry. Enter CASTROLSYNTEC. This also gives you $10,000.

NERF N-STRIKE

BLACK HEART VENGEANCE
Select Codes from the Main menu and enter BHDETA8.

CRUSHER SAD-G
Select Codes from the Main menu and enter CRUSH14.

FIREFLY ELITE
Select Codes from the Main menu and enter HELIOX6.

GOLIATHAN NITRO
Select Codes from the Main menu and enter FIERO2.

HABANERO
Select Codes from the Main menu and enter 24KGCON4.

HYDRA
Select Codes from the Main menu and enter HRANGEL3.

LONGSHOT STREET
Select Codes from the Main menu and enter LONGST5.

MAVERICK CRYSTAL
Select Codes from the Main menu and enter CRISTOL10.

MAVERICK MIDNIGHT
Select Codes from the Main menu and enter MAVMID7.

MERCURIO
Select Codes from the Main menu and enter RSMERC9.

SEMPER FIRE ULTRA
Select Codes from the Main menu and enter CROMO1.

SPARTAN NCS-12
Select Codes from the Main menu and enter THISIS12.

STAMPEDE
Select Codes from the Main menu and enter DOGIE15.

VULCAN MAGMA
Select Codes from the Main menu and enter MAGMA3.

NHL 2K9

3RD JERSEYS
At the Codes menu enter R6y34bsH52.

NICKTOONS: ATTACK OF THE TOYBOTS

DAMAGE BOOST

Select Cheats from the Extras menu. Choose Enter Cheat Code and enter 456645.

INVULNERABILITY

Select Cheats from the Extras menu. Choose Enter Cheat Code and enter 313456.

UNLOCK EXO-HUGGLES 9000

Select Cheats from the Extras menu. Choose Enter Cheat Code and enter 691427.

UNLOCK MR. HUGGLES

Select Cheats from the Extras menu. Choose Enter Cheat Code and enter 654168.

UNLIMITED LOBBER GOO

Select Cheats from the Extras menu. Choose Enter Cheat Code and enter 118147.

UNLIMITED SCATTER GOO

Select Cheats from the Extras menu. Choose Enter Cheat Code and enter 971238.

UNLIMITED SPLITTER GOO

Select Cheats from the Extras menu. Choose Enter Cheat Code and enter 854511.

PRINCE OF PERSIA RIVAL SWORDS

BABY TOY WEAPON

Pause the game and enter the following code. Use the D-pad for the directions.

Left, Left, Right, Right, Z, Nunchuck down, Nunchuck down, Z, Up, Down

CHAINSAW

Pause the game and enter the following code. Use the D-pad for the directions.

Up, Up, Down, Down, Left, Right, Left, Right, Z, Nunchuck down, Z, Nunchuck down

SWORDFISH

Pause the game and enter the following code. Use the D-pad for the directions.

Up, Down, Up, Down, Left, Right, Left, Right, Z, Nunchuck down, Z, Nunchuck down

TELEPHONE SWORD

Pause the game and enter the following code. Use the D-pad for the directions.

Right, Left, Right, Left, Down, Down, Up, Up, Z, Nunchuck Down, Z, Z, Nunchuck Down, Nunchuck Down

RAMPAGE: TOTAL DESTRUCTION

ALL MONSTERS

At the Main menu, press Minus + Plus to access the Cheat menu and enter 141421.

INVULNERABLE TO ATTACKS

At the Main menu, press Minus + Plus to access the Cheat menu and enter 986960.

ALL SPECIAL ABILITIES

At the Main menu, press Minus + Plus to access the Cheat menu and enter 011235.

ALL LEVELS

At the Main menu, press Minus + Plus to access the Cheat menu and enter 271828.

CPU VS CPU DEMO

At the Main menu, press Minus + Plus to access the cheat menu and enter 082864.

FAST CPU VS CPU DEMO

At the Main menu, press Minus + Plus to access the Cheat menu and enter 874098.

ONE-HIT DESTROYS BUILDINGS

At the Main menu, press Minus + Plus to access the Cheat menu and enter 071767.

OPENING MOVIE

At the Main menu, press Minus + Plus to access the Cheat menu and enter 667300.

ENDING MOVIE

At the Main menu, press Minus + Plus to access the Cheat menu and enter 667301.

CREDITS

At the Main menu, press Minus + Plus to access the Cheat menu and enter 667302.

VERSION INFORMATION

At the Main menu, press Minus + Plus to access the Cheat menu and enter 314159.

CLEAR CHEATS

At the Main menu, press Minus + Plus to access the Cheat menu and enter 000000.

RATATOUILLE

Select Gusteau's Shop from the Extras menu. Choose Secrets, select the appropriate code number, and then enter the code. Once the code is entered, select the cheat you want to activate it.

CODE NUMBER	CODE	EFFECT
1	Pieceocake	Very Easy difficulty mode
2	Myhero	No impact and no damage from enemies
3	Shielded	No damage from enemies
4	Spyagent	Move undetected by any enemy
5	Ilikeonions	Fart every time Remy jumps
6	Hardfeelings	Head butt when attacking instead of tailswipe
7	Slumberparty	Multiplayer mode
8	Gusteauart	All Concept Art
9	Gusteauship	All four championship modes
10	Mattelme	All single player and multiplayer minigames
11	Gusteauvid	All Videos
12	Gusteaures	All Bonus Artworks
13	Gusteaudream	All Dream Worlds in Gusteau's Shop
14	Gusteauslide	All Slides in Gusteau's Shop
15	Gusteaulevel	All single player minigames
16	Gusteaucombo	All items in Gusteau's Shop
17	Gusteaupot	5,000 Gusteau points
18	Gusteaujack	10,000 Gusteau points
19	Gusteauomni	50,000 Gusteau points

RAYMAN RAVING RABBIDS 2

FUNKYTOWN

Play each game at least once.

RABBID COSTUMES

Costumes are unlocked as you score 12,000 points in certain games, as well as when you shoot the correct rabbid in the shooting games.

COSTUME	MINIGAME	HOW TO UNLOCK
Cossack	Chess	Earn 12,000 points
Crash Test Dummy	Shopping Cart Downhill	Earn 12,000 points
Cupid	Burgerinnii	Earn 12,000 points
Doctor	Anesthetics	Earn 12,000 points
Fireman	Paris, Pour Troujours	Shoot fireman rabbid
French Maid	Little Chemist	Earn 12,000 points
Fruit-Hat Dancer	Year of the Rabbids	Shoot rabbid wearing fruit hat
Gingerbread	Hot Cake	Earn 12,000 points
HAZE Armor	Big City Fights	Shoot rabbid with armor
Indiana Jones	Rolling Stone	Earn 12,000 points
Jet Trooper	Greatest Hits	Earn 12,000 points
Ken	RRR Xtreme Beach Volleyball	Earn 12,000 points
Martian	Bumper Cars	Earn 12,000 points
Party Girl	Paris, Mon Amour	Once inside boat, shoot girl rabbid

COSTUME	MINIGAME	HOW TO UNLOCK
Raider's	American Football	Earn 12,000 points
Sam Fisher	Rabbid School	Earn 12,000 points
Samurai	The Office	Earn 12,000 points
Space	Year of the Rabbids	Earn 12,000 points
Spider-	Spider Rabbid	Play the "Spider Rabbid" Game
TMNT, Leonardo	Usual Rabbids	Earn 12,000 points
Transformer	Plumber Rabbids	Earn 12,000 points
Vegas Showgirl	Burp	Earn 12,000 points
Voodoo	Voodoo Rabbids	Earn 12,000 points
Wrestler	Greatest Hits	Shoot rabbid in green outfit

RESIDENT EVIL: THE UMBRELLA CHRONICLES

UNLIMITED AMMO

Earn S rank in all scenarios on hard difficulty.

ARCHIVE ITEMS

Defeat the following scenarios with the indicated rank to earn that item. Get an S rank to get both A and S items.

SCENARIO	A RANK	S RANK
Train Derailment 1	Mixing Set	Briefcase
Train Derailment 2	Statue of Evil/Good	Relief of Discipline/ Obedience/Unity
Train Derailment 3	Blue/Green Leech Charm	Sterilizing Agent
Beginnings 1	Motherboard	Valve Handle
Beginnings 2	Fire/Water Key	Microfilm A/B
Mansion Incident 1	Lighter/Lockpick	Great Eagle/Wolf Medal
Mansion Incident 2	Sun/Star/Moon Crest	V-Jolt
Mansion Incident 3	MO Disc	Fuel Canteen
Nightmare 1	Cylinder Shaft	Hex Crank
Nightmare 2	Last Book, Vol. 1/2	Emblem/Gold Emblem
Rebirth 1	Clark/Gail X-Ray	Slide Cartridge
Rebirth 2	Blue/Red/Yellow Gemstone	Death Mask
Raccoon's Destruction 1	S.T.A.R.S. Card (Jill's)	Book of Wisdom/Future Compass
Raccoon's Destruction 2	Joint N/S Plug	Lighter Fluid
Raccoon's Destruction 3	Crystal/Obsidian/Amber Ball	Chronos Key
Death's Door	Picture (Ada and Jon)	S.T.A.R.S. Card (Brad's)
Fourth Survivor	G-virus	Eagle/Serpent/Jaguar Stone
Umbrella's End 1	Plastic Bomb/Detonator	Square Crank
Umbrella's End 2	Blue/Red/Green Chemical	Ink Ribbon
Umbrella's End 3	Vaccine	Medium Base
Dark Legacy 1	King/Knight/Bishop/Rook Plug	Battery
Dark Legacy 2	Film A/B/D/C	Spade/Diamond/Club/ Heart Key

ROCK BAND

UNLOCK ALL SONGS

At the Title screen, press Red, Yellow, Blue, Red, Red, Blue, Blue, Red, Yellow, Blue. This code disables saving.

RUBIK'S PUZZLE WORLD

ALL LEVELS AND CUBIES

At the Main menu, press A, B, B, A, A.

SAMBA DE AMIGO

UNLOCK EVERYTHING

At the Title screen, press 1, 1, 1, B, A, 1, 1, 1, B, A.

SCARFACE: THE WORLD IS YOURS

MAX AMMO

Pause the game, select Cheats and enter AMMO.

REFILL HEALTH

Pause the game, select Cheats and enter MEDIK.

BULLDOZER

Pause the game, select Cheats and enter DOZER.

INCREASE GANG HEAT

Pause the game, select Cheats and enter GOBALLS.

DECREASE GANG HEAT

Pause the game, select Cheats and enter NOBALLS.

INCREASE COP HEAT

Pause the game, select Cheats and enter DONUT.

DECREASES COP HEAT

Pause the game, select Cheats and enter FLYSTRT.

FILL BALLS METER

Pause the game, select Cheats and enter FPATCH.

GRAY SUIT TONY WITH SUNGLASSES

Pause the game, select Cheats and enter GRAYSH.

TOGGLE RAIN

Pause the game, select Cheats and enter RAINY.

SHREK THE THIRD

10,000 GOLD COINS

At the gift shop, press Up, Up, Down, Up, Right, Left.

SIMANIMALS

FERRET

Begin a game in an unlocked forest area, press 2 to pause, and select Enter Codes. Enter Ferret.

PANDA

Begin a game in an unlocked forest area, press 2 to pause, and select Enter Codes. Enter PANDA.

RED PANDA

Begin a game in an unlocked forest area, press 2 to pause, and select Enter Codes. Enter Red Panda.

SIMCITY CREATOR

EGYPTIAN BUILDING SET

Name your city Mummy's desert.

GREEK BUILDING SET

Name your city Ancient culture.

JUNGLE BUILDING SET

Name your city Become wild.

SCI-FI BUILDING SET

Name your city Future picture.

THE SIMPSONS GAME

UNLIMITED POWER FOR ALL CHARACTERS

At the Extras menu, press Plus, Left, Right, Plus, Minus, Z.

ALL MOVIES

At the Extras menu, press Minus, Left, Minus, Right, Plus, C.

ALL CLICHÉS

At the Extras menu, press Left, Minus, Right, Plus, Right, Z.

THE SIMS 2: CASTAWAY

CHEAT GNOME

During a game, press B, Z, Up, Down, B. You can now use this Gnome to get the following:

MAX ALL MOTIVES

During a game, press Minus, Plus, Z, Z, A.

MAX CURRENT INVENTORY

During a game, press Left, Right, Left, Right, A.

MAX RELATIONSHIPS

During a game, press Z, Plus, A, B, 2.

ALL RESOURCES

During a game, press A, A, Down, Down, A.

ALL CRAFTING PLANS

During a game, press Plus, Plus, Minus, Minus, Z.

ADD 1 TO SKILL

During a game, press 2, Up, Right, Z, Right.

SPACE HARRIER

CONTINUE AFTER GAME OVER

At the Game Over screen, press Up, Up, Down, Down, Left, Right, Left, Right, Down, Up, Down, Up.

SPEED RACER

INVULNERABILITY

Select Enter Code from the Options menu and enter A, B, A, Up, Left, Down, Right.

UNLIMITED BOOST

Select Enter Code from the Options menu and enter B, A, Down, Up, B, A, Down.

LAST 3 CARS

Select Enter Code from the Options menu and enter 1, 2, 1, 2, B, A, Plus.

GRANITE CAR

Select Enter Code from the Options menu and enter B, Up, Minus, Plus, 1, Up, Plus.

MONSTER TRUCK

Select Enter Code from the Options menu and enter B, Up, Minus, 2, B, Up, Minus.

AGGRESSIVE OPPONENTS

Select Enter Code from the Options menu and enter Up, Left, Down, Right, Up, Left, Down.

PACIFIST OPPONENTS

Select Enter Code from the Options menu and enter Up, Right, Down, Left, Up, Right, Down.

TINY OPPONENTS

Select Enter Code from the Options menu and enter B, A, Left, Down, Minus, Up, Minus.

HELIUM

Select Enter Code from the Options menu and enter Minus, Up, Minus, 2, Minus, Up, Minus.

MOON GRAVITY

Select Enter Code from the Options menu and enter Up, Plus, Up, Right, Minus, Up, Minus.

OVERKILL

Select Enter Code from the Options menu and enter A, Minus, Plus, Down, Up, Plus, 1.

PSYCHEDELIC

Select Enter Code from the Options menu and enter Left, A, Right, Down, B, Up, Minus.

SPIDER-MAN: FRIEND OR FOE

NEW GREEN GOBLIN AS A SIDEKICK

While standing in the Helicarrier between levels, press Left, Down, Right, Right, Down, Left.

SANDMAN AS A SIDEKICK

While standing in the Helicarrier between levels, press Right, Right, Right, Up, Down, Left.

VENOM AS A SIDEKICK

While standing in the Helicarrier between levels, press Left, Left, Right, Up, Down, Down.

5000 TECH TOKENS

While standing in the Helicarrier between levels, press Up, Up, Down, Down, Left, Right.

SPONGEBOB SQUAREPANTS: CREATURE FROM THE KRUSTY KRAB

30,000 EXTRA Z'S

Select Cheat Codes from the Extras menu and enter ROCFISH.

PUNK SPONGEBOB IN DIESEL DREAMING

Select Cheat Codes from the Extras menu and enter SPONGE. Select Activate Bonus Items to enable this bonus item.

HOT ROD SKIN IN DIESEL DREAMING

Select Cheat Codes from the Extras menu and enter HOTROD. Select Activate Bonus Items to enable this bonus item.

PATRICK TUX IN STARFISHMAN TO THE RESCUE

Select Cheat Codes from the Extras menu and enter PATRICK. Select Activate Bonus Items to enable this bonus item.

SPONGEBOB PLANKTON IN SUPER-SIZED PATTY

Select Cheat Codes from the Extras menu and enter PANTS. Select Activate Bonus Items to enable this bonus item.

PATRICK LASER COLOR IN ROCKET RODEO

Select Cheat Codes from the Extras menu and enter ROCKET. Select Activate Bonus Items to enable this bonus item.

PATRICK ROCKET SKIN COLOR IN ROCKET RODEO

Select Cheat Codes from the Extras menu and enter SPACE. Select Activate Bonus Items to enable this bonus item.

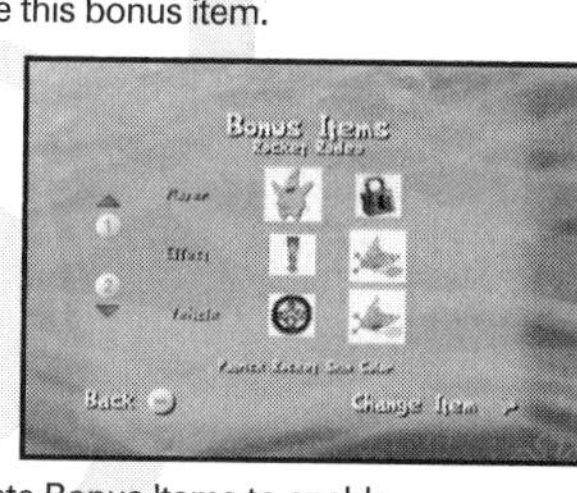

PLANKTON ASTRONAUT SUIT IN REVENGE OF THE GIANT PLANKTON MONSTER

Select Cheat Codes from the Extras menu and enter ROBOT. Select Activate Bonus Items to enable this bonus item.

PLANKTON EYE LASER COLOR IN REVENGE OF THE GIANT PLANKTON MONSTER

Select Cheat Codes from the Extras menu and enter LASER. Select Activate Bonus Items to enable this bonus item.

PIRATE PATRICK IN ROOFTOP RUMBLE

Select Cheat Codes from the Extras menu and enter PIRATE. Select Activate Bonus Items to enable this bonus item.

HOVERCRAFT VEHICLE SKIN IN HYPNOTIC HIGHWAY - PLANKTON

Select Cheat Codes from the Extras menu and enter HOVER. Select Activate Bonus Items to enable this bonus item.

SPONGEBOB SQUAREPANTS FEATURING NICKTOONS: GLOBS OF DOOM

When entering the following codes, the order of the characters going down is: SpongeBob SquarePants, Nicolai Technus, Danny Phantom, Dib, Zim, Tlaloc, Tak, Beautiful Gorgeous, Jimmy Neutron, Plankton. These names are shortened to the first name in the following.

ATTRACT COINS

Using the Upgrade Machine on the bottom level of the lair, select "Input cheat codes here". Enter Tlaloc, Plankton, Danny, Plankton, Tak. Coins are attracted to you making them much easier to collect.

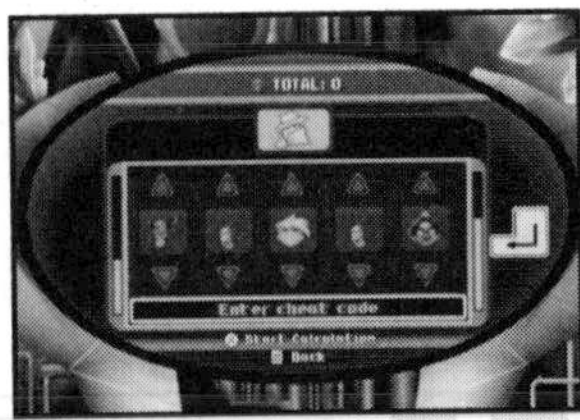

DON'T LOSE COINS

Using the Upgrade Machine on the bottom level of the lair, select "Input cheat codes here." Enter Plankton, Jimmy, Beautiful, Jimmy, Plankton. You don't lose coins when you get knocked out.

GOO HAS NO EFFECT

Using the Upgrade Machine on the bottom level of the lair, select "Input cheat codes here". Enter Danny, Danny, Danny, Nicolai, Nicolai. Goo does not slow you down.

MORE GADGET COMBO TIME

Using the Upgrade Machine on the bottom level of the lair, select "Input cheat codes here". Enter SpongeBob, Beautiful, Danny, Plankton, Nicolai. You have more time to perform gadget combos.

SSX BLUR

ALL CHARACTERS

Select Cheats from the Options menu and enter NoHolds.

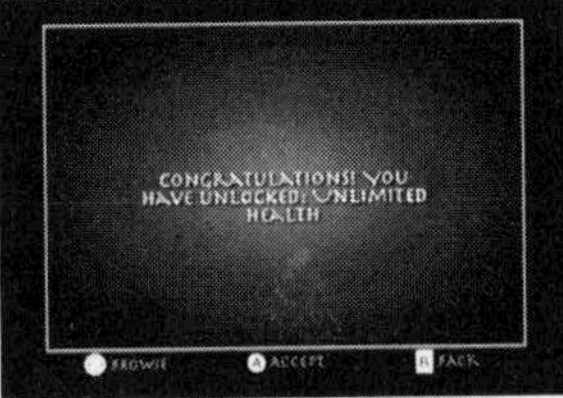

ENTIRE MOUNTAIN UNLOCKED

Select Cheats from the Options menu and enter MasterKey.

ALL OUTFITS

Select Cheats from the Options menu and enter ClothShop.

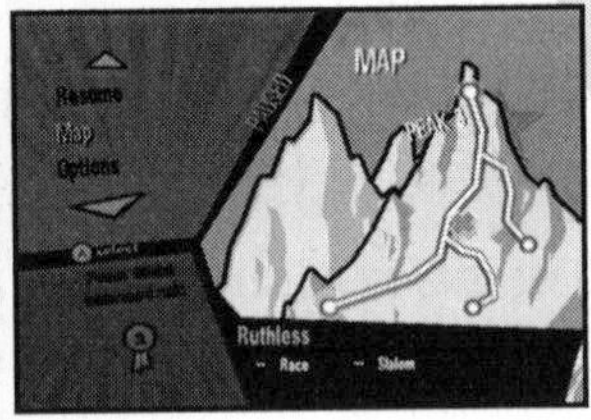

YETI OUTFIT

Select Cheats from the Options menu and enter WildFur.

STAR WARS: THE FORCE UNLEASHED

CHEATS

Once you have accessed the Rogue Shadow, select Enter Code from the Extras menu. Now you can enter the following codes:

CHEAT	CODE
Invincibility	CORTOSIS
Unlimited Force	VERGENCE
1,000,000 Force Points	SPEEDER
All Force Powers	TYRANUS
Max Force Power Level	KATARN
Max Combo Level	COUNTDOOKU
Stronger Lightsaber	LIGHTSABER

COSTUMES

Once you have accessed the Rogue Shadow, select Enter Code from the Extras menu. Now you can enter the following codes:

COSTUME	CODE
All Costumes	GRANDMOFF
501st Legion	LEGION
Aayla Secura	AAYLA
Admiral Ackbar	ITSATWAP
Anakin Skywalker	CHOSENONE
Asajj Ventress	ACOLYTE
Ceremonial Jedi Robes	DANTOOINE
Chop'aa Notimo	NOTIMO
Classic stormtrooper	TK421
Count Dooku	SERENNO
Darth Desolous	PAUAN
Darth Maul	ZABRAK
Darth Phobos	HIDDENFEAR
Darth Vader	SITHLORD
Drexl Roosh	DREXLROOSH
Emperor Palpatine	PALPATINE
General Rahm Kota	MANDALORE
Han Solo	NERFHERDER
Heavy trooper	SHOCKTROOP
Juno Eclipse	ECLIPSE
Kento's Robe	WOOKIEE
Kleef	KLEEF
Lando Calrissian	SCOUNDREL
Luke Skywalker	T16WOMPRAT
Luke Skywalker (Yavin)	YELLOWJCKT
Mace Windu	JEDIMASTER
Mara Jade	MARAJADE
Maris Brook	MARISBROOD
Navy commando	STORMTROOP
Obi Wan Kenobi	BENKENOBI
Proxy	HOLOGRAM
Qui Gon Jinn	MAVERICK
Shaak Ti	TOGRUTA
Shadow trooper	INTHEDARK
Sith Robes	HOLOCRON
Sith Stalker Armor	KORRIBAN
Twi'lek	SECURA

STRONG BAD'S COOL GAME FOR ATTRACTIVE PEOPLE EPISODE 1: HOMESTAR RUINER

COBRA MODE IN SNAKE BOXER 5

At the Snake Boxer 5 title screen, press Up, Up, Down, Up, Plus.

SUPER MARIO GALAXY

PLAY AS LUIGI
Collect all 120 stars and fight Bowser. After the credits you will get a message that Luigi is playable.

GRAND FINALE GALAXY
Collect all 120 stars with Luigi and beat Bowser.

STAR 121
Collect 100 purple coins.

SURF'S UP

ALL CHAMPIONSHIP LOCATIONS
Select Cheat Codes from the Extras menu and enter FREEVISIT.

ALL LEAF SLIDE STAGES
Select Cheat Codes from the Extras menu and enter GOINGDOWN.

ALL MULTIPLAYER LEVELS
Select Cheat Codes from the Extras menu and enter MULTIPASS.

ALL BOARDS
Select Cheat Codes from the Extras menu and enter MYPRECIOUS.

ASTRAL BOARD
Select Cheat Codes from the Extras menu and enter ASTRAL.

MONSOON BOARD
Select Cheat Codes from the Extras menu and enter MONSOON.

TINE SHOCKWAVE BOARD
Select Cheat Codes from the Extras menu and enter TINYSHOCKWAVE.

ALL CHARACTER CUSTOMIZATIONS
Select Cheat Codes from the Extras menu and enter TOPFASHION.

PLAY AS ARNOLD
Select Cheat Codes from the Extras menu and enter TINYBUTSTRONG.

PLAY AS ELLIOT
Select Cheat Codes from the Extras menu and enter SURPRISEGUEST.

PLAY AS GEEK
Select Cheat Codes from the Extras menu and enter SLOWANDSTEADY.

PLAY AS TANK EVANS
Select Cheat Codes from the Extras menu and enter IMTHEBEST.

PLAY AS TATSUHI KOBAYASHI
Select Cheat Codes from the Extras menu and enter KOBAYASHI.

PLAY AS ZEKE TOPANGA
Select Cheat Codes from the Extras menu and enter THELEGEND.

ALL VIDEOS AND SPEN GALLERY
Select Cheat Codes from the Extras menu and enter WATCHAMOVIE.

ART GALLERY
Select Cheat Codes from the Extras menu and enter NICEPLACE.

TENCHU: SHADOW ASSASSINS

ALL NORMAL ITEMS
At the Title screen, hold C + Z and quickly press Up, Left, Down, Right, Up, Left, Down, Right, Right, 1, 2.

ALL SECRET ITEMS
At the Title screen, hold C + Z and quickly press Up, Right, Down, Left, Up, Right, Down, Left, Left, 1, 2.

MAX ITEMS
At the Title screen, hold C + Z and quickly press Down, Up, Down, Up, Right, Left, Right, Left, Left, 1.

ALL MISSIONS/ASSIGNMENTS
At the Title screen, hold C + Z and quickly press Left, Left, Left, Left, Right, Right, Right, Right, 1, 2.

FULL SWORD GAUGE
At the Title screen, hold C + Z and quickly press Up, Down, Up, Down, Left, Right, Left, Right, Right, 1, 2.

THRILLVILLE: OFF THE RAILS

$50,000
During a game, press C, Z, B, C, Z, B, A.

500 THRILL POINTS
During a game, press Z, C, B, Z, C, B, C.

ALL MISSIONS
During a game, press C, Z, B, C, Z, B, Z.

ALL PARKS
During a game, press C, Z, B, C, Z, B, C.

ALL RIDES
During a game, press C, Z, B, C, Z, B, B.

ALL MINIGAMES
During a game, press C, Z, B, C, Z, B, Right.

TIGER WOODS PGA TOUR 07

ALL CHARACTERS
Select Password from the Options menu and enter gameface.

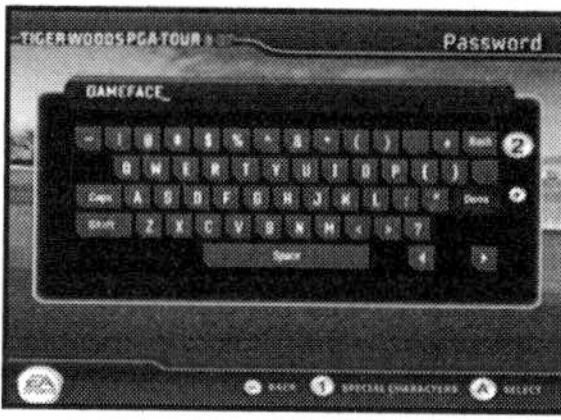

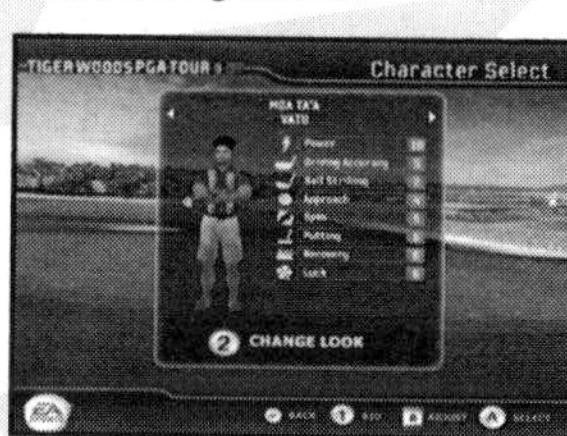

UNLOCK ADIDAS ITEMS
Select Password from the Options menu and enter three stripes.

UNLOCK BRIDGESTONE ITEMS
Select Password from the Options menu and enter shojiro.

UNLOCK COBRA ITEMS
Select Password from the Options menu and enter snakeking.

UNLOCK EA SPORTS ITEMS
Select Password from the Options menu and enter inthegame.

UNLOCK GRAFALLOY ITEMS
Select Password from the Options menu and enter just shafts.

UNLOCK MACGREGOR ITEMS
Select Password from the Options menu and enter mactec.

UNLOCK MIZUNO ITEMS
Select Password from the Options menu and enter rihachinrzo.

UNLOCK NIKE ITEMS
Select Password from the Options menu and enter justdoit.

UNLOCK OAKLEY ITEMS
Select Password from the Options menu and enter jannard.

UNLOCK PGA TOUR ITEMS
Select Password from the Options menu and enter lightning.

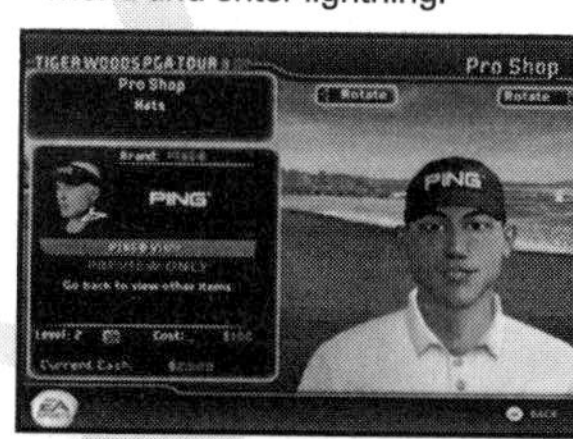

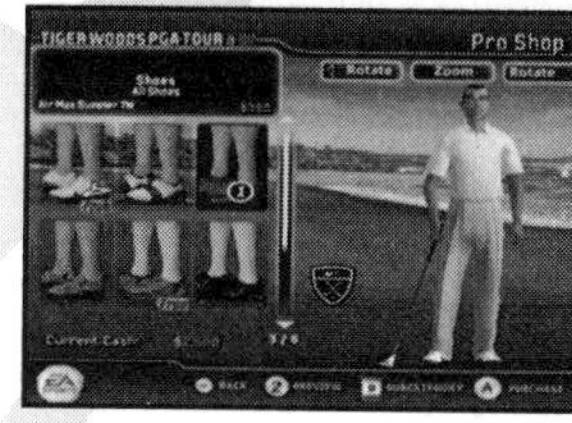

UNLOCK PING ITEMS
Select Password from the Options menu and enter solheim.

UNLOCK PRECEPT ITEMS
Select Password from the Options menu and enter guys are good.

UNLOCK TAYLORMADE ITEMS
Select Password from the Options menu and enter mradams.

TIGER WOODS PGA TOUR 08

ALL CLUBS
Select Passwords from the Options and enter PROSHOP.

ALL GOLFERS
Select Passwords from the Options and enter GAMEFACE.

BRIDGESTONE ITEMS
Select Passwords from the Options and enter NOTJUSTTIRES.

BUICK ITEMS
Select Passwords from the Options and enter THREESTRIPES.

CLEVELAND GOLF ITEMS
Select Passwords from the Options and enter CLEVELAND.

COBRA ITEMS
Select Passwords from the Options and enter SNAKEKING.

EA ITEMS
Select Passwords from the Options and enter INTHEGAME.

GRAFALLOY ITEMS
Select Passwords from the Options and enter JUSTSHAFTS.

MIZUNO ITEMS
Select Passwords from the Options and enter RIHACHINRIZO.

NIKE ITEMS
Select Passwords from the Options and enter JUSTDOIT.

PRECEPT ITEMS
Select Passwords from the Options and enter GUYSAREGOOD.

TIGER WOODS PGA TOUR 09 ALL-PLAY

SPECTATORS BIG HEAD MODE
Select EA SPORTS Extras from My Tiger '09, choose Password and enter cephalus.

TMNT

CHALLENGE MAP 2
At the Main menu, hold Z and press A, A, A, 1, A.

DON'S BIG HEAD GOODIE
At the Main menu, hold Z and press 1, A, C, 2.

TONY HAWK'S DOWNHILL JAM

BOARDS

BOARD	COMPLETE EVENT
Street Issue	Street Issue Slalom (Tier 1)
Solar	Tourist Trap (Tier 1)
Chaos	Vista Point Race (Random)
Kuni	Hong Kong Race (Tier 2)
Red Rascal	San Francisco Elimination (Tier 3)
Cruiser	Grind Time (Tier 4)
Illuminate	Machu Pichu Top to Bottom Tricks (Tier 4)
Dark Sign	He-Man Club/Girl Power (Tier 5)
Spooky	Clearance Sale (Tier 6)
Black Icer	Precision Shopping Slalom (Tier 7)
Ripper	Del Centro Slalom (Tier 7)
Dispersion	Machu Picchu Top to Bottom Race (Tier 7)
Makonga	Mall Rats (Tier 8)
Goddess of Speed	The Hills Are Alive Tricks (Tier 9)
Dragon	Swiss Elimination (Tier 9)

OUTFITS

CHARACTER	OUTFIT	COMPLETE EVENT
Gunnar	High-G Armor	Gunnar's Threads (Tier 1)
Kyla	Shooting Star	Cuzco Challenge Race (Tier 2)
Tony	Business Camouflage	Mountain High Race (Random)
Budd	The Bohemian	Catacombs Slalom (Tier 2)
Tiffany	Baby Blue	Tourist Spot Slalom (Tier 2)
Ammon	Money Suit	Edinburgh Full Tricks (Tier 3)
Jynx	Black Tuesday	Road to Cuzco Race (Tier 3)
Jynx	Graveyard Casual	Cable Car Tricks (Random)
Crash	Bombs Away	Fallen Empire Race (Tier 4)
MacKenzie	Spitfire Squadron	Edinburgh Full Race (Tier 4)
Gunnar	Street Creds	Favela Rush (Tier 4)
Crash	Brace for Impact	Out of the Woods Race (Tier 5)
Kyla	Touchdown	Clear the Streets (Tier 5)
Tony	Mariachi Loco	Out of the Woods Tricks (Random)
MacKenzie	Killer Bee	High Street Slalom (Tier 6)
Ammon	Tommy T	Seaside Village Race (Tier 6)
Budd	Power of Chi	Rome Elimination (Tier 6)
Crash	Space Monkey	Lift Off (Tier 7)
Jynx	Funeral Fun	Del Centro Race (Tier 7)
Budd	Toys for Bob	Waterfront Race (Random)
MacKenzie	Street Combat	Parking Lot Shuffle (Tier 7)
Gunnar	Black Knight	Park It Anywhere (Tier 7)
Tiffany	Nero Style	Rome Burning (Tier 7)
Tiffany	Military Chic	Shopping Spree (Tier 8)
Ammon	Tan Suit	Saturday Matinee (Tier 9)
Tony	Downhill Jam	Hills Are Alive Race (Tier 9)
Kyla	Alpine Red	San Francisco Full Slalom (Tier 9)

SKATERS

SKATER	COMPLETE EVENT
Kevin Staab	Kevin's Challenge (Random)
MacKenzie	MacKenzie's Challenge (Tier 2)
Crash	Crash Test (Tier 3)
Armando Gnutbagh	Unknown Skater (Tier 10)

CHEAT CODES

Select Cheat Codes from the Options menu and enter the following cheats. Select Toggle Cheats to enable/disable them.

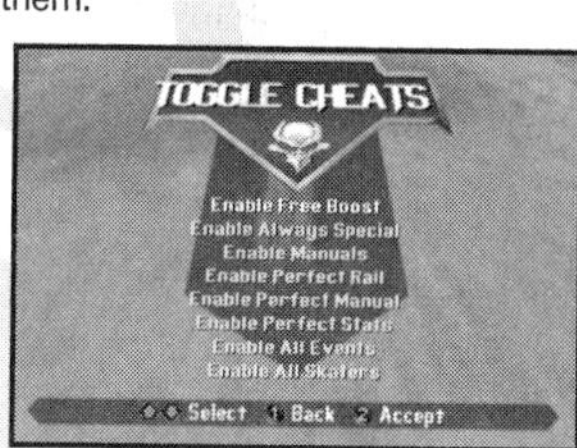

FREE BOOST
Enter OOTBAGHFOREVER.

ALWAYS SPECIAL
Enter POINTHOGGER.

UNLOCK MANUALS
Enter IMISSMANUALS.

PERFECT RAIL
Enter LIKETILTINGAPLATE.

PERFECT MANUAL
Enter TIGHTROPEWALKER.

PERFECT STATS
Enter IAMBOB.

EXTREME CAR CRASHES
Enter WATCHFORDOORS.

FIRST-PERSON SKATER
Enter FIRSTPERSONJAM.

SHADOW SKATER
Enter CHIMNEYSWEEP.

DEMON SKATER
Enter EVILCHIMNEYSWEEP.

MINI SKATER
Enter DOWNTHERABBITHOLE.

GIGANTO-SKATER
Enter IWANNABETALLTALL.

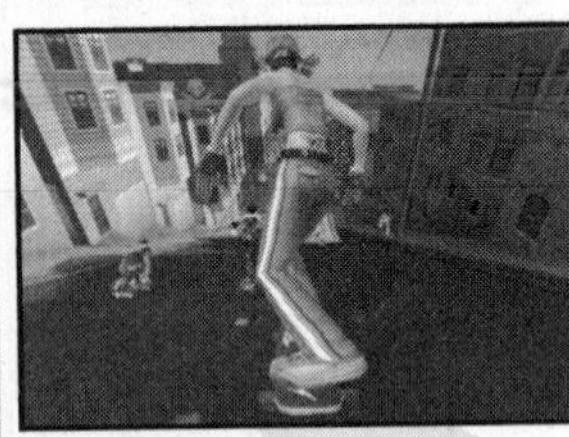

INVISIBLE BOARD
Enter LOOKMANOBOARD.

INVISIBLE SKATER
Enter NOWYOUSEEME.

PICASSO SKATER
Enter FOURLIGHTS.

CHIPMUNK VOICES
Enter HELLOHELIUM.
Enter DISPLAYCOORDINATES.

LARGE BIRDS
Enter BIRDBIRDBIRDBIRD.

REALLY LARGE BIRDS
Enter BIRDBIRDBIRDBIRDBIRD.

TINY PEOPLE
Enter SHRINKTHEPEOPLE.

*There is no need to toggle on the following cheats. They take effect after entering them.

ALL EVENTS
Enter ADVENTURESOFKWANG.

ALL SKATERS
Enter IMINTERFACING.

ALL BOARDS/OUTFITS
Enter RAIDTHEWOODSHED.

ALL MOVIES
Enter FREEBOZZLER.

TONY HAWK'S PROVING GROUND

Select Cheat Codes from the Options and enter the following cheats. Some codes need to be enabled by selecting Cheats from the Options during a game.

UNLOCK	CHEAT
Bosco	MOREMILK
Cam	NOTACAMERA
Cooper	THECOOP
Eddie X	SKETCHY
El Patinador	PILEDRIVER
Eric	FLYAWAY
Judy Nails	LOVEROCKNROLL
Mad Dog	RABBIES
MCA	INTERGALACTIC
Mel	NOTADUDE
Rube	LOOKSSMELLY
Spence	DAPPER
Shayne	MOVERS
TV Producer	SHAKER
FDR	THEPREZPARK
Lansdowne	THELOCALPARK
Air & Space Museum	THEINDOORPARK
All Fun Items	OVERTHETOP
All Game Movies	WATCHTHIS
All Rigger Pieces	IMGONNABUILD
All specials unlocked and in player's special list	LOTSOFTRICKS
Full Stats	BEEFEDUP
Give player +50 skill points	NEEDSHELP

The following cheats lock you out of the Leaderboards:

UNLOCK	CHEAT
Perfect Manual	STILLAINTFALLIN
Perfect Rail	AINTFALLIN
Unlimited Focus	MYOPIC

You can not use the Video Editor with the following cheats:

UNLOCK	CHEAT
Invisible Man	THEMISSING
Mini Skater	TINYTATER

TRANSFORMERS: THE GAME

INFINITE HEALTH

At the Main menu, press Left, Left, Up, Left, Right, Down, Right.

INFINITE AMMO

At the Main menu, press Up, Down, Left, Right, Up, Up, Down.

NO MILITARY OR POLICE

At the Main menu, press Right, Left, Right, Left, Right, Left, Right.

ALL MISSIONS

At the Main menu, press Down, Up, Left, Right, Right, Right, Up, Down.

BONUS CYBERTRON MISSIONS

At the Main menu, press Right, Up, Up, Down, Right, Left, Left.

GENERATION 1 SKIN: JAZZ

At the Main menu, press Left, Up, Down, Down, Left, Up, Right.

GENERATION 1 SKIN: MEGATRON

At the Main menu, press Down, Left, Left, Down, Right, Right, Up.

GENERATION 1 SKIN: OPTIMUS PRIME

At the Main menu, press Down, Right, Left, Up, Down, Down, Left.

GENERATION 1 SKIN: ROBOVISION OPTIMUS PRIME

At the Main menu, press Down, Down, Up, Up, Right, Right, Right.

GENERATION 1 SKIN: STARSCREAM

At the Main menu, press Right, Down, Left, Left, Down, Up, Up.

GENERATION 1 SKIN: MEGATRON

At the Main menu, press Down, Left, Left, Down, Right, Right, Up.

GENERATION 1 SKIN: OPTIMUS PRIME

At the Main menu, press Down, Right, Left, Up, Down, Down, Left.

GENERATION 1 SKIN: ROBOVISION OPTIMUS PRIME

At the Main menu, press Down, Down, Up, Up, Right, Right, Right.

GENERATION 1 SKIN: STARSCREAM

At the Main menu, press Right, Down, Left, Left, Down, Up, Up.

ULTIMATE SHOOTING COLLECTION

ROTATE DISPLAY ON SIDE IN TATE MODE

At the Main menu, press Left, Right, Left, Right, Up, Up, 1, 2.

WALL-E

The following cheats will disable saving. The five possible characters starting with Wall-E and going down are: Wall-E, Auto, EVE, M-O, GEL-A Steward.

ALL BONUS FEATURES UNLOCKED

Select Cheats from the Bonus Features menu and enter Wall-E, Auto, EVE, GEL-A Steward.

ALL GAME CONTENT UNLOCKED

Select Cheats from the Bonus Features menu and enter M-O, Auto, GEL-A Steward, EVE.

ALL SINGLE PLAYER LEVELS UNLOCKED

Select Cheats from the Bonus Features menu and enter Auto, GEL-A Steward, M-O, Wall-E.

ALL MULTIPLAYER MAPS UNLOCKED

Select Cheats from the Bonus Features menu and enter EVE, M-O, Wall-E, Auto.

ALL HOLIDAY COSTUMES UNLOCKED

Select Cheats from the Bonus Features menu and enter Auto, Auto, GEL-A Steward, GEL-A Steward.

ALL MULTIPLAYER COSTUMES UNLOCKED

Select Cheats from the Bonus Features menu and enter GEL-A Steward, Wall-E, M-O, Auto.

UNLIMITED HEALTH UNLOCKED

Select Cheats from the Bonus Features menu and enter Wall-E, M-O, Auto, M-O.

WALL-E: MAKE ANY CUBE AT ANY TIME

Select Cheats from the Bonus Features menu and enter Auto, M-O, Auto, M-O.

WALL-EVE: MAKE ANY CUBE AT ANY TIME

Select Cheats from the Bonus Features menu and enter M-O, GEL-A Steward, EVE, EVE.

WALL-E WITH A LASER GUN AT ANY TIME

Select Cheats from the Bonus Features menu and enter Wall-E, EVE, EVE, Wall-E.

WALL-EVE WITH A LASER GUN AT ANY TIME

Select Cheats from the Bonus Features menu and enter GEL-A Steward, EVE, M-O, Wall-E.

WALL-E: PERMANENT SUPER LASER UPGRADE

Select Cheats from the Bonus Features menu and enter Wall-E, Auto, EVE, M-O.

EVE: PERMANENT SUPER LASER UPGRADE

Select Cheats from the Bonus Features menu and enter EVE, Wall-E, Wall-E, Auto.

CREDITS

Select Cheats from the Bonus Features menu and enter Auto, Wall-E, GEL-A Steward, M-O.

WII SPORTS

BOWLING BALL COLOR

After selecting your Mii, hold the following direction on the D-pad and press A at the warning screen:

DIRECTION	COLOR
Up	Blue
Right	Gold
Down	Green
Left	Red

NO HUD IN GOLF

Hold 2 as you select a course to disable the power meter, map, and wind speed meter.

BLUE TENNIS COURT

After selecting your Mii, hold 2 and press A at the warning screen.

WWE SMACKDOWN! VS. RAW 2008

HBK AND HHH'S DX OUTFIT

Select Cheat Codes from the Options and enter DXCostume69K2.

KELLY KELLY'S ALTERNATE OUTFIT

Select Cheat Codes from the Options and enter KellyKG12R.

NINTENDO Wii

NINTENDO Wii: VIRTUAL CONSOLE

For the Virtual Console games, a Classic Controller may be needed to enter some codes.

ADVENTURES OF LOLO

PASSWORDS

LEVEL	PASSWORD
1-2	BCBT
1-3	BDBR
1-4	BGBQ
1-5	BHBP
2-1	BJBM
2-2	BKBL
2-3	BLBK
2-4	BMBJ
2-5	BPBH
3-1	BQBG
3-2	BRBD
3-3	BTBC
3-4	BVBB
3-5	BYZZ
4-1	BZZY
4-2	CBZV
4-3	CCZT
4-4	CDZR
4-5	CGZQ
5-1	CHZP
5-2	CJZM
5-3	CKZL
5-4	CLZK
5-5	CMZJ
6-1	CPZH
6-2	CQZG
6-3	CRZD
6-4	CTZC
6-5	CVZB
7-1	CYYZ
7-2	CZYY
7-3	DBYV
7-4	DCYT
7-5	DDYR
8-1	DGYQ
8-2	DHYP
8-3	DJYM
8-4	DKYL
8-5	DLYK
9-1	DMYJ
9-2	DPYH
9-3	DQYG
9-4	DRYD
9-5	DTYC
10-1	DVYB
10-2	DYVZ
10-3	DZVY
10-4	GBVV
10-5	GCVT

ADVENTURES OF LOLO 2

MORE DIFFICULTIES

Enter PROA, PROB, PROC, or PROD as a password.

PASSWORDS

LEVEL	PASSWORD
1-1	PPHP
1-2	PHPK
1-3	PQPD
1-4	PVPT
1-5	PRPJ
2-5	PCPZ
2-5	PLPY
2-5	PBPM
2-5	PGPG
2-5	PZPC
3-1	PYPL
3-2	PMPB
3-3	PJPR
3-4	PTPV
3-5	PDPQ
4-1	PKPH
4-2	HPPP
4-3	HHKK
4-4	HQKD
4-5	HVKT
5-1	HRKJ
5-2	HBKM
5-3	HLKY
5-4	HCKZ
5-5	HGKG
6-1	HZKC
6-2	HYKL
6-3	HMKB
6-4	HJKR
6-5	HTKV
7-1	HDKQ
7-2	HKKH

LEVEL	PASSWORD
7-3	QPKP
7-4	QHDK
7-5	QQDD
8-1	QVDT
8-2	QRDJ
8-3	QBDM
8-4	QLDY
8-5	QCDZ
9-1	QGDG
9-2	QZDC
9-3	QYDL
9-4	QMDB
9-5	QJDR
10-1	QTDV
10-2	QDDQ
10-3	QKDH
10-4	VPDP
10-5	VHTK

ALTERED BEAST

LEVEL SELECT

At the Title screen, press B + Start.

BEAST SELECT

At the Title screen, hold A + B + C + Down/Left and press Start.

SOUND TEST

At the Title screen, hold A + C + Up/Right and press Start.

BOMBERMAN '93

PASSWORDS

LEVEL	PASSWORD
A-1	CBCCBBDB
A-2	DDCDBBGB
A-3	FFDDBBJB
A-4	GHFDBCLB
A-5	GJFDBCMB
A-6	HKFDBCNB
A-7	HLFDBCPB
A-8	JNFDBCQB
B-1	GCDDCCKB
B-2	HFFFCCMB
B-3	JGFFCCNB
B-4	JHFFCCPB
B-5	KKGFCCRB
B-6	LLGFCCSB
B-7	LMGFCCTB
B-8	CKFFCHBC
C-1	LFGFFCQB
C-2	LGGFFCRB
C-3	MHGFFCSB
C-4	DFGFFHBC
C-5	DGGFFHCC
C-6	FHGFFJFC
C-7	GKGFFJGC
C-8	GLGFFJHC
D-1	GBGFKJFC
D-2	HDGFKJGC
D-3	HFGFKJHC
D-4	JGGFKJJC
D-5	JHGFKJKC
D-6	KKHFKJLC
D-7	KLHFKJMC
D-8	LMHFKJNC
E-1	NFHFTJQC
E-2	PGJFTJSC
E-3	PHJFTJTC
E-4	GFHFTDBD
E-5	GGHFTDCD
E-6	HHHFTDDD
E-7	JKHGTDGD
E-8	KLJGTDJD
F-1	KCJGTJGD
F-2	LDKGTJJD
F-3	LFKGTJKD
F-4	MHLGTJLD
F-5	MJLGTHLD
F-6	MKLGTJND
F-7	NLLGTJPD
F-8	QNMHTJSD
G-1	JBLHTXBF
G-2	KCMHTXDF
G-3	KDMHTXFF
G-4	LGNHTXHF
G-5	MHNHTXJF
G-6	MJNHTXKF
G-7	NLPHTXLF
G-8	NMPHTXMF

CHEW MAN FU

GAME COMPLETE PASSWORDS

Select Password and enter 573300 or 441300.

COMIX ZONE

STAGE SELECT

At the Jukebox menu, press C on the following numbers:
14, 15, 18, 5, 13, 1, 3, 18, 15, 6
A voice says "Oh Yeah" when entered correctly. Then, press C on 1 through 6 to warp to that stage.

INVINCIBLE

At the Jukebox menu, press C on the following numbers:
3, 12, 17, 2, 2, 10, 2, 7, 7, 11
A voice says "Oh Yeah" when entered correctly.

CREDITS

At the Options menu press A + B + C.

DONKEY KONG COUNTRY 2: DIDDY'S KONG QUEST

SOUND TEST

Highlight Two Player and press Down (x5).

CHEAT MODE

Press Down (x5) again after getting Sound Test to access the cheat mode. Now you can enter the following:

50 LIVES

Press Y, A, Select, A, Down, Left, A, Down.

HARD MODE

Press B, A, Right, Right, A, Left, A, X. This gets rid of the barrels.

DR. ROBOTNIK'S MEAN BEAN MACHINE

EASY PASSWORDS

STAGE	PASSWORD
02: Frankly	Red Bean, Red Bean, Red Bean, Has Bean
03: Humpty	Clear Bean, Purple Bean, Clear Bean, Green Bean
04: Coconuts	Red Bean, Clear Bean, Has Bean, Yellow Bean
05: Davy Sprocket	Clear Bean, Blue Bean, Blue Bean, Purple Bean
06: Skweel	Clear Bean, Red Bean, Clear Bean, Purple Bean
07: Dynamight	Purple Bean, Yellow Bean, Red Bean, Blue Bean
08: Grounder	Yellow Bean, Purple Bean, Has Bean, Blue Bean
09: Spike	Yellow Bean, Purple Bean, Has Bean, Blue Bean
10: Sir Ffuzy-Logik	Red Bean, Yellow Bean, Clear Bean, Has Bean
11: Dragon Breath	Green Bean, Purple Bean, Blue Bean, Clear Bean
12: Scratch	Red Bean, Has Bean, Has Bean, Yellow Bean
13: Dr. Robotnik	Yellow Bean, Has Bean, Blue Bean, Blue Bean

NORMAL PASSWORDS

STAGE	PASSWORD
02: Frankly	Has Bean, Clear Bean, Yellow Bean, Yellow Bean
03: Humpty	Blue Bean, Clear Bean, Red Bean, Yellow Bean
04: Coconuts	Yellow Bean, Blue Bean, Clear Bean, Purple Bean
05: Davy Sprocket	Has Bean, Green Bean, Blue Bean, Yellow Bean
06: Skweel	Green Bean, Purple Bean, Purple Bean, Yellow Bean
07: Dynamight	Purple Bean, Blue Bean, Green Bean, Has Bean
08: Grounder	Green Bean, Has Bean, Clear Bean, Yellow Bean
09: Spike	Blue Bean, Purple Bean, Has Bean, Has Bean
10: Sir Ffuzy-Logik	Has Bean, Red Bean, Yellow Bean, Clear Bean
11: Dragon Breath	Clear Bean, Red Bean, Red Bean, Blue Bean
12: Scratch	Green Bean, Green Bean, Clear Bean, Yellow Bean
13: Dr. Robotnik	Purple Bean, Yellow Bean, Has Bean, Clear Bean

HARD PASSWORDS

STAGE	PASSWORD
02: Frankly	Clear Bean, Green Bean, Yellow Bean, Yellow Bean
03: Humpty	Yellow Bean, Purple Bean, Clear Bean, Purple Bean
04: Coconuts	Blue Bean, Green Bean, Clear Bean, Blue Bean
05: Davy Sprocket	Red Bean, Purple Bean, Green Bean, Green Bean
06: Skweel	Yellow Bean, Yellow Bean, Clear Bean, Green Bean
07: Dynamight	Purple Bean, Clear Bean, Blue Bean, Blue Bean
08: Grounder	Clear Bean, Yellow Bean, Has Bean, Yellow Bean
09: Spike	Purple Bean, Blue Bean, Blue Bean, Green Bean
10: Sir Ffuzy-Logik	Clear Bean, Green Bean, Red Bean, Yellow Bean
11: Dragon Breath	Blue Bean, Yellow Bean, Yellow Bean, Has Bean
12: Scratch	Green Bean, Clear Bean, Clear Bean, Blue Bean
13: Dr. Robotnik	Has Bean, Clear Bean, Purple Bean, Has Bean

HARDEST PASSWORDS

STAGE	PASSWORD
02: Frankly	Blue Bean, Blue Bean, Green Bean, Yellow Bean
03: Humpty	Green Bean, Yellow Bean, Green Bean, Clear Bean
04: Coconuts	Purple Bean, Purple Bean, RedBean, Has Bean
05: Davy Sprocket	Green Bean, Red Bean, Purple Bean, Blue Bean
06: Skweel	Purple Bean, Clear Bean, Green Bean, Yellow Bean
07: Dynamight	Blue Bean, Purple Bean, Green Bean, Has Bean
08: Grounder	Clear Bean, Purple Bean, Yellow Bean, Has Bean
09: Spike	Purple Bean, Green Bean, Has Bean, Clear Bean
10: Sir Ffuzy-Logik	Green Bean, Blue Bean, Yellow Bean, Has Bean
11: Dragon Breath	Green Bean, Purple Bean, Has Bean, Red Bean
12: Scratch	Red Bean, Green Bean, Has Bean, Blue Bean
13: Dr. Robotnik	Red Bean, Red Bean, Clear Bean, Yellow Bean

DUNGEON EXPLORER

PLAY AS PRINCESS AKI

Enter JBBNJ HDCOG as a password.

PLAY AS THE HERMIT

Enter IMGAJ MDPAI as a password.

HOMING WEAPON

Enter HOMIN GAAAA as a password.

CHANGE NAMES

Enter CHECK NAMEA as a password.

INVINCIBILITY

Enter DEBDE DEBDA as a password, then press Plus + 2.

JUMP TO ANY LOCATION

After enabling the Invincibility code, enter one of the 15 bushes in front of Axis castle to jump to the following locations:

LOCATION	BUSH (STARTING FROM LEFT)
Natas	1
Balamous Tower	2
Rotterroad	3
Mistose Dungeon	4
Ratonix Dungeon	5
Reraport Maze	6
Rally Maze	7
Bullbeast	8
Melba Village	9
After Gutworm	10
Nostalgia Dungeon	11
Water Castle	12
Road to Cherry Tower	13
Stonefield	14
Karma Castle	15

ECCO THE DOLPHIN

DEBUG MENU

Pause the game with Ecco facing the screen and press Right, B, C, B, C, Down, C, Up.

INFINITE AIR

Enter LIFEFISH as a password.

PASSWORDS

LEVEL	PASSWORD
The Undercaves	WEFIDNMP
The Vents	BQDPXJDS
The Lagoon	JNSBRIKY
Ridge Water	NTSBZTKB
Open Ocean	YWGTTJNI
Ice Zone	HZIFZBMF
Hard Water	LRFJRQLI
Cold Water	UYNFRQLC
Island Zone	LYTIOQLZ
Deep Water	MNOPOQLR
The Marble	RJNTQQLZ
The Library	RTGXQQLE

LEVEL	PASSWORD
Deep City	DDXPQQLJ
City of Forever	MSDBRQLA
Jurassic Beach	IYCBUNLB
Pteranodon Pond	DMXEUNLI
Origin Beach	EGRIUNLB
Trilobite Circle	IELMUNLB
Dark Water	RKEQUNLN
City of Forever 2	HPQIGPLA
The Tube	JUMFKMLB
The Machine	GXUBKMLF
The Last Fight	TSONLMLU

F-ZERO X

ALL TRACKS, VEHICLES, AND DIFFICULTIES

At the mode select, press Up on the D-pad, L, R, Up on the Right control stick, X, Y, ZR, Plus.

GOLDEN AXE

LEVEL SELECT

At the character select in Arcade mode, hold Down/Left and press B+Start.

START WITH 9 CONTINUES

At the character select in Arcade mode, hold Down/Left and then hold A+C. Release the buttons and select a character.

GRADIUS

MAX OUT WEAPONS

Pause the game and press Up, Up, Down, Down, Left, Right, Left, Right, B, A.

GRADIUS III

FULL POWER-UP

Pause the game and press Up, Up, Down, Down, L, R, L, R, B, A.

SUICIDE

Pause the game and press Up, Up, Down, Down, Left, Right, Left, Right, B, A.

ICE HOCKEY

NO GOALIES

At the title screen, hold A + B on controllers 1 and 2. Then, press start on controller 1.

MILITARY MADNESS

PASSWORDS

LEVEL	PASSWORD
01	REVOLT
02	ICARUS
03	CYRANO
04	RAMSEY
05	NEWTON
06	SENECA
07	SABINE
08	ARATUS
09	GALIOS
10	DARWIN
11	PASCAL
12	HALLEY
13	BORMAN
14	APOLLO
15	KAISER
16	NECTOR

LEVEL	PASSWORD
17	MILTON
18	IRAGAN
19	LIPTUS
20	INAKKA
21	TETROS
22	ARBINE
23	RECTOS
24	YEANTA
25	MONOGA
26	ATTAYA
27	DESHTA
28	NEKOSE
29	ERATIN
30	SOLCIS
31	SAGINE
32	WINNER

SOUND TEST

Enter ONGAKU as a password.

RISTAR

Select Passwords from the Options menu and enter the following:

LEVEL SELECT

ILOVEU

BOSS RUSH MODE

MUSEUM

TIME ATTACK MODE

DOFEEL

TOUGHER DIFFICULTY

SUPER

ONCHI MUSIC

MAGURO. Activate this from the Sound Test.

CLEARS PASSWORD

XXXXXX

GAME COPYRIGHT INFO

AGES

SOLOMON'S KEY

CONTINUE GAME

At the Game Deviation Value screen, hold Up + A + B.

SONIC THE HEDGEHOG

LEVEL SELECT

At the Title screen, press Up, Down, Left, Right. A sound of a ring being collected plays if the code is entered correctly. Hold A and press Start to access the Level Select.

CONTROL MODE

At the Title screen, press Up, C, Down, C, Left, C, Right, C. Then, hold A and press Start.

DEBUG MODE

After entering the Control Mode, hold A and press Start. Press A to change Sonic into another sprite. Press B to change back to Sonic. Press C to place that sprite. Pause the game and press A to restart. Hold B for slow motion and press C to advance a frame.

CHANGE DEMO

During the demo, hold C. Sonic will start making mistakes.

WARIO'S WOODS

HARD BATTLES

Highlight VS. Computer Mode, hold Left and press Start.

PLAYSTATION 3

PLAYSTATION® 3

GAMES

OVERLOAD

BAJA: EDGE OF CONTROL

CAREER COMPLETE 100%

Select Cheat Codes from the Options menu and enter SHOWTIME.

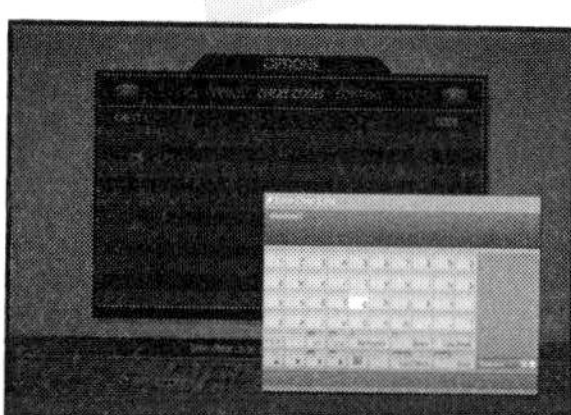

INSTALL ALL PARTS

Select Cheat Codes from the Options menu and enter SUPERMAX.

BATTLEFIELD: BAD COMPANY

M60

Select Unlocks from the Multiplayer menu, press Start and enter try4ndrunf0rcov3r.

QBU88

Select Unlocks from the Multiplayer menu, press Start and enter your3mynextt4rget.

UZI

Select Unlocks from the Multiplayer menu, press Start and enter cov3r1ngthecorn3r.

BEJEWELED 2

TOGGLE CLASSIC STYLE GEMS

During a game, hold L1 + L2 + R1 + R2 and press ⊗.

TOGGLE GAME BORDERS

During a game, hold L1 + L2 + R1 + R2 and press ◉.

THE BIGS

START A ROOKIE WITH HIGHER STATS

When you create a rookie, name him HOT DOG. His stats will be higher than when you normally start.

BIONIC COMMANDO REARMED

The following challenge rooms can be found in the Challenge Room list. Only one code can be active at a time.

AARON SEDILLO'S CHALLENGE ROOM (CONTEST WINNER)

At the Title screen, Right, Down, Left, Up, L1, R1, Triangle, Triangle, X, X, Start.

EUROGAMER CHALLENGE ROOM

At the Title screen, press Down, Up, Down, Up, Left, L1, Square, L1, Square, Triangle, Start.

GAMESRADAR CHALLENGE ROOM

At the Title screen, R1, Triangle, Square, Square, Up, Down, L1, L1, Up, Down, Start.

IGN CHALLENGE ROOM

At the Title screen, Up, Down, Triangle, Square, Square, Triangle, Down, Up, L1, L1, Start.

BLAZING ANGELS: SQUADRONS OF WWII

ALL MISSIONS AND PLANES UNLOCKED

At the Main menu, hold L2 + R2, and press Square, L1, R1, Triangle, Triangle, R1, L1, Square.

GOD MODE

Pause the game, hold L2, and press Square, Triangle, Triangle, Square. Release L2, hold R2 and press Triangle, Square, Square, Triangle. Re-enter the code to disable it.

INCREASED DAMAGE WITH ALL WEAPONS

Pause the game, hold L2, and press L1, L1, R1. Release L2, hold R2, and press R1, R1, L1. Re-enter the code to disable it.

BOLT

Many of the following cheats can be toggled on/off by pausing the game and selecting Cheats.

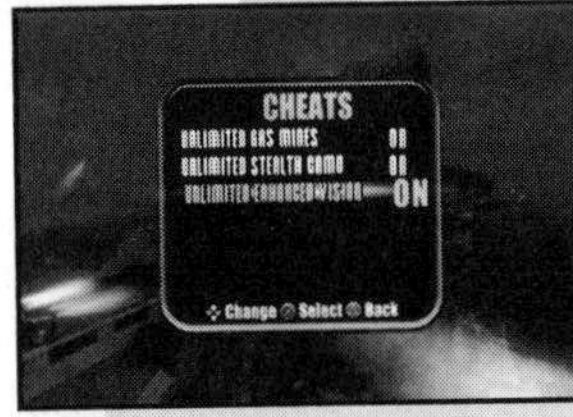

LEVEL SELECT

Select Cheats from the Extras menu and enter Right, Up, Left, Right, Up, Right.

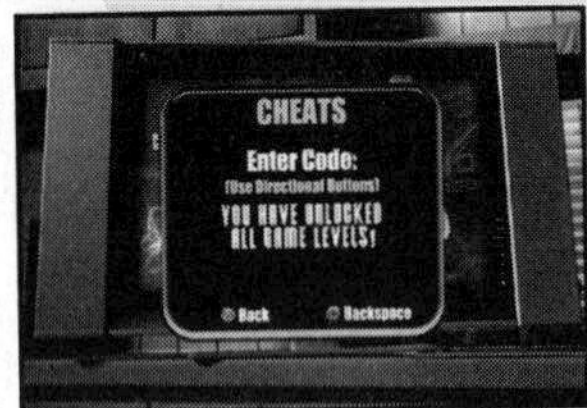

ALL MINIGAMES

Select Cheats from the Extras menu and enter Right, Up, Right, Right.

UNLIMITED ENHANCED VISION

Select Cheats from the Extras menu and enter Left, Right, Up, Down.

UNLIMITED GROUND POUND

Select Cheats from the Extras menu and enter Right, Up, Right, Up, Left, Down.

UNLIMITED INVULNERABILITY

Select Cheats from the Extras menu and enter Down, Down, Up, Left.

UNLIMITED GAS MINES

Select Cheats from the Extras menu and enter Right, Left, Left, Up, Down, Right.

UNLIMITED LASER EYES

Select Cheats from the Extras menu and enter Left, Left, Up, Right.

UNLIMITED STEALTH CAMO

Select Cheats from the Extras menu and enter Left, Down (x3).

UNLIMITED SUPERBARK

Select Cheats from the Extras menu and enter Right, Left, Left, Up, Down, Up.

BROTHERS IN ARMS: HELL'S HIGHWAY

ALL CHAPTERS

Select Enter Code from the Options and enter gimmechapters.

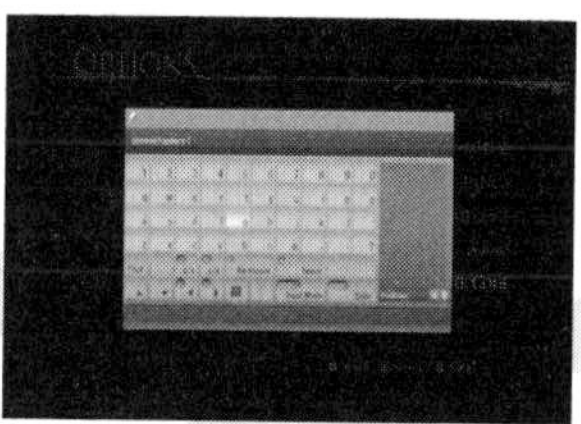

ALL RECON POINTS

Select Enter Code from the Options and enter 0zndrbicra.

KILROY DETECTOR

Select Enter Code from the Options and enter sh2vyivnzf.

TWO MULTIPLAYER SKINS

Select Enter Code from the Options and enter hi9wtpxsuk.

BURNOUT PARADISE

BEST BUY CAR

Pause the game and select Sponsor Product Code from the Under the Hood menu. Enter Bestbuy. Need A License to use this car offline.

CIRCUIT CITY CAR

Pause the game and select Sponsor Product Code from the Under the Hood menu. Enter Circuitcity. Need Burnout Paradise License to use this car offline.

GAMESTOP CAR

Pause the game and select Sponsor Product Code from the Under the Hood menu. Enter Gamestop. Need A License to use this car offline.

WALMART CAR

Pause the game and select Sponsor Product Code from the Under the Hood menu. Enter Walmart. Need Burnout Paradise License to use this car offline.

"STEEL WHEELS" GT

Pause the game and select Sponsor Product Code from the Under the Hood menu. Enter G23X 5K8Q GX2V 04B1 or E60J 8Z7T MS8L 51U6.

LICENSES

LICENSE	NUMBER OF WINS NEEDED
D	2
C	7
B	16
A	26
Burnout Paradise	45
Elite License	All events

CALL OF DUTY 3

ALL CHAPTERS & BONUS CONTENT

At the Chapter Select screen, hold Select and press Right, Right, Left, Left, ●, ●.

CALL OF DUTY 4: MODERN WARFARE

ARCADE MODE

After a complete playthrough of the game, Arcade Mode becomes available from the Main menu.

UNLOCKABLE CHEATS

After completing the game, cheats are unlocked based on how many intelligence pieces were gathered. These cheats cannot be used during Arcade Mode. These cheats may also disable the ability to earn Achievements.

CHEAT	INTEL ITEMS	DESCRIPTION
CoD Noir	2	Black and white
Photo-Negative	4	Inverses colors
Super Contrast	6	Increases contrast
Ragtime Warfare	8	Black and white, scratches fill screen, double speed, piano music
Cluster Bombs	10	Four extra grenade explosions after frag grenade explodes.
A Bad Year	15	Enemies explode into a bunch of old tires when killed.
Slow-Mo Ability	20	Melee button enables/disables slow-motion mode.
Infinite Ammo	30	Unlimited ammo and no need to reload. Doesn't work for single-shot weapons such as RPG.

CARS MATER-NATIONAL

ALL ARCADE RACES, MINI-GAMES, AND WORLDS

Select Codes/Cheats from the options and enter PLAYALL.

ALL CARS

Select Codes/Cheats from the options and enter MATTEL07.

ALTERNATE LIGHTNING MCQUEEN COLORS

Select Codes/Cheats from the options and enter NCEDUDZ.

ALL COLORS FOR OTHERS

Select Codes/Cheats from the options and enter PAINTIT.

UNLIMITED TURBO

Select Codes/Cheats from the options and enter ZZOOOOM.

EXTREME ACCELERATION

Select Codes/Cheats from the options and enter 0TO200X.

EXPERT MODE

Select Codes/Cheats from the options and enter VRYFAST.

ALL BONUS ART

Select Codes/Cheats from the options and enter BUYTALL.

CONAN

PROMOTIONAL UNLOCKABLE #1 CONCEPT ART

Go to the Concept Art menu in Extras and press Up, Down, Up, Down, Left, Right, Left, Right, ■, ▲.

PROMOTIONAL UNLOCKABLE #2 CONCEPT ART

Go to the Concept Art menu in Extras and press Up, Down, Left, Left, ■, ■, ■.

PROMOTIONAL UNLOCKABLE #3 CONCEPT ART

Go to the Concept Art menu in Extras and press L3, L3, ▲, ▲, ■, R3.

PROMOTIONAL UNLOCKABLE #4 CONCEPT ART

Go to the Concept Art menu in Extras and press Left, ■, Left, ▲, Down, R3, R3.

PROMOTIONAL UNLOCKABLE #5 CONCEPT ART

Go to the Concept Art menu in Extras and press Right, Right, Left, Left, Up, Down, Up, Down, ■, ■.

PROMOTIONAL UNLOCKABLE #6 CONCEPT ART

Go to the Concept Art menu in Extras and press ▲, ▲, L3, ■, ■, R3, Up, Down.

THE DARKNESS

DARKLING OUTFITS

Even Darklings can make a fashion statement. Support your mini minions with an ensemble fit for murderous monsters by collecting these fun and colorful outfits.

OUTFIT	MENTIONED IN	AREA	LOCATION
Potato Sack	Chapter 1	Chinatown	Sitting against alley wall near metro exit
Jungle	Chapter 1	Hunters Point Alley	Inside hidden room
Roadworker	Chapter 3	City Hall station	Inside train car
Lumberjack	Side Objectives	Cutrone objective	Inside Cutrone's apartment
Fireman	Side Objectives	Pajamas objective	Inside room 261
Construction	Side Objectives	Mortarello objective	Inside room of last mission
Baseball	N/A	Dial: 555-4263	N/A
Golfshirt	N/A	Dial: 555-5664	N/A

PHONE NUMBERS

Dialing 'D' for Darkness isn't the only number to punch on a telephone. Sure, you called every number you found on those hard-to-get Collectibles, but you certainly haven't found *all* of the phone numbers. Pay close to attention to the environment as you hunt down Uncle Paulie. Chances are, you overlooked a phone number or two without even knowing it as you ripped out a goon's heart. All 25 'secret' phone numbers are scattered throughout New York and can be seen on anywhere from flyers and storefronts to garbage cans and posters. Dial 18 of the 25 numbers on a phone—in no specific order—to unlock the final secret of the game.

PHONE NUMBERS
555-6118
555-1847
555-6667
555-4569
555-9985
555-1037
555-1206
555-9528
555-3285

PHONE NUMBERS
555-5723
555-8024
555-6322
555-9132
555-6893
555-2402
555-6557
555-2309
555-4372

PHONE NUMBERS
555-9723
555-5289
555-6205
555-7658
555-1233
555-3947
555-9562
555-7934
555-7892

PHONE NUMBERS
555-8930
555-3243
555-3840
555-2349
555-6325
555-4565
555-9898
555-7613
555-6969

DEAD SPACE

REFILL STASIS AND KINESIS ENERGY

Pause the game and press ■, ▲, ▲, ■, ▲.

REFILL OXYGEN

Pause the game and press ■, ■, ▲ (x3).

ADD 2 POWER NODES

Pause the game and press ▲, ■ (x3), ▲. This code can only be used once.

ADD 5 POWER NODES

Pause the game and press ▲, ■, ▲, ■, ■, ▲, ■, ■, ▲, ■, ■, ▲. This code can only be used once.

1,000 CREDITS

Pause the game and press ■ (x3), ▲, ■. This code can only be used once.

2,000 CREDITS

Pause the game and press ■ (x3), ▲, ▲. This code can only be used once.

5,000 CREDITS

Pause the game and press ■ (x3), ▲, ■, ▲. This code can only be used once.

10,000 CREDITS

Pause the game and press ■, ▲ (x3), ■, ■, ▲. This code can only be used once.

DEF JAM: ICON

IT'S GOING DOWN BY YUNG JOC

At the Title Screen, after "Press Start Button" appears, press Down, ●, ⊗, Right.

MAKE IT RAIN BY FAT JOE AND FIGHT AS FAT JOE

At the Title Screen, after "Press Start Button" appears, press ●, Up, Right, Left, ■.

DESTROY ALL HUMANS! PATH OF THE FURON

After entering the following codes, select Customize from the Options to activate them.

60'S APPEARANCE

Select Unlock Content from Extras and enter M13Ni95L.

70'S APPEARANCE

Select Unlock Content from Extras and enter S63bf2kd.

BIKER OUTFIT

Select Unlock Content from Extras and enter 1gb57M2x.

CHEF OUTFIT

Select Unlock Content from Extras and enter 51c24KiW.

GANGSTER OUTFIT

Select Unlock Content from Extras and enter J5d99bPz.

KUNG FU OUTFIT

Select Unlock Content from Extras and enter Ly11r98H.

MIME OUTFIT

Select Unlock Content from Extras and enter 7qd33J1n.

VELVET OUTFIT

Select Unlock Content from Extras and enter F9sT5v88.

SAUCER ATTACHMENTS

Select Unlock Content from Extras and enter V81fvUW3.

SAUCER SKINS

Select Unlock Content from Extras and enter X91mw7zp.

EAT LEAD: THE RETURN OF MATT HAZARD

MAXIMUM HAZARD DIFFICULTY

At the difficulty select, press Up, Up, Down, Down, Left, Right, Left, Right.

FAR CRY 2

BONUS MISSIONS

Select Promotional Content from the Additional Content menu and enter the following codes. Each code gives four or six extra missions.

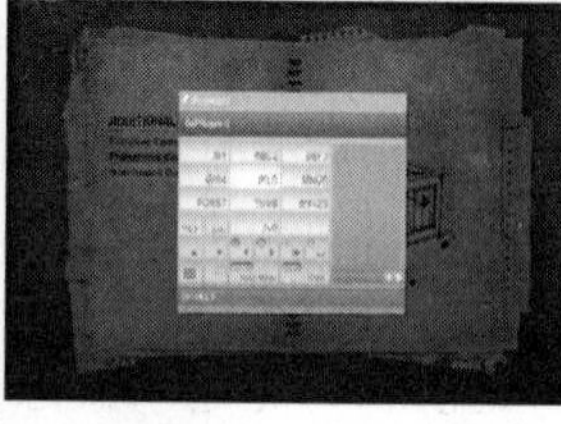

6aPHuswe
Cr34ufrE
2Eprunef
JeM8SpaW
tr99pUkA

F.E.A.R.

ALL MISSIONS

Enter F3ARDAY1 as your profile name.

FIGHT NIGHT ROUND 3

ALL VENUES

Create a champ with a first name of NEWVIEW.

FRACTURE

EXCLUSIVE PRE-ORDER SKIN

Pause the game and press Up, Right, Left, Down, Up, Left, Right, Down.

FULL AUTO 2: BATTLELINES

ALL CARS

Select Cheat Codes from Extras and enter 47GIV3MECARS.

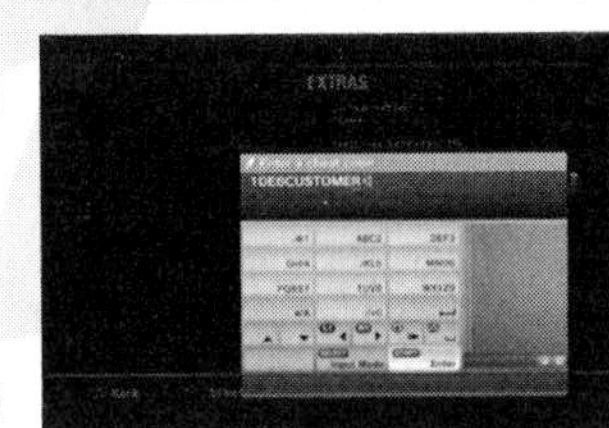

ALL MISSIONS

Select Cheat Codes from Extras and enter IMFEDUPWITHTHIS.

SCEPTRE AND MINI-ROCKETS

Select Cheat Codes from Extras and enter 10E6CUSTOMER. This vehicle and weapon become available in Arcade Mode and Head to Head.

THE GODFATHER: THE DON'S EDITION

The following codes can be used only once every five minutes.

$5,000

Pause the game and press ■, ▲, ■, ■, ▲, L3.

FULL AMMO

Pause the game and press ▲, Left, ▲, Right, ■, R3.

FULL HEALTH

Pause the game and press Left, ■, Right, ▲, Right, L3.

ALL MOVIES

At the Main menu, press ▲, ■, ▲, ■, ■, L3.

THE GODFATHER II

These codes can only be used once every few minutes.

$5,000

While in Don view, press ■, ▲, ■, ■, ▲, L3.

FULL HEALTH

While in Don view, press Left, ■, Right, ▲, Right, L3.

FULL AMMO

While in Don view, press ▲, Left, ▲, Right, ■, R3.

GRAND THEFT AUTO IV

CHEATS

Call the following phone numbers with Niko's phone to activate the cheats. Some cheats may affect the missions and achievements.

VEHICLE	PHONE NUMBER
Change weather	468-555-0100
Get weapons	486-555-0100
Get different weapons	486-555-0150

VEHICLE	PHONE NUMBER
Raise wanted level	267-555-0150
Remove wanted level	267-555-0100
Restore armor	362-555-0100
Restore health	482-555-0100
Restore armor, health, and ammo	482-555-0100

SPAWN VEHICLES

Call the following phone numbers with Niko's phone to spawn the corresponding vehicle.

VEHICLE	PHONE NUMBER
Annihilator	359-555-0100
Cognoscenti	227-555-0142
Comet	227-555-0175
FIB Buffalo	227-555-0100
Jetmax	938-555-0100
NRG-900	625-555-0100
Sanchez	625-555-0150
SuperGT	227-555-0168
Turismo	227-555-0147

MAP LOCATIONS

Access a computer in-game and enter the following URL: www.whattheydonotwantyoutoknow.com.

GRID

ALL DRIFT CARS

Select Bonus Codes from the Options. Then choose Enter Code and enter TUN58396.

ALL MUSCLE CARS

Select Bonus Codes from the Options. Then choose Enter Code and enter MUS59279.

BUCHBINDER EMOTIONAL ENGINEERING BMW 320SI

Select Bonus Codes from the Options. Then choose Enter Code and enter F93857372. You can use this in Race Day or in GRID World once you've started your own team.

EBAY MOTORS MUSTANG

Select Bonus Codes from the Options. Then choose Enter Code and enter DAFJ55E01473M0. You can use this in Race Day or in GRID World once you've started your own team.

GAMESTATION BMW 320SI

Select Bonus Codes from the Options. Then choose Enter Code and enter G29782655. You can use this in Race Day or in GRID World once you've started your own team.

MICROMANIA PAGANI ZONDA R

Select Bonus Codes from the Options. Then choose Enter Code and enter M38572343. You can use this in Race Day or in GRID World once you've started your own team.

PLAY.COM ASTON MARTIN DBR9

Select Bonus Codes from the Options. Then choose Enter Code and enter P47203845. You can use this in Race Day or in GRID World once you've started your own team.

GUITAR HERO III: LEGENDS OF ROCK

To enter the following cheats, strum the guitar with the given buttons held. For example, if it says Yellow + Orange, hold Yellow and Orange as you strum. Air Guitar, Precision Mode, and Performance Mode can be toggled on and off from the Cheats menu. You can also change between five different levels of Hyperspeed at this menu.

UNLOCK EVERYTHING

Select Cheats from the Options. Choose Enter Cheat and enter Green + Red + Blue + Orange, Green + Red + Yellow + Blue, Green + Red + Yellow + Orange, Green + Yellow + Blue + Orange, Green + Red + Yellow + Blue, Red + Yellow + Blue + Orange, Green + Red + Yellow + Blue, Green + Yellow + Blue + Orange, Green + Red + Yellow + Blue, Green + Red + Yellow + Orange, Green + Red + Yellow + Orange, Green + Red + Yellow + Blue, Green + Red + Yellow + Orange. No sounds play while this code is entered.

An easier way to show this code is by representing Green as 1 down to Orange as 5. For example, if you have 1345, you would hold down Green + Yellow + Blue + Orange while strumming. 1245 + 1234 + 1235 + 1345 + 1234 + 2345 + 1234 + 1345 + 1234 + 1235 + 1235 + 1234 + 1235.

ALL SONGS

Select Cheats from the Options. Choose Enter Cheat and enter Yellow + Orange, Red + Blue, Red + Orange, Green + Blue, Red + Yellow, Yellow + Orange, Red + Yellow, Red + Blue, Green + Yellow, Green + Yellow, Yellow + Blue, Yellow + Blue, Yellow + Orange, Yellow + Orange, Yellow + Blue, Yellow, Red, Red + Yellow, Red, Yellow, Orange.

NO FAIL

Select Cheats from the Options. Choose Enter Cheat and enter Green + Red, Blue, Green + Red, Green + Yellow, Blue, Green + Yellow, Red + Yellow, Orange, Red + Yellow, Green + Yellow, Yellow, Green + Yellow, Green + Red.

AIR GUITAR

Select Cheats from the Options. Choose Enter Cheat and enter Blue + Yellow, Green + Yellow, Green + Yellow, Red + Blue, Red + Blue, Red + Yellow, Red + Yellow, Blue + Yellow, Green + Yellow, Green + Yellow, Red + Blue, Red + Blue, Red + Yellow, Red + Yellow, Green + Yellow, Green + Yellow, Red + Yellow, Red + Yellow.

HYPERSPEED

Select Cheats from the Options. Choose Enter Cheat and enter Orange, Blue, Orange, Yellow, Orange, Blue, Orange, Yellow.

PERFORMANCE MODE

Select Cheats from the Options. Choose Enter Cheat and enter Red + Yellow, Red + Blue, Red + Orange, Red + Blue, Red + Yellow, Green + Blue, Red + Yellow, Red + Blue.

EASY EXPERT

Select Cheats from the Options. Choose Enter Cheat and enter Green + Red, Green + Yellow, Yellow + Blue, Red + Blue, Blue + Orange, Yellow + Orange, Red + Yellow, Red + Blue.

PRECISION MODE

Select Cheats from the Options. Choose Enter Cheat and enter Green + Red, Green + Red, Green + Red, Red + Yellow, Red + Yellow, Red + Blue, Red + Blue, Yellow + Blue, Yellow + Orange, Yellow + Orange, Green + Red, Green + Red, Green + Red, Red + Yellow, Red + Yellow, Red + Blue, Red + Blue, Yellow + Blue, Yellow + Orange, Yellow + Orange.

BRET MICHAELS SINGER

Select Cheats from the Options. Choose Enter Cheat and enter Green + Red, Green + Red, Green + Red, Green + Blue, Green + Blue, Green + Blue, Red + Blue, Red, Red, Red, Red + Blue, Red, Red, Red, Red + Blue, Red, Red, Red.

GUITAR HERO: AEROSMITH

Select Cheats from the Options menu and enter the following. To do this, strum the guitar with the given buttons held. For example, if it says Yellow + Orange, hold Yellow and Orange as you strum. Air Guitar, Precision Mode, and Performance Mode can be toggled on and off from the Cheats menu. You can also change between five different levels of Hyperspeed at this menu.

ALL SONGS

Red + Yellow, Green + Red, Green + Red, Red + Yellow, Red + Yellow, Green + Red, Red + Yellow, Red + Yellow, Green + Red, Green + Red, Red + Yellow, Red + Yellow, Green + Red, Red + Yellow, Red + Blue. This code does not unlock Pandora's Box.

AIR GUITAR

Red + Yellow, Green + Red, Red + Yellow, Red + Yellow, Red + Blue, Red + Blue, Red + Blue, Red + Blue, Red + Blue, Yellow + Blue, Yellow + Blue, Yellow + Orange

HYPERSPEED

Yellow + Orange, Yellow + Orange, Yellow + Orange, Yellow + Orange, Yellow + Orange, Red + Yellow, Red + Yellow, Red + Yellow, Red + Yellow, Red + Blue, Red + Blue, Red + Blue, Red + Blue, Red + Blue, Yellow + Blue, Yellow + Orange, Yellow + Orange.

NO FAIL

Select Cheats from the Options. Choose Enter Cheat and enter Green + Red, Blue, Green + Red, Green + Yellow, Blue, Green + Yellow, Red + Yellow, Orange, Red + Yellow, Green + Yellow, Yellow, Green + Yellow, Green + Red.

PERFORMANCE MODE

Green + Red, Green + Red, Red + Orange, Red + Blue, Green + Red, Green + Red, Red + Orange, Red + Blue.

PRECISION MODE

Red + Yellow, Red + Blue, Red + Blue, Red + Yellow, Red + Yellow, Yellow + Blue, Yellow + Blue, Yellow + Blue, Red + Blue, Red + Yellow, Red + Blue, Red + Blue, Red + Yellow, Red + Yellow, Yellow + Blue, Yellow + Blue, Yellow + Blue, Red + Blue.

GUITAR HERO: METALLICA

Once entered, the cheats must be activated in the Cheats menu.

METALLICA COSTUMES

Select Cheats from Settings and enter Green, Red, Yellow, Blue, Blue, Yellow, Red, Green.

HYPERSPEED

Select Cheats from Settings and enter Green, Blue, Red, Yellow, Yellow, Red, Green, Green.

PERFORMANCE MODE

Select Cheats from Settings and enter Yellow, Yellow, Blue, Red, Blue, Green, Red, Red.

INVISIBLE ROCKER

Select Cheats from Settings and enter Green, Red, Yellow (x3), Blue, Blue, Green.

AIR INSTRUMENTS

Select Cheats from Settings and enter Red, Red, Blue, Yellow, Green (x3), Yellow.

ALWAYS DRUM FILL

Select Cheats from Settings and enter Red (x3), Blue, Blue, Green, Green, Yellow.

AUTO KICK

Select Cheats from Settings and enter Yellow, Green, Red, Blue (x4), Red. With this cheat activated, the bass pedal is automatically hit.

ALWAYS SLIDE

Select Cheats from Settings and enter Green, Green, Red, Red, Yellow, Red, Yellow, Blue. All Guitar Notes Become Touch Pad Sliding Notes.

BLACK HIGHWAY

Select Cheats from Settings and enter Yellow, Red, Green, Red, Green, Red, Red, Blue.

FLAME COLOR

Select Cheats from Settings and enter Green, Red, Green, Blue, Red, Red, Yellow, Blue.

GEM COLOR

Select Cheats from Settings and enter Blue, Red, Red, Green, Red, Green, Red, Yellow.

STAR COLOR

Select Cheats from Settings and enter Press Red, Red, Yellow, Red, Blue, Red, Red, Blue.

ADDITIONAL LINE 6 TONES

Select Cheats from Settings and enter Green, Red, Yellow, Blue, Red, Yellow, Blue, Green.

VOCAL FIREBALL

Select Cheats from Settings and enter Red, Green, Green, Yellow, Blue, Green, Yellow, Green.

GUITAR HERO WORLD TOUR

The following cheats can be toggled on and off at the Cheats menu.

QUICKPLAY SONGS

Select Cheats from the Options menu, choose Enter New Cheat and press Blue, Blue, Red, Green, Green, Blue, Blue, Yellow.

ALWAYS SLIDE

Select Cheats from the Options menu, choose Enter New Cheat and press Green, Green, Red, Red, Yellow, Red, Yellow, Blue.

AT&T BALLPARK

Select Cheats from the Options menu, choose Enter New Cheat and press Yellow, Green, Red, Red, Green, Blue, Red, Yellow.

AUTO KICK

Select Cheats from the Options menu, choose Enter New Cheat and press Yellow, Green, Red, Blue (x4), Red.

EXTRA LINE 6 TONES

Select Cheats from the Options menu, choose Enter New Cheat and press Green, Red, Yellow, Blue, Red, Yellow, Blue, Green.

FLAME COLOR

Select Cheats from the Options menu, choose Enter New Cheat and press Green, Red, Green, Blue, Red, Red, Yellow, Blue.

GEM COLOR

Select Cheats from the Options menu, choose Enter New Cheat and press Blue, Red, Red, Green, Red, Green, Red, Yellow.

STAR COLOR

Select Cheats from the Options menu, choose Enter New Cheat and press Red, Red, Yellow, Red, Blue, Red, Red, Blue.

AIR INSTRUMENTS

Select Cheats from the Options menu, choose Enter New Cheat and press Red, Red, Blue, Yellow, Green (x3), Yellow.

HYPERSPEED

Select Cheats from the Options menu, choose Enter New Cheat and press Green, Blue, Red, Yellow, Yellow, Red, Green, Green. These show up in the menu as HyperGuitar, HyperBass, and HyperDrums.

PERFORMANCE MODE

Select Cheats from the Options menu, choose Enter New Cheat and press Yellow, Yellow, Blue, Red, Blue, Green, Red, Red.

INVISIBLE ROCKER

Select Cheats from the Options menu, choose Enter New Cheat and press Green, Red, Yellow (x3), Blue, Blue, Green.

VOCAL FIREBALL

Select Cheats from the Options menu, choose Enter New Cheat and press Red, Green, Green, Yellow, Blue, Green, Yellow, Green.

AARON STEELE!

Select Cheats from the Options menu, choose Enter New Cheat and press Blue, Red, Yellow (x5), Green.

JONNY VIPER

Select Cheats from the Options menu, choose Enter New Cheat and press Blue, Red, Blue, Blue, Yellow (x3), Green.

NICK

Select Cheats from the Options menu, choose Enter New Cheat and press Green, Red, Blue, Green, Red, Blue, Blue, Green.

RINA

Select Cheats from the Options menu, choose Enter New Cheat and press Blue, Red, Green, Green, Yellow (x3), Green.

IRON MAN

CLASSIC ARMOR
Clear One Man Army vs. Mercs.

EXTREMIS ARMOR
Clear One Man Army vs. Maggia.

MARK II ARMOR
Clear One Man Army vs. Ten Rings.

HULKBUSTER ARMOR
Clear One Man Army vs. AIM-X. Can also be unlocked when clear game save data from Incredible Hulk is stored on the same console.

CLASSIC MARK I ARMOR
Clear One Man Army vs. AIM.

ULTIMATE ARMOR
Clear Mission 13: Showdown.

JUICED 2: HOT IMPORT NIGHTS

ASCARI KZ1
Select Cheats and Codes from the DNA Lab menu and enter KNOX. Defeat the challenge to earn the car.

AUDI TT 1.8L QUATTRO
Select Cheats and Codes from the DNA Lab menu and enter YTHZ. Defeat the challenge to earn the car.

BMW Z4 ROADSTER
Select Cheats and Codes from the DNA Lab menu and enter GVDL. Defeat the challenge to earn the car.

FRITO-LAY INFINITI G35
Select Cheats and Codes from the DNA Lab menu and enter MNCH. Defeat the challenge to earn the car.

HOLDEN MONARO
Select Cheats and Codes from the DNA Lab menu and enter RBSG. Defeat the challenge to earn the car.

HYUNDAI COUPE 2.7L V6
Select Cheats and Codes from the DNA Lab menu and enter BSLU. Defeat the challenge to earn the car.

INFINITI G35
Select Cheats and Codes from the DNA Lab menu and enter MRHC. Defeat the challenge to earn the car.

KOENIGSEGG CCX
Select Cheats and Codes from the DNA Lab menu and enter KDTR. Defeat the challenge to earn the car.

MITSUBISHI PROTOTYPE X
Select Cheats and Codes from the DNA Lab menu and enter DOPX. Defeat the challenge to earn the car.

NISSAN 350Z
Select Cheats and Codes from the DNA Lab menu and enter PRGN. Defeat the challenge to earn the car.

NISSAN SKYLINE R34 GT-R
Select Cheats and Codes from the DNA Lab menu and enter JWRS. Defeat the challenge to earn the car.

SALEEN S7
Select Cheats and Codes from the DNA Lab menu and enter WIKF. Defeat the challenge to earn the car.

SEAT LEON CUPRA R
Select Cheats and Codes from the DNA Lab menu and enter FAMQ. Defeat the challenge to earn the car.

KUNG FU PANDA

UNLIMITED CHI
Select Cheats from the Extra menu and enter Down, Right, Left, Up, Down.

INVULNERABILITY
Select Cheats from the Extra menu and enter Down, Down, Right, Up, Left.

FULL UPGRADES
Select Cheats from the Extra menu and enter Left, Right, Down, Left, Up.

FULL AWESOME METER
Select Cheats from the Extra menu and enter Up, Down, Up, Right, Left. This gives Po 4X damage.

MULTIPLAYER CHARACTERS
Select Cheats from the Extra menu and enter Left, Down, Left, Right, Down.

OUTFITS
Select Cheats from the Extra menu and enter Right, Left, Down, Up, Right.

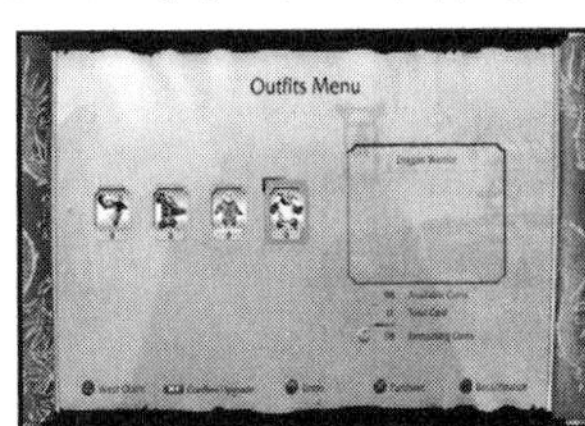

LAIR

CHICKEN VIDEO
At the Cheat menu, enter chicken.

COFFEE VIDEO
At the Cheat menu, enter 686F7420636F66666565.

UNLOCKS STABLE OPTION FOR ALL LEVELS
At the Cheat menu, enter koelsch. Saving is disabled with this code.

THE LEGEND OF SPYRO: DAWN OF THE DRAGON

UNLIMITED LIFE
Pause the game, hold L1 and press Right, Right, Down, Down, Left with the Left Analog Stick.

UNLIMITED MANA
Pause the game, hold R1 and press Up, Right, Up, Left, Down with the Left Analog Stick.

MAXIMUM XP
Pause the game, hold R1 and press Left, Right, Right, Up, Up with the Left Analog Stick.

ALL ELEMENTAL UPGRADES
Pause the game, hold L1 and press Left, Up, Down, Up, Right with the Left Analog Stick.

LEGENDS OF WRESTLEMANIA

ANIMAL'S SECOND COSTUME
Select Cheat Codes from the Options menu and enter TheRoadWarriorAnimal.

BRUTUS BEEFCAKE'S SECOND COSTUME
Select Cheat Codes from the Options menu and enter BrutusTheBarberShop!.

IRON SHEIK'S SECOND COSTUME
Select Cheat Codes from the Options menu and enter IronSheikCamelClutch.

JIMMY HART'S SECOND COSTUME
Select Cheat Codes from the Options menu and enter WithManagerJimmyHart.

KOKO B WARE'S SECOND COSTUME
Select Cheat Codes from the Options menu and enter TheBirdmanKokoBWare!.

THE ROCK'S SECOND COSTUME
Select Cheat Codes from the Options menu and enter UnlockTheRockBottom!.

SGT. SLAUGHTER'S SECOND COSTUME
Select Cheat Codes from the Options menu and enter CobraClutchSlaughter.

SHAWN MICHAEL'S SECOND COSTUME
Select Cheat Codes from the Options menu and enter ShawnsSweetChinMusic.

UNDERTAKER'S SECOND COSTUME
Select Cheat Codes from the Options menu and enter UndertakersTombstone.

LEGO BATMAN

BATCAVE CODES

Using the computer in the Batcave, select Enter Code and enter the following:

CHARACTERS

CHARACTER	CODE
Alfred	ZAQ637
Batgirl	JKR331
Bruce Wayne	BDJ327
Catwoman (Classic)	M1AAWW
Clown Goon	HJK327
Commissioner Gordon	DDP967
Fishmonger	HGY748
Freeze Girl	XVK541
Joker Goon	UTF782
Joker Henchman	YUN924
Mad Hatter	JCA283
Man-Bat	NYU942
Military Policeman	MKL382
Nightwing	MVY759
Penguin Goon	NKA238
Penguin Henchman	BJH782
Penguin Minion	KJP748
Poison Ivy Goon	GTB899
Police Marksman	HKG984
Police Officer	JRY983
Riddler Goon	CRY928
Riddler Henchman	XEU824
S.W.A.T.	HTF114
Sailor	NAV592
Scientist	JFL786
Security Guard	PLB946
The Joker (Tropical)	CCB199
Yeti	NJL412
Zoo Sweeper	DWR243

VEHICLES

VEHICLE	CODE
Bat-Tank	KNTT4B
Bruce Wayne's Private Jet	LEA664
Catwoman's Motorcycle	HPL826
Garbage Truck	DUS483
Goon Helicopter	GCH328
Harbor Helicopter	CHP735
Harley Quinn's Hammer Truck	RDT637
Mad Hatter's Glider	HS000W
Mad Hatter's Steamboat	M4DM4N
Mr. Freeze's Iceberg	ICYICE
The Joker's Van	JUK657
Mr. Freeze's Kart	BCT229
Penguin Goon Submarine	BTN248
Police Bike	LJP234
Police Boat	PLC999
Police Car	KJL832
Police Helicopter	CWR732
Police Van	MAC788
Police Watercraft	VJD328
Riddler's Jet	HAHAHA
Robin's Submarine	TTF453
Two-Face's Armored Truck	EFE933

CHEATS

CHEAT	CODE
Always Score Multiply	9LRGNB
Fast Batarangs	JRBDCB
Fast Walk	ZOLM6N
Flame Batarang	D8NYWH
Freeze Batarang	XPN4NG
Extra Hearts	ML3KHP
Fast Build	EVG26J
Immune to Freeze	JXUDY6
Invincibility	WYD5CP
Minikit Detector	ZXGH9J
More Batarang Targets	XWP645
Piece Detector	KHJ554
Power Brick Detector	MMN786
Regenerate Hearts	HJH7HJ
Score x2	N4NR3E
Score x4	CX9MAT
Score x6	MLVNF2
Score x8	WCCDB9
Score x10	18HW07

LEGO INDIANA JONES: THE ORIGINAL ADVENTURES

CHARACTERS

Approach the blackboard in the Classroom and enter the following codes.

CHARACTER	CODE
Bandit	12N68W
Bandit Swordsman	1MK4RT
Barranca	04EM94
Bazooka Trooper (Crusade)	MK83R7
Bazooka Trooper (Raiders)	S93Y5R
Belloq	CHN3YU
Belloq (Jungle)	TDR197
Belloq (Robes)	VEO29L
British Commander	B73EUA
British Officer	VJ5TI9
British Soldier	DJ5I2W
Captain Katanga	VJ3TT3
Chatter Lal	ENW936
Chatter Lal (Thuggee)	CNH4RY
Chen	3NK48T
Colonel Dietrich	2K9RKS
Colonel Vogel	8EAL4H
Dancing Girl	C7EJ21
Donovan	3NFTU8
Elsa (Desert)	JSNRT9
Elsa (Officer)	VMJ5US
Enemy Boxer	8246RB
Enemy Butler	VJ48W3
Enemy Guard	VJ7R51
Enemy Guard (Mountains)	YR47WM
Enemy Officer	572E61
Enemy Officer (Desert	2MK45O
Enemy Pilot	B84ELP
Enemy Radio Operator	1MF94R
Enemy Soldier (Desert)	4NSU7Q
Fedora	V75YSP
First Mate	0GIN24
Grail Knight	NE6THI

CHARACTER	CODE
Hovitos Tribesman	H0V1SS
Indiana Jones (Desert Disguise)	4J8S4M
Indiana Jones (Officer)	VJ85OS
Jungle Guide	24PF34
Kao Kan	WMO46L
Kazim	NRH23J
Kazim (Desert)	3M29TJ
Lao Che	2NK479
Maharajah	NFK5N2
Major Toht	13NS01
Masked Bandit	N48SF0
Mola Ram	FJUR31
Monkey Man	3RF6YJ
Pankot Assassin	2NKT72
Pankot Guard	VN28RH
Sherpa Brawler	VJ37WJ
Sherpa Gunner	ND762W
Slave Child	0E3ENW
Thuggee	VM683E
Thuggee Acolyte	T2R3F9
Thuggee Slave Driver	VBS7GW
Village Dignitary	KD48TN
Village Elder	4682E1
Willie (Dinner Suit)	VK93R7
Willie (Pajamas)	MEN4IP
Wu Han	3NSLT8

EXTRAS

Approach the blackboard in the Classroom and enter the following codes. Some cheats need to be enabled by selecting Extras from the Pause menu.

CHEAT	CODE
Artifact Detector	VIKED7
Beep Beep	VNF59Q
Character Treasure	VIES2R
Disarm Enemies	VKRNS9
Disguises	4ID1N6
Fast Build	V83SLO
Fast Dig	378RS6
Fast Fix	FJ59WS
Fertilizer	B1GW1F
Ice Rink	33GM7J
Parcel Detector	VUT673
Poo Treasure	WWQ1SA
Regenerate Hearts	MDLP69
Secret Characters	3X44AA
Silhouettes	3HE85H
Super Scream	VN3R7S
Super Slap	0P1TA5
Treasure Magnet	H86LA2
Treasure x10	VI3PS8
Treasure x2	VM4TS9
Treasure x4	VLWEN3
Treasure x6	V84RYS
Treasure x8	A72E1M

LEGO STAR WARS: THE COMPLETE SAGA

The following still need to be purchased after entering the codes.

CHARACTERS

ADMIRAL ACKBAR
At the bar in Mos Eisley Cantina, select Enter Code and enter ACK646.

BATTLE DROID (COMMANDER)
At the bar in Mos Eisley Cantina, select Enter Code and enter KPF958.

BOBA FETT (BOY)
At the bar in Mos Eisley Cantina, select Enter Code and enter GGF539.

BOSS NASS
At the bar in Mos Eisley Cantina, select Enter Code and enter HHY697.

CAPTAIN TARPALS
At the bar in Mos Eisley Cantina, select Enter Code and enter QRN714.

COUNT DOOKU
At the bar in Mos Eisley Cantina, select Enter Code and enter DDD748.

DARTH MAUL
At the bar in Mos Eisley Cantina, select Enter Code and enter EUK421.

EWOK
At the bar in Mos Eisley Cantina, select Enter Code and enter EWK785.

GENERAL GRIEVOUS
At the bar in Mos Eisley Cantina, select Enter Code and enter PMN576.

GREEDO
At the bar in Mos Eisley Cantina, select Enter Code and enter ZZR636.

IG-88
At the bar in Mos Eisley Cantina, select Enter Code and enter GIJ989.

IMPERIAL GUARD
At the bar in Mos Eisley Cantina, select Enter Code and enter GUA850.

JANGO FETT
At the bar in Mos Eisley Cantina, select Enter Code and enter KLJ897.

KI-ADI MUNDI
At the bar in Mos Eisley Cantina, select Enter Code and enter MUN486.

LUMINARA
At the bar in Mos Eisley Cantina, select Enter Code and enter LUM521.

PADMÉ
At the bar in Mos Eisley Cantina, select Enter Code and enter VBJ322.

R2-Q5
At the bar in Mos Eisley Cantina, select Enter Code and enter EVILR2.

STORMTROOPER
At the bar in Mos Eisley Cantina, select Enter Code and enter NBN431.

TAUN WE
At the bar in Mos Eisley Cantina, select Enter Code and enter PRX482.

VULTURE DROID
At the bar in Mos Eisley Cantina, select Enter Code and enter BDC866.

WATTO
At the bar in Mos Eisley Cantina, select Enter Code and enter PLL967.

ZAM WESELL
At the bar in Mos Eisley Cantina, select Enter Code and enter 584HJF.

SKILLS

DISGUISE
At the bar in Mos Eisley Cantina, select Enter Code and enter BRJ437.

FORCE GRAPPLE LEAP
At the bar in Mos Eisley Cantina, select Enter Code and enter CLZ738.

VEHICLES

DROID TRIFIGHTER
At the bar in Mos Eisley Cantina, select Enter Code and enter AAB123.

IMPERIAL SHUTTLE
At the bar in Mos Eisley Cantina, select Enter Code and enter HUT845.

TIE INTERCEPTOR
At the bar in Mos Eisley Cantina, select Enter Code and enter INT729.

TIE FIGHTER
At the bar in Mos Eisley Cantina, select Enter Code and enter DBH897.

ZAM'S AIRSPEEDER
At the bar in Mos Eisley Cantina, select Enter Code and enter UUU875.

LINGER IN SHADOWS

CREDITS AND HIDDEN PART
At the Title screen, press L3 + R3.

MADDEN NFL 07

MADDEN CARDS

Select Madden Cards from My Madden. Then select Madden Codes and enter the following:

CARD	PASSWORD
#199 Gold Lame Duck Cheat	5LAWO0
#200 Gold Mistake Free Cheat	XL7SP1
#210 Gold QB on Target Cheat	WROA0R
#220 Super Bowl XLI Gold	RLA9R7
#221 Super Bowl XLII Gold	WRLUF8
#222 Super Bowl XLIII Gold	NIEV4A
#223 Super Bowl XLIV Gold	M5AB7L
#224 Aloha Stadium Gold	YI8P8U
#225 1958 Colts Gold	B57QLU
#226 1966 Packers Gold	1PL1FL
#227 1968 Jets Gold	MIE6WO
#228 1970 Browns Gold	CL2TOE
#229 1972 Dolphins Gold	NOEB7U
#230 1974 Steelers Gold	YO0FLA
#231 1976 Raiders Gold	MOA11I
#232 1977 Broncos Gold	C8UM7U
#233 1978 Dolphins Gold	VIU0O7
#234 1980 Raiders Gold	NLAPH3
#235 1981 Chargers Gold	COAGI4
#236 1982 Redskins Gold	WL8BRI
#237 1983 Raiders Gold	H0EW71
#238 1984 Dolphins Gold	M1AM1E
#239 1985 Bears Gold	QOETO8
#240 1986 Giants Gold	ZI8S2L
#241 1988 49ers Gold	SP2A8H
#242 1990 Eagles Gold	2L4TRO
#243 1991 Lions Gold	J1ETRI
#244 1992 Cowboys Gold	W9UVI9
#245 1993 Bills Gold	DLA3I7
#246 1994 49ers Gold	DR7EST
#247 1996 Packers Gold	F8LUST
#248 1998 Broncos Gold	FIES95
#249 1999 Rams Gold	S9OUSW
#250 Bears Pump Up the Crowd	B1OUPH
#251 Bengals Cheerleader	DRL2SW
#252 Bills Cheerleader	1PLUYO
#253 Broncos Cheerleader	3ROUJO
#254 Browns Pump Up the Crowd	T1UTOA
#255 Buccaneers Cheerleader	S9EWRI
#256 Cardinals Cheerleader	57IEPI
#257 Chargers Cheerleader	F7UHL8
#258 Chiefs Cheerleader	PRI5SL
#259 Colts Cheerleader	1R5AMI
#260 Cowboys Cheerleader	Z2ACHL
#261 Dolphins Cheerleader	C5AHLE
#262 Eagles Cheerleader	PO7DRO
#263 Falcons Cheerleader	37USPO
#264 49ers Cheerleader	KL0CRL
#265 Giants Pump Up the Crowd	C4USPI
#266 Jaguars Cheerleader	MIEH7E
#267 Jets Pump Up the Crowd	C0LUXI
#268 Lions Pump Up the Crowd	3LABLU
#269 Packers Pump Up the Crowd	4HO7VO
#270 Panthers Cheerleader	F2IASP
#282 All AFC Team Gold	PRO9PH
#283 All NFC Team Gold	RLATH7

MAJOR LEAGUE BASEBALL 2K7

MICKEY MANTLE ON THE FREE AGENTS LIST

Select Enter Cheat Code from the My 2K7 menu and enter themick.

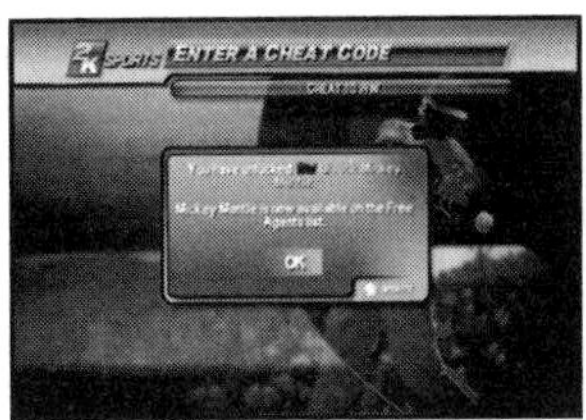

ALL CHEATS

Select Enter Cheat Code from the My 2K7 menu and enter Black Sox.

ALL EXTRAS

Select Enter Cheat Code from the My 2K7 menu and enter Game On.

UNLOCK EVERYTHING

Select Enter Cheat Code from the My 2K7 menu and enter Derek Jeter. This does not unlock the Topps cheats.

MIGHTY MICK CHEAT

Select Enter Cheat Code from the My 2K7 menu and enter mightymick.

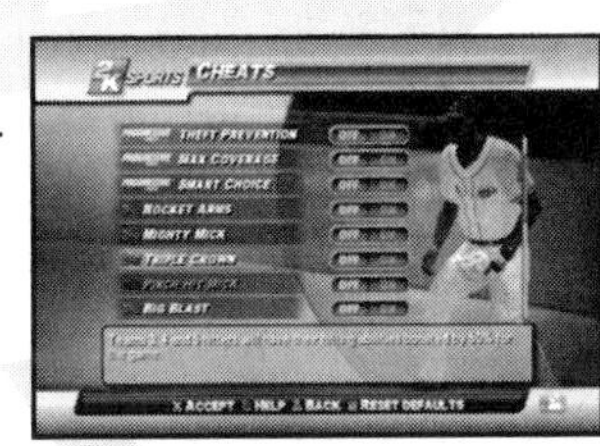

TRIPLE CROWN CHEAT

Select Enter Cheat Code from the My 2K7 menu and enter triplecrown.

BIG BLAST CHEAT

Select Enter Cheat Code from the My 2K7 menu and enter m4murder.

MARVEL ULTIMATE ALLIANCE

UNLOCK ALL SKINS

At the Team menu, press Up, Down, Left, Right, Left, Right, Start.

UNLOCKS ALL HERO POWERS

At the Team menu, press Left, Right, Up, Down, Up, Down, Start.

ALL HEROES TO LEVEL 99

At the Team menu, press Up, Left, Up, Left, Down, Right, Down, Right, Start.

UNLOCK ALL HEROES

At the Team menu, press Up, Up, Down, Down, Left, Left, Left, Start.

UNLOCK DAREDEVIL

At the Team menu, press Left, Left, Right, Right, Up, Down, Up, Down, Start.

UNLOCK SILVER SURFER

At the Team menu, press Down, Left, Left, Up, Right, Up, Down, Left, Start.

GOD MODE

During gameplay, press Up, Down, Up, Down, Up, Left, Down, Right, Start.

TOUCH OF DEATH

During gameplay, press Left, Right, Down, Down, Right, Left, Start.

SUPER SPEED

During gameplay, press Up, Left, Up, Right, Down, Right, Start.

FILL MOMENTUM

During gameplay, press Left, Right, Right, Left, Up, Down, Down, Up, Start.

UNLOCK ALL COMICS

At the Review menu, press Left, Right, Right, Left, Up, Up, Right, Start.

UNLOCK ALL CONCEPT ART

At the Review menu, press Down, Down, Down, Right, Right, Left, Down, Start.

UNLOCK ALL CINEMATICS

At the Review menu, press Up, Left, Left, Up, Right, Right, Up, Start.

UNLOCK ALL LOAD SCREENS

At the Review menu, press Up, Down, Right, Left, Up, Up Down, Start.

UNLOCK ALL COURSES

At the Comic Missions menu, press Up, Right, Left, Down, Up, Right, Left, Down, Start.

MEDAL OF HONOR: AIRBORNE

Using the following cheats disables saves. During a game, hold L1 + R1, and press Square, Circle, Triangle, X, X. This brings up an Enter Cheat screen. Now you can enter the following:

FULL AMMO

Hold L1 + R1 and press Circle, Circle, Triangle, Square, X, Triangle.

FULL HEALTH

Hold L1 + R1 and press Triangle, Square, Square, Triangle, X, Circle.

MERCENARIES 2: WORLD IN FLAMES

To use Cheat Mode, you must update the game by being online when the game is started. The cheats will keep you from earning trophies, but anything earned up to that point remains. You can still save with the cheats, but be careful if you want to earn trophies. Quit the game without saving to return to normal.

CHEAT MODE

Access your PDA by pressing Select. Press L2, R2, R2, L2, R2, L2, L2, R2, R2, R2, L2 and close the PDA. You then need to accept the agreement that says trophies are disabled. Now you can enter the following cheats.

INVINCIBILITY

Access your PDA and press Up, Down, Left, Down, Right, Right. This activates invincibility for you and anyone that joins your game.

INFINITE AMMO

Access your PDA and press Up, Down, Left, Right, Left, Left.

GIVE ALL VEHICLES

Access your PDA and press Up, Down, Left, Right, Right, Left.

GIVE ALL SUPPLIES

Access your PDA and press Left, Right, Right, Left, Up, Up, Left, Up.

GIVE ALL AIRSTRIKES (EXCEPT NUKE)

Access your PDA and press Right, Left, Down, Up, Right, Left, Down, Up.

GIVE NUKE

Access your PDA and press Up, Up, Down, Down, Left, Right, Left, Right.

FILL FUEL

Access your PDA and press Up, Up, Up, Down, Down, Down.

ALL COSTUMES

Access your PDA and press Up, Right, Down, Left, Up.

GRAPPLING HOOK

Access your PDA and press Up, Left, Down, Right, Up.

METAL GEAR SOLID 4: GUNS OF THE PATRIOTS

100,000 DREBIN POINTS

At Otacon's computer in Shadow Moses, enter 14893.

OPENING – OLD L.A. 2040 IPOD SONG

At Otacon's computer in Shadow Moses, enter 78925.

POLICENAUTS END TITLE IPOD SONG

At Otacon's computer in Shadow Moses, enter 13462.

You must first defeat the game to use the following passwords.

DESPERATE CHASE IPOD SONG

Select password from the Extras menu and enter thomas.

GEKKO IPOD SONG

Select password from the Extras menu and enter george.

MIDNIGHT SHADOW IPOD SONG

Select password from the Extras menu and enter theodore.

MOBS ALIVE IPOD SONG

Select password from the Extras menu and enter abraham.

DESERT EAGLE - LONG BARREL

Select password from the Extras menu and enter deskyhstyl.

MK. 23 SOCOM PISTOL

Select password from the Extras menu and enter mekakorkkk.

MOSIN NAGANT

Select password from the Extras menu and enter mnsoymsyhn.

TYPE 17 PISTOL

Select password from the Extras menu and enter jmsotsynrn.

ALTAIR COSTUME

Select password from the Extras menu and enter aottrykmyn.

MLB 07: THE SHOW

CLASSIC STADIUMS

At the Main menu, press Down, Up, Right, Down, Up, Left, Down, Up.

GOLDEN/SLIVER ERA PLAYERS

At the Main menu, press Left, Up, Right, Down, Down, Left, Up, Down.

MLB 08: THE SHOW

ALL CLASSIC STADIUMS

At the Main menu, press Down, Right, ●, ■, Left, ▲, Up, L1. The controller will vibrate if entered correctly.

MOTOSTORM

UNLOCK EVERYTHING

At the Main menu, hold L1 + L2 + R1 + R2 + R3 (while pressed Up) + L3 (while pressed Down).

BIG HEADS ON ATVS AND BIKES

Pause the game and hold L1 + L2 + R1 + R2 + R3 (while pressed Right), + L3 (while pressed Left).

MX VS. ATV UNTAMED

ALL RIDING GEAR

Select Cheat Codes from the Options and enter crazylikea.

ALL HANDLEBARS

Select Cheat Codes from the Options and enter nohands.

NASCAR 08

ALL CHASE MODE CARS

Select cheat codes from the Options menu and enter checkered flag.

EA SPORTS CAR

Select cheat codes from the Options menu and enter ea sports car.

FANTASY DRIVERS

Select cheat codes from the Options menu and enter race the pack.

WALMART CAR AND TRACK

Select cheat codes from the Options menu and enter walmart everyday.

NASCAR 09

ALL FANTASY DRIVERS

Select EA Extras from My Nascar, choose Cheat Codes and enter CHECKERED FLAG.

WALMART TRACK AND THE WALMART CAR

Select EA Extras from My Nascar, choose Cheat Codes and enter Walmart Everyday.

NBA 07

2006 CHARLOTTE BOBCATS ALTERNATE JERSEY

Select NBA.com from the Trophy Room. Press ● to bring up the Enter Code screen. Enter JKL846ETK5.

2006 NOK HORNETS ALTERNATE JERSEY

Select NBA.com from the Trophy Room. Press ● to bring up the Enter Code screen. Enter EL2E3T8H58.

2006 NEW JERSEY NETS ALTERNATE JERSEY

Select NBA.com from the Trophy Room. Press ● to bring up the Enter Code screen. Enter NB79D965D2.

2006 UTAH JAZZ ALTERNATE JERSEY

Select NBA.com from the Trophy Room. Press ● to bring up the Enter Code screen. Enter 228GG7585G.

2006 WAS WIZARDS ALTERNATE JERSEY

Select NBA.com from the Trophy Room. Press ● to bring up the Enter Code screen. Enter PL5285F37F.

2007 EASTERN ALL STARS

Select NBA.com from the Trophy Room. Press ● to bring up the Enter Code screen. Enter 5F89RE3H8G.

2007 WESTERN ALL STARS

Select NBA.com from the Trophy Room. Press ● to bring up the Enter Code screen. Enter 2H5E89EH8C.

NBA 09: THE INSIDE

EASTERN ALL-STARS 09 JERSEY

Select Extras from the Progression menu. Then choose nba.com from the Jerseys menu. Press ■ and enter SHPNV2K699.

WESTERN ALL-STARS 09 JERSEY

Select Extras from the Progression menu. Then choose nba.com from the Jerseys menu. Press ■ and enter K8AV6YMLNF.

L.A. LAKERS LATIN NIGHT JERSEY

Select Extras from the Progression menu. Then choose nba.com from the Jerseys menu. Press ■ and enter NMTWCTC84S.

MIAMI HEAT LATIN NIGHT JERSEY

Select Extras from the Progression menu. Then choose nba.com from the Jerseys menu. Press ■ and enter WCTGSA8SPD.

PHOENIX SUNS LATIN NIGHT JERSEY

Select Extras from the Progression menu. Then choose nba.com from the Jerseys menu. Press ■ and enter LKUTSENFJH.

SAN ANTONIO SPURS LATIN NIGHT JERSEY

Select Extras from the Progression menu. Then choose nba.com from the Jerseys menu. Press ■ and enter JFHSY73MYD.

ST. PATRICK'S DAY JERSEYS

Select Codes from the Features menu and enter uclerehanp.

VALENTINE'S DAY JERSEYS

Select Codes from the Features menu and enter amcnreo.

NBA 2K7

ABA BALL

Select Codes from the Features menu and enter payrespect.

ALL-STAR BALL

Select Codes from the Features menu and enter ply8mia.

MAXIMUM DURABILITY

Select Codes from the Features menu and enter ironman.

UNLIMITED STAMINA

Select Codes from the Features menu and enter norest.

+10 DEFENSIVE AWARENESS

Select Codes from the Features menu and enter getstops.

+10 OFFENSIVE AWARENESS

Select Codes from the Features menu and enter inthezone.

2007 ALL-STAR UNIFORMS

Select Codes from the Features menu and enter syt6cii.

BOBCATS SECONDARY

Select Codes from the Features menu and enter bcb8sta.

JAZZ SECONDARY

Select Codes from the Features menu and enter zjb3lau.

NETS SECONDARY

Select Codes from the Features menu and enter nrd4esj.

WIZARDS SECONDARY

Select Codes from the Features menu and enter zw9idla.

ST. PATRICK'S DAY UNIFORMS
Select Codes from the Features menu and enter tpk7sgn.

VALENTINE'S DAY UNIFORMS
Select Codes from the Features menu and enter vdr5lya.

INTERNATIONAL ALL-STARS
Select Codes from the Features menu and enter tns9roi.

NBA 2K TEAM
Select Codes from the Features menu and enter bestsim.

SUPERSTARS
Select Codes from the Features menu and enter rta1spe

TOPPS 2K SPORTS ALL-STARS
Select Codes from the Features menu and enter topps2ksports.

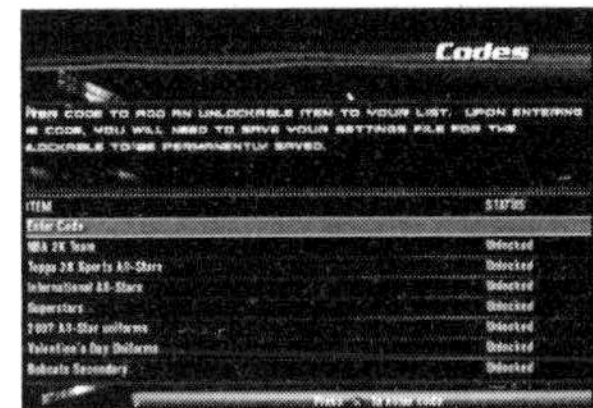

NBA 2K8

ABA BALL
Select Codes from the Features menu and enter Payrespect.

2KSPORTS TEAM
Select Codes from the Features menu and enter 2ksports.

NBA DEVELOPMENT TEAM
Select Codes from the Features menu and enter nba2k.

SUPERSTARS TEAM
Select Codes from the Features menu and enter llmohffaae.

VISUAL CONCEPTS TEAM
Select Codes from the Features menu and enter Vcteam.

2008 ALL STAR NBA JERSEYS
Select Codes from the Features menu and enter haeitgyebs.

BOBCATS RACING JERSEY
Select Codes from the Features menu and enter agtaccsinr.

PACERS SECOND ROAD JERSEY
Select Codes from the Features menu and enter cpares.

NBA 2K9

2K SPORTS TEAM
Select Codes from the Features menu and enter 2ksports.

NBA 2K TEAM
Select Codes from the Features menu and enter nba2k.

SUPERSTARS
Select Codes from the Features menu and enter llmohffaae.

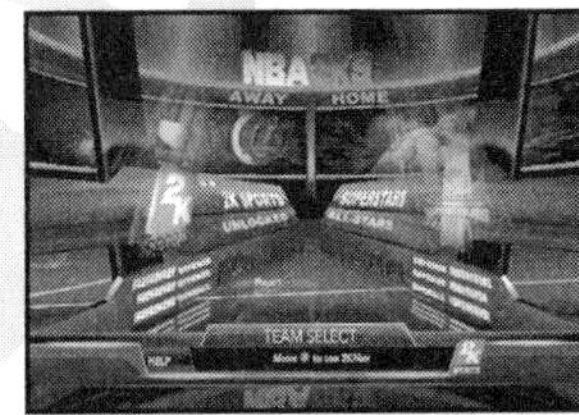

VC TEAM
Select Codes from the Features menu and enter vcteam.

ABA BALL
Select Codes from the Features menu and enter payrespect.

NBA LIVE 07

AIR JORDAN V
Select NBA Codes from My NBA Live 07 and enter PNBBX1EVT5.

AIR JORDAN V
Select NBA Codes from My NBA Live 07 and enter VIR13PC451.

AIR JORDAN V
Select NBA Codes from My NBA Live 07 and enter IB7G8NN91Z.

JORDAN MELO M3
Select NBA Codes from My NBA Live 07 and enter JUL38TC485.

C-BILLUPS ALL-STAR EDITION
Select NBA Codes from My NBA Live 07 and enter BV6877HB9N.

ADIDAS C-BILLUPS VEGAS EDITION
Select NBA Codes from My NBA Live 07 and enter 85NVLDMWS5.

ADIDAS GARNETT BOUNCE ALL-STAR EDITION
Select NBA Codes from My NBA Live 07 and enter HYIOUHCAAN.

ADIDAS GARNETT BOUNCE VEGAS EDITION
Select NBA Codes from My NBA Live 07 and enter KDZ2MQL17W.

ADIDAS GIL-ZERO ALL-STAR EDITION
Select NBA Codes from My NBA Live 07 and enter 23DN1PPOG4.

ADIDAS GIL-ZERO VEGAS EDITION
Select NBA Codes from My NBA Live 07 and enter QQQ3JCUYQ7.

ADIDAS GIL-ZERO MID
Select NBA Codes from My NBA Live 07 and enter 1GSJC8JWRL.

ADIDAS GIL-ZERO MID
Select NBA Codes from My NBA Live 07 and enter 369V6RVU3G.

ADIDAS STEALTH ALL-STAR EDITION
Select NBA Codes from My NBA Live 07 and enter FE454DFJCC.

ADIDAS T-MAC 6 ALL-STAR EDITION
Select NBA Codes from My NBA Live 07 and enter MCJK843NNC.

ADIDAS T-MAC 6 VEGAS EDITION
Select NBA Codes from My NBA Live 07 and enter 84GF7EJG8V.

CHARLOTTE BOBCATS SECOND ROAD JERSEY
Select NBA Codes from My NBA Live 07 and enter WEDX671H7S.

UTAH JAZZ SECOND ROAD JERSEY
Select NBA Codes from My NBA Live 07 and enter VCBI89FK83.

NEW JERSEY NETS SECOND ROAD JERSEY
Select NBA Codes from My NBA Live 07 and enter D4SAA98U5H.

WASHINGTON WIZARDS SECOND ROAD JERSEY
Select NBA Codes from My NBA Live 07 and enter QV93NLKXQC.

EASTERN ALL-STARS 2007 ROAD JERSEY
Select NBA Codes from My NBA Live 07 and enter WOCNW4KL7L.

EASTERN ALL-STARS 2007 HOME JERSEY
Select NBA Codes from My NBA Live 07 and enter 5654ND43N6.

WESTERN ALL-STARS 2007 ROAD JERSEY
Select NBA Codes from My NBA Live 07 and enter XX93BVL20U.

WESTERN ALL-STARS 2007 HOME JERSEY
Select NBA Codes from My NBA Live 07 and enter 993NSKL199.

NBA LIVE 08

ADIDAS GIL-ZERO - ALL-STAR EDITION
Select NBA Codes from My NBA and enter 23DN1PPOG4.

ADIDAS TIM DUNCAN STEALTH - ALL-STAR EDITION
Select NBA Codes from My NBA and enter FE454DFJCC.

NBA LIVE 09

SUPER DUNKS MODE
Use the Sprite vending machine in the practice area and enter spriteslam.

NBA STREET HOMECOURT

ALL TEAMS
At the Main menu, hold R1 + L1 and press Left, Right, Left, Right.

ALL COURTS
At the Main menu, hold R1 + L1 and press Up, Right, Down, Left.

BLACK/RED BALL
At the Main menu, hold R1 + L1 and press Up, Down, Left, Right.

NEED FOR SPEED PROSTREET

$2,000
Select Career and then choose Code Entry. Enter 1MA9X99.

$4,000
Select Career and then choose Code Entry. Enter W2IOLL01.

$8,000
Select Career and then choose Code Entry. Enter L1IS97A1.

$10,000
Select Career and then choose Code Entry. Enter 1MI9K7E1.

$10,000
Select Career and then choose Code Entry. Enter CASHMONEY.

$10,000
Select Career and then choose Code Entry. Enter REGGAME.

AUDI TT
Select Career and then choose Code Entry. Enter ITSABOUTYOU.

CHEVELLE SS
Select Career and then choose Code Entry. Enter HORSEPOWER.

COKE ZERO GOLF GTI
Select Career and then choose Code Entry. Enter COKEZERO.

DODGE VIPER
Select Career and then choose Code Entry. Enter WORLDSLONGESTLASTING.

MITSUBISHI LANCER EVOLUTION
Select Career and then choose Code Entry. Enter MITSUBISHIGOFAR.

UNLOCK ALL BONUSES
Select Career and then choose Code Entry. Enter UNLOCKALLTHINGS.

5 REPAIR MARKERS
Select Career and then choose Code Entry. Enter SAFETYNET.

ENERGIZER VINYL
Select Career and then choose Code Entry. Enter ENERGIZERLITHIUM.

CASTROL SYNTEC VINYL
Select Career and then choose Code Entry. Enter CASTROLSYNTEC. This also gives you $10,000.

NEED FOR SPEED UNDERCOVER

$10,000

Select Secret Codes from the Options menu and enter %%$3/".

DIE-CAST BMW M3 E92

Select Secret Codes from the Options menu and enter)B7@B=.

DIE-CAST LEXUS IS F

Select Secret Codes from the Options menu and enter 0;5M2;.

NEEDFORSPEED.COM LOTUS ELISE

Select Secret Codes from the Options menu and enter -KJ3=E.

DIE-CAST NISSAN 240SX (S13)

Select Secret Codes from the Options menu and enter ?P:COL.

DIE-CAST PORSCHE 911 TURBO

Select Secret Codes from the Options menu and enter >8P:I;.

SHELBY TERLINGUA

Select Secret Codes from the Options menu and enter NeedForSpeedShelbyTerlingua.

DIE-CAST VOLKSWAGEN R32

Select Secret Codes from the Options menu and enter!2ODBJ:.

NHL 08

ALL RBK EDGE JERSEYS

At the RBK Edge Code option, enter h3oyxpwksf8ibcgt.

NHL 2K9

3RD JERSEYS

From the Features menu, enter R6y34bsH52 as a code.

NINJA GAIDEN SIGMA

5 EXTRA MISSIONS IN MISSION MODE.

At the mission mode screen, press Up, Down, Left, Down, Right, Up, □.

THE ORANGE BOX

HALF-LIFE 2

The following codes work for Half-Life 2, Half-Life 2: Episode One, and Half-Life 2: Episode Two.

CHAPTER SELECT

While playing, press Left, Left, Left, Left, L1, Right, Right, Right, Right, R1. Pause the game and select New Game to skip to another chapter.

RESTORE HEALTH (25 POINTS)

While playing, press Up, Up, Down, Down, Left, Right, Left, Right, ○, ✕.

RESTORE AMMO FOR CURRENT WEAPON

While playing, press R1, △, ○, ✕, □, R1, △, □, ✕, ○, R1.

PORTAL

CHAPTER SELECT

While playing, press Left, Left, Left, Left, L1, Right, Right, Right, Right, R1. Pause the game and select New Game to skip to another chapter.

GET A BOX

While playing, press Down, ○, ✕, ○, △, Down, ○, ✕, ○, △.

ENERGY BALL

While playing, press Up, △, △, □, □, ✕, ✕, ○, ○, Up.

PORTAL PLACEMENT ANYWHERE

While playing, press △, ✕, ○, ✕, ○, △, △, ✕, Left, Right.

PORTALGUN ID 0

While playing, press Up, Left, Down, Right, Up, Left, Down, Right, ▲, ▲.

PORTALGUN ID 1

While playing, press Up, Left, Down, Right, Up, Left, Down, Right, ■, ■.

PORTALGUN ID 2

While playing, press Up, Left, Down, Right, Up, Left, Down, Right, ✖, ✖.

PORTALGUN ID 3

While playing, press Up, Left, Down, Right, Up, Left, Down, Right, ●, ●.

UPGRADE PORTALGUN

While playing, press ■, ●, L1, R1, Left, Right, L1, R1, L2, R2.

PRINCE OF PERSIA

SANDS OF TIME PRINCE/FARAH SKINS

Select Skin Manager from the Extras menu. Press ▲ and enter 52585854. This gives you the Sands of Time skin for the Prince and Farah from Sands of Time for the Princess. Access them from the Skin Manager

PRINCE ALTAIR IBN LA-AHAD SKIN

Create an Ubisoft account. Then select "Altair Skin for Prince" to unlock.

RATATOUILLE

Select Gusteau's Shop from the Extras menu. Choose Secrets, select the appropriate code number, and then enter the code. Once the code is entered, select the cheat you want to activate it.

CODE NUMBER	CODE	EFFECT
1	Pieceocake	Very Easy difficulty mode.
2	Myhero	No impact and no damage from enemies.
3	Shielded	No damage from enemies .
4	Spyagent	Move undetected by any enemy.
5	Ilikeonions	Fart every time Remy jumps.
6	Hardfeelings	Head butt when attacking instead of tailswipe.
7	Slumberparty	Multiplayer mode .
8	Gusteauart	All Concept Art .
9	Gusteauship	All four championship modes .
10	Mattelme	All single player and multiplayer minigames.
11	Gusteauvid	All Videos .
12	Gusteaures	All Bonus Artworks.
13	Gusteaudream	All Dream Worlds in Gusteau's Shop.
14	Gusteauslide	All Slides in Gusteau's Shop.
15	Gusteaulevel	All single player minigames.
16	Gusteaucombo	All items in Gusteau's Shop.
17	Gusteaupot	5,000 Gusteau points.
18	Gusteaujack	10,000 Gusteau points.
19	Gusteauomni	50,000 Gusteau points.

RATCHET & CLANK FUTURE: TOOLS OF DESTRUCTION

CHALLENGE MODE

After defeating the game, you can replay it in Challenge Mode with all of Ratchet's current upgraded weapons and armor.

SKILL POINTS

Complete the following objectives to earn skill points. Each one is worth 10 to 40 points and you can use these points to unlock Cheats in the Cheats menu. The list below lists the skill points with a location and description.

SKILL POINT	LOCATION	DESCRIPTION
Smashing Good Time	Cobalia	Destroy all crates and consumer bots in the trade port and gel factory.
I Should Have Gone Down in a Barrel	Cobalia	Jump into each of the two gel waterfall areas in Cobalia gel factory.
Giant Hunter	Cobalia	Kill several Basilisk Leviathans in the Cobalia wilderness.
Wrench Ninja 3	Stratus City	Use only the Omniwrench to get through the level to the Robo-Wings segment.
We Don't Need No Stinkin' Bridges!	Stratus City	Cross the tri-pad sequence using gel-cube bounces.
Surface-to-Air Plasma Beasts	Stratus City	Take out several flying targets using a specific weapon.
Been Around	Stratus City	Take off from every Robo-wing launch pad in Stratus City.
Collector's Addition	Voron	Be very thorough in your collection of goodies.
Minesweeper	Voron	Clear out a bunch of mines.
What's That, R2?	Voron	Barrel roll multiple times.
I Think I'm Gonna Be Sick	IFF	Ride the ferris wheel for 5 loops without getting off or taking damage.
Fast and the Fire-ious	IFF	Use the Charge Boots to cross the bridge to the arena without being burned.
One Heckuva Peephole	IFF	Return after receiving the Geo-laser and complete the Geo-laser setup.
Alphabet City	Apogee	Teleport to each of the six asteroids in alphabetical order.
Knock You Down to Size	Apogee	Wrench Slam 5 centipedes.
Dancin' with the Stars	Apogee	Make 5 enemies dance at once on an asteroid.
Taste o' Yer Own Medicine	Pirate Base	Destroy all of the Shooter Pirates with the Combuster.
Preemptive Strike	Pirate Base	Destroy all of the "sleeping bats" while they are still sleeping.
It's Mutant-E Cap'n!	Pirate Base	Change 5 pirates into penguins in one blast.
You Sunk My Battleship!	Rakar	Shoot down a large percentage of the big destroyers.
Pretty Lights	Rakar	Complete the level without destroying any of the snatchers that fire beams at Ratchet.
I've Got Places To Be	Rakar	Destroy the boss in under 2:30.
The Consumer Is Not (Always) Right	Rykan V	Destroy a bunch of consumer bots in the level.
Live Strong	Rykan V	Complete the Gryo Cycle in 1:45.
Untouchable	Rykan V	Don't take damage in the Gyro-Cycle.
It Sounded Like a Freight Train	Sargasso	Get 10 Swarmers in one tornado.
Head Examiner	Sargasso	Land on all of the dinosaur heads in Sargasso.
Extinction	Sargasso	Kill all of the Sargasso Predators.
Lombaxes Don't Like Cold	Iris	Break all the breakable icicles.
Mow Down Ho-Down	Iris	Use turrets to destroy 10 dancing pirates.
Dancin' on the Ceiling	Zordoom	Successfully use a Groovitron while on a Magboot surface.
Seared Ahi	Zordoom	Use the Pyroblaster on 3 Drophid creatures after freeing them from their robotic suits.
Shocking Ascent	Zordoom	Destroy all enemies on the elevator using just the Shock Ravager.
Expert Marksman	Borag	Kill 75% of all of the enemies.
Can't Touch This	Borag	Don't take damage before fighting the boss.
Pyoo, Pyoo!	Borag	Complete the level without secondary fire.

SKILL POINT	LOCATION	DESCRIPTION
Dead Aim	Kerchu	Destroy several destructible towers while on the pirate barge.
Fire With Fire	Kerchu	Kill a few Kerchu Flamethrowers with the Pyro Blaster.
Rocket Jump	Kerchu	Successfully jump over a row of three rockets while on the grindrail during the boss fight in Kerchu City.
Your Friendly Neighborhood...	Slag Fleet	Destroy 5 enemies while on the grav ramp before Slag's ship.
Turret Times Two	Slag Fleet	Destroy at least 2 pirates with each turret in the level.
Six Gun Salute	Slag Fleet	Get six pirates in a row to salute Ratchet while in the Pirate Disguise.
Gotta Catch 'Em All	Cragmite Ruins	Hit all Cragmite soldiers with the Mag-Net Launcher.
Ratchet and Goliath	Cragmite Ruins	Destroy multiple walkers using just the Nano-Swarmers.
Ratchet &...Not Clank?!	Cragmite Ruins	Use Mr. Zurkon in Cragmite's Ratchet-only segment.
Stay Still So I Can Shoot You!	Meridian	Use strafe-flip 10 times while fighting the Cragmite soldiers.
Now Boarding...	Meridian	Complete the Gyro-Cycle in 55 seconds.
Low Flying Howls	Meridian	Fly under an electrified barrier in the Robo-wings segment.
Extreme Alien Makeover	Fastoon2	Turn 10 Cragmites into penguins.
Empty Bag o' Tricks	Fastoon2	Complete the level without using any devices.
Nowhere to Hide	Fastoon2	Destroy every piece of breakable cover.
No, Up Your Arsenal	Global	Upgrade every weapon to the max.
Roflcopter	Global	Turn enemies into penguins, then use the Visicopter to destroy the penguins.
Stir Fry	Global	Kill 2 different enemy types using the Shock Ravager while they are trapped in a tornado.
Golden Children	Overall	Find all of the Gold Bolts.
Sacagawea	Global	Complete all of the maps 100%, leaving no area undiscovered.
Cheapskate	Global	Purchase a single Combustor round.
Everybody Dance Now	Global	Make every type of enemy in the game dance.
F5 on the Fujita Scale	Global	Pick up more than 10 enemies with one tornado.
Chorus line	Global	Get 10+ enemies to dance together.
Happy Feet	Global	Get several penguins to dance on-screen.
Disco Inferno	Global	Use the Groovitron followed by the Pyro Blaster.
Bolts in the Bank	Global	Sell a bunch of Leviathan Souls to the Smuggler.
It's Like the North Pole Here	Global	Have at least 12-15 enemies and/or citizens turned into penguins at one time.
Say Hello to My Little Friend	Global	Kill 15 enemies with one RYNO shot.
For the Hoard!	Global	Get every item.
Promoted to Inspector	Global	Get every gadget.
Global Thermonuclear War	Global	Get every weapon.
It's Even Better the Second Time!	Global	Complete Challenge Mode.
The Hardest of Core	Global	Get all skill points and everything else in the game.

RESISTANCE: FALL OF MAN

HARD DIFFICULTY

Complete the game on Medium difficulty.

SUPERHUMAN DIFFICULTY

Complete the game on Hard difficulty.

SKILL POINTS

You can access the Skill Points and Rewards menus during gameplay by pressing START to access the Pause Menu, then selecting EXTRAS.

ENEMIES

NAME	LEVEL ACQUIRED	DESCRIPTION
Hybrid	The Gauntlet	After defeating first set of Hybrids.
Leaper	A Lone Survivor	After defeating first few Leapers.
Crawler	A Lone Survivor	After the cinematic and FPNICS.
Menial	Fate Worse Than Death	After the first room.
Cocoon	Conversion	At the third checkpoint.
Carrier	Fate Worse Than Death	At the window when you first see the Carriers.
Howler	Path of Least Resistance	After defeating the Howlers at the end of the level.
Steelhead	Cathedral	After defeating the first two Steelheads in the church.
Titan	Conduits	After defeating the Titan at the beginning of Conduits.
Slipskull	No Way Out	After defeating all three Slipskulls in the burrower room.
Leaper Pod	No Way Out or 61	After finding the Leaper Pods for the first time.
Gray Jack	Angel	After the cryo room.
Hardfang	Evacuation	After defeating the first Hardfang in the cafeteria.
Roller	Into the Depths	After defeating the Rollers in the room with the tunnel in the floor.
Widowmaker	Ice and Iron	After defeating the first Widowmaker.
Hybrid 2.0	Angel's Lair	After the first wave of Hybrids in the node.
Angel	Angel's Lair	After defeating the first Angel on the bridge.

VEHICLES

NAME	LEVEL ACQUIRED	DESCRIPTION
Hawk	The Gauntlet	Player automatically starts with this.
Kingfisher	Path of Least Resistance	At the start of the level.
Sabertooth	A Lone Survivor	After getting inside the tank.
Dropship	Hunted Down	After spotting a Dropship in the parking lot area.
Stalker	Outgunned	After spotting the first one in Outgunned.
Burrower	No Way Out	After spotting the first one in No Way Out.
Lynx	Common Ground	After getting inside the Lynx.
Goliath	Giant Slayer	After spotting the first one.

WEAPONS—1ST PLAYTHROUGH

NAME	LEVEL ACQUIRED	DESCRIPTION
M5A2 Carbine	The Gauntlet	Automatically unlocked at start of the game.
Frag Grenade	The Gauntlet	Automatically unlocked at start of the game.
Bullseye	The Gauntlet	In the alleyway after checkpoint 2.
Shotgun	Fate Worse Than Death or 32 or 40	Fate Worse Than Death: Behind the stairs in the outdoor area. Hunted Down: Behind the bar. Hunted Down: In the docks area. Path of Least Resistance: Forced here on the stairs between hill 1 and 2.
Auger	Cathedral	After defeating the first two advanced Hybrids.
Fareye	Conduits	After defeating the large Hybrid and reaching checkpoint 1.
Hailstorm	Search and Rescue	After leaving the first area.
Sapper	A Disturbing Discovery	At the back of the first mech factory.
LAARK	In a Darker Place	On the ground in the first room.
Bullseye Mark 2	Angel's Lair	After leaving the first room and going into the node.

WEAPONS—2ND PLAYTHROUGH

NAME	LEVEL ACQUIRED	DESCRIPTION
Reapers	The Gauntlet	Inside the house at the bottom of the hill.
Backlash Grenade	Cathedral	After crossing alley just past the cathedral; it's the first room on the left.
Arc Charger	No Way Out	At the end of the long hallway prior to the burrower.
L11-Dragon	Evacuation	Before the first elevator leading to the hangar.
Splitter	A Desperate Gambit	At checkpoint 1, near the big windows.

LOCATIONS

NAME	LEVEL ACQUIRED	DESCRIPTION
York	The Gauntlet	Unlocked at the start of the level.
Grimsby	Fate Worse Than Death	Unlocked at the start of the level.
Manchester	Path of Least Resistance	Unlocked at the start of the level.
Nottingham	Into the Fire	Unlocked at the start of the level.
Cheshire	No Way Out	Unlocked at the start of the level.
Somerset	Search and Rescue	Unlocked at the start of the level.
Bristol	Devil at the Door	Unlocked at the start of the level.
Bracknell	Into the Depths	Unlocked at the start of the level.
London	A Desperate Gambit	Unlocked at the start of the level.
Thames	Burning Bridges	Unlocked at the start of the level.
Tower	Angel's Lair	Unlocked at the start of the level.

REWARDS

NAME	HOW TO UNLOCK
Concept Art Pack 1	10 points
Concept Art Pack 2	20 points
The Mighty Wrench - Gives allies wrench	40 points
Flip Levels	70 points
Clank Backpacks	100 points
MP Mechanic Skin	126 points
MP Soldier Skin	Beat game on Superhuman mode.
MP Soldier head skin	Beat game on Superhuman mode and collect all Skill Points.
Movie player	Beat game once.

ROBERT LUDLUM'S THE BOURNE CONSPIRACY

AUTOMATIC SHOTGUNS REPLACE SIMI-AUTOS

Select Cheats from the Main menu, press ●, and then enter alwaysanobjective.

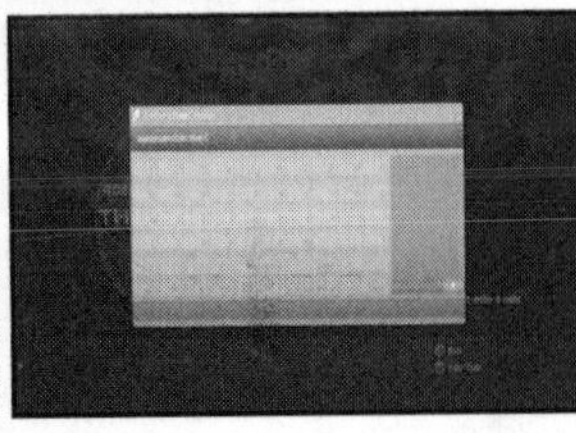

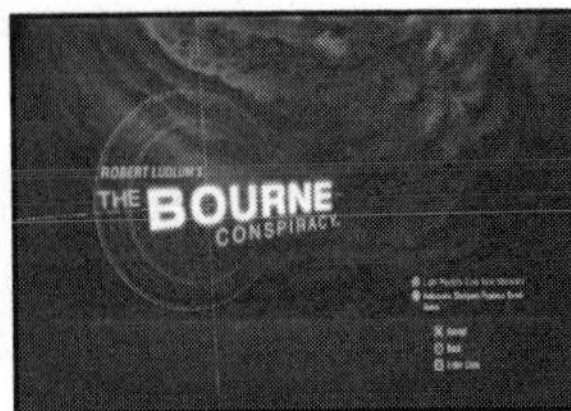

LIGHT MACHINE GUNS HAVE SILENCERS

Select Enter Code from the Cheats screen and enter whattheymakeyougive.

EXTRAS UNLOCKED – CONCEPT ART

Select Enter Code from the Cheats screen and enter lastchancemarie. Select Concept Art from the Extras menu.

EXTRAS UNLOCKED – MUSIC TRACKS

Select Enter Code from the Cheats screen and enter jasonbourneisdead. This unlocks Treadstone Appointment and Manheim Suite in the Music Selector found in the Extras menu.

ROCK BAND

ALL SONGS

At the Title screen, press Red, Yellow, Blue, Red, Red, Blue, Blue, Red, Yellow, Blue. Saving and all network features are disabled with this code.

TRANSPARENT INSTRUMENTS

Complete the hall of fame concert with that instrument.

GOLD INSTRUMENT

Complete the solo tour with that instrument.

SILVER INSTRUMENT

Complete the bonus tour with that instrument.

ROCK BAND 2

Most of these codes disable saving, achievements, and Xbox LIVE play. The first code listed is with the guitar and the second is an alternative using a controller.

UNLOCK ALL SONGS

Select Modify Game from the Extras menu, choose Enter Unlock Code and press Red, Yellow, Blue, Red, Red, Blue, Blue, Red, Yellow, Blue or ●, ▲, ■, ●, ●, ■, ■, ●, ▲, ■. Toggle this cheat on or off from the Modify Game menu.

SELECT VENUE SCREEN

Select Modify Game from the Extras menu, choose Enter Unlock Code and press Blue, Orange, Orange, Blue, Yellow, Blue, Orange, Orange, Blue, Yellow or ■, L1, L1, ■, ▲, ■, L1, L1, ■, ▲. Toggle this cheat on or off from the Modify Game menu.

NEW VENUES ONLY

Select Modify Game from the Extras menu, choose Enter Unlock Code and press Red, Red, Red, Red, Yellow, Yellow, Yellow, Yellow or ● (x4), ▲ (x4). Toggle this cheat on or off from the Modify Game menu.

PLAY THE GAME WITHOUT A TRACK

Select Modify Game from the Extras menu, choose Enter Unlock Code and press Blue, Blue, Red, Red, Yellow, Yellow, Blue, Blue or ■, ■, ●, ●, ▲, ▲, ■, ■. Toggle this cheat on or off from the Modify Game menu.

AWESOMENESS DETECTION

Select Modify Game from the Extras menu, choose Enter Unlock Code and press Yellow, Blue, Orange, Yellow, Blue, Orange, Yellow, Blue, Orange or ▲, ■, L1, ▲, ■, L1, ▲, ■, L1. Toggle this cheat on or off from the Modify Game menu.

STAGE MODE

Select Modify Game from the Extras menu, choose Enter Unlock Code and press Blue, Yellow, Red, Blue, Yellow, Red, Blue, Yellow, Red or ▲, ●, ■, ▲, ●, ■, ▲, ●. Toggle this cheat on or off from the Modify Game menu.

ROCK REVOLUTION

ALL CHARACTERS

At the Main menu, press ●, ■, ●, ■, ●, ■, ●, ▲, ■.

ALL VENUES

At the Main menu, press ■, ●, ▲, ●, ■, ●, ▲, ■, ▲.

SAINTS ROW 2

CHEAT CODES

Select Dial from the Phone menu and enter these numbers followed by the Call button. Activate the cheats by selecting Cheats from the Phone menu. Enabling a cheat prevents the acquisition of Achievements

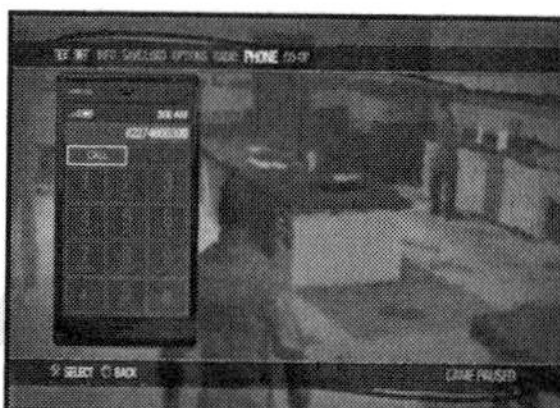

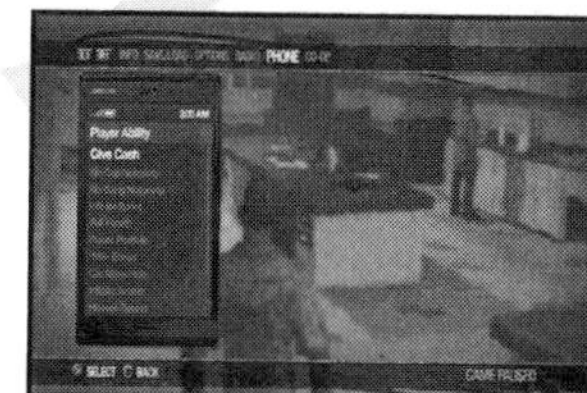

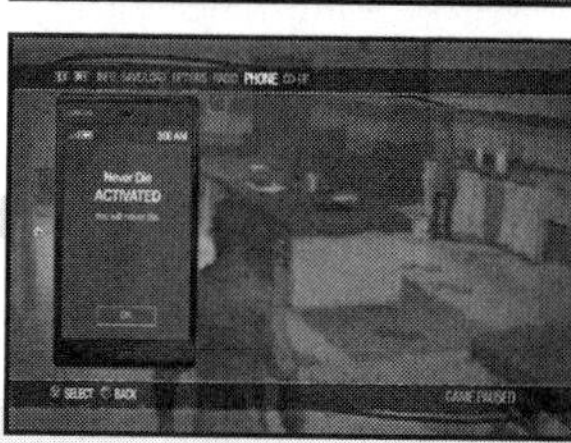

PLAYER ABILITY

Give Cash	#2274666399
No Cop Notoriety	#50
No Gang Notoriety	#51
Infinite Sprint	#6
Full Health	#1
Player Pratfalls	#5
Milk Bones	#3
Car Mass Hole	#2
Infinite Ammo	#11
Heaven Bound	#12
Add Police Notoriety	#4
Add Gang Notoriety	#35
Never Die	#36
Unlimited Clip	#9

VEHICLES

Repair Car	#1056
Venom Classic	#1079
Five-0	#1055
Stilwater Municipal	#1072
Baron	#1047
Attrazione	#1043
Zenith	#1081
Vortex	#1080
Phoenix	#1064
Bootlegger	#1049
Raycaster	#1068
Hollywood	#1057
Justice	#1058
Compton	#1052
Eiswolf	#1053
Taxi	#1074
Ambulance	#1040
Backhoe	#1045
Bagboy	#1046
Rampage	#1067
Reaper	#1069
The Job	#1075
Quota	#1066
FBI	#1054
Mag	#1060
Bulldog	#1050
Quasar	#1065
Titan	#1076
Varsity	#1078
Anchor	#1041
Blaze	#1044
Sabretooth	#804
Sandstorm	#805
Kaneda	#801
Widowmaker	#806
Kenshin	#802
Melbourne	#803
Miami	#826
Python	#827
Hurricane	#825
Shark	#828
Skipper	#829
Mongoose	#1062
Superiore	#1073
Tornado	#713
Horizon	#711
Wolverine	#714
Snipes 57	#712
Bear	#1048
Toad	#1077
Kent	#1059
Oring	#1063
Longhauler	#1061
Atlasbreaker	#1042
Septic Avenger	#1070
Shaft	#1071
Bulldozer	#1051

WEAPONS

AR-50	#923
K6	#935

VEHICLES CONT.

GDHC	#932
NR4	#942
44	#921
Tombstone	#956
T3K	#954
VICE9	#957
AS14 Hammer	#925
12 Gauge	#920
SKR-9	#951
McManus 2010	#938
Baseball Bat	#926
Knife	#936
Molotov	#940
Grenade	#933
Nightstick	#941
Pipebomb	#945
RPG	#946
Crowbar	#955
Pimp Cane	#944
AR200	#922
AR-50/Grenade Launcher	#924
Chainsaw	#927
Fire Extinguisher	#928
Flamethrower	#929
Flashbang	#930
GAL43	#931
Kobra	#934
Machete	#937
Mini-gun	#939
Pepperspray	#943
Annihilator RPG	#947
Samurai Sword	#948
Satchel Charge	#949
Shock Paddles	#950
Sledgehammer	#952
Stungun	#953
XS-2 Ultimax	#958
Pimp Slap	#969

WEATHER

Clear Skies	#78669
Heavy Rain	#78666
Light Rain	#78668
Overcast	#78665
Time Set Midnight	#2400
Time Set Noon	#1200
Wrath Of God	#666

WORLD

Super Saints	#8
Super Explosions	#7
Evil Cars	#16
Pedestrian War	#19
Drunk Pedestrians	#15
Raining Pedestrians	#20
Low Gravity	#18

SEGA SUPERSTARS TENNIS

UNLOCK CHARACTERS

Complete the following missions to unlock the corresponding character.

CHARACTER	COMPLETE THIS MISSION
Alex Kidd	Mission 1 of Alex Kidd's World
Amy Rose	Mission 2 of Sonic the Hedgehog's World
Gilius	Mission 1 of Golden Axe's World
Gum	Mission 12 of Jet Grind Radio's World
Meemee	Mission 8 of Super Monkey Ball's World
Pudding	Mission 1 of Space Channel 5's World
Reala	Mission 2 of NiGHTs' World
Shadow The Hedgehog	Mission 14 of Sonic the Hedgehog's World

SILENT HILL: HOMECOMING

YOUNG ALEX COSTUME

At the Title screen, press Up, Up, Down, Down, Left, Right, Left, Right, ●.

THE SIMPSONS GAME

After unlocking the following, the outfits can be changed at the downstairs closet in the Simpson's house. The Trophies can be viewed at different locations in the house: Bart's room, Lisa's room, Marge's room, and the garage.

BART'S OUTFITS AND TROPHIES (POSTER COLLECTION)

At the Main menu, press Right, Left, ■, ■, ▲, R3.

HOMER'S OUTFITS AND TROPHIES (BEER BOTTLE COLLECTION)

At the Main menu, press Left, Right, ▲, ▲, ■, L3.

LISA'S OUTFITS AND TROPHIES (DOLLS)

At the Main menu, press ■, ▲, ■, ■, ■, ▲, L3.

MARGE'S OUTFITS AND TROPHIES (HAIR PRODUCTS)

At the Main menu, press ▲, ■, ▲, ▲, ■, R3.

SKATE

BEST BUY CLOTHES

At the Main menu, press Up, Down, Left, Right, ■, R1, ▲, L1.

SKATE 2

BIG BLACK

Select Enter Cheat from the Extras menu and enter letsdowork.

3D MODE

Select Enter Cheat from the Extras menu and enter strangeloops. Use glasses to view in 3D.

SOCOM: U.S. NAVY SEALS CONFRONTATION

AMELI MACHINE GUN

Select Spain as your clan country.

FAMAS G2 ASSAULT RIFLE

Select France as your clan country.

GMP SUBMACHINE GUN

Select Germany as your clan country.

IW-80 A2 ASSAULT RIFLE

Select U.K. as your clan country.

SCFR-LW ASSAULT RIFLE

Select U.S. as your clan country.

SOLDIER OF FORTUNE: PAYBACK

ACR-2 SNIPER RIFLE

At the difficulty select, press Up, Up, Down, Left, Right, Right, Down.

STAR WARS: THE FORCE UNLEASHED

CHEAT CODES

Pause the game and select Input Code. Here you can enter the following codes. Activating any of the following cheat codes will disable some unlockables, and you will be unable to save your progress.

CHEAT	CODE
All Force Powers at Max Power	KATARN
All Force Push Ranks	EXARKUN
All Saber Throw Ranks	ADEGAN
All Repulse Ranks	DATHOMIR
All Saber Crystals	HURRIKANE
All Talents	JOCASTA
Deadly Saber	LIGHTSABER

COMBOS

Pause the game and select Input Code. Here you can enter the following codes. Activating any of the following cheat codes will disable some unlockables, and you will be unable to save your progress.

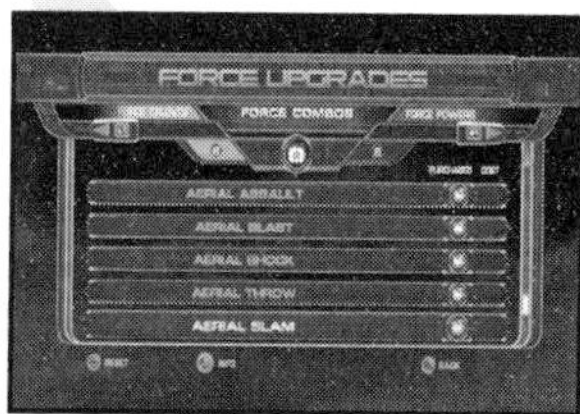

COMBO	CODE
All Combos	MOLDYCROW
Aerial Ambush	VENTRESS
Aerial Assault	EETHKOTH
Aerial Blast	YADDLE
Impale	BRUTALSTAB
Lightning Bomb	MASSASSI
Lightning Grenade	RAGNOS
Saber Slam	PLOKOON
Saber Sling	KITFISTO
Sith Saber Flurry	LUMIYA
Sith Slash	DARAGON
Sith Throw	SAZEN
New Combo	FREEDON
New Combo	MARAJADE

ALL DATABANK ENTRIES

Pause the game and select Input Code. Enter OSSUS.

MIRRORED LEVEL

Pause the game and select Input Code. Enter MINDTRICK. Re-enter the code to return level to normal.

SITH MASTER DIFFICULTY

Pause the game and select Input Code. Enter SITHSPAWN.

COSTUMES

Pause the game and select Input Code. Here you can enter the following codes.

COSTUME	CODE
All Costumes	SOHNDANN
Bail Organa	VICEROY
Ceremonial Jedi Robes	DANTOOINE
Drunken Kota	HARDBOILED
Emperor	MASTERMIND
Incinerator Trooper	PHOENIX
Jedi Adventure Robe	HOLOCRON
Kashyyyk Trooper	TK421GREEN
Kota	MANDALORE
Master Kento	WOOKIEE
Proxy	PROTOTYPE
Scout Trooper	FERRAL
Shadow Trooper	BLACKHOLE
Sith Stalker Armor	KORRIBAN
Snowtrooper	SNOWMAN
Stormtrooper	TK421WHITE
Stormtrooper Commander	TK421BLUE

STREET FIGHTER IV

ALTERNATE STAGES

At the stage select, hold L1 or R1 and select a stage.

STUNTMAN IGNITION

3 PROPS IN STUNT CREATOR MODE

Select Cheats from Extras and enter COOLPROP.

ALL ITEMS UNLOCKED FOR CONSTRUCTION MODE

Select Cheats from Extras and enter NOBLEMAN.

MVX SPARTAN

Select Cheats from Extras and enter fastride.

ALL CHEATS

Select Cheats from Extras and enter Wearefrozen. This unlocks the following cheats: Slo-mo Cool, Thrill Cam, Vision Switcher, Nitro Addiction, Freaky Fast, and Ice Wheels.

ALL CHEATS

Select Cheats from Extras and enter Kungfoopete.

ICE WHEELS CHEAT

Select Cheats from Extras and enter IceAge.

NITRO ADDICTION CHEAT

Select Cheats from Extras and enter TheDuke.

VISION SWITCHER CHEAT

Select Cheats from Extras and enter GFXMODES.

SUPER PUZZLE FIGHTER II TURBO HD REMIX

PLAY AS AKUMA
At the character select, highlight Hsien-Ko and press Down.

PLAY AS DAN
At the character select, highlight Donovan and press Down.

PLAY AS DEVILOT
At the character select, highlight Morrigan and press Down.

PLAY AS ANITA
At the character select, hold L1 + R1 and choose Donovan.

PLAY AS HSIEN-KO'S TALISMAN
At the character select, hold L1 + R1 and choose Hsien-Ko.

PLAY AS MORRIGAN AS A BAT
At the character select, hold L1 + R1 and choose Morrigan.

SUPER STREET FIGHTER II TURBO HD REMIX

The following codes give you the classic fighters in Classic Arcade Mode. Select the character, quickly enter the given code, and select him/her again.

CLASSIC BALROG
Right, Left, Left, Right

CLASSIC BLANKA
Left, Right (x3)

CLASSIC CAMMY
Up, Up, Down, Down

CLASSIC CHUN-LI
Down (x3), Up

CLASSIC DEE JAY
Down, Down, Up, Up

CLASSIC DHALSIM
Down, Up (x3)

CLASSIC E. HONDA
Up (x3), Down

CLASSIC FEI LONG
Left, Left, Right, Right

CLASSIC GUILE
Up, Down (x3)

CLASSIC KEN
Left (x3), Right

CLASSIC M. BISON
Down, Up, Up, Down

CLASSIC RYU
Right (x3), Left

CLASSIC SAGAT
Up, Down (x3), Up

CLASSIC T. HAWK
Right, Right, Left, Left

CLASSIC VEGA
Left, Right, Right, Left

CLASSIC ZANGIEF
Left, Right (x3)

SURF'S UP

ALL CHAMPIONSHIP LOCATIONS
Select Cheat Codes from the Extras menu and enter FREEVISIT.

ALL LEAF SLIDE STAGES
Select Cheat Codes from the Extras menu and enter GOINGDOWN.

ALL MULTIPLAYER LEVELS
Select Cheat Codes from the Extras menu and enter MULTIPASS.

ALL BOARDS
Select Cheat Codes from the Extras menu and enter MYPRECIOUS.

ASTRAL BOARD
Select Cheat Codes from the Extras menu and enter ASTRAL.

MONSOON BOARD
Select Cheat Codes from the Extras menu and enter MONSOON.

TINE SHOCKWAVE BOARD
Select Cheat Codes from the Extras menu and enter TINYSHOCKWAVE.

ALL CHARACTER CUSTOMIZATIONS
Select Cheat Codes from the Extras menu and enter TOPFASHION.

PLAY AS ARNOLD
Select Cheat Codes from the Extras menu and enter TINYBUTSTRONG.

PLAY AS ELLIOT
Select Cheat Codes from the Extras menu and enter SURPRISEGUEST.

PLAY AS GEEK
Select Cheat Codes from the Extras menu and enter SLOWANDSTEADY.

PLAY AS TANK EVANS
Select Cheat Codes from the Extras menu and enter IMTHEBEST.

PLAY AS TATSUHI KOBAYASHI
Select Cheat Codes from the Extras menu and enter KOBAYASHI.

PLAY AS ZEKE TOPANGA
Select Cheat Codes from the Extras menu and enter THELEGEND.

ALL VIDEOS AND SPEN GALLERY
Select Cheat Codes from the Extras menu and enter WATCHAMOVIE.

ART GALLERY
Select Cheat Codes from the Extras menu and enter NICEPLACE.

TIGER WOODS PGA TOUR 08

ALL COURSES
Select Password from EA Sports Extras and enter greensfees.

ALL GOLFERS
Select Password from EA Sports Extras and enter allstars.

TIMESHIFT

KRONE IN MULTIPLAYER
Select Multiplayer from the Options menu. Highlight Model and press △ to get to Krone. Press Y and enter RXYMCPENCJ.

TOMB RAIDER: UNDERWORLD

BULLETPROOF LARA
During a game, hold L2 and press ✕, R2, △, R2, □, L1.

ONE-SHOT KILL
During a game, hold L2 and press △, ✕, △, □, L1, ○.

SHOW ENEMY HEALTH
During a game, hold L2 and press □, ○, ✕, L1, R2, △.

TOM CLANCY'S ENDWAR

EUROPEAN ENFORCER CORPS
Go to Community and Extras, highlight VIP and press △. Enter EUCA20.

RUSSIAN SPETZNAZ BATTALION
Go to Community and Extras, highlight VIP and press △. Enter SPZT17.

RUSSIAN SPETZNAZ GUARD BRIGADE
Go to Community and Extras, highlight VIP and press △. Enter SPZA39.

US JOINT STRIKE FORCE BATTALION
Go to Community and Extras, highlight VIP and press △. Enter JSFA35.

TOM CLANCY'S HAWX

A-12 AVENGER II
At the hangar, hold L2 and press □, L1, □, R1, △, □.

F-18 HARV
At the hangar, hold L2 and press L1, △, L1, △, L1, □.

FB-22 STRIKE RAPTOR
At the hangar, hold L2 and press R1, □, R1, □, R1, △.

TOM CLANCY'S RAINBOW SIX VEGAS

SUPER RAGDOLL

Pause the game, hold L2 and press X, X, Circle, Circle, Square, Square, Triangle, Triangle, X, Circle, Square, Triangle.

THIRD PERSON MODE

Pause the game, hold L2 and press Square, Circle, Square, Circle, L3, L3, Triangle, X, Triangle, X, R3, R3.

BIG HEAD

Pause the game, hold L2 and press Circle, Square, X, Triangle, L3, Triangle, X, Square, Circle, R3.

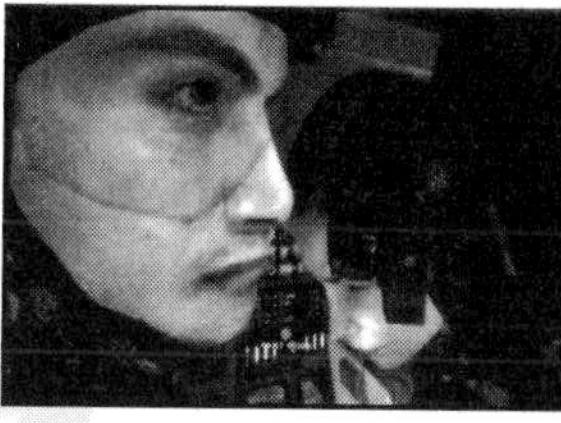

ONE HIT KILLS

Pause the game, hold L2 and press L3, R3, L3, R3, X, Circle, L3, R3, L3, R3 Square, Triangle.

TOM CLANCY'S RAINBOW SIX VEGAS 2

GI JOHN DOE MODE

Pause the game, hold the R1 and press L3, L3, X, R3, R3, Circle, L3, L3, Square, R3, R3, Triangle.

SUPER RAGDOLL

Pause the game, hold the R1 and press X, X, Circle, Circle, Square, Square, Triangle, Triangle, X, Circle, Square, Triangle.

THIRD PERSON MODE

Pause the game, hold the R1 and press Square, Circle, Square, Circle, L3, L3, Triangle, X, Triangle, X, R3, R3.

TAR-21 ASSAULT RIFLE

At the Character Customization screen, hold R1 and press Down, Down, Up, Up, Square, Circle, Square, Circle, Triangle, Up, Up, Triangle.

MULTIPLAYER MAP: COMCAST EVENT

Select Extras from the Main menu. Choose Comcast Gift and enter Comcast Faster.

TONY HAWK'S PROJECT 8

SPONSOR ITEMS

As you progress through Career mode and move up the rankings, you gain sponsors and each comes with its own Create-a-skater item.

RANK REQUIRED	CAS ITEM UNLOCKED
Rank 040	Adio Kenny V2 Shoes
Rank 050	Quiksilver_Hoody_3
Rank 060	Birdhouse Tony Hawk Deck
Rank 080	Vans No Skool Gothic Shoes
Rank 100	Volcom Scallero Jacket
Rank 110	eS Square One Shoes
Rank 120	Almost Watch What You Say Deck
Rank 140	DVS Adage Shoe
Rank 150	Element Illuminate Deck
Rank 160	Etnies Sheckler White Lavender Shoes
Complete Skateshop Goal	Stereo Soundwave Deck

SKATERS

All of the skaters, except for Tony Hawk, must be unlocked by completing challenges in the Career Mode. They are useable in Free Skate and 2 Player modes.

SKATER	HOW TO UNLOCK
Tony Hawk	Always Unlocked
Lyn-z Adams Hawkins	Complete Pro Challenge
Bob Burquist	Complete Pro Challenge
Dustin Dollin	Complete Pro Challenge
Nyjah Huston	Complete Pro Challenge
Bam Margera	Complete Pro Challenge
Rodney Mullen	Complete Pro Challenge
Paul Rodriguez	Complete Pro Challenge
Ryan Sheckler	Complete Pro Challenge
Daewon Song	Complete Pro Challenge
Mike Vallely	Complete Pro Challenge
Stevie Willams	Complete Pro Challenge
Travis Barker	Complete Pro Challenge
Kevin Staab	Complete Pro Challenge
Zombie	Complete Pro Challenge
Christaian Hosoi	Rank #1
Jason Lee	Complete Final Tony Hawk Goal
Photographer	Unlock Shops
Security Guard	Unlock School
Bum	Unlock Car Factory
Beaver Mascot	Unlock High School
Real Estate Agent	Unlock Downtown
Filmer	Unlock High School
Skate Jam Kid	Rank #4
Dad	Rank #1
Colonel	All Gaps
Nerd	Complete School Spirit Goal

CHEAT CODES

Select Cheat Codes from the Options and enter the following codes. In game you can access some codes from the Options menu.

CHEAT CODE	RESULTS
plus44	Unlocks Travis Barker
hohohosoi	Unlocks Christian Hosoi
notmono	Unlocks Jason Lee
mixitup	Unlocks Kevin Staab
strangefellows	Unlocks Dad & Skater Jam Kid
themedia	Unlocks Photog Girl & Filmer
militarymen	Unlocks Colonel & Security Guard
Cheat Code	Results
jammypack	Unlocks Always Special
balancegalore	Unlocks Perfect Rail
frontandback	Unlocks Perect Manual
shellshock	Unlocks Unlimited Focus
shescaresme	Unlocks Big Realtor
birdhouse	Unlocks Inkblot deck
allthebest	Full stats
needaride	All decks unlocked and free, except for Inkblot Deck and Gamestop Deck
yougotitall	All specials unlocked and in player's special list and set as owned in skate shop
wearelosers	Unlocks Nerd and a Bum
manineedadate	Unlocks Beaver Mascot
suckstobedead	Unlocks Officer Dick
HATEDANDPROUD	Unlocks the Vans item

TONY HAWK'S PROVING GROUND

Select Cheat Codes from the Options and enter the following cheats. Some codes need to be enabled by selecting Cheats from the Options during a game.

UNLOCK	CHEAT
Unlocks Boneman	CRAZYBONEMAN
Unlocks Bosco	MOREMILK
Unlocks Cam	NOTACAMERA
Unlocks Cooper	THECOOP
Unlocks Eddie X	SKETCHY
Unlocks El Patinador	PILEDRIVER
Unlocks Eric	FLYAWAY
Unlocks Mad Dog	RABBIES
Unlocks MCA	INTERGALACTIC
Unlocks Mel	NOTADUDE
Unlocks Rube	LOOKSSMELLY
Unlocks Spence	DAPPER
Unlocks Shayne	MOVERS
Unlocks TV Producer	SHAKER
Unlock FDR	THEPREZPARK
Unlock Lansdowne	THELOCALPARK
Unlock Air & Space Museum	THEINDOORPARK
Unlocks all Fun Items	OVERTHETOP
Unlocks all CAS items	GIVEMESTUFF
Unlocks all Decks	LETSGOSKATE
Unlock all Game Movies	WATCHTHIS
Unlock all Lounge Bling Items	SWEETSTUFF
Unlock all Lounge Themes	LAIDBACKLOUNGE
Unlock all Rigger Pieces	IMGONNABUILD
Unlock all Video Editor Effects	TRIPPY
Unlock all Video Editor Overlays	PUTEMONTOP
All specials unlocked and in player's special list	LOTSOFTRICKS
Full Stats	BEEFEDUP
Give player +50 skill points	NEEDSHELP

The following cheats lock you out of the Leaderboards:

UNLOCK	CHEAT
Unlocks Perfect Manual	STILLAINTFALLIN
Unlocks Perfect Rail	AINTFALLIN
Unlock Super Check	BOOYAH
Unlocks Unlimited Focus	MYOPIC
Unlock Unlimited Slash Grind	SUPERSLASHIN
Unlocks 100% branch completion in NTT	FOREVERNAILED
No Bails	ANDAINTFALLIN

You can not use the Video Editor with the following cheats:

UNLOCK	CHEAT
Invisible Man	THEMISSING
Mini Skater	TINYTATER
No Board	MAGICMAN

TRANSFORMERS: THE GAME

INFINITE HEALTH
At the Main menu, press Left, Left, Up, Left, Right, Down, Right.

INFINITE AMMO
At the Main menu, press Up, Down, Left, Right, Up, Up, Down.

NO MILITARY OR POLICE
At the Main menu, press Right, Left, Right, Left, Right, Left, Right.

ALL MISSIONS
At the Main menu, press Down, Up, Left, Right, Right, Right, Up, Down.

BONUS CYBERTRON MISSIONS
At the Main menu, press Right, Up, Up, Down, Right, Left, Left.

GENERATION 1 SKIN: JAZZ
At the Main menu, press Left, Up, Down, Down, Left, Up, Right.

GENERATION 1 SKIN: MEGATRON
At the Main menu, press Down, Left, Left, Down, Right, Right, Up.

GENERATION 1 SKIN: OPTIMUS PRIME
At the Main menu, press Down, Right, Left, Up, Down, Down, Left.

GENERATION 1 SKIN: ROBOVISION OPTIMUS PRIME
At the Main menu, press Down, Down, Up, Up, Right, Right, Right.

GENERATION 1 SKIN: STARSCREAM
At the Main menu, press Right, Down, Left, Left, Down, Up, Up.

UNCHARTED: DRAKE'S FORTUNE

DRAKE'S BASEBALL T-SHIRT
At the costume select, press Left, Right, Down, Up, Triangle, R1, L1, Square.

MAKING A CUTSCENE - GRAVE ROBBING
At the rewards screen, highlight Making a Cutscene - Grave Robbing and press Left, R2, Right, Up, L2, Triangle, Square, Down.

MAKING A CUTSCENE - TIME'S UP
At the rewards screen, highlight Making a Cutscene - Time's Up and press L1, Right, Square, Down, Left, Triangle, R1, Up.

CONCEPT ART - BONUS 1
At the rewards screen, highlight Concept Art - Bonus 1 and press L2, Right, Up, Square, Left, Triangle, R1, Down.

CONCEPT ART - BONUS 2
At the rewards screen, highlight Concept Art - Bonus 2 and press Square, L1, Right, Left, Down, R2, Triangle, Up.

VIRTUA FIGHTER 5

WATCH MODE
Select Exhibition Mode, then at the character select, hold L1 + R1 and press X.

WALL-E

The following cheats will disable saving. The five possible characters starting with Wall-E and going down are: Wall-E, Auto, EVE, M-O, GEL-A Steward.

ALL BONUS FEATURES UNLOCKED
Select Cheats from the Bonus Features menu and enter Wall-E, Auto, EVE, GEL-A Steward.

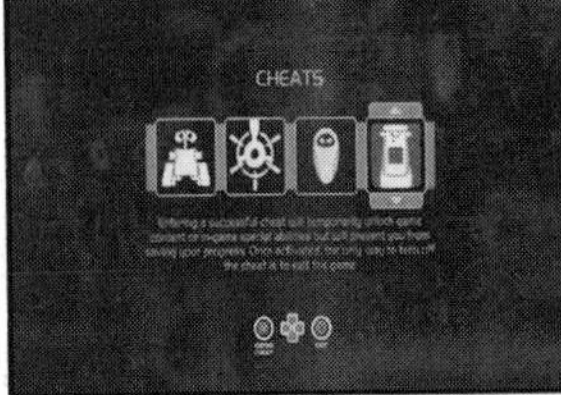

ALL GAME CONTENT UNLOCKED
Select Cheats from the Bonus Features menu and enter M-O, Auto, GEL-A Steward, EVE.

ALL SINGLE PLAYER LEVELS UNLOCKED

Select Cheats from the Bonus Features menu and enter Auto, GEL-A Steward, M-O, Wall-E.

ALL MULTIPLAYER MAPS UNLOCKED

Select Cheats from the Bonus Features menu and enter EVE, M-O, Wall-E, Auto.

ALL HOLIDAY COSTUMES UNLOCKED

Select Cheats from the Bonus Features menu and enter Auto, Auto, GEL-A Steward, GEL-A Steward.

ALL MULTIPLAYER COSTUMES UNLOCKED

Select Cheats from the Bonus Features menu and enter GEL-A Steward, Wall-E, M-O, Auto.

UNLIMITED HEALTH UNLOCKED

Select Cheats from the Bonus Features menu and enter Wall-E, M-O, Auto, M-O.

WALL-E: MAKE ANY CUBE AT ANY TIME

Select Cheats from the Bonus Features menu and enter Auto, M-O, Auto, M-O.

WALL-EVE: MAKE ANY CUBE AT ANY TIME

Select Cheats from the Bonus Features menu and enter M-O, GEL-A Steward, EVE, EVE.

WALL-E WITH A LASER GUN AT ANY TIME

Select Cheats from the Bonus Features menu and enter Wall-E, EVE, EVE, Wall-E.

WALL-EVE WITH A LASER GUN AT ANY TIME

Select Cheats from the Bonus Features menu and enter GEL-A Steward, EVE, M-O, Wall-E.

WALL-E: PERMANENT SUPER LASER UPGRADE

Select Cheats from the Bonus Features menu and enter Wall-E, Auto, EVE, M-O.

EVE: PERMANENT SUPER LASER UPGRADE

Select Cheats from the Bonus Features menu and enter EVE, Wall-E, Wall-E, Auto.

CREDITS

Select Cheats from the Bonus Features menu and enter Auto, Wall-E, GEL-A Steward, M-O.

WANTED: WEAPONS OF FATE

HEALTH IMPROVEMENT

Select Secret Codes and enter 0100 1100.

ONE SHOT ONE KILL

Select Secret Codes and enter 0111 0010.

PLAY WITH SPECIAL SUIT

Select Secret Codes and enter 0110 0001.

SUPER WEAPONS

Select Secret Codes and enter 0100 1111.

UNLIMITED ADRENALINE

Select Secret Codes and enter 0110 1101.

UNLIMITED AMMO

Select Secret Codes and enter 0110 1111.

PLAY AS AIRPLANE BODYGUARD

Select Secret Codes and enter 0101 0111.

PLAY AS CROSS
Select Secret Codes and enter 0101 0100.

PLAY AS JANICE
Select Secret Codes and enter 0100 0100.

PLAY AS WESLEY
Select Secret Codes and enter 0100 0011.

CINEMATIC MODE
Select Secret Codes and enter 0111 0100.

CLOSE COMBAT MODE
Select Secret Codes and enter 0110 0101.

HEADSHOT MODE
Select Secret Codes and enter 0110 0111.

WORLD SERIES OF POKER 2008: BATTLE FOR THE BRACELETS

PHILLIP J. HELLMUTH
Enter BEATTHEBRAT as the player name.

WWE SMACKDOWN! VS. RAW 2008

HBK AND HHH'S DX OUTFIT
Select Cheat Codes from the Options and enter DXCostume69K2.

KELLY KELLY'S ALTERNATE OUTFIT
Select Cheat Codes from the Options and enter KellyKG12R.

BRET HART
Complete the March 31, 1996 Hall of Fame challenge by defeating Bret Hart with Shawn Michaels in a One-On-One 30-Minute Iron Man Match on Legend difficulty. Purchase from WWE Shop for $210,000.

MICK FOLEY
Complete the June 28, 1998 Hall of Fame challenge by defeating Mick Foley with The Undertaker in a Hell In a Cell Match on Legend difficulty. Purchase from WWE Shop for $210,000.

MR. MCMAHON
Win or successfully defend a championship (WWE or World Heavyweight) at WrestleMania in WWE 24/7 GM Mode. Purchase from WWE Shop for $110,000.

THE ROCK
Complete the April 1, 2001 Hall of Fame challenge by defeating The Rock with Steve Austin in a Single Match on Legend Difficulty. Purchase from WWE Shop for $210,000.

STEVE AUSTIN
Complete the March 23, 1997 Hall of Fame challenge by defeating Steve Austin with Bret Hart in a Submission Match on Legend Difficulty. Purchase from WWE Shop for $210,000.

TERRY FUNK
Complete the April 13, 1997 Hall of Fame challenge by defeating Tommy Dreamer, Sabu and Sandman with any Superstar in an ECW Extreme Rules 4-Way Match on Legend difficulty. Purchase from WWE Shop for $210,000.

MR. MCMAHON BALD
Must unlock Mr. McMahon as a playable character first. Purchase from WWE Shop for $60,000.

WWE SMACKDOWN VS. RAW 2009

BOOGEYMAN
Select Cheat Codes from My WWE and enter BoogeymanEatsWorms!!.

GENE SNITSKY
Select Cheat Codes from My WWE and enter UnlockSnitskySvR2009.

HAWKINS & RYDER
Select Cheat Codes from My WWE and enter Ryder&HawkinsTagTeam.

JILLIAN HALL
Select Cheat Codes from My WWE and enter PlayAsJillianHallSvR.

LAYLA
Select Cheat Codes from My WWE and enter UnlockECWDivaLayla09.

RIC FLAIR
Select Cheat Codes from My WWE and enter FlairWoooooooooooooo.

TAZZ
Select Cheat Codes from My WWE and enter UnlockECWTazzSvR2009.

VINCENT MCMAHON
Select Cheat Codes from My WWE and enter VinceMcMahonNoChance.

HORNSWOGGLE AS MANAGER
Select Cheat Codes from My WWE and enter HornswoggleAsManager.

CHRIS JERICHO COSTUME B
Select Cheat Codes from My WWE and enter AltJerichoModelSvR09.

CM PUNK COSTUME B
Select Cheat Codes from My WWE and enter CMPunkAltCostumeSvR!.

REY MYSTERIO COSTUME B
Select Cheat Codes from My WWE and enter BooyakaBooyaka619SvR.

SATURDAY NIGHT'S MAIN EVENT ARENA
Select Cheat Codes from My WWE and enter SatNightMainEventSvR.

PLAYSTATION 2

PLAYSTATION® 2

GAMES

AMPLITUDE

BLUR

During a game, press R3 (x4), L3 (x4), then R3.

MONKEY NOTES

During a game, press L3 (x4), R3 (x4), then L3. Quit the game and go back into the song to see the effect. Re-enter the code to disable it.

RANDOM NOTE PLACEMENT

During a game, press ⊗, ⊗, Left, Left, R3, R3, Right, Right. Quit the game and go back into the song to see the effect. Re-enter the code to disable it.

CHANGE SHAPE OF TRACK LAYOUT

During the game, press L3 (x3), R3 (x3), L3, R3, and L3. Quit the game and go back into the song to see the effect. Enter it once for a tunnel appearance and a second time for a Tempest-style look. Enter the code a third time to disable it.

APE ESCAPE: PUMPED & PRIMED

ALL GADGETS

Complete Story Mode. At the mode select, hold R1 + L1 + R2 + L2 to access the password screen. Enter Go Wild!.

DISABLE ALL GADGETS CHEAT

Complete Story Mode. At the mode select, hold R1 + L1 + R2 + L2 to access the password screen. Enter Limited!.

NORMAL DIFFICULTY

Complete Story Mode. At the mode select, hold R1 + L1 + R2 + L2 to access the password screen. Enter NORMAL!.

HARD DIFFICULTY

Complete Story Mode. At the mode select, hold R1 + L1 + R2 + L2 to access the password screen. Enter HARD!.

AVATAR: THE LAST AIRBENDER—THE BURNING EARTH

1 HIT DISHONOR

At the Main menu, press L1 and select Code Entry. Enter 28260.

ALL BONUS GAME

At the Main menu, press L1 and select Code Entry. Enter 99801.

ALL GALLERY ITEMS

At the Main menu, press L1 and select Code Entry. Enter 85061.

DOUBLE DAMAGE

At the Main menu, press L1 and select Code Entry. Enter 90210.

INFINITE HEALTH

At the Main menu, press L1 and select Code Entry. Enter 65049.

MAX LEVEL

At the Main menu, press L1 and select Code Entry. Enter 89121.

UNLIMITED SPECIAL ATTACKS

At the Main menu, press L1 and select Code Entry. Enter 66206.

AVATAR: THE LAST AIRBENDER—INTO THE INFERNO

ALL CHAPTERS
Select Game Secrets at Ember Islands and enter 52993833.

MAX COINS
Select Game Secrets at Ember Islands and enter 66639224.

ALL ITEMS AVAILABLE AT SHOP
Select Game Secrets at Ember Islands and enter 34737253.

ALL CONCEPT ART
Select Game Secrets at Ember Islands and enter 27858343.

BEN 10: ALIEN FORCE THE GAME

LEVEL LORD
Enter Gwen, Kevin, Big Chill, Gwen as a code.

INVINCIBILITY
Enter Kevin, Big Chill, Swampfire, Kevin as a code.

ALL COMBOS
Enter Swampfire, Gwen, Kevin, Ben as a code.

INFINITE ALIENS
Enter Ben, Swampfire, Gwen, Big Chill as a code.

BEN 10: PROTECTOR OF EARTH

INVINCIBILITY
Select a game from the Continue option. Go to the Map Selection screen, press Start and choose Extras. Select Enter Secret Code and enter XLR8, Heatblast, Wildvine, Fourarms.

ALL COMBOS
Select a game from the Continue option. Go to the Map Selection screen, press Start and choose Extras. Select Enter Secret Code and enter Cannonblot, Heatblast, Fourarms, Heatblast.

ALL LOCATIONS
Select a game from the Continue option. Go to the Map Selection screen, press Start and choose Extras. Select Enter Secret Code and enter Heatblast, XLR8, XLR8, Cannonblot.

DNA FORCE SKINS
Select a game from the Continue option. Go to the Map Selection screen, press Start and choose Extras. Select Enter Secret Code and enter Wildvine, Fourarms, Heatblast, Cannonbolt.

DARK HEROES SKINS
Select a game from the Continue option. Go to the Map Selection screen, press Start and choose Extras. Select Enter Secret Code and enter Cannonbolt, Cannonbolt, Fourarms, Heatblast.

ALL ALIEN FORMS
Select a game from the Continue option. Go to the Map Selection screen, press Start and choose Extras. Select Enter Secret Code and enter Wildvine, Fourarms, Heatblast, Wildvine.

MASTER CONTROL
Select a game from the Continue option. Go to the Map Selection screen, press Start and choose Extras. Select Enter Secret Code and enter Cannonbolt, Heatblast, Wildvine, Fourarms.

BOLT

Some of the following cheats can be toggled on/off by selecting Cheats from the Pause menu.

ALL GAME LEVELS

Select Cheats from the Extras menu and enter Right, Up, Left, Right, Up, Right.

ALL MINI GAMES

Select Cheats from the Extras menu and enter Right, Up, Right, Right.

ENHANCED VISION

Select Cheats from the Extras menu and enter Left, Right, Up, Down.

UNLIMITED GAS MINES

Select Cheats from the Extras menu and enter Right, Left, Left, Up, Down, Right.

UNLIMITED GROUND POUND

Select Cheats from the Extras menu and enter Right, Up, Right, Up, Left, Down.

UNLIMITED INVULNERABILITY

Select Cheats from the Extras menu and enter Down, Down, Up, Left.

UNLIMITED LASER EYES

Select Cheats from the Extras menu and enter Left, Left, Up, Right.

UNLIMITED STEALTH CAMO

Select Cheats from the Extras menu and enter Left, Down, Down, Down.

UNLIMITED SUPERBARK

Select Cheats from the Extras menu and enter Right, Left, Left, Up, Down, Up.

BRATZ: FOREVER DIAMONDZ

1000 BLINGZ

While in the Bratz Office, use the Cheat computer to enter SIZZLN.

2000 BLINGZ

While in the Bratz Office, use the Cheat computer to enter FLAUNT.

PET TREATS

While in the Bratz Office, use the Cheat computer to enter TREATZ.

GIFT SET A

While in the Bratz Office, use the Cheat computer to enter STYLIN.

GIFT SET B

While in the Bratz Office, use the Cheat computer to enter SKATIN.

GIFT SET C

While in the Bratz Office, use the Cheat computer to enter JEWELZ.

GIFT SET E

While in the Bratz Office, use the Cheat computer to enter DIMNDZ.

BROTHERS IN ARMS: EARNED IN BLOOD

ALL LEVELS AND REWARDS

Create a profile with the name 2ndsquad.

BULLY

The following codes must be entered with a controller plugged into port 2:

FULL HEALTH

During a game, hold L1 and press R2, R2, R2.

ALL WEAPONS

During a game, hold L1 and press Up, Up, Up, Up.

INFINITE AMMO

During a game, hold L1 and press Up, Down, Up, Down.

MAX AMMO

During a game, hold L1 and press Up, Up.

MONEY

During a game, hold L1 and press Triangle, Square, Circle, X.

ALL CLOTHES

During a game, press L1, L1, R1, L1, L1, L1, R1, R1.

ALL GYM GRAPPLE MOVES

During a game, hold L1 and press Up, Left, Down, Down, Triangle, Square, X, X.

ALL HOBO FIGHTING MOVES

During a game, hold L1 and press Up, Left, Down, Right, Triangle, Square, X, Circle.

CAPCOM CLASSICS COLLECTION VOL. 2

UNLOCK EVERYTHING

At the Title screen, press Left, Right, Up, Down, L1, R1, L1, R1. This code unlocks Cheats, Tips, Art, and Sound Tests.

CARS MATER-NATIONAL

ALL ARCADE RACES, MINI-GAMES, AND WORLDS

Select Codes/Cheats from the options and enter PLAYALL.

ALL CARS

Select Codes/Cheats from the options and enter MATTEL07.

ALTERNATE LIGHTNING MCQUEEN COLORS

Select Codes/Cheats from the options and enter NCEDUDZ.

ALL COLORS FOR OTHERS

Select Codes/Cheats from the options and enter PAINTIT.

UNLIMITED TURBO

Select Codes/Cheats from the options and enter ZZOOOOM.

EXTREME ACCELERATION

Select Codes/Cheats from the options and enter 0TO200X.

EXPERT MODE

Select Codes/Cheats from the options and enter VRYFAST.

ALL BONUS ART

Select Codes/Cheats from the options and enter BUYTALL.

CORALINE

BUTTON EYE CORALINE

Select Cheats from Options and enter Cheese.

CRASH OF THE TITANS

BIG HEAD CRASH

Pause the game, hold R1, and press Square, Square, Triangle, X. Re-enter the code to disable.

SHADOW CRASH

Pause the game, hold R1, and press Triangle, Square, Triangle, Square. Re-enter the code to disable.

THE DA VINCI CODE

GOD MODE

Select Codes from the Options menu and enter VITRUVIAN MAN.

EXTRA HEALTH

Select Codes from the Options menu and enter SACRED FEMININE.

MISSION SELECT

Select Codes from the Options menu and enter CLOS LUCE 1519.

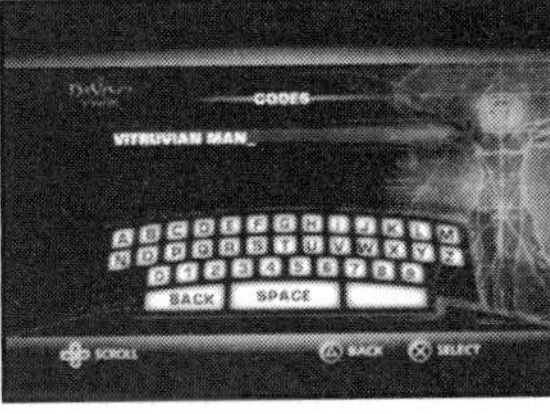

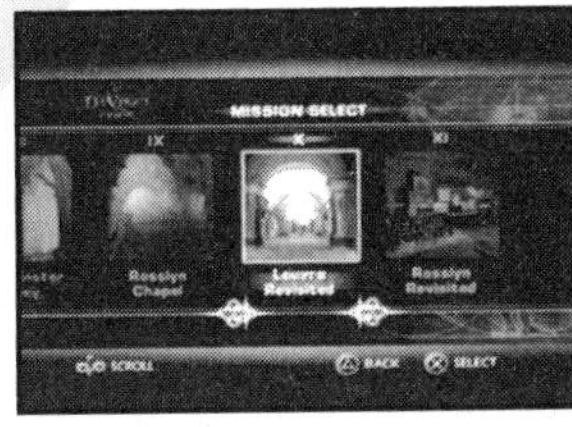

1-HIT FIST KILL

Select Codes from the Options menu and enter PHILLIPS EXETER.

1-HIT WEAPON KILL

Select Codes from the Options menu and enter ROYAL HOLLOWAY.

ALL VISUAL DATABASE

Select Codes from the Options menu and enter APOCRYPHA.

ALL VISUAL DATABASE & CONCEPT ART

Select Codes from the Options menu and enter ET IN ARCADIA EGO.

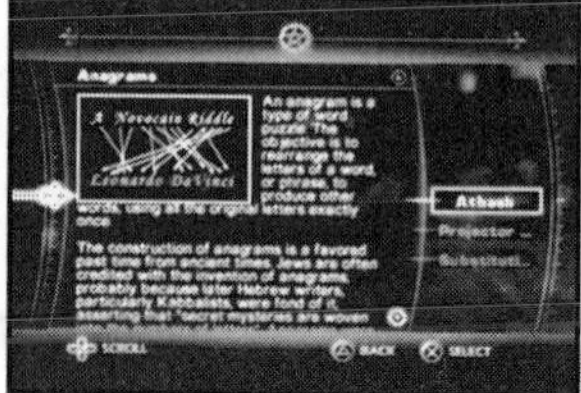

DESTROY ALL HUMANS! 2

SALAD DAYS WITH POX & CRYPTO

Pause the game and select Archives. Then press and hold L3 and press ⊗, ■, ▲, ●, ■, ●, ▲, ⊗, ⊗.

DRAGON BALL Z: SAGAS

PENDULUM ROOMS

Select Options from the Main menu and press Up, Down, Up, Down, Left, Right, Left, Right, Select, Start, Select, Start, ■, ●, ■, ●, ⊗, ⊗, Start. When entered correctly, the message "Pendulum Rooms Unlocked" will appear on-screen. This unlocks the Pendulum mode, all Extras, all Sagas, and all Upgrades.

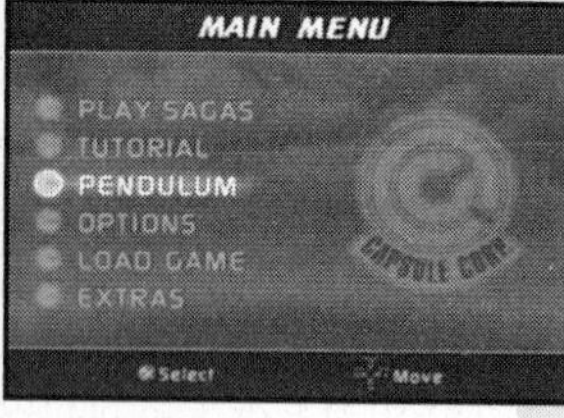

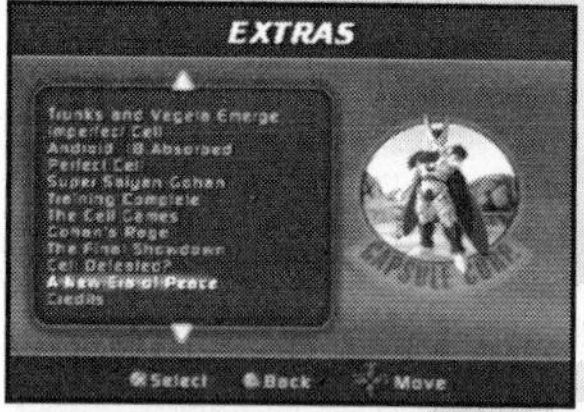

INVINCIBILITY

Pause the game, select Controller and press Down, ⊗, Select, Start, Right, ■, Left, ●, Up, ▲.

ALL UPGRADES

Pause the game, select Controller and press Up, Left, Down, Right, Select, Start, ■, ⊗, ●, ▲.

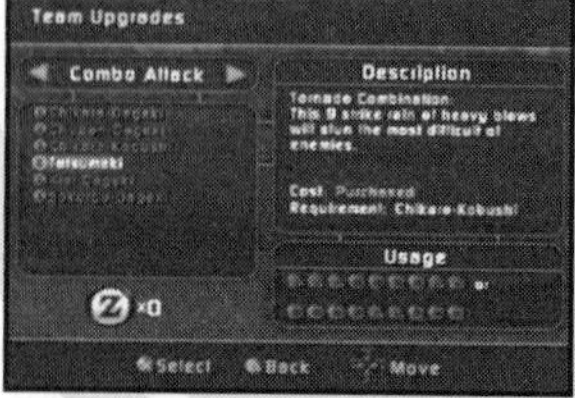

DUEL MASTERS

ALL LOCATIONS

At the Map screen, hold R3 and press ● (x3).

4 OF EVERY CARD & UNLOCK CHUCK IN ARCADE MODE

At the Deck Building screen, hold R3 and press L1, L1, L1.

PLAYER 1 LOSES SHIELD

During a duel, hold R3 and press ▲, ■, ⊗. Release R3.

PLAYER 2 LOSES SHIELD

During a duel, hold R3 and press ▲, ●, ⊗. Release R3.

PLAYER 1 GAINS SHIELD
During a duel, hold R3 and press ⊗, ■, ▲. Release R3.

PLAYER 2 GAINS SHIELD
During a duel, hold R3 and press ⊗, ●, ▲. Release R3.

PLAYER 1 WINS
During a duel, hold R3 and press L1, R1, L1.

PLAYER 2 WINS
During a duel, hold R3 and press R1, L1, R1.

TURN OFF DECK OUTS
During a duel, hold R3 and press ■ (x3).

ERAGON

FURY MODE
Pause the game, hold L1 + L2 + R1 + R2 and press ■, ■, ●, ●.

FIGHT NIGHT ROUND 3

ALL VENUES
Select Create Champ and change the first name to NEWVIEW.

FLATOUT 2

ALL CARS & 1,000,000 CREDITS
Select Enter Code from the Extras menu and enter GIEVEPIX.

1,000,000 CREDITS
Select Enter Code from the Extras menu and enter GIVECASH.

PIMPSTER CAR
Select Enter Code from the Extras menu and enter RUTTO.

FLATMOBILE CAR
Select Enter Code from the Extras menu and enter WOTKINS.

MOB CAR
Select Enter Code from the Extras menu and enter BIGTRUCK.

SCHOOL BUS
Select Enter Code from the Extras menu and enter GIEVCARPLZ.

ROCKET CAR
Select Enter Code from the Extras menu and enter KALJAKOPPA.

TRUCK
Select Enter Code from the Extras menu and enter ELPUEBLO.

GRADIUS V

You can use one of these for each level completed.

DOUBLE SHOT POWER

After the first boss, pause the game and press Up, Up, Down, Down, Left, Right, Left, Right, L2, R2.

LASER POWER

After the first boss, pause the game and press Up, Up, Down, Down, Left, Right, Left, Right, L1, R1.

GRAFFITI KINGDOM

PLAY AS FAKE PASTEL IN VS BOSSES

After completing the game, select VS Mode. Then hold L2 + R1 while selecting VS Bosses.

PLAY AS FAKE PIXEL IN VS BOSSES

After completing the game, select VS Mode. Then hold L1 + L2 while selecting VS Bosses.

PLAY AS PASTEL IN VS BOSSES

After completing the game, select VS Mode. Then hold L1 + R1 while selecting VS Bosses.

PLAY AS PIXEL IN VS BOSSES

After completing the game, select VS Mode. Then hold L1 + R2 while selecting VS Bosses.

FAKE PASTEL VS PASTEL IN 2-PLAYER TOURNAMENT

After completing the game, select VS Mode. Then hold L1 + L2 + R1 while selecting 2 Player Tournament.

FAKE PASTEL VS PIXEL IN 2-PLAYER TOURNAMENT

After completing the game, select VS Mode. Then hold L2 + R1 while selecting 2 Player Tournament.

FAKE PIXEL VS FAKE PASTEL IN 2-PLAYER TOURNAMENT

After completing the game, select VS Mode. Then hold L2 + R2 while selecting 2 Player Tournament.

FAKE PIXEL VS PIXEL IN 2-PLAYER TOURNAMENT

After completing the game, select VS Mode. Then hold L1 + L2 while selecting 2 Player Tournament.

PASTEL VS FAKE PASTEL IN 2-PLAYER TOURNAMENT

After completing the game, select VS Mode. Then hold L1 + R1 while selecting 2 Player Tournament.

PASTEL VS FAKE PIXEL IN 2-PLAYER TOURNAMENT

After completing the game, select VS Mode. Then hold R1 + R2 while selecting 2 Player Tournament.

PIXEL VS FAKE PIXEL IN 2-PLAYER TOURNAMENT

After completing the game, select VS Mode. Then hold L1 + R2 while selecting 2 Player Tournament.

GRAND THEFT AUTO: SAN ANDREAS

During a game, enter the following cheats:

FULL HEALTH, FULL ARMOR & $250,000

Press R1, R2, L1, ⊗, Left, Down, Right, Up, Left, Down, Right, Up.

INFINITE LUNG CAPACITY

Press Down, Left, L1, Down, Down, R2, Down, L2, Down.

0 FAT & 0 MUSCLE

Press △, Up, Up, Left, Right, ■, ●, Right.

MAXIMUM MUSCLES

Press △, Up, Up, Left, Right, ■, ●, Left.

MAXIMUM FAT

Press △, Up, Up, Left, Right, ■, ●, Down.

BIG JUMPS
Press Up, Up, △, △, Up, Up, Left, Right, □, R2, R2.

BIG BUNNY HOPS ON BMX
Press △, □, ○, ○, □, ○, ○, L1, L2, L2, R1, R2.

SUICIDE
Press Right, L2, Down, R1, Left, Left, R1, L1, L2, L1.

FASTER GAMEPLAY
Press △, Up, Right, Down, L2, L1, □.

SLOWER GAMEPLAY
Press △, Up, Right, Down, □, R2, R1.

FASTER TIME
Press ○, ○, L1, □, L1, □, □, □, L1, △, ○, △.

BLACK CARS
Press ○, L2, Up, R1, Left, ⊗, R1, L1, Left, ○.

PINK CARS
Press ○, L1, Down, L2, Left, ⊗, R1, L1, Right, ○.

FAST CARS
Press Up, L1, R1, Up, Right, Up, ⊗, L2, ⊗, L1.

TAXIS HAVE NITROUS & HOP WITH L3
Press Up, ⊗, △, ⊗, △, ⊗, □, R2, Right.

INVISIBLE VEHICLES
Press △, L1, △, R2, □, L1, L1.

INVINCIBLE VEHICLE
Press L1, L2, L2, Up, Down, Down, Up, R1, R2, R2.

DRIVE-BY WHILE DRIVING
Press Up, Up, □, L2, Right, ⊗, R1, Down, R2, ○.

GREEN STOPLIGHTS
Press Right, R1, Up, L2, L2, Left, R1, L1, R1, R1.

AGGRESSIVE TRAFFIC
Press R2, ○, R1, L2, Left, R1, L1, R2, L2.

LESS TRAFFIC
Press ⊗, Down, Up, R2, Down, △, L1, △, Left.

FASTER CARS
Press Right, R1, Up, L2, L2, Left, R1, L1, R1, R1.

BETTER CAR HANDLING
Press △, R1, R1, Left, R1, L1, R2, L1.

CARS FLOAT
Press Right, R2, ○, R1, L2, □, R1, R2.

CARS FLY
Press Up, Down, L1, R1, L1, Right, Left, L1, Left.

ALL CARS EXPLODE
Press R2, L2, R1, L1, L2, R2, □, △, ○, △, L2, L1.

FLYING BOATS
Press R2, ○, Up, L1, Right, R1, Right, Up, □, △.

PEDESTRIANS ATTACK YOU
Press Down, Up, Up, Up, ⊗, R2, R1, L2, L2.

PEDESTRIANS ATTACK EACH OTHER
Press Down, Left, Up, Left, ⊗, R2, R1, L2, L1.

PEDESTRIANS CARRY WEAPONS
Press R2, R1, ⊗, △, ⊗, △, Up, Down.

ELVISES EVERYWHERE
Press L1, Circle, Triangle, L1, L1, Square, L2, Up, Down, Left.

CJ IS A CLOWN, CIVILIANS IN FAST FOOD APPAREL & MORE!
Press Triangle, Triangle, L1, Square, Square, Circle, Square, Down, Circle.

PEOPLE IN SWIMSUITS
Press Up, Up, Down, Down, Square, Circle, L1, R1, Triangle, Down.

GANGS
Press L2, Up, R1, R1, Left, R1, R1, R2, Right, Down.

REDUCE WANTED LEVEL
Press R1, R1, Circle, R2, Up, Down, Up, Down, Up, Down.

RAISE WANTED LEVEL
Press R1, R1, Circle, R2, Left, Right, Left, Right, Left, Right.

CLEAR WEATHER
Press R2, X, L1, L1, L2 (x3), Triangle.

SUNNY WEATHER
Press R2, X, L1, L1, L2 (x3), Down.

FOGGY WEATHER
Press R2, X, L1, L1, L2 (x3), X.

CLOUDY WEATHER
Press R2, X, L1, L1, L2 (x3), Square.

RAINY WEATHER
Press R2, X, L1, L1, L2 (x3), Circle.

WEAPON SET 1
Press R1, R2, L1, R2, Left, Down, Right, Up, Left, Down, Right, Up.

WEAPON SET 2
Press R1, R2, L1, R2, Left, Down, Right, Up, Left, Down, Down, Left.

WEAPON SET 3
Press R1, R2, L1, R2, Left, Down, Right, Up, Left, Down, Down, Down.

PARACHUTE
Press Left, Right, L1, L2, R1, R2, R2, Up, Down, Right, L1.

JETPACK
Press L1, L2, R1, R2, Up, Down, Left, Right, L1, L2, R1, R2, Up, Down, Left, Right.

BLOODRING BANGER
Press Down, R1, Circle, L2, L2, X, R1, L1, Left, Left.

CADDY
Press Circle, L1, Up, R1, L2, X, R1, L1, Circle, X.

DOZER
Press R2, L1, L1, Right, Right, Up, Up, X, L1, Left.

HOTRING RACER 1
Press R1, Circle, R2, Right, L1, L2, X, X, Square, R1.

HOTRING RACER 2
Press R2, L1, Circle, Right, L1, R1, Right, Up, Circle, R2.

HYDRA
Press Triangle, Triangle, Square, Circle, X, L1, L1, Down, Up.

GRAND THEFT AUTO: VICE CITY STORIES

Enter the following cheats during a game.

$250000
Press Up, Down, Left, Right, ⊗, ⊗, L1, R1.

ARMOR
Press Up, Down, Left, Right, ■, ■, L1, R1.

HEALTH
Press Up, Down, Left, Right, ●, ●, L1, R1.

NEVER WANTED
Press Up, Right, ▲, ▲, Down, Left, ●, ●.

LOWER WANTED LEVEL
Press Up, Right, ▲, ▲, Down, Left, ⊗, ⊗.

RAISE WANTED LEVEL
Press Up, Right, ■, ■, Down, Left, ●, ●.

WEAPON SET 1
Press Left, Right, ⊗, Up, Down, ■, Left, Right.

WEAPON SET 2
Press Left, Right, ■, Up, Down, ▲, Left, Right.

WEAPON SET 3
Press Left, Right, ▲, Up, Down, ●, Left, Right.

SPAWN RHINO
Press Up, L1, Down, R1, Left, L1, Right, R1.

SPAWN TRASHMASTER
Press Down, Up, Right, ▲, L1, ▲, L1, ▲.

BLACK CARS
Press L1, R1, L1, R1, Left, ●, Up, ⊗.

CHROME CARS
Press Right, Up, Left, Down, ▲, ▲, L1, R1.

CARS AVOID YOU
Press Up, Up, Right, Left, ▲, ●, ●, ■.

DESTROY ALL CARS
Press L1, R1, R, Left, Right, ■, Down, R1.

GUYS FOLLOW YOU
Press Right, L1, Down, L1, ●, Up, L1, ■.

NO TRACTION
Press Down, Left, Up, L1, R1, ▲, ●, ⊗.

PEDESTRIAN GETS INTO YOUR VEHICLE
Press Down, Up, Right, L1, L1, ■, Up, L1.

PEDESTRIANS ATTACK YOU
Press Down, ▲, Up, ⊗, L1, R1, L1, R1.

PEDESTRIANS HAVE WEAPONS
Press Up, L1, Down, R1, Left, ●, Right, ▲.

PEDESTRIANS RIOT
Press R1, L1, L1, Down, Left, ●, Down, L1.

SUICIDE
Press Right, Right, ●, ●, L1, R1, Down, ⊗.

UPSIDE DOWN 1
Press ■, ■, ■, L1, L1, R1, Left, Right.

UPSIDE DOWN 2
Press Left, Left, Left, R1, R1, L1, Right, Left.

FASTER CLOCK
Press R1, L1, L, Down, Up, ⊗, Down, L1.

FASTER GAMEPLAY
Press Left, Left, R1, R1, Up, ▲, Down, ⊗.

SLOWER GAMEPLAY
Press Left, Left, ●, ●, Down, Up, ▲, ⊗.

CLEAR WEATHER
Press Left, Down, R1, L1, Right, Up, Left, ⊗.

FOGGY WEATHER
Press Left, Down, ▲, ⊗, Right, Up, Left, L1.

OVERCAST WEATHER
Press Left, Down, L1, R1, Right, Up, Left, ■.

RAINY WEATHER
Press Left, Down, L1, R1, Right, Up, Left, ▲.

SUNNY WEATHER
Press Left, Down, R1, L1, Right, Up, Left, ●.

GRAN TURISMO 4

EXTRA TRACKS FOR ARCADE MODE

Play through the indicated number of days to unlock the corresponding track in Arcade Mode.

DAYS	UNLOCKS
15	Deep Forest Raceway
29	Opera Paris
43	Fuji Speedway 80s
57	Special Stage Route 5
71	Suzuka Circuit
85	Twin Ring Motegi Road Course East Short
99	Grand Valley Speedway
113	Hong Kong
127	Suzuka Circuit West Course
141	Fuji Speedway 2005 GT
155	Ice Arena
169	Apricot Hill Raceway
183	Cote d Azur
197	Tahiti Maze
211	Twin Ring Motegi Road Course
225	George V Paris
239	Cathedral Rocks Trail I
253	Costa di Amalfi
267	Circuit de la Sarthe 1
281	Autumn Ring
309	Chamonix
309	Infineon Raceway Stock Car Course
323	Fuji Speedway 2005 F
337	Tsukuba Circuit Wet
351	Circuit de la Sarthe 2 (not chicaned)

GUITAR HERO

UNLOCK ALL CHEATS

At the Main menu, press Yellow, Orange, Blue, Blue, Orange, Yellow, Yellow.

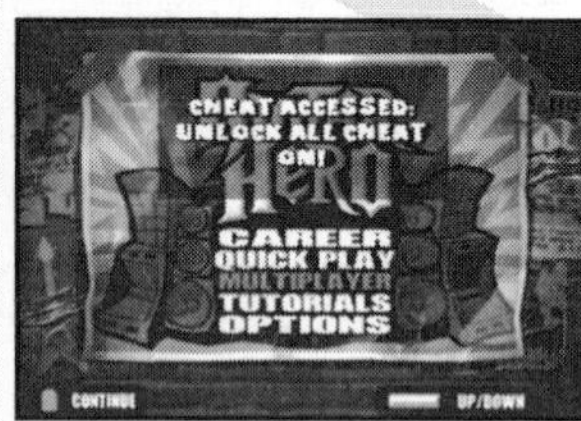

GUITAR HERO GUITAR CHEAT

At the Main menu, press Blue, Orange, Yellow, Blue, Blue.

CROWD METER CHEAT

At the Main menu, press Yellow, Blue, Orange, Orange, Blue, Blue, Yellow, Orange.

MONKEY HEAD CROWD

At the Main menu, press Blue, Orange, Yellow, Yellow, Yellow, Blue, Orange.

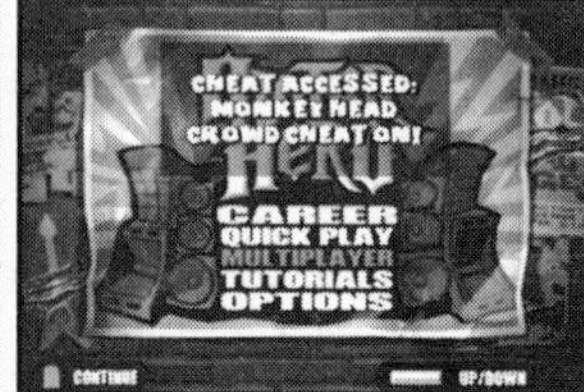

SKULL HEAD CROWD

At the Main menu, press Orange, Yellow, Blue, Blue, Orange, Yellow, Blue, Blue.

AIR GUITAR CHEAT

At the Main menu, press Orange, Orange, Blue, Yellow, Orange.

NO VENUE CHEAT

At the Main menu, press Blue, Yellow, Orange, Blue, Yellow, Orange.

GUITAR HERO II

AIR GUITAR

At the Main menu, press Yellow, Yellow, Blue, Orange, Yellow, Blue.

EYEBALL HEAD CROWD

At the Main menu, press Blue, Orange, Yellow, Orange, Yellow, Orange, Blue.

MONKEY HEAD CROWD

At the Main menu, press Orange, Blue, Yellow, Yellow, Orange, Blue, Yellow, Yellow.

FLAMING HEAD

At the Main menu, press Orange, Yellow, Orange, Orange, Yellow, Orange, Yellow, Yellow.

HORSE HEAD

At the Main menu, press Blue, Orange, Orange, Blue, Orange, Orange, Blue, Orange, Orange, Blue.

HYPER SPEED DEACTIVATE

At the Main menu, press Orange, Blue, Orange, Yellow, Orange, Blue, Orange, Yellow.

PERFORMANCE MODE

At the Main menu, press Yellow, Yellow, Blue, Yellow, Yellow, Orange, Yellow, Yellow.

GUITAR HERO III: LEGENDS OF ROCK

To enter the following cheats, strum the guitar with the given buttons held. For example, if it says Yellow + Orange, hold Yellow and Orange as you strum. Some cheats can be toggled on and off from the Cheats menu. You can also change between five different levels of Hyperspeed at this menu.

UNLOCK EVERYTHING

Select Cheats from the Options. Choose Enter Cheat and enter Green + Red + Blue + Orange, Green + Red + Yellow + Blue, Green + Red + Yellow + Orange, Green + Yellow + Blue + Orange, Green + Red + Yellow + Blue, Red + Yellow + Blue + Orange, Green + Red + Yellow + Blue, Green + Yellow + Blue + Orange, Green + Red + Yellow + Blue, Green + Red + Yellow + Orange, Green + Red + Yellow + Orange, Green + Red + Yellow + Blue, Green + Red + Yellow + Orange. No sounds play while this code is entered.

An easier way to show this code is by representing Green as 1 down to Orange as 5. For example, if you have 1345, you would hold down Green + Yellow + Blue + Orange while strumming. 1245 + 1234 + 1235 + 1345 + 1234 + 2345 + 1234 + 1345 + 1234 + 1235 + 1235 + 1234 + 1235.

ALL SONGS

Select Cheats from the Options. Choose Enter Cheat and enter Yellow + Orange, Red + Blue, Red + Orange, Green + Blue, Red + Yellow, Yellow + Orange, Red + Yellow, Red + Blue, Green + Yellow, Green + Yellow, Yellow + Blue, Yellow + Blue, Yellow + Orange, Yellow + Orange, Yellow + Blue, Yellow, Red, Red + Yellow, Red, Yellow, Orange.

ANO FAIL

Select Cheats from the Options. Choose Enter Cheat and enter Green + Red, Blue, Green + Red, Green + Yellow, Blue, Green + Yellow, Red + Yellow, Orange, Red + Yellow, Green + Yellow, Yellow, Green + Yellow, Green + Red.

AIR GUITAR

Select Cheats from the Options. Choose Enter Cheat and enter Blue + Yellow, Green + Yellow, Green + Yellow, Red + Blue, Red + Blue, Red + Yellow, Red + Yellow, Blue + Yellow, Green + Yellow, Green + Yellow, Red + Blue, Red + Blue, Red + Yellow, Red + Yellow, Green + Yellow, Green + Yellow, Red + Yellow, Red + Yellow.

HYPERSPEED

Select Cheats from the Options. Choose Enter Cheat and enter Orange, Blue, Orange, Yellow, Orange, Blue, Orange, Yellow.

PERFORMANCE MODE

Select Cheats from the Options. Choose Enter Cheat and enter Red + Yellow, Red + Blue, Red + Orange, Red + Blue, Red + Yellow, Green + Blue, Red + Yellow, Red + Blue.

EASY EXPERT

Select Cheats from the Options. Choose Enter Cheat and enter Green + Red, Green + Yellow, Yellow + Blue, Red + Blue, Blue + Orange, Yellow + Orange, Red + Yellow, Red + Blue.

PRECISION MODE

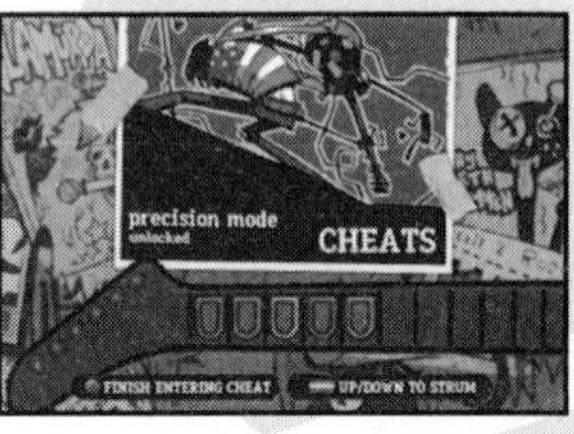

Select Cheats from the Options. Choose Enter Cheat and enter Green + Red, Green + Red, Green + Red, Red + Yellow, Red + Yellow, Red + Blue, Red + Blue, Yellow + Blue, Yellow + Orange, Yellow + Orange, Green + Red, Green + Red, Green + Red, Red + Yellow, Red + Yellow, Red + Blue, Red + Blue, Yellow + Blue, Yellow + Orange, Yellow + Orange.

LARGE GEMS

Select Cheats from the Options. Choose Enter Cheat and enter Green, Red, Green, Yellow, Green, Blue, Green, Orange, Green, Blue, Green, Yellow, Green, Red, Green, Green + Red, Red + Yellow, Green + Red, Yellow + Blue, Green + Red, Blue + Orange, Green + Red, Yellow + Blue, Green + Red, Red + Yellow, Green + Red, Green + Yellow.

GUITAR HERO: AEROSMITH

At the Main menu, select "Options", "Cheats", "Enter New Cheat", then enter one of the following codes to unlock the corresponding cheat option. Note: Each note or chord must be strummed. Press Green at the "Cheats" menu to turn off a particular cheat.

AIR GUITAR

Press Red + Yellow, Green + Red, [Red + Yellow] two times, [Red + Blue] five times, [Yellow + Blue] two times, Yellow + Orange.

HYPERSPEED

YO, YO, YO, YO, YO, RY, RY, RY, RY, RB, RB, RB, RB, RB, YB, YO, YO

NO FAIL

Press Green + Red, Blue, Green + Red, Green + Yellow, Blue, Green + Yellow, Red + Yellow, Orange, Red + Yellow, Green + Yellow, Yellow, Green + Yellow.

ALL SONGS

Press Red + Yellow, [Green + Red] two times, [Red + Yellow] two times, Green + Red, [Red + Yellow] two times, [Green + Red] two times, [Red + Yellow].

GUITAR HERO ENCORE: ROCKS THE 80S

UNLOCK EVERYTHING

At the Main menu, press Blue, Orange, Yellow, Red, Orange, Yellow, Blue, Yellow, Red, Yellow, Blue, Yellow, Red, Yellow, Blue, Yellow.

HYPERSPEED

At the Main menu, press Yellow, Blue, Orange, Orange, Blue, Yellow, Yellow, Orange.

PERFORMANCE MODE

At the Main menu, press Blue, Blue, Orange, Yellow, Yellow, Blue, Orange, Blue.

AIR GUITAR

At the Main menu, press Yellow, Blue, Yellow, Orange, Blue, Blue.

EYEBALL HEAD CROWD

At the Main menu, press Yellow, Blue, Orange, Orange, Orange, Blue, Yellow.

MONKEY HEAD CROWD

At the Main menu, press Blue, Blue, Orange, Yellow, Blue, Blue, Orange, Yellow.

FLAME HEAD

At the Main menu, press Yellow, Orange, Yellow, Orange, Yellow, Orange, Blue, Orange.

HORSE HEAD

At the Main menu, press Blue, Orange, Orange, Blue, Yellow, Blue, Orange, Orange, Blue, Yellow.

GUITAR HERO: METALLICA

METALLICA COSTUMES

Select Cheats from Settings and enter Green, Red, Yellow, Blue, Blue, Yellow, Red, Green.

HYPERSPEED

Select Cheats from Settings and enter Green, Blue, Red, Yellow, Yellow, Red, Green, Green.

PERFORMANCE MODE

Select Cheats from Settings and enter Yellow, Yellow, Blue, Red, Blue, Green, Red, Red.

INVISIBLE ROCKER

Select Cheats from Settings and enter Green, Red, Yellow (x3), Blue, Blue, Green.

AIR INSTRUMENTS

Select Cheats from Settings and enter Red, Red, Blue, Yellow, Green (x3), Yellow.

ALWAYS DRUM FILL

Select Cheats from Settings and enter Red (x3), Blue, Blue, Green, Green, Yellow.

AUTO KICK

Select Cheats from Settings and enter Yellow, Green, Red, Blue (x4), Red. With this cheat activated, the bass pedal is automatically hit.

ALWAYS SLIDE

Select Cheats from Settings and enter Green, Green, Red, Red, Yellow, Red, Yellow, Blue. All Guitar Notes Become Touch Pad Sliding Notes.

BLACK HIGHWAY

Select Cheats from Settings and enter Yellow, Red, Green, Red, Green, Red, Red, Blue.

FLAME COLOR

Select Cheats from Settings and enter Green, Red, Green, Blue, Red, Red, Yellow, Blue.

GEM COLOR

Select Cheats from Settings and enter Blue, Red, Red, Green, Red, Green, Red, Yellow.

STAR COLOR

Select Cheats from Settings and enter Press Red, Red, Yellow, Red, Blue, Red, Red, Blue.

ADDITIONAL LINE 6 TONES

Select Cheats from Settings and enter Green, Red, Yellow, Blue, Red, Yellow, Blue, Green.

VOCAL FIREBALL

Select Cheats from Settings and enter Red, Green, Green, Yellow, Blue, Green, Yellow, Green.

GUITAR HERO WORLD TOUR

ALL SONGS IN QUICK PLAY

At the Cheats menu, select Enter New Cheat and press Blue, Blue, Red, Green, Green, Blue, Blue, Yellow.

AIR INSTRUMENTS

At the Cheats menu, select Enter New Cheat and press Red, Red, Blue, Yellow, Green, Green, Green, Yellow.

ALWAYS SLIDE

At the Cheats menu, select Enter New Cheat and press Green, Green, Red, Red, Yellow, Red, Yellow, Blue.

AT&T BALL PARK

At the Cheats menu, select Enter New Cheat and press Yellow, Green, Red, Red, Green, Blue, Red, Yellow.

AUTO KICK

At the Cheats menu, select Enter New Cheat and press Yellow, Green, Red, Blue, Blue, Blue, Blue, Red.

EXTRA LINE 6 TONES

At the Cheats menu, select Enter New Cheat and press Green, Red, Yellow, Blue, Red, Yellow, Blue, Green.

FLAME COLORS

At the Cheats menu, select Enter New Cheat and press Green, Red, Green, Blue, Red, Red, Yellow, Blue.

GEM COLORS

At the Cheats menu, select Enter New Cheat and press Blue, Red, Red, Green, Red, Green, Red, Yellow.

HYPER SPEED

At the Cheats menu, select Enter New Cheat and press Green, Blue, Red, Yellow, Yellow, Red, Green, Green.

INVISIBLE ROCKER

At the Cheats menu, select Enter New Cheat and press Green, Red, Yellow, Yellow, Yellow, Blue, Blue, Green.

PERFORMANCE MODE

At the Cheats menu, select Enter New Cheat and press Yellow, Yellow, Blue, Red, Blue, Green, Red, Red.

STAR COLORS

At the Cheats menu, select Enter New Cheat and press Red, Red, Yellow, Red, Blue, Red, Red, Blue.

AARON STEELE

At the Cheats menu, select Enter New Cheat and press Blue, Red, Yellow, Yellow, Yellow, Yellow, Yellow, Green.

JOHNNY VIPER

At the Cheats menu, select Enter New Cheat and press Blue, Red, Blue, Blue, Yellow, Yellow, Yellow, Green.

NICK

At the Cheats menu, select Enter New Cheat and press Green, Red, Blue, Green, Red, Blue, Blue, Green.

RINA

At the Cheats menu, select Enter New Cheat and press Blue, Red, Green, Green, Yellow, Yellow, Yellow, Green.

VOCAL FIREBALL

At the Cheats menu, select Enter New Cheat and press Red, Green, Green, Yellow, Blue, Green, Yellow, Green.

HOT SHOTS GOLF FORE!

Select Password from the Options menu and enter the following codes to enable these cheats.

ALL CHARACTERS IN VS MODE
Enter REZTWS.

PRICE REDUCTION SALE IN SHOP
Enter MKJEFQ.

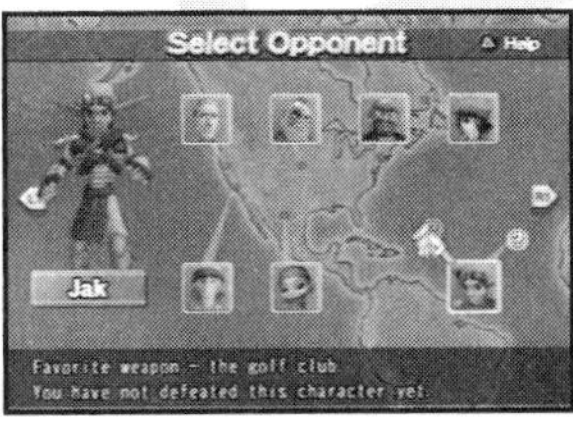

ALOHA BEACH RESORT COURSE IN SHOP
Enter XSREHD.

BAGPIPE CLASSIC COURSE IN SHOP
Enter CRCNHZ.

BLUE LAGOON C.C. COURSE IN SHOP
Enter WVRJQS.

DAY DREAM G.C. IN SHOP
Enter OQUTNA.

MINI-GOLF 2 G.C. IN SHOP
Enter RVMIRU.

SILKROAD CLASSIC COURSE IN SHOP
Enter ZKOGJM.

UNITED FOREST G.C. IN SHOP
Enter UIWHLZ.

WESTERN VALLEY COUNTRY CLUB COURSE IN SHOP
Enter LIBTFL.

WILD GREEN C.C. COURSE IN SHOP
Enter YZLOXE.

CAPSULE 01 IN SHOP
Enter WXAFSJ.

CAPSULE 2 IN SHOP
Enter OEINLK.

CAPSULE 3 IN SHOP
Enter WFKVTG.

CAPSULE 4 IN SHOP
Enter FCAVDO.

CAPSULE 5 IN SHOP
Enter YYPOKK.

CAPSULE 6 IN SHOP
Enter GDQDOF.

CAPSULE 7 IN SHOP
Enter HHXKPV.

CAPSULE 8 IN SHOP
Enter UOKXPS.

CAPSULE 9 IN SHOP
Enter LMIRYD.

CAPSULE 10 IN SHOP
Enter MJLJEQ.

CAPSULE 11 IN SHOP
Enter MHNCQI

LOWER TOURNEY STAGE
Enter XKWGFZ.

CADDIE CLANK IN SHOP
Enter XCQGWJ.

CADDIE DAXTER IN SHOP
Enter WSIKIN.

CADDIE KAYLA IN SHOP
Enter MZIMEL.

CADDIE KAZ IN SHOP
Enter LNNZJV.

CADDIE MOCHI IN SHOP
Enter MYPWPA.

CADDIE SIMON IN SHOP
Enter WRHZNB.

CADDIE SOPHIE IN SHOP
Enter UTWIVQ.

BEGINNER'S BALL IN SHOP
Enter YFQJJI.

BIR AIR BALL IN SHOP
Enter CRCGKR.

INFINITY BALL IN SHOP
Enter DJXBRG.

PIN HOLE BALL IN SHOP
Enter VZLSGP.

SIDESPIN BALL IN SHOP
Enter JAYQRK.

TURBO SPIN BALL IN SHOP
Enter XNETOK.

100T HAMMER CLUB (B-CLASS) IN SHOP
Enter NFSNHR.

UPGRADE 100T HAMMER CLUB (A-CLASS) IN SHOP
Enter BVLHSI.

UPGRADE 100T HAMMER CLUB (S-CLASS) IN SHOP
Enter MCSRUK.

BIG AIR CLUB (B-CLASS) IN SHOP
Enter DLJMFZ.

UPGRADE BIG AIR CLUB (A-CLASS) IN SHOP
Enter TOSXUJ.

UPGRADE BIG AIR CLUB (S-CLASS) IN SHOP
Enter JIDTQI.

INFINITY CLUB IN SHOP
Enter RZTQGV.

UPGRADE INFINITY CLUB (A-CLASS) IN SHOP
Enter WTGFOR.

UPGRADE INFINITY CLUB (S-CLASS) IN SHOP
Enter EIPCUL.

PIN HOLE CLUB (B-CLASS) IN SHOP
Enter DGHFRP.

UPGRADE PIN HOLE CLUB (A-CLASS) IN SHOP
Enter TTIMHT.

UPGRADE PIN HOLE CLUB (S-CLASS) IN SHOP
Enter RBXVEL.

UPGRADE TURBO SPIN CLUB (A-CLASS) IN SHOP
Enter NIWKWP.

UPGRADE TURBO SPIN CLUB (S-CLASS) IN SHOP
Enter DTIZAB.

EXTRA POSE CAM IN SHOP
Enter UEROOK.

EXTRA SWING CAM IN SHOP
Enter RJIFQS.

EXTRA VIDEO IN SHOP
Enter DPYHIU.

HECKLETS IN SHOP
Enter DIXWFE.

HSG CD/VOICE IN SHOP
Enter UITUGF.

HSG CD/MUSIC IN SHOP
Enter PAJXLI.

HSG RULES IN SHOP
Enter FKDHDS.

LANDING GRID IN SHOP
Enter MQTIMV.

REPLAY CAM A IN SHOP
Enter PVJEMF.

REPLAY CAM B IN SHOP
Enter EKENCR.

REPLAY CAM C IN SHOP
Enter ZUHHAC.

MENU CHARACTER BRAD IN SHOP
Enter ZKJSIO.

MENU CHARACTER PHOEBE IN SHOP
Enter LWVLCB.

MENU CHARACTER RENEE IN SHOP
Enter AVIQXS.

WALLPAPER SET 2 IN SHOP
Enter RODDHQ.

MIKE'S COSTUME IN SHOP
Enter YKCFEZ.

LIN'S COSTUME IN SHOP
Enter BBLSKQ.

MEL'S COSTUME IN SHOP
Enter ARFLCR.

PHOEBE'S COSTUME IN SHOP
Enter GJBCHY.

IRON MAN

ARMOR SELECTION

Iron Man's different armor suits are unlocked by completing certain missions. Refer to the following tables for when each is unlocked. After selecting a mission to play, you get the opportunity to pick the armor you wish to use.

COMPLETE MISSION	SUIT UNLOCKED
1: Escape	Mark I
2: First Flight	Mark II
3: Fight Back	Mark III
6: Flying Fortress	Comic Tin Can
9: Home Front	Classic
13: Showdown	Silver Centurion

CONCEPT ART

Concept Art is unlocked after finding certain numbers of Weapon Crates.

CONCEPT ART UNLOCKED	NUMBER OF WEAPON CRATES FOUND
Environments Set 1	6
Environments Set 2	12
Iron Man	18
Environments Set 3	24
Enemies	30
Environments Set 4	36
Villains	42
Vehicles	48
Covers	50

JUICED 2: HOT IMPORT NIGHTS

ASCARI KZ1

Select Cheats and Codes from the DNA Lab menu and enter KNOX. Defeat the challenge to earn the car.

NISSAN SKYLINE R34 GT-R

Select Cheats and Codes from the DNA Lab menu and enter JWRS. Defeat the challenge to earn the car.

KARAOKE REVOLUTION VOLUME 3

BANANA MICROPHONE

Score gold at each venue in Showtime mode. At the Extras menu, press Down, Up, Left, Right, Square, Circle, Square, Circle at Cheat Collection 1.

BIG EYED CHARACTER

Score gold at each venue in Showtime mode. At the Extras menu, press Circle, Circle, Square, Square, Down, Left, Left, Down at Cheat Collection 1.

DWAYNE DOLL MICROPHONE

Score gold at each venue in Showtime mode. At the Extras menu, press Square, Square, R3, Circle, Up, Down, Right, Left at Cheat Collection 1.

TOOTHBRUSH MICROPHONE

Score gold at each venue in Showtime mode. At the Extras menu, press L2, L2, Square, Circle, Down, Up, Left, L3 at Cheat Collection 1.

BIG HEAD CHARACTER

Score gold at each venue in Showtime mode. At the Extras menu, press Circle, Square, Circle, Square, Up, Right, Down, Left at Cheat Collection 2.

FISH MICROPHONE

Score gold at each venue in Showtime mode. At the Extras menu, press Square, Down, Up, Left, Square, Square, L2, L1 at Cheat Collection 2.

MERCURY CHARACTER

Score gold at each venue in Showtime mode. At the Extras menu, press Down, Down, Right, Left, Right, Left, Square, Circle at Cheat Collection 2.

WRAITH CHARACTER

Score gold at each venue in Showtime mode. At the Extras menu, press L2, L2, Right, Right, Circle, Square, R1, R1 at Cheat Collection 2.

GLASS CHARACTER

Score gold at each venue in Showtime mode. At the Extras menu, press Down, L2, R1, R2, L1, Circle, Square, Circle at Cheat Collection 3.

ICE CREAM MICROPHONE

Score gold at each venue in Showtime mode. At the Extras menu, press Square, Circle, Square, Circle, R2, L2, R1, L1 at Cheat Collection 3.

OIL SLICK CHARACTER

Score gold at each venue in Showtime mode. At the Extras menu, press L3, L3, R2, R1, L2, L1, Down, Up at Cheat Collection 3.

SMALL HEAD CHARACTER

Score gold at each venue in Showtime mode. At the Extras menu, press ◉, R2, L2, R1, L1, Down, Down, Up at Cheat Collection 3.

ALIEN CROWD

Score gold at each venue in Showtime mode. At the Extras menu, press Up, Up, Down, ◉, ◉, L2, R2, ▣ at Cheat Collection 4.

PIRATE CROWD

Score gold at each venue in Showtime mode. At the Extras menu, press Down, L2, L2, R2, R2, ▣, ◉, ▣ at Cheat Collection 4.

ROBOT CROWD

Score gold at each venue in Showtime mode. At the Extras menu, press L3, Down, Down, R1, ◉, ▣, ◉, ▣ at Cheat Collection 4.

TOUGH AUDIO CROWD

Score gold at each venue in Showtime mode. At the Extras menu, press ◉, L1, L2, R1, R2, Right, Right, Down at Cheat Collection 4.

ZOMBIE CROWD

Score gold at each venue in Showtime mode. At the Extras menu, press ▣, ▣, ◉, ◉, Up, Right, Right, Up at Cheat Collection 4.

KATAMARI DAMACY

COMETS

Finish a "Make a Star" level under a certain time to earn a comet.

LEVEL	FINISH WITHIN
Make a Star 1	1 minute
Make a Star 2	3 minutes
Make a Star 3	4 minutes
Make a Star 4	6 minutes
Make a Star 5	8 minutes
Make a Star 6	8 minutes
Make a Star 7	8 minutes
Make a Star 8	12 minutes
Make a Star 9	15 minutes
Make the Moon	20 minutes

KUNG FU PANDA

INVULNERABILITY

Select Cheats from the Extras menu and enter Down, Down, Right, Up, Left.

INFINITE CHI

Select Cheats from the Extras menu and enter Down, Right, Left, Up, Down.

BIG HEAD MODE

Select Cheats from the Extras menu and enter Down, Up, Left, Right, Right.

ALL MULTIPLAYER CHARACTERS

Select Cheats from the Extras menu and enter Left, Down, Left, Right, Down.

DRAGON WARRIOR OUTFIT IN MULTIPLAYER

Select Cheats from the Extras menu and enter Left, Down, Right, Left, Up.

THE LEGEND OF SPYRO: DAWN OF THE DRAGON

INFINITE HEALTH

Pause the game, hold L1 and press Right, Right, Down, Down, Left with the Left Analog Stick.

INFINITE MANA

Pause the game, hold L1 and press Up, Right, Up, Left, Down with the Left Analog Stick.

MAX XP

Pause the game, hold L1 and press Up, Left, Left, Down, Up with the Left Analog Stick.

ALL ELEMENTAL UPGRADES

Pause the game, hold L1 and press Left, Up, Down, Up, Right with the Left Analog Stick.

LEGO BATMAN

BATCAVE CODES

Using the computer in the Batcave, select Enter Code and enter the following:

CHARACTERS

CHARACTER	CODE
Alfred	ZAQ637
Batgirl	JKR331
Bruce Wayne	BDJ327
Catwoman (Classic)	M1AAWW
Clown Goon	HJK327
Commissioner Gordon	DDP967
Fishmonger	HGY748
Freeze Girl	XVK541
Joker Goon	UTF782
Joker Henchman	YUN924
Mad Hatter	JCA283
Man-Bat	NYU942
Military Policeman	MKL382
Nightwing	MVY759
Penguin Goon	NKA238
Penguin Henchman	BJH782
Penguin Minion	KJP748
Poison Ivy Goon	GTB899
Police Marksman	HKG984
Police Officer	JRY983
Riddler Goon	CRY928
Riddler Henchman	XEU824
S.W.A.T.	HTF114
Sailor	NAV592
Scientist	JFL786
Security Guard	PLB946
The Joker (Tropical)	CCB199
Yeti	NJL412
Zoo Sweeper	DWR243

VEHICLES

VEHICLE	CODE
Bat-Tank	KNTT4B
Bruce Wayne's Private Jet	LEA664
Catwoman's Motorcycle	HPL826
Garbage Truck	DUS483
Goon Helicopter	GCH328
Harbor Helicopter	CHP735
Harley Quinn's Hammer Truck	RDT637
Mad Hatter's Glider	HS000W
Mad Hatter's Steamboat	M4DM4N
Mr. Freeze's Iceberg	ICYICE
The Joker's Van	JUK657
Mr. Freeze's Kart	BCT229
Penguin Goon Submarine	BTN248
Police Bike	LJP234
Police Boat	PLC999
Police Car	KJL832
Police Helicopter	CWR732
Police Van	MAC788
Police Watercraft	VJD328
Riddler's Jet	HAHAHA
Robin's Submarine	TTF453
Two-Face's Armored Truck	EFE933

CHEATS

CHEAT	CODE
Always Score Multiply	9LRGNB
Fast Batarangs	JRBDCB
Fast Walk	ZOLM6N
Flame Batarang	D8NYWH
Freeze Batarang	XPN4NG
Extra Hearts	ML3KHP
Fast Build	EVG26J
Immune to Freeze	JXUDY6
Invincibility	WYD5CP
Minikit Detector	ZXGH9J
More Batarang Targets	XWP645
Piece Detector	KHJ554
Power Brick Detector	MMN786
Regenerate Hearts	HJH7HJ
Score x2	N4NR3E
Score x4	CX9MAT
Score x6	MLVNF2
Score x8	WCCDB9
Score x10	18HW07

LEGO STAR WARS II: THE ORIGINAL TRILOGY

EACH TROOPER
At Mos Eisley Canteena, select Enter Code and enter UCK868. You must still select Characters and purchase this character for 20,000 studs.

BEN KENOBI (GHOST)
At Mos Eisley Canteena, select Enter Code and enter BEN917. You must still select Characters and purchase this character for 1,100,000 studs.

BESPIN GUARD
At Mos Eisley Canteena, select Enter Code and enter VHY832. You must still select Characters and purchase this character for 15,000 studs.

BIB FORTUNA
At Mos Eisley Canteena, select Enter Code and enter WTY721. You must still select Characters and purchase this character for 16,000 studs.

BOBA FETT
At Mos Eisley Canteena, select Enter Code and enter HLP221. You must still select Characters and purchase this character for 175,000 studs.

DEATH STAR TROOPER
At Mos Eisley Canteena, select Enter Code and enter BNC332. You must still select Characters and purchase this character for 19,000 studs.

EWOK
At Mos Eisley Canteena, select Enter Code and enter TTT289. You must still select Characters and purchase this character for 34,000 studs.

GAMORREAN GUARD
At Mos Eisley Canteena, select Enter Code and enter YZF999. You must still select Characters and purchase this character for 40,000 studs.

GONK DROID
At Mos Eisley Canteena, select Enter Code and enter NFX582. You must still select Characters and purchase this character for 1,550 studs.

GRAND MOFF TARKIN
At Mos Eisley Canteena, select Enter Code and enter SMG219. You must still select Characters and purchase this character for 38,000 studs.

GREEDO
At Mos Eisley Canteena, select Enter Code and enter NAH118. You must still select Characters and purchase this character for 60,000 studs.

HAN SOLO (HOOD)
At Mos Eisley Canteena, select Enter Code and enter YWM840. You must still select Characters and purchase this character for 20,000 studs.

IG-88
At Mos Eisley Canteena, select Enter Code and enter NXL973. You must still select Characters and purchase this character for 30,000 studs.

IMPERIAL GUARD
At Mos Eisley Canteena, select Enter Code and enter MMM111. You must still select Characters and purchase this character for 45,000 studs.

IMPERIAL OFFICER
At Mos Eisley Canteena, select Enter Code and enter BBV889. You must still select Characters and purchase this character for 28,000 studs.

IMPERIAL SHUTTLE PILOT
At Mos Eisley Canteena, select Enter Code and enter VAP664. You must still select Characters and purchase this character for 29,000 studs.

IMPERIAL SPY
At Mos Eisley Canteena, select Enter Code and enter CVT125. You must still select Characters and purchase this character for 13,500 studs.

JAWA
At Mos Eisley Canteena, select Enter Code and enter JAW499. You must still select Characters and purchase this character for 24,000 studs.

LOBOT
At Mos Eisley Canteena, select Enter Code and enter UUB319. You must still select Characters and purchase this character for 11,000 studs.

PALACE GUARD
At Mos Eisley Canteena, select Enter Code and enter SGE549. You must still select Characters and purchase this character for 14,000 studs.

REBEL PILOT
At Mos Eisley Canteena, select Enter Code and enter CYG336. You must still select Characters and purchase this character for 15,000 studs.

REBEL TROOPER (HOTH)
At Mos Eisley Canteena, select Enter Code and enter EKU849. You must still select Characters and purchase this character for 16,000 studs.

SANDTROOPER
At Mos Eisley Canteena, select Enter Code and enter YDV451. You must still select Characters and purchase this character for 14,000 studs.

SKIFF GUARD
At Mos Eisley Canteena, select Enter Code and enter GBU888. You must still select Characters and purchase this character for 12,000 studs.

SNOWTROOPER
At Mos Eisley Canteena, select Enter Code and enter NYU989. You must still select Characters and purchase this character for 16,000 studs.

STORMTROOPER
At Mos Eisley Canteena, select Enter Code and enter PTR345. You must still select Characters and purchase this character for 10,000 studs.

THE EMPEROR
At Mos Eisley Canteena, select Enter Code and enter HHY382. You must still select Characters and purchase this character for 275,000 studs.

TIE FIGHTER
At Mos Eisley Canteena, select Enter Code and enter HDY739. You must still select Characters and purchase this item for 60,000 studs.

TIE FIGHTER PILOT
At Mos Eisley Canteena, select Enter Code and enter NNZ316. You must still select Characters and purchase this character for 21,000 studs.

TIE INTERCEPTOR
At Mos Eisley Canteena, select Enter Code and enter QYA828. You must still select Characters and purchase this item for 40,000 studs.

TUSKEN RAIDER
At Mos Eisley Canteena, select Enter Code and enter PEJ821. You must still select Characters and purchase this character for 23,000 studs.

UGNAUGHT
At Mos Eisley Canteena, select Enter Code and enter UGN694. You must still select Characters and purchase this character for 36,000 studs.

MADDEN NFL 07

MADDEN CARDS
Select Madden Cards from My Madden. Then select Madden Codes and enter the following:

CARD	PASSWORD
#199 Gold Lame Duck Cheat	5LAWO0
#200 Gold Mistake Free Cheat	XL7SP1
#210 Gold QB on Target Cheat	WROA0R
#220 Super Bowl XLI Gold	RLA9R7
#221 Super Bowl XLII Gold	WRLUF8
#222 Super Bowl XLIII Gold	NIEV4A
#223 Super Bowl XLIV Gold	M5AB7L
#224 Aloha Stadium Gold	YI8P8U
#225 1958 Colts Gold	B57QLU
#226 1966 Packers Gold	1PL1FL
#227 1968 Jets Gold	MIE6WO
#228 1970 Browns Gold	CL2TOE
#229 1972 Dolphins Gold	NOEB7U

CARD	PASSWORD
#230 1974 Steelers Gold	YO0FLA
#231 1976 Raiders Gold	MOA11I
#232 1977 Broncos Gold	C8UM7U
#233 1978 Dolphins Gold	VIU0O7
#234 1980 Raiders Gold	NLAPH3
#235 1981 Chargers Gold	COAGI4
#236 1982 Redskins Gold	WL8BRI
#237 1983 Raiders Gold	H0EW71
#238 1984 Dolphins Gold	M1AM1E
#239 1985 Bears Gold	QOETO8
#240 1986 Giants Gold	ZI8S2L
#241 1988 49ers Gold	SP2A8H
#242 1990 Eagles Gold	2L4TRO
#243 1991 Lions Gold	J1ETRI
#244 1992 Cowboys Gold	W9UVI9
#245 1993 Bills Gold	DLA3I7
#246 1994 49ers Gold	DR7EST
#247 1996 Packers Gold	F8LUST
#248 1998 Broncos Gold	FIES95
#249 1999 Rams Gold	S9OUSW
#250 Bears Pump Up the Crowd	B1OUPH
#251 Bengals Cheerleader	DRL2SW
#252 Bills Cheerleader	1PLUYO
#253 Broncos Cheerleader	3ROUJO
#254 Browns Pump Up the Crowd	T1UTOA
#255 Buccaneers Cheerleader	S9EWRI
#256 Cardinals Cheerleader	57IEPI
#257 Chargers Cheerleader	F7UHL8
#258 Chiefs Cheerleader	PRI5SL
#259 Colts Cheerleader	1R5AMI
#260 Cowboys Cheerleader	Z2ACHL
#261 Dolphins Cheerleader	C5AHLE
#262 Eagles Cheerleader	PO7DRO
#263 Falcons Cheerleader	37USPO
#264 49ers Cheerleader	KL0CRL
#265 Giants Pump Up the Crowd	C4USPI
#266 Jaguars Cheerleader	MIEH7E
#267 Jets Pump Up the Crowd	COLUXI
#268 Lions Pump Up the Crowd	3LABLU
#269 Packers Pump Up the Crowd	4HO7VO
#270 Panthers Cheerleader	F2IASP
#282 All AFC Team Gold	PRO9PH
#283 All NFC Team Gold	RLATH7

MAJOR LEAGUE BASEBALL 2K8

BIG HEAD MODE

Select Enter Cheat Code from the My 2K8 menu and enter Black Sox. This unlocks the Smart Choice cheat. Go to My Cheats to toggle the cheat on and off.

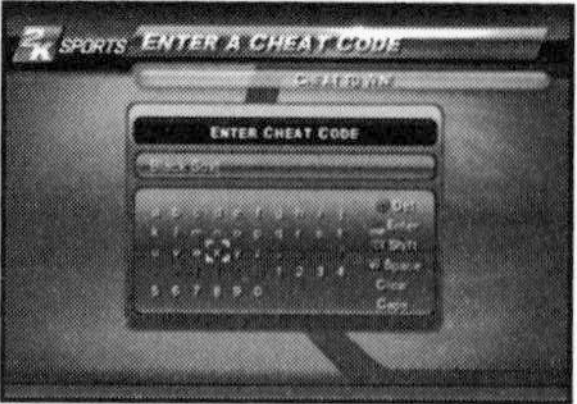

MAJOR LEAGUE BASEBALL 2K9

BIG HEADS

At the Cheats menu, enter Black Sox.

MANHUNT 2

EXTRA LEVEL AS LEO
Defeat the game.

RELIVE SCENE
Defeat the game. This allows you to replay any level.

MARC ECKO'S GETTING UP: CONTENTS UNDER PRESSURE

ALL LEVELS
Select Codes from the Options menu and enter IPULATOR.

INFINITE HEALTH
Select Codes from the Options screen and enter MARCUSECKOS.

MAX HEALTH
Select Codes from the Options screen and enter BABYLONTRUST.

INFINITE SKILLS
Select Codes from the Options screen and enter FLIPTHESCRIPT.

MAX SKILLS
Select Codes from the Options screen and enter VANCEDALLISTER.

ALL COMBAT UPGRADES
Select Codes from the Options menu and enter DOGTAGS.

ALL CHARACTERS IN VERSUS MODE
Select Codes from the Options menu and enter STATEYOURNAME.

ALL VERSUS ARENAS
Select Codes from the Options menu and enter WORKBITCH.

ALL ART
Select Codes from the Options menu and enter SIRULLY.

ALL BLACK BOOK
Select Codes from the Options menu and enter SHARDSOFGLASS.

ALL IPOD
Select Codes from the Options menu and enter GRANDMACELIA.

ALL LEGENDS
Select Codes from the Options menu and enter NINESIX.

ALL MOVIES
Select Codes from the Options menu and enter DEXTERCROWLEY.

MEDAL OF HONOR: VANGUARD

EXTRA ARMOR
Pause the game and press Up, Down, Up, Down to get the Enter Cheat Code message. Then, press Right, Left, Right, Down, Up, Right.

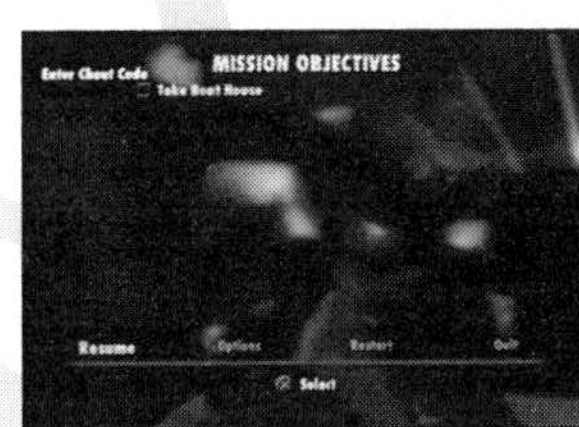

MERCENARIES 2: WORLD IN FLAMES

$1,000,000
At the Faction menu, press Right, Down, Left, Up, Up, Left, Down, Right.

INFINITE AMMO
At the Faction menu, press Right, Left, Right, Right, Left, Right, Left, Left.

INFINITE HEALTH
At the Faction menu, press Press Up, Down, Up, Down, Left, Right, Left, Right.

ALL FACTIONS TO NEUTRAL
At the Faction menu, press Up, Up, Up, Up, Down, Down, Right, Left.

MLB 07: THE SHOW

CLASSIC STADIUMS

At the Main menu, press Down, Up, Right, Down, Up, Left, Down, Up.

GOLDEN/SLIVER ERA PLAYERS

At the Main menu, press Left, Up, Right, Down, Down, Left, Up, Down.

MLB 08: THE SHOW

ALL CLASSIC STADIUMS

At the Main menu, press Down, Right, ●, ■, Left, ▲, Up, L1. The controller will vibrate if entered correctly.

ALL GOLDEN & SILVER ERA PLAYERS IN EXHIBITION

At the Main menu, press L1, L2, ■, ■, ▲, ●, Down. The controller will vibrate if entered correctly.

MLB POWER PROS

VIEW MLB PLAYERS AT CREATED PLAYERS MENU

Select View or Delete Custom Players/Password Display from the My Data menu. Press Up, Up, Down, Down, Left, Right, Left Right, L1, R1.

ALVIN LOCKHART'S BATTING STANCE AND PITCHING FORM

At the Main menu, press Right, Left, Up, Down, Down, Right, Right, Up, Up, Left, Down, Left. These will be available at the shop.

MVP 07 NCAA BASEBALL

ALL CHALLENGE ITEMS

In Dynasty Mode, create a player with the name David Hamel.

MX VS. ATV UNTAMED

EVERYTHING

Select Cheat Codes from the Options menu and enter YOUGOTIT.

1000000 STORE POINTS

Select Cheat Codes from the Options menu and enter MANYZEROS.

50CC BIKE CLASS

Select Cheat Codes from the Options menu and enter LITTLEGUY.

ALL BIKES

Select Cheat Codes from the Options menu and enter ONRAILS.

ALL CHALLENGES

Select Cheat Codes from the Options menu and enter MORESTUFF.

ALL FREESTYLE TRACKS

Select Cheat Codes from the Options menu and enter ALLSTYLE.

ALL GEAR

Select Cheat Codes from the Options menu and enter WELLDRESSED.

ALL MACHINES

Select Cheat Codes from the Options menu and enter MCREWHEELS.

ALL RIDERS

Select Cheat Codes from the Options menu and enter WHOSTHAT.

ALL TRACKS

Select Cheat Codes from the Options menu and enter FREETICKET.

MONSTER TRUCK

Select Cheat Codes from the Options menu and enter PWNAGE.

NARUTO: ULTIMATE NINJA 2

In Naruto's house, select Input Password. Here you are able to enter an element, then three signs. Enter the following here:

1,000 RYO

Water, Hare, Monkey, Monkey
Water, Ram, Horse, Dog
Water, Horse, Horse, Horse
Water, Rat, Rooster, Boar
Water, Rat, Monkey, Rooster
Fire, Rat, Dragon, Dog

5,000 RYO

Water, Tiger, Dragon, Tiger
Water, Snake, Rooster, Horse

10,000 RYO

Fire, Tiger, Tiger, Rooster
Fire, Tiger, Dragon, Hare

NASCAR 08

ALL CHASE MODE CARS

Select cheat codes from the options menu and enter checkered flag.

EA SPORTS CAR

Select cheat codes from the options menu and enter ea sports car.

FANTASY DRIVERS

Select cheat codes from the options menu and enter race the pack.

WALMART CAR AND TRACK

Select cheat codes from the options menu and enter walmart everyday.

NASCAR 09

WALMART TRACK AND THE WALMART CAR

In Chase for the Sprint Cup, enter the driver's name as WalMart EveryDay.

NBA 07

2006 CHARLOTTE BOBCATS ALTERNATE JERSEY

Select NBA.com from the Trophy Room. Press ◉ to bring up the Enter Code screen. Enter JKL846ETK5.

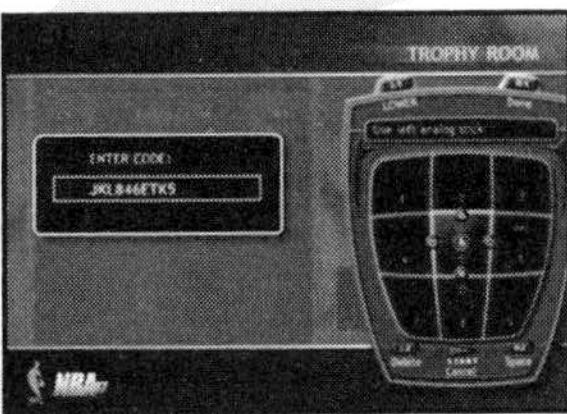

2006 NOK HORNETS ALTERNATE JERSEY

Select NBA.com from the Trophy Room. Press ◉ to bring up the Enter Code screen. Enter EL2E3T8H58.

2006 NEW JERSEY NETS ALTERNATE JERSEY

Select NBA.com from the Trophy Room. Press ◉ to bring up the Enter Code screen. Enter NB79D965D2.

2006 UTAH JAZZ ALTERNATE JERSEY

Select NBA.com from the Trophy Room. Press ◉ to bring up the Enter Code screen. Enter 228GG7585G.

2006 WAS WIZARDS ALTERNATE JERSEY

Select NBA.com from the Trophy Room. Press ◉ to bring up the Enter Code screen. Enter PL5285F37F.

2007 EASTERN ALL STARS

Select NBA.com from the Trophy Room. Press ◉ to bring up the Enter Code screen. Enter 5F89RE3H8G.

2007 WESTERN ALL STARS

Select NBA.com from the Trophy Room. Press ◉ to bring up the Enter Code screen. Enter 2H5E89EH8C.

NBA 09 THE INSIDE

ALL-STAR 09 EAST

Select Trophy Room from the Options. Press L1, then ◉, and enter SHPNV2K699.

ALL-STAR 09 WEST

Select Trophy Room from the Options. Press L1, then ◉, and enter K8AV6YMLNF.

ALL TROPHIES

Select Trophy Room from the Options. Press L1, then ◉, and enter K@ZZ@@M!.

LA LAKERS LATIN NIGHTS

Select Trophy Room from the Options. Press L1, then ◉, and enter NMTWCTC84S.

MIAMI HEAT LATIN NIGHTS

Select Trophy Room from the Options. Press L1, then ◉, and enter WCTGSA8SPD.

PHOENIX SUNS LATIN NIGHTS

Select Trophy Room from the Options. Press L1, then ◉, and enter LKUTSENFJH.

SAN ANTONIO LATIN NIGHTS

Select Trophy Room from the Options. Press L1, then ◉, and enter JFHSY73MYD.

NBA 2K8

2K SPORTS TEAM

Select Codes from the Features menu and enter 2ksports.

NBA DEVELOPMENT TEAM

Select Codes from the Features menu and enter nba2k.

VISUAL CONCEPTS TEAM

Select Codes from the Features menu and enter vcteam.

ABA BALL

Select Codes from the Features menu and enter payrespect.

NBA LIVE 08

ADIDAS GIL II ZERO SHOE CODES

Select NBA Codes from My NBA Live and enter the following:

SHOES	CODE
Agent Zero	ADGILLIT6BE
Black President	ADGILLIT7BF
Cuba	ADGILLIT4BC
Cust0mize Shoe	ADGILLIT5BD
GilWood	ADGILLIT1B9
TS Lightswitch Away	ADGILLIT0B8
TS Lightswitch Home	ADGILLIT2BA

PENNANT CODES

Go to My Shrine and select Pennants. Press Select and enter the following:

PENNANT	CODE
#200 1st & 15 Cheat	Thanks
#201 Blink Cheat	For
#202 Boing Cheat	Registering
#204 Butter Fingers Cheat	With EA
#205 Crossed The Line Cheat	Tiburon
#206 Cuffed Cheat	EA Sports
#207 Extra Credit Cheat	Touchdown
#208 Helium Cheat	In The Zone
#209 Hurricane Cheat	Turnover
#210 Instant FrePlay Cheat	Impact
#211 Jumbalaya Cheat	Heisman
#212 Molasses Cheat	Game Time
#213 Nike Free Cheat	Break Free
#214 Nike Magnigrip Cheat	Hand Picked
#215 Nike Pro Cheat	No Sweat
#219 QB Dud Cheat	Elite 11
#221 Steel Toe Cheat	Gridiron
#222 Stiffed Cheat	NCAA
#223 Super Dive Cheat	Upset
#226 Tough As Nail Cheats	Offense
#228 What A Hit Cheat	Blitz
#229 Kicker Hex Cheat	Sideline
#273 2004 All-American Team	Fumble
#274 All-Alabama Team	Roll Tide
#276 All-Arkansas Team	Woopigsooie
#277 All-Auburn Team	War Eagle
#278 All-Clemson Team	Death Valley
#279 All-Colorado Team	Glory
#281 All-FSU Team	Uprising
#282 All-Georgia Team	Hunker Down
#283 All-Iowa Team	On Iowa
#285 All-LSU Team	Geaux Tigers
#287 All-Michigan Team	Go Blue
#288 All-Mississippi State Team	Hail State
#289 All-Nebraska Team	Go Big Red
#291 All-Notre Dame Team	Golden Domer
#292 All-Ohio State Team	Killer Nuts
#293 All-Oklahoma Team	Boomer
#294 All-Oklahoma State Team	Go Pokes
#296 All-Penn State Team	We Are
#298 All-Purdue Team	Boiler Up
#300 All-Tennessee Team	Big Orange
#301 All-Texas Team	Hook Em
#302 All-Texas A&M Team	Gig Em
#303 All-UCLA Team	Mighty
#304 All-USC Team	Fight On
#305 All-Virginia Team	Wahoos
#307 All-Washington Team	Bow Down
#308 All-Wisconsin Team	U Rah Rah
#344 MSU Mascot Team	Mizzou Rah
#385 Wyo Mascot	All Hail
#386 Zips Mascot	Hail WV

NEED FOR SPEED PROSTREET

$2,000
Select Career and then choose Code Entry. Enter 1MA9X99.

$4,000
Select Career and then choose Code Entry. Enter W2IOLL01.

$8,000
Select Career and then choose Code Entry. Enter L1IS97A1.

$10,000
Select Career and then choose Code Entry. Enter 1MI9K7E1.

$10,000
Select Career and then choose Code Entry. Enter CASHMONEY.

$10,000
Select Career and then choose Code Entry. Enter REGGAME.

AUDI TT
Select Career and then choose Code Entry. Enter ITSABOUTYOU.

CHEVELLE SS
Select Career and then choose Code Entry. Enter HORSEPOWER.

COKE ZERO GOLF GTI
Select Career and then choose Code Entry. Enter COKEZERO.

DODGE VIPER
Select Career and then choose Code Entry. Enter WORLDSLONGESTLASTING.

MITSUBISHI LANCER EVOLUTION
Select Career and then choose Code Entry. Enter MITSUBISHIGOFAR.

UNLOCK ALL BONUSES
Select Career and then choose Code Entry. Enter UNLOCKALLTHINGS.

5 REPAIR MARKERS
Select Career and then choose Code Entry. Enter SAFETYNET.

ENERGIZER VINYL
Select Career and then choose Code Entry. Enter ENERGIZERLITHIUM.

CASTROL SYNTEC VINYL
Select Career and then choose Code Entry. Enter CASTROLSYNTEC. This also gives you $10,000.

NHL 08

ALL RBK EDGE JERSEYS
At the RBK Edge Code option, enter h3oyxpwksf8ibcgt.

NHL 09

UNLOCK 3RD JERSEYS
At the Cheat menu, enter xe6377uyrwm48frf.

NICKTOONS: ATTACK OF THE TOYBOTS

DAMAGE BOOST
Select Cheats from the Extras menu. Choose Enter Cheat Code and enter 456645.

INVULNERABILITY
Select Cheats from the Extras menu. Choose Enter Cheat Code and enter 313456.

UNLOCK EXO-HUGGLES 9000
Select Cheats from the Extras menu. Choose Enter Cheat Code and enter 691427.

UNLOCK MR. HUGGLES
Select Cheats from the Extras menu. Choose Enter Cheat Code and enter 654168.

UNLIMITED LOBBER GOO
Select Cheats from the Extras menu. Choose Enter Cheat Code and enter 118147.

UNLIMITED SCATTER GOO
Select Cheats from the Extras menu. Choose Enter Cheat Code and enter 971238.

UNLIMITED SPLITTER GOO
Select Cheats from the Extras menu. Choose Enter Cheat Code and enter 854511.

OVER THE HEDGE

COMPLETE LEVELS

Pause the game, hold L1 + R1 and press △, ○, △, ○, ○, □.

ALL MINI-GAMES

Pause the game, hold L1 + R1 and press △, ○, △, △, □, □.

MORE HP FROM FOOD

Pause the game, hold L1 + R1 and press △, ○, △, ○, □, △.

ALWAYS POWER PROJECTILE

Pause the game, hold L1 + R1 and press △, ○, △, ○, □, ○.

BONUS COMIC 14

Pause the game, hold L1 + R1 and press △, ○, □, □, ○, △.

BONUS COMIC 15

Pause the game, hold L1 + R1 and press △, △, □, ○, □, ○.

PRINCE OF PERSIA: THE TWO THRONES

BABY TOY HAMMER WEAPON

Pause the game and press Left, Left, Right, Right, ○ □, □, ○, Up, Down.

CHAINSAW WEAPON

Pause the game and press Up, Up, Down, Down, Left, Right, Left, Right, ○, □, ○, □.

SWORDFISH WEAPON

Pause the game and press Up, Down, Up, Down, Left, Right, Left, Right, ○, □, ○, □.

TELEPHONE OF SORROW WEAPON

Pause the game and press Left, Right, Left, Right, ○, □, ○, ○, □, □.

RATATOUILLE

Select Gusteau's Shop from the Extras menu. Choose Secrets, select the appropriate code number, and then enter the code. Once the code is entered, select the cheat you want to activate it.

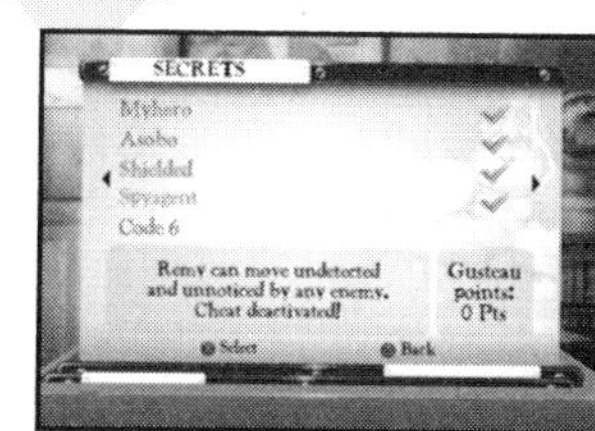

CODE #	CODE	EFFECT
1	Pieceocake	Very Easy difficulty mode
2	Myhero	no impact and no damage from enemies
3	Asobo	Plays the Asobo logo
4	Shielded	No damage from enemies
5	Spyagent	Move undetected by any enemy
6	Ilikeonions	Fart every time Remy jumps
7	Hardfeelings	Head butt when attacking instead of tailswipe
8	Slumberparty	Multiplayer mode
9	Gusteauart	All Concept Art
10	Gusteauship	All four championship modes
11	Mattelme	All single player and multiplayer minigames
12	Gusteauvid	All Videos
13	Gusteaures	All Bonus Artworks
14	Gusteaudream	All Dream Worlds in Gusteau's Shop
15	Gusteauslide	All Slides in Gusteau's Shop
16	Gusteaulevel	All single player minigames
17	Gusteaucombo	All items in Gusteau's Shop
18	Gusteaupot	5,000 Gusteau points
19	Gusteaujack	10,000 Gusteau points
20	Gusteauomni	50,000 Gusteau points

RATCHET AND CLANK: UP YOUR ARSENAL

DUEL BLADE LASER SWORD

Pause the game and press ●, ■, ●, ■, Up, Down, Left, Left.

QWARK'S ALTERNATE COSTUME

Start a game of Qwark Vid-Comic and press Up, Up, Down, Down, Left, Right, ●, ●, ■.

PIRATE VS NINJA MINI-GAME

At the Qwark Comics Issue select, press ■ to bring up a password screen. Enter _MEGHAN_ as a password.

4-PLAYER BOMB MINI-GAME

At the Qwark Comics Issue select, press ■ to bring up a password screen. Enter YING_TZU as a password. Press Start, Select to return to Starship Phoenix.

SLY 2: BAND OF THIEVES DEMO

At the Title screen, hold L1 + L2 + R1 + R2.

RESERVOIR DOGS

UNLIMITED AMMO

Select Cheats from the Extras menu and press R2, L2, ●, L2, ⊗, R2.

ALL LEVELS

Select Cheats from the Extras menu and press L2, R2, L2, R2, L1, R1.

ART GALLERY

Select Cheats from the Extras menu and press ●, ⊗, L2, R2, ●, ⊗.

MOVIE GALLERY

Select Cheats from the Extras menu and press L1, L1, ●, ⊗, L1, R1.

RESIDENT EVIL 4

ALTERNATE TITLE SCREEN

Complete the game.

MATILDA

Complete the game.

MERCENARIES

Complete the game.

PROFESSIONAL DIFFICULTY

Complete the game.

SEPERATE WAYS

Complete the game.

ASHLEY'S ARMOR OUTFIT

Defeat Separate Ways.

LEON'S GANGSTER OUTFIT

Defeat Separate Ways.

ROBOTS

BIG HEAD

Pause the game and press Up, Down, Down, Up, Right, Right, Left, Right.

UNLIMITED HEALTH

Pause the game and press Up, Right, Down, Up, Left, Down, Right, Left.

UNLIMITED SCRAP

Pause the game and press Down, Down, Left, Up, Up, Right, Up, Down.

ROCK BAND

ALL SONGS

At the Title screen, press Red, Yellow, Blue, Red, Red, Blue, Blue, Red, Yellow, Blue. Using this code disables the ability to save your game.

SAMURAI JACK: THE SHADOW OF AKU

MAXIMUM HEALTH

During a game, hold Left on the Left Analog Stick + Right on the Right Analog Stick and press ×, ○, △, □.

MAXIMUM ZEN

During a game, hold Left on the Left Analog Stick + Right on the Right Analog Stick and press ○, ×, □, △.

CRYSTAL SWORD

During a game, press Left on the Left Analog Stick Down + Up on the Right Analog Stick and press ×, ○, □, △.

FIRE SWORD

During a game, press Down on the Left Analog Stick + Up on the Right Analog Stick and press □, ×, ○, △.

LIGHTNING SWORD

During a game, press Down on the Left Analog Stick + Up on the Right Analog Stick and press ○, ×, △, □.

SCARFACE: THE WORLD IS YOURS

After entering the following Cheats, highlight the cheat and press A to "DO IT."

MAX AMMO

Pause the game, select Cheats and enter AMMO.

REFILL HEALTH

Pause the game, select Cheats and enter MEDIK.

FILL BALLS METER

Pause the game, select Cheats and enter FPATCH.

KILL TONY

Pause the game, select Cheats and enter KILTONY.

DECREASE COP HEAT

Pause the game, select Cheats and enter FLYSTRT.

INCREASE COP HEAT

Pause the game, select Cheats and enter DONUT.

DECREASE GANG HEAT

Pause the game, select Cheats and enter NOBALLS.

INCREASE GANG HEAT

Pause the game, select Cheats and enter GOBALLS.

REPAIR TONY'S VEHICLE

Pause the game, select Cheats and enter TBURGLR.

SPAWN ARIEL MK III

Pause the game, select Cheats and enter OLDFAST.

SPAWN BACINARI

Pause the game, select Cheats and enter 666999.

SPAWN BODOG STAMPEDE
Pause the game, select Cheats and enter BUMMER.

SPAWN BULLDOZER
Pause the game, select Cheats and enter DOZER.

SPAWN ODIN VH88
Pause the game, select Cheats and enter DUMPER.

BLACK SUIT TONY
Pause the game, select Cheats and enter BLACK.

BLUE PINSTRIPE SUIT TONY WITH SHADES
Pause the game, select Cheats and enter BLUESH.

GRAY SUIT TONY
Pause the game, select Cheats and enter GRAY.

GRAY SUIT TONY WITH SHADES
Pause the game, select Cheats and enter GRAYSH.

HAWAIIAN SHIRT TONY
Pause the game, select Cheats and enter HAWAII.

HAWAIIAN SHIRT TONY WITH SHADES
Pause the game, select Cheats and enter HAWAIIG.

SANDY SHIRT TONY
Pause the game, select Cheats and enter SANDY.

SANDY SHIRT TONY WITH SHADES
Pause the game, select Cheats and enter SANDYSH.

WHITE SUIT TONY
Pause the game, select Cheats and enter WHITE.

WHITE SUIT TONY WITH SHADES
Pause the game, select Cheats and enter WHITESH.

CHANGE TIME OF DAY
Pause the game, select Cheats and enter MARTHA.

TOGGLE LIGHTNING
Pause the game, select Cheats and enter SHAZAAM.

TOGGLE RAIN
Pause the game, select Cheats and enter RAINY.

BREAL "THE WORLD IS YOURS" MUSIC TRACK
Pause the game, select Cheats and enter TUNEME.

SEGA GENESIS COLLECTION

Before using the following cheats, select the ABC Control option. This sets the controller to the following: ■ is A, ✖ is B, ● is C.

ALTERED BEAST

OPTIONS MENU
At the title screen, hold B and press Start.

LEVEL SELECT
After enabling the Options menu, select a level from the menu. At the title screen, hold A and press Start.

BEAST SELECT
At the title screen, hold A + B + C + Down/Left and then press Start

SOUND TEST
At the title screen, hold A + C + Up/Right and press Start.

COMIX ZONE

INVINCIBILITY
At the jukebox screen, press C on the following sounds:
3, 12, 17, 2, 2, 10, 2, 7, 7, 11

LEVEL SELECT
At the jukebox screen, press C on the following sounds:
14, 15, 18, 5, 13, 1, 3, 18, 15, 6
Press C on the desired level.

ECCO THE DOLPHIN

INVINCIBILITY

When the level name appears, hold A + Start until the level begins.

DEBUG MENU

Pause the game with Ecco facing the screen and press Right, B, C, B, C, Down, C, Up.

INFINITE AIR

Enter LIFEFISH as a password.

PASSWORDS

LEVEL	PASSWORD
The Undercaves	WEFIDNMP
The Vents	BQDPXJDS
The Lagoon	JNSBRIKY
Ridge Water	NTSBZTKB
Open Ocean	YWGTTJNI
Ice Zone	HZIFZBMF
Hard Water	LRFJRQLI
Cold Water	UYNFRQLC
Island Zone	LYTIOQLZ
Deep Water	MNOPOQLR
The Marble	RJNTQQLZ
The Library	RTGXQQLE
Deep City	DDXPQQLJ
City of Forever	MSDBRQLA
Jurassic Beach	IYCBUNLB
Pteranodon Pond	DMXEUNLI
Origin Beach	EGRIUNLB
Trilobite Circle	IELMUNLB
Dark Water	RKEQUNLN
City of Forever 2	HPQIGPLA
The Tube	JUMFKMLB
The Machine	GXUBKMLF
The Last Fight	TSONLMLU

FLICKY

ROUND SELECT

Begin a new game. Before the first round appears, hold A + C + Up + Start. Press Up or Down to select a Round.

GAIN GROUND

LEVEL SELECT

At the Options screen, press A, C, B, C.

GOLDEN AXE

LEVEL SELECT

Select Arcade Mode. At the character select, hold Down/Left + B and press Start. Press Up or Down to select a level.

RISTAR

Select Passwords from the Options menu and enter the following:

LEVEL SELECT

ILOVEU

BOSS RUSH MODE

MUSEUM

TIME ATTACK MODE

DOFEEL

TOUGHER DIFFICULTY

SUPER

ONCHI MUSIC

MAGURO. Activate this from the Sound Test.

CLEARS PASSWORD

XXXXXX

GAME COPYRIGHT INFO

AGES

SONIC THE HEDGEHOG

LEVEL SELECT

At the title screen, press Up, Down, Left, Right. Hold A and press Start.

SONIC THE HEDGEHOG 2

LEVEL SELECT

Select Sound Test from the options. Press C on the following sounds in order: 19, 65, 09, 17. At the title screen, hold A and press Start.

VECTORMAN

DEBUG MODE

At the options screen, press A, B, B, A, Down, A, B, B, A.

REFILL LIFE

Pause the game and press A, B, Right, A, C, A, Down, A, B, Right, A.

VECTORMAN 2

LEVEL SELECT

Pause the game and press Up, Right, A, B, A, Down, Left, A, Down.

EXTRA LIFE

Pause the game and press Right, Up, B, A, Down, Up, B, Down, Up, B. Repeat for more lives.

FULL ENERGY

Pause the game and press B, A, B, A, Left, Up, Up.

NEW WEAPON

Pause the game and press C, A, Left, Left, Down, A, Down. Repeat for more weapons.

SEGA SUPERSTARS TENNIS

UNLOCK CHARACTERS

Complete the following missions to unlock the corresponding character.

CHARACTER	COMPLETE THIS MISSION
Alex Kidd	Mission 1 of Alex Kidd's World
Amy Rose	Mission 2 of Sonic the Hedgehog's World
Gilius	Mission 1 of Golden Axe's World
Gum	Mission 12 of Jet Grind Radio's World
Meemee	Mission 8 of Super Monkey Ball's World
Pudding	Mission 1 of Space Channel 5's World
Reala	Mission 2 of NiGHTs' World
Shadow The Hedgehog	Mission 14 of Sonic the Hedgehog's World

SHAMAN KING: POWER OF SPIRIT

VERSUS MODE

Complete all 20 episodes in Story Mode.

MASKED MERIL IN VERSUS MODE

Press Select on Meril.

MATILDA IN VERSUS MODE

Press Select on Kanna.

MARION FAUNA IN VERSUS MODE

Press Select on Matilda.

ZEKE ASAKURA IN VERSUS MODE

Press Select on Yoh Asakura.

SHREK THE THIRD

10,000 GOLD COINS

At the gift shop, press Up, Up, Down, Up, Right, Left.

SILENT HILL: ORIGINS

CODEBREAKER SUIT

During a game, press Up, Up, Down, Down, Left, Right, Left, Right, ⊗, ●. You must first finish the game to get this suit.

THE SIMPSONS GAME

UNLIMITED POWER FOR ALL CHARACTERS

At the Extras menu, press ○, Left, Right, ○, □, L1.

ALL CLICHÉS.

At the Extras menu, press Left, □, Right, ○, Right, L1.

ALL MOVIES

At the Extras menu, press □, Left, □, Right, ○, R1.

THE SIMS 2: CASTAWAY

CHEAT GNOME

During a game, press R1, L1, Down, □, R2. You can now use this Gnome to get the following:

EXCLUSIVE VEST AND TANKTOP

Pause the game and go to Fashion and Grooming. Press □, R2, R2, △, Down.

MAX ALL MOTIVES

During a game, press R2, Up, X, □, L1.

MAX CURRENT INVENTORY

During a game, press Left, Right, □, R2, □.

MAX RELATIONSHIPS

During a game, press L1, Up, R2, Left, △.

ALL RESOURCES

During a game, press □, △, Down, X, Left.

ALL CRAFTING PLANS

During a game, press X, △, L2, □, R1.

ADD 1 TO SKILL

During a game, press △, L1, L1, Left, △.

THE SIMS 2: PETS

CHEAT GNOME

During a game, press L1, L1, R1, ✕, ✕, Up.

GIVE SIM PET POINTS

After activating the Cheat Gnome, press △, ○, ✕, □, L1, R1 during a game. Select the Gnome to access the cheat.

ADVANCE 6 HOURS

After activating the Cheat Gnome, press Up, Left, Down, Right, R1 during a game. Select the Gnome to access the cheat.

GIVE SIM SIMOLEONS

After activating the Cheat Gnome, enter the Advance 6 Hours cheat. Access the Gnome and exit. Enter the cheat again. Now, Give Sim Simoleons should be available from the Gnome.

CAT AND DOG CODES

When creating a family, press □ to Enter Unlock Code. Enter the following for new fur patterns.

FUR PATTERN/CAT OR DOG	UNLOCK CODE
Bandit Mask Cats	EEGJ2YRQZZAIZ9QHA64
Bandit Mask Dogs	EEGJ2YRQZQARQ9QHA64
Black Dot Cats	EEGJ2YRZQQ1IQ9QHA64
Black Dot Dogs	EEGJ2YRQZZ1IQ9QHA64
Black Smiley Cats	EEGJ2YRQQZ1RQ9QHA64
Black Smiley Dogs	EEGJ2YRZQQARQ9QHA64
Blue Bones Cats	EEGJ2YRQZZARQ9QHA64
Blue Bones Dogs	EEGJ2YRZZZ1IZ9QHA64
Blue Camouflage Cats	EEGJ2YRZZQ1IQ9QHA64
Blue Camouflage Dogs	EEGJ2YRZZZ1RQ9QHA64
Blue Cats	EEGJ2YRQZZAIQ9QHA64
Blue Dogs	EEGJ2YRQQQ1IZ9QHA64

FUR PATTERN/CAT OR DOG	UNLOCK CODE
Blue Star Cats	EEGJ2YRQQZ1IZ9QHA64
Blue Star Dogs	EEGJ2YRQZQ1IQ9QHA64
Deep Red Cats	EEGJ2YRQQQAIQ9QHA64
Deep Red Dogs	EEGJ2YRQZQ1RQ9QHA64
Goofy Cats	EEGJ2YRQZQ1IZ9QHA64
Goofy Dogs	EEGJ2YRZZZARQ9QHA64
Green Cats	EEGJ2YRZQQAIZ9QHA64
Green Dogs	EEGJ2YRQZQAIQ9QHA64
Green Flower Cats	EEGJ2YRZQZAIQ9QHA64
Green Flower Dogs	EEGJ2YRQZZ1RQ9QHA64
Light Green Cats	EEGJ2YRZZQ1RQ9QHA64
Light Green Dogs	EEGJ2YRZQQ1RQ9QHA64
Navy Hearts Cats	EEGJ2YRZQZ1IQ9QHA64
Navy Hearts Dogs	EEGJ2YRQQZ1IQ9QHA64
Neon Green Cats	EEGJ2YRZZQAIQ9QHA64
Neon Green Dogs	EEGJ2YRZQQAIQ9QHA64
Neon Yellow Cats	EEGJ2YRZZQARQ9QHA64
Neon Yellow Dogs	EEGJ2YRQQQAIZ9QHA64
Orange Diagonal Cats	EEGJ2YRQQZAIQ9QHA64
Orange Diagonal Dogs	EEGJ2YRZQZ1IZ9QHA64
Panda Cats	EEGJ2YRQZQAIZ9QHA64
Pink Cats	EEGJ2YRQZZ1IZ9QHA64
Pink Dogs	EEGJ2YRZQZ1RQ9QHA64
Pink Vertical Strip Cats	EEGJ2YRQQQARQ9QHA64
Pink Vertical Strip Dogs	EEGJ2YRZZZAIQ9QHA64
Purple Cats	EEGJ2YRQQZARQ9QHA64
Purple Dogs	EEGJ2YRQQZAIZ9QHA64
Star Cats	EEGJ2YRZQZARQ9QHA64
Star Dogs	EEGJ2YRZQZAIZ9QHA64
White Paws Cats	EEGJ2YRQQQ1RQ9QHA64
White Paws Dogs	EEGJ2YRZQQ1IZ9QHA64
White Zebra Stripe Cats	EEGJ2YRZZQ1IZ9QHA64
White Zebra Stripe Dogs	EEGJ2YRZZZ1IQ9QHA64
Zebra Stripes Dogs	EEGJ2YRZZQAIZ9QHA64

SLY 3: HONOR AMONG THIEVES

TOONAMI PLANE

While flying the regular plane, pause the game and press R1, R1, Right, Down, Down, Right.

RESTART EPISODES

Pause the game during the Episode and enter the following codes to restart that Episode. You must first complete that part of the Episode to use the code.

EPISODE	CODE
Episode 1, Day 1	Left, R2, Right, L1, R2, L1
Episode 1, Day 2	Down, L2, Up, Left, R2, L2
Episode 2, Day 1	Right, L2, Left, Up, Right, Down
Episode 2, Day 2	Down, Up, R1, Up, R2, L2
Episode 3, Day 1	R2, R1, L1, Left, L1, Down
Episode 3, Day 2	L2, R1, R2, L2, L1, Up
Episode 4, Day 1	Left, Right, L1, R2, Right, R2
Episode 4, Day 2	L1, Left, L2, Left, Up, L1
Episode 5, Day 1	Left, R2, Right, Up, L1, R2
Episode 5, Day 2	R2, R1, L1, R1, R2, R1
Operation Laptop Retrieval	L2, Left, R1, L2, L1, Down
Operation Moon Crash	L2, Up, Left, L1, L2, L1
Operation Reverse Double Cross	Right, Left, Up, Left, R2, Left
Operation Tar Be-Gone	Down, L2, R1, L2, R1, Right
Operation Turbo Dominant Eagle	Down, Right, Left, L2, R1, Right
Operation Wedding Crasher	L2, R2, Right, Down, L1, R2

SOCOM 3: U.S. NAVY SEALS

DISPLAY COORDINATES

Pause the game and press Square, Triangle, Circle, Circle, L1, Triangle, Circle, Circle, Triangle, Square.

SOCOM U.S. NAVY SEALS: COMBINED ASSAULT

SHOW COORDINATES

Pause the game and press Square, Triangle, Circle, Circle, L1, Triangle, Circle, Circle, Triangle, Square.

THE SOPRANOS: ROAD TO RESPECT

INFINITE AMMO

During a game, hold L2 + R2 and press Circle, Square, X, Square, Triangle, Triangle.

INFINITE RESPECT

During a game, hold L2 + R2 and press X, Square, X, Square, Triangle, Triangle.

SPIDER-MAN: FRIEND OR FOE

NEW GREEN GOBLIN AS A SIDEKICK

While standing in the Helicarrier between levels, press Left, Down, Right, Right, Down, Left.

SANDMAN AS A SIDEKICK

While standing in the Helicarrier between levels, press Right, Right, Right, Up, Down, Left.

VENOM AS A SIDEKICK

While standing in the Helicarrier between levels, press Left, Left, Right, Up, Down, Down.

5000 TECH TOKENS

While standing in the Helicarrier between levels, press Up, Up, Down, Down, Left, Right.

THE SPIDERWICK CHRONICLES

INVULNERABILITY

During the game, hold L1 + R1 and press Triangle, Triangle, Triangle, Triangle, X, X, Triangle, Triangle.

HEAL

During the game, hold L1 + R1 and press Triangle, Square, X, Circle, Triangle, Square, X, Circle.

COMBAT LOADOUT

During the game, hold L1 + R1 and press Triangle, Triangle, X, X, Square, Circle, Square, Circle.

INFINITE AMMO

During the game, hold L1 + R1 and press Square, Square, Square, Circle, X, X, X, Triangle.

FIELD GUIDE UNLOCKED

During the game, hold L1 + R1 and press Circle, Circle, Circle, Square, Triangle, Triangle, Triangle, X.

SPRITE A

During the game, hold L2 + R2 and press Triangle, X, Circle, Square, X, Triangle, Square, Circle.

SPRITE B

During the game, hold L2 + R2 and press X, X, Triangle, Square, Square, Circle, Triangle, X.

SPRITE C

During the game, hold L2 + R2 and press Circle, Triangle, Square, X, Circle, Triangle, Square, X.

SPONGEBOB SQUAREPANTS: CREATURE FROM THE KRUSTY KRAB

30,000 EXTRA Z'S

Select Cheat Codes from the Extras menu and enter ROCFISH.

PUNK SPONGEBOB IN DIESEL DREAMING

Select Cheat Codes from the Extras menu and enter SPONGE. Select Activate Bonus Items to enable this bonus item.

HOT ROD SKIN IN DIESEL DREAMING

Select Cheat Codes from the Extras menu and enter HOTROD. Select Activate Bonus Items to enable this bonus item.

PATRICK TUX IN STARFISHMAN TO THE RESCUE

Select Cheat Codes from the Extras menu and enter PATRICK. Select Activate Bonus Items to enable this bonus item.

SPONGEBOB PLANKTON IN SUPER-SIZED PATTY

Select Cheat Codes from the Extras menu and enter PANTS. Select Activate Bonus Items to enable this bonus item.

PATRICK LASER COLOR IN ROCKET RODEO

Select Cheat Codes from the Extras menu and enter ROCKET. Select Activate Bonus Items to enable this bonus item.

PATRICK ROCKET SKIN COLOR IN ROCKET RODEO

Select Cheat Codes from the Extras menu and enter SPACE. Select Activate Bonus Items to enable this bonus item.

PLANKTON EYE LASER COLOR IN REVENGE OF THE GIANT PLANKTON MONSTER

Select Cheat Codes from the Extras menu and enter LASER. Select Activate Bonus Items to enable this bonus item.

PIRATE PATRICK IN ROOFTOP RUMBLE

Select Cheat Codes from the Extras menu and enter PIRATE. Select Activate Bonus Items to enable this bonus item.

HOVERCRAFT VEHICLE SKIN IN HYPNOTIC HIGHWAY—PLANKTON

Select Cheat Codes from the Extras menu and enter HOVER. Select Activate Bonus Items to enable this bonus item.

SPONGEBOB SQUAREPANTS FEATURING NICKTOONS: GLOBS OF DOOM

When entering the following codes, the order of the characters going down is: SpongeBob SquarePants, Nicolai Technus, Danny Phantom, Dib, Zim, Tlaloc, Tak, Beautiful Gorgeous, Jimmy Neutron, Plankton. These names are shortened to the first name in the following.

ATTRACT COINS

Using the Upgrade Machine on the bottom level of the lair, select "Input cheat codes here". Enter Tlaloc, Plankton, Danny, Plankton, Tak. Coins are attracted to you making them much easier to collect.

DON'T LOSE COINS

Using the Upgrade Machine on the bottom level of the lair, select "Input cheat codes here". Enter Plankton, Jimmy, Beautiful, Jimmy, Plankton. You don't lose coins when you get knocked out.

GOO HAS NO EFFECT

Using the Upgrade Machine on the bottom level of the lair, select "Input cheat codes here". Enter Danny, Danny, Danny, Nicolai, Nicolai. Goo does not slow you down.

MORE GADGET COMBO TIME

Using the Upgrade Machine on the bottom level of the lair, select "Input cheat codes here". Enter SpongeBob, Beautiful, Danny, Plankton, Nicolai. You have more time to perform gadget combos.

SPY HUNTER: NOWHERE TO RUN

SPY HUNTER ARCADE

You must activate the machine when you come across it in the safe house on Level 7 (Cleaning Up).

SSX ON TOUR

NEW THREADS
Select Cheats from the Extras menu and enter FLYTHREADS.

THE WORLD IS YOURS
Select Cheats from the Extras menu and enter BACKSTAGEPASS.

SHOW TIME (ALL MOVIES)
Select Cheats from the Extras menu and enter THEBIGPICTURE.

BLING BLING (INFINITE CASH)
Select Cheats from the Extras menu and enter LOOTSNOOT.

FULL BOOST, FULL TIME
Select Cheats from the Extras menu and enter ZOOMJUICE.

MONSTERS ARE LOOSE (MONSTER TRICKS)
Select Cheats from the Extras menu and enter JACKALOPESTYLE.

SNOWBALL FIGHT
Select Cheats from the Extras menu and enter LETSPARTY.

FEEL THE POWER (STAT BOOST)
Select Cheats from the Extras menu and enter POWERPLAY.

CHARACTERS ARE LOOSE
Select Cheats from the Extras menu and enter ROADIEROUNDUp.

UNLOCK CONRAD
Select Cheats from the Extras menu and enter BIGPARTYTIME.

UNLOCK MITCH KOOBSKI
Select Cheats from the Extras menu and enter MOREFUNTHANONE.

UNLOCK NIGEL
Select Cheats from the Extras menu and enter THREEISACROWD.

UNLOCK SKI PATROL
Select Cheats from the Extras menu and enter FOURSOME.

STAR TREK: ENCOUNTERS

ALL LEVELS AND SHIPS
Get a high score in Onslaught Mode and enter your name as 4jstudios.

ALL CREW CARDS
Get a high score in Onslaught Mode and enter your name as Bethesda.

STAR WARS: BATTLEFRONT II

INFINITE AMMO
Pause the game, hold L2 + R2 and press Up, Down, Left, Down, Down, Left, Down, Down, Left, Down, Down, Down, Left, Right.

INVINCIBILITY
Pause the game, hold L2 + R2 and press Up, Up, Up, Left, Down, Down, Down, Left, Up, Up, Up, Left, Right.

NO HUD
Pause the game, hold L2 + R2 and press Up, Up, Up, Up, Left, Up, Up, Down, Left, Down, Up, Up, Left, Right. Re-enter the code to enable the HUD again.

ALTERNATE SOLDIERS
Pause the game, hold L2 + R2 and press Down, Down, Down, Up, Up, Left, Down, Down, Down, Down, Down, Left, Up, Up, Up, Left.

ALTERNATE SOUNDS
Pause the game, hold L2 + R2 and press Up, Up, Up, Left, Up, Down, Up, Up, Left, Down, Down, Down, Left, Up, Down, Down, Left, Right.

FUNNY MESSAGES WHEN REBELS DEFEATED
Pause the game, hold L2 + R2 and press Up, Down, Left, Down, Left, Right.

PLAYSTATION 2

STAR WARS EPISODE III: REVENGE OF THE SITH

INFINITE FORCE
Select Codes from the Settings menu and enter KAIBURR.

INFINITE HEALTH
Select Codes from the Settings menu and enter XUCPHRA.

QUICK HEALTH & FORCE RESTORATION
Select Codes from the Settings menu and enter BELSAVIS.

ALL STORY, BONUS & CO-OP MISSIONS AND DUELISTS
Select Codes from the Settings menu and enter 021282.

ALL STORY MISSIONS
Select Codes from the Settings menu and enter KORRIBAN.

ALL BONUS MISSIONS
Select Codes from the Settings menu and enter NARSHADDAA.

ALL DUEL ARENAS
Select Codes from the Settings menu and enter TANTIVIEV.

ALL DUELISTS
Select Codes from the Settings menu and enter ZABRAK.

ALL POWERS & MOVES
Select Codes from the Settings menu and enter JAINA.

SUPER LIGHTSABER MODE
Select Codes from the Settings menu and enter SUPERSABERS.

TINY DRIOD MODE
Select Codes from the Settings menu and enter 071779.

ALL REPLAY MOVIES
Select Codes from the Settings menu and enter COMLINK.

ALL CONCEPT ART
Select Codes from the Settings menu and enter AAYLASECURA.

STAR WARS: THE FORCE UNLEASHED

CHEATS
Once you have accessed the Rogue Shadow, select Enter Code from the Extras menu. Now you can enter the following:

CHEAT	CODE
Invincibility	CORTOSIS
Unlimited Force	VERGENCE
1,000,000 Force Points	SPEEDER
All Force Powers	TYRANUS
Max Force Power Level	KATARN
Max Combo Level	COUNTDOOKU
Stronger Lightsaber	LIGHTSABER

COSTUMES
Once you have accessed the Rogue Shadow, select Enter Code from the Extras menu. Now you can enter the following codes:

COSTUME	CODE
All Costumes	GRANDMOFF
501st Legion	LEGION
Aayla Secura	AAYLA
Admiral Ackbar	ITSATWAP
Anakin Skywalker	CHOSENONE
Asajj Ventress	ACOLYTE
Ceremonial Jedi Robes	DANTOOINE
Chop'aa Notimo	NOTIMO
Classic stormtrooper	TK421
Count Dooku	SERENNO
Darth Desolous	PAUAN
Darth Maul	ZABRAK
Darth Phobos	HIDDENFEAR
Darth Vader	SITHLORD
Drexl Roosh	DREXLROOSH
Emperor Palpatine	PALPATINE
General Rahm Kota	MANDALORE

OVERLOAD

COSTUME	CODE
Han Solo	NERFHERDER
Heavy trooper	SHOCKTROOP
Juno Eclipse	ECLIPSE
Kento's Robe	WOOKIEE
Kleef	KLEEF
Lando Calrissian	SCOUNDREL
Luke Skywalker	T16WOMPRAT
Luke Skywalker (Yavin)	YELLOWJCKT
Mace Windu	JEDIMASTER
Mara Jade	MARAJADE
Maris Brook	MARISBROOD
Navy commando	STORMTROOP
Obi Wan Kenobi	BENKENOBI
Proxy	HOLOGRAM
Qui Gon Jinn	MAVERICK
Shaak Ti	TOGRUTA
Shadow trooper	INTHEDARK
Sith Robes	HOLOCRON
Sith Stalker Armor	KORRIBAN
Twi'lek	SECURA

STREET FIGHTER ALPHA ANTHOLOGY

STREET FIGHTER ALPHA

PLAY AS DAN

At the character select screen in Arcade Mode, hold the Start button and place the cursor on the Random Select space then input one of the following commands within 1 second:
LP LK MK HK HP MP
HP HK MK LK LP MP
LK LP MP HP HK MK
HK HP MP LP LK HK

PLAY AS M.BISON

At the character select screen, hold the Start button, place the cursor on the random select box, and input:
1P side: Down, Down, Back, Back, Down, Back, Back + LP + HP
2P side: Down, Down, Forward, Forward, Down, Forward, Forward + LP + HP

PLAY AS AKUMA

At the character select screen, hold the Start button, place the cursor on the random select box, and input:
1P side: Down, Down, Down, Back, Back, Back + LP + HP
2P side: Down, Down, Down, Forward, Forward, Forward + LP + HP

AKUMA MODE

Select your character in Arcade mode, then press and hold Start + MP + MK as the character selection screen ends.

RYU AND KEN VS. M.BISON

On both the 1p and 2p side in Arcade mode, press and hold Start, then:
1P side: place the cursor on Ryu and input Up, Up, release Start, Up, Up + LP
2P side: place the cursor on Ken and input Up, Up, release Start, Up, Up + HP

LAST BOSS MODE

Select Arcade mode while holding ■, ✖, and R1.

DRAMATIC BATTLE MODE

Select Dramatic Battle mode while holding ■, ✖, and R2.

RANDOM BATTLE MODE

Select Versus mode while holding ■, ✖, and R2.

STREET FIGHTER ALPHA 2

PLAY AS ORIGINAL CHUN-LI

Highlight Chun-Li on the character select screen, hold the Start button for 3 seconds, then select Chun-Li normally.

PLAY AS SHIN AKUMA

Highlight Akuma on the character select screen, hold the Start button for 3 seconds, then select Akuma normally.

PLAY AS EVIL RYU

Highlight Ryu on the character select screen, hold the Start button, input Forward, Up, Down, Back, then select Ryu normally.

PLAY AS EX DHALSIM

Highlight Dhalsim on the character select screen, hold the Start button, input Back, Down, Forward, Up, then select Dhalsim normally.

PLAY AS EX ZANGIEF

Highlight Zangief on the character select screen, hold the Start button, input Down, Back, Back, Back, Back, Up, Up, Forward, Forward, Forward, Forward, Down, then select Zangief normally.

LAST BOSS MODE

Select Arcade mode while holding the ■, ●, and R1 buttons.

DRAMATIC BATTLE MODE

Select Dramatic Battle mode while holding the ■ + ✖ + R2.

SELECT SPECIAL ROUTE IN SURVIVAL MODE

Select Survival Battle while holding the R1 or R2.

RANDOM BATTLE MODE

Select Versus mode while holding the ■ + ✖ + R2.

STREET FIGHTER ALPHA 2 GOLD

PLAY AS EX RYU

Highlight Ryu and press the Start button once before selecting normally.

PLAY AS EVIL RYU

Highlight Ryu and press the Start button twice before selecting normally.

PLAY AS ORIGINAL CHUN-LI

Highlight Chun-Li and press the Start button once before selecting normally.

PLAY AS EX CHUN-LI

Highlight Chun-Li and press the Start button twice before selecting normally.

PLAY AS EX KEN

Highlight Ken and press the Start button once before selecting normally.

PLAY AS EX DHALSIM

Highlight Dhalsim and press the Start button once before selecting normally.

PLAY AS EX ZANGIEF

Highlight Zangief and press the Start button once before selecting normally.

PLAY AS EX SAGAT

Highlight Sagat and press the Start button once before selecting normally.

PLAY AS EX M.BISON

Highlight M.Bison and press the Start button once before selecting normally.

PLAY USING SAKURA'S ALTERNATE COLORS

Highlight Sakura and press the Start button five times before selecting normally.

PLAY AS SHIN AKUMA

Highlight Akuma and press the Start button five times before selecting normally.

PLAY AS CAMMY

Highlight M.Bison and press the Start button twice before selecting normally.

HIDDEN MODES

LAST BOSS MODE

Select Arcade mode while holding Square + Circle + R1.

SELECT SPECIAL ROUTE IN SURVIVAL MODE

Select Survival Battle while holding the R1 or R2.

DRAMATIC BATTLE MODE

Select Dramatic Battle mode while holding Square + X + R2.

RANDOM BATTLE MODE

Select Versus mode while holding Square + X + R2.

STREET FIGHTER ALPHA 3

PLAY AS BALROG

Highlight Karin for one second, then move the cursor to the random select box and hold Start before selecting normally.

PLAY AS JULI

Highlight Karin for one second, then move the cursor to the random select box and press Up, or Down, while selecting normally.

PLAY AS JUNI

Highlight Karin for one second, then move the cursor to the random select box and press Back, or Forward, while selecting normally.

CLASSICAL MODE

Press and hold HP + HK while starting game.

SPIRITED MODE

Press and hold MP + MK while starting game.

SAIKYO MODE

Press and hold LP + LK while starting game.

SHADALOO MODE

Press and hold LK + MK + HK while starting game.

SELECT SPECIAL ROUTE IN SURVIVAL MODE

Select Survival mode while holding R1 or R2.

DRAMATIC BATTLE MODE

Select Dramatic Battle mode while holding Square + X + R2.

RANDOM BATTLE MODE

Select Versus mode while holding Square + X + R2.

STUNTMAN IGNITION

3 PROPS IN STUNT CREATOR MODE

Select Cheats from Extras and enter COOLPROP.

ALL ITEMS UNLOCKED FOR CONSTRUCTION MODE

Select Cheats from Extras and enter NOBLEMAN.

MVX SPARTAN

Select Cheats from Extras and enter fastride.

ALL CHEATS

Select Cheats from Extras and enter Wearefrozen. This unlocks the following cheats: Slo-mo Cool, Thrill Cam, Vision Switcher, Nitro Addiction, Freaky Fast, and Ice Wheels.

ALL CHEATS

Select Cheats from Extras and enter Kungfoopete.

ICE WHEELS CHEAT

Select Cheats from Extras and enter IceAge.

NITRO ADDICTION CHEAT

Select Cheats from Extras and enter TheDuke.

VISION SWITCHER CHEAT

Select Cheats from Extras and enter GFXMODES.

THE SUFFERING: TIES THAT BIND

SUICIDE
During gameplay, hold L1 + R1 + ⊗ and press Down, Down, Down, Down.

SHOTGUN & AMMO
During gameplay, hold L1 + R1 + ⊗ and press Left, Left, Left, Down, Down, Down.

MOLOTOV COCKTAILS
During gameplay, hold L1 + R1 + ⊗ and press Down, Down, Down, Up, Up, Up.

FULL FLASHLIGHT
During gameplay, hold L1 + R1 + ⊗ and press Up, Left, Down, Right, Up, Right, Down, Left, R2.

FULL AMMO CURRENT WEAPON
During gameplay, hold L1 + R1 + ⊗ and press Right, Right, Down, Up, Left, Right, Left, Left, R2.

FULL AMMO CURRENT THROWN
During gameplay, hold L1 + R1 + ⊗ and press Left, Left, Up, Down, Right, Left, Right, Right, R2.

FULL INSANITY
During gameplay, hold L1 + R1 + ⊗ and press Right, Right, Right, R2, Left, Left, Right, Left, R2.

FULL HEALTH
During gameplay, hold L1 + R1 + ⊗ and press Down, Down, Down, R2, Up, Up, Down, Up, R2.

ARSENAL
During gameplay, hold L1 + R1 + ⊗ and press Down, Right, Up, Left, Down, R2, Left, Left, Right, Right, R2, Down, Up, Left, Right, R2.

INVINCIBILITY
During gameplay, hold L1 + R1 + ⊗ and press Down, Up, Down, Up.

MINUS 50 REP
During gameplay, hold L1 + R1 + ⊗ and press Left, Left, Down, Up.

PLUS 50 REP
During gameplay, hold L1 + R1 + ⊗ and press Up, Up, Right, Up.

FULL BLOOD
During gameplay, hold L1 + R1 + ⊗ and press Up, Down, Left, Right.

ZERO BLOOD
During gameplay, hold L1 + R1 + ⊗ and press Down, Up, Right, Left.

SHRAPNEL
During gameplay, hold L1 + R1 + ⊗ and press Right, Right, Right, Left, Left, Left.

MAX EVIL REP
During gameplay, hold L1 + R1 + ⊗ and press Left, Down, Left, Down, Left, Down, R2.

MAX GOOD REP
During gameplay, hold L1 + R1 + ⊗ and press Up, Right, Up, Right, Up, Right, R2.

FULL BOTTLES
During gameplay, hold L1 + R1 + ⊗ and press Right, Right, Up, Up, R2, Left, Right, R2, Right, Up, Right, R2.

SUPER BAD DUDE
During gameplay, hold L1 + R1 + ⊗ and press Down, Up, Down, Left, Right, Left, R2, Up, Left, Down, Right, Up, Right, Down, Left, R2, Down, Down, Down, R2, R2.

PROJECTOR STATE
During gameplay, hold L1 + R1 + ⊗ and press Up, R2, Left, R2, Down, R2, Right, R2.

DREAM STATE
During gameplay, hold L1 + R1 + ⊗ and press Left, Left, R2, Right, Right, R2, Up, Up, R2, Down, Down, R2.

ALL NOTES
During gameplay, hold L1 + R1 + ⊗ and press Right, Left, Up, Left, R2, Right, Down, Right.

ALL MAPS
During gameplay, hold L1 + R1 + ⊗ and press Left, Right, Down, Right, R2, Left, Up, Left.

SUPERMAN RETURNS

GOD MODE
Pause the game, select Options and press Up, Up, Down, Down, Left, Right, Left, Right, ●, ■.

INFINITE CITY HEALTH
Pause the game, select Options and press ●, Right, ●, Right, Up, Left, Right, ●.

ALL POWER-UPS
Pause the game, select Options and press Left, ●, Right, ■, Down, ●, Up, Down, ■, ●, ■.

ALL UNLOCKABLES
Pause the game, select Options and press Left, Up, Right, Down, ●, ■, ●, Up, Right, ■.

FREE ROAM AS BIZARRO
Pause the game, select Options and press Up, Right, Down, Right, Up, Left, Down, Right, Up.

SUZUKI TT SUPERBIKES

CHEAT SCREEN
At the Main menu, press R1, R2, L1, L2, R1, R2, L1, L2. Now you can enter the following:

ALL EVENTS
Enter BORN FREE.

RED BULL MAD SUNDAY EVENTS
Enter SUNDAYSUNDAY.

ALL HELMETS
Enter SKID LIDS.

ALL LEATHERS
Enter COLORED HIDE.

ALL BIKES
Enter ROCKETS.

ALL WHEELS
Enter TIRE CITY.

ALL COLLECTION BOOK
Enter COUCH POTATO.

TAITO LEGENDS

EXTRA GAMES
At the Title screen, press L1, R1, R2, L2, Select, Start.

TAK AND THE GUARDIANS OF GROSS

INVULNERABILITY
Select Cheat Codes from the Extras menu and enter KRUNKIN.

INFINITE NOVA
Select Cheat Codes from the Extras menu and enter CAKEDAY.

WEAK ENEMIES
Select Cheat Codes from the Extras menu and enter CODMODE.

ALL LEVELS
Select Cheat Codes from the Extras menu and enter GUDGEON.

ALL MINIGAMES
Select Cheat Codes from the Extras menu and enter CURLING.

ALL AWARDS
Select Cheat Codes from the Extras menu and enter SNEAKER.

ALL CONCEPT ART
Select Cheat Codes from the Extras menu and enter FRIVERS.

RAINBOW TRAIL
Select Cheat Codes from the Extras menu and enter UNICORN.

TAK: THE GREAT JUJU CHALLENGE

BONUS SOUND EFFECTS
In Juju's Potions, select Universal Card and enter the following for Bugs, Crystals and Fruits respectively: 20, 17, 5.

BONUS SOUND EFFECTS 2
In Juju's Potions, select Universal Card and enter the following for Bugs, Crystals and Fruits respectively: 50, 84, 92.

BONUS MUSIC TRACK 1
In Juju's Potions, select Universal Card and enter the following for Bugs, Crystals and Fruits respectively: 67, 8, 20.

BONUS MUSIC TRACK 2
In Juju's Potions, select Universal Card and enter the following for Bugs, Crystals and Fruits respectively: 6, 18, 3.

MAGIC PARTICLES
In Juju's Potions, select Universal Card and enter the following for Bugs, Crystals and Fruits respectively: 24, 40, 11.

MORE MAGIC PARTICLES
In Juju's Potions, select Universal Card and enter the following for Bugs, Crystals and Fruits respectively: 48, 57, 57.

VIEW JUJU CONCEPT ART
In Juju's Potions, select Universal Card and enter the following for Bugs, Crystals and Fruits respectively: 33, 22, 28.

VIEW VEHICLE ART
In Juju's Potions, select Universal Card and enter the following for Bugs, Crystals and Fruits respectively: 11, 55, 44.

VIEW WORLD ART
In Juju's Potions, select Universal Card and enter the following for Bugs, Crystals and Fruits respectively: 83, 49, 34.

TEENAGE MUTANT NINJA TURTLES 3: MUTANT NIGHTMARE

INVINCIBILITY
Select Passwords from the Options menu and enter MDLDSSLR.

HEALTH POWER-UPS BECOME SUSHI
Select Passwords from the Options menu and enter SLLMRSLD.

NO HEALTH POWER-UPS
Select Passwords from the Options menu and enter DMLDMRLD.

ONE HIT DEFEATS TURTLE
Select Passwords from the Options menu and enter LDMSLRDD.

MAX OUGI
Select Passwords from the Options menu and enter RRDMLSDL.

UNLIMITED SHURIKEN
Select Passwords from the Options menu and enter LMDRRMSR.

NO SHURIKEN
Select Passwords from the Options menu and enter LLMSRDMS.

DOUBLE ENEMY ATTACK
Select Passwords from the Options menu and enter MSRLSMML.

DOUBLE ENEMY DEFENSE
Select Passwords from the Options menu and enter SLRMLSSM.

TEST DRIVE UNLIMITED

ALL CARS AND MONEY
At the Main menu, press Triangle, Circle, L1, R1, Triangle.

THRILLVILLE: OFF THE RAILS

ALL PARKS
While in a park, press Square, Circle, Triangle, Square, Circle, Triangle, Square.

ALL RIDES IN PARK
While in a park, press Square, Circle, Triangle, Square, Circle, Triangle, Triangle.

$50.000
While in a park, press Square, Circle, Triangle, Square, Circle, Triangle, X.

MISSION COMPLETE
While in a park, press Square, Circle, Triangle, Square, Circle, Triangle, Circle.

TIGER WOODS PGA TOUR 07

ALL CHARACTERS
Select Password from the Options menu and enter gameface.

UNLOCK ADIDAS ITEMS
Select Password from the Options menu and enter three stripes.

UNLOCK BRIDGESTONE ITEMS
Select Password from the Options menu and enter shojiro.

UNLOCK COBRA ITEMS
Select Password from the Options menu and enter snakeking.

UNLOCK EA SPORTS ITEMS
Select Password from the Options menu and enter inthegame.

UNLOCK GRAFALLOYE ITEMS
Select Password from the Options menu and enter just shafts.

UNLOCK MACGERGOR ITEMS
Select Password from the Options menu and enter mactec.

UNLOCK MIZUNO ITEMS
Select Password from the Options menu and enter rihachinrzo.

UNLOCK NIKE ITEMS
Select Password from the Options menu and enter justdoit.

UNLOCK OAKLEY ITEMS
Select Password from the Options menu and enter jannard.

UNLOCK PGA TOUR ITEMS
Select Password from the Options menu and enter lightning.

UNLOCK PING ITEMS
Select Password from the Options menu and enter solheim.

UNLOCK PRECEPT ITEMS
Select Password from the Options menu and enter guys are good.

UNLOCK TAYLORMADE ITEMS
Select Password from the Options menu and enter mradams.

TIGER WOODS PGA TOUR 08

ALL GOLFERS
Select Passwords from the Options and enter GAMEFACE.

BRIDGESTONE ITEMS
Select Passwords from the Options and enter SHOJIRO.

COBRA ITEMS
Select Passwords from the Options and enter SNAKEKING.

GRAFALLOY ITEMS
Select Passwords from the Options and enter JUSTSHAFTS.

MACGREGOR ITEMS
Select Passwords from the Options and enter MACTEC.

MIZUNO ITEMS
Select Passwords from the Options and enter RIHACHINRIZO.

NIKE ITEMS
Select Passwords from the Options and enter JUSTDOIT.

OAKLEY ITEMS
Select Passwords from the Options and enter JANNARD.

PING ITEMS
Select Passwords from the Options and enter SOLHEIM.

PRECEPT ITEMS
Select Passwords from the Options and enter GUYSAREGOOD.

TAYLORMADE ITEMS
Select Passwords from the Options and enter MRADAMS.

TIGER WOODS PGA TOUR 09

$1,000,000
Select Passwords from the Extras menu and enter JACKPOT.

MAX SKILL POINTS
Select Passwords from the Extras menu and enter IAMRUBBISH.

ALL CLOTHING & EQUIPMENT
Select Passwords from the Extras menu and enter SHOP2DROP.

ALL PGA TOUR EVENTS
Select Passwords from the Extras menu and enter BEATIT.

ALL COVER STORIES
Select Passwords from the Extras menu and enter HEADLINER.

TIM BURTON'S THE NIGHTMARE BEFORE CHRISTMAS: OOGIE'S REVENGE

ALL LEVELS
At the Title screen, press L1, L2, L1, L2, L3, R1, R2, R1, R2, R3.

INVINCIBILITY
During a game, press Right, Left, L3, R3, Left, Right, R3, L3.

UPGRADE SOUL ROBBER
During a game, press Up, Right, Left, Down, R3, L3.

UNLIMITED POWER FOR PUMPKIN KING
During a game, press Left, Down, Right, Up, Right, Down, Left, Up.

UNLIMITED SANTA JACK PRESENTS
During a game, press Down, Left, Right, Up, L3, R3.

ONE BUTTON MUSICAL BATTLES
During a boss fight, press Left, Up, Right, Down, Left, R3, L3.

PUMPKIN JACK AND SANTA JACK COSTUMES
During a game, press Down, Up, Right, Left, L3, R3.

UNLOCK DANCING JACK, PHANTOM JACK, PJ JACK, AND THESPIAN JACK
At Jack's house, press Up, Down, Left, Right, R3, L3.

UNLOCK STATUE COLLECTION
At Jack's house, press Up, Up, R3, Up.

TMNT

DON'S BIG HEAD GOODIE

At the Main menu, hold L1 and press ○, △, ×, □.

CHALLENGE MAP 2

At the Main menu, hold L1 and press ×, ×, ○, ×.

TOMB RAIDER: LEGEND

You must unlock the following codes in the game before using them.

BULLETPROOF

During gameplay, hold L1 and press ×, R1, △, R1, □, L2.

DRAIN ENEMY HEALTH

During gameplay, hold L1 and press □, ○, ×, L2, R1, △.

INFINITE ASSAULT RIFLE AMMO

During gameplay, hold L2 and press ×, ○, ×, L1, □, △.

INFINITE GRENADE LAUNCHER AMMO

During gameplay, hold L2 and press L1, △, R1, ○, L1, □.

INFINITE SHOTGUN AMMO

During gameplay, hold L2 and press R1, ○, □, L1, □, ×.

INFINITE SMG AMMO

During gameplay, hold L2 and press ○, △, L1, R1, ×, ○.

EXCALIBUR

During gameplay, hold L2 and press △, ×, ○, R1, △, L1.

ONE-SHOT KILL

During gameplay, hold L1 and press △, ×, △, □, L2, ○.

NO TEXTURE MODE

During gameplay, hold L1 and press L2, ×, ○, ×, △, R1.

TOMB RAIDER: UNDERWORLD

BULLETPROOF LARA

During a game, hold L2 and press ×, R2, △, R2, □, L1.

ONE-SHOT KILL

During a game, hold L2 and press △, ×, △, □, L1, ○.

SHOW ENEMY HEALTH

During a game, hold L2 and press □, ○, ×, L1, R2, △.

TOM CLANCY'S SPLINTER CELL CHAOS THEORY

ALL SOLO LEVELS

At the Solo menu, hold L1 + L2 + R1 + R2 and press □ (x5), ○ (x5).

ALL COOP LEVELS

At the Coop menu, hold L1 + L2 + R1 + R2 and press □ (x5), ○ (x5).

TEAM PICTURE

At the Main menu, press R2, ○ (x5), □.

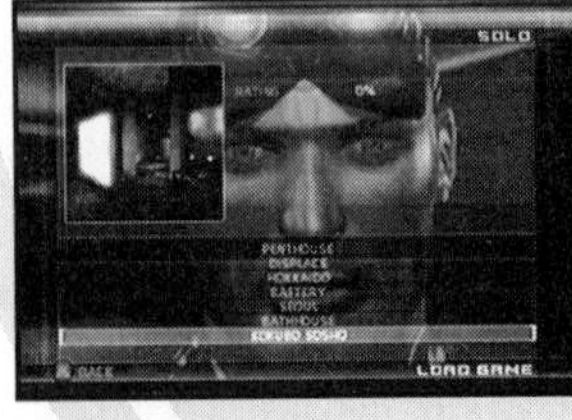

TONY HAWK'S DOWNHILL JAM

CHEAT CODES

Select Cheat Codes from the Options menu and enter the following cheats. Select Toggle Cheats to enable/disable them.

FREE BOOST

Enter OOTBAGHFOREVER.

ALWAYS SPECIAL

Enter POINTHOGGER.

UNLOCK MANUALS

Enter IMISSMANUALS.

PERFECT RAIL

Enter LIKETILTINGAPLATE.

PERFECT MANUAL
Enter TIGHTROPEWALKER.

PERFECT STATS
Enter IAMBOB.

FIRST-PERSON SKATER
Enter FIRSTPERSONJAM.

SHADOW SKATER
Enter CHIMNEYSWEEP.

DEMON SKATER
Enter EVILCHIMNEYSWEEP.

MINI SKATER
Enter DOWNTHERABBITHOLE.

GIGANTO-SKATER
Enter IWANNABETALLTALL.

INVISIBLE SKATER
Enter NOWYOUSEEME.

FREE BOOST
Enter OOTBAGHFOREVER.

ALWAYS SPECIAL
Enter POINTHOGGER.

UNLOCK MANUALS
Enter IMISSMANUALS.

PERFECT RAIL
Enter LIKETILTINGAPLATE.

PERFECT MANUAL
Enter TIGHTROPEWALKER.

PERFECT STATS
Enter IAMBOB.

FIRST-PERSON SKATER
Enter FIRSTPERSONJAM.

SHADOW SKATER
Enter CHIMNEYSWEEP.

DEMON SKATER
Enter EVILCHIMNEYSWEEP.

MINI SKATER
Enter DOWNTHERABBITHOLE.

GIGANTO-SKATER
Enter IWANNABETALLTALL.

INVISIBLE SKATER
Enter NOWYOUSEEME.

SKATE AS A WORK OF ART
Enter FOURLIGHTS.

DISPLAY COORDINATES
Enter DISPLAYCOORDINATES.

LARGE BIRDS
Enter BIRDBIRDBIRDBIRD.

ESPECIALLY LARGE BIRDS
Enter BIRDBIRDBIRDBIRDBIRD.

TINY PEOPLE
Enter SHRINKTHEPEOPLE.
*There is no need to toggle on the following cheats. They take effect after entering them.

ALL EVENTS
Enter ADVENTURESOFKWANG.

ALL SKATERS
Enter IMINTERFACING.

ALL BOARDS/OUTFITS
Enter RAIDTHEWOODSHED.

ALL MOVIES
Enter FREEBOZZLER.

TONY HAWK'S PROVING GROUND

CHEAT CODES

Select Cheat Codes from the Options and enter the following cheats. Some codes need to be enabled by selecting Cheats from the Options during a game.

UNLOCK	CHEAT
Unlocks Bosco	MOREMILK
Unlocks Cam	NOTACAMERA
Unlocks Cooper	THECOOP
Unlocks Eddie X	SKETCHY
Unlocks El Patinador	PILEDRIVER
Unlocks Eric	FLYAWAY
Unlocks Judy Nails	LOVEROCKNROLL
Unlocks Mad Dog	RABBIES
Unlocks MCA	INTERGALACTIC
Unlocks Mel	NOTADUDE
Unlocks Rube	LOOKSSMELLY
Unlocks Spence	DAPPER
Unlocks Shayne	MOVERS
Unlocks TV Producer	SHAKER
Unlock FDR	THEPREZPARK
Unlock Lansdowne	THELOCALPARK
Unlock Air & Space Museum	THEINDOORPARK

UNLOCK	CHEAT
Unlocks all Fun Items	OVERTHETOP
Unlock all Game Movies	WATCHTHIS
Unlock all Rigger Pieces	IMGONNABUILD
All specials unlocked and in player's special list	LOTSOFTRICKS
Full Stats	BEEFEDUP
Give player +50 skill points	NEEDSHELP
Unlocks Perfect Manual	STILLAINTFALLIN
Unlocks Perfect Rail	AINTFALLIN
Unlocks Unlimited Focus	MYOPIC
Invisible Man	THEMISSING
Mini Skater	TINYTATER

TOTAL OVERDOSE: A GUNSLINGER'S TALE IN MEXICO

CHEAT MODE
Hold L1 + R1 + L2 + R2 + L3 + R3 for a few seconds, then you can enter the following codes.

RESTORE HEALTH
Press ⊗, ⊡, ⊙, △.

ALL LOCO MOVES
During a game, hold L1 + L2 + L3 + R1 + R2 + R3 for three seconds. Then press ⊙, ⊙, L2, R2.

MAXIMUM HEALTH
During a game, hold L1 + L2 + L3 + R1 + R2 + R3 for three seconds. Then press ⊗, ⊡, ⊙, △.

MAXIMUM OF REWINDINGS
During a game, hold L1 + L2 + L3 + R1 + R2 + R3 for three seconds. Then press R1, R2, L2, ⊗.

FREE ALL WEAPONS
During a game, hold L1 + L2 + L3 + R1 + R2 + R3 for three seconds. Then press △, L1, R2, ⊡.

TRANSFORMERS: THE GAME

INFINITE HEALTH
At the Main menu, press Left, Left, Up, Left, Right, Down, Right.

INFINITE AMMO
At the Main menu, press Up, Down, Left, Right, Up, Up, Down.

NO MILITARY OR POLICE
At the Main menu, press Right, Left, Right, Left, Right, Left, Right.

ALL MISSIONS
At the Main menu, press Down, Up, Left, Right, Right, Right, Up, Down.

BONUS CYBERTRON MISSIONS
At the Main menu, press Right, Up, Up, Down, Right, Left, Left.

GENERATION 1 SKIN: JAZZ
At the Main menu, press Left, Up, Down, Down, Left, Up, Right.

GENERATION 1 SKIN: MEGATRON
At the Main menu, press Down, Left, Left, Down, Right, Right, Up.

GENERATION 1 SKIN: OPTIMUS PRIME
At the Main menu, press Down, Right, Left, Up, Down, Down, Left.

GENERATION 1 SKIN: ROBOVISION OPTIMUS PRIME
At the Main menu, press Down, Down, Up, Up, Right, Right, Right.

GENERATION 1 SKIN: STARSCREAM
At the Main menu, press Right, Down, Left, Left, Down, Up, Up.

TWISTED METAL: HEAD ON - EXTRA TWISTED EDITION

Hold L1 + R1 + L2 + R2 during gameplay, then press the button combination. Do the same thing to turn it off.

INVULNERABILITY
During a game, hold L1 + R1 + L2 + R2 and press Up, Down, Left, Right, Right, Left, Down, Up.

TRADE WEAPONS FOR HEALTH
During a game, hold L1 + R1 + L2 + R2 and press △, ⊗, ⊡, ⊙.

INFINITE WEAPONS

During a game, hold L1 + R1 + L2 + R2 and press Triangle, Triangle, Down, Down.

KILLER WEAPONS

During a game, hold L1 + R1 + L2 + R2 and press X, X, Up, Up.

MEGA GUNS

During a game, hold L1 + R1 + L2 + R2 and press X, Triangle, X, Triangle.

RADIAL BLAST

During a game, hold L1 + R1 + L2 + R2 and press Left, Left, Up, Down, Left, Right.

ULTIMATE SPIDER-MAN

ALL CHARACTERS

Pause the game and select Controller Setup from the Options menu. Press Right, Down, Right, Down, Left, Up, Left, Right.

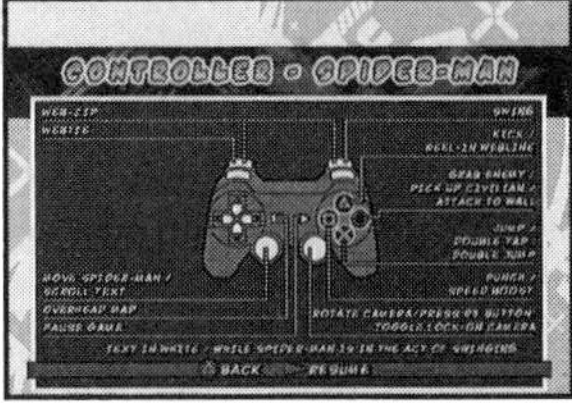

ALL COVERS

Pause the game and select Controller Setup from the Options menu. Press Left, Left, Right, Left, Up, Left, Left, Down.

ALL CONCEPT ART

Pause the game and select Controller Setup from the Options menu. Press Down, Down, Down, Up, Down, Up, Left, Left.

ALL LANDMARKS

Pause the game and select Controller Setup from the Options menu. Press Up, Right, Down, Left, Down, Up, Right, Left.

URBAN CHAOS: RIOT RESPONSE

At the Main menu, press Up, Up, Down, Down, Circle, Down, Up, Circle. This opens the Cheat screen. Select Add Cheat and enter the following:

ALL LEVELS & EMERGENCIES

Enter KEYTOTHECITY.

TERROR MODE

Enter BURNERSREVENGE.

ASSUALT RIFLE MK. 3 WITH INFINITE SHELLS

Enter ULTIMATEPOWER.

MINI-GUN

Enter MINIFUN.

PISTOL MK. 4

Enter ZEROTOLERANCE.

ENHANCED STUN GUN

Enter FRYINGTIME.

BURNING BULLETS

Enter BURNINGBULLET.

DISCO CHEAT

Enter DANCINGFEET.

HEADLESS CHEAT

Enter KEEPYOURHEAD.

SQUEAKY VOICES

Enter WHATWASTHAT.

VICTORIOUS BOXERS 2: FIGHTING SPRIRT

EXTRA CHARACTERS IN EXHIBITION
Select Password from the Options menu and enter NEL SAZ UMA.

BROCCOMAN IN EXHIBITION MODE
Select Password from the Options menu and enter BRC MAN EXH.

LUNSAKU PAUDY, JUNICHI HOTTA & HIROSHI YAMANAKA
Select Password from the Options menu and enter ALL *ST ARS.

KAMOGAWA, NEKOTA AND HAMA IN EXHIBITION MODE
Select Password from the Options menu and enter MRS AND MAN.

DATE VS. RAMIREZ MATCH IN STORY MODE
Select Password from the Options menu and enter DAT EVS RMZ.

TAKAMURA VS. YAJIMA MATCH IN STORY MODE
Select Password from the Options menu and enter ASA CT3 CLR.

EXTRA STAGES
Select Password from the Options menu and enter DAM ATA MAQ.

THE WARRIORS

100% COMPLETE
During gameplay, press L1, Select, ■, Down, L2, Right.

99 CREDITS IN ARMIES OF THE NIGHT
During the Armies of the Night mini-game, press Up, Up, Down, Down, Left, Right.

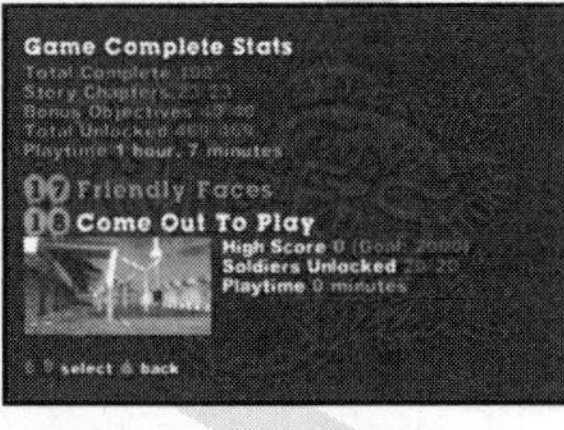

$200, FLASH, & SPRAY PAINT
During gameplay, press R1, R2, L1, ✖, Down, L1.

UNBREAKABLE BAT
During gameplay, press L3, L3, ●, Up, ●, Select.

BRASS KNUCKLES
During gameplay, press ●, ●, ●, L1, Select, ▲.

KNIFE
During gameplay, press Down, Down, Select, Up, Up, L3.

MACHETE
During gameplay, press L1, ✖, R1, R1, Select, R2.

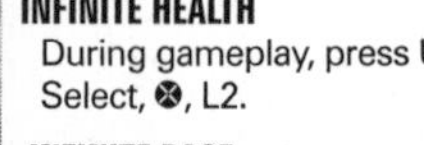

INFINITE HEALTH
During gameplay, press Up, ▲, L3, Select, ✖, L2.

INFINITE RAGE
During gameplay, press ■, ●, ▲, Select, ✖, Left.

INFINITE SPRINT
During gameplay, press Down, ■, left, ✖, L1, Select.

COMPLETE MISSION
During gameplay, press Down, ■, ✖, Select, R1, Left.

BAT
During gameplay, press ■, R2, Down, Down, L1, L1.

PIPE
During gameplay, press R2, ●, Select, Up, L1, Right.

STEEL-TOE BOOTS
During gameplay, press R3, R2, R1,

BUM ADVICE UPGRADE
During gameplay, press ●, ●, Down, R2, L2, ●.

COMBAT STAMINA UPGRADE
During gameplay, press ⊗, L1, Down, ■, Up, ⊗.

FLASH CAPACITY UPGRADE
During gameplay, press L2, ⊗, R2, L1, L1, ●.

FLASH UPGRADE
During gameplay, press Down, Left, Up, Up, ■, Right.

SPRINT STAMINA UPGRADE
During gameplay, press L2, Select, Select, Select, Select, ▲.

CUFF DROPS
During gameplay, press Up, ⊗, Up, Select, L3, L1.

CUFF KEY DROPS
During gameplay, press Left, ⊗, ⊗, R2, L1, Down.

UNCUFF SELF
During gameplay, press ▲, ▲, ▲, Select, ▲, R1.

LOSE THE POLICE
During gameplay, press Up, Select, ⊗, ▲, ▲, ■.

HOBO ALLIANCE
During gameplay, press R1, R1, L1, R1, L1, Up.

WEAPONS DEALER
During gameplay, press Right, R1, ●, ⊗, Select, ■.

HOBO ALLIANCE
During gameplay, press R1, R1, L1, R1, L1, Up.

WEAPONS DEALER
During gameplay, press Right, R1, ●, ⊗, Select, ■.

WAY OF THE SAMURAI 2

MORE CHARACTER MODELS
At the Character Customization screen, highlight Name and press L1, R2, R1, L2, L1, R2, R1, L2, ■. Press Right or Left to change character models.

WWE SMACKDOWN! VS. RAW 2008

HBK AND HHH'S DX OUTFIT
Select Cheat Codes from the Options and enter DXCostume69K2.

KELLY KELLY'S ALTERNATE OUTFIT
Select Cheat Codes from the Options and enter KellyKG12R.

WWE SMACKDOWN VS. RAW 2009

BOOGEYMAN
Select Cheat Codes from My WWE and enter BoogeymanEatsWorms!!.

GENE SNITSKY
Select Cheat Codes from My WWE and enter UnlockSnitskySvR2009.

HAWKINS & RYDER
Select Cheat Codes from My WWE and enter Ryder&HawkinsTagTeam.

JILLIAN HALL
Select Cheat Codes from My WWE and enter PlayAsJillianHallSvR.

LAYLA
Select Cheat Codes from My WWE and enter UnlockECWDivaLayla09.

RIC FLAIR
Select Cheat Codes from My WWE and enter FlairWoooooooooooooo.

TAZZ
Select Cheat Codes from My WWE and enter UnlockECWTazzSvR2009.

VINCENT MCMAHON
Select Cheat Codes from My WWE and enter VinceMcMahonNoChance.

HORNSWOGGLE AS MANAGER
Select Cheat Codes from My WWE and enter HornswoggleAsManager.

CHRIS JERICHO COSTUME B
Select Cheat Codes from My WWE and enter AltJerichoModelSvR09.

CM PUNK COSTUME B
Select Cheat Codes from My WWE and enter CMPunkAltCostumeSvR!.

REY MYSTERIO COSTUME B
Select Cheat Codes from My WWE and enter BooyakaBooyaka619SvR.

SATURDAY NIGHT'S MAIN EVENT ARENA
Select Cheat Codes from My WWE and enter SatNightMainEventSvR.

X-MEN: THE OFFICIAL GAME

DANGER ROOM ICEMAN

At the Cerebro Files menu, press Right, Right, Left, Left, Down, Up, Down, Up, Start.

DANGER ROOM NIGHTCRAWLER

At the Cerebro Files menu, press Up, Up, Down, Down, Left, Right, Left, Right, Start.

DANGER ROOM WOLVERINE

At the Cerebro Files menu, press Down, Down, Up, Up, Right, Left, Right, Left, Start.

YS: THE ARK OF NAPISHTIM

Enter the cheat codes as follows:

1. **Select New Game.**
2. **Select Cheat to enter the Cheat Room.**
3. **To activate Cheat Mode, strike the colored crystals in this sequence: Red, Blue, Yellow, Red, Blue, Yellow. The sequence appears at the top left as you strike each crystal.**
4. **Perform a Downward Thrust strike on the center pedestal to complete the code and activate Cheat Mode.**
5. **You can now use the same method to enter one of the cheat codes listed below, then exit the Cheat Room.**
6. **The game selection buttons are now red. Games saved with the Cheat Mode enabled will appear in red.**

CLEARFLAG

Hit the crystals in the following order: Red, Red, Red, Red, Blue, Blue, Blue, Blue, Yellow, Yellow, Yellow, Yellow, Blue, Blue, Yellow, Yellow, Red, Red. Turns on all special features normally available only after you've completed the game once—Nightmare Mode, Time Attack, and Red Spirit Monuments. **Note:** When enabled, Red Spirit Monuments appear after you reach Port Rimorge. They allow you to warp between the Rehdan Village and Port Rimorge monuments to save travel time.

OPENING MOVIE WITH ENGLISH VOICE/ ENGLISH TEXT

Hit the crystals in the following order: Blue, Blue, Yellow, Red.

OPENING MOVIE WITH ENGLISH VOICE/ JAPANESE TEXT

Hit the crystals in the following order: Blue, Blue, Blue, Yellow, Red.

OPENING MOVIE WITH JAPANESE VOICE/ ENGLISH TEXT

Hit the crystals in the following order: Blue, Blue, Blue, Blue, Yellow, Red.

OPENING MOVIE WITH JAPANESE VOICE/ NO TEXT

Hit the crystals in the following order: Blue, Yellow, Red.

ALTERNATE OPENING MOVIE

Hit the crystals in the following order: Red, Blue, Red.

BEACH MOVIE WITH ENGLISH VOICE/ ENGLISH TEXT

Hit the crystals in the following order: Blue, Blue, Red, Yellow

BEACH MOVIE WITH ENGLISH VOICE/ JAPANESE TEXT

Hit the crystals in the following order: Blue, Blue, Blue, Red, Yellow.

BEACH MOVIE WITH JAPANESE VOICE/ ENGLISH TEXT

Hit the crystals in the following order: Blue, Red, Red, Yellow.

BEACH MOVIE WITH JAPANESE VOICE/ JAPANESE TEXT

Hit the crystals in the following order: Blue, Red, Yellow.

ROMUN FLEET ENTRANCE ANIME MOVIE

Hit the crystals in the following order: Blue, Red, Yellow, Red, Red, Yellow, Blue, Blue, Blue.

ROMUN FLEET ENTRANCE CG MOVIE

Hit the crystals in the following order: Blue, Red, Yellow, Red, Red, Yellow, Blue.

ROMUN FLEET DESTROYED ANIME MOVIE

Hit the crystals in the following order: Blue, Red, Yellow, Red, Red, Yellow, Red, Red, Red.

ROMUN FLEET DESTROYED CG MOVIE

Hit the crystals in the following order: Blue, Red, Yellow, Red, Red, Yellow, Red.

NAPISHTIM DESTROYED MOVIE WITH ENGLISH VOICE/ENGLISH TEXT

Hit the crystals in the following order: Blue, Red, Yellow, Red, Red, Blue, Yellow, Yellow.

NAPISHTIM DESTROYED MOVIE WITH ENGLISH VOICE/JAPANESE TEXT

Hit the crystals in the following order: Blue, Red, Yellow, Red, Red, Blue, Yellow, Yellow, Yellow.

NAPISHTIM DESTROYED MOVIE WITH JAPANESE VOICE/ENGLISH TEXT

Hit the crystals in the following order: Blue, Red, Yellow, Red, Red, Blue, Yellow, Yellow, Yellow, Yellow.

NAPISHTIM DESTROYED MOVIE WITH JAPANESE VOICE/JAPANESE TEXT

Hit the crystals in the following order: Blue, Red, Yellow, Red, Red, Blue, Yellow.

OLHA IN BIKINI

Hit the crystals in the following order: Blue, Blue, Blue, Blue, Blue, Yellow, Yellow, Yellow, Red, Blue, Yellow, Yellow, Red, Red, Red.

OLHA DEMO AFTER CLEARING TIME ATTACK ON HARD (JAPANESE)

Hit the crystals in the following order: Red, Red, Red, Red, Red, Blue, Blue, Blue, Yellow, Red, Blue, Blue, Yellow, Yellow, Yellow.

GAME IN JAPANESE

Hit the crystals in the following order: Yellow, Yellow, Red, Blue.

LEVEL 10

Hit the crystals in the following order: Red, Blue, Blue, Red, Red, Blue.

LEVEL 20

Hit the crystals in the following order: Red, Blue, Blue, Red, Red, Blue, Blue.

LEVEL 30

Hit the crystals in the following order: Red, Red, Blue, Blue, Red, Red, Blue, Blue.

LEVEL 40

Hit the crystals in the following order: Red, Red, Blue, Red, Red, Blue, Blue, Yellow.

LEVEL 60

Hit the crystals in the following order: Red, Red, Blue, Blue, Yellow, Yellow, Red, Red, Blue, Blue, Yellow, Yellow.

HALF PRICE ITEMS

Hit the crystals in the following order: Yellow, Yellow, Blue, Blue, Red, Red, Red, Yellow, Yellow, Yellow, Red, Red, Blue, Blue.

20 ITEM TOOL MAX INCREASE

Hit the crystals in the following order: Yellow, Yellow, Red, Red, Blue, Blue, Yellow, Red.

MAXED OUT BLIRANTE SWORD

Hit the crystals in the following order: Blue, Blue, Yellow, Yellow, Yellow, Red, Blue, Red, Red, Red, Yellow, Yellow.

MAXED OUT LIVART SWORD

Hit the crystals in the following order: Blue, Blue, Blue, Yellow, Yellow, Red, Blue, Red, Red, Yellow, Yellow, Yellow.

MAXED OUT ERICCIL SWORD

Hit the crystals in the following order: Blue, Yellow, Yellow, Red, Red, Red, Blue, Blue, Blue, Red, Red, Yellow.

MAXED OUT ALL 3 SWORDS

Hit the crystals in the following order: Blue, Yellow, Red, Blue, Blue, Blue, Red, Red, Red, Yellow, Yellow, Yellow, Blue, Yellow, Red.

ALTERNATE ENDING MOVIES

In the Rehdan Village (Festival at Night): Toksa and Nahrya look toward Adol as he walks by.

At the Entrance of the Village: Isha runs toward the back, then returns.

On the Tres Mares: The cat is on the front of the ship.

ENDING CHANGE CRITERIA

Direction Calman is facing: Faces Adol if he has gotten the Gold Locket.

Number of Pikkards: Found all four pikkards and returned them to Emilio.

XBOX®

GAMES

ALIEN HOMINID

ALL LEVELS, MINI-GAMES, AND HATS

Select Player 1 Setup or Player 2 Setup and change the name to ROYGBIV.

HATS FOR 2-PLAYER GAME

Go to the Options menu and rename your alien one of the following:

ALIEN	HAT STYLE	HAT NUMBER
ABE	Top Hat	#11
APRIL	Blond Wig	#4
BEHEMOTH	Red Cap	#24
CLETUS	Hunting Hat	#3
DANDY	Flower Petal Hat	#13
GOODMAN	Black Curly Hair	#7
GRRL	Flowers	#10
PRINCESS	Tiara	#12
SUPERFLY	Afro	#6
TOMFULP	Brown Messy Hair	#2

AVATAR: THE LAST AIRBENDER

ALL TREASURE MAPS

Select Code Entry from the Extras menu and enter 37437.

1 HIT DISHONOR

Select Code Entry from the Extras menu and enter 54641.

DOUBLE DAMAGE

Select Code Entry from the Extras menu and enter 34743.

UNLIMITED COPPER

Select Code Entry from the Extras menu and enter 23637.

UNLIMITED CHI

Select Code Entry from the Extras menu and enter 24463.

UNLIMITED HEALTH

Select Code Entry from the Extras menu and enter 94677.

NEVERENDING STEALTH

Select Code Entry from the Extras menu and enter 53467.

CHARACTER CONCEPT ART GALLERY

Select Code Entry from the Extras menu and enter 97831.

THE BARD'S TALE

During a game, hold L + R and enter the following:

EVERYTHING ON (SILVER AND ADDERSTONES)

Up, Up, Down, Down, Left, Right, Left, Right

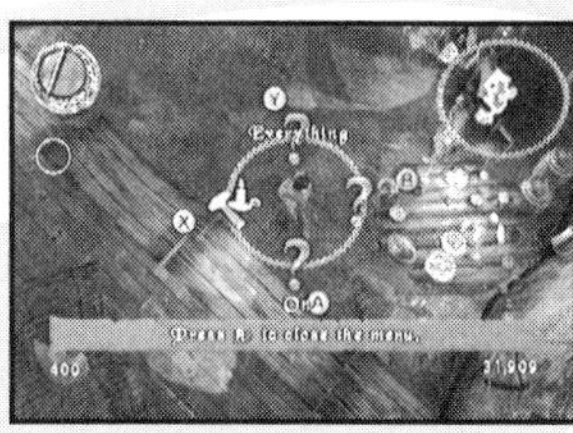

FULL HEALTH AND MANA

Left, Left, Right, Right, Up, Down, Up, Down

CAN'T BE HURT

Right, Left, Right, Left, Up, Down, Up, Down

CAN'T BE STRUCK

Left, Right, Left, Right, Up, Down, Up, Down

DAMAGE X100

Up, Down, Up, Down, Left, Right, Left, Right

BATTLEFIELD 2: MODERN COMBAT

ALL WEAPONS

During gameplay, hold Black + White and press Right, Right, Down, Up, Left, Left.

BLAZING ANGELS: SQUADRONS OF WWII

ALL MISSIONS, MEDALS, & PLANES

At the Main menu, hold Left Trigger + Right Trigger and press X, White, Black, Y, Y, Black, White, X.

GOD MODE

Pause the game, hold Left Trigger and press X, Y, Y, X. Release Left Trigger, hold Right Trigger and press Y, X, X, Y. Re-enter the code to disable it.

DAMAGE INCREASED

Pause the game, hold Left Trigger and press White, White, Black. Release Left Trigger, hold Right Trigger and press Black, Black, White. Re-enter the code to disable it.

CAPCOM CLASSICS COLLECTION

ALL LOCKS OPENED

At the Title screen, press Left Trigger, Right Trigger, Up on Right Thumbstick, Down on Right Thumbstick, Left Trigger, Right Trigger, Up on Left Thumbstick, Down on Left Thumbstick, Left Trigger, Right Trigger, Up, Down.

CARS

UNLOCK EVERYTHING

Select Cheat Codes from the Options menu and enter IF900HP.

ALL CHARACTERS

Select Cheat Codes from the Options menu and enter YAYCARS.

ALL CHARACTER SKINS

Select Cheat Codes from the Options menu and enter R4MONE.

ALL MINI-GAMES AND COURSES

Select Cheat Codes from the Options menu and enter MATTL66.

MATER'S COUNTDOWN CLEAN-UP MINI-GAME & MATER'S SPEEDY CIRCUIT

Select Cheat Codes from the Options menu and enter TRGTEXC.

FAST START

Select Cheat Codes from the Options menu and enter IMSPEED.

INFINITE BOOST

Select Cheat Codes from the Options menu and enter VROOOOM.

ART

Select Cheat Codes from the Options menu and enter CONC3PT.

VIDEOS

Select Cheat Codes from the Options menu and enter WATCHIT.

THE CHRONICLES OF NARNIA: THE LION, THE WITCH AND THE WARDROBE

ENABLE CHEATS

At the Title screen, press A and hold Left Trigger + Right Trigger and press Down, Down, Right, Up. The text should turn green when entered correctly. When this occurs, you can enter the following codes.

LEVEL SELECT

At the wardrobe, hold Left Trigger and press Up, Up, Right, Right, Up, Right, Down.

ALL BONUS LEVELS

At the Bonus Drawer, hold Left Trigger and press Down, Down, Right, Right, Down, Right, Up.

LEVEL SKIP
During gameplay, hold Left Trigger and press Down, Left, Down, Left, Down, Right, Down, Right, Up.

INVINCIBILITY
During gameplay, hold Left Trigger and press Down, Up, Down, Right, Right.

RESTORE HEALTH
During gameplay, hold Left Trigger and press Down, Left, Left, Right.

10,000 COINS
During gameplay, hold Left Trigger and press Down, Left, Right, Down, Down.

ALL ABILITIES
During gameplay, hold Left Trigger and press Down, Left, Right, Left, Up.

FILL COMBO METER
During gameplay, hold Left Trigger and press Up, Up, Right, Up.

COLD WAR

INVULNERABILITY
Pause the game and press X, White, Y, Black, Left.

WIN CURRENT LEVEL
Pause the game and press X, White, Y, Black, X.

ALL ITEMS, GADGETS, & TECH POINTS
Pause the game and press X, White, Y, Black, Y.

COMMANDOS STRIKE FORCE

MISSION SELECT
Enter TRUCO as a profile name.

UNLIMITED AMMO
Pause the game, hold Left Trigger + Right Trigger and press A, Y, A, B, X, Y.

CONSTANTINE

BIG DEMON HEADS
Press Back to get to the Journal and press Black, Left, Right, Left, Left, Right, Left, Black.

BIG WEAPON MODE
Press Back to get to the Journal and press Left, X, X, X, Y, Y, Y.

INFINITE AMMO
Press Back to get to the Journal and press Left, Right, Left, X, Y, X, X, Y, Y, X, Y, X, X, Y, Y.

INFINITE SPELL SOUL ENERGY
Press Back to get to the Journal and press Left, Right, Right, Left, Left, Right, Right, Left, Y, Y.

RAPID FIRE SHOTGUN
Press Back to get to the Journal and press White, Left, Black, Left, Y, X, Y, X.

SHOOT LARGE FIREBALLS
Press Back to get to the Journal and press Y, Y, Y, Left, Right, Right, Left, Left, Right.

EXPLOSIVE HOLY BOMBS
Press Back to get to the Journal and press Right, Left, X, Y, X, Y, Left, Right.

DANCE DANCE REVOLUTION ULTRAMIX 3

ALL SONGS
Select Credits from the Options menu and play the Credits mini-game, then press the opposite of what the game indicates. (For example, press Up when it says Down and so on. Or, if it says Left + Right, press Up + Down.) You'll hear applause when the code is entered correctly.

THE DA VINCI CODE

GOD MODE
Select Codes from the Options menu and enter VITRUVIAN MAN.

EXTRA HEALTH
Select Codes from the Options menu and enter SACRED FEMININE.

MISSION SELECT
Select Codes from the Options menu and enter CLOS LUCE 1519.

1-HIT FIST KILL
Select Codes from the Options menu and enter PHILLIPS EXETER.

ONE-HIT WEAPON KILL

Select Codes from the Options menu and enter ROYAL HOLLOWAY.

ALL VISUAL DATABASE

Select Codes from the Options menu and enter APOCRYPHA.

ALL VISUAL DATABASE & CONCEPT ART

Select Codes from the Options menu and enter ET IN ARCADIA EGO.

DEF JAM: FIGHT FOR NY

Select Cheats from the Extras menu and enter the following:

100 REWARD POINTS

Enter NEWJACK, THESOURCE, CROOKLYN, DUCKETS, or GETSTUFF. You can only enter each code once.

UNLOCK SONG: "AFTERHOURS" BY NYNE

Enter LOYALTY.

UNLOCK SONG: "ANYTHING GOES" BY C-N-N

Enter MILITAIN.

UNLOCK SONG: "BUST" BY OUTKAST

Enter BIGBOI.

UNLOCK SONG: "BLINDSIDE" BY BAXTER

Enter CHOPPER.

UNLOCK SONG: "COMP" BY COMP

Enter CHOCOCITY.

UNLOCK SONG: "DRAGON HOUSE" BY CHIANG

Enter AKIRA.

UNLOCK SONG: "GET IT NOW" BY BLESS

Enter PLATINUMB.

UNLOCK SONG: "KOTO" BY CHIANG

Enter GHOSTSHELL.

UNLOCK SONG: "LIL' BRO" BY RIC-A-CHE

Enter GONBETRUBL.

UNLOCK SONG: "MAN UP" BY STICKY FINGAZ

Enter KIRKJONES.

UNLOCK SONG: "MOVE!" BY PUBLIC ENEMY

Enter RESPECT.

UNLOCK SONG: "O. G. ORIGINAL GANGSTER" BY ICE T

Enter POWER.

UNLOCK SONG: "POPPA LARGE" BY ULTRAMAGNETIC MC'S

Enter ULTRAMAG.

UNLOCK SONG: "SIEZE THE DAY" BY BLESS

Enter SIEZE.

UNLOCK SONG: "TAKE A LOOK AT MY LIFE" BY FAT JOE

Enter CARTAGENA.

UNLOCK SONG: "WALK WITH ME" BY JOE BUDDEN

Enter PUMP.

DESTROY ALL HUMANS! 2

SALAD DAYS WITH POX & CRYPTO MOVIE

Pause the game and select Archives. Hold Left Thumbstick and press A, X, Y, B, X, B, Y, A, A.

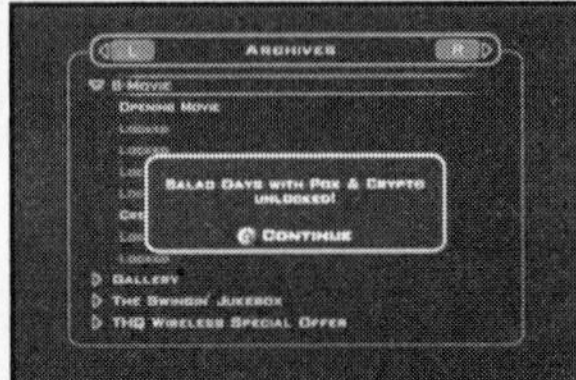

DRAGON BALL Z: SAGAS

ALL UPGRADES

Pause the game, select Controller and press Up, Left, Down, Right, Back, Start, Y, X, A, B.

INVINCIBILITY

Pause the game, select Controller and press Down, A, Up, Y, Back, Start, Right, X, Left, B.

DRIV3R

At the Main menu, enter the following cheats. Then select Cheats from the Options menu to toggle them on and off.

ALL MISSIONS

Enter X, X, Y, Y, R, R, L.

ALL WEAPONS

Enter L, L, X, Y, Y, R, R.

UNLIMITED AMMO

Enter R, R, L, L, X, Y, Y.

INVINCIBILITY (TAKE A RIDE)

Enter X, Y, L, R, L, R, R.

IMMUNITY

Enter X, Y, R, R, L, L, Y.

ALL VEHICLES

Enter X, X, Y, Y, L, R, L.

EA SPORTS ARENA FOOTBALL

BIG BALL

While at the line of scrimmage, press Left Trigger + Y, Up, Up.

SMALL BALL

While at the line of scrimmage, press Left Trigger + Y, Down, Down.

NORMAL SIZE BALL

While at the line of scrimmage, press Left Trigger + Y, Up, Down.

MAX STATS IN QUICK PLAY

Load a profile with the name IronMen. This will maximize all players' stats in Quick Play.

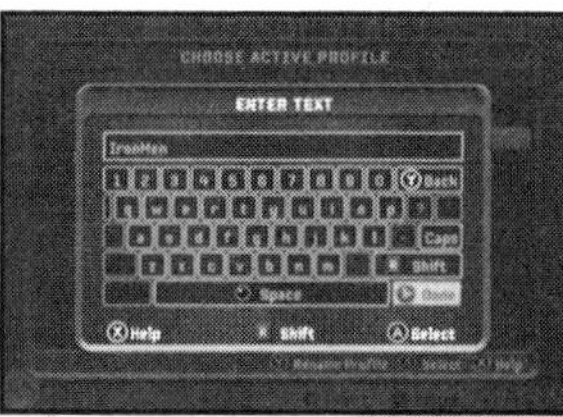

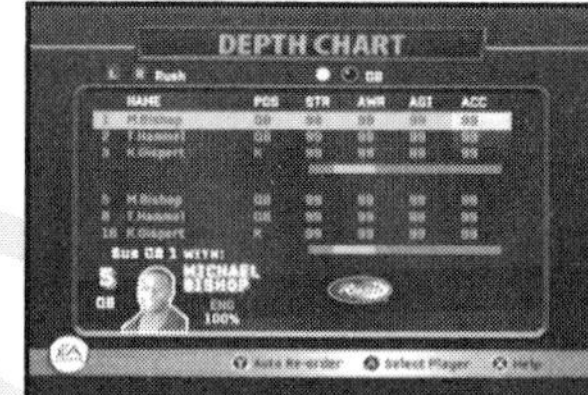

ERAGON

FURY MODE

Pause the game, hold Left Trigger + Right Trigger and press X, X, B, B.

FAR CRY: INSTINCTS—EVOLUTION

ALL MAPS

Enter GiveMeTheMaps at the Cheats menu.

FERAL ATTACKS (EARLY LEVELS)

Enter FeralAttack at the Cheats menu.

RESTORE HEALTH

Enter ImJackCarver at the Cheats menu.

INFINITE AMMO

Enter UnleashHell at the Cheats menu.

INFINITE ADRENALINE

Enter BloodLust at the cheats menu.

FLATOUT 2

ALL CARS AND 1,000,000 CREDITS

Select Enter Code from Extras and enter GIEVEPIX.

1,000,000 CREDITS

Select Enter Code from the Extras and enter GIVECASH.

PIMPSTER CAR

Select Enter Code from Extras and enter RUTTO.

FLATMOBILE CAR

Select Enter Code from Extras and enter WOTKINS.

MOB CAR

Select Enter Code from the Extras and enter BIGTRUCK.

SCHOOL BUS

Select Enter Code from Extras and enter GIEVCARPLZ.

ROCKET CAR

Select Enter Code from Extras and enter KALJAKOPPA.

TRUCK

Select Enter Code from the Extras and enter ELPUEBLO.

FULL SPECTRUM WARRIOR: TEN HAMMERS

ALL LEVELS

Enter FULLSPECTRUMPWNAGE at the Cheat menu.

THE GODFATHER

$5,000

Pause the game and press X, Y, X, X, Y, Left Thumbstick.

FULL AMMO

Pause the game and press Y, Left, Y, Right, X, Right Thumbstick.

FULL HEALTH

Pause the game and press Left, X, Right, Y, Right, Left Thumbstick.

UNLOCK ENTIRE FILM ARCHIVE

After loading a game and before joining the family, press Y, X, Y, X, X, Left Thumbstick. Select Film Archive to view films.

GRAND THEFT AUTO 3

BETTER VEHICLE HANDLING

Press Right Trigger, Left Trigger, Black, Left Trigger, Left, Right Trigger, Right Trigger, Y while *outside* your vehicle. This code makes all vehicles handle better. When entered correctly, press the Left Thumbstick to cause the vehicle to hop.

VEHICLE HEALTH

Press Black, Black, Left Trigger, Right Trigger, Left, Down, Right, Up, Left, Down, Right, Up while *inside* a vehicle. The car will remain damaged, but it will stop smoking and retain its perfect "health" status.

EXPLODE ALL VEHICLES

Press White, Black, Left Trigger, Right Trigger, White, Black, Y, X, B, Y, White, Left Trigger.

RHINO

Press B (x6), Right Trigger, White, Left Trigger, Y, B, Y.

INVISIBLE CAR CHASSIS

Press Left Trigger, Left Trigger, X, Black, Y, Left Trigger, Y.

FLYING VEHICLES

Press Right, Black, B, Right Trigger, White, Down, Left Trigger, Right Trigger.

FOGGY

Press Left Trigger, White, Right Trigger, Black, Black, Right Trigger, White, A.

CLOUDY

Press Left Trigger, White, Right Trigger, Black, Black, Right Trigger, White, X.

RAIN

Press Left Trigger, White, Right Trigger, Black, Black, Right Trigger, White, B.

NORMAL WEATHER

Press Left Trigger, White, Right Trigger, Black, Black, Right Trigger, White, Y.

PEDESTRIANS RIOT

Press Down, Up, Left, Up, A, Right Trigger, Black, White, Left Trigger. Please note that this code is irreversible, so do NOT enter the code and save your game.

PEDESTRIANS OUT TO GET YOU

Press Down, Up, Left, Up, A, Right Trigger, Black, Left Trigger, White. Please note that this code is irreversible, so do NOT enter the code and save your game.

PEDESTRIANS PACKING HEAT

Press Black, Right Trigger, Y, A, White, Left Trigger, Up, Down. Please note that this code is irreversible, so do NOT enter the code and save your game.

WANTED LEVEL INCREASE

Press Black, Black, Left Trigger, Black, Left, Right, Left, Right, Left to increase your Wanted Level by two each time the code is entered.

WANTED LEVEL DECREASE

Press Black, Black, Left Trigger, Black, Up, Down, Up, Down, Up, Down to decrease your Wanted Level.

WEAPON CHEAT

Press Black, Black, Left Trigger, Black, Left, Down, Right, Up, Left, Down, Right, Up. Continue to enter the code until the maximum ammo capacity of 9999 is reached for each weapon. When a weapon reaches its maximum ammo capacity, its ammunition supply becomes infinite.

CHANGE CHARACTER MODEL

Press Right, Down, Left, Up, Left Trigger, White, Up, Left, Down, Right. Please note that this code is irreversible, so do NOT enter the code and save your game.

HEALTH CHEAT

Press Black, Black, Left Trigger, Right Trigger, Left, Down, Right, Up, Left, Down, Right, Up.

ARMOR CHEAT

Press Black, Black, Left Trigger, White, Left, Down, Right, Up, Left, Down, Right, Up.

MONEY CHEAT ($250,000)

Press Black, Black, Left Trigger, Left Trigger, Left, Down, Right, Up, Left, Down, Right, Up.

INCREASED GORE FACTOR

Press X, Left Trigger, B, Down, Left Trigger, Right Trigger, Y, Right, Left Trigger, A to make victims lose body parts.

SLOW MOTION

Press Y, Up, Right, Down, X, Right Trigger, Black. Enter this cheat three times for even more slowdown.

FASTER GAMEPLAY

Press Y, Up, Right, Down, X, Left Trigger, White. Enter this cheat three times for even faster gameplay.

INCREASE TIME

Press B (x3), X (x5), Left Trigger, Y, B, Y. Enter this cheat a second time to return to "normal" time.

GRAND THEFT AUTO: VICE CITY

Enter the following cheats during gameplay. Note that some of these codes may affect your gameplay, so don't save your game unless you want the code to stay in effect.

HEALTH CHEAT

Press Right Trigger, Black, Left Trigger, B, Left, Down, Right, Up, Left, Down, Right, Up.

ARMOR CHEAT

Press Right Trigger, Black, Left Trigger, A, Left, Down, Right, Up, Left, Down, Right, Up.

LOW GRAVITY

Press Right, Black, B, Right Trigger, White, Down, Left Trigger, Right Trigger.

BETTER DRIVING

Press Y, Right Trigger, Right Trigger, Left, Right Trigger, Left Trigger, Black, Left Trigger. Press the Left Thumbstick to jump.

SUICIDE

Press Right, White, Down, Right Trigger, Left, Left, Right Trigger, Left Trigger, White, Left Trigger.

WANTED LEVEL UP 2 STARS

Press Right Trigger, Right Trigger, B, Black, Left, Right, Left, Right, Left, Right.

WANTED LEVEL DOWN 2 STARS

Press Right Trigger, Right Trigger, B, Black, Up, Down, Up, Down, Up, Down.

SLOW MOTION

Press Y, Up, Right, Down, X, Black, Right Trigger.

SPEED UP TIME

Press B, B, Left Trigger, X, Left Trigger, X, X, X, Left Trigger, Y, B, Y.

BLACK CARS

Press B, White, Up, Right Trigger, Left, A, Right Trigger, Left Trigger, Left, B.

PINK CARS

Press B, Left Trigger, Down, White, Left, A, Right Trigger, Left Trigger, Right, B.

CHANGE WHEELS

Press Right Trigger, A, Y, Right, Black, X, Up, Down, X.

CAR SPEED X2

Press Right Trigger, Black, Left Trigger, L, Left, Down, Right, Up, Left, Down, Right, Up.

CARS FLOAT

Press Right, Black, B, Right Trigger, White, X, Right Trigger, Black.

ALL CARS EXPLODE

Press Black, White, Right Trigger, Left Trigger, White, Black, X, Y, B, Y, White, Left Trigger.

ROBOCOPS

Press B, Left Trigger, Down, White, Left, A, Right Trigger, Left Trigger, Right, A.

CARS DON'T STOP

Press Black, B, Right Trigger, White, Left, Right Trigger, Left Trigger, Black, White.

PEDESTRIANS RIOT

Press Down, Left, Up, Left, A, Black, Right Trigger, White, Left Trigger.

PEDESTRIANS ATTACK

Press Down, Up (x3), A, Black, Right Trigger, White, White.

ARMED PEDESTRIANS

Press Black, Right Trigger, A, Y, A, Y, Up, Down.

WOMEN WITH GUNS

Press Right, Left Trigger, B, White, Left, A, Right Trigger, Left Trigger, Left Trigger, A.

WOMEN FOLLOW YOU

Press B, A, Left Trigger, Left Trigger, Black, A, A, B, Y.

MEDIA LEVEL METER

Press Black, B, Up, Left Trigger, Right, Right Trigger, Right, Up, X, Y.

The following codes provide one weapon for each weapon class:

WEAPONS SET 1

Press Black, Black, Right Trigger, Black, Left Trigger, Black, Left, Down, Right, Up, Left Down, Right, Up.

WEAPONS SET 2

Press Right Trigger, Black, Left Trigger, Black, Left, Down, Right, Up, Left, Down, Down, Left.

WEAPONS SET 3

Press Right Trigger, Black, Left Trigger, Black, Left, Down, Right, Up, Left, Down, Down, Down.

CLEAR WEATHER

Press Black, A, Left Trigger, Left Trigger, White, White, White, Down.

SUNNY

Press Black, A, Left Trigger, Left Trigger, White (x3), Y.

OVERCAST
Press Black, A, Left Trigger, Left Trigger, White (x3), X.

RAIN
Press Black, A, Left Trigger, Left Trigger, White (x3), B.

FOG
Press Black, A, Left Trigger, Left Trigger, White (x3), A.

RED LEATHER
Press Right, Right, Left, Up, Left Trigger, White, Left, Up, Down, Right.

CANDY SUXXX
Press B, Black, Down, Right Trigger, Left, Right, Right Trigger, Left Trigger, A, White.

HILARY KING
Press Right Trigger, B, Black, Left Trigger, Right, Right Trigger, Left Trigger, A, Black.

KEN ROSENBERG
Press Right, Left Trigger, Up, White, Left Trigger, Right, Right Trigger, Left Trigger, A, R.

LANCE VANCE
Press B, White, Left, A, Right Trigger, Left Trigger, A, Left Trigger.

LOVE FIST 1
Press Down, Left Trigger, Down, White, Left, A, Right Trigger, Left Trigger, A, A.

LOVE FIST 2
Press Right Trigger, White, Black, Left Trigger, Right, Black, Left, A, X, Left Trigger.

MERCEDES
Press Black, Left Trigger, Up, Left Trigger, Right, Right Trigger, Right, Up, B, Y.

PHIL CASSADY
Press Right, Right Trigger, Up, Black, Left Trigger, Right, Right Trigger, Left Trigger, Right, B.

RICARDO DIAZ
Press Left Trigger, White, Right Trigger, Black, Down, Left Trigger, Black, White.

SONNY FORELLI
Press B, Left Trigger, B, White, Left, A, Right Trigger, Left Trigger, A, A.

BLOODRING BANGER
Press Up, Right, Right, Left Trigger, Right, Up, X, White.

BLOODRING BANGER
Press Down, Right Trigger, B, White, White, A, Right Trigger, Left Trigger, Left, Left.

CADDY
Press B, Left Trigger, Up, Right Trigger, White, A, Right Trigger, Left Trigger, B, A.

HOTRING RACER 1
Press Black, Left Trigger, B, Right, Left Trigger, Right Trigger, Right, Up, B, Black.

HOTRING RACER 2
Press Right Trigger, B, Black, Right, Left Trigger, White, A, A, X, Right Trigger.

LOVE FIST LIMO
Press Black, Up, White, Left, Left, Right Trigger, Left Trigger, B, Right.

RHINO TANK
Press B, B, Left Trigger, B (x3), Left Trigger, White, Right Trigger, Y, B, Y.

ROMERO'S HEARSE
Press Down, Black, Down, Right Trigger, White, Left, Right Trigger, Left Trigger, Left, Right.

SABRE TURBO
Press Right, White, Down, White, White, A, Right Trigger, Left Trigger, B, Left.

TRASHMASTER
Press B, Right Trigger, B, Right Trigger, Left, Left, Right Trigger, Left Trigger, B, Right.

GRAND THEFT AUTO: SAN ANDREAS

During gameplay, enter the following cheats:

FULL HEALTH, FULL ARMOR, & $250,000
Press Right Trigger, Black, Left Trigger, A, Left , Down, Right, Up, Left, Down, Right, Up.

INFINITE HEALTH
Press Down, A, Right, Left, Right, Right Trigger, Right, Down, Up, Y.

INFINITE AMMO
Press Left Trigger, Right Trigger, X, Right Trigger, Left, Black, Right Trigger, Left, X, Down, Left Trigger, Left Trigger.

INFINITE LUNG CAPACITY
Press Down, Left, Left Trigger, Down, Down, Black, Down, White, Down.

MAX RESPECT
Press Left Trigger, Right Trigger, Y, Down, Black, A, Left Trigger, Up, White, White, Left Trigger, Left Trigger.

MAX SEX APPEAL
Press B, Y, Y, Up, B, Right Trigger, White, Up, Y, Left Trigger, Left Trigger, Left Trigger

MAX VEHICLE STATS
Press X, White, A, Right Trigger, White, White, Left, Right Trigger, Right, Left Trigger, Left Trigger, Left Trigger.

0 FAT AND 0 MUSCLE
Press Y, Up, Up, Left, Right, X, B, Right.

MAXIMUM MUSCLES
Press Y, Up, Up, Left, Right, X, B, Left.

MAXIMUM FAT
Press Y, Up, Up, Left, Right, X, B, Down.

BIG JUMPS
Press Up, Up, Y, Y, Up, Up, Left, Right, X, Black, Black.

BIG BUNNY HOPS ON BMX
Press Y, X, B, B, X, B, B, Left Trigger, White, White, Right Trigger, Black

SUICIDE
Press Right, White, Down, Right Trigger, Left, Left, Right Trigger, Left Trigger, White, Left Trigger.

MIDNIGHT
Press X, Left Trigger, Right Trigger, Right, A, Up, Left Trigger, Left, Left.

FASTER GAMEPLAY
Press Y, Up, Right, Down, White, Left Trigger, X.

SLOWER GAMEPLAY
Press Y, Up, Right, Down, X, Black, Right Trigger.

FASTER TIME
Press B, B, Left Trigger, X, Left Trigger, X, X, X, Left Trigger, Y, B, Y.

JUNK CARS
Press White, Right, Left Trigger, Up, A, Left Trigger, White, Black, Right Trigger, Left Trigger, Left Trigger, Left Trigger.

FARM VEHICLES
Press Left Trigger, Left Trigger, Right Trigger, Right Trigger White, Left Trigger, Black, Down, Left, Up.

BLACK CARS
Press B, White, Up, Right Trigger, Left, A, Right Trigger, Left Trigger, Left, B.

PINK CARS
Press B, Left Trigger, Down, White, Left, A, Right Trigger, Left Trigger, Right, B.

FAST CARS
Press Up, Left Trigger, Right Trigger, Up, Right, Up, A, White, A, Left Trigger.

NITROUS FOR ALL CARS
Press Left, Y, Right Trigger, Left Trigger, Up, X, Y, Down, B, White, Left Trigger, Left Trigger.

NITROUS FOR TAXIS & HOP
Press Up, A, Y, A, Y, A, X, Black, Right.

INVISIBLE VEHICLES
Press Y, Left Trigger, Y, Black, X, Left Trigger, Left Trigger.

INVINCIBLE VEHICLE
Press Left Trigger, White, White, Up, Down, Down, Up, Right Trigger, Black, Black.

DRIVE-BY WHILE DRIVING
Press Up, Up, X, White, Right, A, Right Trigger, Down, Black, B.

GREEN STOPLIGHTS
Press Right, Right Trigger, Up, White, White, Left, Right Trigger, Left Trigger, Right Trigger, Right Trigger.

AGGRESSIVE DRIVERS
Press Right, Black, Up, Up, Black, B, X, Black, Left Trigger, Right, Down, Left Trigger.

AGGRESSIVE TRAFFIC
Press Black, B, Right Trigger, White, Left, Right Trigger, Left Trigger, Black, White.

LESS TRAFFIC
Press A, Down, Up, Black, Down, Y, Left Trigger, Y, Left.

FASTER CARS
Press Right, Right Trigger, Up, White, White, Left, Right Trigger, Left Trigger, Right Trigger, Right Trigger.

BETTER HANDLING CARS
Press Y, Right Trigger, Right Trigger, Left, Right Trigger, Left Trigger, Black, Left Trigger.

FLOATING CARS
Press Right, Black, B, Right Trigger, White, X, Right Trigger, Black.

FLYING CARS
Press X, Down, White, Up, Left Trigger, B, Up, A, Left.

EXPLODING CARS
Press Black, White, Right Trigger, Left Trigger, White, Black, X, Y, B, Y, White, Left Trigger.

FLYING BOATS
Press Black, B, Up, Left Trigger, Right, Right Trigger, Right, Up, X, Y.

PEDESTRIANS ATTACK
Press Down, Up, Up, Up, A, Black, Right Trigger, White, White.

PEDESTRIANS ATTACK WITH GUNS
Press A, Left Trigger, Up, X, Down, A, White, Y, Down, Right Trigger, Left Trigger, Left Trigger.

PEDESTRIANS ATTACK EACH OTHER
Press Down, Left, Up, Left, A, Black, Right Trigger, White, Left Trigger.

PEDESTRIANS CARRY WEAPONS
Press Black, Right Trigger, A, Y, A, Y, Up, Down.

ELVIS IS EVERYWHERE
Press Left Trigger, B, Y, Left Trigger, Left Trigger, X, White, Up, Down, Left.

ATTRACT LADIES OF THE NIGHT
Press X, Right, X, X, White, A, Y, A, Y.

LADIES OF THE NIGHT PAY YOU
Press Right, White, White, Down, White, Up, Up, White, Black.

MULTIPLE UNLOCKABLES
When this code is entered, CJ turns into a Clown, civilians appear in fast food apparel and as clowns, there are BF Injections, HotDogs and so on. Press Y, Y, Left Trigger, X, X, B, X, Down, B.

PEOPLE IN SWIMSUITS
Press Up, Up, Down, Down, X, B, Left Trigger, Right Trigger, Y, Down.

GANGS
Press White, Up, Right Trigger, Right Trigger, Left, Right Trigger, Right Trigger, Black, Right, Down.

DECREASE WANTED LEVEL
Press Right Trigger, Right Trigger, B, Black, Up, Down, Up, Down, Up, Down.

INCREASE WANTED LEVEL
Press Right Trigger, Right Trigger, B, Black, Right, Left, Right, Left, Right, Left.

CLEAR WEATHER
Press Black, A, Left Trigger, Left Trigger, White, White, White, X.

NIGHT
Press Black, A, Left Trigger, Left Trigger, White, White, White, Y.

SUNNY WEATHER
Press Black, A, Left Trigger, Left Trigger, White, White, White, Down.

ORANGE SKY
Press Left, Left, White, Right Trigger, Right, X, X, Left Trigger, White, A.

FOGGY WEATHER
Press Black, A, Left Trigger, Left Trigger, White, White, White, A.

CLOUDY WEATHER
Press White, Down, Down, Left, X, Left, Black, X, A, Right Trigger, Left Trigger, Left Trigger.

OVERCAST
Press Black, A, Left Trigger, Left Trigger, White, White, White, X.

SAND STORM
Press Up, Down, Left Trigger, Left Trigger, White, White, Left Trigger, White, Right Trigger, Black.

RAINY WEATHER
Press Black, A, Left Trigger, Left Trigger, White, White, White, B.

HITMAN RANK
Press Down, X, A, Left, Right Trigger, Black, Left, Down, Down, Left Trigger, Left Trigger, Left Trigger.

WEAPONS SET 1
Press Right Trigger, Black, Left Trigger, Black, Left, Down, Right, Up, Left, Down, Right, Up.

WEAPONS SET 2
Press Right Trigger, Black, Left Trigger, Black, Left, Down, Right, Up, Left, Down, Down, Left.

WEAPONS SET 3
Press Right Trigger, Black, Left Trigger, Black, Left, Down, Right, Up, Left , Down, Down, Down.

PARACHUTE
Press Left, Right, Left Trigger, White, Right Trigger, Black, Black, Up, Down, Right, Left Trigger.

JETPACK
Press Left, Right, Left Trigger, White, Right Trigger, Black, Up, Down, Left, Right.

BLOODRING BANGER
Press Down, Right Trigger, B, White, White, A, Right Trigger, Left Trigger, Left, Left.

CADDY
Press B, Left Trigger, Up, Right Trigger, White, A, Right Trigger, Left Trigger, B, A.

DOZER
Press Black, Left Trigger, Left Trigger, Right, Right, Up, Up, A, Left Trigger, Left.

HOTRING RACER 1
Press Right Trigger, B, Black, Right, Left Trigger, White, A, A, X, Right Trigger.

HOTRING RACER 2
Press Black, Left Trigger, B, Right, Left Trigger, Right Trigger, Right, Up, B, Black.

HUNTER
Press B, A, Left Trigger, B, B, Left Trigger, B, Right Trigger, Black, White, Left Trigger, Left Trigger.

HYDRA
Press Y, Y, X, B, A, Left Trigger, Left Trigger, Down, Up.

MONSTER
Press Right, Up, Right Trigger, Right Trigger, Right Trigger, Down, Y, Y, A, B, Left Trigger, Left Trigger.

QUADBIKE
Press Left, Left, Down, Down, Up, Up, X, B, Y, Right Trigger, Black.

RANCHER
Press Up, Right, Right, Left Trigger, Right, Up, X, White.

RHINO
Press B, B, Left Trigger, B, B, B, Left Trigger, White, Right Trigger, Y, B, Y.

ROMERO
Press Down, Black, Down, Right Trigger, White, Left, Right Trigger, Left Trigger, Left, Right.

STRETCH
Press Black, Up, White, Left, Left, Right Trigger, Left Trigger, B, Right.

STUNTPLANE
Press B, Up, Left Trigger, White, Down, Right Trigger, Left Trigger, Left Trigger, Left, Left, A, Y.

TANKER
Press Right Trigger, Up, Left, Right, Black, Up, Right, X, Right, White, Left Trigger, Left Trigger.

TRASHMASTER
Press B, Right Trigger, B, Right Trigger, Left, Left, Right Trigger, Left Trigger, B, Right.

VORTEX
Press Y, Y, X, B, A, Left Trigger, White, Down, Down.

THE INCREDIBLE HULK: ULTIMATE DESTRUCTION

You must first collect a specific comic in the game to activate each code. After collecting the appropriate comic, you can enter the following. If you don't have the comic and enter the code, you get the following message: "That code cannot be activated…yet". You can access the cheats on the Code Input screen.

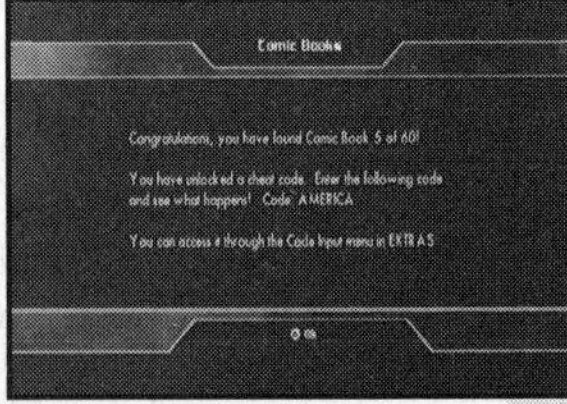

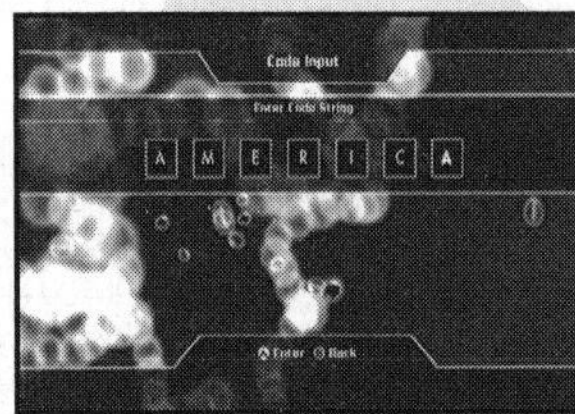

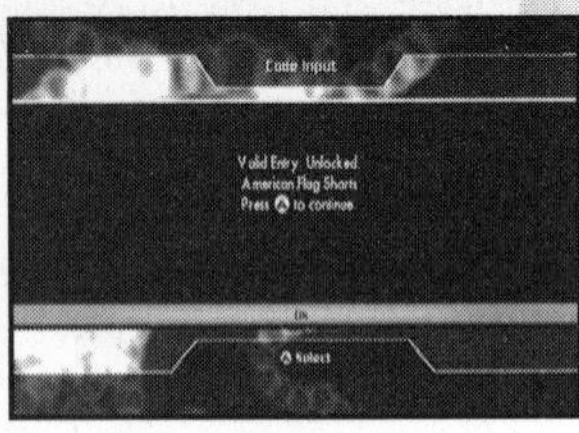

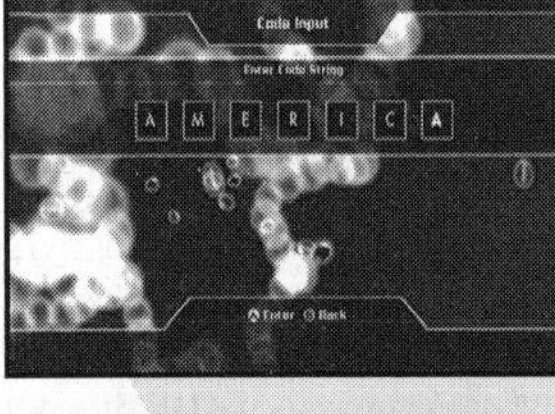

UNLOCKED: CABS GALORE
Select Code Input from the Extras menu and enter CABBIES.

UNLOCKED: GORILLA INVASION
Select Code Input from the Extras menu and enter KINGKNG.

UNLOCKED: MASS TRANSIT
Select Code Input from the Extras menu and enter TRANSIT.

UNLOCKED: 5000 SMASH POINTS
Select Code Input from the Extras menu and enter SMASH5.

UNLOCKED: 10000 SMASH POINTS
Select Code Input from the Extras menu and enter SMASH10.

UNLOCKED: 15000 SMASH POINTS
Select Code Input from the Extras menu and enter SMASH15.

UNLOCKED: AMERICAN FLAG SHORTS
Select Code Input from the Extras menu and enter AMERICA.

UNLOCKED: CANADIAN FLAG SHORTS
Select Code Input from the Extras menu and enter OCANADA.

UNLOCKED: FRENCH FLAG SHORTS
Select Code Input from the Extras menu and enter Drapeau.

UNLOCKED: GERMAN FLAG SHORTS
Select Code Input from the Extras menu and enter DEUTSCH.

UNLOCKED: ITALIAN FLAG SHORTS
Select Code Input from the Extras menu and enter MUTANDA.

UNLOCKED: JAPANESE FLAG SHORTS
Select Code Input from the Extras menu and enter FURAGGU.

UNLOCKED: SPANISH FLAG SHORTS
Select Code Input from the Extras menu and enter BANDERA.

UNLOCKED: UK FLAG SHORTS
Select Code Input from the Extras menu and enter FSHNCHP.

UNLOCKED: COW MISSILES
Select Code Input from the Extras menu and enter CHZGUN.

UNLOCKED: DOUBLE HULK'S DAMAGE
Select Code Input from the Extras menu and enter DESTROY.

UNLOCKED: DOUBLE POWER COLLECTABLES
Select Code Input from the Extras menu and enter BRINGIT.

UNLOCKED: BLACK AND WHITE
Select Code Input from the Extras menu and enter RETRO.

UNLOCKED: SEPIA
Select Code Input from the Extras menu and enter HISTORY.

UNLOCKED: ABOMINATION
Select Code Input from the Extras menu and enter VILLAIN.

UNLOCKED: GRAY HULK
Select Code Input from the Extras menu and enter CLASSIC.

UNLOCKED: JOE FIXIT SKIN
Select Code Input from the Extras menu and enter SUITFIT.

UNLOCKED: WILD TRAFFIC
Select Code Input from the Extras menu and enter FROGGIE.

UNLOCKED: LOW GRAVITY
Select Code Input from the Extras menu and enter PILLOWS.

JAMES BOND 007: EVERYTHING OR NOTHING

CHEATS
To access the following codes, you must first earn the given number of Platinum. Upon doing so, pause the game and enter the corresponding code.

EFFECT	PLATINUM	CODE
Golden Gun	1	B, Y, A, B, Y
Improved Traction	3	B, A, A, X, Y
Improved Battery	5	B, X, X, A, B
Double Ammunition	7	B, B, A, B, Y
Double Damage	9	B, Y, Y, X, B
Full Ammunition	11	B, B, Y, X, X
Cloak	13	B, Y, A, Y, X
Full Battery	15	B, Y, Y, A, B
All Weapons	17	B, Y, A, A, B
Unlimited Battery	19	B, X, B, X, Y
Unlimited Ammo	23	B, A, X, A, Y
Slow Motion Driving	25	B, X, Y, A, Y
Platinum Gun	27	B, X, X, B, A

LEGO STAR WARS II: THE ORIGINAL TRILOGY

BEACH TROOPER
At Mos Eisley Canteena, select Enter Code and enter UCK868. You still need to select Characters and purchase this character for 20,000 studs.

BEN KENOBI (GHOST)
At Mos Eisley Canteena, select Enter Code and enter BEN917. You still need to select Characters and purchase this character for 1,100,000 studs.

BESPIN GUARD
At Mos Eisley Canteena, select Enter Code and enter VHY832. You still need to select Characters and purchase this character for 15,000 studs.

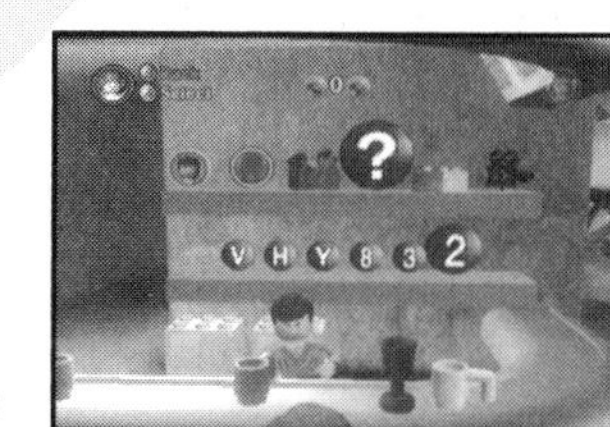

BIB FORTUNA
At Mos Eisley Canteena, select Enter Code and enter WTY721. You still need to select Characters and purchase this character for 16,000 studs.

BOBA FETT
At Mos Eisley Canteena, select Enter Code and enter HLP221. You still need to select Characters and purchase this character for 175,000 studs.

DEATH STAR TROOPER
At Mos Eisley Canteena, select Enter Code and enter BNC332. You still need to select Characters and purchase this character for 19,000 studs.

EWOK
At Mos Eisley Canteena, select Enter Code and enter TTT289. You still need to select Characters and purchase this character for 34,000 studs.

GAMORREAN GUARD
At Mos Eisley Canteena, select Enter Code and enter YZF999. You still need to select Characters and purchase this character for 40,000 studs.

GONK DROID
At Mos Eisley Canteena, select Enter Code and enter NFX582. You still need to select Characters and purchase this character for 1,550 studs.

GRAND MOFF TARKIN
At Mos Eisley Canteena, select Enter Code and enter SMG219. You still need to select Characters and purchase this character for 38,000 studs.

GREEDO
At Mos Eisley Canteena, select Enter Code and enter NAH118. You still need to select Characters and purchase this character for 60,000 studs.

HAN SOLO (HOOD)
At Mos Eisley Canteena, select Enter Code and enter YWM840. You still need to select Characters and purchase this character for 20,000 studs.

IG-88
At Mos Eisley Canteena, select Enter Code and enter NXL973. You still need to select Characters and purchase this character for 30,000 studs.

IMPERIAL GUARD
At Mos Eisley Canteena, select Enter Code and enter MMM111. You still need to select Characters and purchase this character for 45,000 studs.

IMPERIAL OFFICER
At Mos Eisley Canteena, select Enter Code and enter BBV889. You still need to select Characters and purchase this character for 28,000 studs.

IMPERIAL SHUTTLE PILOT
At Mos Eisley Canteena, select Enter Code and enter VAP664. You still need to select Characters and purchase this character for 29,000 studs.

IMPERIAL SPY
At Mos Eisley Canteena, select Enter Code and enter CVT125. You still need to select Characters and purchase this character for 13,500 studs.

JAWA
At Mos Eisley Canteena, select Enter Code and enter JAW499. You still need to select Characters and purchase this character for 24,000 studs.

LOBOT
At Mos Eisley Canteena, select Enter Code and enter UUB319. You still need to select Characters and purchase this character for 11,000 studs.

PALACE GUARD
At Mos Eisley Canteena, select Enter Code and enter SGE549. You still need to select Characters and purchase this character for 14,000 studs.

REBEL PILOT
At Mos Eisley Canteena, select Enter Code and enter CYG336. You still need to select Characters and purchase this character for 15,000 studs.

REBEL TROOPER (HOTH)
At Mos Eisley Canteena, select Enter Code and enter EKU849. You still need to select Characters and purchase this character for 16,000 studs.

SANDTROOPER

At Mos Eisley Canteena, select Enter Code and enter YDV451. You still need to select Characters and purchase this character for 14,000 studs.

SKIFF GUARD

At Mos Eisley Canteena, select Enter Code and enter GBU888. You still need to select Characters and purchase this character for 12,000 studs.

SNOWTROOPER

At Mos Eisley Canteena, select Enter Code and enter NYU989. You still need to select Characters and purchase this character for 16,000 studs.

STROMTROOPER

At Mos Eisley Canteena, select Enter Code and enter PTR345. You still need to select Characters and purchase this character for 10,000 studs.

THE EMPEROR

At Mos Eisley Canteena, select Enter Code and enter HHY382. You still need to select Characters and purchase this character for 275,000 studs.

TIE FIGHTER

At Mos Eisley Canteena, select Enter Code and enter HDY739. You still need to select Characters and purchase this character for 60,000 studs.

TIE FIGHTER PILOT

At Mos Eisley Canteena, select Enter Code and enter NNZ316. You still need to select Characters and purchase this character for 21,000 studs.

TIE INTERCEPTOR

At Mos Eisley Canteena, select Enter Code and enter QYA828. You still need to select Characters and purchase this character for 40,000 studs.

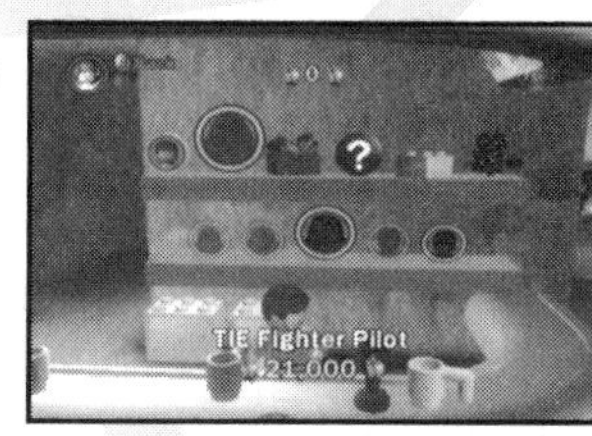

TUSKEN RAIDER

At Mos Eisley Canteena, select Enter Code and enter PEJ821. You still need to select Characters and purchase this character for 23,000 studs.

UGNAUGHT

At Mos Eisley Canteena, select Enter Code and enter UGN694. You still need to select Characters and purchase this character for 36,000 studs.

MADDEN NFL 07

MADDEN CARDS

Select Madden Cards from My Madden. Then select Madden Codes and enter the following:

CARD	PASSWORD
#199 Gold Lame Duck Cheat	5LAWO0
#200 Gold Mistake Free Cheat	XL7SP1
#210 Gold QB on Target Cheat	WROA0R
#220 Super Bowl XLI Gold	RLA9R7
#221 Super Bowl XLII Gold	WRLUF8
#222 Super Bowl XLIII Gold	NIEV4A
#223 Super Bowl XLIV Gold	M5AB7L
#224 Aloha Stadium Gold	YI8P8U
#225 1958 Colts Gold	B57QLU
#226 1966 Packers Gold	1PL1FL
#227 1968 Jets Gold	MIE6WO
#228 1970 Browns Gold	CL2TOE
#229 1972 Dolphins Gold	NOEB7U
#230 1974 Steelers Gold	YOOFLA
#231 1976 Raiders Gold	MOA11I
#232 1977 Broncos Gold	C8UM7U
#233 1978 Dolphins Gold	VIU0O7
#234 1980 Raiders Gold	NLAPH3
#235 1981 Chargers Gold	COAGI4
#236 1982 Redskins Gold	WL8BRI
#237 1983 Raiders Gold	H0EW71

CARD	PASSWORD
#238 1984 Dolphins Gold	M1AM1E
#239 1985 Bears Gold	QOETO8
#240 1986 Giants Gold	ZI8S2L
#241 1988 49ers Gold	SP2A8H
#242 1990 Eagles Gold	2L4TRO
#243 1991 Lions Gold	J1ETRI
#244 1992 Cowboys Gold	W9UVI9
#245 1993 Bills Gold	DLA3I7
#246 1994 49ers Gold	DR7EST
#247 1996 Packers Gold	F8LUST
#248 1998 Broncos Gold	FIES95
#249 1999 Rams Gold	S9OUSW
#250 Bears Pump Up the Crowd	B1OUPH
#251 Bengals Cheerleader	DRL2SW
#252 Bills Cheerleader	1PLUYO
#253 Broncos Cheerleader	3ROUJO
#254 Browns Pump Up the Crowd	T1UTOA
#255 Buccaneers Cheerleader	S9EWRI
#256 Cardinals Cheerleader	57IEPI
#257 Chargers Cheerleader	F7UHL8
#258 Chiefs Cheerleader	PRI5SL
#259 Colts Cheerleader	1R5AMI
#260 Cowboys Cheerleader	Z2ACHL
#261 Dolphins Cheerleader	C5AHLE
#262 Eagles Cheerleader	PO7DRO
#263 Falcons Cheerleader	37USPO
#264 49ers Cheerleader	KL0CRL
#265 Giants Pump Up the Crowd	C4USPI
#266 Jaguars Cheerleader	MIEH7E
#267 Jets Pump Up the Crowd	COLUXI
#268 Lions Pump Up the Crowd	3LABLU
#269 Packers Pump Up the Crowd	4HO7VO
#270 Panthers Cheerleader	F2IASP
#282 All AFC Team Gold	PRO9PH
#283 All NFC Team Gold	RLATH7

MAJOR LEAGUE BASEBALL 2K7

MICKEY MANTLE ON THE FREE AGENTS LIST

Select Enter Cheat Code from the My 2K7 menu and enter themick.

ALL CHEATS

Select Enter Cheat Code from the My 2K7 menu and enter Black Sox.

ALL EXTRAS

Select Enter Cheat Code from the My 2K7 menu and enter Game On.

UNLOCK EVERYTHING

Select Enter Cheat Code from the My 2K7 menu and enter Derek Jeter. This does not unlock the Topps cheats.

MIGHTY MICK CHEAT

Select Enter Cheat Code from the My 2K7 menu and enter mightymick.

TRIPLE CROWN CHEAT

Select Enter Cheat Code from the My 2K7 menu and enter triplecrown.

PINCH HIT MICK CHEAT

Select Enter Cheat Code from the My 2K7 menu and enter phmantle.

BIG BLAST CHEAT

Select Enter Cheat Code from the My 2K7 menu Rand enter m4murder.

MANHUNT

CHEAT CODES

The following codes cannot be used until they are unlocked. To unlock them, you must earn a five-star rating (which is only possible on Hardcore mode) in each pair of two consecutive scenes. After unlocking the codes, enter them at the Title screen.

EFFECT	CODE
Runner	White, White, L, White, Left, Right, Left, Right (Scenes 01 and 02)
Silence	R, L, White, L, Right, Left (x3) (Scenes 03 and 04)
Regenerate	White, Right, B, White, Black, Down, B, Left (Scenes 05 and 06)
Helium Hunters	R, R, Y, B, X, Black, L, Down (Scenes 07 and 08)
Fully Equipped	R, White, L, Black, Down, Up, Left, Up (Scenes 09 and 10)
Super Punch	L, Y (x3), B (x3), R (Scenes 11 and 12)
Rabbit Skin	Left, R, R, Y, R, R, X, L (Scenes 13 and 14)
Monkey Skin	X, X, White, Down, Y, X, B, Down (Scenes 15 and 16)
Invisibility	X (x3), Down, X, Down, B, Up (Scenes 17 and 18)
Piggsy Skin	Up, Down, Left, Left, R, White, L, L (Scenes 19 and 20)

GOD MODE

After defeating the game on Fetish mode, press Down, Down, B, Up, X, Y, X, White, Up, Up, L, Y.

MARC ECKO'S GETTING UP: CONTENTS UNDER PRESSURE

ALL LEVELS

Select Codes from the Options menu and enter IPULATOR.

INFINITE HEALTH

Select Codes from the Options menu and enter MARCUSECKOS.

MAX HEALTH

Select Codes from the Options menu and enter BABYLONTRUST.

INFINITE SKILLS

Select Codes from the Options menu and enter FLIPTHESCRIPT.

MAX SKILLS

Select Codes from the Options menu and enter VANCEDALLISTER.

ALL COMBAT UPGRADES

Select Codes from the Options menu and enter DOGTAGS.

ALL CHARACTERS IN VERSUS MODE

Select Codes from the Options menu and enter STATEYOURNAME.

ALL VERSUS ARENAS

Select Codes from the Options menu and enter WORKBITCH.

ALL ART

Select Codes from the Options menu and enter SIRULLY.

ALL BLACK BOOK

Select Codes from the Options menu and enter SHARDSOFGLASS.

ALL IPOD

Select Codes from the Options menu and enter GRANDMACELIA.

ALL LEGENDS

Select Codes from the Options menu and enter NINESIX.

ALL MOVIES

Select Codes from the Options menu and enter DEXTERCROWLEY.

NARC

ALL DRUGS

During a game, press R, L, R, L, R, L, Left Thumbstick.

ALL WEAPONS

During a game, press R, L, R, L, R, L, Right Thimbstick.

INVINCIBILITY

During a game, press R, L, R, L, R, L, A.

SHOW HIDDEN STASHES
During a game, press R, L, R, L, R, L, Left.

UNLIMITED AMMO FOR CURRENT WEAPON
During a game, press R, L, R, L, R, L, Down.

THE REFINERY
During a game, press R, L, R, L, R, L, X.

NASCAR 07

$10,000,000
In Fight to the Top mode, enter your name as GiveMe More.

10,000,000 FANS
In Fight to the Top mode, enter your name as AllBow ToMe.

PRESTIGE LEVEL 10 WITH 2,000,000 POINTS
In Fight to the Top mode, enter your name as Outta MyWay.

100% TEAM PRESTIGE
In Fight to the Top mode, enter your name as MoMoney BlingBling.

ALL CHASE PLATES
In Fight to the Top mode, enter your name as ItsAll ForMe.

OLD SPICE TRACKS AND CARS
In Fight to the Top mode, enter your name as KeepCool SmellGreat.

WALMART TRACK AND CARS
In Fight to the Top mode, enter your name as Walmart EveryDay.

NBA 2K7

MAX DURABILITY
Select Codes from the Features menu and enter ironman.

UNLIMITED STAMINA
Select Codes from the Features menu and enter norest.

+10 DEFFENSIVE AWARENESS
Select Codes from the Features menu and enter getstops.

+10 OFFENSIVE AWARENESS
Select Codes from the Features menu and enter inthezone.

TOPPS 2K SPORTS ALL-STARS
Select Codes from the Features menu and enter topps2ksports.

ABA BALL
Select Codes from the Features menu and enter payrespect.

NBA LIVE 07

ADIDAS ARTILLERY II BLACK & THE RBK ANSWER 9 VIDEO
Select NBA Codes from My NBA Live and enter 99B6356HAN.

ADIDAS ARTILLERY II
Select NBA Codes and enter NTGNFUE87H.

ADIDAS BTB LOW AND THE MESSAGE FROM ALLEN IVERSON VIDEO
Select NBA Codes and enter 7FB3KS9JQ0.

ADIDAS C-BILLUPS
Select NBA Codes and enter BV6877HB9N.

ADIDAS C-BILLUPS BLACK
Select NBA Codes and enter 85NVLDMWS5.

ADIDAS CAMPUS LT
Select NBA Codes and enter CLT2983NC8.

ADIDAS CRAZY 8
Select NBA Codes and enter CC98KKL814.

ADIDAS EQUIPMENT BBALL
Select NBA Codes and enter 22OIUJKMDR.

ADIDAS GARNETT BOUNCE
Select NBA Codes and enter HYIOUHCAAN.

ADIDAS GARNETT BOUNCE BLACK
Select NBA Codes and enter KDZ2MQL17W.

ADIDAS GIL-ZERO
Select NBA Codes and enter 23DN1PPOG4.

ADIDAS GIL-ZERO BLACK
Select NBA Codes and enter QQQ3JCUYQ7.

ADIDAS GIL-ZERO MID
Select NBA Codes and enter 1GSJC8JWRL.

ADIDAS GIL-ZERO MID BLACK
Select NBA Codes and enter 369V6RVU3G.

ADIDAS STEALTH
Select NBA Codes and enter FE454DFJCC.

ADIDAS T-MAC 6
Select NBA Codes and enter MCJK843NNC.

ADIDAS T-MAC 6 WHITE
Select NBA Codes and enter 84GF7EJG8V.

AIR JORDAN V
Select NBA Codes and enter PNBBX1EVT5.

AIR JORDAN V
Select NBA Codes and enter VIR13PC451.

AIR JORDAN V
Select NBA Codes and enter IB7G8NN91Z.

JORDAN MELO M3
Select NBA Codes and enter JUL38TC485.

CHARLOTTE BOBCATS 2006-07 ALTERNATE JERSEY
Select NBA Codes and enter WEDX671H7S.

UTAH JAZZ 2006-07 ALTERNATE JERSEY
Select NBA Codes and enter VCBI89FK83.

NEW JERSEY NETS 2006-07 ALTERNATE JERSEY
Select NBA Codes and enter D4SAA98U5H.

WASHINGTON WIZARDS 2006-07 ALTERNATE JERSEY
Select NBA Codes and enter QV93NLKXQC.

EASTERN ALL-STARS 2006-07 ROAD JERSEY
Select NBA Codes and enter WOCNW4KL7L.

EASTERN ALL-STARS 2006-07 HOME JERSEY
Select NBA Codes and enter 5654ND43N6.

WESTERN ALL-STARS 2006-07 ROAD JERSEY
Select NBA Codes and enter XX93BVL20U.

WESTERN ALL-STARS 2006-07 HOME JERSEY
Select NBA Codes and enter 993NSKL199.

NCAA FOOTBALL 07

PENNANT CODES
Select Pennant Collection from My NCAA, then press Select to enter the following codes.

CODE NAME	ENTER
#16 Baylor	Sic Em
#16 Nike Speed TD	Light Speed
#63 Illinois	Oskee Wow
#160 Texas Tech	Fight
#200 First and Fifteen	Thanks
#201 Blink	For
#202 Boing	Registering
#204 Butter Fingers	With EA
#205 Crossed the Line	Tiburon
#206 Cuffed	EA Sports

CODE NAME	ENTER
#207 Extra Credit	Touchdown
#208 Helium	In The Zone
#209 Hurricane	Turnover
#210 Instant Freeplay	Impact
#211 Jumbalaya	Heisman
#212 Molasses	Game Time
#213 Nike Free	Break Free
#214 Nike Magnigrip	Hand Picked
#215 Nike Pro	No Sweat
#219 QB Dud	Elite 11
#221 Steel Toe	Gridiron

CODE NAME	ENTER
#222 Stiffed	NCAA
#223 Super Dive	Upset
#224 Take Your Time	Football
#225 Thread & Needle	06
#226 Tough As Nails	Offense
#227 Trip	Defense
#228 What a Hit	Blitz
#229 Kicker Hex	Sideline
#273 2004 All-Americans	Fumble
#274 All-Alabama	Roll Tide
#276 All-Arkansas	Woopigsooie
#277 All-Auburn	War Eagle
#278 All-Clemson	Death Valley
#279 All-Colorado	Glory
#280 All-Florida	Great To Be
#281 All-FSU	Uprising
#282 All-Georgia	Hunker Down
#283 All-Iowa	On Iowa
#284 All-Kansas State	Victory
#285 All-LSU	Geaux Tigers
#286 All-Miami	Raising Cane
#287 All-Michigan	Go Blue
#288 All-Mississippi State	Hail State
#289 All-Nebraska	Go Big Red
#290 All-North Carolina	Rah Rah
#291 All-Notre Dame	Golden Domer
#292 All-Ohio State	Killer Nuts

CODE NAME	ENTER
#293 All-Oklahoma	Boomer
#294 All-Oklahoma State	Go Pokes
#295 All-Oregon	Quack Attack
#296 All-Penn State	We Are
#297 All-Pittsburgh	Lets Go Pitt
#298 All-Purdue	Boiler Up
#299 All-Syracuse	Orange Crush
#300 All-Tennessee	Big Orange
#301 All-Texas	Hook Em
#302 All-Texas A&M	Gig Em
#303 All-UCLA	MIGHTY
#304 All-USC	Fight On
#305 All-Virginia	Wahoos
#306 All-Virginia Tech	Tech Triumph
#307 All-Washington	Bow Down
#308 All-Wisconsin	U Rah Rah
#311 Ark Mascot	Bear Down
#329 GT Mascot	RamblinWreck
#333 ISU Mascot	Red And Gold
#335 KU Mascot	Rock Chalk
#341 Minn Mascot	Rah Rah Rah
#344 Mizzou Mascot	Mizzou Rah
#346 MSU Mascot	Go Green
#349 NCSU Mascot	Go Pack
#352 NU Mascot	Go Cats
#360 S Car Mascot	Go Carolina
#371 UK Mascot	On On UK
#382 Wake Forest	Go Deacs Go
#385 WSU Mascot	All Hail
#386 WVU Mascot	Hail WV

NEED FOR SPEED UNDERGROUND 2

ALL CIRCUIT TRACKS
At the Main menu, press Down, Right Trigger, Right Trigger, Right Trigger, Black, Black, Black, X.

BEST BUY VINYL
At the Main menu, press Up, Down, Up, Down, Down, Up, Right, Left.

BURGER KING VINYL
At the Main menu, press Up, Up, Up, Up, Down, Up, Up, Left.

H2 CAPONE
At the Main menu, press Up, Left, Up, Up, Down, Left, Down, Left.

NISSIAN SKYLINE
At the Main menu, press Down, Down, Left Trigger, White, Left Trigger, White, Left Trigger, Down.

LEVEL 1 PERFORMANCE PARTS
At the Main menu, press Left Trigger, Right Trigger, Left Trigger, Right Trigger, Left, Left, Right, Up.

LEVEL 2 PERFORMANCE PARTS
At the Main menu, press Right Trigger, Right Trigger, Left Trigger, Right Trigger, Left, Right, Up, Down.

LEVEL 1 VISUAL PARTS
At the Main menu, press Right Trigger, Right Trigger, Up, Down, Left Trigger, Left Trigger, Up, Down.

LEVEL 2 VISUAL PARTS
At the Main menu, press Left Trigger, Right Trigger, Up, Down, Left Trigger, Up, Up, Down.

NFL HEAD COACH

CLOWN
Name your coach Red Nose.

JOHN MADDEN
Name your coach John Madden.

SANTA CLAUS
Name your coach Merry Christmas.

SUPER BOWL ALWAYS AT HOMETOWN
Name your coach Hometown Hero.

NINJA GAIDEN

ORIGINAL BLUE NINJA COSTUME

Highlight New Game and press Left Trigger + Right Trigger, then press the A button.

OUTRUN 2

Select OutRun Challenge and go to the Gallery screen. Choose Enter Code and input the following.

ALL CARS

Enter DREAMING.

ALL MISSION STAGES

Enter THEJOURNEY.

BONUS TRACKS

Enter TIMELESS.

REVERSE TRACKS

Enter DESREVER.

ALL MUSIC

Enter RADIOSEGA.

ORIGINAL OUTRUN

Enter NINETEEN86.

ALL CARDS

Enter BIRTHDAY.

OVER THE HEDGE

COMPLETE LEVELS

Pause the game, hold Left Trigger + Right Trigger and press Y, B, Y, B, B, X.

ALL MINIGAMES

Pause the game, hold Left Trigger + Right Trigger and press Y, B, Y, Y, X, X.

ALL MOVES

Pause the game, hold Left Trigger + Right Trigger and press Y, B, Y, X, X, B.

EXTRA DAMAGE

Pause the game, hold Left Trigger + Right Trigger and press Y, B, Y, B, Y, X.

MORE HP FROM FOOD

Pause the game, hold Left Trigger + Right Trigger and press Y, B, Y, B, X, Y.

ALWAYS POWER PROJECTILE

Pause the game, hold Left Trigger + Right Trigger and press Y, B, Y, B, X, B.

BONUS COMIC 14

Pause the game, hold Left Trigger + Right Trigger and press Y, B, X, X, B, Y.

BONUS COMIC 15

Pause the game, hold Left Trigger + Right Trigger and press Y, Y, X, B, X, B.

PAINKILLER: HELL WARS

GOD MODE

During a game, hold White + L and press B.

TOGGLE DEMON MODE

During a game, hold White + L and press X.

PARIAH

ALL AMMO

Select Cheat Codes from the Settings menu and press Down, Up, Down, Y

GOD MODE

Select Cheat Codes from the Settings menu and press Up, Left Trigger, X, Left Trigger.

ALL SINGLE-PLAYER LEVELS

Select Cheat Codes from the Settings menu and press Y, Down, Right Trigger, Down.

LOCATION STATUS

Select Cheat Codes from the Settings menu and press X, Right, Left Trigger, Left.

BEST BUY MULTIPLAYER LEVEL

Select Cheat Codes from the Settings menu and press Left Trigger, Black, White, Right Trigger.

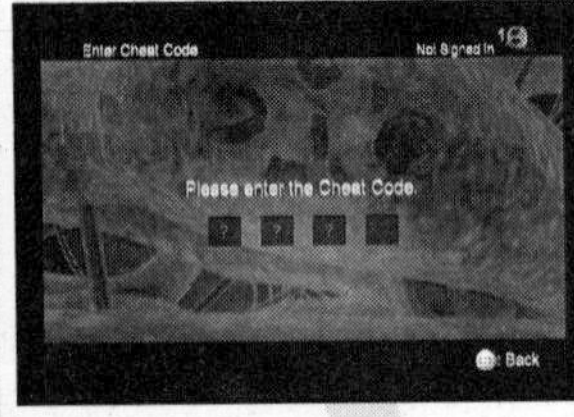

EB MULTIPLAYER LEVEL

Select Cheat Codes from the Settings menu and press White, Y, X, Black.

GAMESTOP MULTIPLAYER LEVEL

Select Cheat Codes from the Settings menu and press Left, Left Trigger, X, Left.

TOYS 'R' US MULTIPLAYER LEVEL

Select Cheat Codes from the Settings menu and press Left, Up, White, Black.

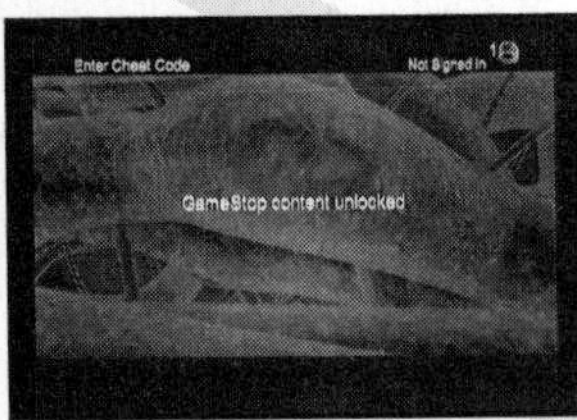

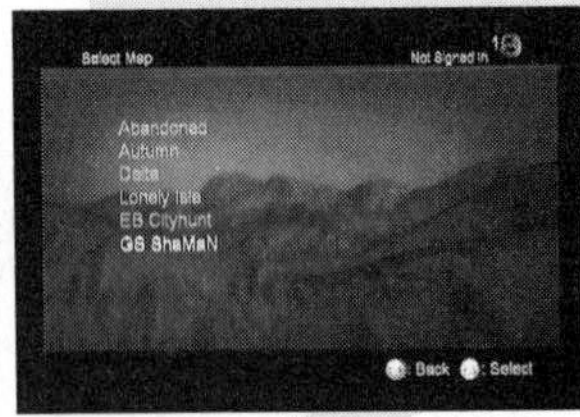

PRINCE OF PERSIA: THE TWO THRONES

BABY TOY HAMMER WEAPON

Pause the game and press Left, Left, Right, Right, Y, X, X, Y, Up, Down.

CHAINSAW WEAPON

Pause the game and press Up, Up, Down, Down, Left, Right, Left, Right, Y, X, Y, X.

SWORDFISH WEAPON

Pause the game and press Up, Down, Up, Down, Left, Right, Y, X, Y, X.

TELEPHONE OF SORROW WEAPON

Pause the game and press Right, Left, Right, Left, Down, Down, Up, Up, Y, X, Y, Y, X, X.

PSYCHONAUTS

ALL POWERS

During a game, hold Left Trigger + Right Trigger and press B, B, Y, White, Left Thumbstick, Y.

9999 LIVES

During a game, hold Left Trigger + Right Trigger and press Left Thumbstick, White, White, B, A, Right Thumbstick.

9999 AMMO (BLAST, CONFUSION)

During a game, hold Left Trigger + Right Trigger and press Right Thumbstick, A, Left Thumbstick, Left Thumbstick, Y, B.

GLOBAL ITEMS (NO PSI-BALL COLORIZER, NO DREAM FLUFFS)

During a game, hold Left Trigger + Right Trigger and press Right Thumbstick, B, White, White, Left Thumbstick, Y.

ALL POWERS UPGRADED (MAX RANK)

During a game, hold Left Trigger + Right Trigger and press Left Thumbstick, Right Thumbstick, Left Thumbstick, White, B, White.

9999 ARROWHEADS

During a game, hold Left Trigger + Right Trigger and press A, Right Thumbstick, Right Thumbstick, White, Y, X.

INVINCIBILITY

During a game, hold Left Trigger + Right Trigger and press B, White, B, B, Y, Black.

WEIRD TEXT

During a game, hold Left Trigger + Right Trigger and press White, A, click Left Thumbstick, White, White, B.

RESERVOIR DOGS

ALL LEVELS

Select Cheats from the Extras menu and enter Black, White, Black, White, Left Trigger, Right Trigger, Start.

ADRENALINE RUSH-INFINITE ADRENALINE

Select Cheats from the Extras menu and enter A, Left Trigger, Y, A, Left Trigger, A, Start.

BATTERING RAM-INSTANT CRASH

Select Cheats from the Extras menu and enter Black, Black, A, A, Y, White, Start.

BULLETPROOF-INFINITE HEALTH

Select Cheats from the Extras menu and enter Left Trigger, Right Trigger, Y, Y, Right Trigger, Y, Start.

FULLY LOADED-INFINITE AMMO

Select Cheats from the Extras menu and enter White, Black, Y, Black, A, White, Start.

MAGIC BULLET-ONE SHOT KILLS

Select Cheats from the Extras menu and enter Right Trigger, Black, Y, A, Right Trigger, A, Start.

TIME OUT-INFINITE TIMER

Select Cheats from the Extras menu and enter Right Trigger, Right Trigger, White, Y, A, Black, Start.

ART GALLERY

Select Cheats from the Extras menu and enter Y, A, Black, White, Y, A, Start.

MOVIE GALLERY

Select Cheats from the Extras menu and enter Left Trigger, Left Trigger, Y, A, Left Trigger, Right Trigger, Start.

ROBOTS

BIG HEAD FOR RODNEY

Pause the game and press Up, Down, Down, Up, Right, Right, Left, Right.

UNLIMITED HEALTH

Pause the game and press Up, Right, Down, Up, Left, Down, Right, Left.

UNLIMITED SCRAP

Pause the game and press Down, Down, Left, Up, Up, Right, Up, Down.

SCARFACE: THE WORLD IS YOURS

After entering the following cheats, highlight the cheat and press A to "DO IT."

MAX AMMO
Pause the game, select Cheats and enter AMMO.

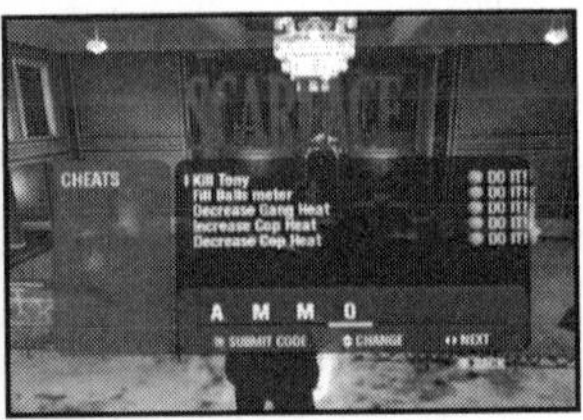

REFILL HEALTH
Pause the game, select Cheats and enter MEDIK.

FILL BALLS METER
Pause the game, select Cheats and enter FPATCH.

KILL TONY
Pause the game, select Cheats and enter KILTONY.

DECREASE COP HEAT
Pause the game, select Cheats and enter FLYSTRT.

INCREASE COP HEAT
Pause the game, select Cheats and enter DONUT.

DECREASE GANG HEAT
Pause the game, select Cheats and enter NOBALLS.

INCREASE GANG HEAT
Pause the game, select Cheats and enter GOBALLS.

REPAIR TONY'S VEHICLE
Pause the game, select Cheats and enter TBURGLR.

SPAWN ARIEL MK III
Pause the game, select Cheats and enter OLDFAST.

SPAWN BACINARI
Pause the game, select Cheats and enter 666999.

SPAWN BODOG STAMPEDE
Pause the game, select Cheats and enter BUMMER.

SPAWN BULLDOZER
Pause the game, select Cheats and enter DOZER.

SPAWN ODIN VH88
Pause the game, select Cheats and enter DUMPER.

BLACK SUIT TONY
Pause the game, select Cheats and enter BLACK.

BLUE PINSTRIPE SUIT TONY WITH SHADES
Pause the game, select Cheats and enter BLUESH.

GRAY SUIT TONY
Pause the game, select Cheats and enter GRAY.

GRAY SUIT TONY WITH SHADES
Pause the game, select Cheats and enter GRAYSH.

HAWAIIAN SHIRT TONY
Pause the game, select Cheats and enter HAWAII.

HAWAIIAN SHIRT TONY WITH SHADES
Pause the game, select Cheats and enter HAWAIIG.

SANDY SHIRT TONY
Pause the game, select Cheats and enter SANDY.

SANDY SHIRT TONY WITH SHADES
Pause the game, select Cheats and enter SANDYSH.

WHITE SUIT TONY
Pause the game, select Cheats and enter WHITE.

WHITE SUIT TONY WITH SHADES
Pause the game, select Cheats and enter WHITESH.

CHANGE TIME OF DAY
Pause the game, select Cheats and enter MARTHA.

TOGGLE LIGHTNING
Pause the game, select Cheats and enter SHAZAAM.

TOGGLE RAIN
Pause the game, select Cheats and enter RAINY.

BREAL "THE WORLD IS YOURS" MUSIC TRACK
Pause the game, select Cheats and enter TUNEME.

SKIP CURRENT WEEK IN CAMPAIGN MODE

At the US Map, press Start for the Options. Then select Cheat Menu and press X, Y, X, B, A.

WIN CIVIL WAR IN CAMPAIGN MODE

At the US Map, press Start for the Options. Then select Cheat Menu and press X, B, A, B, Y.

$100,000

At the US Map, press Start for the Options. Then select Cheat Menu and press X, X, A, A, Y.

ARCADIA PLAINS

At the US Map, press Start for the Options. Then select Cheat Menu and press B, X, X, X, A.

ARIZONA TERRITORY

At the US Map, press Start for the Options. Then select Cheat Menu and press B, X, X, A, X.

CAROLINAS

At the US Map, press Start for the Options. Then select Cheat Menu and press B, X, Y, X, A.

CENTRAL CASCADES

At the US Map, press Start for the Options. Then select Cheat Menu and press B, X, X, X, Y.

CENTRAL HEARTLAND

At the US Map, press Start for the Options. Then select Cheat Menu and press B, X, X, B, Y.

CUMBERLANDS

At the US Map, press Start for the Options. Then select Cheat Menu and press B, X, Y, X, Y.

DAKOTAS

At the US Map, press Start for the Options. Then select Cheat Menu and press B, X, X, B, X.

EASTERN SHENANDOAH

At the US Map, press Start for the Options. Then select Cheat Menu and press B, X, Y, Y, B.

FLORIDA

At the US Map, press Start for the Options. Then select Cheat Menu and press B, X, Y, X, B.

GREAT BASIN

At the US Map, press Start for the Options. Then select Cheat Menu and press B, X, X, Y, A.

GREAT LAKES

At the US Map, press Start for the Options. Then select Cheat Menu and press B, X, X, B, A.

GREAT PLAINS

At the US Map, press Start for the Options. Then select Cheat Menu and press B, X, X, B, B.

MISSISSIPPI DELTA

At the US Map, press Start for the Options. Then select Cheat Menu and press B, X, Y, X, X.

NEW MEXICO

At the US Map, press Start for the Options. Then select Cheat Menu and press B, X, X, Y, B.

NEW YORK

At the US Map, press Start for the Options. Then select Cheat Menu and press B, X, Y, Y, Y.

NORTHERN CALIFORNIA

At the US Map, press Start for the Options. Then select Cheat Menu and press B, X, X, Y, X.

NORTHERN CASCADES

At the US Map, press Start for the Options. Then select Cheat Menu and press B, X, X, X, B.

NORTHERN NEW ENGLAND

At the US Map, press Start for the Options. Then select Cheat Menu and press B, X, Y, Y, A.

NORTHERN TEXAS

At the US Map, press Start for the Options. Then select Cheat Menu and press B, X, X, A, A.

OHIO VALLEY

At the US Map, press Start for the Options. Then select Cheat Menu and press B, X, Y, Y, X.

OKLAHOMA GRASSLANDS

At the US Map, press Start for the Options. Then select Cheat Menu and press B, X, X, A, Y.

SOUTHEASTERN CASCADES

At the US Map, press Start for the Options. Then select Cheat Menu and press B, X, X, X, X.

SOUTHERN CALIFORNIA

At the US Map, press Start for the Options. Then select Cheat Menu and press B, X, X, Y, Y.

SOUTHERN TEXAS

At the US Map, press Start for the Options. Then select Cheat Menu and press B, X, X, A, B.

SID MEIER'S PIRATES!

FOOD NEVER DWINDLES
Name your character Sweet Tooth.

INVINCIBLE SHIP
Name your character Bloody Bones Baz.

JEFF BRIGGS AS ABBOTT
Name your character Firaxis.

SNAPPY DRESSER
Name your character Bonus Frag.

BEST SHIP AND FULL CREW
Name your character D.Gackey.

FLEET IS TWICE AS FAST
Name your character Sprinkler.

HIGHEST MORALE
Name your character B.Caudizzle.

DUELING INVINCIBILITY
Name your character Dragon Ma.

SID MEIER AS MYSTERIOUS STRANGER
Name your character Max Remington.

SONIC HEROES

METAL CHARACTERS IN 2-PLAYER
After selecting a level in 2-Player mode, hold A + Y.

SPY VS SPY

ALL CLASSIC MAPS
Enter RETROSPY at the password screen.

ALL STORY MODE LEVELS
Enter ANTONIO at the password screen.

ALL LEVELS FOR SINGLE-PLAYER MODERN MODE
Enter PROHIAS at the password screen.

ALL MULTIPLAYER MAPS
Enter MADMAG at the password screen.

ALL OUTFITS
Enter DISGUISE at the password screen.

ALL WEAPONS
Enter WRKBENCH at the password screen.

INVULNERABILITY
Enter ARMOR at the password screen.

SUPER DAMAGE
Enter BIGGUNZ at the password screen.

PERMANENT FAIRY IN MODERN MODE
Enter FAIRY at the password screen.

NO DROPPED ITEMS WHEN KILLED
Enter NODROP at the password screen.

INVISIBLE HUD
Enter BLINK at the password screen.

ALL MOVIES
Enter SPYFLIX at the password screen.

CONCEPT ART
Enter SPYPICS at the password screen.

SSX ON TOUR

NEW THREADS
Select Cheats from the Extras menu and enter FLYTHREADS.

THE WORLD IS YOURS
Select Cheats from the Extras menu and enter BACKSTAGEPASS.

SHOW TIME (ALL MOVIES)
Select Cheats from the Extras menu and enter THEBIGPICTURE.

BLING BLING (INFINITE CASH)
Select Cheats from the Extras menu and enter LOOTSNOOT.

FULL BOOST, FULL TIME
Select Cheats from the Extras menu and enter ZOOMJUICE.

MONSTERS ARE LOOSE (MONSTER TRICKS)
Select Cheats from the Extras menu and enter JACKALOPESTYLE.

SNOWBALL FIGHT
Select Cheats from the Extras menu and enter LETSPARTY.

FEEL THE POWER (STAT BOOST)
Select Cheats from the Extras menu and enter POWERPLAY.

CHARACTERS ARE LOOSE
Select Cheats from the Extras menu and enter ROADIEROUNDUp.

UNLOCK CONRAD
Select Cheats from the Extras menu and enter BIGPARTYTIME.

UNLOCK MITCH KOOBSKI
Select Cheats from the Extras menu and enter MOREFUNTHANONE.

UNLOCK NIGEL
Select Cheats from the Extras menu and enter THREEISACROWD.

UNLOCK SKI PATROL
Select Cheats from the Extras menu and enter FOURSOME.

STAR WARS KNIGHTS OF THE OLD REPUBLIC II: THE SITH LORDS

CHANGE VOICES
Add a controller to the controller port 4 and press Black or White to raise and lower character voices.

STOLEN

LEVEL SKIP
At the Title screen, press Right Trigger, Left Trigger, Start + Down.

99 OF ALL ITEMS
During gameplay, go to Equipment and press Right Trigger, Left Trigger, Right.

SUPERMAN RETURNS: THE VIDEOGAME

INFINITE STAMINA

Pause the game, select Options and press Up, Up, Down, Down, Left, Right, Left, Right, Y, X.

INFINITE CITY HEALTH

Pause the game, select Options and press Y, Right, Y, Right, Up, Left, Right, Y.

ALL MOVES

Pause the game, select Options and press Left, Y, Right, X, Down, Y, Up, Down, X, Y, X.

ALL COSTUMES, TROPHIES AND THEATER ITEMS

Pause the game, select Options and press Left, Up, Right, Down, Y, X, Y, Up, Right, X.

TAK: THE GREAT JUJU CHALLENGE

BONUS SOUND EFFECTS

In Juju's Potions, select Universal Card and enter the following numbers for Bugs, Crystals and Fruits: 20, 17, 5.

BONUS SOUND EFFECTS 2

In Juju's Potions, select Universal Card and enter the following numbers for Bugs, Crystals and Fruits: 50, 84, 92.

BONUS MUSIC TRACK 1

In Juju's Potions, select Universal Card and enter the following numbers for Bugs, Crystals and Fruits: 67, 8, 20.

BONUS MUSIC TRACK 2

In Juju's Potions, select Universal Card and enter the following numbers for Bugs, Crystals and Fruits: 6, 18, 3.

MAGIC PARTICLES

In Juju's Potions, select Universal Card and enter the following numbers for Bugs, Crystals and Fruits: 24, 40, 11.

MORE MAGIC PARTICLES

In Juju's Potions, select Universal Card and enter the following numbers for Bugs, Crystals and Fruits: 48, 57, 57.

VIEW JUJU CONCEPT ART

In Juju's Potions, select Universal Card and enter the following numbers for Bugs, Crystals and Fruits: Art 33, 22, 28.

VIEW VEHICLE ART

In Juju's Potions, select Universal Card and enter the following numbers for Bugs, Crystals and Fruits: 11, 55, 44.

VIEW WORLD ART

In Juju's Potions, select Universal Card and enter the following numbers for Bugs, Crystals and Fruits: 83, 49, 34.

THRILLVILLE

$50,000

During a game, press X, B, Y, X, B, Y, A. Repeat this code as much as desired.

ALL PARKS

During a game, press X, B, Y, X, B, Y, X.

ALL RIDES

During a game, press X, B, Y, X, B, Y, Y. Some rides still need to be researched.

COMPLETE MISSIONS

During a game, press X, B, Y, X, B, Y, B. Then, at the Missions menu, highlight a mission and press X to complete that mission. Some missions have Bronze, Silver, and Gold objectives. For these missions the first press of X earns the Bronze, the second earns the Silver, and the third earns the Gold.

TIGER WOODS PGA TOUR 07

NIKE ITEMS

Select the Password option and enter JUSTDOIT.

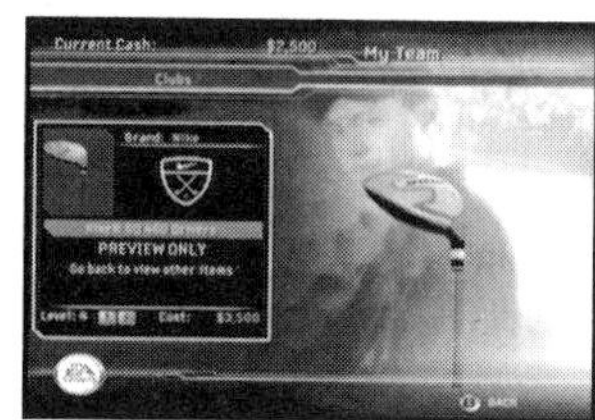

TOMB RAIDER: LEGEND

You must unlock the following codes in the game before using them.

BULLETPROOF

During gameplay, hold Left Trigger and press A, Right Trigger, Y, Right Trigger, X, Black.

DRAIN ENEMY HEALTH

During gameplay, hold Left Trigger and press X, B, A, Black, Right Trigger, Y.

INFINITE ASSAULT RIFLE AMMO

During gameplay, hold Black and press A, B, A, Left Trigger, X, Y.

INFINITE GRENADE LAUNCHER AMMO

During gameplay, hold Black and press Left Trigger, Y, Right Trigger, B, Left Trigger, X.

INFINITE SHOTGUN AMMO

During gameplay, hold Black and press Right Trigger, B, X, Left Trigger, X, A.

INFINITE SMG AMMO

During gameplay, hold Black and press B, Y, Left Trigger, Right Trigger, A, B.

EXCALIBUR

During gameplay, hold Black and press Y, A, B, Right Trigger, Y, Left Trigger.

SOUL REAVER

During gameplay, hold Black and press A, Right Trigger, B, Right Trigger, Left Trigger, X.

NO TEXTURE MODE

During gameplay, hold Left Trigger and press Black, A, B, A, Y, Right Trigger.

TONY HAWK'S AMERICAN WASTELAND

ALWAYS SPECIAL

Select Cheat Codes from the Options menu and enter uronfire. Pause the game and select Cheats from the Game Options to enable the cheat.

PERFECT RAIL

Select Cheat Codes from the Options menu and enter grindxpert. Pause the game and select Cheats from the Game Options to enable the cheat.

PERFECT SKITCH

Select Cheat Codes from the Options menu and enter h!tchar!de. Pause the game and select Cheats from the Game Options to enable the cheat.

PERFECT MANUAL

Select Cheat Codes from the Options menu and enter 2wheels!. Pause the game and select Cheats from the Game Options to enable the cheat.

MOON GRAVITY

Select Cheat Codes from the Options menu and enter 2them00n. Pause the game and select Cheats from the Game Options to enable the cheat.

MAT HOFFMAN

Select Cheat Codes from the Options screen and enter the_condor.

JASON ELLIS

Select Cheat Codes from the Options menu and enter sirius-dj.

TOTAL OVERDOSE: A GUNSLINGER'S TALE IN MEXICO

CHEAT MODE

Hold Left Trigger + Right Trigger + White + Black + Left Thumbstick + Right Thumbstick for a few seconds. Now enter any of the following cheats.

RESTORE HEALTH

Press A, X, B, Y.

ALL LOCO MOVES

Press B, B, White, Black.

MAXIMUM REWINDING

Press Right Trigger, Black, White, A.

ALL WEAPONS

Press Y, Left Trigger, Black, X.

TY THE TASMANIAN TIGER 3: NIGHT OF THE QUINKAN

100,000 OPALS

During a game, press Start, Start, Y, Start, Start, Y, B, A, B, A.

ALL RINGS

During a game, press Start, Start, Y, Start, Start, Y, B, X, B, X.

ULTIMATE SPIDER-MAN

ALL CHARACTERS

Pause the game and select Controller Setup from the Options menu. Press Right, Down, Right, Down, Left, Up, Left, Right.

ALL COVERS

Pause the game and select Controller Setup from the Options menu. Press Left, Left, Right, Left, Up, Left, Left, Down.

ALL CONCEPT ART

Pause the game and select Controller Setup from the Options menu. Press Down, Down, Down, Up, Down, Up, Left, Left.

ALL LANDMARKS

Pause the game and select Controller Setup from the Options menu. Press Up, Right, Down, Left, Down, Up, Right, Left.

THE WARRIORS

100% COMPLETE

During gameplay, press Right Trigger, Back, X, Down, Left Trigger, Right.

99 CREDITS IN ARMIES OF THE NIGHT

During the Armies of the Night mini-game, press Up, Up, Down, Down, Left, Right.

$200, FLASH, & SPRAY PAINT

During gameplay, press Black, Left Thumbstick, Right Trigger, A, Down, R.

INFINITE HEALTH

During gameplay, press Up, Y, White, Back, A, Left Trigger, Down, X, Left, A, Right Trigger, Back.

INFINITE RAGE

During gameplay, press X, B, Y, Back, A, Left.

INFINITE SPRINT

During gameplay, press Down, X, Left, A, R, Back.

COMPLETE MISSION

During gameplay, press Down, X, A, Back, Back, Left.

BAT

During gameplay, press X, Left Thumbstick, Down, Down, Right Trigger, Right Trigger.

UNBREAKABLE BAT

During gameplay, press White, White, B, Up, B, Back.

BRASS KNUCKLES

During gameplay, press B, B, B, R, Back, Y.

KNIFE

During gameplay, press Down, Down, Back, Up, Up, White.

MACHETE

During gameplay, press Right Trigger, A, Black, Black, Back, Left Thumbstick.

PIPE

During gameplay, press Left Thumbstick, B, Back, Up, Right Trigger, Right.

STEEL-TOE BOOTS

During gameplay, press Click Right Thumbstick, Click Left Thumbstick, Black, White, Left Trigger, Right Trigger.

BUM ADVICE UPGRADE

During gameplay, press B, B, Down, Click Left Thumbstick, Left Trigger, B.

COMBAT STAMINA UPGRADE

During gameplay, press A, Right Trigger, Down, X, Up, A.

FLASH CAPACITY UPGRADE

During gameplay, press Left Trigger, A, Click Left Thumbstick, Right Trigger, Right Trigger, B.

FLASH UPGRADE

During gameplay, press Down, Left, Up, Up, X, Right.

SPRINT STAMINA UPGRADE

During gameplay, press Left Trigger, Back, Back, Back, Back, Y.

CUFF DROPS

During gameplay, press Up, A, Up, Back, White, Right Trigger.

CUFF KEY DROPS

During gameplay, press Left, A, A, Click Left Thumbstick, Right Trigger, Down.

UNCUFF SELF

During gameplay, press Y, Y, Y, Back, Y, Black.

LOSE THE POLICE

During gameplay, press Up, Back, A, Y, Y, B.

HOBO ALLIANCE

During gameplay, press Black, Black, Right Trigger, Black, Right Trigger, Up.

WEAPONS DEALER

During gameplay, press Right, Black, B, A, Back, X.

X-MEN: THE OFFICIAL GAME

DANGER ROOM ICEMAN

At the Cerebro Files menu, press Right, Right, Left, Left, Down, Up, Down, Up, Start.

DANGER ROOM NIGHTCRAWLER

At the Cerebro Files menu, press Up, Up, Down, Down, Left, Right, Left, Right, Start.

DANGER ROOM WOLVERINE

At the Cerebro Files menu, press Down, Down, Up, Up, Right, Left, Right, Left, Start.

YU-GI-OH! THE DAWN OF DESTINY

COSMO QUEEN CARD IN DECK

Enter your name as KONAMI.

TRI-HORN DRAGON CARD IN DECK

Enter your name as HEARTOFCARDS.

ZERA THE MANT CARD IN DECK

Enter your name as XBOX.

GAMECUBE™

GAMES

ANIMAL CROSSING

TOM NOOK PASSWORDS

Talk to Tom Nook and select the Other Things option. Then, select Say Code and enter the following passwords. You will be able to enter only three at a time.

PASSWORD	ITEM
CbDahLBdaDh98d 9ub8ExzZKwu7Zl	Balloon Fight NES Game
1n5%N%8JUjE5fj lEcGr4%ync5eUp	Baseball NES Game
Crm%h4BNRyu98d 9uu8exzZKwu7Zl	Clu Clu Land NES Game
bA5PC%8JUjE5fj ljcGr4%ync5EUp	DK Jr. Math NES Game
2n5@N%8JUjE5fj ljcGr4%ync5EUp	Donkey Kong NES Game
3%Q4fhMTRByAY3 05yYAK9zNHxLd7	Excitebike NES Game
Crm%h4BNRbu98d 9un8exzZKwo7Zl	Golf NES Game
bA5PC%8JUjE5fj 1EcGr4%ync5eup	Wario's Woods NES Game
Wn2&SAVAcglC7N POudE2Tk8JHyUH	10,000 Bells from Project Hyrule
WB2&pARAcnOwnU jMCK%hTk8JHyrT	30,000 Bells from Project Hyrule
#SbaUlRmw#gwkY BK66q#LGscTY%2	? Block
IboOBCeHz3YbIC B5igPvQYsfMZMd	Block Flooring
1mWYg6lfB@&q75 8XzSNKpfWj76ts	Brick Block
4UT6T6L89ZnOW3 dw&%jtL3qjLZBf	Cannon
4UT6T948GZnOW3 dw#%jtLEqj5ZBf	Fire Flower
4UT6T6L89ZnOW3 dwU%jtL3qjLZBf	Flagpole
1mWYg6lfB@&q7z 8XzSNwpfij76ts	Green Pipe
BCQ4iZFK%i5xqo SnyrjcrwAeDMkQ	Luigi Trophy
QI6DLEnhm23CqH zrUHk3cXd#HOr9	Mushroom Mural
4UF6T948GZ3ZW3 dw#%jtLEqj5ZBf	Starman
1LhOwvrDA23fmt dsgnvzbClBAsyd	Station Model 1

LETTER TO VILLAGER PASSWORDS

For the following codes, send the password to one of the animals living in your town. Only include the password in the body of the letter. Be sure to include a line break between the two lines of code.

PASSWORD	ITEM
rSbaUIRmwUgwkA 1K6tq#LMscTY%2	Coin
rSbaUIAmwUgwkY 1K6tq#LGscTY%2	Koopa Shell
ECzihy%rtHbHuk o3XIP3lslEql#K	Mario Trophy
#SbaUIRmw#gwkY Bh66qeLMscTY%2	Super Mushroom

BATMAN BEGINS

GALLERY OF FEAR
Finish the game on any difficulty mode.

ALL MOVIES AND INTERVIEWS
Finish the game on any difficulty mode.

ALTERNATE COSTUMES
Finish the game on any difficulty mode.

PROTOTYPE BATMOBILE
Finish the game on any difficulty mode.

BRATZ: FOREVER DIAMONDZ

1000 BLINGZ
While in the Bratz Office, use the Cheat computer to enter SIZZLN.

2000 BLINGZ
While in the Bratz Office, use the Cheat computer to enter FLAUNT.

PET TREATS
While in the Bratz Office, use the Cheat computer to enter TREATZ.

GIFT SET A
While in the Bratz Office, use the Cheat computer to enter STYLIN.

GIFT SET B
While in the Bratz Office, use the Cheat computer to enter SKATIN.

GIFT SET C
While in the Bratz Office, use the Cheat computer to enter JEWELZ.

GIFT SET E
While in the Bratz Office, use the Cheat computer to enter DIMNDZ.

CARS

UNLOCK EVERYTHING
Select Cheat Codes from the Options screen and enter IF900HP.

ALL CHARACTERS
Select Cheat Codes from the Options screen and enter YAYCARS.

ALL CHARACTER SKINS
Select Cheat Codes from the Options screen and enter R4MONE.

ALL MINI-GAMES AND COURSES
Select Cheat Codes from the Options screen and enter MATTL66.

MATER'S COUNTDOWN CLEAN-UP MINI-GAME AND MATER'S SPEEDY CIRCUIT
Select Cheat Codes from the Options menu and enter TRGTEXC.

FAST START
Select Cheat Codes from the Options menu and enter IMSPEED.

INFINITE BOOST
Select Cheat Codes from the Options menu and enter VROOOOM.

ART
Select Cheat Codes from the Options menu and enter CONC3PT.

VIDEOS
Select Cheat Codes from the Options menu and enter WATCHIT.

THE CHRONICLES OF NARNIA: THE LION, THE WITCH AND THE WARDROBE

ENABLE CHEATS
At the Title screen, press A then hold L + R and press Down, Down, Right, Up. When entered correctly, the text turns green. Now you can enter the following:

LEVEL SELECT
At the wardrobe, hold L and press Up, Up, Right, Right, Up, Right, Down.

ALL BONUS LEVELS
At the Bonus Drawer, hold L and press Down, Down, Right, Right, Down, Right, Up.

LEVEL SKIP
During gameplay, hold L and press Down, Left, Down, Left, Down, Right, Down, Right, Up.

INVINCIBILITY
During gameplay, hold L and press Down, Up, Down, Right, Right.

RESTORE HEALTH
During gameplay, hold L and press Down, Left, Left, Right.

10,000 COINS
During gameplay, hold L and press Down, Left, Right, Down, Down.

ALL ABILITIES
During gameplay, hold L and press Down, Left, Right, Left, Up.

FILL COMBO METER
During gameplay, hold L and press Up, Up, Right, Up.

CURIOUS GEORGE

CURIOUS GEORGE GOES APE
Pause the game, hold Z and press B, B, A, Y, B.

UNLIMITED BANANAS
Pause the game, hold Z and press A, X, X, Y, A.

ROLLERSKATES & FEZ HAT
Pause the game, hold Z and press X, A, A, A, B.

UPSIDE DOWN GRAVITY MODE
Pause the game, hold Z and press Y, Y, B, A, A.

ICE AGE 2: THE MELTDOWN

ALL BONUSES
Pause the game and press Down, Left, Up, Down, Down, Left, Right, Right.

LEVEL SELECT
Pause the game and press Up, Right, Right, Left, Right, Right, Down, Down.

UNLIMITED PEBBLES
Pause the game and press Down, Down, Left, Up, Up, Right, Up, Down.

INFINITE ENERGY
Pause the game and press Down, Left, Right, Down, Down, Right, Left, Down.

INFINITE HEALTH
Pause the game and press Up, Right, Down, Up, Left, Down, Right, Left.

THE INCREDIBLE HULK: ULTIMATE DESTRUCTION

You must collect a specific comic in the game to activate each code. After collecting the appropriate comic, you can enter the following codes. If you don't have the comic and enter the code, you receive a message "That code cannot be activated... yet". Enter the cheats at the Code Input screen.

UNLOCKED: CABS GALORE
Select Code Input from the Extras menu and enter CABBIES.

UNLOCKED: GORILLA INVASION
Select Code Input from the Extras menu and enter kingkng.

UNLOCKED: MASS TRANSIT
Select Code Input from the Extras menu and enter TRANSIT.

UNLOCKED: 5000 SMASH POINTS
Select Code Input from the Extras menu and enter SMASH5.

UNLOCKED: 10000 SMASH POINTS
Select Code Input from the Extras menu and enter SMASH10.

UNLOCKED: 15000 SMASH POINTS
Select Code Input from the Extras menu and enter SMASH15.

UNLOCKED: AMERICAN FLAG SHORTS
Select Code Input from the Extras menu and enter AMERICA.

UNLOCKED: CANADIAN FLAG SHORTS
Select Code Input from the Extras menu and enter OCANADA.

UNLOCKED: FRENCH FLAG SHORTS
Select Code Input from the Extras menu and enter Drapeau.

UNLOCKED: GERMAN FLAG SHORTS
Select Code Input from the Extras menu and enter DEUTSCH.

UNLOCKED: ITALIAN FLAG SHORTS
Select Code Input from the Extras menu and enter MUTANDA.

UNLOCKED: JAPANESE FLAG SHORTS
Select Code Input from the Extras menu and enter FURAGGU.

UNLOCKED: SPANISH FLAG SHORTS
Select Code Input from the Extras menu and enter BANDERA.

UNLOCKED: UK FLAG SHORTS
Select Code Input from the Extras menu and enter FSHNCHP.

UNLOCKED: COW MISSILES
Select Code Input from the Extras menu and enter CHZGUN.

UNLOCKED: DOUBLE HULK'S DAMAGE
Select Code Input from the Extras menu and enter DESTROY.

UNLOCKED: DOUBLE POWER COLLECTABLES
Select Code Input from the Extras menu and enter BRINGIT.

UNLOCKED: BLACK AND WHITE
Select Code Input from the Extras menu and enter RETRO.

UNLOCKED: SEPIA
Select Code Input from the Extras menu and enter HISTORY.

UNLOCKED: ABOMINATION
Select Code Input from the Extras menu and enter VILLAIN.

UNLOCKED: GRAY HULK
Select Code Input from the Extras menu and enter CLASSIC.

UNLOCKED: JOE FIXIT SKIN
Select Code Input from the Extras menu and enter SUITFIT.

UNLOCKED: WILD TRAFFIC
Select Code Input from the Extras menu and enter FROGGIE.

UNLOCKED: LOW GRAVITY
Select Code Input from the Extras menu and enter PILLOWS.

LEGO STAR WARS II: THE ORIGINAL TRILOGY

BEACH TROOPER
At Mos Eisley Canteena, select Enter Code and enter UCK868. You must then select Characters and purchase this character for 20,000 studs.

BEN KENOBI (GHOST)
At Mos Eisley Canteena, select Enter Code and enter BEN917. You must then select Characters and purchase this character for 1,100,000 studs.

BESPIN GUARD
At Mos Eisley Canteena, select Enter Code and enter VHY832. You must then select Characters and purchase this character for 15,000 studs.

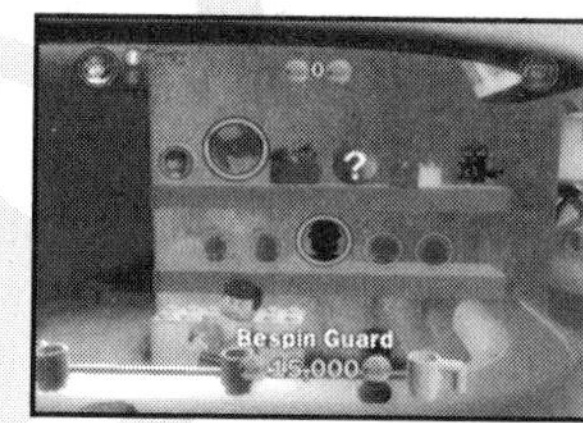

BIB FORTUNA
At Mos Eisley Canteena, select Enter Code and enter WTY721. You must then select Characters and purchase this character for 16,000 studs.

BOBA FETT
At Mos Eisley Canteena, select Enter Code and enter HLP221. You must then select Characters and purchase this character for 175,000 studs.

DEATH STAR TROOPER
At Mos Eisley Canteena, select Enter Code and enter BNC332. You must then select Characters and purchase this character for 19,000 studs.

EWOK
At Mos Eisley Canteena, select Enter Code and enter TTT289. You must then select Characters and purchase this character for 34,000 studs.

GAMORREAN GUARD

At Mos Eisley Canteena, select Enter Code and enter YZF999. You must then select Characters and purchase this character for 40,000 studs.

GONK DROID

At Mos Eisley Canteena, select Enter Code and enter NFX582. You must then select Characters and purchase this character for 1,550 studs.

GRAND MOFF TARKIN

At Mos Eisley Canteena, select Enter Code and enter SMG219. You must then select Characters and purchase this character for 38,000 studs.

GREEDO

At Mos Eisley Canteena, select Enter Code and enter NAH118. You must then select Characters and purchase this character for 60,000 studs.

HAN SOLO (HOOD)

At Mos Eisley Canteena, select Enter Code and enter YWM840. You must then select Characters and purchase this character for 20,000 studs.

IG-88

At Mos Eisley Canteena, select Enter Code and enter NXL973. You must then select Characters and purchase this character for 30,000 studs.

IMPERIAL GUARD

At Mos Eisley Canteena, select Enter Code and enter MMM111. You must then select Characters and purchase this character for 45,000 studs.

IMPERIAL OFFICER

At Mos Eisley Canteena, select Enter Code and enter BBV889. You must then select Characters and purchase this character for 28,000 studs.

IMPERIAL SHUTTLE PILOT

At Mos Eisley Canteena, select Enter Code and enter VAP664. You must then select Characters and purchase this character for 29,000 studs.

IMPERIAL SPY

At Mos Eisley Canteena, select Enter Code and enter CVT125. You must then select Characters and purchase this character for 13,500 studs.

JAWA

At Mos Eisley Canteena, select Enter Code and enter JAW499. You must then select Characters and purchase this character for 24,000 studs.

LOBOT

At Mos Eisley Canteena, select Enter Code and enter UUB319. You must then select Characters and purchase this character for 11,000 studs.

PALACE GUARD

At Mos Eisley Canteena, select Enter Code and enter SGE549. You must then select Characters and purchase this character for 14,000 studs.

REBEL PILOT

At Mos Eisley Canteena, select Enter Code and enter CYG336. You must then select Characters and purchase this character for 15,000 studs.

REBEL TROOPER (HOTH)

At Mos Eisley Canteena, select Enter Code and enter EKU849. You must then select Characters and purchase this character for 16,000 studs.

SANDTROOPER

At Mos Eisley Canteena, select Enter Code and enter YDV451. You must then select Characters and purchase this character for 14,000 studs.

SKIFF GUARD

At Mos Eisley Canteena, select Enter Code and enter GBU888. You must then select Characters and purchase this character for 12,000 studs.

SNOWTROOPER

At Mos Eisley Canteena, select Enter Code and enter NYU989. You must then select Characters and purchase this character for 16,000 studs.

STORMTROOPER

At Mos Eisley Canteena, select Enter Code and enter PTR345. You must then select Characters and purchase this character for 10,000 studs.

THE EMPEROR

At Mos Eisley Canteena, select Enter Code and enter HHY382. You must then select Characters and purchase this character for 275,000 studs.

TIE FIGHTER

At Mos Eisley Canteena, select Enter Code and enter HDY739. You must then select Characters and purchase this item for 60,000 studs.

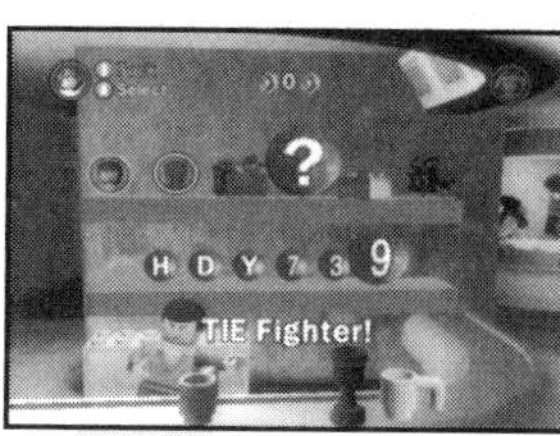

TIE FIGHTER PILOT

At Mos Eisley Canteena, select Enter Code and enter NNZ316. You must then select Characters and purchase this character for 21,000 studs.

TIE INTERCEPTOR

At Mos Eisley Canteena, select Enter Code and enter QYA828. You must then select Characters and purchase this item for 40,000 studs.

TUSKEN RAIDER

At Mos Eisley Canteena, select Enter Code and enter PEJ821. You must then select Characters and purchase this character for 23,000 studs.

UGNAUGHT

At Mos Eisley Canteena, select Enter Code and enter UGN694. You must then select Characters and purchase this character for 36,000 studs.

MADDEN NFL 07

MADDEN CARDS

Select Madden Cards from My Madden. Then select Madden Codes and enter the following:

CARD	PASSWORD
#199 Gold Lame Duck Cheat	5LAWO0
#200 Gold Mistake Free Cheat	XL7SP1
#210 Gold QB on Target Cheat	WROA0R
#220 Super Bowl XLI Gold	RLA9R7
#221 Super Bowl XLII Gold	WRLUF8
#222 Super Bowl XLIII Gold	NIEV4A
#223 Super Bowl XLIV Gold	M5AB7L
#224 Aloha Stadium Gold	YI8P8U
#225 1958 Colts Gold	B57QLU
#226 1966 Packers Gold	1PL1FL
#227 1968 Jets Gold	MIE6WO
#228 1970 Browns Gold	CL2TOE
#229 1972 Dolphins Gold	NOEB7U
#230 1974 Steelers Gold	YO0FLA
#231 1976 Raiders Gold	MOA11I
#232 1977 Broncos Gold	C8UM7U
#233 1978 Dolphins Gold	VIU0O7
#234 1980 Raiders Gold	NLAPH3
#235 1981 Chargers Gold	COAGI4
#236 1982 Redskins Gold	WL8BRI
#237 1983 Raiders Gold	H0EW71
#238 1984 Dolphins Gold	M1AM1E
#239 1985 Bears Gold	QOETO8
#240 1986 Giants Gold	ZI8S2L
#241 1988 49ers Gold	SP2A8H
#242 1990 Eagles Gold	2L4TRO
#243 1991 Lions Gold	J1ETRI
#244 1992 Cowboys Gold	W9UVI9
#245 1993 Bills Gold	DLA3I7
#246 1994 49ers Gold	DR7EST
#247 1996 Packers Gold	F8LUST
#248 1998 Broncos Gold	FIES95
#249 1999 Rams Gold	S9OUSW
#250 Bears Pump Up the Crowd	B1OUPH
#251 Bengals Cheerleader	DRL2SW

CARD	PASSWORD
#252 Bills Cheerleader	1PLUYO
#253 Broncos Cheerleader	3ROUJO
#254 Browns Pump Up the Crowd	T1UTOA
#255 Buccaneers Cheerleader	S9EWRI
#256 Cardinals Cheerleader	57IEPI
#257 Chargers Cheerleader	F7UHL8
#258 Chiefs Cheerleader	PRI5SL
#259 Colts Cheerleader	1R5AMI
#260 Cowboys Cheerleader	Z2ACHL
#261 Dolphins Cheerleader	C5AHLE
#262 Eagles Cheerleader	PO7DRO
#263 Falcons Cheerleader	37USPO
#264 49ers Cheerleader	KL0CRL
#265 Giants Pump Up the Crowd	C4USPI
#266 Jaguars Cheerleader	MIEH7E
#267 Jets Pump Up the Crowd	C0LUXI
#268 Lions Pump Up the Crowd	3LABLU
#269 Packers Pump Up the Crowd	4HO7VO
#270 Panthers Cheerleader	F2IASP
#282 All AFC Team Gold	PRO9PH
#283 All NFC Team Gold	RLATH7

MARIO GOLF: TOADSTOOL TOUR

At the Title screen, press Start + Z to access the Password screen. Enter the following to open the bonus tournaments.

TARGET BULLSEYE TOURNAMENT

Enter CEUFPXJ1.

HOLLYWOOD VIDEO TOURNAMENT

Enter BJGQBULZ.

CAMP HYRULE TOURNAMENT

Enter 0EKW5G7U.

BOWSER BADLANDS TOURNAMENT

Enter 9L3L9KHR.

BOWSER JR.'S JUMBO TOURNAMENT

Enter 2GPL67PN.

MARIO OPEN TOURNAMENT

Enter GGAA241H.

PEACH'S INVITATIONAL TOURNAMENT

Enter ELBUT3PX.

MARIO POWER TENNIS

EVENT MODE

At the Title screen, press Z + Start.

MARIO SUPERSTAR BASEBALL

STAR DASH MINI GAME

Complete Star difficulty on all mini-games.

BABY LUIGI

Complete Challenge Mode with Yoshi.

DIXIE KONG

Complete Challenge Mode with Donkey Kong.

HAMMER BRO

Complete Challenge Mode with Bowser.

MONTY MOLE

Complete Challenge Mode with Mario.

PETEY PIRANHA

Complete Challenge Mode with Wario.

TOADETTE

Complete Challenge Mode with Peach.

KOOPA CASTLE STADIUM

Complete Challenge Mode.

PIKMIN 2

TITLE SCREEN

At the Title screen, press the following for a variety of options.

Press R to make the Pikmin form the word NINTENDO.
Press L to go back to PIKMIN 2.
Press X to get a beetle.
Use the C-Stick to move the beetle around.
Press L to dispose of the Beetle.
Press Y to get a Chappie.
Use the C-Stick to move the Chappie around.
Press Z to eat the Pikmin.
Press L to dispose of the Chappie.

PRINCE OF PERSIA: THE TWO THRONES

BABY TOY HAMMER WEAPON

Pause the game and press Left, Left, Right, Right, A, Y, Y, A, Up, Down.

CHAINSAW WEAPON

Pause the game and press Up, Up, Down, Down, Left, Right, Left, Right, A, Y, A, Y.

SWORDFISH WEAPON

Pause the game and press Up, Down, Up, Down, Left, Right, Left, Right, A, Y, A, Y.

TELEPHONE OF SORROW WEAPON

Pause the game and press Right, Left, Right, Left, Down, Down, Up, Up, A, Y, A, A, Y, Y.

THE SIMS 2: PETS

CHEAT GNOME

During a game, press L, L, R, A, A, Up.

ADVANCE 6 HOURS

After activating the Cheat Gnome, press Up, Left, Down, Right, R during a game. Select the Gnome to access the cheat.

GIVE SIM SIMOLEONS

After activating the Cheat Gnome, enter the Advance 6 Hours cheat. Access the Gnome and exit. Enter the cheat again. Now, Give Sim Simoleons should be available from the Gnome.

CAT AND DOG CODES

When creating a family, press X to Enter Unlock Code. Enter the following for new fur patterns.

FUR PATTERN/CAT OR DOG	UNLOCK CODE
Bandit Mask Cats	EEGJ2YRQZZAIZ9QHA64
Bandit Mask Dogs	EEGJ2YRQZQARQ9QHA64
Black Dot Cats	EEGJ2YRZQQ1IQ9QHA64
Black Dot Dogs	EEGJ2YRQZZ1IQ9QHA64
Black Smiley Cats	EEGJ2YRQQZ1RQ9QHA64
Black Smiley Dogs	EEGJ2YRZQQARQ9QHA64
Blue Bones Cats	EEGJ2YRQZZARQ9QHA64
Blue Bones Dogs	EEGJ2YRZZZ1IZ9QHA64
Blue Camouflage Cats	EEGJ2YRZZQ1IQ9QHA64
Blue Camouflage Dogs	EEGJ2YRZZZ1RQ9QHA64
Blue Cats	EEGJ2YRQZZAIQ9QHA64
Blue Dogs	EEGJ2YRQQQ1IZ9QHA64
Blue Star Cats	EEGJ2YRQQZ1IZ9QHA64
Blue Star Dogs	EEGJ2YRQZQ1IQ9QHA64
Deep Red Cats	EEGJ2YRQQQAIQ9QHA64
Deep Red Dogs	EEGJ2YRQZQ1RQ9QHA64
Goofy Cats	EEGJ2YRQZQ1IZ9QHA64
Goofy Dogs	EEGJ2YRZZZARQ9QHA64
Green Cats	EEGJ2YRZQQAIZ9QHA64
Green Dogs	EEGJ2YRQZQAIQ9QHA64
Green Flower Cats	EEGJ2YRZQZAIQ9QHA64

FUR PATTERN/CAT OR DOG	UNLOCK CODE
Green Flower Dogs	EEGJ2YRQZZ1RQ9QHA64
Light Green Cats	EEGJ2YRZZQ1RQ9QHA64
Light Green Dogs	EEGJ2YRZQQ1RQ9QHA64
Navy Hearts Cats	EEGJ2YRZQZ1IQ9QHA64
Navy Hearts Dogs	EEGJ2YRQQZ1IQ9QHA64
Neon Green Cats	EEGJ2YRZZQAIQ9QHA64
Neon Green Dogs	EEGJ2YRZQQAIQ9QHA64
Neon Yellow Cats	EEGJ2YRZZQARQ9QHA64
Neon Yellow Dogs	EEGJ2YRQQQAIZ9QHA64
Orange Diagonal Cats	EEGJ2YRQQZAIQ9QHA64
Orange Diagonal Dogs	EEGJ2YRZQZ1IZ9QHA64
Panda Cats	EEGJ2YRQZQAIZ9QHA64
Pink Cats	EEGJ2YRQZZ1IZ9QHA64
Pink Dogs	EEGJ2YRZQZ1RQ9QHA64
Pink Vertical Strip Cats	EEGJ2YRQQQARQ9QHA64
Pink Vertical Strip Dogs	EEGJ2YRZZZAIQ9QHA64
Purple Cats	EEGJ2YRQQZARQ9QHA64
Purple Dogs	EEGJ2YRQQZAIZ9QHA64
Star Cats	EEGJ2YRZQZARQ9QHA64
Star Dogs	EEGJ2YRZQZAIZ9QHA64
White Paws Cats	EEGJ2YRQQQ1RQ9QHA64
White Paws Dogs	EEGJ2YRZQQ1IZ9QHA64
White Zebra Stripe Cats	EEGJ2YRZZQ1IZ9QHA64
White Zebra Stripe Dogs	EEGJ2YRZZZ1IQ9QHA64
Zebra Stripes Dogs	EEGJ2YRZZQAIZ9QHA64

SSX ON TOUR

NEW THREADS
Select Cheats from the Extras menu and enter FLYTHREADS.

THE WORLD IS YOURS
Select Cheats from the Extras menu and enter BACKSTAGEPASS.

SHOW TIME (ALL MOVIES)
Select Cheats from the Extras menu and enter THEBIGPICTURE.

BLING BLING (INFINITE CASH)
Select Cheats from the Extras menu and enter LOOTSNOOT.

FULL BOOST, FULL TIME
Select Cheats from the Extras menu and enter ZOOMJUICE.

MONSTERS ARE LOOSE (MONSTER TRICKS)
Select Cheats from the Extras menu and enter JACKALOPESTYLE.

SNOWBALL FIGHT
Select Cheats from the Extras menu and enter LETSPARTY.

FEEL THE POWER (STAT BOOST)
Select Cheats from the Extras menu and enter POWERPLAY.

CHARACTERS ARE LOOSE
Select Cheats from the Extras menu and enter ROADIEROUNDUP.

UNLOCK CONRAD
Select Cheats from the Extras menu and enter BIGPARTYTIME.

UNLOCK MITCH KOOBSKI
Select Cheats from the Extras menu and enter MOREFUNTHANONE.

UNLOCK NIGEL
Select Cheats from the Extras menu and enter THREEISACROWD.

UNLOCK SKI PATROL
Select Cheats from the Extras menu and enter FOURSOME.

LEVEL SELECT (COOPERATIVE MODE)
Enter SWGRCQPL, then enter UCHEATED.

ALL SINGLE-PLAYER MISSIONS
Enter HYWSC!WS, then enter NONGAMER.

ALL SINGLE-PLAYER MISSIONS & BONUS MISSIONS
Enter EEQQ?YPL, then enter CHE!ATER.

BEGGAR'S CANYON RACE (COOPERATIVE MODE)
Enter FRLL!CSF, then enter FARMBOY?.

ASTEROID FIELD MISSION (COOPERATIVE MODE)
Enter RWALPIGC, then enter NOWAYOUT.

DEATH STAR ESCAPE MISSION (COOPERATIVE MODE)
Enter YFCEDFRH, then enter DSAGAIN?.

ENDURANCE MISSION (COOPERATIVE MODE)
Enter WPX?FGC!, then enter EXCERSIZ.

ALL SHIPS (VERSUS MODE)
Enter W!WSTPQB, then enter FREEPLAY.

MILLENNIUM FALCON
Enter QZCRPTG!, then enter HANSRIDE.

NABOO STARFIGHTER
Enter RTWCVBSH, then enter BFNAGAIN.

SLAVE I
Enter TGBCWLPN, then enter ZZBOUNTY.

TIE BOMBER
Enter JASDJWFA, then enter !DABOMB!.

TIE HUNTER
Enter FRRVBMJK, then enter LOOKOUT!.

TIE FIGHTER (COOPERATIVE MODE)
Enter MCKEMAKD, then enter ONESHOT!.

TIE ADVANCE IN COOPERATIVE
Enter VDX?WK!H, then enter ANOKSHIP.

RUDY'S CAR
Enter AXCBPRHK, then enter WHATTHE?.

CREDITS
Enter LOOKMOM!. This option is available in the Special Features menu.

STAR WARS ARCADE GAME
Enter RTJPFC!G, then enter TIMEWARP.

EMPIRE STRIKES BACK ARCADE GAME
Enter !H!F?HXS, then enter KOOLSTUF.

DOCUMENTARY
Enter THEDUDES.

ART GALLERY
Enter !KOOLART.

MUSIC HALL
Enter HARKHARK.

BLACK & WHITE
Enter NOCOLOR?.

TAK: THE GREAT JUJU CHALLENGE

BONUS SOUND EFFECTS
In Juju's Potions, select Universal Card and enter the following numbers for Bugs, Crystals and Fruit: 20, 17, 5.

BONUS SOUND EFFECTS 2
In Juju's Potions, select Universal Card and enter the following numbers for Bugs, Crystals and Fruit: 50, 84, 92.

BONUS MUSIC TRACK 1
In Juju's Potions, select Universal Card and enter the following numbers for Bugs, Crystals and Fruit: 67, 8, 20.

BONUS MUSIC TRACK 2
In Juju's Potions, select Universal Card and enter the following numbers for Bugs, Crystals and Fruit: 6, 18, 3.

MAGIC PARTICLES
In Juju's Potions, select Universal Card and enter the following numbers for Bugs, Crystals and Fruit: 24, 40, 11.

MORE MAGIC PARTICLES
In Juju's Potions, select Universal Card and enter the following numbers for Bugs, Crystals and Fruit: 48, 57, 57.

VIEW JUJU CONCEPT ART
In Juju's Potions, select Universal Card and enter the following numbers for Bugs, Crystals and Fruit: Art 33, 22, 28.

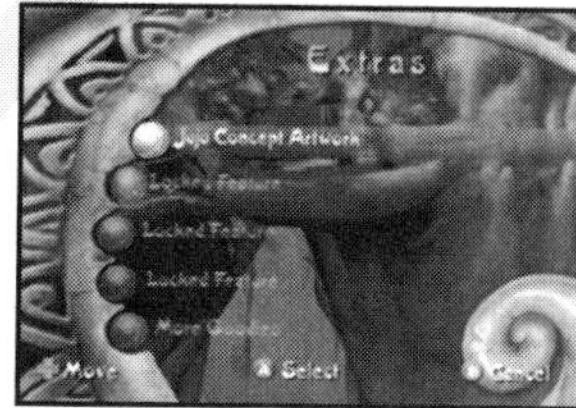

VIEW VEHICLE ART

In Juju's Potions, select Universal Card and enter the following numbers for Bugs, Crystals and Fruit: 11, 55, 44.

VIEW WORLD ART

In Juju's Potions, select Universal Card and enter the following numbers for Bugs, Crystals and Fruit: 83, 49, 34.

ULTIMATE SPIDER-MAN

ALL CHARACTERS

Pause the game and select Controller Setup from the Options menu. Press Right, Down, Right, Down, Left, Up, Left, Right.

ALL COVERS

Pause the game and select Controller Setup from the Options menu. Press Left, Left, Right, Left, Up, Left, Left, Down.

ALL CONCEPT ART

Pause the game and select Controller Setup from the Options menu. Press Down, Down, Down, Up, Down, Up, Left, Left.

ALL LANDMARKS

Pause the game and select Controller Setup from the Options menu. Press Up, Right, Down, Left, Down, Up, Right, Left.

X-MEN: THE OFFICIAL GAME

DANGER ROOM ICEMAN

At the Cerebro Files menu, press Right, Right, Left, Left, Down, Up, Down, Up, Start.

DANGER ROOM NIGHTCRAWLER

At the Cerebro Files menu, press Up, Up, Down, Down, Left, Right, Left, Right, Start.

DANGER ROOM WOLVERINE

At the Cerebro Files menu, press Down, Down, Up, Up, Right, Left, Right, Left, Start.

NINTENDO DS™

GAMES

ADVANCE WARS: DAYS OF RUIN

UNLOCK COS

Complete the following missions to unlock the corresponding CO.

COMPLETE MISSION	CO UNLOCKED
12	Tasha
13	Gage
14	Forthsythe
20	Waylon
21	Greyfield
24	Penny
25	Tabitha
26	Caulder

ADVANCE WARS: DUAL STRIKE

ADVANCE WARS MAP

Select Map from the Design Room menu and immediately press and hold L + R. This reveals a map that spells out Advance Wars.

ADVANCE WARPAPER

Insert Advance Wars into the GBA slot of your Nintendo DS. Start Advance Wars: Dual Strike. Select Battle maps and purchase Advance Warpaper. Select Display from the Design Room and choose Classic 1.

HACHI'S LAND

Insert Advance Wars into the GBA slot of your Nintendo DS. Start Advance Wars: Dual Strike. Select Battle Maps and purchase Hachi's Land for 1.

NELL'S LAND

Insert Advance Wars into the GBA slot of your Nintendo DS. Start Advance Wars: Dual Strike. Select Battle Maps and purchase Nell's Land for 1.

ADVANCE WARPAPER 2

Insert Advance Wars 2: Black Hole Rising into the GBA slot of your Nintendo DS. Start Advance Wars: Dual Strike. Select Battle maps and purchase Advance Warpaper 2. Select Display from the Design Room and choose Classic 2.

LASH'S LAND

Insert Advance Wars 2: Black Hole Rising into the GBA slot of your Nintendo DS. Start Advance Wars: Dual Strike. Select Battle Maps and purchase Lash's Land for 1.

STRUM'S LAND

Insert Advance Wars 2: Black Hole Rising into the GBA slot of your Nintendo DS. Start Advance Wars: Dual Strike. Select Battle Maps and purchase Strum's Land for 1.

ANIMANIACS: LIGHTS, CAMERA, ACTION!

SKIP LEVEL
Pause the game and press L, L, R, R, Down, Down.

DISABLE TIME
Pause the game and press L, R, Left, Left, Up, Up.

KINGSIZE PICK-UPS
Pause the game and press Right, Right, Right, Left, Left, Left, R, L.

PASSWORDS

LEVEL	PASSWORD
1	Wakko, Wakko, Wakko, Wakko, Wakko
2	Dot, Yakko, Brain, Wakko, Pinky
3	Yakko, Dot, Wakko, Wakko, Brain
4	Pinky, Yakko, Yakko, Dot, Brain
5	Pinky, Pinky, Yakko, Wakko, Wakko
6	Brain, Dot, Brain, Pinky, Yakko
7	Brain, Pinky, Wakko, Pinky, Brain
8	Brain Pinky, Pinky, Wakko, Wakko
9	Dot, Dot, Yakko, Pinky, Wakko
10	Brain, Dot, Brain, Yakko, Wakko
11	Akko, Yakko, Pinky, Dot, Dot
12	Pinky, Pinky, Brain, Dot, Wakko
13	Yakko, Wakko, Pinky, Wakko, Brain
14	Pinky, Wakko, Brain, Wakko, Yakko
15	Dot, Pinky, Wakko, Wakko, Yakko

BEN 10: PROTECTOR OF EARTH

GWEN 10 SKINS
At the level select, press Left, Right, Left, Right, L, R, Select.

GALACTIC ENFORCER SKINS
At the level select, press A, B, X, Y, L, R, Select.

ULTRA BEN SKINS
At the level select, press Up, Right, Down, Left, A, B, Select.

BRAIN AGE: TRAIN YOUR BRAIN IN MINUTES A DAY

BRAIN AGE CHECK SELECTION MENU
At the Daily Training Menu, hold Select while choosing Brain Age Check.

TOP 3 LISTS
At the Daily Training Menu, hold Select while choosing Graph.

BRAIN VOYAGE

ALL GOLD MEDALS
At the World Map, press A, B, Up, L, L, Y.

INFINITE COINS
At the World Tour Mode, press L, Up, X, Up, R, Y.

BUBBLE BOBBLE REVOLUTION

BONUS LEVELS IN CLASSIC MODE
At the Classic Mode title screen, press L, R, L, R, L, R, Right, Select. Touch the door at Level 20.

POWER UP! MODE IN CLASSIC VERSION
At the Classic Mode title screen, press Select, R, L, Left, Right, R, Select, Right.

SUPER BUBBLE BOBBLE IN CLASSIC VERSION
You must first defeat the boss with two players. Then at the Classic Mode title screen, press Left, R, Left, Select, Left, L, Left, Select.

BUST-A-MOVE DS

DARK WORLD
Complete the game then press A Left Right A at the Title screen.

SOUND TEST
At the Main menu, press Select, A, B, Left, Right, A, Select, Right.

CALL OF DUTY: WORLD AT WAR

ALL CAMPAIGN AND CHALLENGE MISSIONS
At the War Room Options screen, press Y, X, Y, Y, X, Y, X, X, Y.

CARS

SECRET MUSIC TRACK FOR RAMONE'S STYLE
At the Title screen, press Up, Down, Up, Down, A, B, X, Y.

EVERYTHING EXCEPT HIDDEN MUSIC
At the Title screen, press Up, Up, Down, Down, Left, Right, Left, Right, B, A, B.

CARTOON NETWORK RACING

The following codes will disable the ability to save:

UNLOCK EVERYTHING
Select Nickname from the Options and enter GIMMIE.

ENABLES ALL HAZARDS AND PICKUPS IN TIME TRIAL
Select Nickname from the Options and enter AAARGH.

ROCKETS TURN NON-INVULNERABLE OPPONENTS INTO STONE
Select Nickname from the Options and enter STONEME.

UNLIMITED DUMB ROCKETS
Select Nickname from the Options and enter ROCKETMAN.

UNLIMITED SUPERPOWER ENERGY
Select Nickname from the Options and enter SPINACH.

TOP-DOWN VIEW
Select Nickname from the Options and enter IMACOPTER.

CASTLEVANIA: DAWN OF SORROW

POTION
Complete Boss Rush Mode.

RPG
Complete Boss Rush Mode in less than 5 minutes.

DEATH'S ROBE
Complete Boss Rush Mode in less than 6 minutes.

TERROR BEAR
Complete Boss Rush Mode in less than 7 minutes.

NUNCHAKUS
Complete Boss Rush Mode in less than 8 minutes.

CASTLEVANIA: PORTRAIT OF RUIN

JAPANESE VOICEOVERS
At the Main menu, hold L and press A.

THE CHRONICLES OF NARNIA: THE LION, THE WITCH AND THE WARDROBE

RESTORE HEALTH

At the Main menu, press Left, Right, Up, Down, A (x4).

INVINCIBILITY

At the Main menu, press A, Y, X, B, Up, Up, Down, Down.

ARMOR

At the Main menu, press A, X, Y, B, Up, Up, Up, Down.

EXTRA MONEY

At the Main menu, press Up, X, Up, X, Down, B, Down, B.

ALL BLESSINGS

At the Main menu, press Left, Up, A, B, Right, Down, X, Y.

MAXIMUM ATTRIBUTES

At the Main menu, press Left, B, Up, Y, Down, X, Right, A.

MAX SKILLS

At the Main menu, press A, Left, Right, B, Down, Up, X, X.

STRONGER ATTACKS

At the Main menu, press A, Up, B, Down, X, X, Y, Y.

CODE LYOKO

CODELYOKO.COM SECRET FILES

Enter the following as Secret Codes on the My Secret Album page of www.codelyoko.com:

SECRET FILE	CODE
Dark Enemies Wallpaper	9L8Q
Desert Sketch	6G7T
Fight Video	4M9P
FMV Ending	5R5K
Forest Sketch	8C3X
Ice Sketch	2F6U
Mountain Sketch	7E5V
Overbike	3Q4L
Overboard	8P3M
Overwing	8N2N
Scorpion Video	9H8S
Scorpion Wallpaper	3D4W
Sector 5 Sketch	5J9R
Ulrich	9A9Z
Yumi	4B2Y

CONTRA 4

SUPER C

10 LIVES

At the title screen, press Right, Left, Down, Up, B, Y.

SOUND TEST

As the logo fades in to the title screen, hold Y + B and press Start.

CONTRA

30 LIVES

At the title screen, press Up, Up, Down, Down, Left, Right Left, Right, Y, B.

UPGRADE WEAPONS

Pause the game and press Up, Up, Down, Down, Left, Right Left, Right, B, A, Start. This code can be used once per life. If you enter it a second time, you will die.

DINOSAUR KING

STONE CIRCLE PASSWORDS

Defeat the game to unlock the Stone Circle in South Euro. Now you can enter the following passwords to unlock dinosaurs. Find the level 1 dinosaur in a chest at the shrine.

009 DASPLETEOSARUS
Enter Grass, Water, Lightning, Lightning, Earth, Earth, Water, Wind.

012 SIAMOTYRRANUS
Enter Fire, Wind, Fire, Water, Wind, Grass, Fire, Water.

025 JOBARIA
Enter Water, Lightning, Lightning, Earth, Fire, Earth, Fire, Wind.

029 TRICERATOPS
Enter Lightning, Fire, Lightning, Fire, Water, Lightning, Grass, Earth.

038 MONOCLONIUS
Enter Lightning, Earth, Water, Water, Grass, Fire, Earth, Wind.

046 EUOPLOCEPHALUS
Enter Earth, Earth, Grass, Water, Wind, Earth, Wind, Fire.

058 ALTIRHINUS
Enter Wind, Fire, Fire, Fire, Lightning, Earth, Water, Grass.

061 CARNOTAURUS
Enter Earth, Wind, Water, Lightning, Fire, Wind, Wind, Water.

EX ACE/EX CHOMP
Enter Lightning, Grass, Fire, Earth, Water, Water, Lightning, Fire. This gives you Ace if you are playing as Rex and Chomp as Max.

EX MINI-KING
Enter Lightning, Wind, Earth, Lightning, Grass, Wind, Fire, Water.

EX PARIS
Enter Grass, Water, Water, Earth, Wind, Grass, Lightning, Lightning.

EX SAUROPHAGANAX
Enter Fire, Water, Earth, Grass, Wind, Lightning, Fire, Water.

EX SPINY
Enter Water, Earth, Fire, Water, Fire, Grass, Wind, Earth.

EX TANK
Enter Earth, Grass, Earth, Water, Wind, Water, Grass, Fire.

EX TERRY
Enter Fire, Lightning, Wind, Wind, Water, Fire, Fire, Earth.

DISGAEA DS

ETNA MODE
At the Main menu, highlight New Game and press X, Y, B, X, Y, B, A.

DRAGLADE

CHARACTERS

CHARACTER	TO UNLOCK
Asuka	Defeat Daichi's story
Gyamon	Defeat Guy's story
Koki	Defeat Hibito's story
Shura	Defeat Kairu's story

HIDDEN QUEST: SHADOW OF DARKNESS
Defeat Story Mode with all of the main characters. This unlocks this hidden quest in Synethesia.

ZEKE
Complete all of the quests including Shadow of Darkness to unlock Zeke in wireless battle.

DRAGON QUEST HEROES: ROCKET SLIME

KNIGHTRO TANK IN MULTIPLAYER
While inside the church, press Y, L, L, Y, R, R, Y, Up, Down, Select.

THE NEMESIS TANK IN MULTIPLAYER
While inside the church, press Y, R, R, up, L, L, Y, Down, Down, Down, Y, Select.

DRAGON QUEST MONSTERS: JOKER

CAPTAIN CROW

As you travel between the islands on the sea scooters, you are occasionally attacked by pirates. Find out which route the pirates are located on the bulletin board in any scoutpost den. When you face them between Infant Isle and Celeste Isle, Captain Crow makes an appearance. Defeat him and he forces himself into your team.

SOLITAIRE'S CHALLENGE

After completing the main game, load your game back up for a new endeavor. The hero is in Solitaire's office where she proposes a new non-stop challenge known as Solitaire's Challenge.

METAL KING SLIME

Acquire 100 different skills for your library and talk to the woman in Solitaire's office.

METAL KAISER SLIME

Acquire 150 different skills for your library and talk to the woman in Solitaire's office.

LEOPOLD

Acquire all of the skills for your library and talk to the woman in Solitaire's office.

LIQUID METAL SLIME

Collect 100 monsters in your library and talk to the man in Solitaire's office.

GRANDPA SLIME

Collect 200 monsters in your library and talk to the man in Solitaire's office.

EMPYREA

Collect all of the monsters in your library and talk to the man in Solitaire's office.

TRODE AND ROBBIN' HOOD

Complete both the skills and monster libraries and talk to both the man and woman in Solitaire's office.

DRAWN TO LIFE

HEAL ALL DAMAGE

During a game, press Start, hold L and press Y, X, Y, X, Y, X, A.

INVINCIBLITY

During a game, press Start, hold L and press A, X, B, B, Y.

ALIEN TEMPLATES

During a game, press Start, hold L and press X, Y, B, A, A.

ANIMAL TEMPLATES

During a game, press Start, hold L and press B, B, A, A, X.

ROBOT TEMPLATES

During a game, press Start, hold L and press Y, X, Y, X, A.

SPORTS TEMPLATES

During a game, press Start, hold L and press Y, A, B, A, X.

DRAWN TO LIFE: SPONGEBOB SQUAREPANTS EDITION

9,999,999 REWARD COINS

Select Cheat Entry and enter Down, Down, B, B, Down, Left, Up, Right, A.

ELEBITS: THE ADVENTURES OF KAI & ZERO

BIG RED BONUS OMEGA

Select Download Additional Omegas from the Extra menu. Choose Download Data and press B, Y, Up, L, Right, R, Down, Left, X, A.

FINAL FANTASY FABLES: CHOCOBO TALES

OMEGA – WAVE CANNON CARD

Select Send from the Main Menu and then choose Download Pop-Up Card. Press L, L, Up, B, B, Left.

GODZILLA UNLEASHED: DOUBLE SMASH

ANGUIRUS
Defeat Hedorah Terrorizes San Francisco.

DESTOROYAH
Defeat Monster Island, The Final Battle.

FIRE RODAN
Defeat Biollante Attacks Paris.

KING GHIDORAH
Defeat Mecha King Ghidorah Ravages Bangkok.

GRAND THEFT AUTO: CHINATOWN WARS

FULL HEALTH AND ARMOR
During a game, press L, L, R, A, A, B, B, R.

FULL ARMOR
During a game, press L, L, R, B, B, A, A, R.

INCREASE WANTED LEVEL
During a game, press L, L, R, Y, Y, X, X, R.

DECREASE WANTED LEVEL
During a game, press R, X, X, Y, Y, R, L, L.

EXPLOSIVE PISTOL ROUND
During a game, press L, R, X, Y, A, B, Up, Down.

WEAPONS SET 1
During a game, press R, Up, B, Down, Left, R, B, Right. This gives you the Pistol, Nightstick, Minigun, Assault Rifle, Micro SMG, Stubby Shotgun, and Grenades with max ammo.

WEAPONS SET 2
During a game, press R, Up, A, Down, Left, R, A, Right. This gives you the Twin Pistol, Teaser, Flame Thrower, Carbine Rifle, SMG, Double Barreled Shotgun, and Molotovs with max ammo.

WEAPONS SET 3
During a game, press R, Up, Y, Down, Left, R, Y, Right. This gives you the Revolver, Chainsaw, Flame Thrower, Carbine Rifle, SMG, Double Barreled Shotgun, and Proximity Mines with max ammo.

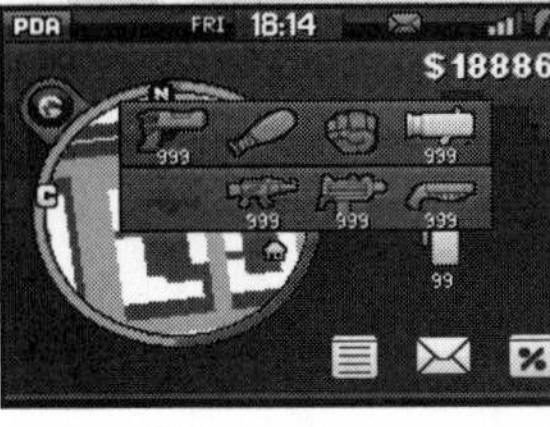

WEAPONS SET 4
During a game, press R, Up, X, Down, Left, R, X, Right. This gives you the Pistol, Baseball Bat, Carbine Rifle, RPG, Micro SMG, Shotgun, and Flashbangs with max ammo.

WEATHER: SUNNY
During a game, press Up, Down, Left, Right, A, B, L, R.

WEATHER: CLOUDY
During a game, press Up, Down, Left, Right, X, Y, L, R.

WEATHER: RAIN
During a game, press Up, Down, Left, Right, Y, A, L, R.

WEATHER: HEAVY RAIN
During a game, press Up, Down, Left, Right, A, X, R, L.

WEATHER: THUNDERSTORMS
During a game, press Up, Down, Left, Right, B, Y, R, L.

GRID

UNLOCK ALL
Select Cheat Codes from the Options and enter 233558.

INVULNERABILITY
Select Cheat Codes from the Options and enter 161650.

DRIFT MASTER
Select Cheat Codes from the Options and enter 789520.

PERFECT GRIP
Select Cheat Codes from the Options and enter 831782.

HIGH ROLLER
Select Cheat Codes from the Options and enter 401134.

GHOST CAR
Select Cheat Codes from the Options and enter 657346.

TOY CARS
Select Cheat Codes from the Options and enter 592014.

MM MODE
Select Cheat Codes from the Options and enter 800813.

IZUNA: LEGEND OF THE UNEMPLOYED NINJA

PATH OF TRAILS BONUS DUNGEON
After completing the game, touch the crystal from the beginning.

JACKASS THE GAME

CHANGE MUSIC
Press A + Y + Up.

JAKE HUNTER: DETECTIVE CHRONICLES

PASSWORDS
Select Password from the Main menu and enter the following:

UNLOCKABLE	PASSWORD
1 Password Info	AAAA
2 Visuals	LEET
3 Visuals	GONG
4 Visuals	CARS
5 Movies	ROSE
6 Jukebox	BIKE
7 Hints	HINT

JAM SESSIONS

BONUS SONGS
At the Free Play menu, press Up, Up, Down, Down, Left, Right, Left, Right. This unlocks I'm Gonna Miss Her by Brad Paisley, Needles and Pins by Tom Petty, and Wild Thing by Jimi Hendrix.

JUICED 2: HOT IMPORT NIGHTS

$5000
At the Cheat menu, enter HSAC.

ALL CARS
At the Cheat menu, enter SRAC.

ALL RACES
At the Cheat menu, enter EDOM.

ALL TRACKS
At the Cheat menu, enter KART.

JUMBLE MADNESS

FEBRUARY 31 PUZZLE
For Daily Jumble and Jumble Crosswords, select the square under February 28, 2009.

KIRBY: CANVAS CURSE

JUMP GAME
Defeat the game with all five characters, then select the game file to get Jump Game next to the Options on the Main menu.

LEGO BATMAN

ALFRED PENNYWORTH
Use the computer in the Batcave, select Enter Code and enter ZAQ637.

BATGIRL
Use the computer in the Batcave, select Enter Code and enter JKR331.

BRUCE WAYNE
Use the computer in the Batcave, select Enter Code and enter BDJ327.

CLASSIC CATWOMAN
Use the computer in the Batcave, select Enter Code and enter M1AAWW.

CLOWN GOON
Use the computer in the Batcave, select Enter Code and enter HJK327.

COMMISSIONER GORDON
Use the computer in the Batcave, select Enter Code and enter DDP967.

FISHMONGER
Use the computer in the Batcave, select Enter Code and enter HGY748.

FREEZE GIRL
Use the computer in the Batcave, select Enter Code and enter XVK541.

FREEZE HENCHMAN
Use the computer in the Batcave, select Enter Code and enter NJL412.

JOKER GOON
Use the computer in the Batcave, select Enter Code and enter UTF782.

JOKER HENCHMAN
Use the computer in the Batcave, select Enter Code and enter YUN924.

NIGHTWING
Use the computer in the Batcave, select Enter Code and enter MVY759.

TROPICAL JOKER
Use the computer in the Batcave, select Enter Code and enter CCB199.

1 MILLION STUDS
At the Main menu, press X, Y, B, B, Y, X, L, L, R, R, Up, Down, Left, Right, Start, Select.

3 MILLION STUDS
At the Main menu, press Up, Up, B, Down, Down, X, Left, Left, Y, L, R, L, R, B, Y, X, Start, Select.

ALL CHARACTERS
At the Main menu, press X, Up, B, Down, Y, Left, Start, Right, R, R, L, R, R, Down, Down, Up, Y, Y, Y, Start, Select.

ALL EPISODES AND FREE PLAY MODE
At the Main menu, press Right, Up, R, L, X, Y, Right, Left, B, L, R, L, Down, Down, Up, Y, Y, X, X, B, B, Up, Up, L, R, Start, Select.

ALL EXTRAS
At the Main menu, press Up, Down, L, R, L, R, L, Left, Right, X, X, Y, Y, B, B, L, Up, Down, L, R, L, R, Up, Up, Down, Start, Select.

LEGO INDIANA JONES: THE ORIGINAL ADVENTURES

You should hear a confirmation sound after the following codes are entered.

ALL CHARACTERS

At the Title screen, press X, Up, B, Down, Y, Left, Start, Right, R, R, L, R, R, Down, Down, Up, Y, Y, Y, Start, Select.

ALL EPISODES AND FREE PLAY MODE

Right, Up, R, L, X, Y, Right, Left, B, L, R, L, Down, Down, Up, Y, Y, X, X, B, B, Up, Up, L, R, Start, Select.

ALL EXTRAS

Up, Down, L, R, L, R, L, Left, Right, X, X, Y, Y, B, B, L, Up, Down, L, R, L, R, Up, Up, Down, Start, Select.

1,000,000 STUDS

At the Title screen, press X, Y, B, B, Y, X, L, L, R, R, Up, Down, Left, Right, Start, Select.

3,000,000 STUDS

At the Title screen, press Up, Up, B, Down, Down, X, Left, Left, Y, L, R, L, R, B, Y, X, Start, Select.

LEGO STAR WARS: THE COMPLETE SAGA

3,000,000 STUDS

At the main menu, press Start, Start, Down, Down, Left, Left, Up, Up, Select. This cheat can only be used once.

DEBUG MENUS

At the main menu, press Up, Left, Down, Right, Up, Left, Down, Right, Up, Left, Down, Right, R, L, Start, Select.

BONUS TOUCH GAME 1

At the main menu, press Up, Up, Down, L, L, R, R.

LEGO STAR WARS II: THE ORIGINAL TRILOGY

10 STUDS

At the Mos Eisley cantina, enter 4PR28U.

OBI WAN GHOST

At the Mos Eisley cantina, enter BEN917.

LITTLEST PET SHOP: GARDEN

GIRAFFE PET

Select Passwords from the Options and enter LPSTRU. It is available in the Meow Market.

LITTLEST PET SHOP: JUNGLE

GIRAFFE PET

Select Passwords from the Options and enter LPSTRU. It is available in the Meow Market.

LOCK'S QUEST

REPLACE CLOCKWORKS WITH KINGDOM FORCE

After completing the game, hold R and select your profile.

ENDING STORY

After completing the game, hold L and select your profile.

LUNAR KNIGHTS

SOUND DATA (BOKTAI)

With Boktai in the GBA slot, purchase this from the General Store in Acuna.

SOUND DATA (BOKTAI 2)

With Boktai 2 in the GBA slot, purchase this from the General Store in Acuna.

MARIO PARTY DS

BOSS BASH

Complete Story Mode.

EXPERT CPU DIFFICULTY LEVEL

Complete Story Mode.

MUSIC AND VOICE ROOM

Complete Story Mode.

SCORE SCUFFLE

Complete Story Mode.

TRIANGLE TWISTER PUZZLE MODE

Complete Story Mode.

MEGAMAN BATTLE NETWORK 5: DOUBLE TEAM

NUMBERMAN CODES

When the Numberman machine is available in Higsby's Shop, enter the following codes.

CODE	ENTER
Area Steal *	99428938
Dark Recovery *	91182599
DoroTsunamiBall *	78234329
Leaders Raid L	01285874
Lord of Chaos X	39285712
MagmaSeed *	29387483
NumberBall *	64836563
P. Battle Pack 1	22323856
P. Battle Pack 2	66426428
P.Attack+3	76820385
P.Chip+50	48582829
P.HP+100	28475692
P.HP+50	53891756
Super Kitakaze *	29486933
Sword *	12495783
TP Chip	85375720
Tsunami Hole *	19283746
Unlocker	15733751

NUMBERMAN NAVI CUSTOMIZER PROGRAM

Enter the following codes in the Numberman Lotto Number.

CODE	ENTER
Attack Max Yellow	63231870
Beat Blue	79877132
BodyPack Green	30112002
BustPack Blue	80246758
Charge Max White	87412146
HP+200 Pink	90630807
HP+300 Pink	48785625
HP+300 White	13926561
HP+400 Pink	03419893
HP+400 Yellow	45654128
HP+500 Pink	50906652
HP+500 White	72846472
Mega Folder 2 Green	97513648
Rush Yellow	09609807
SoulT+1 Yellow	28256341
Speed Max Pink	36695497
Spin Blue	12541883

CODE	ENTER
Spin Green	78987728
Spin Red	30356451
Tango Green	54288793

METROID PRIME PINBALL

PHAZON MINES

Complete Omega Pirate in Multi Mission Mode.

PHENDRANA DRIFTS

Complete Thardus in Multi Mission Mode.

MY JAPANESE COACH

UNLOCK LESSONS

Look up the word cheat in the dictionary. Touch the V next to the verb to open the conjugation chart. Hold L + R for a few seconds. You should hear the word cheat in Japanese. Return to the Main menu, go to Options, then Sound. Pressing R will advance you one lesson, and pressing L will advance you to the beginning of the next lesson group.

MYSIMS KINGDOM

SAMURAI ARMOR

Pause the game and press Y, X, Right, Left, L, R, Down, Up.

SAMURAI HELMET

Pause the game and press X, Y, R, L, X, Y, R, L.

PUNK BOTTOM

Pause the game and press Left, R, L, Right, Y, Y, X, X.

PUNK TOP

Pause the game and press Up, X, Down, Y, Left, L, Right, R.

MY WORD COACH

WORD POPPERS MINIGAME

After reaching 200 word successes, at the options menu, press A, B, X, Y, A, B.

N+

ATARI BONUS LEVELS

Select Unlockables from the Main menu, hold L + R and press A, B, A, B, A, A, B.

NARUTO: PATH OF THE NINJA

After defeating the game, talk to Knohamaru on the roof of the Ninja Academy. He allows you go get certain cheats by tapping four successive spots on the touch screen in order. There are 12 different spots on the screen, we have numbered them from left to right, top to bottom as follows:

1	2	3	4
5	6	7	8
9	10	11	12

Now enter the following by touching the four spots in the order given.

UNLOCK	CODE
4th Hokage's Sword	4, 7, 11, 5
Fuji Fan	8, 11, 2, 5
Jiraiya	11, 3, 1, 6
Rajin's Sword	7, 6, 5, 11
Rasengan	9, 2, 12, 7

NARUTO: PATH OF THE NINJA 2

CHARACTER PASSWORDS

Talk to Konohamaru at the school to enter the following passwords. You must first complete the game for the passwords to work.

CHARACTER	PASSWORD
Gaara	DKFIABJL
Gai	IKAGDEFL
Iruka	JGDLKAIB
Itachi Uchiha	GBEIDALF
Jiraiya	EBJDAGFL
Kankuro	ALJKBEDG
Kyuubi Naruto	GJHLBFDE
Orochimaru	AHFBLEJG

NEW SUPER MARIO BROS.

PLAY AS LUIGI IN SINGLE-PLAYER MODE

At the Select a File screen, press and hold L + R while selecting a saved game.

SECRET CHALLENGE MODE

While on the map, pause the game and press L, R, L, R, X, X, Y, Y.

THE NEW YORK TIMES CROSSWORDS

BLACK & WHITE

At the Main menu, press Up, Up, Down, Down, B, B, Y, Y.

NICKTOONS: ATTACK OF THE TOYBOTS

DANNY PHANTOM 2

Select Unlock Code from the Options and enter Tak, Jimmy, Zim, El Tigre.

SPONGEBOB 2

Select Unlock Code from the Options and enter Patrick, Jenny, Timmy, Tak.

PEGGLE: DUAL SHOT

Q LEVEL 10

Send the trial game to another DS.

PHINEAS AND FERB

STOP CANDACE

At the Title screen, press X, Y, L, R, Select.

DOUBLE SPEED

At the Title screen, press A, B, L, R, Select.

PIRATES OF THE CARIBBEAN: DEAD MAN'S CHEST

10 GOLD
During a game, press Right, X, X, Right, Left.

INVINCIBILITY
During a game, press Up, Down, Left, Right (x5), Left, Right, Up, Down, Left, Right, Up (x5), Left.

UNLIMITED POWER
During a game, press Up, Up, Down, Down, Left, Right, Left, Right, L, R.

RESTORE HEALTH
During a game, press Y, Y, Select, Left, Right, Left, Right, Left.

RESTORE SAVVY
During a game, press X, X, Select, Up, Down, Up, Down, Up.

GHOST FORM MODE
During a game, press Y, X, Y, X, Y, X.

SEASICKNESS MODE
During a game, press X, X, Y, X, X, Y.

SILLY WEAPONS
During a game, press Y, Y, X, Y (x3).

AXE
During a game, press Left, L, L, Down, Down, Left, Up, Up, Down, Down.

BLUNDERBUSS
During a game, press Down, L, L, Down (x3).

CHICKEN
During a game, press Right, L, L, Up, Down, Down.

EXECUTIONER AXE
During a game, press Right, L, L, Up, Down, Up, Right, Right, Left (x2).

PIG
During a game, press Right, R, R, Down, Up, Up.

PISTOL
During a game, press Down, L, L, Down, Down, Right.

RIFLE
During a game, press Left, L, L, Up (x3).

FAST MUSIC
During a game, press Y, Select, Y (x4).

SLOW MUSIC
During a game, press Y, Select, X (x4).

DISABLE CHEATS
During a game, press X (x6).

POKEMON MYSTERY DUNGEON: EXPLORERS OF DARKNESS/ TIME

Select Wonder Mail before starting your game, and then enter the following passwords to add a mission to your Job List. These are listed by the reward you receive for completing the mission.

Each password can only be used once. There are many possible passwords, here we list some examples. These passwords work on Explorers of Darkness and Explorers of Time.

ACCESSORY

ACCESSORY	PASSWORD
Gold Ribbon	5+KPKXT9RYP754&M2-58&&1-
Golden Mask	@QYPSJ@-N-J%TH6=4-SK32CR
Joy Ribbon	597C6#873795@Q6=F+TSQ68J
Mobile Scarf	R2MQ0X0&&-RN+64#4S0R+&-1
Miracle Chest	FX199P@CW@-XK54Q%4628XT#
No-Stick Cap	1@484PJ7NJW@XCHC2&-+H=@P
Pecha Scarf	8%2R-T&T1F-KR5#08P#&T=@=
Persim Band	TCX#TJQ0%#46Q6MJYMH2S#C9
Power Band	FHSM5950-2QNFTH9S-JM3Q9F
Racket Band	-F773&1XM0FRJT7Y@PJ%9C40
Special Band	752PY8M-Q1NHY#QX92836MHT
Stamina Band	F9RM4Y6W1&2T7@%SWF=R0NK&
X-Ray Specs	C#7H-#P2J9QPHCFPM5F674H=
Wonder Chest	0@R#3-+&7SC2K3@4NQ0-JQX9
Zinc Band	@WWHK8X18@C+C8KTN51H#213

ITEM

ITEM	PASSWORD
Beauty Scarf	@+CWF98#5CPYR13RJ#3YWKS5
Calcium	Y=59NRNS-#M2%C25725NJMQQ
Coronet Rock	S%9@47NTYP#Y105SR#%QH9MX
Dawn Stone	N54=MK=FSH1FCR8=R@HN14#Y
Deepseascale	WT192-H2=K@-WTJ3=JJ64C16
Deepseatooth	WQCM0-H=QH&-W+JP7FKT4CP+
Dusk Stone	X0=-JQ&X1X4KRY=8Y=23M=FH
Electrilizer	4SJYCFNX0-N@JN%NQ#+7-Q7#
Frozen Rock	YT&8WY&+278+2QJT@53TM3M8
Heal Seed	TWTN%RFRK+39-P#M2X+CXQS#
Joy Seed	PQS39&-7WC+R&QJQM2Y@@1KN
Leaf Stone	NP96N4K0HW3CJX8#FNK%=F&+
Link Box	&%8FXT9C76F4Q4SP5F8X3RW%
Lost Loot	J%0+F18XW5%P-9@&17+F8P9M
Lunar Ribbon	%-94RKFY%505XXMMC=FYK45N
Magmarizer	=TK+0KH72MNJNRW5P@RS&Y6=
Max Elixir	4Q9F-K6X66YW5TJY6MXK+RX7
Metal Coat	NP3SMTH-T&TMQFY@N1Q&SFNK
Mossy Rock	@JH#ST1&S14W3T2XJ8=7KR+7
Mystery Part	PXJ634F44Q3FQW&KYRX538+=
Oval Stone	@&FYQ977C#0YN-77TM&=X&+Q
Razor Claw	6JK2T26&MPC7&%-HWRXK2&-W
Reviver Seed	W+P0MYKJFNN3&Q%&-J12J2QH
Secret Slab	K=&4Q=@908N7=X&XHQ+Q1-CS
Shiny Stone	69-HHQX%K@#%7+5SMSPSQP#2
Sun Ribbon	7C8W308RYJ2XM@&QTYSJ%3=9
Thunderstone	+4QQK3PY84Y39P&=KN3=@XYR
Vile Seed	8#8%4496C#=JKRX9M&RKQW4%
Zinc	X=S#N&RNYSP9R2S01HT4MP8&

TM

TM	PASSWORD
Attract	Y@=JC48#K4SQ0NS9#S7@32%3
Blizzard	Y#ST42FMC4H+NM@M=T999#PR
Brick Break	@MF=%8400Y8X#T8FCTQC5XTS
Brine	9C04WP5XXN@=4NPFR08SS&03
Calm Mind	SH&YH&96C%&JK9Y0H99%3WM9
Dig	SQ96Y08RXJJXMJJ7=SSQK3K3
Embargo	1PQ7K%JX#4=HFHXPPK%7K04H
Energy Ball	5016-@1X8@&5H46#51M&+-XC
Fire Blast	W0T+NF98J13+F&NN=XNR&J-7
Flamethrower	JQ78%-CK%1PTP-77M740=F98
Flash	FS272Y61F1@MNN8FCSSTJ6TP
Gyro Ball	C#S@Y4%9YFQ+SQ6WRK36@1N0
Iron Tail	8+R006Y-&X57XX#&N-PT@R&6
Overheat	F=X5&K=FYJ3FC-N-@QXK34QJ
Payback	K3%0=W61FQCMN-FPHP=J5&W3
Poison Jab	S==YMX%92R54TSK6=F8%-%MN
Protect	Q#6762JK@967H#CMX#RQ3&M3
Psych Up	6=49WKH72&-JN%14SKNF&40N
Recycle	M@56C+=@H%K13WF4Q%RJ2JP9
Reflect	F=YTCK297HC02MT+MF13SQ4W
Rest	KR=WT#JC#@+HFS5K0JJM-0-2
Roar	C&0FWPTCRMKT&7NQ@N0&RQS+
Rock Slide	CN%+TMSHM0&3#&5YC4M1#C@2
Skill Swap	-H4TNNKY&1-P%4HSJY&XHW%Q
Sleep Talk	1M5972RY8X6NCC3CPPRS0K8J
Swords Dance	=633=JSY147RT=&0R9PJJ1FM
Thunder	WKY&7==@HR2%32YX6755JQ85
Vacuum-Cut	7PS2#26WN7HNX83M23J6F@C5
X-Scissor	S6P&198+-5QYR&22FJMKW1XF

PRINCESS NATASHA

ALL GADGETS
Select Codes from the Extras menu and enter OLEGSGIZMO.

EXTRA LEVELS
Select Codes from the Extras menu and enter SMASHROBOT.

INFINITE LIVES
Select Codes from the Extras menu and enter CRUSHLUBEK.

RACE DRIVER: CREATE & RACE

ALL CHALLENGES
Select Cheat Codes from Extras and enter 942785.

ALL CHAMPIONSHIPS
Select Cheat Codes from Extras and enter 761492.

ALL REWARDS
Select Cheat Codes from Extras and enter 112337.

FREE DRIVE
Select Cheat Codes from Extras and enter 171923.

NO DAMAGE
Select Cheat Codes from Extras and enter 505303.

EASY STEERING
Select Cheat Codes from Extras and enter 611334.

MINIATURE CARS
Select Cheat Codes from Extras and enter 374288.

MM VIEW
Select Cheat Codes from Extras and enter 467348.

RETRO GAME CHALLENGE

COSMIC GATE

HARD MODE
At the Title screen, press Down, Down, B, B, A, A, Start.

POWERED-UP INFINITY
Pause the game and press Up, Up, A, B. This cheat can only be used once per game.

SHIP POWER-UP
Pause the game and press Up, Up, A, A, B, B.

CONTINUE GAME
At the Game Over screen, press Left + Start. You will continue the game with a score of 000.

HAGGLE MAN CODES *UPDATED*

FULL HEALTH
Pause the game and press Down, Right, Up, Left, B, B, B, B, A, A, A, A.

SCROLLS APPEAR
Pause the game and press Up, Right, Down, Left, A, A, A, A, B, B, B, B.

INFINITE TIME
Before a level, hold Up/Left and press A + B.

HAGGLE MAN 2

STAGE SELECT
At the Title screen, hold A and press Up, Up, Right, Right, Right, Down, Down, Left, Left, Left.

FULL POWER
Pause the game and press Up, Down, Up, Down, B, B, A, A.

SCROLLS APPEAR
Pause the game and press Down, Up, Down, Up, A, A, B, B.

CONTINUE
At the Game Over screen, hold Left and press Start.

HAGGLE MAN 3

99 LIVES
Pause the game and press A, B, A, B, Left, Right, Left, Right.

9999 GEARS
Pause the game and press B, A, B, A, Right, Left, Right, Left.

WARP TO BOSS
Pause the game and press B, B, A, A, Left, Left, Right, Right.

RALLY KING

INVINCIBILITY
At the Title screen, press Select + Left.

CARS DISAPPEAR
At the Title screen, hold Select and press Down/Right.

START AT COURSE 2
At the Title screen, press A, B, A, B, Up + Select.

START AT COURSE 3
At the Title screen, press A, B, A, B, Left + Select.

START AT COURSE 4
At the Title screen, press A, B, A, B, Down + Select.

STAR PRINCE

INVINCIBILITY
At the Title screen, hold Up and press A, A, A. Then hold Down and press B, B, B.

CONTINUE
At the Game Over screen, hold Left and press Start.

RIDGE RACER DS

00-AGENT CAR
Finish more than 10 races in Multiplayer.

CADDY CAR
Finish more than 10 races in Multiplayer.

GALAGA '88 CAR
Finish more than 10 races in Multiplayer.

MARIO RACING CAR
Finish more than 10 races in Multiplayer.

POOKA CAR
Finish more than 10 races in Multiplayer.

RED SHIRT RAGE CAR
Finish more than 10 races in Multiplayer.

SHY GUY CAR
Finish more than 10 races in Multiplayer.

GALAGA PAC JAM SONG
Unlock the Pooka car.

MUSHROOM KINGDOM II SONG
Unlock the DK Team Racing car.

RHYTHM HEAVEN

RHYTHM TOYS - TELEPHONE NUMBERS
Enter the following numbers into the telephone in Rhythm Toys to unlock sounds from Rhythm Tengoku:

5553282338
5557325937
5557268724
5557625688

RUBIK'S PUZZLE WORLD

ALL LEVELS AND CUBIES
At the Main menu, press X, Y, Y, X, X.

SHREK SUPERSLAM

ALTERNATE OUTFIT FOR SHREK

Start the game with the GBA version of Shrek SuperSlam in the GBA slot.

SIMCITY CREATOR

99999999 MONEY

Enter MONEYBAGS as a password.

AMERICAN PROSPERITY AGE MAP

Enter NEWWORLD as a password.

ASIA AGE MAP

Enter SAMURAI as a password.

ASIA AGE BONUS MAP

Enter FEUDAL as a password.

DAWN OF CIVILIZATION MAP

Enter ANCIENT as a password.

GLOBAL WARMING MAP

Enter MODERN as a password.

GLOBAL WARMING BONUS MAP

Enter BEYOND as a password.

RENAISSANCE BONUS MAP

Enter HEREANDNOW as a password.

SIMCITY DS

LANDMARK BUILDINGS

Select Landmark Collection from the Museum menu. Choose Password and enter the following:

BUILDING	PASSWORD
Anglican Cathedral (UK)	kipling
Arc de Triomphe (France)	gaugin
Atomic Dome (Japan)	kawabata
Big Ben (UK)	orwell
Bowser Castle (Nintendo)	hanafuda
Brandenburg Gate (Germany)	gropius
Coit Tower	kerouac
Conciergerie (France)	rodin
Daibutsu (Japan)	mishima
Edo Castle (Japan)	shonagon
Eiffel Tower (France)	camus
Gateway Arch (USA)	twain
Grand Central Station (USA)	f.scott
Great Pyramids (Egypt)	mahfouz
Hagia Sofia (Turkey)	ataturk
Helsinki Cathedral (Finland)	kivi
Himeji Castle (Japan)	hokusai
Holstentor (Germany)	durer
Independence Hall (USA)	mlkingjr
Jefferson Memorial (USA)	thompson
Kokkai (Japan)	soseki
LA Landmark (USA)	hemingway
Lincoln Memorial (USA)	melville
Liver Building (UK)	dickens
Melbourne Cricket Ground (Australia)	damemelba
Metropolitan Cath. (UK)	austen
Moai (Chile)	allende
Mt. Fuji (Japan)	hiroshige
National Museum (Taiwan)	yuantlee
Neuschwanstein Castle (Germany)	beethoven
Notre Dame (France)	hugo

BUILDING	PASSWORD
Palace of Fine Arts (USA)	bunche
Palacio Real (Spain)	cervantes
Paris Opera (France)	daumier
Parthenon (Greece)	callas
Pharos of Alexandria (Egypt)	zewail
Building	Password
Rama IX Royal Park (Thailand)	phu
Reichstag (Germany)	goethe
Sagrada Familia (Spain)	dali
Shuri Castle (Japan)	basho
Smithsonian Castle (USA)	pauling
Sphinx (Egypt)	haykal
St Paul's Cathedral (UK)	defoe
St. Basil's Cathedral (Russia)	tolstoy
St. Stephen's Cathedral (Austria)	mozart
Statue of Liberty (USA)	pollack
Stockholm Palace (Sweden)	bergman
Taj Mahal (India)	tagore
Tower of London (UK)	maugham
Trafalgar Square (UK)	joyce
United Nations (UN)	amnesty
United States Capitol (USA)	poe
Washington Monument	capote
Westminster Abbey (UK)	greene
White House (USA)	Steinbeck

THE SIMS 2

MONGOO MONKEY FOR THE CASINO

Start the game with Sims 2 in the GBA slot of your Nintendo DS.

SKATE IT

EMO CRYS

At the Credits screen, press Up, Up, Left, Left, Down, Down, Right, Right.

JACK KNIFE

At the Credits screen, press X, A, X, Y, Up, Left, Down, Right.

JAY JAY

At the Credits screen, press L, R, A, Left, Right, Y, R, L.

LIL' ROB

At the Credits screen, press L, Left, Y, R, Right, A, Up, X.

SPITBALL

At the Credits screen, press Up, Up, Down, Down, L, R, L, R.

SOUL BUBBLES

REVEAL ALL CALABASH LOCATIONS

Pause the game and press A, L, L, R, A, Down, A, R.

ALL LEVELS

At the World Select, press L, Up, X, Up, R, Y.

ALL GALLERY ITEMS

At the Gallery, press B, Up, B, B, L, Y.

SPECTROBES

CARD INPUT SYSTEM

When the Upsilon Cube is unearthed and shown to Aldous, the Card Input System feature becomes available. This will allow you to input data from Spectrobe Cards. These give you new Spectrobes and Custom Parts.

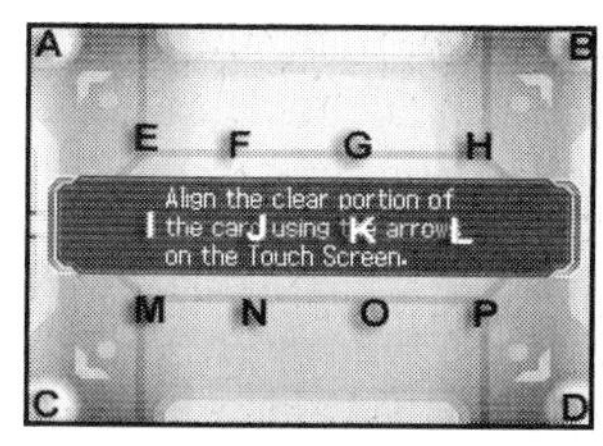

If you get your hands on a Spectrobe Card and the system is unlocked, investigate the card input system in the spaceship's lower deck. Follow the instructions on the upper screen to match the four corner points of the card to the corners of the touch screen. Touch the screen through the seven holes in the card in the order indicated on the card. If the code you input is correct, you receive Spectrobes, custom Parts, minerals or Cubes.

You can input the same card a maximum of four times. This means that you can only obtain four of the same Spectrobes from a single card. Some cards are only able to be inputted once. And some cards cannot be input until you have reached a certain point in the game.

Here we give you the codes without needing the actual cards. There are 16 different spots that are used for these codes. These spots are labeled on the following image as A through P.

The following table gives you a seven character code which refers to the spots you touch in order. The first four characters have you touching the four corners and the final three are spots among the 12 in the middle. To get Cyclone Geo, Hammer Geo, Ice Geo, Plasma Geo, or Thunder Geo; you must first beat the game.

EFFECT	CODE
Aobasat Apex	BACD HEP
Cyclone Geo	CDAB LGM
Danaphant Tuska	ABDC ELI
Danilob	DABC GLO
Emerald Mineral	BACD FKN
Grilden Biblad	ABDC FIH
Grildragos Drafly	CDAB MHK
Gristar	BACD EJN
Effect	Code
Hammer Geo	ABDC ELH
Harumitey Lazos	DABC ILM
Ice Geo	CDAB HEK
Inataflare Auger	ABDC IGH
Inkalade	ABDC GLP
Iota Cube	ABDC OHE
Komainu	CDAB HMJ
Kugaster Sonara	DABC LOE
Mossax Jetspa (Custom Color 1)	BACD JML
Naglub	ABDC EJM
Plasma Geo	BACD KLE
Rho Cube	BACD PNI
Ruby Mineral	CDAB FKO
Samukabu	ABDC OIL
Samurite Voltar	BACD LHM
Sapphire Mineral	ABDC FJO
Segulos Propos	CDAB KIH
Seguslice	CDAB GKP
Shakor Bristle	DABC MLK
Sigma Cube	CDAB PML
Tau Cube	DABC LIF
Thunder Geo	DABC MEL
Vilagrisp (Custom Part)	DABC EIN
Vilakroma	BACD NLM
Vilakroma (Custom Color 1)	CDAB LJI
Vilakroma (Custom Color 2)	DABC EGP
Windora	ABDC MGP
Windora (Custom Color 1)	DABC EHG
Windora (Custom Color 2)	CDAB JPM
Windora Ortex	BACD IPG
Windora Ortex (Custom Color 1)	ABDC MPH
Windora Ortex (Custom Color 2)	DABC MGH
Windora Sordina	CDAB PEO

EFFECT	CODE
Windora Sordina (Custom Color 1)	BACD MOH
Windora Sordina (Custom Color 2)	ABDC LEN
Wing Geo (must beat game	DABC MNP

SPONGEBOB SQUAREPANTS FEATURING NICKTOONS: GLOBS OF DOOM

INFINITE HEALTH

Select Unlock Codes from the Options and enter Tak, Tlaloc, Jimmy Neutron, Beautiful Gorgeous.

INSTANT KO

Select Unlock Codes from the Options and enter Dib, Tak, Beautiful Gorgeous, Plankton.

EXTRA ATTACK

Select Unlock Codes from the Options and enter Dib, Plankton, Technus, Jimmy Neutron.

EXTRA DEFENSE

Select Unlock Codes from the Options and enter Zim, Danny Phantom, Plankton, Beautiful Gorgeous.

MAX DEFENSE

Select Unlock Codes from the Options and enter Plankton, Dib, Beautiful Gorgeous, Plankton.

ITEMS +

Select Unlock Codes from the Options and enter Danny Phantom, Beautiful Gorgeous, Jimmy Neutron, Technus.

ITEMS ++

Select Unlock Codes from the Options and enter SpongeBob, Tlaloc, SpongeBob, Danny Phantom.

NO HEALTH ITEMS

Select Unlock Codes from the Options and enter Tak, SpongeBob, Technus, Danny Phantom.

LOWER PRICES

Select Unlock Codes from the Options and enter Tlaloc, Zim, Beautiful Gorgeous, SpongeBob.

SUPER BEAUTIFUL GORGEOUS

Select Unlock Codes from the Options and enter Beautiful Gorgeous, Technus, Jimmy Neutron, Beautiful Gorgeous.

SUPER DANNY PHANTOM

Select Unlock Codes from the Options and enter Danny Phantom, Zim, Danny Phantom, Beautiful Gorgeous.

SUPER DIB

Select Unlock Codes from the Options and enter Zim, Plankton, Dib, Plankton.

SUPER JIMMY

Select Unlock Codes from the Options and enter Technus, Danny Phantom, Jimmy Neutron, Technus.

SUPER PLANKTON

Select Unlock Codes from the Options and enter Tak, Plankton, Dib, Technus.

SUPER SPONGEBOB

Select Unlock Codes from the Options and enter Technus, SpongeBob, Technus, Tlaloc.

SUPER TAK

Select Unlock Codes from the Options and enter Danny Phantom, Jimmy Neutron, Tak, Tlaloc.

SUPER TECHNUS

Select Unlock Codes from the Options and enter Danny Phantom, Technus, Tak, Technus.

SUPER TLALOC

Select Unlock Codes from the Options and enter Tlaloc, Beautiful Gorgeous, Dib, SpongeBob.

SUPER ZIM

Select Unlock Codes from the Options and enter Plankton, Zim, Technus, SpongeBob.

SUPER JETPACK

Select Unlock Codes from the Options and enter Beautiful Gorgeous, Tlaloc, Jimmy Neutron, Jimmy Neutron.

COLORLESS ENEMIES

Select Unlock Codes from the Options and enter Technus, Jimmy Neutron, Tlaloc, Plankton.

BLUE ENEMIES

Select Unlock Codes from the Options and enter Beautiful Gorgeous, Zim, Plankton, Technus.

RED ENEMIES
Select Unlock Codes from the Options and enter SpongeBob, Tak, Jimmy Neutron, Danny Phantom.

DIFFICULT ENEMIES
Select Unlock Codes from the Options and enter SpongeBob, Dib, Dib, Technus.

DIFFICULT BOSSES
Select Unlock Codes from the Options and enter Plankton, Beautiful Gorgeous, Technus, Tlaloc.

INVINCIBLE PARTNER
Select Unlock Codes from the Options and enter Plankton, Tak, Beautiful Gorgeous, SpongeBob.

STAR WARS: THE FORCE UNLEASHED

INCREASED HEALTH
Select Unleashed Codes from the Extras menu and enter QSSPVENXO.

MAX OUT FORCE POWERS
Select Unleashed Codes from the Extras menu and enter CPLOOLKBF.

UNLIMITED FORCE ENERGY
Select Unleashed Codes from the Extras menu and enter TVENCVMJZ.

MORE POWERFUL LIGHTSABER
Select Unleashed Codes from the Extras menu and enter lightsaber.

UBER LIGHTSABER
Select Unleashed Codes from the Extras menu and enter MOMIROXIW.

ROM KOTA
Select Unleashed Codes from the Extras menu and enter mandalore.

CEREMONIAL JEDI ROBES
Select Unleashed Codes from the Extras menu and enter CURSEZRUX.

DAD'S ROBES
Select Unleashed Codes from the Extras menu and enter wookiee.

DARTH VADER'S COSTUME
Select Unleashed Codes from the Extras menu and enter HRMXRKVEN.

KENTO'S ROBE
Select Unleashed Codes from the Extras menu and enter KBVMSEVNM.

KOTA'S OUTFIT
Select Unleashed Codes from the Extras menu and enter EEDOPVENG.

SITH ROBE
Select Unleashed Codes from the Extras menu and enter ZWSFVENXA.

SITH ROBES
Select Unleashed Codes from the Extras menu and enter holocron.

SITH STALKER ARMOR
Select Unleashed Codes from the Extras menu and enter CPLZKMZTD.

SUPER PRINCESS PEACH

MINI-GAME
At the Title screen, hold R and press Start.

TAMAGOTCHI CONNECTION: CORNER SHOP 3

DOUBLE LAYERED CAKE
Select Enter Code from the Special menu and enter R6194BJD6F.

TOM CLANCY'S SPLINTER CELL CHAOS THEORY

UNLIMITED AMMO/GADGETS
Defeat the game.

CHARACTER SKINS
Defeat the game.

TONY HAWK'S DOWNHILL JAM

ALWAYS SNOWSKATE
Select Buy Stuff from the Skateshop. Choose Enter Code and enter SNOWSK8T.

MIRRORED MAPS
Select Buy Stuff from the Skateshop. Choose Enter Code and enter MIRRORBALL.

ABOMINABLE SNOWMAN OUTFIT
Select Buy Stuff from the Skateshop. Choose Enter Code and enter BIGSNOWMAN.

ZOMBIE SKATER OUTFIT
Select Buy Stuff from the Skateshop. Choose Enter Code and enter ZOMBIEALIVE.

TRAUMA CENTER: UNDER THE KNIFE

X1: KYRIAKI MISSION
Defeat the game. Find the X Missions under Challenge Mode.

X2: DEFTERA MISSION
Defeat X1: Kyriaki Mission. Find the X Missions under Challenge Mode.

X3: TRITI MISSION
Defeat X2: Deftera Mission. Find the X Missions under Challenge Mode.

X4: TETARTI MISSION
Defeat X3: Triti Mission. Find the X Missions under Challenge Mode.

X5: PEMPTI MISSION
Defeat X4: Tetarti Mission. Find the X Missions under Challenge Mode.

X6: PARAKEVI MISSION
Defeat X5: Pempti Mission. Find the X Missions under Challenge Mode.

X7: SAVATO MISSION
Defeat X6: Parakevi Mission. Find the X Missions under Challenge Mode.

ULTIMATE MORTAL KOMBAT

VS CODES
At the VS screen, each player must use LP, BLK, and LK to enter the following codes:

EFFECT	PLAYER 1	PLAYER 2
You are now entering the realm	642	468
Blocking Disabled	020	020
Dark Kombat	448	844
Infinite Run	466	466
Play in Kahn's Kave	004	700
Play in the Kombat Temple	600	N/A
Play in the Soul Chamber	123	901
Play on Jade's Deset	330	033
Play on Kahn's Tower	880	220
Play on Noob Saibot Dorfen	050	050
Play on Rooftops	343	343
Play on Scislac Busorez	933	933
Play on Subway	880	088
Play on the Belltower	091	190
Play on the Bridge	077	022
Play on the Graveyard	666	333
Play on the Pit 3	820	028

EFFECT	PLAYER 1	PLAYER 2
Play on the Street	079	035
Play on the Waterfront	002	003
Play Scorpions Lair	666	444
Player 1 Half Power	033	N/A
Player 1 Quarter Power	707	N/A
Player 2 Half Power	N/A	033
Player 2 Quarter Power	N/A	707
Power Bars Disabled	987	123
Random Kombat	444	444
Revision 1.2	999	999
Sans Power	044	440
Silent Kombat	300	300
Throwing Disabled	100	100
Throwing Encouraged	010	010
Winner of round fights Motaro	969	141
Winner of round fights Noob Saibot	769	342
Winner of round fights Shao Kahn	033	564
Winner of round fights Smoke	205	205

UNLOCK ERMAC, MILEENA, CLASSIC SUB-ZERO

At the Ultimate Kombat Kode screen input the following codes:
(Note: To easily access the Ultimate Kombat Kode screen just get defeated and dont continue)

CLASSIC SUB-ZERO

At the Ultimate Kombat Kode screen, enter 81835. You can reach this screen by losing and not continuing.

ERMAC

At the Ultimate Kombat Kode screen, enter 12344. You can reach this screen by losing and not continuing.

MILEENA

At the Ultimate Kombat Kode screen, enter 22264. You can reach this screen by losing and not continuing.

HUMAN SMOKE

Select ROBO Smoke. Hold Block + Run + High Punch + High Kick + Back before the fight begins.

WORLD CHAMPIONSHIP POKER

UNLOCK CASINOS

At the Title screen, press Y, X, Y, B, L, R. Then press the following direction:

DIRECTION	CASINO
Left	Amazon
Right	Nebula
Down	Renaissance

YU-GI-OH! NIGHTMARE TROUBADOUR

CREDITS

Unlock the Password Machine by defeating the Expert Cup. Enter the Duel Shop and select the Slot Machine, then enter 00000375.

SOUND TEST

Unlock the Password Machine by defeating the Expert Cup. Enter the Duel Shop and select the Slot Machine, then enter 57300000.

YU-GI-OH! WORLD CHAMPIONSHIP 2007

CARD PASSWORDS

Select Password from the Shop and enter one of the Card Passwords. You must already have that card or have it in a pack list for the password to work.

Refer to the Card List for YU-GI-OH! GX TAG FORCE for PSP. All cards may not be available in World Championship 2007.

YU-GI-OH! WORLD CHAMPIONSHIP 2008

CARD PASSWORDS

Enter the following in the password machine to receive the corresponding card. You need to have the card already to use the password.

CARD	PASSWORD
7	67048711
7 Colored Fish	23771716
7 Completed	86198326
A Feint Plan	68170903
A Hero Emerges	21597117
Abyss Soldier	18318842
Acid Rain	21323861
Acid Trap Hole	41356845
Adhesive Explosive	53828196
Agido	16135253
Airknight Parshath	18036057
Aitsu	48202661
Alkana Knight Joker	06150044
Alligator's Sword	64428736
Alligator's Sword Dragon	03366982
Alpha the Magnet Warrior	99785935
Altar for Tribute	21070956
Amazon Archer	91869203
Amazoness Archers	67987611
Amazoness Blowpiper	73574678
Amazoness Chain Master	29654737
Amazoness Fighter	55821894
Amazoness Paladin	47480070
Amazoness Spellcaster	81325903
Amazoness Swords Woman	94004268
Amazoness Tiger	10979723
Amphibian Beast	67371383
Amplifier	00303660
Anti-Spell	53112492
Aqua Madoor	85639257
Aqua Spirit	40916023
Archfiend of Gilfer	50287060
Armed Changer	90374791
Armed Ninja	09076207
Armored Glass	21070956
Armored Zombie	20277860
Array of Revealing Light	69296555
Arsenal Bug	42364374
Arsenal Robber	55348096
Assault on GHQ	62633180
Asura Priest	02134346
Attack and Receive	63689843
Autonomous Action Unit	71453557
Axe of Despair	40619825
Axe Raider	48305365
B. Skull Dragon	11901678
Baby Dragon	88819587

CARD	PASSWORD
Back to Square One	47453433
Backfire	82705573
Bad Reaction to Simochi	40633297
Bait Doll	07165085
Ballista of Rampart Smashing	00242146
Banisher of the Light	61528025
Banner of Courage	10012614
Bark of The Dark Ruler	41925941
Baron of the Fiend Sword	86325596
Barrel Behind the Door	78783370
Barrel Dragon	81480460
Battery Charger	61181383
Batteryman AA	63142001
Batteryman C	19733961
Batteryman D	55401221
Battle Ox	05053103
Battle Warrior	55550921
Beast Fangs	46009906
Beast Soul Swap	35149085
Beastking of the Swamps	99426834
Beautiful Headhuntress	16899564
Beckoning Light	16255442
Berfomet	77207191
Berserk Gorilla	39168895
Beta the Magnet Warrior	39256679
Bickuribox	25655502
Big Bang Shot	61127349
Big Eye	16768387
Big Shield Gardna	65240384
Birdface	45547649
Black Illusion Ritual	41426869
Black Luster Ritual	55761792
Black Luster Soldier	72989439
Black Magic Ritual	76792184
Black Pendant	65169794
Bladefly	28470714
Blast Held by a Tribute	89041555
Blast Magician	21051146
Blast Sphere	26302522
Blast with Chain	98239899
Blasting the Ruins	21466326
Blessings of the Nile	30653173
Blowback Dragon	25551951
Blue Medicine	20871001
Blue-Eyes Toon Dragon	53183600
Blue-Eyes Ultimate Dragon	23995346
Blue-Eyes White Dragon	80906030
Blue-Eyes White Dragon	80906030
Book of Taiyou	38699854
Bottomless Trap Hole	29401950
Bowganian	52090844
Bracchio-Raidus	16507828
Brain Control	87910978
Breaker the Magical Warrior	71413901
Breath of Light	20101223
Bright Castle	82878489
Burning Land	24294108
Burning Spear	18937875
Burst Return	27191436
Burst Stream of Destruction	17655904
Buster Rancher	84740193
Cannon Soldier	11384280
Cannonball Spear Shellfish	95614612

CARD	PASSWORD
Card Destruction	72892473
Card of Sanctity	04266498
Card Shuffle	12183332
Castle of Dark Illusions	00062121
Castle Walls	44209392
Catapult Turtle	95727991
Ceasefire	36468556
Celtic Guardian	91152256
Cemetery Bomb	51394546
Centrifugal Field	01801154
Cestus of Dagla	28106077
Chain Destruction	01248895
Chain Disappearance	57139487
Chain Energy	79323590
Chaos Command Magician	72630549
Chaos End	61044390
Chaos Greed	97439308
Chimera the Flying Mythical Beast	04796100
Chiron the Mage	16956455
Chorus of Sanctuary	81380218
Chthonian Alliance	46910446
Chthonian Blast	18271561
Chthonian Polymer	72287557
Clay Charge	22479888
Cocoon of Evolution	40240595
Coffin Seller	65830223
Cold Wave	60682203
Command Knight	10375182
Conscription	31000575
Continuous Destruction Punch	68057622
Contract with Exodia	33244944
Contract with the Dark Master	96420087
Convulsion of Nature	62966332
Copycat	26376390
Cosmo Queen	38999506
Covering Fire	74458486
Crass Clown	93889755
Crawling Dragon #2	38289717
Crimson Sunbird	46696593
Crush Card Virus	57728570
Curse of Anubis	66742250
Curse of Darkness	84970821
Curse of Dragon	28279543
Curse of the Masked Beast	94377247
Cursed Seal of the Forbidden Spell	58851034
Cyber Raider	39978267
Cyber Shield	63224564
Cyber-Tech Alligator	48766543
D.D. Borderline	60912752
D.D. Designator	33423043
D.D. Assailant	70074904
D.D. Dynamite	08628798
D.D. Trap Hole	05606466
D.D. Warrior	37043180
D.D. Warrior Lady	07572887
D. Tribe	02833249
Dark Artist	72520073
Dark Deal	65824822
Dark Dust Spirit	89111398
Dark Elf	21417692
Dark Energy	04614116
Dark Factory of Mass Production	90928333
Dark Jeroid	90980792

CARD	PASSWORD
Dark Magic Attack	02314238
Dark Magic Curtain	99789342
Dark Magician	46986414
Dark Magician Girl	38033121
Dark Magician of Chaos	40737112
Dark Master - Zorc	97642679
Dark Mimic LV1	74713516
Dark Mimic LV3	01102515
Dark Mirror Force	20522190
Dark Necrofear	31829185
Dark Paladin	98502113
Dark Rabbit	99261403
Dark Room of Nightmare	85562745
Dark Sage	92377303
Dark Snake Syndrome	47233801
Dark Spirit of the Silent	93599951
Dark World Lightning	93554166
Darkness Approaches	80168720
Dark-Piercing Light	45895206
Deck Devastation Virus	35027493
Decoy Dragon	02732323
Dedication through Light and Darkness	69542930
De-Fusion	95286165
Delta Attacker	39719977
Despair from the Dark	71200730
De-Spell	19159413
Destiny Board	94212438
Destruction Ring	21219755
Dian Keto the Cure Master	84257639
Dice Re-Roll	83241722
Different Dimension Capsule	11961740
Different Dimension Dragon	50939127
Different Dimension Gate	56460688
Diffusion Wave-Motion	87880531
Dimension Fusion	23557835
Dimension Wall	67095270
Dimensional Prison	70342110
Dimensionhole	22959079
Disappear	24623598
Disarmament	20727787
Divine Sword - Phoenix Blade	31423101
Divine Wrath	49010598
DNA Surgery	74701381
Doomcaliber Knight	78700060
Double Coston	44436472
Double Snare	03682106
Double Spell	24096228
Dragged Down into the Grave	16435235
Dragon Capture Jar	50045299
Dragon Seeker	28563545
Dragon Treasure	01435851
Dragonic Attack	32437102
Dragon's Mirror	71490127
Draining Shield	43250041
Dramatic Rescue	80193355
Dream Clown	13215230
Drill Bug	88733579
Driving Snow	00473469
Drop Off	55773067
Dunames Dark Witch	12493482
Dust Barrier	31476755
Dust Tornado	60082867
Earth Chant	59820352

CARD	PASSWORD
Earthbound Spirit's Invitation	65743242
Earthquake	82828051
Eatgaboon	42578427
Ectoplasmer	97342942
Ekibyo Drakmord	69954399
Electro-Whip	37820550
Elegant Egotist	90219263
Elemental Hero Avian	21844576
Elemental Hero Burstinatrix	58932615
Elemental Hero Clayman	84327329
Elemental Hero Flame Wingman	35809262
Elemental Hero Rampart Blaster	47737087
Elemental Hero Sparkman	20721928
Elemental Hero Thunder Giant	61204971
Embodiment of Apophis	28649820
Emergency Provisions	53046408
Enchanted Arrow	93260132
Enchanting Fitting Room	30531525
Enemy Controller	98045062
Energy Drain	56916805
Enervating Mist	26022485
Enraged Battle Ox	76909279
Eradicating Aerosol	94716515
Eternal Drought	56606928
Eternal Rest	95051344
Exarion Universe	63749102
Exchange	05556668
Exhausting Spell	95451366
Exodia Necross	12600382
Exodia the Forbidden One	33396948
Fairy Box	21598948
Fairy King Truesdale	45425051
Fairy Meteor Crush	97687912
Fairy's Hand Mirror	17653779
Fake Trap	03027001
Feather Shot	19394153
Feather Wind	71060915
Fengsheng Mirror	37406863
Feral Imp	41392891
Fiend Comedian	81172176
Fiend Skull Dragon	66235877
Fiend's Hand Mirror	58607704
Fiend's Sanctuary	24874630
Final Countdown	95308449
Final Destiny	18591904
Firewing Pegasus	27054370
Fissure	66788016
Flame Cerebrus	60862676
Flame Manipulator	34460851
Flame Swordsman	40502030
Flying Kamakiri #1	84834865
Foolish Burial	81439173
Forced Ceasefire	97806240
Forest	87430998
Fortress Whale	62337487
Fortress Whale's Oath	77454922
Frozen Soul	57069605
Fulfillment of the Contract	48206762
Full Salvo	70865988
Fusilier Dragon, the Duel-Mode Beast	51632798
Fusion Gate	24094653
Fusion Sage	26902560
Fusion Sword Murasame Blade	37684215

CARD	PASSWORD
Gaia Power	56594520
Gaia the Dragon Champion	66889139
Gaia the Fierce Knight	06368038
Gamma the Magnet Warrior	11549357
Garoozis	14977074
Garuda the Wind Spirit	12800777
Gazelle the King of Mythical Beasts	05818798
Gear Golem the Moving Fortress	30190809
Gearfried the Iron Knight	00423705
Gearfried the Swordmaster	57046845
Gemini Elf	69140098
Generation Shift	34460239
Germ Infection	24668830
Getsu Fuhma	21887179
Giant Flea	41762634
Giant Germ	95178994
Giant Rat	97017120
Giant Red Seasnake	58831685
Giant Soldier of Stone	13039848
Giant Trunade	42703248
Gigantes	47606319
Gilasaurus	45894482
Gilford the Legend	69933858
Gilford the Lightning	36354007
Gil Garth	38445524
Goblin Attack Force	78658564
Goblin Fan	04149689
Goblin King	18590133
Goblin Thief	45311864
Goblin's Secret Remedy	11868825
Goddess of Whim	67959180
Goddess with the Third Eye	53493204
Gokibore	15367030
Gorgon's Eye	52648457
Graceful Dice	74137509
Gradius' Option	14291024
Granadora	13944422
Grand Tiki Elder	13676474
Gravedigger Ghoul	82542267
Gravekeeper's Assailant	25262697
Gravekeeper's Cannonholder	99877698
Gravekeeper's Chief	62473983
Gravekeeper's Commandant	17393207
Gravekeeper's Curse	50712728
Gravekeeper's Guard	37101832
Gravekeeper's Servant	16762927
Gravekeeper's Spear Soldier	63695531
Gravekeeper's Spy	24317029
Gravekeeper's Vassal	99690140
Gravekeeper's Watcher	26084285
Gravity Axe - Grarl	32022366
Gravity Bind	85742772
Great Moth	14141448
Greed	89405199
Green Baboon, Defender of the Forest	46668237
Greenkappa	61831093
Ground Collapse	90502999
Gust	73079365
Gust Fan	55321970
Gyaku-Gire Panda	09817927
Hammer Shot	26412047
Hand Collapse	74519184
Hannibal Necromancer	05640330

CARD	PASSWORD
Harpie Lady	76812113
Harpie Lady 1	91932350
Harpie Lady 2	27927359
Harpie Lady 3	54415063
Harpie Lady Sisters	12206212
Harpies' Hunting Ground	75782277
Harpie's Pet Dragon	52040216
Headless Knight	5434080
Heart of Clear Water	64801562
Heart of the Underdog	35762283
Heavy Mech Support Platform	23265594
Heavy Slump	52417194
Heavy Storm	19613556
Helpoemer	76052811
Hercules Beetle	52584282
Hero Kid	32679370
Hero Signal	22020907
Hidden Book of Spell	21840375
Hieroglyph Lithograph	10248192
Hinotama	46130346
Hiro's Shadow Scout	81863068
Hitotsu-Me Giant	76184692
Horn Imp	69669405
Horn of Light	38552107
Horn of the Unicorn	64047146
Hoshiningen	67629977
House of Adhesive Tape	15083728
Human-Wave Tactics	30353551
Illusionist Faceless Mage	28546905
Impenetrable Formation	96631852
Inferno	74823665
Inferno Fire Blast	52684508
Infinite Cards	94163677
Infinite Dismissal	54109233
Injection Fairy Lily	79575620
Insect Armor with Laser Cannon	03492538
Insect Barrier	23615409
Insect Imitation	96965364
Insect Queen	91512835
Inspection	16227556
Interdimensional Matter Transporter	36261276
Invigoration	98374133
Jack's Knight	90876561
Jade Insect Whistle	95214051
Jam Breeding Machine	21770260
Jam Defender	21558682
Jar of Greed	83968380
Jigen Bakudan	90020065
Jinzo	77585513
Jinzo #7	77585513
Jowgen the Spiritualist	41855169
Jowls of Dark Demise	05257687
Judge Man	30113682
Judgment of the Pharaoh	55948544
Just Desserts	24068492
Kabazauls	51934376
Kabazauls	51934376
Kanan the Swordsmistress	12829151
Killer Needle	88979991
Kinetic Soldier	79853073
King of the Skull Servants	36021814
King of the Swamp	79109599
King Tiger Wanghu	83986578

CARD	PASSWORD
King's Knight	64788463
Koitsu	69456283
Krokodilus	76512652
Kryuel	82642348
Kunai with Chain	37390589
Kuriboh	40640057
Kycoo the Ghost Destroyer	88240808
Labyrinth of Nightmare	66526672
Labyrinth Tank	99551425
Larvae Moth	87756343
Laser Cannon Armor	77007920
Last Day of the Witch	90330453
Launcher Spider	87322377
Lava Battleguard	20394040
Lava Golem	00102380
Left Arm of the Forbidden One	07902349
Left Leg of the Forbidden One	44519536
Legacy of Yata-Garasu	30461781
Legendary Sword	61854111
Level Conversion Lab	84397023
Level Limit - Area A	54976796
Level Limit - Area B	03136426
Level Modulation	61850482
Level Up!	25290459
Light of Judgment	44595286
Lighten the Load	37231841
Lightforce Sword	49587034
Lightning Vortex	69162969
Little Chimera	68658728
Luminous Soldier	57482479
Luminous Spark	81777047
Luster Dragon	11091375
Machine Duplication	63995093
Machine King	46700124
Mad Sword Beast	79870141
Mage Power	83746708
Magic Cylinder	62279055
Magic Drain	59344077
Magic Formula	67227834
Magic Jammer	77414722
Magical Arm Shield	96008713
Magical Dimension	28553439
Magical Explosion	32723153
Magical Hats	81210420
Magical Stone Excavation	98494543
Magical Thorn	53119267
Magician of Black Chaos	30208479
Magician of Faith	31560081
Magician's Circle	00050755
Magician's Unite	36045450
Magician's Valkyria	80304126
Maha Vailo	93013676
Maharaghi	40695128
Maiden of the Aqua	17214465
Major Riot	09074847
Malevolent Catastrophe	01224927
Malevolent Nuzzler	99597615
Malfunction	06137091
Malice Dispersion	13626450
Man-Eater Bug	54652250
Man-Eating Treasure Chest	13723605
Manga Ryu-Ran	38369349
Marauding Captain	02460565

CARD	PASSWORD
Marie the Fallen One	57579381
Marshmallon	31305911
Marshmallon Glasses	66865880
Mask of Brutality	82432018
Mask of Darkness	28933734
Mask of Dispel	20765952
Mask of Restrict	29549364
Mask of the Accursed	56948373
Mask of Weakness	57882509
Masked Sorcerer	10189126
Mass Driver	34906152
Master Kyonshee	24530661
Mataza the Zapper	22609617
Mausoleum of the Emperor	80921533
Mechanicalchaser	07359741
Mega Ton Magical Cannon	32062913
Megamorph	22046459
Melchid the Four-Faced Beast	86569121
Meltiel, Sage of the Sky	49905576
Mesmeric Control	48642904
Messenger of Peace	44656491
Metal Detector	75646520
Metal Reflect Slime	26905245
Metalmorph	68540058
Metalzoa	50705071
Meteor Black Dragon	90660762
Meteor Dragon	64271667
Michizure	37580756
Micro Ray	18190572
Millennium Shield	32012841
Milus Radiant	07489323
Mind Control	37520316
Mind Crush	15800838
Miracle Dig	63434080
Miracle Kids	55985014
Miracle Restoring	68334074
Mirror Force	44095762
Mispolymerization	58392024
Mist body	47529357
Moisture Creature	75285069
Mokey Mokey	27288416
Mokey Mokey King	13803864
Mokey Mokey Smackdown	01965724
Molten Destruction	19384334
Monster Gate	43040603
Monster Recovery	93108433
Monster Reincarnation	74848038
Mooyan Curry	58074572
Morphing Jar	33508719
Morphing Jar #2	79106360
Mother Grizzly	57839750
Mountain	50913601
Muka Muka	46657337
Multiplication of Ants	22493811
Multiply	40703222
Mushroom Man	14181608
My Body as a Shield	69279219
Mysterious Puppeteer	54098121
Mystic Box	25774450
Mystic Horseman	68516705
Mystic Probe	49251811
Mystic Swordsman LV2	47507260
Mystic Swordsman LV4	74591968

CARD	PASSWORD
Mystic Swordsman LV6	60482781
Mystic Tomato	83011277
Mystical Elf	15025844
Mystical Moon	36607978
Mystical Refpanel	35563539
Mystical Sheep #1	30451366
Mystical Space Typhoon	05318639
Narrow Pass	40172183
Necrovalley	47355498
Needle Wall	38299233
Needle Worm	81843628
Negate Attack	14315573
Neo the Magic Swordsman	50930991
Newdoria	04335645
Next to be Lost	07076131
Nightmare Wheel	54704216
Nimble Momonga	22567609
Nitro Unit	23842445
Non Aggression Area	76848240
Non-Fusion Area	27581098
Non-Spellcasting Area	20065549
Numinous Healer	02130625
Nuvia the Wicked	12953226
Obnoxious Celtic Guard	52077741
Ojama Black	79335209
Ojama Delta Hurricane!!	08251996
Ojama Green	12482652
Ojama King	90140980
Ojama Trio	29843091
Ojama Yellow	42941100
Ojamagic	24643836
Ojamuscle	98259197
Ominous Fortunetelling	56995655
Ookazi	19523799
Opti-Camouflage Armor	44762290
Order to Charge	78986941
Order to Smash	39019325
Otohime	39751093
Overpowering Eye	60577362
Panther Warrior	42035044
Paralyzing Potion	50152549
Parasite Paracide	27911549
Parrot Dragon	62762898
Patrician of Darkness	19153634
Pendulum Machine	24433920
Penguin Knight	36039163
Penguin Soldier	93920745
Perfectly Ultimate Great Moth	48579379
Petit Moth	58192742
Pharaoh's Treasure	63571750
Pigeonholing Books of Spell	96677818
Pikeru's Second Sight	58015506
Pinch Hopper	26185991
Pitch-Black Power Stone	34029630
Poison Fangs	76539047
Poison of the Old Man	08842266
Polymerization	35550694
Pot of Avarice	67169062
Premature Burial	70828912
Prepare to Strike Back	04483989
Prevent Rat	00549481
Princess of Tsurugi	51371017
Prohibition	43711255

CARD	PASSWORD
Protector of the Sanctuary	24221739
Pumpking the King of Ghosts	29155212
Queen's Knight	25652259
Rabid Horseman	94905343
Radiant Jeral	84177693
Radiant Mirror Force	21481146
Raigeki Break	04178474
Rapid-Fire Magician	06337436
Ray of Hope	82529174
Ready for Intercepting	31785398
Really Eternal Rest	28121403
Reaper of the Cards	33066139
Reckless Greed	37576645
Recycle	96316857
Red Archery Girl	65570596
Red Medicine	38199696
Red-Eyes B. Chick	36262024
Red-Eyes Black Dragon	74677422
Red-Eyes Black Metal Dragon	64335804
Reflect Bounder	02851070
Reinforcement of the Army	32807846
Reinforcements	17814387
Release Restraint	75417459
Relieve Monster	37507488
Relinquished	64631466
Remove Trap	51482758
Respect Play	08951260
Restructer Revolution	99518961
Reversal Quiz	05990062
Reverse Trap	77622396
Revival Jam	31709826
Right Arm of the Forbidden One	70903634
Right Leg of the Forbidden One	08124921
Rigorous Reaver	39180960
Ring of Magnetism	20436034
Riryoku Field	70344351
Rising Energy	78211862
Rite of Spirit	30450531
Ritual Weapon	54351224
Robbin' Goblin	88279736
Robbin' Zombie	83258273
Robotic Knight	44203504
Rock Bombardment	20781762
Rocket Warrior	30860696
Rod of Silence - Kay'est	95515060
Rogue Doll	91939608
Roll Out!	91597389
Royal Command	33950246
Royal Decree	51452091
Royal Magical Library	70791313
Royal Oppression	93016201
Royal Surrender	56058888
Royal Tribute	72405967
Rude Kaiser	26378150
Rush Recklessly	70046172
Ryu Kokki	57281778
Ryu-Kishin	15303296
Ryu-Ran	02964201
Sage's Stone	13604200
Saggi the Dark Clown	66602787
Sakuretsu Armor	56120475
Salamandra	32268901
Salvage	96947648

CARD	PASSWORD
Sangan	26202165
Sasuke Samurai #3	77379481
Sasuke Samurai #4	64538655
Satellite Cannon	50400231
Second Coin Toss	36562627
Sengenjin	76232340
Serial Spell	49398568
Serpentine Princess	71829750
Seven Tools of the Bandit	03819470
Shadow Ghoul	30778711
Shadow of Eyes	58621589
Share the Pain	56830749
Shield & Sword	52097679
Shield Crush	30683373
Shift	59560625
Shifting Shadows	59237154
Shinato, King of a Higher Plane	86327225
Shinato's Ark	60365591
Shining Abyss	87303357
Shining Angel	95956346
Shooting Star Bow - Ceal	95638658
Shrink	55713623
Silver Bow and Arrow	01557499
Simultaneous Loss	92219931
Skilled Dark Magician	73752131
Skilled White Magician	46363422
Skull Dice	00126218
Skull Servant	32274490
Skull-Mark Ladybug	64306248
Skyscraper	63035430
Slate Warrior	78636495
Slot Machine	03797883
Smashing Ground	97169186
Smoke Grenade of the Thief	63789924
Snake Fang	00596051
Sogen	86318356
Solar Ray	44472639
Solemn Judgment	41420027
Solemn Wishes	35346968
Sorcerer of the Doomed	49218300
Soul Absorption	68073522
Soul Demolition	76297408
Soul Exchange	68005187
Soul of Purity and Light	77527210
Soul of the Pure	47852924
Soul Release	05758500
Soul Resurrection	92924317
Soul Reversal	78864369
Soul Taker	81510157
Spark Blaster	97362768
Spatial Collapse	20644748
Special Hurricane	42598242
Spell Absorption	51481927
Spell Reproduction	29228529
Spell Vanishing	29735721
Spellbinding Circle	18807108
Spell-stopping Statute	10069180
Spiral Spear Strike	49328340
Spirit Message "A"	94772232
Spirit Message "I"	31893528
Spirit Message "L"	30170981
Spirit Message "N"	67287533
Spirit of Flames	13522325

CARD	PASSWORD
Spirit of the Pharaoh	25343280
Spirit's Invitation	92394653
Spiritual Earth Art - Kurogane	70156997
Spiritual Energy Settle Machine	99173029
Spiritual Fire Art - Kurenai	42945701
Spiritual Water Art - Aoi	06540606
Spiritual Wind Art - Miyabi	79333300
Spiritualism	15866454
St. Joan	21175632
Staunch Defender	92854392
Steel Ogre Grotto #2	90908427
Steel Scorpion	13599884
Stim-Pack	83225447
Stone Statue of the Aztecs	31812496
Stop Defense	63102017
Stray Lambs	60764581
Stumbling	34646691
Swamp Battleguard	40453765
Swift Gaia the Fierce Knight	16589042
Sword of Deep-Seated	98495314
Sword of the Soul-Eater	05371656
Swords of Concealing Light	12923641
Swords of Revealing Light	72302403
Swordsman of Landstar	03573512
System Down	07672244
Tailor of the Fickle	43641473
Terraforming	73628505
The A. Forces	00403847
The Agent of Force - Mars	91123920
The Agent of Judgement - Saturn	91345518
The Big March of Animals	01689516
The Bistro Butcher	71107816
The Cheerful Coffin	41142615
The Creator	61505339
The Creator Incarnate	97093037
The Dark Door	30606547
The Earl of Demise	66989694
The Fiend Megacyber	66362965
The First Sarcophagus	31076103
The Flute of Summoning Kuriboh	20065322
The Forgiving Maiden	84080938
The Gross Ghost of Fled Dreams	68049471
The Illusory Gentleman	83764996
The Inexperienced Spy	81820689
The Last Warrior from Another Planet	86099788
The Law of the Normal	66926224
The League of Uniform Nomenclature	55008284
The Little Swordsman of Aile	25109950
The Masked Beast	49064413
The Portrait's Secret	32541773
The Regulation of Tribe	00296499
The Reliable Guardian	16430187
The Rock Spirit	76305638
The Sanctuary in the Sky	56433456
The Second Sarcophagus	04081094
The Secret of the Bandit	99351431
The Shallow Grave	43434803
The Snake Hair	29491031
The Spell Absorbing Life	99517131
The Statue of Easter Island	10261698
The Third Sarcophagus	78697395
The Unhappy Girl	27618634
The Unhappy Maiden	51275027

CARD	PASSWORD
The Warrior Returning Alive	95281259
The Wicked Worm Beast	06285791
Thestalos the Firestorm Monarch	26205777
Thousand Dragon	41462083
Thousand Energy	05703682
Thousand Knives	63391643
Thousand-Eyes Idol	27125110
Threatening Roar	36361633
Three-Headed Geedo	78423643
Thunder Crash	69196160
Thunder Dragon	31786629
Thunder Nyan Nyan	70797118
Time Machine	80987696
Time Wizard	06285791
Token Feastevil	83675475
Toon Alligator	59383041
Toon Cannon Soldier	79875176
Toon Dark Magician Girl	90960358
Toon Defense	43509019
Toon Gemini Elf	42386471
Toon Goblin Attack Force	15270885
Toon Masked Sorcerer	16392422
Toon Mermaid	65458948
Toon Summoned Skull	91842653
Toon Table of Contents	89997728
Toon World	15259703
Tornado	61068510
Tornado Wall	18605135
Torpedo Fish	90337190
Tower of Babel	94256039
Tragedy	35686187
Transcendent Wings	25573054
Trap Hole	04206964
Trap Jammer	19252988
Trap Master	46461247
Tremendous Fire	46918794
Triage	30888983
Triangle Ecstasy Spark	12181376
Triangle Power	32298781
Tribute Doll	02903036
Tribute to the Doomed	79759861
Tri-Horned Dragon	39111158
Twin Swords of Flashing Light - Tryce	21900719
Twin-Headed Behemoth	43586926
Twin-Headed Thunder Dragon	54752875
Two-Headed King Rex	94119974
Two-Pronged Attack	83887306
Tyhone	72842870
Type Zero Magic Crusher	35346968
UFO Turtle	60806437
Ultimate Offering	80604091
Ultra Evolution Pill	22431243
Umiiruka	82999629
Union Attack	60399954
United We Stand	56747793
Unity	14731897
Upstart Goblin	70368879
Uraby	01784619
Valkyrion the Magna Warrior	75347539
Versago the Destroyer	50259460
Vile Germs	39774685
Vorse Raider	14898066
Waboku	12607053

CARD	PASSWORD
Wall of Illusion	13945283
Wall of Revealing Light	17078030
Wall Shadow	63162310
Warrior Elimination	90873992
Warrior Lady of the Wasteland	05438492
Wasteland	98239899
Weapon Change	10035717
Weather Report	72053645
Weed Out	28604635
White Magical Hat	15150365
White-Horned Dragon	73891874
Wicked-Breaking Flamberge - Baou	68427465
Widespread Ruin	77754944
Wild Nature's Release	61166988
Winged Dragon, Guardian of the Fortress #1	87796900
Winged Kuriboh	57116033
Winged Kuriboh LV10	98585345
Witch's Apprentice	80741828
Wolf	49417509
Wolf Axwielder	56369281
Woodland Sprite	06979239
World Suppression	12253117
Xing Zhen Hu	76515293
Yamata Dragon	76862289
Yami	59197169
Yellow Luster Shield	04542651
Yu-Jo Friendship	81332143
Zaborg the Thunder Monarch	51945556
Zero Gravity	83133491
Zoa	24311372
Zolga	16268841
Zombie Warrior	31339260

PLAYSTATION® PORTABLE

GAMES

300: MARCH TO GLORY

25,000 KLEOS

Pause the game and press Down, Left, Down, Left, Up, Left. You can only use this code once.

ATV OFFROAD FURY: BLAZIN' TRAILS

UNLOCK EVERYTHING EXCEPT THE FURY BIKE

Select Player Profile from the Options menu. Choose Enter Cheat and enter All Access.

1500 CREDITS

Select Player Profile from the Options menu. Choose Enter Cheat and enter $moneybags$.

ALL RIDER GEAR

Select Player Profile from the Options menu. Choose Enter Cheat and enter Duds.

TIRES

Select Player Profile from the Options menu. Choose Enter Cheat and enter Dubs.

MUSIC VIDEOS

Select Player Profile from the Options menu. Choose Enter Cheat and enter Billboards.

BEN 10: ALIEN FORCE THE GAME

LEVEL LORD

Enter Gwen, Kevin, Big Chill, Gwen as a code.

INVINCIBILITY

Enter Kevin, Big Chill, Swampfire, Kevin as a code.

ALL COMBOS

Enter Swampfire, Gwen, Kevin, Ben as a code.

INFINITE ALIENS

Enter Ben, Swampfire, Gwen, Big Chill as a code.

BEN 10: PROTECTOR OF EARTH

INVINCIBILITY
Select a game from the Continue option. Go to the Map Selection screen, press Start and choose Extras. Select Enter Secret Code and enter XLR8, Heatblast, Wildvine, Fourarms.

ALL COMBOS
Select a game from the Continue option. Go to the Map Selection screen, press Start and choose Extras. Select Enter Secret Code and enter Cannonblot, Heatblast, Fourarms, Heatblast.

ALL LOCATIONS
Select a game from the Continue option. Go to the Map Selection screen, press Start and choose Extras. Select Enter Secret Code and enter Heatblast, XLR8, XLR8, Cannonblot.

DNA FORCE SKINS
Select a game from the Continue option. Go to the Map Selection screen, press Start and choose Extras. Select Enter Secret Code and enter Wildvine, Fourarms, Heatblast, Cannonbolt.

DARK HEROES SKINS
Select a game from the Continue option. Go to the Map Selection screen, press Start and choose Extras. Select Enter Secret Code and enter Cannonbolt, Cannonbolt, Fourarms, Heatblast.

ALL ALIEN FORMS
Select a game from the Continue option. Go to the Map Selection screen, press Start and choose Extras. Select Enter Secret Code and enter Wildvine, Fourarms, Heatblast, Wildvine.

MASTER CONTROL
Select a game from the Continue option. Go to the Map Selection screen, press Start and choose Extras. Select Enter Secret Code and enter Cannonbolt, Heatblast, Wildvine, Fourarms.

BLITZ: OVERTIME

The following codes only work for Quick Play mode.

BALL TRAILS ALWAYS ON
Select Extras from the menu and enter ONFIRE.

BEACH BALL
Select Extras from the menu and enter BOUNCY.

DOUBLE UNLEASH ICONS
Select Extras from the menu and enter PIPPED.

STAMINA DISABLED
Select Extras from the menu and enter NOTTIRED.

SUPER CLASH MODE
Select Extras from the menu and enter CLASHY.

SUPER UNLEASH CLASH MODE
Select Extras from the menu and enter BIGDOGS.

INSTANT WIN IN CAMPAIGN MODE
Select Extras from the menu and enter CHAMPS. In Campaign mode, highlight a team and press ■, ■, ▲ to win against that team.

TWO PLAYER CO-OP MODE
Select Extras from the menu and enter CHUWAY.

BROTHERS IN ARMS D-DAY

LEVEL SELECT
Enter JUNESIX as your profile name.

BURNOUT LEGENDS

COP RACER
Earn a Gold in all Pursuit events.

FIRE TRUCK
Earn a Gold in all Crash Events.

GANGSTER BOSS
Earn Gold in all Race events.

CAPCOM CLASSICS COLLECTION REMIXED

UNLOCK EVERYTHING

At the title screen, press Left on D-pad, Right on D-pad, Left on Analog stick, Right on Analog stick, ■, ●, Up on D-pad, Down on D-pad.

CAPCOM PUZZLE WORLD

SUPER BUSTER BROS.

LEVEL SELECT IN TOUR MODE

At the Main menu, highlight Tour Mode, hold Down and press ✖.

SUPER PUZZLE FIGHTER

PLAY AS AKUMA

At the character select, highlight Hsien-Ko and press Down.

PLAY AS DAN

At the character select, highlight Donovan and press Down.

PLAY AS DEVILOT

At the character select, highlight Morrigan and press Down.

PLAY AS ANITA

At the character select, hold L + R and choose Donovan.

PLAY AS HSIEN-KO'S TALISMAN

At the character select, hold L + R and choose Hsien-Ko.

PLAY AS MORRIGAN AS A BAT

At the character select, hold L + R and choose Morrigan.

CARS

BONUS SPEEDWAY (REVERSED) IN CUSTOM RACE

At the Main menu, hold L and press ✖, ■, ▲, ✖, ▲, ■.

ALL CARS, PAINTJOBS, TRACKS, MOVIE CLIPS AND MODES

At the Main menu, hold L and press ▲, ■, ✖, ●, ▲, ✖, ■, ▲, ●, ✖.

UNLIMITED NITROUS

At the Main menu, hold L and ✖, ■, ●, ●, ●, ▲, ■, ✖.

CASTLEVANIA: THE DRACULA X CHRONICLES

ORIGINAL RONDO OF BLOOD

LEVEL SELECT

Enter X-X!V''Q as your player name

SYMPHONY OF THE NIGHT

PLAY AS ALUCARD WITH 99 LUCK AND LAPIS LAZULI

Start a new game with the name X-X!V''Q.

PLAY AS ALUCARD WITH AXE LORD ARMOR

After clearing the game once, start a new game with the name AXEARMOR.

PLAY AS MARIA RENARD

After clearing the game once, start a new game with the name MARIA.

PLAY AS RICHTER BELMONT

After clearing the game once, start a new game with the name RICHTER.

CRASH: MIND OVER MUTANT

A cheat can be deactivated by re-entering the code.

FREEZE ENEMIES WITH TOUCH

Pause the game, hold R and press Down, Down, Down, Up.

ENEMIES DROP X4 DAMAGE

Pause the game, hold R and press Up, Up, Up, Left.

ENEMIES DROP PURPLE FRUIT

Pause the game, hold R and press Up, Down, Down, Up.

ENEMIES DROP SUPER KICK

Pause the game, hold R and press Up, Right, Down, Left.

ENIMIES DROP WUMPA FRUIT

Pause the game, hold R and press Right, Right, Right, Up.

SHADOW CRASH

Pause the game, hold R and press Left, Right, Left, Right.

DEFORMED CRASH

Pause the game, hold R and press Left, Left, Left, Down.

CRASH TAG TEAM RACING

FASTER VEHICLES

At the Main menu, hold L + R and press Circle, Circle, Triangle, Triangle.

1-HIT KO

At the Main menu, hold L + R and press X, Circle, Circle, X.

DISABLE HUD

At the Main menu, hold L + R and press X, Square, Triangle, Circle.

CHICKEN HEADS

At the Main menu, hold L + R and press X, Circle, Circle, Square.

JAPANESE CRASH

At the Main menu, hold L + R and press Square, Circle, Square, Circle.

DRIVE A BLOCK VEHICLE

At the Main menu, hold L + R and press Circle, Circle, Triangle, Square.

CRISIS CORE-FINAL FANTASY VII

NEW GAME+

After completing the game, you'll be prompted to make a new save. Loading a game from this new save will begin a New Game+, starting the game over while allowing Zack to retain almost everything he's earned.

The following items transfer to a New Game+:

- Level, Experience, SP, Gil, Playtime, Non-Key Items, Materia, and DMW Completion Rate

The following items do not transfer:

- Key Items, Materia/Accessory Slot Expansion, Ability to SP Convert, DMW Images, Mission Progress, Mail, and Unlocked Shops

DARKSTALKERS CHRONICLE: THE CHAOS TOWER

EX OPTIONS
At the Main menu, hold L and select Options.

MARIONETTE IN ARCADE MODE
At the Character Select screen, highlight ? and press START (x7), then press P or K.

OBORO BISHAMON IN ALL MODES
At the Character Select screen, highlight Bishamon, hold START, and press P or K.

SHADOW IN ARCADE MODE
At the Character Select screen, highlight ? and press START (x5), then press P or K.

DAXTER

THE MATRIX DREAM SEQUENCE
Collect 1 Precursor Orb.

BRAVEHEART DREAM SEQUENCE
Collect 100 Precursor Orbs.

THE LORD OF THE RINGS DREAM SEQUENCE
Collect 200 Precursor Orbs.

INDIANA JONES DREAM SEQUENCE
Collect 300 Precursor Orbs.

THE MATRIX DREAM SEQUENCE 2
Collect 400 Precursor Orbs.

THE LORD OF THE RINGS DREAM SEQUENCE 2
Collect 500 Precursor Orbs.

E3 2005 TRAILER
Collect 600 Precursor Orbs, then pause the game and select Extras from the Secrets menu.

CONCEPT ART
Collect 700 Precursor Orbs, then pause the game and select Extras from the Secrets menu.

INTRO ANIMATIC
Collect 800 Precursor Orbs, then pause the game and select Extras from the Secrets menu.

GAME UNDER CONSTRUCTION
Collect 900 Precursor Orbs, then pause the game and select Extras from the Secrets menu.

BEHIND THE SCENES
Collect 1000 Precursor Orbs, then pause the game and select Extras from the Secrets menu.

PANTS
Earn Gold on The Lord of the Rings Dream Sequence 2, then pause the game and select Cheats from the Secrets menu.

HAT
Earn Gold on the Indiana Jones Dream Sequence, then pause the game and select Cheats from the Secrets menu.

DEATH JR.

CAN'T TOUCH THIS (INVINCIBILITY)
Pause the game, hold L + R and press Up, Up, Down, Down, Left, Left, Right, Right, ■, ▲.

INCREASED HEALTH
Pause the game, hold L + R and press Up, Up, Down, Down, ✕, ●, ▲, ■, ✕, ✕.

WEAPONS UPGRADED (GIVES ALL WEAPONS)
Pause the game, hold L + R and press Up, Up, Down, Down, Left, Right, Left, Right, ✕, ●.

AMMO REFILLED

Pause the game, hold L + R and press △, △, ✕, ✕, □, ○, □, ○, Down, Right.

UNLIMITED AMMO

Pause the game, hold L + R and press △, △, ✕, ✕, □, ○, □, ○, Right, Down.

MY HEAD FEELS FUNNY (BIG HEAD)

Pause the game, hold L + R and press △, ○, ✕, □, △, Up, Right, Down, Left, Up. Re-enter the code for normal head size.

GIANT BLADE (BIG SCYTHE)

Pause the game, hold L + R and press △, □, ✕, ○, △, Up, Left, Down, Right, Up.

FREE SEEP

Pause the game, hold L + R and press Left, Left, Right, Right, Left, Right, Left, Right, ✕, ✕.

A LITTLE MORE HELP (ASSIST EXTENDER)

Pause the game, hold L + R and press Up, Up, Down, Down, △, △, ✕, ✕, △, △.

FREE WIDGET

Pause the game, hold L + R and press Right, Up, Down, Up, △, Up, Left, □, △, Right.

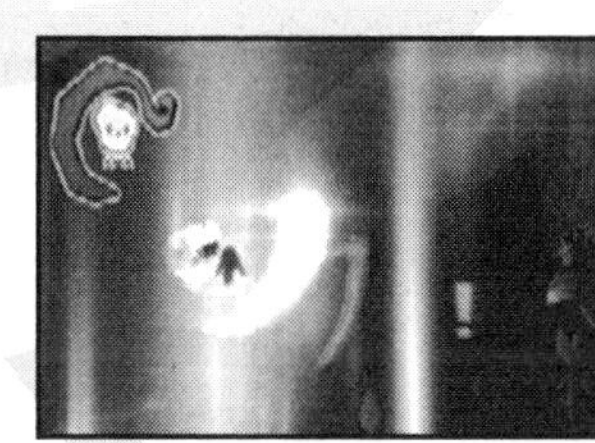

ALL LEVELS & FREE ALL CHARACTERS

Pause the game, hold L + R and press Up (x4), Down (x4), ✕, ✕. Enter a stage and exit back to the museum for the code to take effect.

I'D BUY THAT FOR A DOLLAR (FILL PANDORA ASSIST METER)

Pause the game, hold L + R and press Up, Up, Down, Down, Up, Right, Down, Left, ✕, ✕.

THIS WAS JED'S IDEA (ATTACKS HAVE DIFFERENT NAMES)

Pause the game, hold L + R and press Up, Up, Down, Left, △, △, □, ✕, ○, □.

WEAPON NAMES = NORMAL (WEAPONS HAVE DIFFERENT NAMES)

Pause the game, hold L + R and press Down, Down, Up, Up, Left, Right, Left, Right, □, △.

EYEDOOR SOLIDITY QUESTIONABLE (NO LONGER REQUIRE SOULS)

Pause the game, hold L + R and press Up, Left, Down, Right, Left, △, □, ✕, ○, □.

BUDDY DECALS (BULLET HOLES BECOME PICTURES)

Pause the game, hold L + R and press Up, Right, Down, Left, Up, △, ○, ✕, □, △.

STAGE WARP

Pause the game, hold L + R and enter the following codes to warp to that stage.

STAGE	CODE
Advanced Training	Down, K, Down, K, Down, K, Down, K, Down, I
The Basement	Down, K, Down, K, Down, K, Down, K, Up, J
Basic Training	Up, J, Up, K, Down, K, Down, K, Down, K
Big Trouble in Little Downtown	Up, J, Down, K, Down, K, Down, K, Down, K
Bottom of the Bell Curve	Down, K, Down, K, Down, K, Down, K, Down, J

STAGE	CODE
The Burger Tram	Down, K, Down, K, Down, K, Up, K, Down, K
Burn It Down	Down, K, Up, J, Down, K, Down, K, Down, K
The Corner Store	Down, K, Up, K, Down, K, Down, K, Down, K
Final Battle	Down, K, Down, K, Down, K, Down, J, Up, K
Growth Spurt	Down, K, Down, K, Down, K, Down, K, Up, K
Happy Trails Insanitarium	Down, K, Down, J, Up, K, Down, K, Down, K
Higher Learning	Down, K, Down, K, Down, K, Down, J, Down, K
How a Cow Becomes a Steak	Down, K, Down, K, Down, J, Down, K, Down, K
Inner Madness	Down, K, Down, K, Up, J, Down, K, Down, K
Into the Box	Down, K, Down, K, Down, K, Up, J, Down, K
Moving on Up	Down, J, Up, K, Down, K, Down, K, Down, K
The Museum	Up, K, Down K, Down, K, Down, K, Down, K
My House	Down, K, Down, J, Down, K, Down, K, Down, K
Seep's Hood	Down, J, Down, K, Down, K, Down, K, Down, K
Shock Treatment	Down, K, Down, K, Down, J, Up, K, Down, K
Udder Madness	Down, K, Down, K, Up, K, Down, K, Down, K

DISGAEA: AFTERNOON OF DARKNESS

ETNA MODE

At the Main menu, highlight New Game and press △, □, ○, △, □, ○, ✕.

DRAGON BALL Z: SHIN BUDOKAI

MINI-GAME

At the Main menu, press L and then press R to begin the mini-game.

DUNGEON SIEGE: THRONE OF AGONY

ITEM CODES

Talk to Feydwer and Klaars in Seahaven and enter the following codes. Enter the Master Code and one of the item codes.

ITEM	CODE
Master Code	MPJNKBHAKANLPGHD
Bloodstained Warboots	MHFMCJIFNDHOKLPM
Bolt Flingers	OBMIDNBJNPFKADCL
Enkindled Cleaver	MJPOBGFNLKELLLLP
Malignant Force	JDGJHKPOLNMCGHNC
Polychromatic Shiv	PJJEPCFHEIHAJEEE
Teasha's Ire	GDIMBNLEIGNNLOEG
Traveler's Handbook	PIJNPEGFJJPFALNO

ELITE MODE

Defeat the game to unlock this mode.

EA REPLAY

B.O.B.

PASSWORDS

LEVEL	PASSWORD
Anciena 1	672451
Anciena 2	272578
Anciena 3	652074
Anciena 4	265648
Anciena 5	462893
Anciena 6	583172
Goth 2	171058
Goth 3	950745
Goth 4	472149
Ultraworld 1	743690
Ultraworld 2	103928

LEVEL	PASSWORD
Ultraworld 3	144895
Ultraworld 4	775092
Ultraworld 5	481376

DESERT STRIKE

10 LIVES

At the Desert Strike menu, press □ to bring up the Password screen. Enter BQQQAEZ.

JUNGLE STRIKE

PASSWORDS

Press □ at the Jungle Strike menu to bring up the Password screen. Enter the following:

LEVEL	PASSWORD
Mountains	7LSPFBVWTWP
Night Strike	X4MFB4MHPH4
Puloso City	V6HGY39XVXL
Return Home	N4MK9N6MHM7
River Raid	TGB76MGCZCC
Training Ground	9NHDXMGCZCG
Washington D.C	BXYTNMGCYDB

WING COMMANDER

INVINCIBILITY AND STAGE SELECT

At the Wing Commander menu, press ✕, ○,✕, □, ✕, □, L, ○, R, ○, Start.

ROAD RASH 2

WILD THING MOTORCYCLE

At the title screen, hold Up + □ + ○ and press Start.

FAMILY GUY

ALL STAGES

At the Main menu, press Up, Left, Up, Left, Down, Right, Start.

FINAL FANTASY TACTICS: THE WAR OF THE LIONS

MUSIC TEST MODE

Enter the main character's name as PolkaPolka at the name entry screen.

FLATOUT: HEAD ON

1 MILLION CREDITS

Select Enter Code from the Extras menu and enter GIVECASH.

ALL CARS AND 1 MILLION CREDITS

Select Enter Code from the Extras menu and enter GIEVEPIX.

BIG RIG

Select Enter Code from the Extras menu and enter ELPUEBLO.

BIG RIG TRUCK

Select Enter Code from the Extras menu and enter RAIDERS.

FLATMOBILE CAR

Select Enter Code from the Extras menu and enter WOTKINS.

MOB CAR

Select Enter Code from the Extras menu and enter BIGTRUCK.

PIMPSTER CAR

Select Enter Code from the Extras menu and enter RUTTO.

ROCKET CAR

Select Enter Code from the Extras menu and enter KALJAKOPPA.

SCHOOL BUS

Select Enter Code from the Extras menu and enter GIEVCARPLZ.

FULL AUTO 2: BATTLELINES

ALL CARS

Select Cheats from the Options and press Up, Up, Up, Up, Left, Down, Up, Right, Down, Down, Down, Down.

ALL EVENTS

Select Cheats from the Options and press Start, Left, Select, Right, Right, △, ✕, □, Start, R, Down, Select.

THE GODFATHER: MOB WARS

Each of the following codes will work once every five minutes.

$1000

Pause the game and press □, ○, □, □, ○, L.

FULL AMMO

Pause the game and press ○, Left, ○, Right □, R.

FULL HEALTH

Pause the game and press Left, □, Right, ○, Right, L.

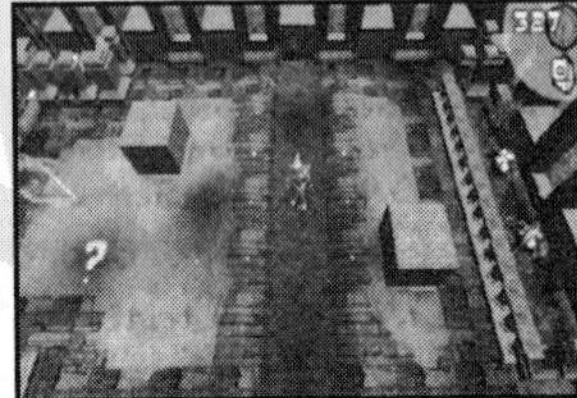

GRADIUS COLLECTION

AALL WEAPONS & POWER-UPS

Pause the game and press Up, Up, Down, Down, Left, Right, Left, Right, L, R. This code can be used once per level.

GRAND THEFT AUTO: LIBERTY CITY STORIES

$250,000

During a game, press L, R, △, L, R, ○, L, R.

FULL HEALTH

During a game, press L, R, ✕, L, R, □, L, R.

FULL ARMOR

During a game, press L, R, ○, L, R, ✕, L, R.

WEAPON SET 1

During a game, press Up, □, □, Down, L, □, □, R.

WEAPON SET 2

During a game, press Up, ○, ○, Down, Left, ○, ○, R.

WEAPON SET 3

During a game, press Up, ✕, ✕, Down, L, ✕, ✕, R.

CHROME PLATED CARS

During a game, press △, R, L, Down, Down, R, R, △.

BLACK CARS

During a game, press ○, ○, R, △, △, L, □, □.

WHITE CARS

During a game, press ✕, ✕, R, ○, ○, L, △, △.

CARS DRIVE ON WATER

During a game, press ○, ✕, Down, ○, ✕, Up, L, L.

PERFECT TRACTION

During a game, press L, Up, L, R, △, ○, Down, ✕.

CHANGE BICYCLE TIRE SIZE

During a game, press ○, Right, ✕, Up, R, ✕, L, □.

AGGRESSIVE DRIVERS

During a game, press □, □, R, ✕, ✕, L, ○, ○.

ALL GREEN LIGHTS

During a game, press △, △, R, □, □, L, ✕, ✕.

DESTROY ALL CARS

During a game, press L, L, Left, L, L, R, ✕, □.

RAISE MEDIA ATTENTION

During a game, press L, Up, R, R, △, □, Down, ✕.

RAISE WANTED LEVEL
During a game, press L, R, Square, L, R, Triangle, L, R.

NEVER WANTED
During a game, press L, L, Triangle, R, R, X, Square, Circle.

CHANGE OUTFIT
During a game, press L, L, L, L, L, Right, Square, Triangle.

BOBBLE HEAD WORLD
During a game, press Down, Down, Down, Circle, Circle, X, L, R.

PEOPLE ATTACK YOU
During a game, press L, L, R, L, L, R, Up, Triangle.

PEOPLE FOLLOW YOU
During a game, press Down, Down, Down, Triangle, Triangle, Circle, L, R.

PEOPLE HAVE WEAPONS
During a game, press R, R, L, R, R, L, R, Circle.

PEOPLE RIOT
During a game, press L, L, R, L, L, R, L, Square.

SPAWN RHINO
During a game, press L, L, L, L, L, R, Triangle, Circle.

SPAWN TRASHMASTER
During a game, press Triangle, Circle, Down, Triangle, Circle, Up, L, L.

FASTER CLOCK
During a game, press L, L, L, L, L, R, Circle, X

FASTER GAMEPLAY
During a game, press R, R, L, R, R, L, Down, X

SLOWER GAMEPLAY
During a game, press R, Triangle, X, R, Square, Circle, L, R.

ALL CHARACTERS, CARS, & ENTIRE CITY (MULTIPLAYER)
During a game, press Up (x3), Triangle, Triangle, Circle, L, R.

43 CHARACTERS & 7 GANGS (MULTIPLAYER)
During a game, press Up (x3), X, X, Square, R, L.

28 CHARACTERS & 4 GANGS (MULTIPLAYER)
During a game, press Up (x3), Circle, Circle, X, L, R.

14 CHARACTERS & 2 GANGS (MULTIPLAYER)
During a game, press Up (x3), Square, Square, Triangle, R, L.

CLEAR WEATHER
During a game, press Up, Down, Circle, Up, Down, Square, L, R.

FOGGY WEATHER
During a game, press Up, Down, Triangle, Up, Down, X, L, R.

OVERCAST WEATHER
During a game, press Up, Down, X, Up, Down, Triangle, L, R.

RAINY WEATHER
During a game, press Up, Down, Square, Up, Down, Circle, L, R.

SUNNY WEATHER
During a game, press L, L, Circle, R, R, Square, Triangle, X

UPSIDE DOWN
During a game, press Down, Down, Down, X, X, Square, R, L.

UPSIDE UP
During a game, press X, X, X, Down, Down, Right, L, R.

RIGHT SIDE UP
During a game, press Triangle, Triangle, Triangle, Up, Up, Right, L, R.

COMMIT SUICIDE
During a game, press L, Down, Left, R, X, Circle, Up, Triangle.

GAME CREDITS
During a game, press L, R, L, R, Up, Down, L, R.

GRAND THEFT AUTO: VICE CITY STORIES

Enter the following cheats during a game.

$250000
Press Up, Down, L, R, X, X, L, R.

ARMOR
Press Up, Down, L, R, Square, Square, L, R.

HEALTH
Press Up, Down, L, R, Circle, Circle, L, R.

NEVER WANTED
Press Up, R, Triangle, Triangle, Down, L, Circle, Circle.

LOWER WANTED LEVEL
Press Up, R, Triangle, Triangle, Down, L, X, X.

RAISE WANTED LEVEL
Press Up, R, Square, Square, Down, L, Circle, Circle.

WEAPON SET 1
Press L, R, X, Up, Down, Square, L, R.

WEAPON SET 2
Press L, R, Square, Up, Down, Triangle, L, R.

WEAPON SET 3
Press L, R, Triangle, Up, Down, Circle, L, R.

SPAWN RHINO
Press Up, L, Down, R, L, L, R, R.

SPAWN TRASHMASTER
Press Down, Up, R, Triangle, L, Triangle, L, Triangle.

BLACK CARS
Press L, R, L, R, L, Circle, Up, X.

CHROME CARS
Press R, Up, L, Down, △, △, L, R.

CARS AVOID YOU
Press Up, Up, R, L, △, ○, ○, □.

DESTROY ALL CARS
Press L, R, R, L, R, □, Down, R.

GUYS FOLLOW YOU
Press R, L, Down, L, ○, Up, L, □.

PERFECT TRACTION
Press Down, Left, Up, L, R, △, ○, ✕. Press Down to jump into a car.

PEDESTRIAN GETS INTO YOUR VEHICLE
Press Down, Up, R, L, L, □, Up, L.

PEDESTRIANS ATTACK YOU
Press Down, △, Up, ✕, L, R, L, R.

PEDESTRIANS HAVE WEAPONS
Press Up, L, Down, R, L, ○, R, △.

PEDESTRIANS RIOT
Press R, L, L, Down, L, ○, Down, L.

SUICIDE
Press R, R, ○, ○, L, R, Down, ✕.

UPSIDE DOWN 1
Press □, □, □, L, L, R, L, R.

UPSIDE DOWN 2
Press L, L, L, R, R, L, R, L.

FASTER CLOCK
Press R, L, L, Down, Up, ✕, Down, L.

FASTER GAMEPLAY
Press L, L, R, R, Up, △, Down, ✕.

SLOWER GAMEPLAY
Press L, L, ○, ○, Down, Up, △, ✕.

CLEAR WEATHER
Press L, Down, R, L, R, Up, L, ✕.

FOGGY WEATHER
Press L, Down, △, ✕, R, Up, L, L.

OVERCAST WEATHER
Press L, Down, L, R, R, Up, L, □.

RAINY WEATHER
Press L, Down, L, R, R, Up, Left, △.

SUNNY WEATHER
Press L, Down, R, L, R, Up, L, ○.

GUN SHOWDOWN

ALL CHAPTERS IN QUICK PLAY
Enter hunter as a profile name.

PLAY AS JENNY
Enter allies as a profile name.

UNLOCKS ALL WEAPONS IN STORY MODE
Enter nedwhite as a profile name. This does not unlock the final weapon.

FASTER GUN FIRING
Enter quivira as a profile name.

INCREASE AMMUNTION CAPACITY
Enter campbell as a profile name.

INFINITE AMMUNITION IN STORY MODE
Enter barton as a profile name.

NEW MULTIPLAYER MAP
Enter badlands as a profile name.

HOT BRAIN

119.99 TEMPERATURE IN ALL 5 CATEGORIES
Select New Game and enter Cheat.

HOT SHOTS GOLF 2

UNLOCK EVERYTHING
Enter 2gsh as your name.

IRON MAN

ARMOR SUITS
Iron Man's different armor suits are unlocked by completing certain missions.

COMPLETE MISSION	SUIT UNLOCKED
1, Escape	Mark I
2, First Flight	Mark II
3, Fight Back	Mark III
5, Maggia Compound	Gold Tin Can
8, Frozen Ship	Classic
11, Island Meltdown	Stealth
13, Showdown	Titanium Man

PSP MINIGAMES

Minigames can be unlocked by completing the following missions. Access the minigames through the Bonus menu.

COMPLETE MISSION	PSP MINIGAME UNLOCKED
1, Escape	Tin Can Challenge 1 + 2
2, First Flight	DEATH RACE: STARK INDUSTRY
3, Fight Back	BOSS FIGHT: DREADNOUGHT
4, Weapons Transport	DEATH RACE: AFGHAN DESERT BOSS FIGHT: WHIPLASH
5, Maggia Compound	DEATH RACE: MAGGIA MANSION
6, Flying Fortress	SPEED KILL: FLYING FORTRESS SURVIVAL: FLYING FORTRESS
7, Nuclear Winter	DEATH RACE: ARTIC CIRCLE
8, Frozen Ship	SPEED KILL: FROZEN SHIP SURVIVAL: FROZEN SHIP
9, Home Front	BOSS FIGHT: TITANIUM MAN
10, Save Pepper	DEATH RACE: DAM BASSIN
11, Island Meltdown	SPEED KILL: GREEK ISLANDS SURVIVAL: GREEK ISLANDS
12, Battlesuit Factory	SPEED KILL: TINMEN FACTORY SURVIVAL: TINMEN FACTORY
13, Showdown	BOSS FIGHT: IRON MONGER

CONCEPT ART

As you progress through the game and destroy the Weapon Crates, bonuses are unlocked. You can find all of these in the Bonus menu once unlocked.

CONCEPT ART UNLOCKED	NUMBER OF WEAPON CRATES FOUND
Environments Set 1	6
Environments Set 2	12
Iron Man	18
Environments Set 3	24
Enemies	30
Environments Set 4	36
Villains	42
Vehicles	48
Covers	50

JUICED 2: HOT IMPORT NIGHTS

LAST MAN STANDING CHALLENGE AND AN ASCARI KZ1

Select Cheats and Challenges from the DNA Lab menu and enter KNOX. Defeat the challenge to earn the Ascari KZ1.

SPECIAL CHALLENGE AND AN AUDI TT 1.8 QUATTRO

Select Cheats and Challenges from the DNA Lab menu and enter YTHZ. Defeat the challenge to earn the Audi TT 1.8 Quattro.

SPECIAL CHALLENGE AND A BMW Z4

Select Cheats and Challenges from the DNA Lab menu and enter GVDL. Defeat the challenge to earn the BMW Z4.

SPECIAL CHALLENGE AND A HOLDEN MONARO

Select Cheats and Challenges from the DNA Lab menu and enter RBSG. Defeat the challenge to earn the Holden Monaro.

SPECIAL CHALLENGE AND A HYUNDAI COUPE 2.7 V6

Select Cheats and Challenges from the DNA Lab menu and enter BSLU. Defeat the challenge to earn the Hyundai Coupe 2.7 V6.

SPECIAL CHALLENGE AND AN INFINITY G35

Select Cheats and Challenges from the DNA Lab menu and enter MRHC. Defeat the challenge to earn the Infinity G35.

SPECIAL CHALLENGE AND AN INFINITY RED G35

Select Cheats and Challenges from the DNA Lab menu and enter MNCH. Defeat the challenge to earn the Infinity G35.

SPECIAL CHALLENGE AND A KOENIGSEGG CCX

Select Cheats and Challenges from the DNA Lab menu and enter KDTR. Defeat the challenge to earn the Koenigsegg CCX.

SPECIAL CHALLENGE AND A MITSUBISHI PROTOTYPE X

Select Cheats and Challenges from the DNA Lab menu and enter DOPX. Defeat the challenge to earn the Mitsubishi Prototype X.

SPECIAL CHALLENGE AND A NISSAN 350Z

Select Cheats and Challenges from the DNA Lab menu and enter PRGN. Defeat the challenge to earn the Nissan 350Z.

SPECIAL CHALLENGE AND A NISSAN SKYLINE R34 GT-R

Select Cheats and Challenges from the DNA Lab menu and enter JWRS. Defeat the challenge to earn the Nissan Skyline R34 GT-R.

SPECIAL CHALLENGE AND A SALEEN S7

Select Cheats and Challenges from the DNA Lab menu and enter WIKF. Defeat the challenge to earn the Saleen S7.

SPECIAL CHALLENGE AND A SEAT LEON CUPRA R

Select Cheats and Challenges from the DNA Lab menu and enter FAMQ. Defeat the challenge to earn the Seat Leon Cupra R.

JUSTICE LEAGUE HEROES

UNLOCK EVERYTHING

Pause the game, hold L + R and press Down, Left, Up, Right.

INVINCIBLE

Pause the game, hold L + R and press Left, Down, Right, Up, Left, Down, Right, Up.

UNLIMITED ENERGY

Pause the game, hold L + R and press Down, Down, Right, Right, Up, Up, Left, Left.

MAX ABILITIES

Pause the game, hold L + R and press Right, Down, Right, Down.

20 FREE SHIELDS

Pause the game, hold L + R and press Up, Up, Down, Down.

25 BOOSTS

Pause the game, hold L + R and press Left, Right, Left, Right.

LEGO BATMAN

BATCAVE CODES

Using the computer in the Batcave, select Enter Code and enter the following:

CHARACTERS

CHARACTER	CODE
Alfred	ZAQ637
Batgirl	JKR331
Bruce Wayne	BDJ327
Catwoman (Classic)	M1AAWW
Clown Goon	HJK327
Commissioner Gordon	DDP967
Fishmonger	HGY748
Freeze Girl	XVK541
Joker Goon	UTF782
Joker Henchman	YUN924
Mad Hatter	JCA283
Man-Bat	NYU942
Military Policeman	MKL382
Nightwing	MVY759
Penguin Goon	NKA238
Penguin Henchman	BJH782
Penguin Minion	KJP748
Poison Ivy Goon	GTB899

CHARACTER	CODE
Police Marksman	HKG984
Police Officer	JRY983
Riddler Goon	CRY928
Riddler Henchman	XEU824
S.W.A.T.	HTF114
Sailor	NAV592
Scientist	JFL786
Security Guard	PLB946
The Joker (Tropical)	CCB199
Yeti	NJL412
Zoo Sweeper	DWR243

VEHICLES

VEHICLE	CODE
Bat-Tank	KNTT4B
Bruce Wayne's Private Jet	LEA664
Catwoman's Motorcycle	HPL826
Garbage Truck	DUS483
Goon Helicopter	GCH328
Harbor Helicopter	CHP735
Harley Quinn's Hammer Truck	RDT637
Mad Hatter's Glider	HS000W
Mad Hatter's Steamboat	M4DM4N
Mr. Freeze's Iceberg	ICYICE
The Joker's Van	JUK657
Mr. Freeze's Kart	BCT229
Penguin Goon Submarine	BTN248
Police Bike	LJP234
Police Boat	PLC999
Police Car	KJL832
Police Helicopter	CWR732
Police Van	MAC788
Police Watercraft	VJD328
Riddler's Jet	HAHAHA
Robin's Submarine	TTF453
Two-Face's Armored Truck	EFE933

CHEATS

CHEAT	CODE
Always Score Multiply	9LRGNB
Fast Batarangs	JRBDCB
Fast Walk	ZOLM6N
Flame Batarang	D8NYWH
Freeze Batarang	XPN4NG
Extra Hearts	ML3KHP
Fast Build	EVG26J
Immune to Freeze	JXUDY6
Invincibility	WYD5CP
Minikit Detector	ZXGH9J
More Batarang Targets	XWP645
Piece Detector	KHJ554
Power Brick Detector	MMN786
Regenerate Hearts	HJH7HJ
Score x2	N4NR3E
Score x4	CX9MAT
Score x6	MLVNF2
Score x8	WCCDB9
Score x10	18HW07

LEGO INDIANA JONES: THE ORIGINAL ADVENTURES

CHARACTERS

Approach the blackboard in the Classroom and enter the following codes.

CHARACTER	CODE
Bandit	12N68W
Bandit Swordsman	1MK4RT
Barranca	04EM94
Bazooka Trooper (Crusade)	MK83R7
Bazooka Trooper (Raiders)	S93Y5R
Belloq	CHN3YU
Belloq (Jungle)	TDR197
Belloq (Robes)	VEO29L
British Commander	B73EUA
British Officer	VJ5TI9
British Soldier	DJ5I2W
Captain Katanga	VJ3TT3
Chatter Lal	ENW936
Chatter Lal (Thuggee)	CNH4RY
Chen	3NK48T
Colonel Dietrich	2K9RKS
Colonel Vogel	8EAL4H
Dancing Girl	C7EJ21
Donovan	3NFTU8
Elsa (Desert)	JSNRT9
Elsa (Officer)	VMJ5US
Enemy Boxer	8246RB
Enemy Butler	VJ48W3
Enemy Guard	VJ7R51
Enemy Guard (Mountains)	YR47WM
Enemy Officer	572E61
Enemy Officer (Desert	2MK45O
Enemy Pilot	B84ELP
Enemy Radio Operator	1MF94R
Enemy Soldier (Desert)	4NSU7Q
Fedora	V75YSP
First Mate	0GIN24
Grail Knight	NE6THI
Hovitos Tribesman	H0V1SS
Indiana Jones (Desert Disguise)	4J8S4M
Indiana Jones (Officer)	VJ85OS
Jungle Guide	24PF34
Kao Kan	WMO46L
Kazim	NRH23J
Kazim (Desert)	3M29TJ
Lao Che	2NK479
Maharajah	NFK5N2
Major Toht	13NS01
Masked Bandit	N48SF0
Mola Ram	FJUR31
Monkey Man	3RF6YJ
Pankot Assassin	2NKT72
Pankot Guard	VN28RH
Sherpa Brawler	VJ37WJ
Sherpa Gunner	ND762W
Slave Child	0E3ENW
Thuggee	VM683E
Thuggee Acolyte	T2R3F9
Thuggee Slave Driver	VBS7GW
Village Dignitary	KD48TN
Village Elder	4682E1

CHARACTER	CODE
Willie (Dinner Suit)	VK93R7
Willie (Pajamas)	MEN4IP
Wu Han	3NSLT8

EXTRAS

Approach the blackboard in the Classroom and enter the following codes. Some cheats need to be enabled by selecting Extras from the pause menu.

CHEAT	CODE
Artifact Detector	VIKED7
Beep Beep	VNF59Q
Character Treasure	VIES2R
Disarm Enemies	VKRNS9
Disguises	4ID1N6
Fast Build	V83SLO
Fast Dig	378RS6
Fast Fix	FJ59WS
Fertilizer	B1GW1F
Ice Rink	33GM7J
Parcel Detector	VUT673
Poo Treasure	WWQ1SA
Regenerate Hearts	MDLP69
Secret Characters	3X44AA
Silhouettes	3HE85H
Super Scream	VN3R7S
Super Slap	0P1TA5
Treasure Magnet	H86LA2
Treasure x10	VI3PS8
Treasure x2	VM4TS9
Treasure x4	VLWEN3
Treasure x6	V84RYS
Treasure x8	A72E1M

LEGO STAR WARS II: THE ORIGINAL TRILOGY

BEACH TROOPER

At Mos Eisley Canteena, select Enter Code and enter UCK868. You still need to select Characters and purchase this character for 20,000 studs.

BEN KENOBI (GHOST)

At Mos Eisley Canteena, select Enter Code and enter BEN917. You still need to select Characters and purchase this character for 1,100,000 studs.

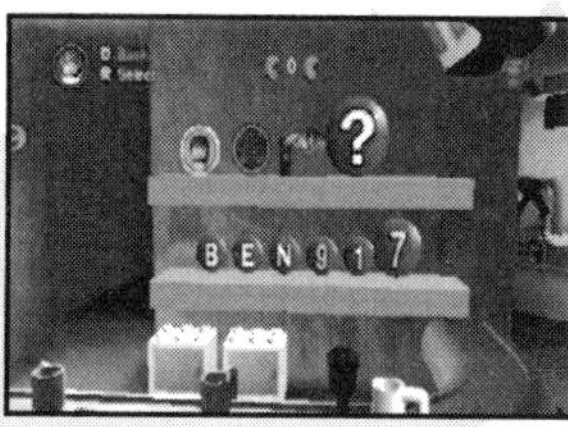

BESPIN GUARD

At Mos Eisley Canteena, select Enter Code and enter VHY832. You still need to select Characters and purchase this character for 15,000 studs.

BIB FORTUNA

At Mos Eisley Canteena, select Enter Code and enter WTY721. You still need to select Characters and purchase this character for 16,000 studs.

BOBA FETT

At Mos Eisley Canteena, select Enter Code and enter HLP221. You still need to select Characters and purchase this character for 175,000 studs.

DEATH STAR TROOPER

At Mos Eisley Canteena, select Enter Code and enter BNC332. You still need to select Characters and purchase this character for 19,000 studs.

EWOK

At Mos Eisley Canteena, select Enter Code and enter TTT289. You still need to select Characters and purchase this character for 34,000 studs.

GAMORREAN GUARD

At Mos Eisley Canteena, select Enter Code and enter YZF999. You still need to select Characters and purchase this character for 40,000 studs.

GONK DROID

At Mos Eisley Canteena, select Enter Code and enter NFX582. You still need to select Characters and purchase this character for 1,550 studs.

GRAND MOFF TARKIN

At Mos Eisley Canteena, select Enter Code and enter SMG219. You still need to select Characters and purchase this character for 38,000 studs.

GREEDO

At Mos Eisley Canteena, select Enter Code and enter NAH118. You still need to select Characters and purchase this character for 60,000 studs.

HAN SOLO (HOOD)

At Mos Eisley Canteena, select Enter Code and enter YWM840. You still need to select Characters and purchase this character for 20,000 studs.

IG-88

At Mos Eisley Canteena, select Enter Code and enter NXL973. You still need to select Characters and purchase this character for 30,000 studs.

IMPERIAL GUARD

At Mos Eisley Canteena, select Enter Code and enter MMM111. You still need to select Characters and purchase this character for 45,000 studs.

IMPERIAL OFFICER

At Mos Eisley Canteena, select Enter Code and enter BBV889. You still need to select Characters and purchase this character for 28,000 studs.

IMPERIAL SHUTTLE PILOT

At Mos Eisley Canteena, select Enter Code and enter VAP664. You still need to select Characters and purchase this character for 29,000 studs.

IMPERIAL SPY

At Mos Eisley Canteena, select Enter Code and enter CVT125. You still need to select Characters and purchase this character for 13,500 studs.

JAWA

At Mos Eisley Canteena, select Enter Code and enter JAW499. You still need to select Characters and purchase this character for 24,000 studs.

LOBOT

At Mos Eisley Canteena, select Enter Code and enter UUB319. You still need to select Characters and purchase this character for 11,000 studs.

PALACE GUARD

At Mos Eisley Canteena, select Enter Code and enter SGE549. You still need to select Characters and purchase this character for 14,000 studs.

REBEL PILOT

At Mos Eisley Canteena, select Enter Code and enter CYG336. You still need to select Characters and purchase this character for 15,000 studs.

REBEL TROOPER (HOTH)

At Mos Eisley Canteena, select Enter Code and enter EKU849. You still need to select Characters and purchase this character for 16,000 studs.

SANDTROOPER

At Mos Eisley Canteena, select Enter Code and enter YDV451. You still need to select Characters and purchase this character for 14,000 studs.

SKIFF GUARD

At Mos Eisley Canteena, select Enter Code and enter GBU888. You still need to select Characters and purchase this character for 12,000 studs.

SNOWTROOPER

At Mos Eisley Canteena, select Enter Code and enter NYU989. You still need to select Characters and purchase this character for 16,000 studs.

STORMTROOPER

At Mos Eisley Canteena, select Enter Code and enter PTR345. You still need to select Characters and purchase this character for 10,000 studs.

THE EMPEROR

At Mos Eisley Canteena, select Enter Code and enter HHY382. You still need to select Characters and purchase this character for 275,000 studs.

TIE FIGHTER

At Mos Eisley Canteena, select Enter Code and enter HDY739. You still need to select Characters and purchase this item for 60,000 studs.

TIE FIGHTER PILOT

At Mos Eisley Canteena, select Enter Code and enter NNZ316. You still need to select Characters and purchase this character for 21,000 studs.

TIE INTERCEPTOR

At Mos Eisley Canteena, select Enter Code and enter QYA828. You still need to select Characters and purchase this item for 40,000 studs.

TUSKEN RAIDER

At Mos Eisley Canteena, select Enter Code and enter PEJ821. You still need to select Characters and purchase this character for 23,000 studs.

UGNAUGHT

At Mos Eisley Canteena, select Enter Code and enter UGN694. You still need to select Characters and purchase this character for 36,000 studs.

MAJOR LEAGUE BASEBALL 2K7

MICKEY MANTLE ON THE FREE AGENTS LIST

Select Enter Cheat Code from the My 2K7 menu and enter themick.

MICKEY PINCH HITS

Select Enter Cheat Code from the My 2K7 menu and enter phmantle.

UNLOCK EVERYTHING

Select Enter Cheat Code from the My 2K7 menu and enter Derek Jeter. This does not unlock the Topps cheats.

ALL CHEATS

Select Enter Cheat Code from the My 2K7 menu and enter Black Sox.

ALL EXTRAS

Select Enter Cheat Code from the My 2K7 menu and enter Game On.

MIGHTY MICK CHEAT

Select Enter Cheat Code from the My 2K7 menu and enter mightymick.

TRIPLE CROWN CHEAT

Select Enter Cheat Code from the My 2K7 menu and enter triplecrown.

BIG BLAST CHEAT

Select Enter Cheat Code from the My 2K7 menu and enter m4murder.

MANHUNT 2

EXTRA LEVEL AS LEO

Defeat the game.

RELIVE SCENE

Defeat the game. This allows you to replay any level.

MARVEL TRADING CARD GAME

COMPLETE CARD LIBRARY

At the Deck menu, select new deck and name it BLVRTRSK.

ALL PUZZLES

At the Deck menu, select new deck and name it WHOWANTSPIE.

MARVEL ULTIMATE ALLIANCE

UNLOCK ALL SKINS

At the Team menu, press Up, Down, Left, Right, Left, Right, Start.

UNLOCK ALL HERO POWERS

At the Team menu, press Left, Right, Up, Down, Up, Down, Start.

ALL HEROES TO LEVEL 99

At the Team menu, press Up, Left, Up, Left, Down, Right, Down, Right, Start.

UNLOCK ALL HEROES

At the Team menu, press Up, Up, Down, Down, Left, Left, Left, Start Unlock Daredevil

At the Team Menu, press Left, Left, Right, Right, Up, Down, Up, Down, Start.

UNLOCK SILVER SURFER

At the Team menu, press Down, Left, Left, Up, Right, Up, Down, Left, Start.

GOD MODE

During gameplay, press Up, Down, Up, Down, Up, Left, Down, Right, Start.

TOUCH OF DEATH

During gameplay, press Left, Right, Down, Down, Right, Left, Start.

SUPER SPEED

During gameplay, press Up, Left, Up, Right, Down, Right, Start.

FILL MOMENTUM

During gameplay, press Left, Right, Right, Left, Up, Down, Down, Up, Start.

UNLOCK ALL COMICS

At the Review menu, press Left, Right, Right, Left, Up, Up, Right, Start.

UNLOCK ALL CONCEPT ART

At the Review menu, press Down, Down, Down, Right, Right, Left, Down, Start.

MEDIEVIL: RESURRECTION

INVINCIBILITY & ALL WEAPONS

Pause the game, hold R and press Down, Up, ■, ▲, ▲, ●, Down, Up, ■, ▲. Pause the game to access the Cheat menu.

CHEAT MENU

Pause the game, hold R and press Down, Up, ■, ▲, ▲, ●, Down, Up, ■+▲. This gives you invincibility and all weapons.

ALL ARTIFACTS AND KEYS

Pause the game and press L + R, ✕, ✕, ●, ■, ▲, ✕.

METAL GEAR ACID 2

CARD NO. 046—STRAND

Enter nojiri as a password.

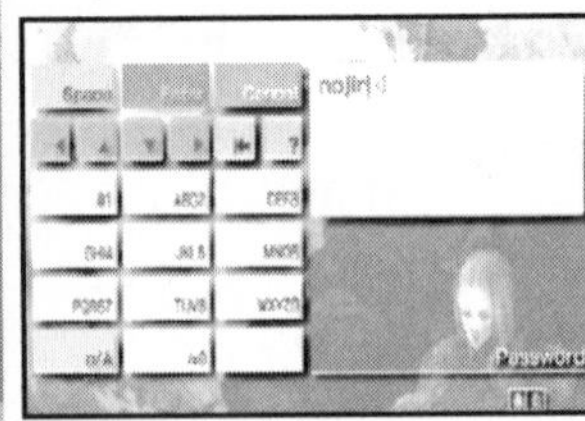

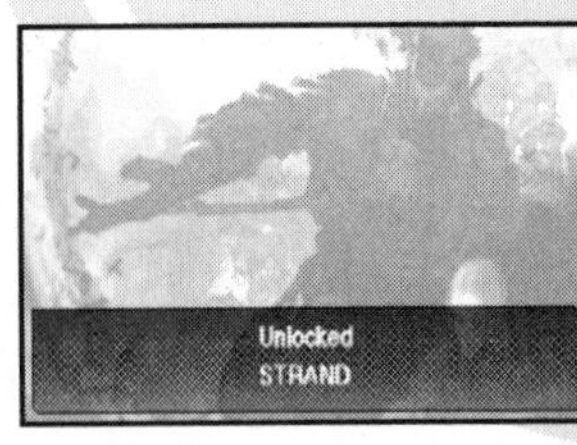

CARD NO. 099—GIJIN-SAN
Enter shinta as a password.

CARD NO. 119—REACTION BLOCK
Enter konami as a password.

CARD NO. 161—VIPER
Enter viper as a password.

CARD NO. 166—MIKA SLAYTON
Enter mika as a password.

CARD NO. 170—KAREN HOJO
Enter karen as a password.

CARD NO. 172—JEHUTY
Enter jehuty as a password.

CARD NO. 187—XM8
Enter xmeight as a password.

CARD NO. 188—MR. SIGINT
Enter signt as a password.

CARD NO. 197—SEA HARRIER
Enter shrrr as a password.

CARD NO. 203—DECOY OCTOPUS
Enter dcy as a password.

CARD NO. 212—ROGER MCCOY
Enter mccy as a password.

CARD NO. 281—REIKO HINOMOTO
Enter hnmt as a password.

CARD NO. 285—AYUMI KINOSHITA
Enter aym as a password.

CARD NO. 286—MEGURU ISHII
Enter mgr as a password.

CARD NO. 287—NATSUME SANO
Enter ntm as a password.

CARD NO. 288—MGS4
Enter nextgen as a password.

CARD NO. 289—EMMA'S PARROT
Enter ginormousj as a password.

CARD NO. 290—BANANA SKIN
Enter ronaldsiu as a password.

CARD NO. 292—POSSESSED ARM
Enter thespaniard as a password.

CARD NO. 293—SOLID EYE
Enter tobidacid as a password.

CARD NO. 294—SOLID SNAKE (MGS4)
Enter snake as a password.

CARD NO. 295—OTACON (MGS4)
Enter otacon as a password.

CARD NO. 296—GEKKO
Enter gekko as a password.

CARD NO. 297—METAL GEAR MK. II (MGS4)
Enter mk2 as a password.

CARD NO. 298—NO SMOKING
Enter smoking as a password.

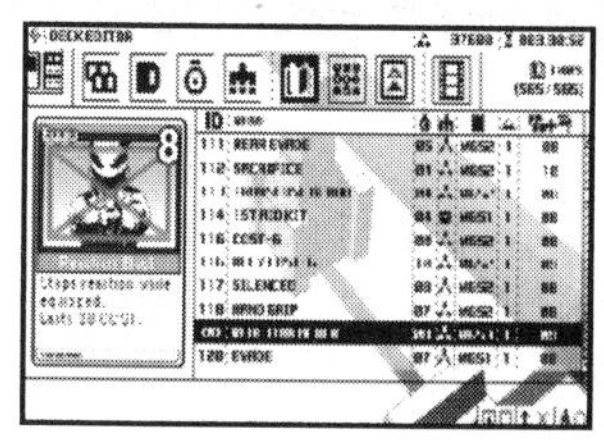

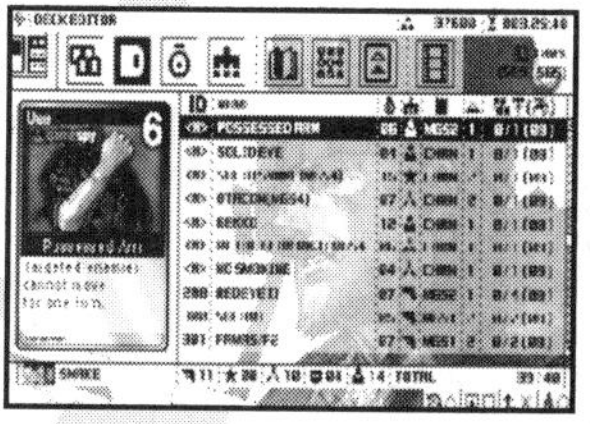

METAL GEAR SOLID: PORTABLE OPS

CUNNINGHAM
Enter JUNKER as a password.

ELISA
Enter THE-L as a password.

EVA
Enter E.APPLE as a password.

GA KO
Enter !TRAUMER as a password.

GENE
Enter ERBE as a password.

NULL
Enter Hunter-n as a password.

OCELOT
Enter R.R.R. as a password.

PARAMEDIC
Enter PM-EMS as a password.

PYTHON
Enter LQ.N2 as a password.

RAIKOV
Enter IVN =RV as a password.

SIGINT
Enter DARPA-1 as a password.

SOKOLOV
Enter SATURNV as a password.

TELIKO
Enter T.F-ACID as a password.

URSULA
Enter PK +ESP as a password.

VENUS
Enter MGA2VE as a password.

ZERO
Enter 1+2-3 as a password.

METAL GEAR SOLID: PORTABLE OPS PLUS

SOLDIER PASSWORDS
Enter the following as a password.

SOLDIER	PASSWORD
Alabama	BB6K768KM9
Alaska	XL5SW5NH9S
Arizona	ZHEFPVV947
Arkansas	VNRE7JNQ8WE
Black Genome	WYNGG3JBP3YS
Blue Genome	9GNPHGFFLH
California	6MSJQYWNCJ8
Colorado	W6TAH498DJ
Connecticut	2N2AB3JV2WA
Delaware	AJRL6E7TT9
Female Scientist 1	3W8WVRGB2LNN
Female Scientist 2	FUC72C463KZ
Female Scientist 3	UCAWYTMXB5V
Female Soldier 1	UZZQYRPXM86

SOLDIER	PASSWORD
Female Soldier 2	QRQQ7GWKHJ
Female Soldier 3	MVNDAZAP8DWE
Florida	A44STZ3BHY5
Fox Soldier 1	FMXT79TPV4U8
Fox Soldier 2	HGMK3WCYURM
Fox Soldier 3	6ZY5NYW4TGK
Georgia	VD5H53JJCRH
Green Genome	TGQ6F5TUHD
GRU Soldier	9V8S7DVYFTR
Gurlukovich's Soldier	6VWM6A22FSS8
Hawaii	TW7ZMZHCBL
Hideochan Soldier	RU8XRCLPUUT
High Official	ADPS2SE5UC8
High Rank Officer 1	DVB2UDTQ5Z
High Rank Officer 2	84ZEC4X5PJ6
High Ranking Officer 3	DTAZ3QRQQDU
High-Tech Soldier	M4MSJ6R87XPP
Idaho	XAFGETZGXHGA
Illinois	QYUVCNDFUPZJ
Indiana	L68JVXVBL8RN
Iowa	B8MW36ZU56S
Kansas	TYPEVDEE24YT
Kentucky	LCD7WGS5X5
KGB Soldier	MNBVYRZP4QH
Louisiana	EHR5VVMHUSG
Maine	T5GYHQABGAC3
Maintenance Crew Member 1	T8EBSRK6F38
Maintenance Crew Member 2	YHQU74J6LLQ
Maintenance Crew Member 3	MFAJMUXZHHKJ
Male Scientist 1	ZFKHJKDEA2
Male Scientist 2	QQ4N3TPCL8PF
Male Scientist 3	CXFCXF4FP9R6
Maryland	L2W9G5N76MH7
Massachusetts	ZLU2S3ULDEVF
Michigan	HGDRBUB5P3SA
Minnesota	EEBBM888ZRA
Mississippi	TBF7H9G6TJH7
Missouri	WJND6M9N738
Montana	9FYUFV29B2Y
Nebraska	MCNB5S5K47H
Nevada	Z9D4UGG8T4U6
New Hampshire	7NQYDQ9Y4KMP
New Jersey	LGHTBU9ZTGR
New Mexico	RGJCMHNLSX
New York	6PV39FKG6X
Normal Soldier Long Sleeve	QK3CMV373Y
Normal Soldier Long Sleeve Magazine Vest	D8RV32E9774
Normal Soldier Short Sleeve	N524ZHU9N4Z
Normal Soldier Short Sleeve Magazine Vest	6WXZA7PTT9Z
North Carolina	JGVT2XV47UZ
North Dakota	T5LSAVMPWZCY
Ocelot Female A	9FS7QYSHZ56N
Ocelot Female B	F94XDZSQSGJ8
Ocelot Female C	CRF8PZGXR28
Ocelot Unit	GE6MU3DXL3X
Ohio	AUWGAXWCA3D
Oklahoma	ZQT75NUJH8A3
Oregon	HKSD3PJ5E5
Pennsylvania	PL8GVVUM4HD
Pink Genome	7WRG3N2MRY2
Red Genome	9CM4SY23C7X8

SOLDIER	PASSWORD
Rhode Island	MMYC99T3QG
Seal	X56YCKZP2V
South Carolina	ZR4465MD8LK
South Dakota	RY3NUDDPMU3
Tengu Soldier	PHHB4TY4J2D
Tennessee	TD2732GCX43U
Texas	QM84UPP6F3
Tsuhan soldier	A9KK7WYWVCV
USSR Female Soldier A	2VXUZQVH9R
USSR Female Soldier B	HPMRFSBXDJ3Y
USSR Female Soldier C	QXQVW9R3PZ
USSR Female Soldier D	GMC3M3LTPVW7
USSR Female Soldier E	5MXVX6UFPMZ5
USSR Female Soldier F	76AWS7WDAV
Utah	V7VRAYZ78GW
Vermont	L7T66LFZ63C8
Virginia	DRTCS77F5N
Washington	G3S4N42WWKTV
Washington DC	Y5YCFYHVZZW
West Virginia	72M8XR99B6
White Genome	QJ4ZTQSLUT8
Wisconsin	K9BUN2BGLMT3
Wyoming	C3THQ749RA
Yellow Genome	CE5HHYGTSSB

MLB 07: THE SHOW

SILVER ERA AND GOLD ERA TEAMS
At the Main menu, press Left, Up, Right, Down, Down, Left, Up, Down.

MAX BREAK PITCHES
Pause the game and press Right, Up, Right, Down, Up, Left, Left, Down.

MAX SPEED PITCHES
Pause the game and press Up, Left, Down, Up, Left, Right, Left, Down.

MLB 08: THE SHOW

CLASSIC FREE AGENTS AT THE PLAYER MOVEMENT MENU
At the Main menu, press Left, Right, Up, Left, Right, Up, Right, Down.

SILVER ERA AND GOLDEN ERA TEAMS
At the Main menu, press Right, Up, Right, Down, Down, Left, Up, Down.

BIG BALL
Pause the game and press Right, Down, Up, Left, Right, Left, Down, Up.

BIG HEAD MODE
Pause the game and press Right, Left, Down, Up, Left, Up, Down, Left.

SMALL HEAD MODE
Pause the game and press Left, Right, Down, Up, Right, Left, Down, Left.

MTX MOTOTRAX

ALL TRACKS
Enter BA7H as a password.

ALL BONUSES
Enter 2468GOA7 as a password.

SUPER SPEED
Enter JIH345 as a password.

MAXIMUM AIR
Enter BFB0020 as a password.

BUTTERFINGER GEAR
Enter B77393 as a password.

LEFT FIELD GEAR
Enter 12345 as a password.

SOBE GEAR
Enter 50BE as a password.

MVP BASEBALL

ALL REWARDS

Select My MVP and create a player with the name Dan Carter.

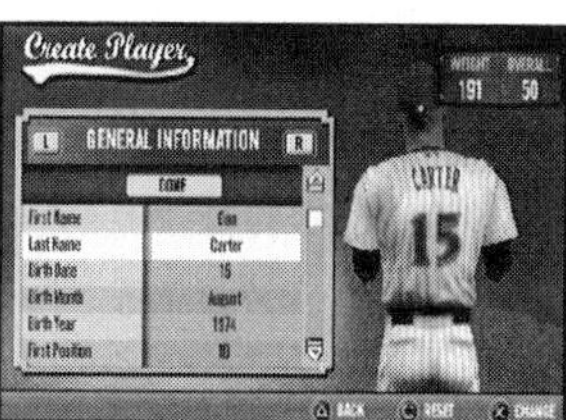

MX VS. ATV UNLEASHED: ON THE EDGE

UNLOCK EVERYTHING

Select Cheat Codes from the Options screen and enter TOOLAZY.

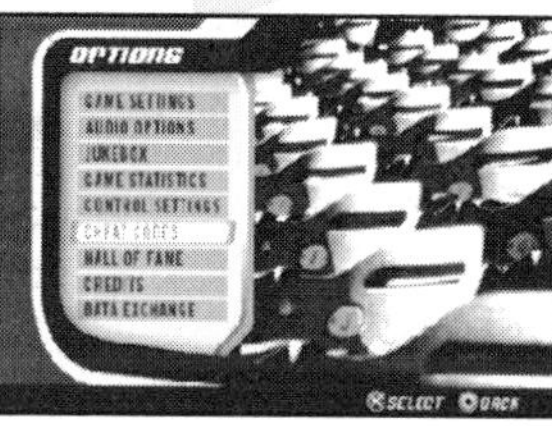

1,000,000 POINTS

Select Cheat Codes from the Options screen and enter BROKEASAJOKE.

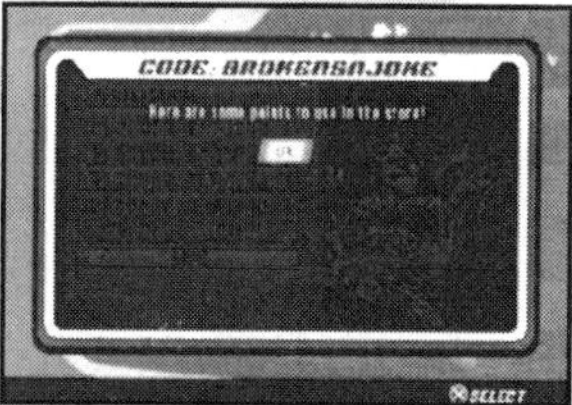

PRO PHYSICS

Select Cheat Codes from the Options screen and enter IAMTOOGOOD.

ALL GEAR

Select Cheat Codes from the Options screen and enter WARDROBE.

ALL BIKES

Select Cheat Codes from the Options screen and enter BRAPP.

50CC BIKE CLASS

Select Cheat Codes from the Options screen and enter MINIMOTO.

500CC BIKE CLASS

Select Cheat Codes from the Options screen and enter BIGBORE.

ALL ATVS

Select Cheat Codes from the Options screen and enter COUCHES.

ALL MACHINES

Select Cheat Codes from the Options screen and enter LEADFOOT.

ALL FREESTYLE TRACKS

Select Cheat Codes from the Options screen and enter HUCKIT.

ALL NATIONAL TRACKS

Select Cheat Codes from the Options screen and enter GOOUTSIDE.

ALL OPEN CLASS TRACKS

Select Cheat Codes from the Options screen and enter NOTMOTO.

ALL SUPERCROSS TRACKS

Select Cheat Codes from the Options screen and enter GOINSIDE.

ALL TRACKS

Select Cheat Codes from the Options screen and enter PITPASS.

N+

25 EXTRA LEVELS

At the Main menu, hold L + R and press ⊗, ●, ⊗, ●, ⊗, ⊗, ●.

NASCAR

ALL CHASE PLATES

Go to Fight to the Top mode. Next, edit the driver's first and last name so that it says ItsAll ForMe. Note that the code is case-sensitive.

$10,000,000

In Fight to the Top mode, enter your driver's name as GiveMe More.

10,000,000 FANS

In Fight to the Top mode, enter your driver's name as AllBow ToMe.

ALL CHASE PLATES

In Fight to the Top mode, enter your driver's name as ItsAll ForMe.

OLD SPICE TRACKS AND CARS

In Fight to the Top mode, enter your driver's name as KeepCool SmellGreat.

NBA BALLERS: REBOUND

VERSUS SCREEN CHEATS

You must enter the following codes at the Vs screen. The ■ button corresponds to the first number in the code, the ▲ is the second number, and the ● button corresponds to the last number. Press the D-pad in any direction to enter the code. The name of the code will appear when entered correctly. Some of the codes will give you the wrong code name when entered.

EFFECT	CODE
Big Head	1 3 4
Pygmy	4 2 5
Alternate Gear	1 2 3
Show Shot Percentage	0 1 2
Expanded Move Set	5 1 2
Super Push	3 1 5
Super Block Ability	1 2 4
Great Handles	3 3 2
Unlimited Juice	7 6 3
Super Steals	2 1 5

EFFECT	CODE
Perfect Free Throws	3 2 7
Better Free Throws	3 1 7
Speedy Players	2 1 3
Alley-Oop Ability	7 2 5
Back-In Ability	1 2 2
Hotspot Ability	6 2 7
Pass 2 Friend Ability	5 3 6
Put Back Ability	3 1 3
Stunt Ability	3 7 4
2x Juice Replenish	4 3 1
Legal Goal Tending	7 5 6
Play As Afro Man	5 1 7
Play As Agent	5 5 7
Play As Business-A	5 3 7
Play As Business-B	5 2 7
Play As Coach	5 6 7
Play As Secretary	5 4 7
Super Back-Ins	2 3 5
Half House	3 6 7
Random Moves	3 0 0
Tournament Mode	0 1 1

PHRASE-OLOGY CODES

Select Phrase-ology from the Inside Stuff option and enter the following to unlock that bonus.

BONUS	PHRASE
All Players and Cinemas	NBA BALLERS TRUE PLAYA
Special Shoe #2	COLD STREAK
Special Shoe #3	LOST YA SHOES

CRIBS

Select Phrase-ology from the Inside Stuff option and enter the following to unlock player cribs.

CRIB	PHRASE
Allen Iverson's Recording Studio	THE ANSWER
Karl Malone's Devonshire Estate	ICE HOUSE
Kobe Bryant's Italian Estate	EURO CRIB
Ben Gordon's Yacht	NICE YACHT
Yao Ming's Childhood Grade School	PREP SCHOOL

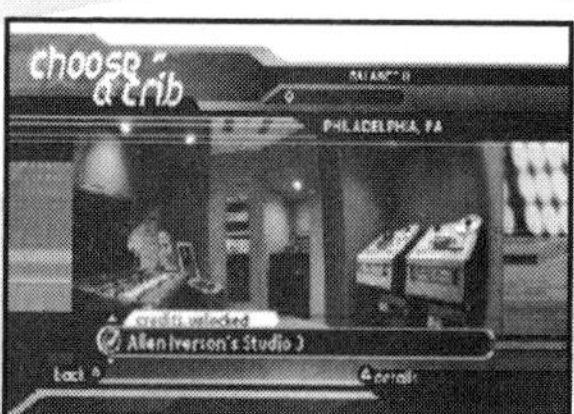

NEOPETS PETPET ADVENTURE: THE WAND OF WISHING

START GAME WITH 5 CHOCOLATE TREATS

Enter treat4u as your Petpet's name. You can then rename your character. The chocolate treats are shaped according to the character you chose.

PAC-MAN WORLD 3

ALL LEVELS AND MAZES

At the Main menu, press Left, Right, Left, Right, ○, Up.

PINBALL HALL OF FAME

CUSTOM BALLS OPTION

Enter CKF as a code.

TILT OPTION

Enter BZZ as a code.

PAYOUT MODE

Enter WGR as a code.

ACES HIGH IN FREEPLAY

Enter UNO as a code.

CENTRAL PARK IN FREEPLAY

Enter NYC as a code.

LOVE MACHINE IN FREEPLAY

Enter HOT as a code.

PLAYBOY TABLE IN FREEPLAY

Enter HEF as a code.

STRIKES 'N SPARES IN FREEPLAY

Enter PBA as a code.

TEE'D OFF IN FREEPLAY

Enter PGA as a code.

XOLTEN IN FREEPLAY

Enter BIG as a code.

PRINNY: CAN I REALLY BE THE HERO?

START A NEW GAME WITH THE ALTERNATE STORYLINE

At the Main menu, highlight New Game and press △, □, ○, △, □, ○, ✕.

POCKET POOL

ALL PICTURES AND VIDEOS

At the Title screen, press L, R, L, L, R, R, L (x3), R (x3), L (x4), R (x4).

SEGA GENESIS COLLECTION

Before using the following cheats, select the ABC Control option. This sets the controller to the following: □ is A, ✕ is B, ○ is C.

ALTERED BEAST

OPTIONS MENU

At the Title screen, hold B and press Start.

LEVEL SELECT

After enabling the Options menu, select a level from the menu. At the Title screen, hold A and press Start.

BEAST SELECT

At the Title screen, hold A + B + C + Down/Left and then press Start

SOUND TEST

At the Title screen, hold A + C + Up/Right and press Start.

COMIX ZONE

INVINCIBILITY

At the Jukebox screen, press C on the following sounds:
3, 12, 17, 2, 2, 10, 2, 7, 7, 11

LEVEL SELECT

At the Jukebox screen, press C on the following sounds:
14, 15, 18, 5, 13, 1, 3, 18, 15, 6
Press C on the desired level.

ECCO THE DOLPHIN

INVINCIBILITY

When the level name appears, hold A + Start until the level begins.

DEBUG MENU

Pause the game with Ecco facing the screen and press Right, B, C, B, C, Down, C, Up.

INFINITE AIR

Enter LIFEFISH as a password.

PASSWORDS

LEVEL	PASSWORD
The Undercaves	WEFIDNMP
The Vents	BQDPXJDS
The Lagoon	JNSBRIKY
Ridge Water	NTSBZTKB
Open Ocean	YWGTTJNI
Ice Zone	HZIFZBMF
Hard Water	LRFJRQLI
Cold Water	UYNFRQLC
Island Zone	LYTIOQLZ
Deep Water	MNOPOQLR
The Marble	RJNTQQLZ
The Library	RTGXQQLE
Deep City	DDXPQQLJ
City of Forever	MSDBRQLA
Jurassic Beach	IYCBUNLB
Pteranodon Pond	DMXEUNLI
Origin Beach	EGRIUNLB
Trilobite Circle	IELMUNLB
Dark Water	RKEQUNLN
City of Forever 2	HPQIGPLA
The Tube	JUMFKMLB
The Machine	GXUBKMLF
The Last Fight	TSONLMLU

FLICKY

ROUND SELECT

Begin a new game. Before the first round appears, hold A + C + Up + Start. Press Up or Down to select a Round.

GAIN GROUND

LEVEL SELECT

At the Options screen, press A, C, B, C.

GOLDEN AXE

LEVEL SELECT

Select Arcade Mode. At the character select, hold Down/Left + B and press Start. Press Up or Down to select a level.

RISTAR

Select Passwords from the Options menu and enter the following:

LEVEL SELECT

ILOVEU

BOSS RUSH MODE

MUSEUM

TIME ATTACK MODE

DOFEEL

TOUGHER DIFFICULTY

SUPER

ONCHI MUSIC

MAGURO. Activate this from the Sound Test.

CLEARS PASSWORD

XXXXXX

GAME COPYRIGHT INFO

AGES

SONIC THE HEDGEHOG

LEVEL SELECT

At the title screen, press Up, Down, Left, Right. Hold A and press Start.

SONIC THE HEDGEHOG 2

LEVEL SELECT

Select Sound Test from the options. Press C on the following sounds in order: 19, 65, 09, 17. At the title screen, hold A and press Start.

VECTORMAN

DEBUG MODE

At the options screen, press A, B, B, A, Down, A, B, B, A.

REFILL LIFE

Pause the game and press A, B, Right, A, C, A , Down, A, B, Right, A.

VECTORMAN 2

LEVEL SELECT

Pause the game and press Up, Right, A, B, A, Down, Left, A, Down.

EXTRA LIFE

Pause the game and press Right, Up, B, A, Down, Up, B, Down, Up, B. Repeat for more lives.

FULL ENERGY

Pause the game and press B, A, B, A, Left, Up, Up.

NEW WEAPON

Pause the game and press C, A, Left, Left, Down, A, Down. Repeat for more weapons.

SHREK THE THIRD

10,000 BONUS COINS

Press Up, Up, Down, Up, Right, Left at the Gift Shop.

SILENT HILL: ORIGINS

CODEBREAKER SUIT

During a game, press Up, Up, Down, Down, Left, Right, Left, Right, ⊗, ●. You must first finish the game to get this suit.

THE SIMPSONS GAME

UNLIMITED POWER FOR ALL CHARACTERS

At the Extras menu, press ▲, Left, Right, ▲, ■, L.

ALL MOVIES

At the Extras menu, press ■, Left, ■, Right, ▲, R.

ALL CLICHÉS

At the Extras menu, press Left, ■, Right, ▲, Right, L.

THE SIMS 2

PERK CHEAT

At the Buy Perks screen, hold L + R + ■. Buy the Cheat Perk to get some money, skills, and more.

THE SIMS 2: CASTAWAY

CHEAT GNOME

During a game, press L, R, Up, ⊗, R. You can now use this Gnome to get the following during Live mode:

ALL PLANS

During a game, press ⊗, R, ⊗, R, ⊗.

ALL CRAFT AND RESOURCES

During a game, press ■, ▲, R, Down, Down, Up.

MAX FOOD AND RESOURCES

During a game, press ■(x4), L.

THE SIMS 2: PETS

CHEAT GNOME

During a game, press L, L, R, ⊗, ⊗, Up. Now you can enter the following cheats:

ADVANCE TIME 6 HOURS

During a game, press Up, L, Down, R, R.

GIVE SIM PET POINTS

During a game, press △, ○, ⊗, □, L, R.

$10,000

During a game, press △, Up, Left, Down, R.

SPIDER-MAN: FRIEND OR FOE

NEW GREEN GOBLIN AS A SIDEKICK

While standing in the Helicarrier between levels, press Left, Down, Right, Right, Down, Left.

SANDMAN AS A SIDEKICK

While standing in the Helicarrier between levels, press Right, Right, Right, Up, Down, Left.

VENOM AS A SIDEKICK

While standing in the Helicarrier between levels, press Left, Left, Right, Up, Down, Down.

5000 TECH TOKENS

While standing in the Helicarrier between levels, press Up, Up, Down, Down, Left, Right.

NEW GOBLIN

At the stage complete screen, hold L + R and press ○, Down, ⊗, Right, □, Up, △, Left.

STAR WARS: THE FORCE UNLEASHED

CHEATS

Once you have accessed the Rogue Shadow, select Enter Code from the Extras menu. Now you can enter the following:

CHEAT	CODE
Invincibility	CORTOSIS
Unlimited Force	VERGENCE
1,000,000 Force Points	SPEEDER
All Force Powers	TYRANUS
Max Force Power Level	KATARN
Max Combo Level	COUNTDOOKU
Amplified Lightsaber Damage	LIGHTSABER

COSTUMES

Once you have accessed the Rogue Shadow, select Enter Code from the Extras menu. Now you can enter the following:

COSTUME	CODE
All Costumes	GRANDMOFF
501st Legion	LEGION
Aayla Secura	AAYLA
Admiral Ackbar	ITSATWAP
Anakin Skywalker	CHOSENONE
Asajj Ventress	ACOLYTE
Ceremonial Jedi Robes	DANTOOINE
Chop'aa Notimo	NOTIMO
Classic stormtrooper	TK421
Count Dooku	SERENNO
Darth Desolous	PAUAN
Darth Maul	ZABRAK
Darth Phobos	HIDDENFEAR
Darth Vader	SITHLORD
Drexl Roosh	DREXLROOSH

COSTUME	CODE
Emperor Palpatine	PALPATINE
General Rahm Kota	MANDALORE
Han Solo	NERFHERDER
Heavy trooper	SHOCKTROOP
Juno Eclipse	ECLIPSE
Kento's Robe	WOOKIEE
Kleef	KLEEF
Lando Calrissian	SCOUNDREL
Luke Skywalker	T16WOMPRAT
Luke Skywalker (Yavin)	YELLOWJCKT
Mace Windu	JEDIMASTER
Mara Jade	MARAJADE
Maris Brook	MARISBROOD
Navy commando	STORMTROOP
Obi Wan Kenobi	BENKENOBI
Proxy	HOLOGRAM
Qui Gon Jinn	MAVERICK
Shaak Ti	TOGRUTA
Shadow trooper	INTHEDARK
Sith Robes	HOLOCRON
Sith Stalker Armor	KORRIBAN
Twi'lek	SECURA

STAR WARS: LETHAL ALLIANCE

ALL LEVELS
Select Create Profile from the Profiles menu and enter HANS0L0.

ALL LEVELS AND REFILL HEALTH WHEN DEPLETED
Select Create Profile from the Profiles menu and enter JD1MSTR.

REFILL HEALTH WHEN DEPLETED
Select Create Profile from the Profiles menu and enter B0BAF3T.

SUPER MONKEY BALL ADVENTURE

ALL CARDS
At the mode select, press Square, Triangle, Circle, Square, Triangle, Circle, Square, Triangle, Circle, Square, Triangle, Circle.

THRILLVILLE: OFF THE RAILS

$50,000
During a game, press Square, Circle, Triangle, Square, Circle, Triangle, X. Repeat this code as much as desired.

ALL PARKS
During a game, press Square, Circle, Triangle, Square, Circle, Triangle, Square.

ALL RIDES
During a game, press Square, Circle, Triangle, Square Circle, Triangle, Triangle. Some rides still need to be researched.

COMPLETE MISSIONS
During a game, press Square, Circle, Triangle, Square, Circle, Triangle, Circle. Then, at the Missions menu, highlight a mission and press Square to complete that mission. Some missions have Bronze, Silver, and Gold objectives. For these missions the first press of Square earns the Bronze, the second earns the Silver, and the third earns the Gold.

TIGER WOODS PGA TOUR 09

UNLOCK PGA TOUR EVENTS
Enter BEATIT as a password.

$1,000,000
Enter JACKPOT as a password.

UNLOCK ALL CLOTHING AND EQUIPMENT
Enter SHOP2DROP as a password.

MAX SKILL POINTS AND ALL CLOTHING AND EQUIPMENT
Enter IAMRUBBISH as a password.

UNLOCK ALL COVER STORIES
Enter HEADLINER as a password.

TOMB RAIDER: LEGEND

You must unlock the following cheats before you can use them.

BULLETPROOF
During a game, hold L and press ✕, R, △, R, □, R.

DRAW ENEMY HEALTH
During a game, hold L and press □, ○, ✕, R, R, △.

INFINITE ASSUALT RIFLE AMMO
During a game, hold L and press ✕, ○, ✕, R, □, △.

INFINITE GRENADE LAUNCHER
During a game, hold L and press R, △, R, ○, R, □.

INFINITE SHOTGUN AMMO
During a game, hold L and press R, ○, □, R, □, ✕.

INFINITE SMG AMMO
During a game, hold L and press ○, △, R, R, ✕, ○.

1-SHOT KILL
During a game, hold L and press △, ✕, △, □, R, ○.

TEXTURELESS MODE
Hold L and press R, ✕, ○, ✕, △, R.

WIELD EXCALIBUR
During a game, hold L and press △, ✕, ○, R, △, R.

TWISTED METAL: HEAD-ON

Note that the following codes will not work for Multiplayer or Online modes.

HEALTH RECHARGED
Hold L + R and press △, ✕, □, ○.

INFINITE AMMO
Hold L + R and press △, △, Down, Down, Left.

INVULNERABLE
Hold L + R and press Right, Left, Down, Up.

INFINITE WEAPONS
Hold L + R and press △, △, Down, Down.

KILLER WEAPONS
Hold L + R and press ✕, ✕, Up, Up.

MEGA GUNS
Hold L + R and press ✕, △, ✕, △

VIRTUA TENNIS 3

ALL COURTS
At the Game Mode screen, press Up, Up, Down, Down, Left, Right, Left, Right.

ALL GEAR
At the Game Mode screen, press Left, Right, ○, Left, Right, ○, Up, Down.

KING & DUKE
At the Game Mode screen, press Up, Up, Down, Down, Left, Right, L, R.

WALL-E

KILL ALL
Select Cheats and then Secret Codes. Enter BOTOFWAR.

UNDETECTED BY ENEMIES
Select Cheats and then Secret Codes. Enter STEALTHARMOR.

LASERS CHANGE COLORS
Select Cheats and then Secret Codes. Enter RAINBOWLAZER.

CUBES ARE EXPLOSIVE
Select Cheats and then Secret Codes. Enter EXPLOSIVEWORLD.

LIGHTEN DARK AREAS
Select Cheats and then Secret Codes. Enter GLOWINTHEDARK.

GOGGLES
Select Cheats and then Secret Codes. Enter BOTOFMYSTERY.

GOLD TRACKS
Select Cheats and then Secret Codes. Enter GOLDENTRACKS.

THE WARRIORS

100% COMPLETION IN STORY MODE

During a game, press L, Select, □, Down, L, Right.

COMPLETE CURRENT MISSION

During a game, press Down, □, ✕, Select, R, Left.

UNLIMITED HEALTH

During a game, press Up, △, R, Select, ✕, L.

UPGRADES STAMINA

During a game, press ✕, L, Down, □, Up, ✕.

UNLIMITED RAGE

During a game, press □, ○, △, Select, ✕, Left.

BRASS KNUCKLES

During a game, press ○, ○, ○, L, Select, △.

HAND CUFFS

During a game, press ✕, Up, Select, L, L.

HAND CUFF KEYS

During a game, press Left, ✕, ✕, R, L, Down.

KNIFE

During a game, press Down, Down, Select, Up, Up, L.

MACHETE

During a game, press L, ✕, R(x2), Select, R.

UNBREAKABLE BAT

During a game, press L, L, ○, Up, ○, Select.

ALL DEALERS

During a game, press right, R, ○, ✕, Select, □.

UPGRADE FLASH CAPACITY

During a game, press L, ✕, R, L, L, ○.

99 CREDITS IN ARMIES OF THE NIGHT

During a game of Armie of the Night, press Up, Up, Down, Down, Left, Right.

WRC: FIA WORLD RALLY CHAMPIONSHIP

UNLOCK EVERYTHING

Create a new profile with the name PADLOCK.

EXTRA AVATARS

Create a new profile with the name UGLYMUGS.

GHOST CAR

Create a new profile with the name SPOOKY.

SUPERCHARGER

Create a new profile with the name MAXPOWER.

TIME TRIAL GHOST CARS

Create a new profile with the name AITRIAL.

BIRD CAMERA

Create a new profile with the name dovecam.

REVERSES CONTROLS

Create a new profile with the name REVERSE.

X-MEN LEGENDS II: RISE OF APOCALYPSE

ALL CHARACTERS
At the Team Management screen, press Right, Left, Left, Right, Up, Up, Up, Start.

LEVEL 99 CHARACTERS
At the Team Management screen, press Up, Down, Up, Down, Left, Up, Left, Right, Start.

ALL SKILLS
At the Team Management screen, press Left, Right, Left, Right, Down, Up, Start.

SUPER SPEED
Pause the game and press Up, Up, Up, Down, Up, Down, Start.

UNLIMITED XTREME POWER
Pause the game and press Left, Down, Right, Down, Up, Up, Down, Up Start.

100,000 TECHBITS
At Forge or Beast's equipment screen, press Up, Up, Up, Down, Right, Right, Start.

ALL CINEMATICS
At the Review menu, press Left, Right, Right, Left, Down, Down, Left, Start.

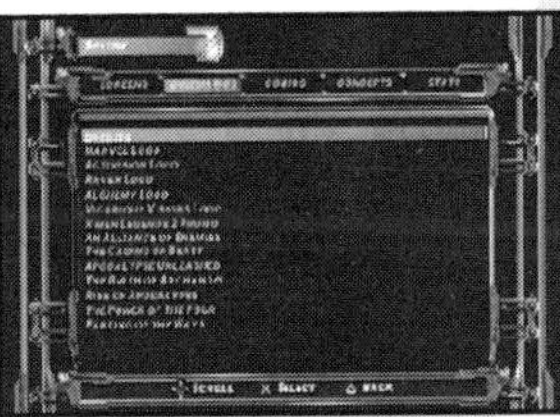

ALL COMIC BOOKS
At the Review menu, press Right, Left, Left, Right, Up, Up, Right, Start.

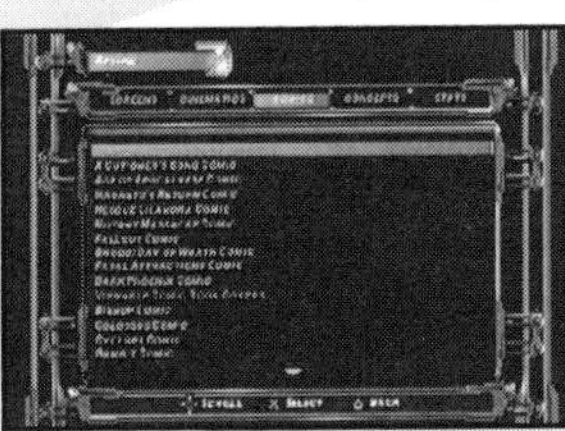

YU-GI-OH! DUEL MONSTERS GX: TAG FORCE 3

MIDDAY CONSTELLATION BOOSTER PACK
At the store, get to the booster pack menu and press Up, Up, Down, Down, Left, Right, Left, Right, ⊗, ●. The pack will now be available at the store.

YU-GI-OH! GX TAG FORCE

BOOSTER PACK

At the card shop, press Up, Up, Down, Down, Left, Right, Left, Right, ⊗, ◉.

RENTAL CARD PASSWORDS

Enter the following in the Password Machine to obtain for rental:

CARD	PASSWORD
30,000-Year White Turtle	11714098
4-Starred Ladybug of Doom	83994646
7	67048711
7 Colored Fish	23771716
7 Completed	86198326
A Cat of Ill Omen	24140059
A Deal with Dark Ruler	06850209
A Feather of the Phoenix	49140998
A Feint Plan	68170903
A Hero Emerges	21597117
A Legendary Ocean	00295517
A Man with Wdjat	51351302
A Rival Appears!	05728014
A Wingbeat of Giant Dragon	28596933
A-Team: Trap Disposal Unit	13026402
Abare Ushioni	89718302
Absolute End	27744077
Absorbing Kid From the Sky	49771608
Abyss Soldier	18318842
Abyssal Designator	89801755
Acid Rain	21323861
Acid Trap Hole	41356845
Acrobat Monkey	47372349
Adhesion Trap Hole	62325062
Adhesive Explosive	53828396
After the Struggle	25345186
Agido	16135253
Airknight Parshath	18036057
Aitsu	48202661
Alkana Knight Joker	06150044
Alpha the Magnet Warrior	99785935
Altar for Tribute	21070956
Amazon Archer	91869203
Amazoness Archers	67987611
Amazoness Blowpiper	73574678
Amazoness Chain Master	29654737
Amazoness Paladin	47480070
Amazoness Swords Woman	94004268
Amazoness Tiger	10979723
Ambulance Rescueroid	98927491
Ambulanceroid	36378213
Ameba	95174353
Amphibian Beast	67371383
Amphibious Bugroth MK-3	64342551
Amplifier	00303660
An Owl of Luck	23927567
Ancient Elf	93221206
Ancient Gear	31557782
Ancient Gear Beast	10509340

CARD	PASSWORD
Ancient Gear Cannon	80045583
Ancient Gear Castle	92001300
Ancient Gear Drill	67829249
Ancient Gear Golem	83104731
Ancient Gear Soldier	56094445
Ancient Lamp	54912977
Ancient Lizard Warrior	43230671
Andro Sphinx	15013468
Anteatereatingant	13250922
Anti-Aircraft Flower	65064143
Anti-Spell	53112492
Apprentice Magician	09156135
Appropriate	48539234
Aqua Madoor	85639257
Aqua Spirit	40916023
Arcane Archer of the Forest	55001420
Archfiend of Gilfer	50287060
Archfiend Soldier	49881766
Archlord Zerato	18378582
Armaill	53153481
Armed Changer	90374791
Armed Dragon LV 3	00980973
Armed Dragon LV 5	46384672
Armed Dragon LV 7	73879377
Armed Dragon LV 10	59464593
Armed Ninja	09076207
Armed Samurai - Ben Kei	84430950
Armor Axe	07180418
Armor Break	79649195
Armored Lizard	15480588
Armored Starfish	17535588
Armored Zombie	20277860
Array of Revealing Light	69296555
Arsenal Bug	42364374
Arsenal Robber	55348096
Arsenal Summoner	85489096
Assault on GHQ	62633180
Astral Barrier	37053871
Asura Priest	02134346
Aswan Apparition	88236094
Atomic Firefly	87340664
Attack and Receive	63689843
Attack Reflector Unit	91989718
Aussa the Earth Charmer	37970940
Autonomous Action Unit	71453557
Avatar of the Pot	99284890
Axe Dragonute	84914462
Axe of Despair	40619825
B. Skull Dragon	11901678
B.E.S. Covered Core	15317640
B.E.S. Crystal Core	22790789
B.E.S. Tetran	44954628
Baby Dragon	88819587
Back to Square One	47453433

CARD	PASSWORD
Backfire	82705573
Backup Soldier	36280194
Bad Reaction to Simochi	40633297
Bait Doll	07165085
Ballista of Rampart Smashing	00242146
Banisher of the Light	61528025
Bark of Dark Ruler	41925941
Barrel Dragon	81480460
Basic Insect	89091579
Battery Charger	61181383
Batteryman AA	63142001
Batteryman C	19733961
Batteryman D	55401221
Battle Footballer	48094997
Battle Ox	05053103
Battle-Scarred	94463200
Bazoo The Soul-Eater	40133511
Beast Soul Swap	35149085
Beaver Warrior	32452818
Beckoning Light	16255442
Beelze Frog	49522489
Begone, Knave	20374520
Behemoth the King of All Animals	22996376
Beiige, Vanguard of Dark World	33731070
Berserk Dragon	85605684
Berserk Gorilla	39168895
Beta the Magnet Warrior	39256679
Bickuribox	25655502
Big Bang Shot	61127349
Big Burn	95472621
Big Core	14148099
Big Eye	16768387
Big Koala	42129512
Big Shield Gardna	65240384
Big Wave Small Wave	51562916
Big-Tusked Mammoth	59380081
Bio-Mage	58696829
Birdface	45547649
Black Illusion Ritual	41426869
Black Luster Soldier - Envoy of the Beginning	72989439
Black Pendant	65169794
Black Tyranno	38670435
Blackland Fire Dragon	87564352
Blade Knight	39507162
Blade Rabbit	58268433
Blade Skater	97023549
Bladefly	28470714
Blast Held By a Tribute	89041555
Blast Magician	21051146
Blast with Chain	98239899
Blasting the Ruins	21466326
Blazing Inpachi	05464695
Blind Destruction	32015116
Blindly Loyal Goblin	35215622
Block Attack	25880422
Blockman	48115277
Blowback Dragon	25551951
Blue-Eyes Shining Dragon	53347303
Blue-Eyes Toon Dragon	53183600

CARD	PASSWORD
Blue-Eyes Ultimate Dragon	23995346
Blue-Eyes White Dragon	89631139
Blue-Winged Crown	41396436
Bokoichi the Freightening Car	08715625
Bombardment Beetle	57409948
Bonding - H2O	45898858
Boneheimer	98456117
Book of Life	02204140
Book of Moon	14087893
Book of Taiyou	38699854
Boss Rush	66947414
Bottom Dweller	81386177
Bottomless Shifting Sand	76532077
Bottomless Trap Hole	29401950
Bountiful Artemis	32296881
Bowganian	52090844
Bracchio-Raidus	16507828
Brain Control	87910978
Brain Jacker	40267580
Branch	30548775
Breaker the Magical Warrior	71413901
Broww, Huntsman of Dark World	79126789
Brron, Mad King of Dark World	06214884
Bubble Blaster	53586134
Bubble Illusion	80075749
Bubble Shuffle	61968753
Bubonic Vermin	06104968
Burning Algae	41859700
Burning Beast	59364406
Burning Land	24294108
Burst Breath	80163754
Burst Return	27191436
Burst Stream of Destruction	17655904
Buster Blader	78193831
Buster Rancher	84740193
Butterfly Dagger - Elma	69243953
Byser Shock	17597059
Call of The Haunted	97077563
Call of the Mummy	04861205
Cannon Soldier	11384280
Cannonball Spear Shellfish	95614612
Card of Safe Return	57953380
Card Shuffle	12183332
Castle of Dark Illusions	00062121
Cat's Ear Tribe	95841282
Catapult Turtle	95727991
Cathedral of Nobles	29762407
Catnipped Kitty	96501677
Cave Dragon	93220472
Ceasefire	36468556
Celtic Guardian	91152256
Cemetery Bomb	51394546
Centrifugal	01801154
Ceremonial Bell	20228463
Cetus of Dagala	28106077
Chain Burst	48276469

CARD	PASSWORD
Chain Destruction	01248895
Chain Disappearance	57139487
Chain Energy	79323590
Chain Thrasher	88190453
Chainsaw Insect	77252217
Change of Heart	04031928
Chaos Command Magician	72630549
Chaos Emperor Dragon-Envoy of the End	82301904
Chaos End	61044390
Chaos Greed	97439308
Chaos Necromancer	01434352
Chaos Sorcerer	09596126
Chaosrider Gutaph	47829960
Charcoal Inpachi	13179332
Charm of Shabti	50412166
Charubin the Fire Knight	37421579
Chiron the Mage	16956455
Chopman the Desperate Outlaw	40884383
Chorus of Sanctuary	81380218
Chthonian Alliance	46910446
Chthonian Blast	18271561
Chthonian Polymer	72287557
Chu-Ske the Mouse Fighter	08508055
Clay Charge	22479888
Cliff the Trap Remover	06967870
Cobra Jar	86801871
Cobraman Sakuzy	75109441
Cold Wave	60682203
Collected Power	07565547
Combination Attack	08964854
Command Knight	10375182
Commander Covington	22666164
Commencement Dance	43417563
Compulsory Evacuation Device	94192409
Confiscation	17375316
Conscription	31000575
Continuous Destruction Punch	68057622
Contract With Exodia	33244944
Contract With the Abyss	69035382
Contract with the Dark Master	96420087
Convulsion of Nature	62966332
Cost Down	23265313
Covering Fire	74458486
Crab Turtle	91782219
Crass Clown	93889755
Creature Swap	31036355
Creeping Doom Manta	52571838
Crimson Ninja	14618326
Criosphinx	18654201
Cross Counter	37083210
Crush D. Gandra	64681432
Cure Mermaid	85802526
Curse of Aging	41398771
Curse of Anubis	66742250
Curse of Darkness	84970821
Curse of Dragon	28279543

CARD	PASSWORD
Curse of the Masked Beast	94377247
Curse of Vampire	34294855
Cyberdark Dragon	40418351
Cyberdark Horn	41230939
Cyberdark Keel	03019642
D - Sheild	62868900
D - Time	99075257
D. D. Assailant	70074904
D. D. Borderline	60912752
D. D. Trainer	86498013
D. D. Warrior Lady	07572887
D.D. Crazy Beast	48148828
D.D. Dynamite	08628798
D.D. Trap Hole	05606466
D.D.M. - Different Dimension Master	82112775
Dancing Fairy	90925163
Dangerous Machine TYPE-6	76895648
Dark Artist	72520073
Dark Bat	67049542
Dark Blade	11321183
Dark Blade the Dragon Knight	86805855
Dark Driceratops	65287621
Dark Dust Spirit	89111398
Dark Elf	21417692
Dark Energy	04614116
Dark Factory of Mass Production	90928333
Dark Flare Knight	13722870
Dark Hole	53129443
Dark Magic Attack	02314238
Dark Magic Ritual	76792184
Dark Magician	46986414
Dark Magician Girl	38033121
Dark Magician of Chaos	40737112
Dark Magician's Tome of Black Magic	67227834
Dark Master - Zorc	97642679
Dark Mirror Force	20522190
Dark Paladin	98502113
Dark Paladin	98502113
Dark Room of Nightmare	85562745
Dark Sage	92377303
Dark Snake Syndrome	47233801
Dark-Piercing Light	45895206
Darkfire Dragon	17881964
Darkfire Soldier #1	05388481
Darkfire Soldier #2	78861134
Darkworld Thorns	43500484
De-Spell	19159413
Deal of Phantom	69122763
Decayed Commander	10209545
Dedication Through Light And Darkness	69542930
Deepsea Shark	28593363
Dekoichi the Battlechanted Locomotive	87621407
Delinquent Duo	44763025
Demotion	72575145
Des Counterblow	39131963
Des Croaking	44883830

CARD	PASSWORD
Des Dendle	12965761
Des Feral Imp	81985784
Des Frog	84451804
Des Kangaroo	78613627
Des Koala	69579761
Des Lacooda	02326738
Des Wombat	09637706
Desert Sunlight	93747864
Destertapir	13409151
Destiny Board	94212438
Destiny Hero - Captain Tenacious	77608643
Destiny Hero - Diamond Dude	13093792
Destiny Hero - Doom Lord	41613948
Destiny Hero - Dreadmaster	40591390
Destiny Signal	35464895
Destroyer Golem	73481154
Destruction Ring	21219755
Dian Keto the Cure Master	84257639
Dice Jar	03549275
Dimension Distortion	95194279
Dimensional Warrior	37043180
Dimenional Fissure	816747482
Disappear	24623598
Disarmament	20727787
Disc Fighter	19612721
Dissolverock	40826495
Divine Dragon Ragnarok	62113340
Divine Wrath	49010598
DNA Surgery	74701381
DNA Transplant	56769674
Doitsu	57062206
Dokurorider	99721536
Dokuroyaiba	30325729
Don Turtle	03493978
Don Zaloog	76922029
Doriado	84916669
Doriado's Blessing	23965037
Dragon Seeker	28563545
Dragon Treasure	01435851
Dragon Zombie	66672569
Dragon's Mirror	71490127
Dragon's Rage	54178050
Dragoness the Wicked Knight	70681994
Draining Shield	43250041
Dream Clown	13215230
Drillago	99050989
Drillroid	71218746
Dunames Dark Witch	12493482
Dust Tornado	60082867
Earth Chant	59820352
Earthbound Spirit	67105242
Earthquake	82828051
Eatgaboon	42578427
Ebon Magician Curran	46128076
Electro-Whip	37820550
Elegant Egotist	90219263
Element Dragon	30314994
Elemental Burst	61411502
Elemental Hero Avian	21844576

CARD	PASSWORD
Elemental Hero Bladedge	59793705
Elemental Hero Bubbleman	79979666
Elemental Hero Burstinatrix	58932615
Elemental Hero Clayman	84327329
Elemental Hero Electrum/Erekshieler	29343734
Elemental Hero Flame Wingman	35809262
Elemental Hero Mariner	14225239
Elemental Hero Necroid Shaman	81003500
Elemental Hero Neos	89943723
Elemental Hero Phoenix Enforcer	41436536
Elemental Hero Shining Flare Wingman	25366484
Elemental Hero Shining Phoenix Enforcer	88820235
Elemental Hero Sparkman	20721928
Elemental Hero Thunder Giant	61204971
Elemental Mistress Doriado	99414158
Elemental Recharge	36586443
Elf's Light	39897277
Emblem of Dragon Destroyer	06390406
Embodiment of Apophis	28649820
Emergency Provisions	53046408
Emes the Infinity	43580269
Empress Judge	15237615
Empress Mantis	58818411
Enchanted Javelin	96355986
Enchanting Mermaid	75376965
Enraged Battle Ox	76909279
Enraged Muka Muka	91862578
Eradicating Aerosol	94716515
Eternal Draught	56606928
Eternal Rest	95051344
Exhausting Spell	95451366
Exile of the Wicked	26725158
Exiled Force	74131780
Exodia Necross	12600382
Exodia the Forbidden One	33396948
Fairy Box	21598948
Fairy Dragon	20315854
Fairy King Truesdale	45425051
Fairy Meteor Crush	97687912
Faith Bird	75582395
Fatal Abacus	77910045
Fenrir	00218704
Feral Imp	41392891
Fiber Jar	78706415
Fiend Comedian	81172176
Fiend Scorpion	26566878
Fiend's Hand	52800428
Fiend's Mirror	31890399
Final Countdown	95308449
Final Destiny	18591904
Final Flame	73134081
Final Ritual of the Ancients	60369732

PSP

CARD	PASSWORD
Fire Darts	43061293
Fire Eye	88435542
Fire Kraken	46534755
Fire Princess	64752646
Fire Reaper	53581214
Fire Sorcerer	27132350
Firegrass	53293545
Firewing Pegasus	27054370
Fireyarou	71407486
Fissure	66788016
Five God Dragon (Five-Headed Dragon)	99267150
Flame Cerebrus	60862676
Flame Champion	42599677
Flame Dancer	12883044
Flame Ghost	58528964
Flame Manipulator	34460851
Flame Swordsman	45231177
Flame Viper	02830619
Flash Assailant	96890582
Flower Wolf	95952802
Flying Fish	31987274
Flying Kamakiri #1	84834865
Flying Kamakiri #2	03134241
Follow Wind	98252586
Foolish Burial	81439173
Forest	87430998
Fortress Whale	62337487
Fortress Whale's Oath	77454922
Frenzied Panda	98818516
Frozen Soul	57069605
Fruits of Kozaky's Studies	49998907
Fuh-Rin-Ka-Zan	01781310
Fuhma Shuriken	09373534
Fulfillment of the Contract	48206762
Fushi No Tori	38538445
Fusion Gate	33550694
Fusion Recovery	18511384
Fusion Sage	26902560
Fusion Weapon	27967615
Fusionist	01641883
Gadget Soldier	86281779
Gagagigo	49003308
Gaia Power	56594520
Gaia the Dragon Champion	66889139
Gaia the Fierce Knight	06368038
Gale Dogra	16229315
Gale Lizard	77491079
Gamble	37313786
Gamma the Magnet Warrior	11549357
Garma Sword	90844184
Garma Sword Oath	78577570
Garoozis	14977074
Garuda the Wind Spirit	12800777
Gatling Dragon	87751584
Gazelle the King of Mythical Beasts	05818798
Gear Golem the Moving Fortress	30190809
Gearfried the Iron Knight	00423705

CARD	PASSWORD
Gearfried the Swordmaster	57046845
Gemini Elf	69140098
Getsu Fuhma	21887179
Giant Axe Mummy	78266168
Giant Germ	95178994
Giant Kozaky	58185394
Giant Orc	73698349
Giant Rat	97017120
Giant Red Seasnake	58831685
Giant Soldier of Stone	13039848
Giant Trunade	42703248
Gift of the Mystical Elf	98299011
Giga Gagagigo	43793530
Giga-Tech Wolf	08471389
Gigantes	47606319
Gigobyte	53776525
Gil Garth	38445524
Gilasaurus	45894482
Giltia the D. Knight	51828629
Girochin Kuwagata	84620194
Goblin Attack Force	78658564
Goblin Calligrapher	12057781
Goblin Elite Attack Force	85306040
Goblin Thief	45311864
Goblin's Secret Remedy	11868825
Gogiga Gagagigo	39674352
Golem Sentry	82323207
Good Goblin Housekeeping	09744376
Gora Turtle	80233946
Graceful Charity	79571449
Graceful Dice	74137509
Gradius	10992251
Gradius' Option	14291024
Granadora	13944422
Grand Tiki Elder	13676474
Granmarg the Rock Monarch	60229110
Gravedigger Ghoul	82542267
Gravekeeper's Cannonholder	99877698
Gravekeeper's Curse	50712728
Gravekeeper's Guard	37101832
Gravekeeper's Servant	16762927
Gravekeeper's Spear Soldier	63695531
Gravekeeper's Spy	24317029
Gravekeeper's Vassal	99690140
Graverobber's Retribution	33737664
Gravity Bind	85742772
Gray Wing	29618570
Great Angus	11813953
Great Long Nose	02356994
Great Mammoth of Goldfine	54622031
Green Gadget	41172955
Gren Maju Da Eiza	36584821
Ground Attacker Bugroth	58314394
Ground Collapse	90502999
Gruesome Goo	65623423
Gryphon Wing	55608151

CARD	PASSWORD
Gryphon's Feather Duster	34370473
Guardian Angel Joan	68007326
Guardian of the Labyrinth	89272878
Guardian of the Sea	85448931
Guardian Sphinx	40659562
Guardian Statue	75209824
Gust Fan	55321970
Gyaku-Gire Panda	09817927
Gyroid	18325492
Hade-Hane	28357177
Hamburger Recipe	80811661
Hammer Shot	26412047
Hamon	32491822
Hand of Nephthys	98446407
Hane-Hane	07089711
Hannibal Necromancer	05640330
Hard Armor	20060230
Harpie Girl	34100324
Harpie Lady 1	91932350
Harpie Lady 2	27927359
Harpie Lady 3	54415063
Harpie Lady Sisters	12206212
Harpie's Brother	30532390
Harpies' Hunting Ground	75782277
Hayabusa Knight	21015833
Headless Knight	05434080
Heart of Clear Water	64801562
Heart of the Underdog	35762283
Heavy Mech Support Platform	23265594
Heavy Storm	19613556
Helios - the Primordial Sun	54493213
Helios Duo Megistus	80887952
Helios Tris Megiste	17286057
Helping Robo for Combat	47025270
Hero Barrier	44676200
HERO Flash!	00191749
Hero Heart	67951831
Hero Kid	32679370
Hero Ring	26647858
Hero Signal	22020907
Hidden Book of Spell	21840375
Hidden Soldier	02047519
Hieracosphinx	82260502
Hieroglyph Lithograph	10248192
High Tide Gyojin	54579801
Hiita the Fire Charmer	00759393
Hino-Kagu-Tsuchi	75745607
Hinotama Soul	96851799
Hiro's Shadow Scout	81863068
Hitotsu-Me Giant	76184692
Holy Knight Ishzark	57902462
Homunculus the Alchemic Being	40410110
Horn of Heaven	98069388
Horn of Light	38552107
Horn of the Unicorn	64047146
Horus The Black Flame Dragon LV 4	75830094
Horus The Black Flame Dragon LV 6	11224103

CARD	PASSWORD
Horus The Black Flame Dragon LV 8	48229808
Hoshiningen	67629977
House of Adhesive Tape	15083728
Howling Insect	93107608
Huge Revolution	65396880
Human-Wave Tactics	30353551
Humanoid Slime	46821314
Humanoid Worm Drake	05600127
Hungry Burger	30243636
Hydrogeddon	22587018
Hyena	22873798
Hyozanryu	62397231
Hyper Hammerhead	02671330
Hysteric Fairy	21297224
Icarus Attack	53567095
Illusionist Faceless Mage	28546905
Impenetrable Formation	96631852
Imperial Order	61740673
Inaba White Rabbit	77084837
Incandescent Ordeal	33031674
Indomitable Fighter Lei Lei	84173492
Infernal Flame Emperor	19847532
Infernal Queen Archfiend	08581705
Inferno	74823665
Inferno Fire Blast	52684508
Inferno Hammer	17185260
Inferno Reckless Summon	12247206
Inferno Tempest	14391920
Infinite Cards	94163677
Infinite Dismissal	54109233
Injection Fairy Lily	79575620
Inpachi	97923414
Insect Armor with Laser Cannon	03492538
Insect Barrier	23615409
Insect Imitation	96965364
Insect Knight	35052053
Insect Princess	37957847
Insect Queen	91512835
Insect Soldiers of the Sky	07019529
Inspection	16227556
Interdimensional Matter Transporter	36261276
Invader From Another Dimension	28450915
Invader of Darkness	56647086
Invader of the Throne	03056267
Invasion of Flames	26082229
Invigoration	98374133
Iron Blacksmith Kotetsu	73431236
Island Turtle	04042268
Jack's Knight	90876561
Jade Insect Whistle	95214051
Jam Breeding Machine	21770260
Jam Defender	21558682
Jar of Greed	83968380
Jar Robber	33784505
Javelin Beetle	26932788
Javelin Beetle Pact	41182875
Jellyfish	14851496

CARD	PASSWORD
Jerry Beans Man	23635815
Jetroid	43697559
Jinzo	77585513
Jinzo #7	32809211
Jirai Gumo	94773007
Jowgen the Spiritualist	41855169
Jowls of Dark Demise	05257687
Judge Man	30113682
Judgment of Anubis	55256016
Just Desserts	24068492
KA-2 Des Scissors	52768103
Kabazauls	51934376
Kagemusha of the Blue Flame	15401633
Kaibaman	34627841
Kaiser Dragon	94566432
Kaiser Glider	52824910
Kaiser Sea Horse	17444133
Kaminari Attack	09653271
Kaminote Blow	97570038
Kamionwizard	41544074
Kangaroo Champ	95789089
Karate Man	23289281
Karbonala Warrior	54541900
Karma Cut	71587526
Kelbek	54878498
Keldo	80441106
Killer Needle	88979991
Kinetic Soldier	79853073
King Dragun	13756293
King Fog	84686841
King of the Skull Servants	36021814
King of the Swamp	79109599
King of Yamimakai	69455834
King Tiger Wanghu	83986578
King's Knight	64788463
Kiryu	84814897
Kiseitai	04266839
Kishido Spirit	60519422
Knight's Title	87210505
Koitsu	69456283
Kojikocy	01184620
Kotodama	19406822
Kozaky	99171160
Kozaky's Self-Destruct Button	21908319
Kryuel	82642348
Kumootoko	56283725
Kurama	85705804
Kuriboh	40640057
Kuwagata Alpha	60802233
Kwagar Hercules	95144193
Kycoo The Ghost Destroyer	88240808
La Jinn The Mystical Genie of The Lamp	97590747
Labyrinth of Nightmare	66526672
Labyrinth Tank	99551425
Lady Assailant of Flames	90147755
Lady Ninja Yae	82005435
Lady of Faith	17358176
Larvas	94675535
Laser Cannon Armor	77007920

CARD	PASSWORD
Last Day of Witch	90330453
Last Turn	28566710
Launcher Spider	87322377
Lava Battleguard	20394040
Lava Golem	00102380
Layard the Liberator	67468948
Left Arm of the Forbidden One	07902349
Left Leg of the Forbidden One	44519536
Legendary Black Belt	96438440
Legendary Flame Lord	60258960
Legendary Jujitsu Master	25773409
Legendary Sword	61854111
Leghul	12472242
Lekunga	62543393
Lesser Dragon	55444629
Lesser Fiend	16475472
Level Conversion Lab	84397023
Level Limit - Area A	54976796
Level Limit - Area B	03136426
Level Modulation	61850482
Level Up	25290459
Levia-Dragon	37721209
Levia-Dragon - Daedalus	37721209
Light of Intervention	62867251
Light of Judgment	44595286
Lighten the Load	37231841
Lightforce Sword	49587034
Lightning Blade	55226821
Lightning Conger	27671321
Lightning Vortex	69162969
Limiter Removal	23171610
Liquid Beast	93108297
Little Chimera	68658728
Little-Winguard	90790253
Lizard Soldier	20831168
Lord of the Lamp	99510761
Lost Guardian	45871897
Luminous Soldier	57282479
Luminous Spark	81777047
Luster Dragon	11091375
Luster Dragon #2	17658803
M-Warrior #1	56342351
M-Warrior #2	92731455
Machine Conversion Factory	25769732
Machine Duplication	63995093
Machine King	46700124
Machine King Prototype	89222931
Machiners Defender	96384007
Machiners Force	58054262
Machiners Sniper	23782705
Machiners Soldier	60999392
Mad Dog of Darkness	79182538
Mad Lobster	97240270
Mad Sword Beast	79870141
Mage Power	83746708
Magic Drain	59344077
Magic Jammer	77414722
Magical Cylinder	62279055
Magical Dimension	28553439
Magical Explosion	32723153

CARD	PASSWORD
Magical Hats	81210420
Magical Labyrinth	64389297
Magical Marionette	08034697
Magical Merchant	32362575
Magical Plant Mandragola	07802006
Magical Scientist	34206604
Magical Thorn	53119267
Magician of Black Chaos	30208479
Magician of Faith	31560081
Magician's Circle	00050755
Magician's Unite	36045450
Magician's Valkyrie	80304126
Magnet Circle	94940436
Maha Vailo	93013676
Maharaghi	40695128
Maiden of the Aqua	17214465
Maji-Gire Panda	60102563
Maju Garzett	08794435
Makiu	27827272
Makyura the Destructor	21593977
Malevolent Nuzzler	99597615
Malfunction	06137095
Malice Ascendant	14255590
Malice Dispersion	13626450
Mammoth Graveyard	40374923
Man Eater	93553943
Man-Eater Bug	54652250
Man-Eating Black Shark	80727036
Man-Eating Treasure Chest	13723605
Man-Thro' Tro	43714890
Manga Ryu-Ran	38369349
Manju of the Ten Thousand Hands	95492061
Manticore of Darkness	77121851
Marauding Captain	02460565
Marie the Fallen One	57579381
Marine Beast	29929832
Marshmallon	31305911
Marshmallon Glasses	66865880
Maryokutai	71466592
Masaki the Legendary Swordsman	44287299
Mask of Brutality	82432018
Mask of Darkness	28933734
Mask of Restrict	29549364
Mask of Weakness	57882509
Masked Dragon	39191307
Masked of the Accursed	56948373
Masked Sorcerer	10189126
Mass Driver	34906152
Master Kyonshee	24530661
Master Monk	49814180
Master of Dragon Knight	62873545
Master of Oz	27134689
Mataza the Zapper	22609617
Mavelus	59036972
Maximum Six	30707994
Mazera DeVille	06133894
Mech Mole Zombie	63545455
Mecha-Dog Marron	94667532
Mechanical Hound	22512237
Mechanical Snail	34442949

CARD	PASSWORD
Mechanical Spider	45688586
Mechanicalchaser	07359741
Meda Bat	76211194
Medusa Worm	02694423
Mefist the Infernal General	46820049
Mega Thunderball	21817254
Mega Ton Magical Cannon	32062913
Megamorph	22046459
Megarock Dragon	71544954
Melchid the Four-Face Beast	86569121
Memory Crusher	48700891
Mermaid Knight	24435369
Messenger of Peace	44656491
Metal Armored Bug	65957473
Metal Dragon	09293977
Metallizing Parasite	07369217
Metalmorph	68540058
Metalzoa	50705071
Metamorphosis	46411259
Meteor B. Dragon	90660762
Meteor Dragon	64271667
Meteor of Destruction	33767325
Meteorain	64274292
Michizure	37580756
Micro-Ray	18190572
Mid Shield Gardna	75487237
Mighty Guard	62327910
Mikazukinoyaiba	38277918
Millennium Golem	47986555
Millennium Scorpion	82482194
Millennium Shield	32012841
Milus Radiant	07489323
Minar	32539892
Mind Control	37520316
Mind Haxorz	75392615
Mind on Air	66690411
Mind Wipe	52718046
Mine Golem	76321376
Minefield Eruption	85519211
Minor Goblin Official	01918087
Miracle Dig	06343408
Miracle Fusion	45906428
Miracle Kid	55985014
Miracle Restoring	68334074
Mirage Dragon	15960641
Mirage Knight	49217579
Mirage of Nightmare	41482598
Mirror Force	44095762
Mirror Wall	22359980
Misfortune	01036974
Mispolymerization	58392024
Mistobody	47529357
Moai Interceptor Cannons	45159319
Mobius the Frost Monarch	04929256
Moisture Creature	75285069
Mokey Mokey	27288416
Mokey Mokey King	13803864
Mokey Mokey Smackdown	01965724

CARD	PASSWORD
Molten Behemoth	17192817
Molten Destruction	19384334
Molten Zombie	04732017
Monk Fighter	03810071
Monster Egg	36121917
Monster Eye	84133008
Monster Gate	43040603
Monster Reborn	83764718
Monster Recovery	93108433
Monster Reincarnation	74848038
Mooyan Curry	58074572
Morale Boost	93671934
Morphing Jar	33508719
Morphing Jar #2	79106360
Mother Grizzly	57839750
Mountain	50913601
Mr. Volcano	31477025
Mudora	82108372
Muka Muka	46657337
Multiplication of Ants	22493811
Multiply	40703222
Musician King	56907389
Mustering of the Dark Scorpions	68191243
Mysterious Puppeteer	54098121
Mystic Horseman	68516705
Mystic Lamp	98049915
Mystic Plasma Zone	18161786
Mystic Swordsman LV 2	47507260
Mystic Swordsman LV 4	74591968
Mystic Swordsman LV 6	60482781
Mystic Tomato	83011277
Mystic Wok	80161395
Mystical Beast Serket	89194033
Mystical Elf	15025844
Mystical Knight of Jackal	98745000
Mystical Moon	36607978
Mystical Sand	32751480
Mystical Sheep #	30451366
Mystical Shine Ball	39552864
Mystical Space Typhoon	05318639
Mystik Wok	80161395
Mythical Beast Cerberus	55424270
Nanobreaker	70948327
Necklace of Command	48576971
Necrovalley	47355498
Needle Ball	94230224
Needle Burrower	98162242
Needle Ceiling	38411870
Needle Wall	38299233
Needle Worm	81843628
Negate Attack	14315573
Nemuriko	90963488
Neo Aqua Madoor	49563947
Neo Bug	16587243
Neo the Magic Swordsman	50930991
Neo-Space	40215635
Neo-Spacian Aqua Dolphin	17955766
Newdoria	04335645
Next to be Lost	07076131
Night Assailant	16226786
Nightmare Horse	59290628

CARD	PASSWORD
Nightmare Penguin	81306586
Nightmare Wheel	54704216
Nightmare's Steelcage	58775978
Nimble Momonga	22567609
Nin-Ken Dog	11987744
Ninja Grandmaster Sasuke	04041838
Ninjitsu Art of Decoy	89628781
Ninjitsu Art of Transformation	70861343
Nitro Unit	23842445
Niwatori	07805359
Nobleman of Crossout	71044499
Nobleman of Extermination	17449108
Nobleman-Eater Bug	65878864
Non Aggression Area	76848240
Non-Fusion Area	27581098
Non-Spellcasting Area	20065549
Novox's Prayer	43694075
Nubian Guard	51616747
Numinous Healer	02130625
Nutrient Z	29389368
Nuvia the Wicked	12953226
O - Oversoul	63703130
Obnoxious Celtic Guardian	52077741
Ocubeam	86088138
Offerings to the Doomed	19230407
Ojama Black	79335209
Ojama Delta Hurricane	08251996
Ojama Green	12482652
Ojama King	90140980
Ojama Trio	29843091
Ojama Yellow	42941100
Ojamagic	24643836
Ojamuscle	98259197
Old Vindictive Magician	45141844
Ominous Fortunetelling	56995655
Oni Tank T-3	66927994
Opti-Camaflauge Armor	44762290
Opticlops	14531242
Option Hunter	33248692
Orca Mega-Fortress of Darkness	63120904
Ordeal of a Traveler	39537362
Order to Charge	78986941
Order to Smash	39019325
Otohime	39751093
Outstanding Dog Marron	11548522
Overdrive	02311603
Oxygeddon	58071123
Painful Choice	74191942
Paladin of White Dragon	73398797
Pale Beast	21263083
Pandemonium	94585852
Pandemonium Watchbear	75375465
Parasite Paracide	27911549
Parasitic Ticky	87978805
Patrician of Darkness	19153634
Patroid	71930383
Penguin Knight	36039163
Penumbral Soldier Lady	64751286

CARD	PASSWORD
People Running About	12143771
Perfect Machine King	18891691
Performance of Sword	04849037
Petit Angel	38142739
Petit Dragon	75356564
Petit Moth	58192742
Phantasmal Martyrs	93224848
Pharaoh's Servant	52550973
Pharonic Protector	89959682
Phoenix Wing Wind Blast	63356631
Photon Generator Unit	66607691
Pikeru's Circle of Enchantment	74270067
Pikeru's Second Sight	58015506
Pinch Hopper	26185991
Pineapple Blast	90669991
Piranha Army	50823978
Pitch-Black Power Stone	34029630
Pitch-Black Warwolf	88975532
Pitch-Dark Dragon	47415292
Poison Draw Frog	56840658
Poison Fangs	76539047
Poison Mummy	43716289
Poison of the Old Man	08842266
Polymerization	24094653
Possessed Dark Soul	52860176
Pot of Avarice	67169062
Pot of Generosity	70278545
Pot of Greed	55144522
Power Bond	37630732
Power Capsule	54289683
Precious Card from Beyond	68304813
Premature Burial	70828912
Prepare to Strike Back	04483989
Prevent Rat	00549481
Prickle Fairy	91559748
Primal Seed	23701465
Princess Curran	02316186
Princess of Tsurugi	51371017
Princess Pikeru	75917088
Protective Soul Ailin	11678191
Protector of the Sanctuary	24221739
Protector of the Throne	10071456
Proto-Cyber Dragon	26439287
Pumpking the King of Ghosts	29155212
Punished Eagle	74703140
Pyramid of Light	53569894
Pyramid Turtle	77044671
Queen's Knight	25652259
Rabid Horseman	94905343
Rafflesia Seduction	31440542
Raging Flame Sprite	90810762
Raigeki	12580477
Raigeki Break	04178474
Rain Of Mercy	66719324
Rainbow Flower	21347810
Rancer Dragonute	11125718
Rapid-Fire Magician	06337436
Rare Metalmorph	12503902
Raregold Armor	07625614

CARD	PASSWORD
Raviel, Lord of Phantasms	69890967
Ray & Temperature	85309439
Ray of Hope	82529174
Re-Fusion	74694807
Ready For Intercepting	31785398
Really Eternal Rest	28121403
Reaper of the Cards	33066139
Reaper of the Nightmare	85684223
Reasoning	58577036
Reborn Zombie	23421244
Reckless Greed	37576645
Recycle	96316857
Red Archery Girl	65570596
Red Gadget	86445415
Red Medicine	38199696
Red Moon Baby	56387350
Red-Eyes B. Chick	36262024
Red-Eyes B. Dragon	74677422
Red-Eyes Black Metal Dragon	64335804
Red-Eyes Darkness Dragon	96561011
Reflect Bounder	02851070
Regenerating Mummy	70821187
Reinforcement of the Army	32807846
Release Restraint	75417459
Relinquished	64631466
Reload	22589918
Remove Trap	51482758
Rescue Cat	14878871
Rescueroid	24311595
Reshef the Dark Being	62420419
Respect Play	08951260
Return from the Different Dimension	27174286
Return of the Doomed	19827717
Reversal of Graves	17484499
Reversal Quiz	05990062
Revival Jam	31709826
Right Arm of the Forbidden One	70903634
Right Leg of the Forbidden One	08124921
Ring of Destruction	83555666
Ring of Magnetism	20436034
Riryoku Field	70344351
Rising Air Current	45778932
Rising Energy	78211862
Rite of Spirit	30450531
Ritual Weapon	54351224
Robbin' Goblin	88279736
Robbin' Zombie	83258273
Robolady	92421852
Robotic Knight	44203504
Roboyarou	38916461
Rock Bombardment	20781762
Rock Ogre Grotto	68846917
Rocket Jumper	53890795
Rocket Warrior	30860696
Rod of the Mind's Eye	94793422
Roll Out	91597389
Root Water	39004808
Rope of Life	93382620

CARD	PASSWORD
Rope of Spirit	37383714
Roulette Barrel	46303688
Royal Command	33950246
Royal Decree	51452091
Royal Keeper	16509093
Royal Knight	68280530
Royal Magical Library	70791313
Royal Surrender	56058888
Royal Tribute	72405967
Ruin, Queen of Oblivion	46427957
Rush Recklessly	70046172
Ryu Kokki	57281778
Ryu Senshi	49868263
Ryu-Kishin Clown	42647539
Ryu-Kishin Powered	24611934
Saber Beetle	49645921
Sacred Crane	30914564
Sacred Phoenix of Nephthys	61441708
Saggi the Dark Clown	66602787
Sakuretsu Armor	56120475
Salamandra	32268901
Salvage	96947648
Samsara	44182827
Sand Gambler	50593156
Sand Moth	73648243
Sangan	26202165
Sanwitch	53539634
Sasuke Samurai	16222645
Sasuke Samurai 2#	11760174
Sasuke Samurai 3#	77379481
Sasuke Samurai 4#	64538655
Satellite Cannon	50400231
Scapegoat	73915051
Scarr, Scout of Dark World	05498296
Science Soldier	67532912
Scroll of Bewitchment	10352095
Scyscraper	63035430
Sea Serpent Warrior of Darkness	42071342
Sealmaster Meisei	02468169
Second Coin Toss	36562627
Second Goblin	19086954
Secret Barrel	27053506
Self-Destruct Button	57585212
Senri Eye	60391791
Serial Spell	49398568
Serpent Night Dragon	66516792
Serpentine Princess	71829750
Servant of Catabolism	02792265
Seven Tools of the Bandit	03819470
Shadow Ghoul	30778711
Shadow Of Eyes	58621589
Shadow Tamer	37620434
Shadowknight Archfiend	09603356
Shadowslayer	20939559
Share the Pain	56830749
Shield & Sword	52097679
Shield Crash	30683373
Shien's Spy	07672244
Shift	59560625
Shifting Shadows	59237154

CARD	PASSWORD
Shinato's Ark	60365591
Shinato, King of a Higher Plane	86327225
Shining Abyss	87303357
Shining Angel	95956346
Shooting Star Bow - Ceal	95638658
Silent Insect	40867519
Silent Magician Lv 4	73665146
Silent Magician Lv 8	72443568
Silent Swordsman LV 3	01995985
Silent Swordsman LV 5	74388798
Silent Swordsman LV 7	37267041
Sillva, Warlord of Dark World	32619583
Silpheed	73001017
Silver Fang	90357090
Simultaneous Loss	92219931
Sinister Serpent	08131171
Sixth Sense	03280747
Skill Drain	82732705
Skilled Dark Magician	73752131
Skilled White Magician	46363422
Skull Archfiend of Lightning	61370518
Skull Descovery Knight	78700060
Skull Dog Marron	86652646
Skull Invitation	98139712
Skull Lair	06733059
Skull Mariner	05265750
Skull Red Bird	10202894
Skull Servant	32274490
Skull Zoma	79852326
Skull-Mark Ladybug	64306248
Skyscraper	63035430
Slate Warrior	78636495
Smashing Ground	97169186
Smoke Grenade of the Thief	63789924
Snatch Steal	45986603
Sogen	86318356
Soitsu	60246171
Solar Flare Dragon	45985838
Solar Ray	44472639
Solemn Judgment	41420027
Solemn Wishes	35346968
Solomon's Lawbook	23471572
Sonic Duck	84696266
Sonic Jammer	84550200
Sorcerer of Dark Magic	88619463
Soul Absorption	68073522
Soul Exchange	68005187
Soul of Purity and Light	77527210
Soul Release	05758500
Soul Resurrection	92924317
Soul Reversal	78864369
Soul Tiger	15734813
Soul-Absorbing Bone Tower	63012333
Souleater	31242786
Souls Of The Forgotten	04920010
Space Mambo	36119641
Spark Blaster	97362768
Sparks	76103675

CARD	PASSWORD
Spatial Collapse	20644748
Spear Cretin	58551308
Spear Dragon	31553716
Spell Canceller	84636823
Spell Economics	04259068
Spell Purification	01669772
Spell Reproduction	29228529
Spell Shield Type-8	38275183
Spell Vanishing	29735721
Spell-Stopping Statute	10069180
Spellbinding Circle	18807108
Spherous Lady	52121290
Sphinx Teleia	51402177
Spiral Spear Strike	49328340
Spirit Barrier	53239672
Spirit Caller	48659020
Spirit Message "A"	94772232
Spirit Message "I"	31893528
Spirit Message "L"	30170981
Spirit Message "N"	67287533
Spirit of Flames	13522325
Spirit of the Breeze	53530069
Spirit of the Harp	80770678
Spirit of the Pharaoh	25343280
Spirit Reaper	23205979
Spirit Ryu	67957315
Spiritual Earth Art - Kurogane	70156997
Spiritual Energy Settle Machine	99173029
Spiritual Fire Art - Kurenai	42945701
Spiritual Water Art - Aoi	06540606
Spiritual Wind Art - Miyabi	79333300
Spiritualism	15866454
St. Joan	21175632
Stamping Destruction	81385346
Star Boy	08201910
Statue of the Wicked	65810489
Staunch Defender	92854392
Stealth Bird	03510565
Steam Gyroid	05368615
Steamroid	44729197
Steel Ogre Grotto #1	29172562
Steel Ogre Grotto #2	90908427
Stim-Pack	83225447
Stop Defense	63102017
Storming Wynn	29013526
Stray Lambs	60764581
Strike Ninja	41006930
Stronghold	13955608
Stumbling	34646691
Success Probability 0%	06859683
Summon Priest	00423585
Summoned Skull	70781052
Summoner of Illusions	14644902
Super Conductor Ttranno	85520851
Super Rejuvenation	27770341
Super Robolady	75923050
Super Roboyarou	01412158
Supply	44072894
Susa Soldier	40473581

CARD	PASSWORD
Swarm of Locusts	41872150
Swarm of Scarabs	15383415
Swift Gaia the Fierce Knight	16589042
Sword Hunter	51345461
Sword of Deep-Seated	98495314
Sword of Dragon's Soul	61405855
Sword of the Soul Eater	05371656
Swords of Concealing Light	12923641
Swords of Revealing Light	72302403
Swordsman of Landstar	03573512
Symbol of Heritage	45305419
System Down	18895832
T.A.D.P.O.L.E	10456559
Tactical Espionage Expert	89698120
Tailor of the Fickle	43641473
Taunt	90740329
Tenkabito Shien	41589166
Terra the Terrible	63308047
Terraforming	73628505
Terrorking Archfiend	35975813
Terrorking Salmon	78060096
Teva	16469012
The Agent of Creation - Venus	64734921
The Agent of Force - Mars	91123920
The Agent of Judgment - Saturn	91345518
The Agent of Wisdom - Mercury	38730226
The All-Seeing White Tiger	32269855
The Big March of Animals	01689516
The Bistro Butcher	71107816
The Cheerful Coffin	41142615
The Creator	61505339
The Creator Incarnate	97093037
The Dark - Hex Sealed Fusion	52101615
The Dark Door	30606547
The Dragon Dwelling in the Cave	93346024
The Dragon's Bead	92408984
The Earl of Demise	66989694
The Earth - Hex Sealed Fusion	88696724
The Emperor's Holiday	68400115
The End of Anubis	65403020
The Eye Of Truth	34694160
The Fiend Megacyber	66362965
The Flute of Summoning Dragon	43973174
The Flute of Summoning Kuriboh	20065322
The Forceful Sentry	42829885
The Forces of Darkness	29826127
The Forgiving Maiden	84080938
The Furious Sea King	18710707
The Graveyard in the Fourth Dimension	88089103
The Gross Ghost of Fled Dreams	68049471

CARD	PASSWORD
The Hunter With 7 Weapons	01525329
The Illusionary Gentleman	83764996
The Immortal of Thunder	84926738
The Kick Man	90407382
The Last Warrior From Another Planet	86099788
The Law of the Normal	66926224
The League of Uniform Nomenclature	55008284
The Legendary Fisherman	03643300
The Light - Hex Sealed Fusion	15717011
The Little Swordsman of Aile	25109950
The Masked Beast	49064413
The Portrait's Secret	32541773
The Regulation of Tribe	00296499
The Reliable Guardian	16430187
The Rock Spirit	76305638
The Sanctuary in the Sky	56433456
The Second Sarcophagus	04081094
The Secret of the Bandit	99351431
The Shallow Grave	43434803
The Spell Absorbing Life	99517131
The Thing in the Crater	78243409
The Third Sarcophagus	78697395
The Trojan Horse	38479725
The Unhappy Girl	27618634
The Unhappy Maiden	51275027
The Warrior returning alive	95281259
Theban Nightmare	51838385
Theinen the Great Sphinx	87997872
Thestalos the Firestorm Monarch	26205777
Thousand Dragon	41462083
Thousand Energy	05703682
Thousand Needles	33977496
Thousand-Eyes Idol	27125110
Thousand-Eyes Restrict	63519819
Threatening Roar	36361633
Three-Headed Geedo	78423643
Throwstone Unit	76075810
Thunder Crash	69196160
Thunder Dragon	31786629
Thunder Nyan Nyan	70797118
Thunder of Ruler	91781589
Time Seal	35316708
Time Wizard	71625222
Timeater	44913552
Timidity	40350910
Token Festevil	83675475
Token Thanksgiving	57182235
Tongyo	69572024
Toon Cannon Soldier	79875176
Toon Dark Magician Girl	90960358
Toon Defense	43509019
Toon Gemini Elf	42386471
Toon Goblin Attack Force	15270885

CARD	PASSWORD
Toon Masked Sorcerer	16392422
Toon Mermaid	65458948
Toon Summoned Skull	91842653
Toon Table of Contents	89997728
Toon World	15259703
Tornado Bird	71283180
Tornado Wall	18605135
Torpedo Fish	90337190
Torrential Tribute	53582587
Total Defense Shogun	75372290
Tower of Babel	94256039
Tradgedy	35686187
Transcendent Wings	25573054
Trap Dustshoot	64697231
Trap Hole	04206964
Trap Jammer	19252988
Treeborn Frog	12538374
Tremendous Fire	46918794
Tri-Horned Dragon	39111158
Triage	30888983
Trial of Nightmare	77827521
Trial of the Princesses	72709014
Triangle Ecstasy Spar	12181376T
Triangle Power	32298781
Tribe-Infecting Virus	33184167
Tribute Doll	02903036
Tribute to The Doomed	79759861
Tripwire Beast	45042329
Troop Dragon	55013285
Tsukuyomi	34853266
Turtle Oath	76806714
Turtle Tiger	37313348
Twin Swords of Flashing Light	21900719
Twin-Headed Behemoth	43586926
Twin-Headed Fire Dragon	78984772
Twin-Headed Thunder Dragon	54752875
Twin-Headed Wolf	88132637
Twinheaded Beast	82035781
Two Thousand Needles	83228073
Two-Man Cell Battle	25578802
Two-Mouth Darkruler	57305373
Two-Pronged Attack	83887306
Tyhone	72842870
Type Zero Magic Crusher	21237481
Tyranno Infinity	83235263
Tyrant Dragon	94568601
UFOroid	07602840
UFOroid Fighter	32752319
Ultimate Insect LV 1	49441499
Ultimate Insect LV 3	34088136
Ultimate Insect LV 5	34830502
Ultimate Insect LV 7	19877898
Ultimate Obedient Fiend	32240937
Ultimate Tyranno	15894048
Ultra Evolution Pill	22431243
Umi	22702055
Umiiruka	82999629
Union Attack	60399954
United Resistance	85936485
United We Stand	56747793

CARD	PASSWORD
Unity	14731897
Unshaven Angler	92084010
Upstart Goblin	70368879
Uraby	01784619
Uria, Lord of Sealing Flames	06007213
V-Tiger Jet	51638941
Valkyrion the Magna Warrior	75347539
Vampire Genesis	22056710
Vampire Lord	53839837
Vampire Orchis	46571052
Vengeful Bog Spirit	95220856
Victory D	44910027
Vilepawn Archfiend	73219648
VW-Tiger Catapult	58859575
VWXYZ-Dragon Catapult Cannon	84243274
W-Wing Catapult	96300057
Waboku	12607053
Wall of Revealing Light	17078030
Wandering Mummy	42994702
Warrior Dai Grepher	75953262
Warrior of Zera	66073051
Wasteland	23424603
Water Dragon	85066822
Water Omotics	02483611
Wave Motion Cannon	38992735
Weed Out	28604635
Whiptail Crow	91996584
Whirlwind Prodigy	15090429
White Dragon Ritual	09786492
White Horn Dragon	73891874
White Magical Hat	15150365
White Magician Pikeru	81383947
White Ninja	01571945
Wicked-Breaking Flameberge-Baou	68427465
Wild Nature's Release	61166988
Winged Dragon, Guardian of the Fortress #1	87796900

CARD	PASSWORD
Winged Kuriboh	57116033
Winged Kuriboh LV1	98585345
Winged Minion	89258225
Winged Sage Falcos	87523462
Wingweaver	31447217
Witch Doctor of Chaos	75946257
Witch of the Black Forest	78010363
Witch's Apprentice	80741828
Witty Phantom	36304921
Wolf Axwielder	56369281
Woodborg Inpachi	35322812
Woodland Sprite	06979239
Worm Drake	73216412
Wroughtweiler	06480253
Wynn the Wind Charmer	37744402
X-Head Cannon	62651957
Xing Zhen Hu	76515293
XY-Dragon Cannon	02111707
XYZ-Dragon Cannon	91998119
XZ-Tank Cannon	99724761
Y-Dragon Head	65622692
Yamata Dragon	76862289
Yami	59197169
Yata-Garasu	03078576
Yellow Gadget	13839120
Yellow Luster Shield	04542651
Yomi Ship	51534754
YZ-Tank Dragon	25119460
Z-Metal Tank	64500000
Zaborg the Thunder Monarch	51945556
Zero Gravity	83133491
Zoa	24311372
Zolga	16268841
Zombie Tiger	47693640
Zombyra the Dark	88472456
Zure, Knight of Dark World	07459013

YU-GI-OH! GX TAG FORCE 2

MIDDDAY CONSTELLATION BOOSTER PACK

When buying booster packs, press Up, Up, Down, Down, Left, Right, Left, Right, ⊗, ◉.

CARD PASSWORDS

CARD	PASSWORD
4-Starred Ladybug of Doom	83994646
7 Colored Fish	23771716
A Cat of Ill Omen	24140059
A Deal With Dark Ruler	06850209
A Feather of the Phoenix	49140998
A Feint Plan	68170903
A Hero Emerges	21597117
A Legendary Ocean	00295517
A Man With Wdjat	51351302
A Rival Appears!	05728014
A Wingbeat of Giant Dragon	28596933

CARD	PASSWORD
A-Team: Trap Disposal Unit	13026402
Abare Ushioni	89718302
Absolute End	27744077
Absorbing Kid From the Sky	49771608
Abyss Soldier	18318842
Abyssal Designator	89801755
Acid Trap Hole	41356845
Acrobat Monkey	47372349
Adhesion Trap Hole	62325062
Adhesive Explosive	53828396
After the Struggle	25345186

CARD	PASSWORD
Agido	16135253
Airknight Parshath	18036057
Aitsu	48202661
Alkana Knight Joker	06150044
Alpha the Magnet Warrior	99785935
Altar for Tribute	21070956
Amazon Archer	91869203
Amazoness Archers	67987611
Amazoness Blowpiper	73574678
Amazoness Chain Master	29654737
Amazoness Paladin	47480070
Amazoness Swords Woman	94004268
Amazoness Tiger	10979723
Ambulance Rescueroid	98927491
Ambulanceroid	36378213
Ameba	95174353
Amphibian Beast	67371383
Amphibious Bugroth MK-3	64342551
Amplifier	00303660
An Owl of Luck	23927567
Ancient Elf	93221206
Ancient Gear	31557782
Ancient Gear Beast	10509340
Ancient Gear Cannon	80045583
Ancient Gear Castle	92001300
Ancient Gear Drill	67829249
Ancient Gear Golem	83104731
Ancient Gear Soldier	56094445
Ancient Lamp	54912977
Ancient Lizard Warrior	43230671
Andro Sphinx	15013468
Anteatereatingant	13250922
Anti-Aircraft Flower	65064143
Anti-Spell	53112492
Apprentice Magician	09156135
Appropriate	48539234
Aqua Madoor	85639257
Aqua Spirit	40916023
Arcane Archer of the Forest	55001420
Archfiend of Gilfer	50287060
Archfiend Soldier	49881766
Archlord Zerato	18378582
Armaill	53153481
Armed Changer	90374791
Armed Dragon LV 3	00980973
Armed Dragon LV 5	46384672
Armed Dragon LV 7	73879377
Armed Dragon LV10	59464593
Armed Ninja	09076207
Armed Samurai - Ben Kei	84430950
Armor Axe	07180418
Armor Break	79649195
Armored Lizard	15480588
Armored Starfish	17535588
Armored Zombie	20277860
Array of Revealing Light	69296555
Arsenal Bug	42364374
Arsenal Robber	55348096
Arsenal Summoner	85489096
Assault on GHQ	62633180
Astral Barrier	37053871
Asura Priest	02134346
Aswan Apparition	88236094
Atomic Firefly	87340664
Attack and Receive	63689843
Attack Reflector Unit	91989718
Aussa the Earth Charmer	37970940
Autonomous Action Unit	71453557
Avatar of the Pot	99284890
Axe Dragonute	84914462
Axe of Despair	40619825
B. Skull Dragon	11901678
B.E.S. Covered Core	15317640
B.E.S. Crystal Core	22790789
B.E.S. Tetran	44954628
Baby Dragon	88819587
Back to Square One	47453433
Backfire	82705573
Backup Soldier	36280194
Bad Reaction to Simochi	40633297
Bait Doll	07165085
Ballista of Rampart Smashing	00242146
Banisher of the Light	61528025
Bark of Dark Ruler	41925941
Barrel Dragon	81480460
Basic Insect	89091579
Battery Charger	61181383
Batteryman AA	63142001
Batteryman C	19733961
Batteryman D	55401221
Battle Footballer	48094997
Battle Ox	05053103
Battle-Scarred	94463200
Bazoo The Soul-Eater	40133511
Beast Soul Swap	35149085
Beaver Warrior	32452818
Beckoning Light	16255442
Beelze Frog	49522489
Begone, Knave	20374520
Behemoth the King of All Animals	22996376
Beiige, Vanguard of Dark World	33731070
Berserk Dragon	85605684
Berserk Gorilla	39168895
Beta the Magnet Warrior	39256679
Bickuribox	25655502
Big Bang Shot	61127349
Big Burn	95472621
Big Core	14148099
Big Koala	42129512
Big Shield Gardna	65240384
Big Wave Small Wave	51562916
Big-Tusked Mammoth	59380081
Bio-Mage	58696829
Birdface	45547649
Black Illusion Ritual	41426869
Black Luster Soldier - Envoy of the Beginning	72989439

CARD	PASSWORD
Black Pendant	65169794
Black Tyranno	38670435
Blackland Fire Dragon	87564352
Blade Knight	39507162
Blade Rabbit	58268433
Blade Skater	97023549
Bladefly	28470714
Blast Held By a Tribute	89041555
Blast Magician	21051146
Blast with Chain	98239899
Blasting the Ruins	21466326
Blazing Inpachi	05464695
Blind Destruction	32015116
Blindly Loyal Goblin	35215622
Block Attack	25880422
Blockman	48115277
Blowback Dragon	25551951
Blue-Eyes Shining Dragon	53347303
Blue-Eyes Toon Dragon	53183600
Blue-Eyes Ultimate Dragon	23995346
Blue-Eyes White Dragon	89631139
Blue-Winged Crown	41396436
Bokoichi the Freightening Car	08715625
Bombardment Beetle	57409948
Bonding - H2O	45898858
Boneheimer	98456117
Book of Life	02204140
Book of Moon	14087893
Book of Taiyou	38699854
Boss Rush	66947414
Bottom Dweller	81386177
Bottomless Shifting Sand	76532077
Bottomless Trap Hole	29401950
Bountiful Artemis	32296881
Bowganian	52090844
Bracchio-Raidus	16507828
Brain Control	87910978
Brain Jacker	40267580
Branch!	30548775
Breaker the Magical Warrior	71413901
Broww, Huntsman of Dark World	79126789
Brron, Mad King of Dark World	06214884
Bubble Blaster	53586134
Bubble Illusion	80075749
Bubble Shuffle	61968753
Bubonic Vermin	06104968
Burning Algae	41859700
Burning Beast	59364406
Burning Land	24294108
Burst Breath	80163754
Burst Return	27191436
Burst Stream of Destruction	17655904
Buster Blader	78193831
Buster Rancher	84740193
Butterfly Dagger - Elma	69243953
Byser Shock	17597059

CARD	PASSWORD
Call of The Haunted	97077563
Call of the Mummy	04861205
Cannon Soldier	11384280
Cannonball Spear Shellfish	95614612
Card of Safe Return	57953380
Card Shuffle	12183332
Castle of Dark Illusions	00062121
Cat's Ear Tribe	95841282
Catapult Turtle	95727991
Cathedral of Nobles	29762407
Catnipped Kitty	96501677
Cave Dragon	93220472
Ceasefire	36468556
Celtic Guardian	91152256
Cemetery Bomb	51394546
Centrifugal	01801154
Ceremonial Bell	20228463
Cetus of Dagala	28106077
Chain Burst	48276469
Chain Destruction	01248895
Chain Disappearance	57139487
Chain Energy	79323590
Chain Thrasher	88190453
Chainsaw Insect	77252217
Change of Heart	04031928
Chaos Command Magician	72630549
Chaos Emperor Dragon - Envoy of the End	82301904
Chaos End	61044390
Chaos Greed	97439308
Chaos Necromancer	01434352
Chaos Sorcerer	09596126
Chaosrider Gutaph	47829960
Charcoal Inpachi	13179332
Charm of Shabti	50412166
Charubin the Fire Knight	37421579
Chiron the Mage	16956455
Chopman the Desperate Outlaw	40884383
Chorus of Sanctuary	81380218
Chthonian Alliance	46910446
Chthonian Blast	18271561
Chthonian Polymer	72287557
Chu-Ske the Mouse Fighter	08508055
Clay Charge	22479888
Cliff the Trap Remover	06967870
Cobra Jar	86801871
Cobraman Sakuzy	75109441
Cold Wave	60682203
Collected Power	07565547
Combination Attack	08964854
Command Knight	10375182
Commander Covington	22666164
Commencement Dance	43417563
Compulsory Evacuation Device	94192409
Confiscation	17375316
Conscription	31000575
Continuous Destruction Punch	68057622
Contract With Exodia	33244944

CARD	PASSWORD
Contract With the Abyss	69035382
Contract with the Dark Master	96420087
Convulsion of Nature	62966332
Cost Down	23265313
Covering Fire	74458486
Crab Turtle	91782219
Crass Clown	93889755
Creature Swap	31036355
Creeping Doom Manta	52571838
Crimson Ninja	14618326
Criosphinx	18654201
Cross Counter	37083210
Crush D. Gandra	64681432
Cure Mermaid	85802526
Curse of Aging	41398771
Curse of Anubis	66742250
Curse of Darkness	84970821
Curse of Dragon	28279543
Curse of the Masked Beast	94377247
Curse of Vampire	34294855
Cyber Dragon	70095154
Cyber End Dragon	01546123
Cyber Twin Dragon	74157028
Cyber-Dark Edge	77625948
Cyber-Stein	69015963
Cyberdark Dragon	40418351
Cyberdark Horn	41230939
Cyberdark Keel	03019642
D - Shield	62868900
D - Time	99075257
D. D. Assailant	70074904
D. D. Borderline	60912752
D. D. Crazy Beast	48148828
D. D. Dynamite	08628798
D. D. M. - Different Dimension Master	82112775
D. D. Trainer	86498013
D. D. Trap Hole	05606466
D. D. Warrior Lady	07572887
Dancing Fairy	90925163
Dangerous Machine TYPE-6	76895648
Dark Artist	72520073
Dark Bat	67049542
Dark Blade	11321183
Dark Blade the Dragon Knight	86805855
Dark Driceratops	65287621
Dark Dust Spirit	89111398
Dark Elf	21417692
Dark Energy	04614116
Dark Factory of Mass Production	90928333
Dark Flare Knight	13722870
Dark Hole	53129443
Dark Magic Attack	02314238
Dark Magic Ritual	76792184
Dark Magician	46986414
Dark Magician Girl	38033121
Dark Magician of Chaos	40737112
Dark Magician's Tome of Black Magic	67227834

CARD	PASSWORD
Dark Master - Zorc	97642679
Dark Mirror Force	20522190
Dark Paladin	98502113
Dark Room of Nightmare	85562745
Dark Sage	92377303
Dark Snake Syndrome	47233801
Dark-Piercing Light	45895206
Darkfire Dragon	17881964
Darkfire Soldier #1	05388481
Darkfire Soldier #2	78861134
Darkworld Thorns	43500484
De-Spell	19159413
Deal of Phantom	69122763
Decayed Commander	10209545
Dedication Through Light And Darkness	69542930
Deepsea Shark	28593363
Dekoichi the Battlechanted Locomotive	87621407
Delinquent Duo	44763025
Demotion	72575145
Des Counterblow	39131963
Des Croaking	44883830
Des Dendle	12965761
Des Feral Imp	81985784
Des Frog	84451804
Des Kangaroo	78613627
Des Koala	69579761
Des Lacooda	02326738
Des Wombat	09637706
Desert Sunlight	93747864
Destertapir	13409151
Destiny Board	94212438
Destiny Hero - Captain Tenacious	77608643
Destiny Hero - Diamond Dude	13093792
Destiny Hero - Doom Lord	41613948
Destiny Hero - Dreadmaster	40591390
Destiny Signal	35464895
Destroyer Golem	73481154
Destruction Ring	21219755
Dian Keto the Cure Master	84257639
Dice Jar	03549275
Dimension Distortion	95194279
Dimensional Warrior	37043180
Disappear	24623598
Disarmament	20727787
Disc Fighter	19612721
Dissolverock	40826495
Divine Dragon Ragnarok	62113340
Divine Wrath	49010598
DNA Surgery	74701381
DNA Transplant	56769674
Doitsu	57062206
Dokurorider	99721536
Dokuroyaiba	30325729
Don Turtle	03493978
Don Zaloog	76922029
Doriado	84916669

CARD	PASSWORD
Doriado's Blessing	23965037
Dragon Seeker	28563545
Dragon Treasure	01435851
Dragon Zombie	66672569
Dragon's Mirror	71490127
Dragon's Rage	54178050
Dragoness the Wicked Knight	70681994
Draining Shield	43250041
Dream Clown	13215230
Drillago	99050989
Drillroid	71218746
Dunames Dark Witch	12493482
Dust Tornado	60082867
Earth Chant	59820352
Earthbound Spirit	67105242
Earthquake	82828051
Eatgaboon	42578427
Ebon Magician Curran	46128076
Electro-Whip	37820550
Elegant Egotist	90219263
Element Dragon	30314994
Elemental Burst	61411502
Elemental Hero Avian	21844576
Elemental Hero Bladedge	59793705
Elemental Hero Bubbleman	79979666
Elemental Hero Burstinatrix	58932615
Elemental Hero Clayman	84327329
Elemental Hero Electrum/Erekshieler	29343734
Elemental Hero Flame Wingman	35809262
Elemental Hero Mariner	14225239
Elemental Hero Necroid Shaman	81003500
Elemental Hero Neos	89943723
Elemental Hero Phoenix Enforcer	41436536
Elemental Hero Shining Flare Wingman	25366484
Elemental Hero Shining Phoenix Enforcer	88820235
Elemental Hero Sparkman	20721928
Elemental Hero Thunder Giant	61204971
Elemental Mistress Doriado	99414158
Elemental Recharge	36586443
Elf's Light	39897277
Emblem of Dragon Destroyer	06390406
Embodiment of Apophis	28649820
Emergency Provisions	53046408
Emes the Infinity	43580269
Empress Judge	15237615
Empress Mantis	58818411
Enchanted Javelin	96355986
Enchanting Mermaid	75376965
Enemy Controller	98045062
Enraged Battle Ox	76909279
Enraged Muka Muka	91862578
Eradicating Aerosol	94716515

CARD	PASSWORD
Eternal Draught	56606928
Eternal Rest	95051344
Exhausting Spell	95451366
Exile of the Wicked	26725158
Exiled Force	74131780
Exodia Necross	12600382
Exodia the Forbidden One	33396948
Fairy Box	21598948
Fairy Dragon	20315854
Fairy King Truesdale	45425051
Fairy Meteor Crush	97687912
Faith Bird	75582395
Fatal Abacus	77910045
Fenrir	00218704
Feral Imp	41392891
Fiber Jar	78706415
Fiend Comedian	81172176
Fiend Scorpion	26566878
Fiend's Hand	52800428
Fiend's Mirror	31890399
Final Countdown	95308449
Final Destiny	18591904
Final Flame	73134081
Final Ritual of the Ancients	60369732
Fire Darts	43061293
Fire Eye	88435542
Fire Kraken	46534755
Fire Princess	64752646
Fire Reaper	53581214
Fire Sorcerer	27132350
Firegrass	53293545
Firewing Pegasus	27054370
Fireyarou	71407486
Fissure	66788016
Five God Dragon (Five Headed Dragon)	99267150
Flame Cerebrus	60862676
Flame Champion	42599677
Flame Dancer	12883044
Flame Ghost	58528964
Flame Manipulator	34460851
Flame Swordsman	45231177
Flame Viper	02830619
Flash Assailant	96890582
Flower Wolf	95952802
Flying Fish	31987274
Flying Kamakiri #1	84834865
Flying Kamakiri #2	03134241
Follow Wind	98252586
Foolish Burial	81439173
Forest	87430998
Fortress Whale	62337487
Fortress Whale's Oath	77454922
Frenzied Panda	98818516
Frozen Soul	57069605
Fruits of Kozaky's Studies	49998907
Fuh-Rin-Ka-Zan	01781310
Fuhma Shuriken	09373534
Fulfillment of the Contract	48206762
Fushi No Tori	38538445

CARD	PASSWORD
Fusion Gate	33550694
Fusion Recovery	18511384
Fusion Sage	26902560
Fusion Weapon	27967615
Fusionist	01641883
Gadget Soldier	86281779
Gagagigo	49003308
Gaia Power	56594520
Gaia the Dragon Champion	66889139
Gaia the Fierce Knight	06368038
Gale Dogra	16229315
Gale Lizard	77491079
Gamble	37313786
Gamma the Magnet Warrior	11549357
Garma Sword	90844184
Garma Sword Oath	78577570
Garoozis	14977074
Garuda the Wind Spirit	12800777
Gatling Dragon	87751584
Gazelle the King of Mythical Beasts	05818798
Gear Golem the Moving Fortress	30190809
Gearfried the Iron Knight	00423705
Gearfried the Swordmaster	57046845
Gemini Elf	69140098
Getsu Fuhma	21887179
Giant Axe Mummy	78266168
Giant Germ	95178994
Giant Kozaky	58185394
Giant Orc	73698349
Giant Rat	97017120
Giant Red Seasnake	58831685
Giant Soldier of Stone	13039848
Giant Trunade	42703248
Gift of the Mystical Elf	98299011
Giga Gagagigo	43793530
Giga-Tech Wolf	08471389
Gigantes	47606319
Gigobyte	53776525
Gil Garth	38445524
Gilasaurus	45894482
Giltia the D. Knight	51828629
Girochin Kuwagata	84620194
Goblin Attack Force	78658564
Goblin Calligrapher	12057781
Goblin Elite Attack Force	85306040
Goblin Thief	45311864
Goblin's Secret Remedy	11868825
Gogiga Gagagigo	39674352
Golem Sentry	82323207
Good Goblin Housekeeping	09744376
Gora Turtle	80233946
Graceful Charity	79571449
Graceful Dice	74137509
Gradius	10992251
Gradius' Option	14291024
Granadora	13944422
Grand Tiki Elder	13676474

CARD	PASSWORD
Granmarg the Rock Monarch	60229110
Gravedigger Ghoul	82542267
Gravekeeper's Cannonholder	99877698
Gravekeeper's Curse	50712728
Gravekeeper's Guard	37101832
Gravekeeper's Servant	16762927
Gravekeeper's Spear Soldier	63695531
Gravekeeper's Spy	24317029
Gravekeeper's Vassal	99690140
Graverobber's Retribution	33737664
Gravity Bind	85742772
Gray Wing	29618570
Great Angus	11813953
Great Long Nose	02356994
Great Mammoth of Goldfine	54622031
Green Gadget	41172955
Gren Maju Da Eiza	36584821
Ground Attacker Bugroth	58314394
Ground Collapse	90502999
Gruesome Goo	65623423
Gryphon Wing	55608151
Gryphon's Feather Duster	34370473
Guardian Angel Joan	68007326
Guardian of the Labyrinth	89272878
Guardian of the Sea	85448931
Guardian Sphinx	40659562
Guardian Statue	75209824
Gust Fan	55321970
Gyaku-Gire Panda	09817927
Gyroid	18325492
Hade-Hane	28357177
Hamburger Recipe	80811661
Hammer Shot	26412047
Hamon	32491822
Hand of Nephthys	98446407
Hane-Hane	07089711
Hannibal Necromancer	05640330
Hard Armor	20060230
Harpie Girl	34100324
Harpie Lady 1	91932350
Harpie Lady 2	27927359
Harpie Lady 3	54415063
Harpie Lady Sisters	12206212
Harpie's Brother	30532390
Harpies' Hunting Ground	75782277
Hayabusa Knight	21015833
Headless Knight	05434080
Heart of Clear Water	64801562
Heart of the Underdog	35762283
Heavy Mech Support Platform	23265594
Heavy Storm	19613556
Helios - The Primordial Sun	54493213
Helios Duo Megistus	80887952
Helios Tris Megiste	17286057

CARD	PASSWORD
Helping Robo for Combat	47025270
Hero Barrier	44676200
HERO Flash!!	00191749
Hero Heart	67951831
Hero Kid	32679370
Hero Ring	26647858
Hero Signal	22020907
Hidden Book of Spell	21840375
Hidden Soldier	02047519
Hieracosphinx	82260502
Hieroglyph Lithograph	10248192
High Tide Gyojin	54579801
Hiita the Fire Charmer	00759393
Hino-Kagu-Tsuchi	75745607
Hinotama Soul	96851799
Hiro's Shadow Scout	81863068
Hitotsu-Me Giant	76184692
Holy Knight Ishzark	57902462
Homunculus the Alchemic Being	40410110
Horn of Heaven	98069388
Horn of Light	38552107
Horn of the Unicorn	64047146
Horus The Black Flame Dragon LV4	75830094
Horus The Black Flame Dragon LV6	11224103
Horus The Black Flame Dragon LV8	48229808
Hoshiningen	67629977
House of Adhesive Tape	15083728
Howling Insect	93107608
Huge Revolution	65396880
Human-Wave Tactics	30353551
Humanoid Slime	46821314
Humanoid Worm Drake	05600127
Hungry Burger	30243636
Hydrogeddon	22587018
Hyena	22873798
Hyozanryu	62397231
Hyper Hammerhead	02671330
Hysteric Fairy	21297224
Icarus Attack	53567095
Illusionist Faceless Mage	28546905
Impenetrable Formation	96631852
Imperial Order	61740673
Inaba White Rabbit	77084837
Incandescent Ordeal	33031674
Indomitable Fighter Lei Lei	84173492
Infernal Flame Emperor	19847532
Infernal Queen Archfiend	08581705
Inferno	74823665
Inferno Fire Blast	52684508
Inferno Hammer	17185260
Inferno Reckless Summon	12247206
Inferno Tempest	14391920
Infinite Cards	94163677
Infinite Dismissal	54109233
Injection Fairy Lily	79575620
Inpachi	97923414

CARD	PASSWORD
Insect Armor with Laser Cannon	03492538
Insect Barrier	23615409
Insect Imitation	96965364
Insect Knight	35052053
Insect Princess	37957847
Insect Queen	91512835
Insect Soldiers of the Sky	07019529
Inspection	16227556
Interdimensional Matter Transporter	36261276
Invader From Another Dimension	28450915
Invader of Darkness	56647086
Invader of the Throne	03056267
Invasion of Flames	26082229
Invigoration	98374133
Iron Blacksmith Kotetsu	73431236
Island Turtle	04042268
Jack's Knight	90876561
Jade Insect Whistle	95214051
Jam Breeding Machine	21770260
Jam Defender	21558682
Jar of Greed	83968380
Jar Robber	33784505
Javelin Beetle	26932788
Javelin Beetle Pact	41182875
Jellyfish	14851496
Jerry Beans Man	23635815
Jetroid	43697559
Jinzo	77585513
Jinzo #7	32809211
Jirai Gumo	94773007
Jowgen the Spiritualist	41855169
Jowls of Dark Demise	05257687
Judge Man	30113682
Judgment of Anubis	55256016
Just Desserts	24068492
KA-2 Des Scissors	52768103
Kabazauls	51934376
Kagemusha of the Blue Flame	15401633
Kaibaman	34627841
Kaiser Dragon	94566432
Kaiser Glider	52824910
Kaiser Sea Horse	17444133
Kaminari Attack	09653271
Kaminote Blow	97570038
Kamionwizard	41544074
Kangaroo Champ	95789089
Karate Man	23289281
Karbonala Warrior	54541900
Karma Cut	71587526
Kelbek	54878498
Keldo	80441106
Killer Needle	88979991
Kinetic Soldier	79853073
King Dragun	13756293
King Fog	84686841
King of the Skull Servants	36021814
King of the Swamp	79109599
King of Yamimakai	69455834

CARD	PASSWORD
King Tiger Wanghu	83986578
King's Knight	64788463
Kiryu	84814897
Kiseitai	04266839
Kishido Spirit	60519422
Knight's Title	87210505
Koitsu	69456283
Kojikocy	01184620
Kotodama	19406822
Kozaky	99171160
Kozaky's Self-Destruct Button	21908319
Kryuel	82642348
Kumootoko	56283725
Kurama	85705804
Kuriboh	40640057
Kuwagata Alpha	60802233
Kwagar Hercules	95144193
Kycoo The Ghost Destroyer	88240808
La Jinn The Mystical Genie of The Lamp	97590747
Labyrinth of Nightmare	66526672
Labyrinth Tank	99551425
Lady Assailant of Flames	90147755
Lady Ninja Yae	82005435
Lady of Faith	17358176
Larvas	94675535
Laser Cannon Armor	77007920
Last Day of Witch	90330453
Last Turn	28566710
Launcher Spider	87322377
Lava Battleguard	20394040
Lava Golem	00102380
Layard the Liberator	67468948
Left Arm of the Forbidden One	07902349
Left Leg of the Forbidden One	44519536
Legendary Black Belt	96438440
Legendary Flame Lord	60258960
Legendary Jujitsu Master	25773409
Legendary Sword	61854111
Leghul	12472242
Lekunga	62543393
Lesser Dragon	55444629
Lesser Fiend	16475472
Level Conversion Lab	84397023
Level Limit - Area A	54976796
Level Limit - Area B	03136426
Level Modulation	61850482
Level Up!	25290459
Levia-Dragon	37721209
Light of Intervention	62867251
Light of Judgment	44595286
Lighten the Load	37231841
Lightforce Sword	49587034
Lightning Blade	55226821
Lightning Conger	27671321
Lightning Vortex	69162969
Limiter Removal	23171610
Liquid Beast	93108297
Little Chimera	68658728

CARD	PASSWORD
Little-Winguard	90790253
Lizard Soldier	20831168
Lord of D.	17985575
Lord of the Lamp	99510761
Lost Guardian	45871897
Luminous Soldier	57282479
Luminous Spark	81777047
Luster Dragon	11091375
Luster Dragon #2	17658803
M-Warrior #1	56342351
M-Warrior #2	92731455
Machine Conversion Factory	25769732
Machine Duplication	63995093
Machine King	46700124
Machine King Prototype	89222931
Machiners Defender	96384007
Machiners Force	58054262
Machiners Sniper	23782705
Machiners Soldier	60999392
Mad Dog of Darkness	79182538
Mad Lobster	97240270
Mad Sword Beast	79870141
Mage Power	83746708
Magic Drain	59344077
Magic Jammer	77414722
Magical Cylinder	62279055
Magical Dimension	28553439
Magical Explosion	32723153
Magical Hats	81210420
Magical Labyrinth	64389297
Magical Marionette	08034697
Magical Merchant	32362575
Magical Plant Mandragola	07802006
Magical Scientist	34206604
Magical Thorn	53119267
Magician of Black Chaos	30208479
Magician of Faith	31560081
Magician's Circle	00050755
Magician's Unite	36045450
Magician's Valkyrie	80304126
Magnet Circle	94940436
Maha Vailo	93013676
Maharaghi	40695128
Maiden of the Aqua	17214465
Maji-Gire Panda	60102563
Maju Garzett	08794435
Makiu	27827272
Makyura the Destructor	21593977
Malevolent Nuzzler	99597615
Malfunction	06137095
Malice Ascendant	14255590
Malice Dispersion	13626450
Mammoth Graveyard	40374923
Man Eater	93553943
Man-Eater Bug	54652250
Man-Eating Black Shark	80727036
Man-Eating Treasure Chest	13723605
Man-Thro' Tro'	43714890
Manga Ryu-Ran	38369349
Manju of the Ten Thousand Hands	95492061

CARD	PASSWORD
Manticore of Darkness	77121851
Marauding Captain	02460565
Marie the Fallen One	57579381
Marine Beast	29929832
Marshmallon	31305911
Marshmallon Glasses	66865880
Maryokutai	71466592
Masaki the Legendary Swordsman	44287299
Mask of Brutality	82432018
Mask of Darkness	28933734
Mask of Restrict	29549364
Mask of Weakness	57882509
Masked Dragon	39191307
Masked of the Accursed	56948373
Masked Sorcerer	10189126
Mass Driver	34906152
Master Kyonshee	24530661
Master Monk	49814180
Master of Dragon Knight	62873545
Master of Oz	27134689
Mataza the Zapper	22609617
Mavelus	59036972
Maximum Six	30707994
Mazera DeVille	06133894
Mech Mole Zombie	63545455
Mecha-Dog Marron	94667532
Mechanical Hound	22512237
Mechanical Snail	34442949
Mechanical Spider	45688586
Mechanicalchaser	07359741
Meda Bat	76211194
Medusa Worm	02694423
Mefist the Infernal General	46820049
Mega Thunderball	21817254
Mega Ton Magical Cannon	32062913
Megamorph	22046459
Megarock Dragon	71544954
Melchid the Four-Face Beast	86569121
Memory Crusher	48700891
Mermaid Knight	24435369
Messenger of Peace	44656491
Metal Armored Bug	65957473
Metal Dragon	09293977
Metallizing Parasite	07369217
Metalmorph	68540058
Metalzoa	50705071
Metamorphosis	46411259
Meteor B. Dragon	90660762
Meteor Dragon	64271667
Meteor of Destruction	33767325
Meteorain	64274292
Michizure	37580756
Micro-Ray	18190572
Mid Shield Gardna	75487237
Mighty Guard	62327910
Mikazukinoyaiba	38277918
Millennium Golem	47986555
Millennium Scorpion	82482194
Millennium Shield	32012841
Milus Radiant	07489323

CARD	PASSWORD
Minar	32539892
Mind Control	37520316
Mind Haxorz	75392615
Mind on Air	66690411
Mind Wipe	52718046
Mine Golem	76321376
Minefield Eruption	85519211
Minor Goblin Official	01918087
Miracle Dig	06343408
Miracle Fusion	45906428
Miracle Kid	55985014
Miracle Restoring	68334074
Mirage Dragon	15960641
Mirage Knight	49217579
Mirage of Nightmare	41482598
Mirror Force	44095762
Mirror Wall	22359980
Misfortune	01036974
Mispolymerization	58392024
Mistobody	47529357
Moai Interceptor Cannons	45159319
Mobius the Frost Monarch	04929256
Moisture Creature	75285069
Mokey Mokey	27288416
Mokey Mokey King	13803864
Mokey Mokey Smackdown	01965724
Molten Behemoth	17192817
Molten Destruction	19384334
Molten Zombie	04732017
Monk Fighter	03810071
Monster Egg	36121917
Monster Eye	84133008
Monster Gate	43040603
Monster Reborn	83764718
Monster Recovery	93108433
Monster Reincarnation	74848038
Mooyan Curry	58074572
Morale Boost	93671934
Morphing Jar	33508719
Morphing Jar #2	79106360
Mother Grizzly	57839750
Mountain	50913601
Mr. Volcano	31477025
Mudora	82108372
Muka Muka	46657337
Multiplication of Ants	22493811
Multiply	40703222
Musician King	56907389
Mustering of the Dark Scorpions	68191243
Mysterious Puppeteer	54098121
Mystic Horseman	68516705
Mystic Lamp	98049915
Mystic Plasma Zone	18161786
Mystic Swordsman LV 2	47507260
Mystic Swordsman LV 4	74591968
Mystic Swordsman LV 6	60482781
Mystic Tomato	83011277
Mystic Wok	80161395
Mystical Beast Serket	89194033
Mystical Elf	15025844

CARD	PASSWORD
Mystical Knight of Jackal	98745000
Mystical Moon	36607978
Mystical Sand	32751480
Mystical Sheep #2	30451366
Mystical Shine Ball	39552864
Mystical Space Typhoon	05318639
Mystik Wok	80161395
Mythical Beast Cerberus	55424270
Nanobreaker	70948327
Necklace of Command	48576971
Necrovalley	47355498
Needle Ball	94230224
Needle Burrower	98162242
Needle Ceiling	38411870
Needle Wall	38299233
Needle Worm	81843628
Negate Attack	14315573
Nemuriko	90963488
Neo Aqua Madoor	49563947
Neo Bug	16587243
Neo the Magic Swordsman	50930991
Neo-Space	40215635
Neo-Spacian Aqua Dolphin	17955766
Newdoria	04335645
Next to be Lost	07076131
Night Assailant	16226786
Nightmare Horse	59290628
Nightmare Penguin	81306586
Nightmare Wheel	54704216
Nightmare's Steelcage	58775978
Nimble Momonga	22567609
Nin-Ken Dog	11987744
Ninja Grandmaster Sasuke	04041838
Ninjitsu Art of Decoy	89628781
Ninjitsu Art of Transformation	70861343
Nitro Unit	23842445
Niwatori	07805359
Nobleman of Crossout	71044499
Nobleman of Extermination	17449108
Nobleman-Eater Bug	65878864
Non Aggression Area	76848240
Non-Fusion Area	27581098
Non-Spellcasting Area	20065549
Novox's Prayer	43694075
Nubian Guard	51616747
Numinous Healer	02130625
Nutrient Z	29389368
Nuvia the Wicked	12953226
O - Oversoul	63703130
Obnoxious Celtic Guardian	52077741
Ocubeam	86088138
Offerings to the Doomed	19230407
Ojama Black	79335209
Ojama Delta Hurricane	08251996
Ojama Green	12482652
Ojama King	90140980
Ojama Trio	29843091

CARD	PASSWORD
Ojama Yellow	42941100
Ojamagic	24643836
Ojamuscle	98259197
Old Vindictive Magician	45141844
Ominous Fortunetelling	56995655
Oni Tank T-34	66927994
Opti-Camaflauge Armor	44762290
Opticlops	14531242
Option Hunter	33248692
Orca Mega-Fortress of Darkness	63120904
Ordeal of a Traveler	39537362
Order to Charge	78986941
Order to Smash	39019325
Otohime	39751093
Outstanding Dog Marron	11548522
Overdrive	02311603
Oxygeddon	58071123
Painful Choice	74191942
Paladin of White Dragon	73398797
Pale Beast	21263083
Pandemonium	94585852
Pandemonium Watchbear	75375465
Parasite Paracide	27911549
Parasitic Ticky	87978805
Patrician of Darkness	19153634
Patroid	71930383
Penguin Knight	36039163
Penumbral Soldier Lady	64751286
People Running About	12143771
Perfect Machine King	18891691
Performance of Sword	04849037
Petit Angel	38142739
Petit Dragon	75356564
Petit Moth	58192742
Phantasmal Martyrs	93224848
Phantom Beast Cross-Wing	71181155
Phantom Beast Thunder-Pegasus	34961968
Phantom Beast Wild-Horn	07576264
Pharaoh's Servant	52550973
Pharonic Protector	89959682
Phoenix Wing Wind Blast	63356631
Photon Generator Unit	66607691
Pikeru's Circle of Enchantment	74270067
Pikeru's Second Sight	58015506
Pinch Hopper	26185991
Pineapple Blast	90669991
Piranha Army	50823978
Pitch-Black Power Stone	34029630
Pitch-Black Warwolf	88975532
Pitch-Dark Dragon	47415292
Poison Draw Frog	56840658
Poison Fangs	76539047
Poison Mummy	43716289
Poison of the Old Man	08842266
Polymerization	24094653
Possessed Dark Soul	52860176

CARD	PASSWORD
Pot of Avarice	67169062
Pot of Generosity	70278545
Pot of Greed	55144522
Power Bond	37630732
Power Capsule	54289683
Precious Card from Beyond	68304813
Premature Burial	70828912
Prepare to Strike Back	04483989
Prevent Rat	00549481
Prickle Fairy	91559748
Primal Seed	23701465
Princess Curran	02316186
Princess of Tsurugi	51371017
Princess Pikeru	75917088
Protective Soul Ailin	11678191
Protector of the Sanctuary	24221739
Protector of the Throne	10071456
Proto-Cyber Dragon	26439287
Pumpking the King of Ghosts	29155212
Punished Eagle	74703140
Pyramid of Light	53569894
Pyramid Turtle	77044671
Queen's Knight	25652259
Rabid Horseman	94905343
Rafflesia Seduction	31440542
Raging Flame Sprite	90810762
Raigeki	12580477
Raigeki Break	04178474
Rain Of Mercy	66719324
Rainbow Flower	21347810
Rallis the Star Bird	41382147
Rancer Dragonute	11125718
Rapid-Fire Magician	06337436
Rare Metalmorph	12503902
Raregold Armor	07625614
Raviel, Lord of Phantasms	69890967
Ray & Temperature	85309439
Ray of Hope	82529174
Re-Fusion	74694807
Ready For Intercepting	31785398
Really Eternal Rest	28121403
Reaper of the Cards	33066139
Reaper of the Nightmare	85684223
Reasoning	58577036
Reborn Zombie	23421244
Reckless Greed	37576645
Recycle	96316857
Red Archery Girl	65570596
Red Gadget	86445415
Red Medicine	38199696
Red Moon Baby	56387350
Red-Eyes B. Chick	36262024
Red-Eyes B. Dragon	74677422
Red-Eyes Black Metal Dragon	64335804
Red-Eyes Darkness Dragon	96561011
Reflect Bounder	02851070
Regenerating Mummy	70821187

CARD	PASSWORD
Reinforcement of the Army	32807846
Release Restraint	75417459
Relinquished	64631466
Reload	22589918
Remove Trap	51482758
Rescue Cat	14878871
Rescueroid	24311595
Reshef the Dark Being	62420419
Respect Play	08951260
Return from the Different Dimension	27174286
Return of the Doomed	19827717
Reversal of Graves	17484499
Reversal Quiz	05990062
Revival Jam	31709826
Right Arm of the Forbidden One	70903634
Right Leg of the Forbidden One	08124921
Ring of Defense	58641905
Ring of Destruction	83555666
Ring of Magnetism	20436034
Riryoku Field	70344351
Rising Air Current	45778932
Rising Energy	78211862
Rite of Spirit	30450531
Ritual Weapon	54351224
Robbin' Goblin	88279736
Robbin' Zombie	83258273
Robolady	92421852
Robotic Knight	44203504
Roboyarou	38916461
Rock Bombardment	20781762
Rock Ogre Grotto	68846917
Rocket Jumper	53890795
Rocket Warrior	30860696
Rod of the Mind's Eye	94793422
Roll Out!	91597389
Root Water	39004808
Rope of Life	93382620
Rope of Spirit	37383714
Roulette Barrel	46303688
Royal Command	33950246
Royal Decree	51452091
Royal Keeper	16509093
Royal Knight	68280530
Royal Magical Library	70791313
Royal Surrender	56058888
Royal Tribute	72405967
Ruin, Queen of Oblivion	46427957
Rush Recklessly	70046172
Ryu Kokki	57281778
Ryu Senshi	49868263
Ryu-Kishin Clown	42647539
Ryu-Kishin Powered	24611934
Saber Beetle	49645921
Sacred Crane	30914564
Sacred Phoenix of Nephthys	61441708
Saggi the Dark Clown	66602787
Sakuretsu Armor	56120475
Salamandra	32268901
Salvage	96947648

CARD	PASSWORD
Samsara	44182827
Sand Gambler	50593156
Sand Moth	73648243
Sangan	26202165
Sanwitch	53539634
Sasuke Samurai	16222645
Sasuke Samurai #2	11760174
Sasuke Samurai #3	77379481
Sasuke Samurai #4	64538655
Satellite Cannon	50400231
Scapegoat	73915051
Scarr, Scout of Dark World	05498296
Science Soldier	67532912
Scroll of Bewitchment	10352095
Scyscraper	63035430
Sea Serpent Warrior of Darkness	42071342
Sealmaster Meisei	02468169
Second Coin Toss	36562627
Second Goblin	19086954
Secret Barrel	27053506
Self-Destruct Button	57585212
Senri Eye	60391791
Serial Spell	49398568
Serpent Night Dragon	66516792
Serpentine Princess	71829750
Servant of Catabolism	02792265
Seven Tools of the Bandit	03819470
Shadow Ghoul	30778711
Shadow Of Eyes	58621589
Shadow Tamer	37620434
Shadowknight Archfiend	09603356
Shadowslayer	20939559
Share the Pain	56830749
Shield & Sword	52097679
Shield Crash	30683373
Shien's Spy	07672244
Shift	59560625
Shifting Shadows	59237154
Shinato's Ark	60365591
Shinato, King of a Higher Plane	86327225
Shining Abyss	87303357
Shining Angel	95956346
Shooting Star Bow - Ceal	95638658
Silent Insect	40867519
Silent Magician Lv4	73665146
Silent Magician Lv8	72443568
Silent Swordsman LV3	01995985
Silent Swordsman LV5	74388798
Silent Swordsman LV7	37267041
Sillva, Warlord of Dark World	32619583
Silpheed	73001017
Silver Fang	90357090
Simorgh, Bird of Divinity	14989021
Simultaneous Loss	92219931
Sinister Serpent	08131171
Sixth Sense	03280747
Skill Drain	82732705

CARD	PASSWORD
Skilled Dark Magician	73752131
Skilled White Magician	46363422
Skull Archfiend of Lightning	61370518
Skull Descovery Knight	78700060
Skull Dog Marron	86652646
Skull Invitation	98139712
Skull Lair	06733059
Skull Mariner	05265750
Skull Red Bird	10202894
Skull Servant	32274490
Skull Zoma	79852326
Skull-Mark Ladybug	64306248
Skyscraper	63035430
Slate Warrior	78636495
Smashing Ground	97169186
Smoke Grenade of the Thief	63789924
Snatch Steal	45986603
Sogen	86318356
Soitsu	60246171
Solar Flare Dragon	45985838
Solar Ray	44472639
Solemn Judgment	41420027
Solemn Wishes	35346968
Solomon's Lawbook	23471572
Sonic Duck	84696266
Sonic Jammer	84550200
Sorcerer of Dark Magic	88619463
Soul Absorption	68073522
Soul Exchange	68005187
Soul of Purity and Light	77527210
Soul Release	05758500
Soul Resurrection	92924317
Soul Reversal	78864369
Soul Tiger	15734813
Soul-Absorbing Bone Tower	63012333
Souleater	31242786
Souls Of The Forgotten	04920010
Space Mambo	36119641
Spark Blaster	97362768
Sparks	76103675
Spatial Collapse	20644748
Spear Cretin	58551308
Spear Dragon	31553716
Spell Canceller	84636823
Spell Economics	04259068
Spell Purification	01669772
Spell Reproduction	29228529
Spell Shield Type-8	38275183
Spell Vanishing	29735721
Spell-Stopping Statute	10069180
Spellbinding Circle	18807108
Spherous Lady	52121290
Sphinx Teleia	51402177
Spiral Spear Strike	49328340
Spirit Barrier	53239672
Spirit Caller	48659020
Spirit Message A	94772232
Spirit Message I	31893528
Spirit Message L	30170981
Spirit Message N	67287533

CARD	PASSWORD
Spirit of Flames	13522325
Spirit of the Breeze	53530069
Spirit of the Harp	80770678
Spirit of the Pharaoh	25343280
Spirit Reaper	23205979
Spirit Ryu	67957315
Spiritual Earth Art - Kurogane	70156997
Spiritual Energy Settle Machine	99173029
Spiritual Fire Art - Kurenai	42945701
Spiritual Water Art - Aoi	06540606
Spiritual Wind Art - Miyabi	79333300
Spiritualism	15866454
St. Joan	21175632
Stamping Destruction	81385346
Star Boy	08201910
Statue of the Wicked	65810489
Staunch Defender	92854392
Stealth Bird	03510565
Steam Gyroid	05368615
Steamroid	44729197
Steel Ogre Grotto #1	29172562
Steel Ogre Grotto #2	90908427
Stim-Pack	83225447
Stop Defense	63102017
Storming Wynn	29013526
Stray Lambs	60764581
Strike Ninja	41006930
Stronghold	13955608
Stumbling	34646691
Success Probability 0%	06859683
Summon Priest	00423585
Summoned Skull	70781052
Summoner of Illusions	14644902
Super Conductor Tyranno	85520851
Super Rejuvenation	27770341
Super Robolady	75923050
Super Roboyarou	01412158
Supply	44072894
Susa Soldier	40473581
Swarm of Locusts	41872150
Swarm of Scarabs	15383415
Swift Gaia the Fierce Knight	16589042
Sword Hunter	51345461
Sword of Deep-Seated	98495314
Sword of Dragon's Soul	61405855
Sword of the Soul Eater	05371656
Swords of Concealing Light	12923641
Swords of Revealing Light	72302403
Swordsman of Landstar	03573512
Symbol of Heritage	45305419
System Down	18895832
T.A.D.P.O.L.E.	10456559
Tactical Espionage Expert	89698120
Tailor of the Fickle	43641473
Taunt	90740329
Tenkabito Shien	41589166

CARD	PASSWORD
Terra the Terrible	63308047
Terraforming	73628505
Terrorking Archfiend	35975813
Terrorking Salmon	78060096
Teva	16469012
The Agent of Creation - Venus	64734921
The Agent of Force - Mars	91123920
The Agent of Judgment - Saturn	91345518
The Agent of Wisdom - Mercury	38730226
The All-Seeing White Tiger	32269855
The Big March of Animals	01689516
The Bistro Butcher	71107816
The Cheerful Coffin	41142615
The Creator	61505339
The Creator Incarnate	97093037
The Dark - Hex Sealed Fusion	52101615
The Dark Door	30606547
The Dragon Dwelling in the Cave	93346024
The Dragon's Bead	92408984
The Earl of Demise	66989694
The Earth - Hex Sealed Fusion	88696724
The Emperor's Holiday	68400115
The End of Anubis	65403020
The Eye Of Truth	34694160
The Fiend Megacyber	66362965
The Flute of Summoning Dragon	43973174
The Flute of Summoning Kuriboh	20065322
The Forceful Sentry	42829885
The Forces of Darkness	29826127
The Forgiving Maiden	84080938
The Furious Sea King	18710707
The Graveyard in the Fourth Dimension	88089103
The Gross Ghost of Fled Dreams	68049471
The Hunter With 7 Weapons	01525329
The Illusionary Gentleman	83764996
The Immortal of Thunder	84926738
The Kick Man	90407382
The Last Warrior From Another Planet	86099788
The Law of the Normal	66926224
The League of Uniform Nomenclature	55008284
The Legendary Fisherman	03643300
The Light - Hex Sealed Fusion	15717011
The Little Swordsman of Aile	25109950
The Masked Beast	49064413
The Portrait's Secret	32541773
The Regulation of Tribe	00296499

CARD	PASSWORD
The Reliable Guardian	16430187
The Rock Spirit	76305638
The Sanctuary in the Sky	56433456
The Second Sarcophagus	04081094
The Secret of the Bandit	99351431
The Shallow Grave	43434803
The Spell Absorbing Life	99517131
The Thing in the Crater	78243409
The Third Sarcophagus	78697395
The Trojan Horse	38479725
The Unhappy Girl	27618634
The Unhappy Maiden	51275027
The Warrior Returning Alive	95281259
Theban Nightmare	51838385
Theinen the Great Sphinx	87997872
Thestalos the Firestorm Monarch	26205777
Thousand Dragon	41462083
Thousand Energy	05703682
Thousand Needles	33977496
Thousand-Eyes Idol	27125110
Thousand-Eyes Restrict	63519819
Threatening Roar	36361633
Three-Headed Geedo	78423643
Throwstone Unit	76075810
Thunder Crash	69196160
Thunder Dragon	31786629
Thunder Nyan Nyan	70797118
Thunder of Ruler	91781589
Time Seal	35316708
Time Wizard	71625222
Timeater	44913552
Timidity	40350910
Token Festevil	83675475
Token Thanksgiving	57182235
Tongyo	69572024
Toon Cannon Soldier	79875176
Toon Dark Magician Girl	90960358
Toon Defense	43509019
Toon Gemini Elf	42386471
Toon Goblin Attack Force	15270885
Toon Masked Sorcerer	16392422
Toon Mermaid	65458948
Toon Summoned Skull	91842653
Toon Table of Contents	89997728
Toon World	15259703
Tornado Bird	71283180
Tornado Wall	18605135
Torpedo Fish	90337190
Torrential Tribute	53582587
Total Defense Shogun	75372290
Tower of Babel	94256039
Tradgedy	35686187
Transcendent Wings	25573054
Trap Dustshoot	64697231
Trap Hole	04206964
Trap Jammer	19252988
Treeborn Frog	12538374
Tremendous Fire	46918794
Tri-Horned Dragon	39111158
Triage	30888983
Trial of Nightmare	77827521
Trial of the Princesses	72709014
Triangle Ecstasy Spark	12181376
Triangle Power	32298781
Tribe-Infecting Virus	33184167
Tribute Doll	02903036
Tribute to The Doomed	79759861
Tripwire Beast	45042329
Troop Dragon	55013285
Tsukuyomi	34853266
Turtle Oath	76806714
Turtle Tiger	37313348
Twin Swords of Flashing Light	21900719
Twin-Headed Beast	82035781
Twin-Headed Behemoth	43586926
Twin-Headed Fire Dragon	78984772
Twin-Headed Thunder Dragon	54752875
Twin-Headed Wolf	88132637
Two Thousand Needles	83228073
Two-Man Cell Battle	25578802
Two-Mouth Darkruler	57305373
Two-Pronged Attack	83887306
Tyhone	72842870
Type Zero Magic Crusher	21237481
Tyranno Infinity	83235263
Tyrant Dragon	94568601
UFOroid	07602840
UFOroid Fighter	32752319
Ultimate Insect LV1	49441499
Ultimate Insect LV3	34088136
Ultimate Insect LV5	34830502
Ultimate Insect LV7	19877898
Ultimate Obedient Fiend	32240937
Ultimate Tyranno	15894048
Ultra Evolution Pill	22431243
Umi	22702055
Umiiruka	82999629
Union Attack	60399954
United Resistance	85936485
United We Stand	56747793
Unity	14731897
Unshaven Angler	92084010
Upstart Goblin	70368879
Uraby	01784619
Uria, Lord of Sealing Flames	06007213
V-Tiger Jet	51638941
Valkyrion the Magna Warrior	75347539
Vampire Genesis	22056710
Vampire Lord	53839837
Vampire Orchis	46571052
Vengeful Bog Spirit	95220856
Victory D	44910027
Vilepawn Archfiend	73219648
VW-Tiger Catapult	58859575
VWXYZ-Dragon Catapult Cannon	84243274

CARD	PASSWORD
W-Wing Catapult	96300057
Waboku	12607053
Wall of Revealing Light	17078030
Wandering Mummy	42994702
Warrior Dai Grepher	75953262
Warrior of Zera	66073051
Wasteland	23424603
Water Dragon	85066822
Water Omotics	02483611
Wave Motion Cannon	38992735
Weed Out	28604635
Whiptail Crow	91996584
Whirlwind Prodigy	15090429
White Dragon Ritual	09786492
White Horn Dragon	73891874
White Magical Hat	15150365
White Magician Pikeru	81383947
White Ninja	01571945
Wicked-Breaking Flameberge-Baou	68427465
Wild Nature's Release	61166988
Winged Dragon, Guardian of the Fortress #1	87796900
Winged Kuriboh	57116033
Winged Kuriboh LV10	98585345
Winged Minion	89258225
Winged Sage Falcos	87523462
Wingweaver	31447217
Witch Doctor of Chaos	75946257
Witch of the Black Forest	78010363
Witch's Apprentice	80741828

CARD	PASSWORD
Witty Phantom	36304921
Wolf Axwielder	56369281
Woodborg Inpachi	35322812
Woodland Sprite	06979239
Worm Drake	73216412
Wroughtweiler	06480253
Wynn the Wind Charmer	37744402
X-Head Cannon	62651957
Xing Zhen Hu	76515293
XY-Dragon Cannon	02111707
XYZ-Dragon Cannon	91998119
XZ-Tank Cannon	99724761
Y-Dragon Head	65622692
Yamata Dragon	76862289
Yami	59197169
Yata-Garasu	03078576
Yellow Gadget	13839120
Yellow Luster Shield	04542651
Yomi Ship	51534754
YZ-Tank Dragon	25119460
Z-Metal Tank	64500000
Zaborg the Thunder Monarch	51945556
Zero Gravity	83133491
Zoa	24311372
Zolga	16268841
Zombie Tiger	47693640
Zombyra the Dark	88472456
Zure, Knight of Dark World	07459013

GAME BOY® ADVANCE

GAMES

ACE COMBAT ADVANCE

COMPLETE GAME WITH ALL PLANES & LEVELS OPEN

Select Enter Code and enter QF9B9F59.

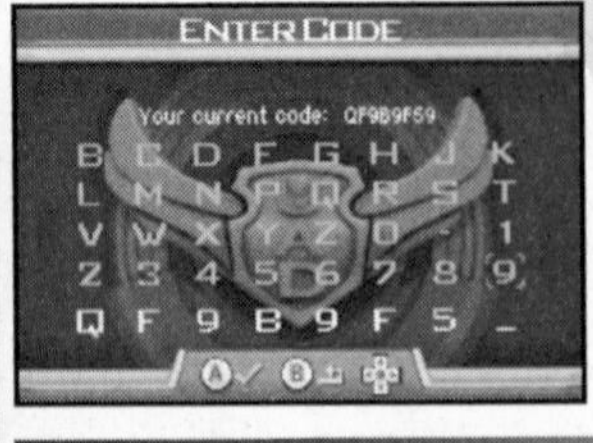

BANJO PILOT

GRUNTY

Defeat Grunty in the Broomstick battle race. Then you can purchase Grunty from Cheato.

HUMBA WUMBA

Defeat Humba Wumba in the Jiggu battle race. Then you can purchase Humba Wumba from Cheato.

JOLLY

Defeat Jolly in the Pumpkin battle race. Then you can purchase Jolly from Cheato.

KLUNGO

Defeat Klungo in the Skull battle race. Then you can purchase Klungo from Cheato.

BARBIE AS THE PRINCESS AND THE PAUPER

PASSWORDS

LEVEL	PASSWORD
1-2	Preminger, Wolfie, Erika, Serafina
1-3	Wolfie, Preminger, Serafina, Preminger
1-4	Preminger, Wolfie, Serfania, Wolfie
Boss 1	Serafina, Woflia. Erika, Preminger
2-1	Princess Anneliese, Preminger, Wolfie, Erika
2-2	Preminger, Princess Anneliese, Wolfie, Erika
2-3	Preminger, Serafina, Preminger, Erika
2-4	Serafina, Erika, Preminger, Wolfie
Boss 2	Preminger, Erika, Serafina, Wolfie
3-1	Wolfie, Preminger, Wolfie, Erika
3-2	Serafina, Preminger, Erika, Serafina
3-3	Erika, Wolfie, Serafina, Princess Anneliese
3-4	Erika, Serafina, Erika, Preminger
Boss 3	Preminger, Serafina, Princess Anneliese, Serafina
4-1	Wolfie, Serafina, Preminger, Serafina
4-2	Preminger, Serafina, Princess Anneliese, Preminger
4-3	Wolfie, Serafina, Erika, Serafina
Boss 4	Erika, Serafina, Princess Anneliese, Wolfie
Final Boss	Erika, Princess Anneliese, Princess Anneliese, Man
Arcade Level	Princess Anneliese, Serafina, Erika, Wolfie

BIONICLE: TALES OF THE TOHUNGA

EVERYTHING BUT THE MINI-GAMES

Enter B9RBRN as a name.

GALI MINI-GAME

Enter 9MA268 as a name.

KOPAKA MINI-GAME

Enter V33673 as a name.

LEWA MINI-GAME

Enter 3LT154 as a name.

ONUA MINI-GAME

Enter 8MR472 as a name.

POHATU MINI-GAME

Enter 5MG834 as a name.

TAHU MINI-GAME

Enter 4CR487 as a name.

CAR BATTLER JOE

BIG BANG

At the Main menu, select Battle League. When the game asks "Use which machine," choose password and enter HAMA!333.

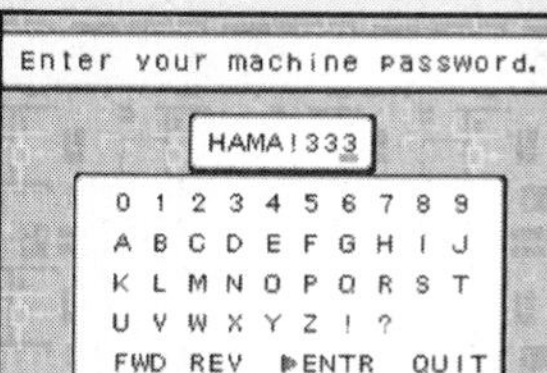

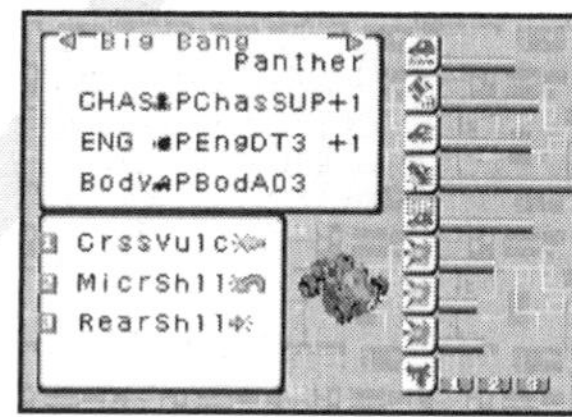

BLUE GALPE EV

At the Main menu, select Battle League. When the game asks "Use which machine," choose password and enter SHISYO!!.

CASEY'S WHLS

At the Main menu, select Battle League. When the game asks "Use which machine," choose password and enter !KOKICHI.

CAVALIER

At the Main menu, select Battle League. When the game asks "Use which machine," choose password and enter CUREWAND.

COPA ZONE23

At the Main menu, select Battle League. When the game asks "Use which machine," choose password and enter CDMACAPA.

EMP FORCE X

At the Main menu, select Battle League. When the game asks "Use which machine," choose password and enter EMPIRE!!.

ISSUE X

At the Main menu, select Battle League. When the game asks "Use which machine," choose password and enter 8998981!.

JOE JIM ZERO

At the Main menu, select Battle League. When the game asks "Use which machine," choose password and enter Todoroki.

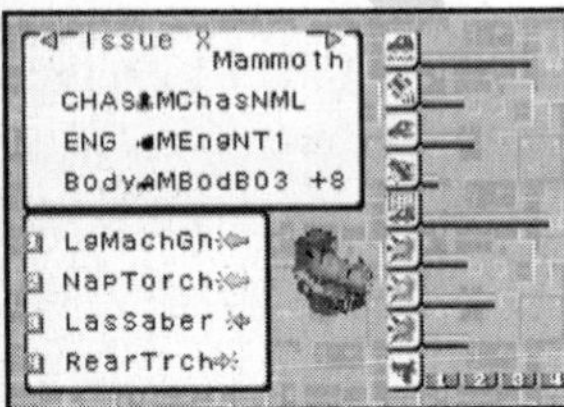

LONG VALLEY

At the Main menu, select Battle League. When the game asks "Use which machine," choose password and enter NAGOYADB.

MATSU K MK4

At the Main menu, select Battle League. When the game asks "Use which machine," choose password and enter MR!HURRY.

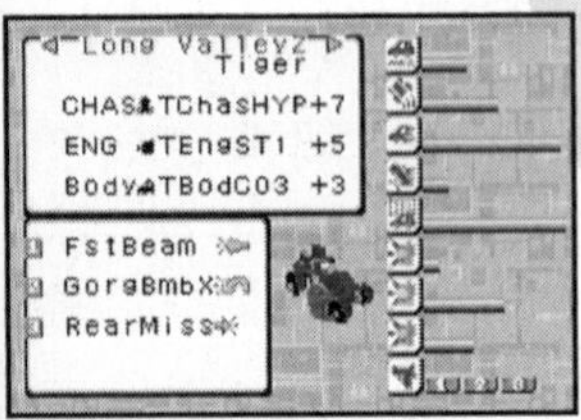

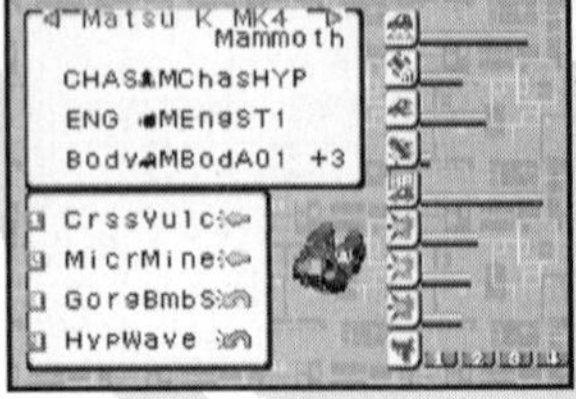

MAX-K

At the Main menu, select Battle League. When the game asks "Use which machine," choose password and enter GANKOMAX.

MEGA M

At the Main menu, select Battle League. When the game asks "Use which machine," choose password and enter M!M!M!M!.

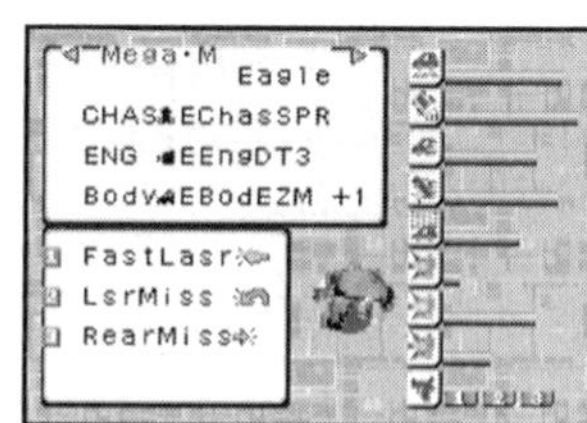

MILLENNIUM90

At the Main menu, select Battle League. When the game asks "Use which machine," choose password and enter 90!60!92.

MRIN'S DREAM

At the Main menu, select Battle League. When the game asks "Use which machine," choose password and enter MARRON!!.

MSSL DOLLY

At the Main menu, select Battle League. When the game asks "Use which machine," choose password and enter KINNIKU!.

PISTON GH

At the Main menu, select Battle League. When the game asks "Use which machine," choose password and enter GO!HOME!.

SOLID WIND

At the Main menu, select Battle League. When the game asks "Use which machine," choose password and enter RED!GUNS.

TAKAH'S LSR

At the Main menu, select Battle League. When the game asks "Use which machine," choose password and enter TK000056.

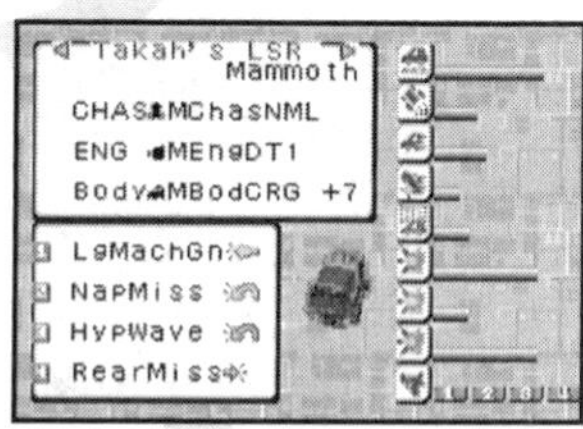

WNN SPECIAL

At the Main menu, select Battle League. When the game asks "Use which machine," choose password and enter BOM!BOM!.

CARS

ALL LEVELS & 90 BOLTS

At the Title screen, press Up, Up, Down, Down, Left, Right, Left, Right, B, A.

ALL CARS

At the Title screen, press Right, Down, Right, B.

ALL CAR COLORS

At the Title screen, press Up, Up, Left, Right, Right, Left, Down, Down.

RADIATOR CAP SECRET CIRCUIT

At the Title screen, press Left, Left, Right, Right, B, B, A.

ALL SCREENSHOTS AT THE DRIVE-IN

At the Title screen, press Left, Down, Right, A.

CASTLEVANIA: ARIA OF SORROW

NO ITEMS

Start a new game with the name NOUSE to use no items in the game.

NO SOULS

Start a new game with the name NOSOUL to use no souls in the game.

CLASSIC NES SERIES: PAC-MAN

PAC-ATTACK PUZZLE MODE

STAGE	PASSWORD
1	STR
2	HNM
3	KST
4	TRT
5	MYX
6	KHL
7	RTS
8	SKB
9	HNT
10	SRY
11	YSK
12	RCF
13	HSM
14	PWW
15	MTN
16	TKY
17	RGH

CT SPECIAL FORCES 3: NAVY OPS

LEVEL PASSWORDS

LEVEL #	ENTER
Level 1-2	5073
Level 2-1	1427
Level 2-2	2438
Level 2-3	7961
Level 2-4	8721
Level 3-1	5986
Level 3-2	2157
Level 3-3	4796
Level 3-4	3496
Level 3-5	1592
Level 3-6	4168
Level 3-7	1364
Level 4-1	7596
Level 4-2	9108
Level 4-3	6124
Level 4-4	7234
Level 4-5	6820
Level 5-1	2394
Level 5-2	4256
Level 5-3	0842

DAREDEVIL: THE MAN WITHOUT FEAR

UNLOCK EVERYTHING

Enter the password 41TK1S6ZNGV.

DK: KING OF SWING

ATTACK BATTLE 3

At the Title screen, press Up + L + A + B to access a password screen. Enter 65942922.

CLIMBING RACE 5

At the Title screen, press Up + L + A + B to access a password screen. Enter 55860327.

OBSTACLE RACE 4

At the Title screen, press Up + L + A + B to access a password screen. Enter 35805225.

UNLOCK TIME ATTACK

Complete the game as DK.

UNLOCK DIDDY MODE

Collect 24 medals as DK.

UNLOCK BUBBLES
Complete Diddy Mode with 24 Medals.

UNLOCK KREMLING
Collect 6 gold medals in Jungle Jam.

UNLOCK KING K. ROOL
Collect 12 gold medals in Jungle Jam.

DONKEY KONG COUNTRY 2: DIDDY KONG'S QUEST

ALL LEVELS
Select Cheats from the Options menu and enter freedom.

START WITH 15 LIVES
Select Cheats from the Options menu and enter helpme.

START WITH 55 LIVES
Select Cheats from the Options menu and enter weakling.

START WITH 10 BANANA COINS
Select Cheats from the Options menu and enter richman.

START WITH 50 BANANA COINS
Select Cheats from the Options menu and enter wellrich.

NO DK OR HALFWAY BARRELS
Select Cheats from the Options menu and enter rockard.

MUSIC PLAYER
Select Cheats from the Options menu and enter onetime.

CREDITS
Select Cheats from the Options menu and enter kredits.

E.T.: THE EXTRA-TERRESTRIAL

PASSWORDS

LEVEL	PASSWORD
2	Up, Up, A, Down, Down, B, R, L
3	Left, Up, Right, Down, L, A, R, B
4	A, Left, B, Right, L, Up, R, Down
5	L, R, R, L, A, Up, B, Left
6	L, Left, R, Right, A, A, B, A
7	B, R, B, L, A, Up, B, Up
8	Up, Up, A, Down, Down, Left, A, B
9	Right, B, B, Left, Up, R, R, L
10	Left, Left, A, L, Right, Right, B, R

FINAL FANTASY I & II: DAWN OF SOULS

FF I TILE GAME

During a game of Final Fantasy I and after you get the ship, hold A and press B about 55 times.

FF II CONCENTRATION GAME

After obtaining the Snowcraft, hold B and press A about 20 times.

FLUSHED AWAY

LEVEL SELECT

Enter 60861775 at the password screen.

GRADIUS GALAXIES

SLOWER

Pause the game and press Left, Right, Up, Down, Left, Left, Right, Start.

ALL WEAPONS

Pause the game and press Up, Up, Down, Down, L, R, L, R, B, A.

SELF-DESTRUCT

Pause the game and press Up, Up, Down, Down, Left, Right, Left, Right, B, A, Start.

GRAND THEFT AUTO

CHEAT MODE/COORDINATES

During a game, press A + B + Start.

ALL WEAPONS

After entering the Cheat Mode code, press Left, Right, Up, Down, A, A.

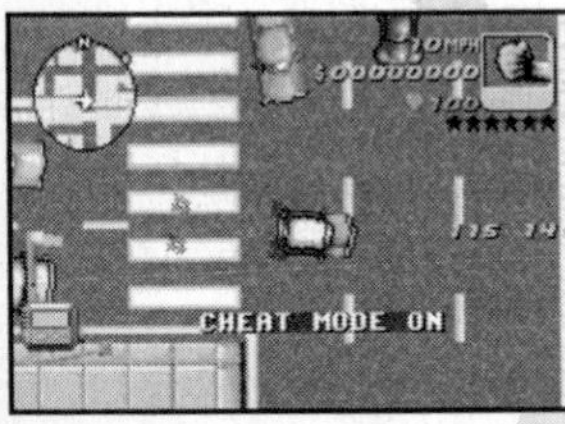

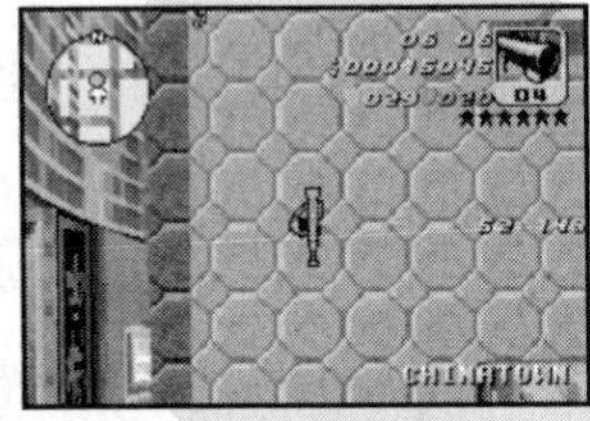

RESTORE ARMOR

After entering the Cheat Mode code, press Left, Right, Up, Down, A, L.

15,000 DOLLARS

After entering the Cheat Mode code, press Left, Right, Up, Down, L, L.

RESTORE HEALTH

After entering the Cheat Mode code, press Left, Right, Up, Down, B, B.

LOWER WANTED LEVEL

After entering the Cheat Mode code, press Left, Right, Up, Down, A, R.

RAISE WANTED LEVEL

After entering the Cheat Mode code, press Left, Right, Up, Down, R, A.

TOGGLE BETWEEN 0 STARS AND 6 STARS

After entering the Cheat Mode code, press Left, Right, Up, Down, R, R.

TOGGLE GANG HOSTILITY

After entering the Cheat Mode code, press Left, Right, Up, Down, B, R.

THE INCREDIBLE HULK

STAGE SKIP

Pause the game and press Down, Right, Down, Right, Left, Left, Left, Up.

THE INCREDIBLES: RISE OF THE UNDERMINER

TUTORIAL

Enter XL9ZMD as a password.

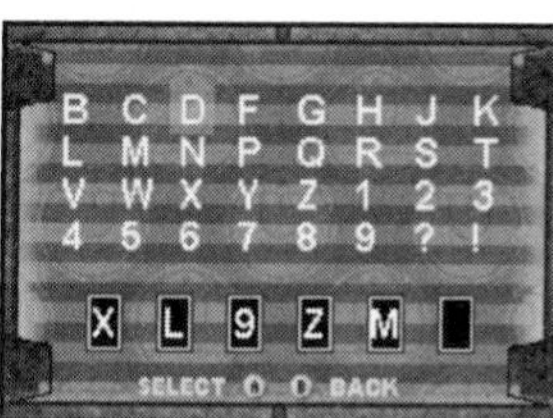

GIANT ROBOT FACTORY 1

Enter G!G1DK as a password.

GIANT ROBOT FACTORY 2

Enter DXY6FK as a password.

GIANT ROBOT FACTORY 3

Enter BBT7FK as a password.

BLIZZARD BACKDOOR 1

Enter ZPGVFK as a password.

BLIZZARD BACKDOOR 2

Enter B94GFK as a password.

BLIZZARD BACKDOOR 3

Enter J2B?FK as a password.

STAGE CORRUPTORATOR 1

Enter QF1XFK as a password.

STAGE CORRUPTORATOR 2

Enter SW3!FK as a password.

STAGE CORRUPTORATOR 3

Enter QQ?7DK as a password.

UNDERMINER

Enter 24NCGK as a password.

JAZZ JACKRABBIT

500 CREDITS

Pause the game and press Right, Left, Right, Left, L, R, Up, Up, R, R, L, L.

1000 CREDITS

Pause the game and press Up, Down, Up, Down, Left, Right, L, R, L, R, R, L.

5000 CREDITS

Pause the game and press Up, Right, Down, Left, L, L, Right, Left, R, R, L, L.

KONG: KING OF ATLANTIS

LEVEL PASSWORDS

Enter the following passwords to unlock certain levels in the game.

LEVEL	PASSWORD
Level 1-2	FJLJBDG
Level 1-3	GGJJJBF
Level 1-4	BFBGLJG
Level 2-1	LDBMLMD
Level 2-2	GMLLDDD
Level 2-3	LDFMLJD
Level 2-4	DGDDGML
Level 3-1	GMMMDFB
Level 3-2	MPFDMLB
Level 3-3	FMJBFFP
Level 3-4	LFGPMGB
Level 4-1	GPPMBGB
Level 4-2	DLBGDPP
Level 4-3	LGFPPJB

LEGO STAR WARS II: THE ORIGINAL TRILOGY

ALDERAAN
At Mos Eisley Cantina, enter 27000 as a code.

BUBBLE BLASTER
At Mos Eisley Cantina, enter 80873 as a code.

CARBONITE CHAMBER
At Mos Eisley Cantina, enter 08433 as a code.

DANCING GIRL
At Mos Eisley Cantina, enter 70546 as a code.

DEATH STAR
At Mos Eisley Cantina, enter 52577 as a code.

DEATH STAR 2
At Mos Eisley Cantina, enter 52583 as a code.

DEATH STAR HANGER
At Mos Eisley Cantina, enter 80500 as a code.

DEATH STAR SUBSECTOR 1
At Mos Eisley Cantina, enter 51999 as a code.

EMPEROR'S LAIR
At Mos Eisley Cantina, enter 20876 as a code.

EWOK VILLAGE
At Mos Eisley Cantina, enter 31299 as a code.

JEDI SPIRIT
At Mos Eisley Cantina, enter 75046 as a code.

MILLENIUM FALCON
At Mos Eisley Cantina, enter 89910 as a code.

MOS EISELY
At Mos Eisley Cantina, enter 82434 as a code.

MOS EISLEY CANTINA
At Mos Eisley Cantina, enter 13197 as a code.

OBI WAN'S HOUSE
At Mos Eisley Cantina, enter 40214 as a code.

SENSOR BALCONY
At Mos Eisley Cantina, enter 61806 as a code.

SITH MODE
At Mos Eisley Cantina, enter 11340 as a code.

THE DARK CAVE
At Mos Eisley Cantina, enter 50250 as a code.

TRASH COMPACTOR
At Mos Eisley Cantina, enter 11911 as a code.

WAMPA CAVE
At Mos Eisley Cantina, enter 42352 as a code.

YODA'S HUT
At Mos Eisley Cantina, enter 06881 as a code.

MADAGASCAR: OPERATION PENGUIN

CHRISTMAS
During gameplay, press Select, Up, L, Left, R, Right, L, Down, R.

MONSTER FORCE

RESTART LEVEL
Pause the game, hold L + R and press A.

FINISH LEVEL
During a game, hold L + R + A and press Up.

PLAY AS MINA OR DREW
At the Character Select screen, hold L + R + B and press Right.

NANCY DREW: HAUNTED MANSION

LEVEL PASSWORDS

LEVEL	PASSWORD
2	Ox, Horse, Tiger, Sheep
3	Rooster, Pig, Rabbit, Dragon
4	Rat, Dog, Monkey, Snake
5	Sheep, Tiger, Horse, Ox
6	Dragon, Rabbit, Pig, Rooster
7	Snake, Monkey, Dog, Rat

NICKTOONS UNITE!

LEVEL 2: FENTON LAB
Select Continue and enter JAZMINE.

LEVEL 3: VLAD'S CHATEAU
Select Continue and enter PAULINA.

LEVEL 4: BIKINI BOTTOM
Select Continue and enter SKULKER.

LEVEL 5: CHUM BUCKET
Select Continue and enter PATRICK.

LEVEL 6: PLANKTON
Select Continue and enter MERMAID.

LEVEL 7: TIMMY'S HOME
Select Continue and enter SCALLOP.

LEVEL 8: DIMMSDALE DUMP
Select Continue and enter BABYSIT.

LEVEL 9: CROCKER'S LOCKER ROOM
Select Continue and enter GODDARD.

LEVEL 10: JIMMY'S LAB
Select Continue and enter ESTEVEZ.

LEVEL 11: SUBTERRANEAN CAVES
Select Continue and enter LIBERTY.

LEVEL 12: PROF CALAMITOUS' LAB
Select Continue and enter SKYLARK.

THE PINBALL OF THE DEAD

BOSS MODE
Enter D0NTN33DM0N3Y as a password.

PRINCESS NATASHA: STUDENT SECRET AGENT

ALL GADGETS
Select Codes from the Extras menu and enter OLEGSGIZMO.

EXTRA LEVELS
Select Codes from the Extras menu and enter SMASHROBOT.

INFINITE LIVES
Select Codes from the Extras menu and enter CRUSHLUBEK.

R-TYPE III: THE THIRD LIGHTNING

PASSWORDS

LEVEL	PASSWORD
2	5bdgb
3	5hhlq
4	5mglt
5	5rflx
6	5wdl0

RACING GEARS ADVANCE

You can enter up to three codes at a time. Note that entering a wrong code resets the codes.

AAA
After selecting the Circuit, hold R and press A, L, B, Right, Right, Up, A. This code eliminates damage.

ARMAGEDDON
After selecting the Circuit, hold R and press B, B, L, Right, Left, Down. This unlocks unlimited ammo.

BLINDSPOT
After selecting the Circuit, hold R and press Right, A, B, B, Left. With this code activated, all opponents become invisible.

CASHCROP
After selecting the Circuit, hold R and press Right, L, Up, A, Left, B. This makes dollar signs worth more.

ENDURANCE
After selecting the Circuit, hold R and press Left, B, A, Right, L, L, Down. This makes the race five laps long.

EQUALIZER
After selecting the Circuit, hold R and press Up, Up, B, Down, A.

HAMBURGER
After selecting the Circuit, hold R and press A, A, L, Left, Right, Up. This code unlocks weapons from the start of the race.

SPRINT
After selecting the Circuit, hold R and press Down, Up, B, Left, Right, A. This makes the race one lap long.

TAXMAN
After selecting the Circuit, hold R and press L, A, B, L, Down, Down. This makes dollar signs worth less.

WUSSY
After selecting the Circuit, hold R and press B, A, B, B, L. This code eliminates weapons.

RATATOUILLE

INVINCIBILITY
Enter X4V!3RJ as a password.

ALL CHAPTERS
Enter H3L!X3! as a password. Press L or R at chapter select screen.

ALL MINI GAMES
Enter JV4ND1Z as a password.

ALL BONUS PICTURES
Enter 3R1CQRR as a password.

RIVER CITY RANSOM EX

Select the status menu and change your name to one of the following.

MAX STATS
DAMAX

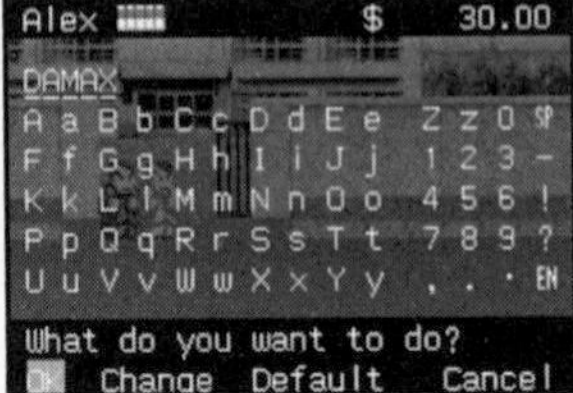

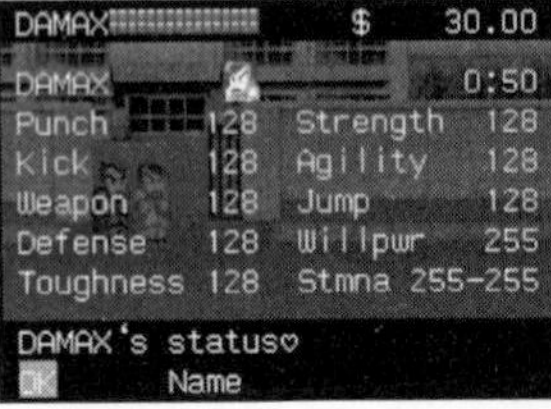

$999999.99
PLAYA

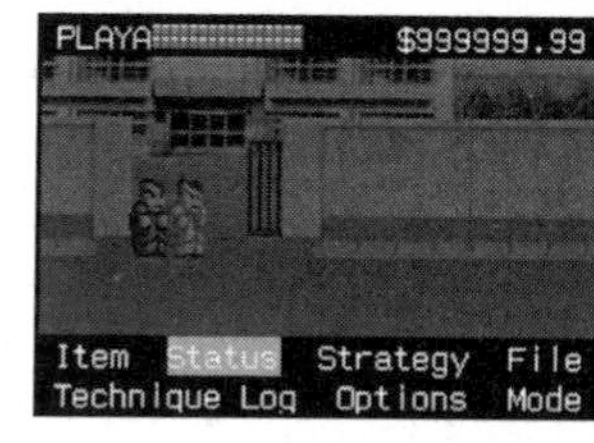

CUSTOM CHAR
XTRA0

CUSTOM SELF
XTRA1

CUSTOM MOVE
XTRA2

CLEAR SAVE
ERAZE

TECHNIQUES 1
FUZZY. This group includes Mach Punch, Dragon Kick, Acro Circus, Grand Slam, Javelin Man, Slick Trick, Nitro Port, Twin Kick, Deadly Shot, Top Spin, Helicopter, Torpedo.

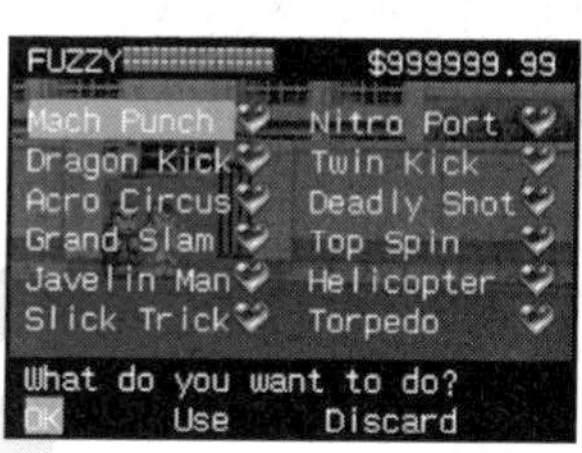

TECHNIQUES 2
WUZZY. This group includes Slap Happy, Pulper, Headbutt, Kickstand, Big Bang, Wheel Throw, Glide Chop, Head Bomb, Chain Chump, Jet Kick, Shuriken, Flip Throw.

TECHNIQUES 3
WAZZA. This group includes Boomerang, Charge It, Bat Fang, Flying Kick, Speed Drop, Bomb Blow, Killer Kick, Bike Kick, Slam Punk, Dragon Knee, God Fist, Hyperguard.

TECHNIQUES 4
BEAR*. This group includes PhoenixWing, Inlines, Springlines, Rocketeers, Air Merc's Narcishoes, Magic Pants, Pandora Box, Skaterz, Custom Fit.

ROCK 'EM SOCK 'EM ROBOTS

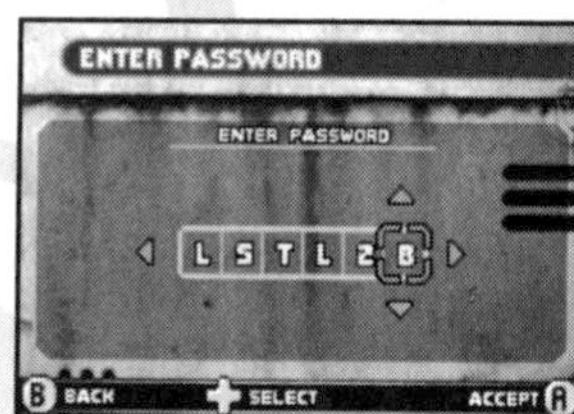

TITLE FIGHT PASSWORDS
Select Passwords from the Select Game Mode screen and enter one of the following.

TITLE FIGHT	PASSWORD
Black Bruiser	LSTL2B
Blue Bomber	B5T32J
Brown Bully	J[]T7KH
Green Grappler	NMTZKQ
Orange Oppressor	2XT9KN
Pink Pummeller	6QT1KK
Purple Pyro	02TX2T
Silver Stretcher	GZTV2K
Yellow Yahoo	W8T52Q
End	3CTNKS

SERIOUS SAM ADVANCE

EASY PASSWORDS

LEVEL	PASSWORD
Amon Thule, Subterranean Palace of the Pharaohs	HEXMODE
Baths of Diocletian	NEED
Caesar's Palace	WAFTY
Gladiator Training School	COINAGE
Praetorian Fort	NORTHERN
Pyramid Entrance Maze	BADDUN
Slave Compound	BOBBINS
Slave Quarters	TOAST
The Forum of Mars	GAMES
The Temple of Herkat Lower	MNIP
Tomb Of Ramses	MEGAMUNT

NORMAL PASSWORDS

LEVEL	PASSWORD
Amon Thule, Subterranean Palace of the Pharaohs	OPEE
Baths OF Diocletian	OWL
Caesar's Palace	MOOPAY
Gladiator Training School	FRYUP
Praetorian Fort	FILLY
Pyramid Entrance Maze	BETTERER
Slave Compound	PILCH
Slave Quarters	BEVIL
The Forum Of Mars	DUCKAROO
The Temple of Herkat Lower	KIPPAGE
Tomb of Ramses	HORSE

HARD PASSWORDS

LEVEL	PASSWORD
Amon Thule, Subterranean Palace of the Pharaohs	WOLF
Baths OF Diocletian	LIMO
Caesar's Palace	MOCKNEY
Gladiator Training School	MADEUP
Praetorian Fort	MIRROR
Pyramid Entrance Maze	CHIPPER
Slave Compound	FORREST
Slave Quarters	BEAK
The Forum Of Mars	FOZZER
The Temple of Herkat Lower	TITHES
Tomb of Ramses	EYE

SPONGEBOB SQUAREPANTS: REVENGE OF THE FLYING DUTCHMAN

DEBUG MODE

Enter the password D3BVG-M0D3.

SPYRO ORANGE: THE CORTEX CONSPIRACY

100 GEMS

At the Mode menu, press L + R, then enter V1S10NS.

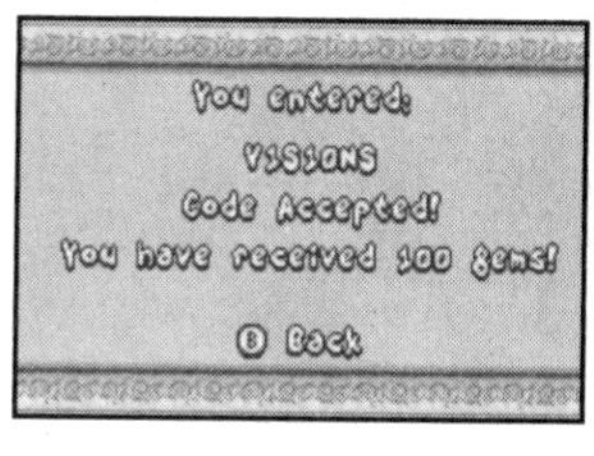

ORANGE GAME

At the Mode menu, press L + R, then enter SP4RX.

PURPLE GAME

At the Mode menu, press L + R, then enter P0RT4L.

ORANGE SPYRO

At the Mode menu, press L + R, then enter SPYR0.

SHEEP MODE

At the Mode menu, press L + R, then enter SH33P.

SHEEP FLAME MODE

At the Mode menu, press L + R, then enter B41S0KV.

CRASH PARTY USA MINI-GAME

Start up your Game Boy Advance and hold L + R.

SPYRO: SEASON OF FLAME

BLUE SPYRO

At the Title screen, press Up, Up, Up, Up, Down, Left, Right, Down, B.

ALL PORTALS

At the Title screen, press Up, Left, Up, Right, Up, Down, Up, Down, B.

ALL WORLDS IN ATLAS

At the Title screen, press Left, Right, Up, Up, Right, Left, Right, Up, B.

ATLAS WARPING

At the Title screen, press Down, Up, Left, Left, Up, Left, Left, Right, B.

INFINITE LIVES

At the Title screen, press Left, Right, Left, Right (x3), Up, Down, B.

INFINITE SHIELD FOR AGENT 9

At the Title screen, press Left, Down, Up, Right, Left, Up, Up, Left, B.

INFINITE AMMO

At the Title screen, press Right, Left, Up, Down, Right, Down, Up, Right, B.

NEVER DROWN

At the Title screen, press Down, Up, Right, Left, Right, Up, Right, Left, B.

ALL BREATH TYPES

At the Title screen, press Right, Down, Up, Right, Left, Up, Right, Down, B.

SUPER CHARGE

At the Title screen, press Left, Left, Down, Up, Up, Right, Left, Left, B.

DRAGON DRAUGHTS MINI-GAME

At the Title screen, press Right, Up, Down, Down, Down, Right, Up, Down, B.

STREET FIGHTER ALPHA 3

ALL FIGHTERS
At the Title screen, press Left, Right, Down, Right, L, L, A, L, L, B, R, A, Up.

ALL MODES
At the Title screen, press A, Up, A, L, R, Right, L, Right, A, Down, Right. Then press L, Right, A, R, Up,L, Right, B, A, Up, Right, Down, Right.

PLAY AS SUPER BISON
At the Character Select screen, hold Start and select Bison.

PLAY AS SHIN AKUMA
At the Character Select screen, hold Start and select Akuma.

ALTERNATE COSTUMES
At the Character Select screen, press L or R.

FINAL BATTLE
At the Speed Select screen, hold A + B.

THAT'S SO RAVEN 2: SUPERNATURAL STYLE

COSTUME MODE
At the Title screen, press Left, Right, Up, Down, B, B, B, Up, Down.

UNLIMITED ENERGY MODE
At the Title screen, press B, B, L, R, Up, Down, Up, Left, Right.

TREASURE PLANET

PASSWORDS

LEVEL	PASSWORD
1	MUSHROOM
2	TRUMPET
3	CLOUDY
4	RABBIT
5	SUNSHINE
6	SPIDER
7	APRON
8	RAINBOW
9	GOOSE
10	ENGLAND
11	MOUNTAIN
12	CAPTAIN
13	SNOWMAN
14	WITCHES
15	MONKEY
16	PRINCESS
17	WINDOW
18	COCONUT
19	FOOTBALL
20	CONCRETE
21	ELEPHANT
22	PHANTOM
23	DRAGON

TRON 2.0: KILLER APP

ALL MINI-GAMES
At the Title screen, press Left, Left, Left, Left, Up, Right, Down, Down, Select.

UNFABULOUS

PASSWORDS

Select Continue and enter the following:

PASSWORD	EFFECT
End of Game	Zach, Brandywine, Addie, Addie
Credits	Geena, Ben, Addie, Ben
Mini Game	Ben, Zach, Ben, Addie

WORLD CHAMPIONSHIP POKER

10 MILLION DOLLAR

Enter the following as a password: 7 Hearts, King Spades, 2 Hearts, Queen Clubs, 9 Hearts, Jack Hearts.

YOSHI TOPSY-TURVY

CHALLENGE MODE & CHALLENGE 1

Defeat Bowser for the second time in Story Mode.

CHALLENGES 2, 3, 4

Complete the Egg Gallery in Story Mode.

FINAL CHALLENGE

Earn all Golds in Story Mode.

YU-GI-OH! ULTIMATE MASTERS: WORLD CHAMPIONSHIP TOURNAMENT 2006

CARD PASSWORDS

Enter the 8-digit codes at the Password screen to unlock that card for purchase. Refer to the Card List for YU-GI-OH! GX TAG FORCE for PSP. All cards may not be available in World Championship Tournament 2006.

DK/BradyGames, a division of Penguin Group (USA) Inc.
800 East 96th Street, 3rd Floor
Indianapolis, IN 46240

ISBN: 978-0-7440-1125-8

Printing Code: The rightmost double-digit number is the year of the book's printing; the rightmost single-digit number is the number of the book's printing. For example, 09-1 shows that the first printing of the book occurred in 2009.

12 11 10 09 4 3 2 1

Manufactured in the United States of America.

BRADYGAMES STAFF

Publisher
David Waybright

Editor-In-Chief
H. Leigh Davis

Licensing Director
Mike Degler

Marketing Director
Debby Neubauer

CREDITS

Senior Development Editor
David Bartley

Code Editor
Michael Owen

Book Designer
Doug Wilkins

Production Designer
Bob Klunder